BASIC
SMALL BUSINESS
MANAGEMENT

BASIC
SMALL BUSINESS
MANAGEMENT

Clifford M. Baumback
University of Iowa

Prentice-Hall, Inc., *Englewood Cliffs, N.J.*   07632

Library of Congress Cataloging in Publication Data

BAUMBACK, CLIFFORD MASON (date)
  Basic small business management.

  Includes bibliographical references and index.
  1. Small business—Management. I. Title.
HD62.7.B37 1983   658'.022   82-18110
ISBN 0-13-066415-4

© 1983 by Prentice-Hall, Inc., Englewood Cliffs, N.J.   07632

All rights reserved.
No part of this book may be reproduced in any form or by any means
without permission in writing from the publisher.

Editorial/production supervision and interior design by Maureen Wilson
Cover design by Diane Saxe
Manufacturing buyer: Ed O'Dougherty

Printed in the United States of America

10 9 8 7 6 5 4 3 2 1

ISBN 0-13-066415-4

Prentice-Hall International, Inc., *London*
Prentice-Hall of Australia Pty. Limited, *Sydney*
Editora Prentice-Hall do Brasil, Ltda., *Rio de Janeiro*
Prentice-Hall Canada Inc., *Toronto*
Prentice-Hall of India Private Limited, *New Delhi*
Prentice-Hall of Japan, Inc., *Tokyo*
Prentice-Hall of Southeast Asia Pte. Ltd., *Singapore*
Whitehall Books Limited, *Wellington, New Zealand*

Contents

Preface   *ix*

Part One
THE WORLD OF SMALL BUSINESS

Role in the Economy   *3*

CHAPTER ONE *What Is a "Small" Business. The Predominance of Small Business. The Make-up of Small Business. Economic Contributions of Small Business. The Franchise Boom. From Small Beginnings . . .*

External or Environmental Problems   *16*

CHAPTER TWO *Capital Shortages. Taxation and Regulations. Product Liability. Patent Abuses. Franchising Abuses. Concern for the Welfare of Small Business. Organized Voices for Small Business*

Success and Failure Factors   *28*

CHAPTER THREE *Causes of Business Failure. Factors in Successful Small Business Management*

Part Two
THE MANAGEMENT PROCESS IN THE SMALLER BUSINESS

Basic Management Functions   *39*

CHAPTER FOUR *Planning. Organizing and Staffing. Directing. Controlling*

Differences in Managing Small and Large Firms   *53*

CHAPTER FIVE *The Strategy of Size. The "One-Man Band" Problem. Education for Small Business Management*

WITHDRAWN

OCT   1983

Special Management Concerns   *62*

CHAPTER SIX   *Time Management.   Community Obligations.   Continuing Management Education.   Management Succession and Business Continuity*

Need for Outside Staff Assistance   *72*

CHAPTER SEVEN   *Clarification of Terms and Concepts.   Government Sources of Business Information.   Nongovernment Sources of Business Information*

Part Three

MANAGING THE PRODUCTION FUNCTION

Providing Physical Facilities   *93*

CHAPTER EIGHT   *Building Requirements.   Obtaining the Equipment.   Arranging the Layout*

Purchasing Goods and Supplies   *107*

CHAPTER NINE   *Determining Inventory Needs.   Locating and Selecting Suppliers.   Negotiating Terms.   Maintaining Favorable Relations with Suppliers.   Receiving, Checking, and Marking Goods.   Follow-up after Purchase*

Controlling Inventories   *123*

CHAPTER TEN   *Dollar Control vs. Unit Control.   Keeping Track of Inventories.   Setting the Quantitative Limits.   Merchandise Control Systems*

Acquiring, Training, and Motivating Employees   *145*

CHAPTER ELEVEN   *The Importance of Job Analysis.   Recruitment and Selection.   Placement.   Training.   Transfers and Promotions.   Remuneration.   Morale Building*

Planning and Controlling Factory Production   *169*

CHAPTER TWELVE   *Planning Production Orders.   Production Order Control.   Flow Control*

Part Four

MANAGING THE DISTRIBUTION FUNCTION

Market Analysis and Business Location   *179*

CHAPTER THIRTEEN   *Selecting the Community.   Selecting the Site. The Retail Location.   Location Requirements in Other Types of Business*

Pricing Methods and Strategies   *204*

CHAPTER FOURTEEN   *Economics of Pricing.   Pricing by
Retailers.   Pricing by Wholesalers.   Pricing by the Service
Establishment.   Pricing for the Small Factory*

Advertising and Sales Promotion   *224*

CHAPTER FIFTEEN   *Customers' Buying Motives.   Advertising.   Window
and Interior Displays.   Special Sales Events.   Personal Selling and Customer
Relations.   Franchising and Other Methods of Distribution.   Government
Assistance Programs.   Public Relations—An Indirect Form of Sales Promotion*

Exporting   *249*

CHAPTER SIXTEEN   *Distribution Channels.   Merchandising to Foreign
Markets.   Government Assistance Programs.   Recommendations for Changes
in Government Policy.   Metric Conversion*

Part Five

MANAGING THE FIRM'S FINANCES

Raising Capital   *261*

CHAPTER SEVENTEEN   *Estimating Capital Needs.   Kinds of
Capital.   Debt vs. Equity Capital.   Sources of Funds*

Credit and Collections   *278*

CHAPTER EIGHTEEN   *Advantages and Disadvantages of Extending
Credit.   Consumer Credit.   Trade Credit*

Accounting Records and Financial Statements   *309*

CHAPTER NINETEEN   *Importance of Financial Records.   The Accounting
Equation.   Basic Accounting Records.   Financial Statements and Their
Interpretation.   Principles of Internal Control.   Computerized Accounting and
Other Record Keeping*

Depreciation and Inventory Valuation   *339*

CHAPTER TWENTY   *Depreciating Capital Assets.   Determining
Inventory Values*

Profit Planning and Cost Control   *350*

CHAPTER TWENTY-ONE   *Demand Forecasting.   Break-even
Analysis.   Incremental Costs and Marginal Income.   Expense Budgeting*

Cash Flows and Capital Expenditures   *372*

CHAPTER TWENTY-TWO   *Importance of Cash Flow.   Investment
Decision Criteria*

Insurance and Risk Management   *384*

CHAPTER TWENTY-THREE   *Insurance Planning.   Loss Reduction or Prevention*

Part Six

THE LEGAL ENVIRONMENT

Types of Legal Business Transactions   *401*

CHAPTER TWENTY-FOUR   *Contracts.   Agency.   Sales.   Negotiable Instruments*

Legal Forms of Business Organization   *409*

CHAPTER TWENTY-FIVE   *The Proprietorship.   The General Partnership.   The Limited Partnership.   The Conventional Corporation. The Tax-Option Corporation*

Government Regulation of Business   *423*

CHAPTER TWENTY-SIX   *Competition.   Price Regulations.   Merchandise Regulations.   Other Consumer Protection Laws.   Environmental Protection.   Labor Legislation.   Restrictions and Permits.   Bankruptcy and Court-approved Debt Settlements*

Taxes and Economic Security Legislation   *444*

CHAPTER TWENTY-SEVEN   *Economic Security Legislation.   Federal Income Taxes.   Federal Excise Taxes.   State and Local Sales Taxes*

Part Seven

LOOKING BACK AND LOOKING AHEAD

Starting a Business   *461*

CHAPTER TWENTY-EIGHT   *The Marketing Plan.   The Organization and Staffing Plan.   The Financial Plan*

Selling (or Buying) a Business   *484*

CHAPTER TWENTY-NINE   *Setting the Price.   Striking a Deal*

Glossary: The Language of Business   *497*

Index   *533*

Preface

Since poor management is at the root of most small business failures, and since approximately half of these failed businesses should never have been started in the first place because their owners were not adequately prepared to manage them, this book—unlike others with similar titles—is written primarily from a managerial rather than an entrepreneurial (or how to get started) perspective. This book is exactly what its title says it is: a book on *basic small business management.*

The rationale for this approach is supported further by the fact that not all managers of small enterprises are entrepreneurs. Although hard data are not available to support the premise, it is also probably true that the number of people with some managerial responsibilities in a small business enterprise is far in excess of the number of entrepreneurial managers. In any case sound management practice is basic to the survival or economic health of any business, owner-managed or not, and so this book takes the larger view.

At the same time, however, the entrepreneurial function is not ignored in this volume. It is given particular focus in the final two chapters. Chapter 28, for example, provides a step-by-step procedure for "Starting a Business," with appropriate cross-references to the body of the text. Instructors and students who wish to teach or study small business management from the perspective of aspiring entrepreneurs can do so, conveniently and without loss of continuity, by starting with this chapter and following its directions; for all others, the chapter serves as a review of what has gone before. Chapter 29 similarly emphasizes the entrepreneurial function by considering the purchase of an ongoing venture as an alternative route to business ownership, as well as the sale of a business from the owner's point of view.

This book was also written from the student's perspective. Liberal use has been made of cartoons and other graphics to clarify or emphasize important concepts and to make the text more enjoyable to read. Further, each chapter begins with a statement of learning objectives and concludes with a concise summary and a glossary of key words and phrases, as well as one or more exercises and/or "cases in point" to illustrate real-life problem situations and to help the student *learn by doing.*

As in any large and creative effort, many people have contributed to the preparation and publication of this volume. Many of them are acknowledged in the text and footnotes. The contributions of others, however, have not been similarly acknowledged and I hasten here to express my appreciation to them also. Deserving of special mention are Maureen Wilson, Prentice-Hall production editor, for her precise editing and supervision, which helped to make the book more readable; Wendell O. Metcalf, retired Chief of Management Assistance in the Small Business Administration, for supplying from his personal files reproduction copies of selected out-of-print SBA illustrations; Linda Knowling, for drawing the original art; Kenneth Lawyer, my friend and colleague, for writing many of the short cases; and Phyllis Irwin and Marguerite Knoedel, for supervising the typing of the manuscript.

CLIFFORD M. BAUMBACK

BASIC
SMALL BUSINESS
MANAGEMENT

Part One

THE WORLD
OF SMALL BUSINESS

The first section of this book is an introduction to the big world of small business. Few students realize how high the probability is that they will someday become involved, directly or indirectly, with a small business enterprise and its management—either as (1) owners of their own businesses, (2) employees of a small business, (3) employees of a large company, the majority of whose customers and suppliers are small business firms, or (4) economists, bankers, legislators, lawyers, or accountants, among many others, who are concerned for one reason or another with the problems and opportunities of small business and the free enterprise system. The three chapters in this introductory section will help prepare you for these future relationships or concerns. After reading them you should have an increased awareness of the nature of "small" business and of the economic, social, and political environment in which small businesses function.

Role
in the Economy

CHAPTER ONE *This is the "what it's all about" chapter. It defines, describes, identifies, and distinguishes the small business. After reading it you should have a better understanding of the role of small businesses and the reasons for their existence. In particular, you will learn that (1) "the economy" is business serving people, providing food, clothing, shelter, utensils, recreational facilities, and so forth, to the public; (2) there are many kinds of business—service (such as insurance or repairs), merchandising (wholesale and retail stores), and manufacturing; and (3) most businesses are small—some small only at their beginnings, others by their natures always small.*

For some, the word "business" conjures up an image of gigantic multinational corporations. For others, it's the family next door who operates the shoe store or the partners who run the hardware store down the street. The community in which you live probably has some big business—the major retailer with stores across the country or the local plant of one of the world's largest firms. But it has vastly more small businesses, and these small businesses are as basic to the local economy as they are numerous.

WHAT IS A "SMALL" BUSINESS?

Thus far the term "small business" has been used generally and without specific and careful definition of what "small" is. But what can we use to accurately measure size? Attempts have been made (as, for example, by the Small Business Administration) to define a small business in terms of (1) employment, (2) asset value, or (3) dollar sales volume. All have proven unsatisfactory in some respect. This irresolution stems largely from the diverse character of varying industries. A firm in one industry may loom large relative to its competitors, yet be small in employment, assets, and sales relative to firms in other industries; or the reverse may be true. And in some circumstances the firm may be small on the basis of employment and large in assets and sales, or vice versa. Additionally, size standards expressed in monetary terms (such as sales and asset value) need to be raised frequently in times of inflation to reflect changes in the value of the dollar. Furthermore, such *quantitative* definitions of a small business leave undemonstrated its *qualitative* distinguishing characteristics.

For these reasons we will cast aside this lack of precision and establish a definition here by indicating the major attributes of a business which has the financial and managerial difficulties which we usually associate with small business.

Characteristically, a **small business** is one that is (1) actively managed by its owners, (2) highly personalized, (3) largely local in its area of operations, (4) of relatively small size within the industry, and (5) largely dependent on internal sources of capital to finance its growth. There are the characteristics which give rise to most of its problems and special needs.

> *A small business is any business in which the owner/manager is able to recall the first names of his or her employees.*

THE PREDOMINANCE OF SMALL BUSINESS

Despite the shortcomings noted above, employment statistics provide the most complete and reliable measure of the small business population currently available. In Table 1-1 it is noted that more than one-third of all the manufacturing firms in the country employ fewer than five persons, or none at all, and that close to two-thirds employ fewer than twenty workers. The employment-size proportions are even greater in merchandising and the service industries. Of the total number of nonfarm businesses of all kinds, 95 percent employ fewer than fifty workers each!

It can reasonably be inferred that firms of such small employment size are independently owned and operated ventures servicing strictly local markets. Although the giant corporations and mass-production firms loom important in terms of productivity and capital investment, it is the small business that actually constitutes the backbone of the nation's economy.

THE MAKE-UP OF SMALL BUSINESS

It is clear from the data in Table 1-1 that small businesses predominate in all private sectors of the economy. The relative importance of the small firm, however, differs considerably from one type of business to another. We shall consider here only the major areas of business activity—the manufacture of products; the distribution of products of all kinds (however produced); and the rendering of services (some of which may involve the use of a product). Together these industries make up approximately 86 percent of the total number of **business firms** employing fewer than fifty workers, distributed as

TABLE 1-1

Percentage Distribution of Business Firms, by Kind of
Business and Employment Size, 1979

INDUSTRY	FEWER THAN 5 EMPLOYEES°	FEWER THAN 10 EMPLOYEES	FEWER THAN 20 EMPLOYEES	FEWER THAN 50 EMPLOYEES
Extractive industries°°	48.5	63.1	76.9	89.5
Manufacturing	34.0	48.6	64.0	80.2
Wholesale trade	47.5	69.1	85.7	96.1
Retail trade	53.0	74.6	87.9	96.4
Contract construction	64.4	81.4	91.6	97.5
Selected services°°°	62.3	79.1	89.4	96.0
All industries	55.3	74.0	86.4	94.9

° Data adjusted to include business firms with no paid employees, estimated by the Social Security Administration at 9 percent of the business population.
°° Mining and quarrying, forestry and fisheries.
°°° Transportation, communications, and public utilities (such as trucking and warehousing, and local and interurban passenger transit); finance, insurance, and real estate (such as banks and other credit agencies, real estate brokers, and insurance carriers and agents); lodging facilities (such as hotels and motels); personal services (such as laundries and dry cleaning plants, and barber and beauty shops); business services (such as advertising agencies, public accounting firms, credit bureaus, and equipment rental); automobile repair and other types of repair services (including garages and parking lots); amusement and recreational services (such as motion picture theaters, billiard parlors, and bowling alleys); and miscellaneous other services. Not included are persons or organizations providing legal services, educational services, medical and other health services, or other skills not used primarily in business.
SOURCE: *County Business Patterns*, 1979, part I; *U.S. Summary*, as reported by the Social Security Administration.

follows: retailing, 34 percent; services, 34 percent; wholesaling, 11 percent; and manufacturing, 7 percent.[1]

Manufacturing

A businesss is considered a **manufacturing enterprise** if it is engaged primarily in receiving materials in one form and, after working on them, distributes them in an altered form. This would include processors of farm

[1] Excluded from this discussion are the extractive industries, which account for less than 1 percent of the total number of small businesses, and contract construction. Although contract construction is an important sector of the small business economy, accounting for close to 13 percent of the total number of firms, this type of economic activity has characteristics of both manufacturing and the service trades, in varying degrees depending on the type of construction. The operating problems of building contractors, for example, are more nearly like those of manufacturers, whereas the service aspect of their work predominates for plumbers, electricians, and carpenters.

products, local craftsmen or artisans, bottling plants, and similar enterprises.

It is the growing concentration of power in manufacturing which, in recent years, has led to some concern for the welfare of small business. Although more than 80 percent of the companies in manufacturing employ fewer than fifty employees, about 75 percent of the total manufacturing employment is concentrated in only 3 percent of the companies. Also noteworthy is the observation that the increase in the number of manufacturing enterprises in recent years has not kept pace with the growth in population (nor with the overall growth in the number of business firms). Between 1969 and 1979, for example, whereas population increased by more than 26 percent, the number of manufacturing firms in operation increased by less than 1 percent. During this same period, manufacturing employment increased by 14 percent and value added by manufacture in constant dollars (that is, after allowing for changes in the price level) increased by more than 44 percent.[2] Thus, in manufacturing, large firms have become relatively larger.

Despite the growing concentration of power in manufacturing, there is still much room in which the small firm can maneuver. Big business is most effective in well-established industries where large markets for low-unit-cost products exist; where technology and mechanization have been developed to a high degree of efficiency, but where huge capital investments are required; and where standardization and simplification (limitation of variety) are desirable policies. However, the mass-production system is often dependent on the small production plant for supplies and components. It is the very existence of the large manufacturers that provides the smaller manufacturers with many of their opportunities.

Some observers comment that our large mass-production industries are essentially assemblers of the products of thousands of small specialized manufacturers. Mass-produced goods such as motor vehicles, airplanes, refrigerators, radios and television sets, and stereophonic equipment have from a few hundred to several thousand component parts, indicating that, on the average, each large concern buys materials and parts from small firms in hundreds of different kinds of businesses.

Thus it is the manufacture of producers' goods (products made for other manufacturers) wherein most of the opportunities exist for the small, independent enterpriser. As big business grows, so does small business.

But opportunities exist also for the small manufacturer in local consumer markets. Some of the more common examples of local manufacturing are

---

[2] Sources of data: U.S. Bureau of Labor Statistics, *Employment and Earnings* (number of employees); U.S. Social Security Administration, *County Business Patterns* (number of establishments and employment-size classification); U.S. Bureau of Economic Analysis, *Survey of Current Business* (value added); and U.S. Bureau of the Census, *Current Population Reports* (population).

printing shops, bakeries, bottling plants, and processed dairy products. These are the ubiquitous industries present in every community that provide needed products for local consumption. As a community grows, so also do the opportunities for the small local manufacturer.

Merchandising

Merchandisers are middlemen in the channel of distribution who actually sell products to the final consumers (**retailers**), or who buy goods for resale to retailers (**wholesalers**).

There are more retail stores in the United States than any other kind of business enterprise; they account for more than 34 percent of the total number of firms of all kinds. Furthermore, most of them are small; some of them can even be described as tiny. In Table 1-1 it is noted that more than five out of ten retail stores have fewer than five paid employees, or none at all, and that 88 percent of them employ fewer than twenty employees. Despite the deep incursions into the market made in recent years by large department stores, chain stores, and mail-order houses, retailing remains largely the bailiwick of the small, independent enterpriser.

Small firms also predominate in wholesaling, though to a lesser degree. A smaller proportion of them employ fewer than twenty persons (86 percent). However, over 20 percent of the firms employ only one person, and over 69 percent have fewer than ten employees!

As in the manufacturing sector of the economy, growth in wholesale trade has not kept pace with the growth in population. Opportunities for the small businessperson in this field are not as great as they once were, owing principally to the absorption of the wholesaling function by franchising organizations, manufacturer's representatives, and large-scale integrated retailers like chain stores, department stores, and mail-order houses.

Just as the mass-production system is dependent on the small specialized manufacturing plant, so also is it dependent on the small merchant. Each retail store handles from a few thousand to well over twenty thousand different items. These small, independent retailers distribute the products of thousands of small manufacturers and about six thousand large manufacturers (five hundred employees or more). A conclusion that at least five hundred different suppliers and several thousand retail dealers serve each large manufacturer is probably very conservative. In addition, most **consumer goods** go through wholesale establishments, the majority of which are small businesses, and each large producer buys services from numerous small and mostly local establishments. Obviously, the small merchant plays a major role in gathering together America's wealth of production and making it available for use.

Service Establishments

The **service businesses** offer literally hundreds of different kinds of services to consumers, to governmental agencies and nonprofit organizations, and to other businesses. They are staffed by technicians and professionally trained people with skills for hire. Most of the common types of service establishments perform work on goods owned by the customer or upon the person of the client. Many others perform services of different kinds, such as banks, insurance companies and underwriters, and real estate brokers.

Except for some notable exceptions in the transportation, communications, and public utilities field (embracing the railroads, airlines, telephone and telegraph companies, light and power companies, and other "natural" monopolies), the dominant characteristic of the service business is its small size. Most require only a small initial investment and depend heavily on close personal supervision. The barber shop, for example, has never achieved mass production, nor has the watchmaker or the lawnmower repairman. Neither the finisher of antique furniture nor the restorer of metal objects can do work mechanically beyond certain preparatory steps. Nor can truckers or carpenters automate their services.

The role played by service industries in the economy is becoming increasingly larger. Between 1969 and 1979 the number of service establishments grew by more than 54 percent. Not only has there been a gain in the number of service establishments, but the *proportion* of such establishments has been rising as well. During this same decade, the proportion of service businesses to the total number of businesses of all kinds rose from 27.7 to 34.3 percent.

An important factor contributing to this growth is that the purchase of services is taking an increasingly larger proportion of the consumer's dollar. Higher incomes and the increased purchasing power available to the average individual has provided the consumer with funds to hire someone else to perform personal and business services. Ironically, this is coupled with increased personal leisure time and the "do-it-yourself" trend. But these may be related; as people have more money, they have more possessions and wider interests which call for an increasing number of services. Perhaps a boat motor will require repair, a frame may be needed for a newly painted picture, or a hand-knit sweater will have to be blocked.

The growth of the service industry can also be attributed to the fact that, since most services are difficult if not impossible to mechanize or automate, productivity per worker is not increasing as rapidly in this industry as in most other sectors of the economy. Consequently, a given increase in the amount of services rendered generates more service enterprises (as well as more employment) than a similar increase in agricultural output or manufacturing output. This is particularly evident in business services, repair services, personal services, and amusement and recreational services.

ECONOMIC CONTRIBUTIONS OF SMALL BUSINESS

Small, independent business is the traditional source of local and national economic growth, furnishing more than 50 percent of all private employment and over 40 percent of the nation's total output of goods and services. Studies have also shown that most of the new jobs created in this country come from small (labor-intensive) companies and not from large (capital-intensive) corporations.

Small business units, however, are even more important to our economy in a *functional* sense, for reasons which we will now examine.

Interdependence of Business

If any one conclusion can be drawn from the preceding discussion, it is this: A basic reality of modern economic life is the interdependence of all business. No modern business is an entity in itself. It must buy from other firms and sell either to different business owners or to consumers in competition with a great many other businesses. This means that there is a place for everyone, if he or she has something worthwhile to offer and is able to offer it in an effective, efficient way. Furthermore, numerous small enterprises are essential to enable a few large ones to concentrate on those activities where their efforts are most effective.

The fact that our economy, with so much mass production, requires great numbers of small wholesalers, retailers, industrial distributors, and other middlemen must be emphasized. The products of our great business "names" are equally available in Gila Bend, Arizona; Chugwater, Wyoming; and Coon Hollow, West Virginia. They are available in thousands of such remote locations only through the invaluable services provided by small independent merchants, gas station operators, and owners of crossroad general stores. Without these middlemen, these regional merchant-sales representatives and their warehouses, mass distribution of our mass production would be impossible.

It is also apparent that the mass producers of automobiles, farm machinery, TV sets, and other electromechanical products of our increasingly affluent society are dependent on thousands of small, independent service establishments for the repair, upkeep, and maintenance of these products. Small enterprises also perform a wide variety of professional, technical, and clerical services both for big business itself and for any other customers in need of their specialized skills and knowledge.

Even in manufacturing, big business and small business work hand in hand. Not only do small firms make most of the component parts that feed our huge assembly lines as well as a wide variety of industrial supplies (such as corrugated boxes and other shipping containers), they are also important users of many of the large firms' products.

The automobile industry provides one of the best illustrations of the basic and far-reaching interdependence of business. When one thinks of this industry, there is a tendency to think only of the "Big Four"—General Motors, Ford, Chrysler, and American Motors. Yet according to the latest count there are more than 3,600 firms classified in this industry. Most of them are parts producers, rather than assemblers, and employ fewer than fifty people. Only 14 percent of them (including the Big Four) employ in excess of 250 workers.

Small businesses are even smaller in the automobile-*related* industries. Of the approximately 112,000 automobile repair shops in the U.S., for example, 66 percent have only one to four employees, or none at all; and of the more than 135,000 service stations, 61 percent are in this size range. Of the 32,000 new-car dealers, 83 percent employ fewer than fifty people.

> *Big business can't prosper without small business to supply its needs and buy its products.*
>
> —DeWitt M. Emery

Maintenance of Competition

In the preceding paragraphs we have stressed the *noncompetitive* aspects of business enterprise, that is, the interdependent or *complementary* nature of the functions and activities of large and small firms. But big and small business also compete with each other in many areas, and it is equally important (if not more so) to preserve competition and our system of free, independent enterprise.

The nation first became concerned about the growing concentration of business power almost one-hundred years ago—in 1890, when Congress enacted the Sherman Act. Subsequent **antitrust legislation** includes the Clayton Act of 1914 and the Wheeler-Lea Act of 1938. In 1953, however, a new, *positive* approach to the problem of growing monopoly power was taken with passage of the Small Business Act, whose purpose is to avert monopoly not by dissolving the giant firms or trusts but by *aiding the smaller businesses.* In passing this act Congress reaffirmed the principle that "the essence of the American system of private enterprise is free competition." "Only through full and free markets, free entry into business, and opportunities for the expression and growth of personal initiative," the preamble to the act continues, "can individual judgment be assured. Indeed, such security and well-being cannot be realized unless the actual and potential capacity of small business is encouraged and developed.

Among other things, the act set up a new department of government—the Small Business Administration. The importance that the federal government attaches to small business and the maintenance of our system of **free enterprise** is further evidenced by the creation of the White House Committee on Small Business and the two standing Congressional Committees on Small Business. Each year, also, the President proclaims one week in May as National Small Business Week, and the Small Business Administration selects the "Small Businessperson of the Year."

The importance of competition in our economy cannot be denied. In an age of rapid change, competition can be the vehicle of change, through innovation or through improvement. Modern competition appears in many forms: price, credit terms, service, product improvement, interindustry struggles concerning substitution and replacement, innovations as to method, and so forth. Basically, it is rivalry for consumer patronage. If a truly free competitive economy is the desired goal of a nation, the continued existence of independent enterprises is imperative. Competitive capitalism insures freedom of enterprise and provides an outlet for individual creative impulses and abilities, as well as a livelihood for a large segment of the population. It is the best insurance that our economy will remain dynamic and provide a continuous stream of innovations, new ideas, experiments, and pioneering efforts.

Innovation

Individuals and small business units provide the major source of new ideas and inventions. Of the patents issued by the U.S. Patent Office in the past twenty-five years, over one-third were issued to individuals and one-fourth to small business firms (partnerships and closely held corporate ventures). Small owner-managed business enterprises are more innovative than are large publicly held corporate enterprises because ingenious people working on new ideas that relate to their own profit are motivated in a more direct way.

In addition, the larger business concentrates on products that have a steady or predictable demand, leaving to the small operator the slower sellers and more risky items. The small business pioneering a new idea naturally does not have a product or service of proven demand. And the difficulty of building adequate sales for something new is so great, in terms of the time and expense required, that frequently several pioneers go bankrupt in the process before one finally succeeds. Only when the small independent enterprise has developed a proven market for the innovation does a larger business become interested in it in a supportive (and often competitive) way.

The small, independent enterpriser will always be important in pioneering some innovation and proving its worth on a small scale until the growth stage, if there is to be one, is reached. At this point the small enterprise may adopt large-scale techniques if the necessary capital can be secured, or sell out to a larger firm better able to finance the larger operation.

THE FRANCHISE BOOM

Even the most casual observer of business today cannot help but be aware of the myriad of fast-food service drive-ins lining the nation's highways and the arterial streets of our urban areas; "Franchise Row"—or the "Franchise Strip"—is a common sight in many of our larger cities and towns. The franchising of small businesses today is "big business."

Franchising is a system for selectively distributing goods or services through outlets owned by the franchisee. Basically, a **franchise** is a patent or trademark license, entitling the holder to market particular products or services under a brand name or trademark according to prearranged terms and conditions.

The brand identification is an important aspect of this form of distribution. It consists of standardization throughout the system. The various outlets in the system are similar as to class of trade, merchandise carried or services rendered, and other factors that have a bearing on joint merchandising and management through common policies. Also, all of the outlets in a franchise system are identified as members of the system. They operate under a common name and/or insignia, and the establishments often have a distinctive appearance common to all members of the system. This standardization is ensured and controlled by the terms of the franchise contract.

Essentially, therefore, a franchise system is a "voluntary" chain, that is, a chain of individually owned businesses. Franchising, in fact, has been the salvation of many independent wholesale and retail merchants in the face of increasing competition from corporate chains and discount operations. By joining a **jobber**-sponsored voluntary chain, for example, an independent retailer can get all the benefits that are available to a corporate chain store: central buying as well as assistance in merchandising, promotion, and management.

There's nothing new about franchising, of course. The automobile, gasoline, and soft-drink industries have been doing it for years; for them it is old hat. The automobile industry, for example, started to franchise dealers in the early 1900s. In the 1920s and 1930s, independent wholesalers of groceries, hardware, automobile accessories, and other products adopted the franchising concept and began to build vast networks of voluntary chains.

Though there is nothing new about the franchising concept, there is a new scope to this method of distribution. In recent years, franchising has spread to businesses as disparate as art galleries, nursing homes, automobile transmission repair shops, muffler shops, gift stores, travel agencies, supper clubs, rental services, part-time secretarial help, computer dating services, diet services, modeling schools, dental technician schools, management consulting, real estate brokerage, and data-processing services. The most rapid growth has been in quick-service food drive-ins dispensing such culinary delights as hamburgers, beefburgers, fried chicken, pizzas, doughnuts, and hot dogs.

The growth of the franchising concept in recent years is nothing short of phenomenal. Franchise sales today account for approximately 15 percent of **gross national product** and over 30 percent of total retail sales.

FROM SMALL BEGINNINGS ...

The economic development of the United States has resulted largely from the efforts of small enterprisers. Most of the large companies of today, including the firms listed in *Fortune*'s list of the 500 largest industrial corporations, as well as our largest and best-known department stores, chain stores, and mail-order houses, were started by **entrepreneurs** with very limited capital: Swift, a local butcher; Ford, a mechanic who built his first cars in a blacksmith shop; Chrysler, a mechanic in a railroad roundhouse who became an automotive engineer; Carnegie, the steel magnate, who saved from his wages as a telegrapher and railroad employee; Gilman, founder of the Great Atlantic & Pacific Tea Company, who started selling tea as a sideline in his hide and leather store; Donald Douglas, who launched his aircraft business in a rented room behind the local barbershop with only $1,000 in cash. Among others, Sears started selling watches by mail in his spare time while a small-town station agent; Montgomery Ward started his business in one small room; Wanamaker began with savings from a small salaried job; Gimbel's started as a frontier trading post; and so on down the list.

Many small businesses today will be the large- and middle-sized businesses of tomorrow. "Mighty oaks from little acorns grow!"

Small opportunities are often the beginning of great enterprises.
—DEMOSTHENES

SUMMING UP

In the United States at the present time there are about six million businesses. By any standard of measurement, most of them can be described as small or even mini-businesses. They predominate in all types of industry and commerce, particularly in retailing and the service trades. An increasing proportion of them are franchised businesses.

Although they are being threatened in some areas (as by large chain stores and discount houses in retailing and the increasing concentration of power in manufacturing), small business enterprises have shown great vitality in others. As noted, they are as relatively important in the context of the total economy as they ever were;

only the form or texture of independent enterprise has changed with the times. Opportunity for those who are energetic and dynamic entrepreneurs is limited only by the limits they place on themselves. The history of American business is filled with examples of successes made from small beginnings.

Independent small businesses play an important role in the nation's economy. They provide the major source of new ideas and inventions. This combined with the competition they provide to each other and to big business accounts for much of America's remarkable economic growth. It is necessary to have a large number of small enterprises if true competition is to exist, if freedom of initiative and business enterprise is to be maintained, and if we are to continue our progress in extending more goods and services to an ever-increasing number of people; big business alone cannot provide these things.

KEY WORDS*

antitrust legislation	manufacturing enterprise
business firm	mass production
constant dollars	merchandisers
consumer goods	producers' goods
entrepreneur	retailer
franchise	service business
free enterprise	small business
gross national product	value added by manufacture
jobber	wholesaler

DISCUSSION QUESTIONS

1. Would you classify the American Motors Corporation as a "small" company? Why or why not?

2. What is meant by the *interdependence of all business?* Give some examples, other than those cited in the text.

3. In your opinion is small business more dependent on big business, or vice versa?

4. How do you account for the rapid growth of franchising in recent years?

* Defined in the Glossary beginning on p. 497. Key words appear in boldface in the text; italicized words used in defining a key word are themselves *key words* listed in this or in preceding and subsequent chapters and should also be consulted for a fuller understanding of the term.

County Business Patterns (source of Table 1-1) are reported for each of the states as well as for the U.S. as a whole. Using the same industry and employment-size classifications shown in Table 1-1:

1. Record on a sheet of paper the number of business establishments of each type and size in the state (or county) in which you live, as reported in the latest annual volume (a copy of this volume is available in your school or public library). Insofar as they can be identified, do not include establishments providing legal services, educational services, medical or other health services, or other skills not used primarily in business.

2. Adjust the establishment data to reflect the approximate number of businesses with *no* employees (estimated by the Social Security Administration at 9 percent); assume that the latter proportion is the same for *each* of the industries in your analysis.

3. Convert these numerical data to percentage distributions in the same manner as illustrated in Table 1-1.

4. What conclusions can you draw from your analysis?

External
or Environmental Problems

CHAPTER TWO *Small businesses have limitations and problems that differ from those of large concerns. Many of these limitations and problems accrue to certain enterprises just because of their small size. This chapter discusses the principal disadvantages of small business size. After reading it you should have an increased awareness of the uncontrollable external realities that form the environment within which the smaller business must operate.*

Although it is poor management (as we shall note in the following chapter) that is at the root of most of its operating difficulties, some of the problems of the smaller business are inherent in the small size of the enterprise rather than in the individual enterpriser. Among the more important of these external or environmental factors are those related to (1) capital shortages, (2) taxation and regulations, (3) product liability, and (4) patent and franchising abuses.

CAPITAL SHORTAGES

Small businesses, as we have noted, account for a major share of the country's gross national product and provide most of the new jobs created in the private sector of the economy. Thus, events or economic conditions (such as double-digit inflation and high bank-loan interest rates) that tend to restrict the flow of funds into small business will surely diminish the nation's rate of economic growth.

The smaller business has serious financial problems in at least three respects: (1) securing funds in small amounts at rates comparable with those paid by larger firms, (2) building and maintaining adequate financial reserves, and (3) securing long-term equity capital.

High Cost of Capital

Small-scale financing is always more expensive per dollar than large-scale financing. It costs just about as much for a banker or other lender to investigate and evaluate a loan application for $1,000 as one for $1,000,000. The former may actually cost more because the applicant for the large loan is often more helpful in providing significant information. So long as the failure rate is higher for small than for big business, the risk of financing and the resulting costs will be higher.

Effect of inflation.   Although the **cost of capital** is higher for the smaller firm in any case, the problem has been compounded in recent years by the rising rate of **inflation.** Inflation affects business **capital** in three major ways:

1. It increases borrowing needs since inventory and accounts receivable increase in value with inflation.

2. It causes interest rates to rise, thus making the increased borrowing needs more expensive.

3. It is usually accompanied by governmental reactions leading to tighter credit. **Tight money** is generally discriminatory to small firms in that they are not well-equipped to compete with larger firms for the diminishing supply of loanable funds.

Inflation, of course, is not selective. However, large corporations, which possess a high degree of **vertical integration,** will fare better in an inflationary period than small businesses, which usually are more specialized (less integrated). Since **federal monetary policy,** rather than **federal fiscal policy,** is normally considered the major weapon against inflation, small businesses are left even more vulnerable; they feel the effects of tight monetary policy more acutely.

Thus a major problem of small business is its inability to obtain adequate financing, either in an absolute sense or because the cost, in terms of interest rates, is often prohibitive. The higher cost of small business borrowing combined with the recent surge in all borrowing costs have put considerable pressure on overall small business profitability.

The two-tiered prime rate.   In an attempt to ease the high costs of small business borrowing, some one hundred banks, at the urging of the Small Business Administration, have initiated rate reduction plans for their small business borrowers. These plans are based on a two-tiered **prime rate,** one rate for large customers and a lower rate for small business borrowers.

Such plans, however, are not based on practical economics. In times of tight and expensive money, it is not feasible for banks to offer their limited funds to their less credit-worthy small business customers at a fraction above cost, while turning away their sounder and/or larger customers. For a two-tiered prime rate plan to be workable, financial incentives in the form of **tax credits** should be provided to banks making loans at the lower small business prime rate (the tax credit not exceeding the bank's potentially higher interest income at the higher prime rate).

Limited Financial Reserves

The effects of both the **business cycle** and our tax system lay additional burdens on smaller businesses, making it difficult for them to build and maintain adequate financial reserves. Heavy taxes on personal incomes in the lower brackets affect the typical small business, which is usually a proprietorship or partnership, although they have no serious impact on larger corporate units. Also, whenever the tax system imposes heavy rates on low-business-profit brackets, the effects are more serious for small than for large business units.

The effects of the business cycle, especially when on the downswing, weigh more heavily on the capital structure of small than of large businesses. However, small business has some compensating advantages, in particular, greater flexibility and relatively lower fixed overhead expenses. Also, the very nature of the recession period of the business cycle—a period of contracting overexpanded business facilities at current prices—may make this pressure on many small businesses desirable. Being more flexible than their large competitors, they may be able to reduce costs and prices to justify continuing operations. If this is not possible, and the ability to stay in business depends on using accumulated capital, small business may actually take a lesser loss by retiring early in the **recession** period of a prolonged business **depression.** In some cases it may even be possible to make a second start later at bargain prices. This resembles the procedure of going through a reorganization of the capital structure, as big firms sometimes do.

The small business has special needs and problems that differ from those of big business when economic activity is changing, either for better or for worse. The fact that limited capital makes it harder for the small owners to withstand a decline in business activity is not always an unmixed evil; but it also restricts their ability to expand rapidly to capitalize fully on opportunities resulting from an upswing in the business cycle.

Limited Sources of Equity Capital

Small firms also tend to have a chronic shortage of **equity capital.** A lender or investor insists on a greater degree of control of the enterprise when financing a small business. This often hampers the management of the small firm and keeps many independents who are unwilling to share control from obtaining the financing they need. When accompanied by high taxes, it becomes a serious matter for the small owner. This problem is more fully discussed in the following section.

TAXATION AND REGULATIONS

Because of the firm's greater reliance on the resources of the entrepreneur and those of the entrepreneur's family and friends as a source of capital,[1] taxation has a greater impact on the small firm than it does on the larger business. High personal income taxes, for example, make it difficult for prospective or incumbent small business owners to acquire initial capital or funds for expansion. Similarly, friends and relatives and other potential private investors are unwilling to furnish funds on an "all risk and no gain" basis—taking all the risk of financing a new or expanding small enterprise but paying most of any tangible gains to the government in taxes. For example, at current tax rates, a 10 percent return on $25,000 invested by a single person would leave after federal taxes only 4½ percent for the individual with a $50,000 income, or only 6 percent with a $25,000 income. In addition, there are in many cases state income taxes to pay.

Lack of Progressivity in Corporate Tax Structure

Even small corporations have heavy tax burdens to contend with. Because corporations are taxed at only slightly **progressive income tax** rates on both the federal and state levels, small businesses are placed at a disadvantage vis-à-vis larger businesses, which are able to take advantage of economies of scale but which are taxed at the same or nearly the same rate. In addition, most small businesses cannot avail themselves of the tax credits and benefits open to larger and more well-heeled firms. Thus in 1979 the largest corporations in the nation paid only an average of 22 percent of their income in taxes, whereas the average effective tax rate on smaller corporations (those below five hundred employees) was almost 40 percent.

Of the forty-five states and the District of Columbia that impose taxes on corporate income, thirty-one have tax structures that are completely nonprogressive—that is, a flat percentage rate is charged, regardless of income level. Of those states which do employ a progressive rate structure, the difference in rates between the lowest and highest brackets is minimal. From the standpoint of small business, this is perhaps the single most onerous element of state tax policy.

Limited Earnings Retention

As noted in the preceding section ("Capital Shortages"), income taxes can be so heavy that the typical small business may find it difficult to retain sufficient profits to set up reserves against bad years, let alone to provide for growth and expansion. This situation is accentuated by the fact that the in-

---

[1] Sources of capital are discussed in Chapter 17, pp. 265–73.

come of the average small business is erratic—up one year, down another—so that it may have to pay at a high rate one year but at a much lower rate the next year.

Important relief would be afforded many small businesses if the Internal Revenue Act were to be amended to permit business firms (like individual tax-payers) to average their net incomes over a period of time, say, five years. In this way, a small firm would not lose the benefit of a lower tax in the poor years and could carry any unused portion forward or backward to apply against the good years.

Inflation-Invoked Changes in Tax Brackets

Income taxes become even more burdensome in times of inflation. Due to inflationary pressures, when a fixed-rate structure is employed, a business may be forced into a higher tax bracket even though there is no change in the real economic position of the business. Inflation-invoked changes in tax brackets are particularly troublesome for small businesses with relatively smaller profit margins.[2]

Serving as a Government Tax Collector

In addition to the taxes levied directly against the firm (if incorporated) or against the entrepreneur (if a proprietor, partner, or shareholder), the business firm is obligated by law to collect sales taxes from customers; and income and social security taxes from employees. The burden of serving as an unpaid tax-collecting agent for the government is greater on the small firm than on the large firm. In a recent study it was found that the time required to compute withholding for federal income and **FICA taxes,** to post employee records and general ledger accounts, to prepare W-2 and W-3 forms, and to prepare quarterly and annual reports ranged from 1.5 to 11.2 hours per year for each employee, the firms with the largest number of employees tending to require the least amount of time per employee.

Taxes as an Impetus to the Merger Movement

The smaller business is also handicapped by existing **inheritance** and **gift tax** laws. Such taxes, combined with high personal income taxes, have given considerable impetus to the **merger** movement. Many small business owners sell out to larger firms in anticipation of death taxes. They have found in mergers an opportunity not only to increase the liquidity of their estates, but also to realize income, in the form of **capital gains,** that they had reinvested in their

---

[2] The Economic Recovery Tax Act of 1981 provides that beginning in 1985 personal income tax brackets will be indexed to the consumer price index; corporate tax brackets, however, will not be indexed.

businesses over the years. Records of the Federal Trade Commission indicate that many of these small firms were earning rates of return in excess of 25 percent on net worth at the time of their merger with large competitors; thus the effect of the merger movement is often to reduce competition by reducing the number of successful enterprises.

There is one difference between a tax collector and a taxidermist: the taxidermist leaves the hide.

—MORTIMER CAPLAN,
Director, Internal Revenue Service,
Time, Feb. 1, 1963

Government Regulation and Paperwork

Added to the problem of overtaxation are those of greatly increased government regulation—both direct regulations imposed on business and the indirect restrictions that come from laws passed to assist labor and others. Paperwork required by the Department of Labor, OSHA, the Equal Opportunity Commission, Environmental Protection Agency, and a host of other bureau-

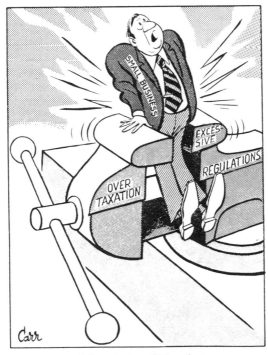

Courtesy of *NAM Reports,* National Association of Manufacturers.

cratic agencies (in addition to the Internal Revenue Service) is costly and time-consuming for the small business operator.

Regulation of business is one of the more visible and conflict-generating forms of government. It crushes the enterprising spirit on which small businesses are founded. It discourages initiative, overburdens the small company with paperwork, and does not leave the owner/manager enough time and productive energy to manage his or her business properly.

OSHA in particular is regarded by many small business operators as a symbol of unresponsiveness on the part of government toward the needs and aspirations of the small business community. Many of OSHA's regulations are applicable only to large firms in hazardous industries. Over 90 percent of businesses with twenty or fewer employees, for example, have *no* accidents or injuries in a given year, and most of the remaining 10 percent have very few. Legislative initiatives are currently underway to stem the flow of environmental restraints and other regulations applied to all firms regardless of size or financial capacity to comply.

The owner/managers of small businesses also feel frustrated by the large amount of duplication that occurs in their interactions with the federal bureaucracy; the same information is often requested or required by as many as five or six different agencies, and the cost of government red tape and paperwork has become increasingly burdensome to them. Their frustration is so great that most of them would just as soon see all data collection centered in one place, despite recent public focus on privacy issues.

Impact of Minimum-Wage Legislation

Federal **minimum-wage** legislation also imposes a particular hardship on smaller businesses, which rely more heavily on teenage and student employment. Since most small firms are labor-intensive, minimum-wage increases have a disproportionately heavy impact on them.

Minimum-wage legislation is also job destructive. In July 1982, for example, when the national unemployment rate for the labor force as a whole was 9.8 percent, the Department of Labor reported that the rate of unemployment among teenage workers was 23 percent! Thus it is the unskilled teenage workers, and the smaller businesses that would normally hire them as apprentices or trainees, who are most seriously affected when statutory hourly minimum-wage rates are increased.

PRODUCT LIABILITY

A basic principle in determining the kind and amount of insurance that a business owner should carry is that the probability that a loss may occur is less important than the possible size of the loss.[3] On the basis of this principle it

[3] Insurance and risk management are discussed in Chapter 23.

would appear that **product liability** is potentially the greatest risk that manu-facturers and the distributors of their products (who, by law, are equally liable) face. The maximum loss that can occur to business property is obviously lim-ited to the value of that property, but in the case of liability for personal in-juries resulting from the use (or even the misuse) of the products that a business firm makes or sells, there is no fixed loss limit.

From the businessperson's point of view, costs associated with liability for the manufacture and sale of defective products have skyrocketed. Insurance premiums, when insurance is even available (which it often is not), have grown disproportionately to the rate of claims paid because of the uncertainty which insurance companies feel. New theories of recovery introduced by courts and record awards by juries make the number of claims difficult for insurers to predict; to be safe, they overcharge. Small businesses, lacking the market dom-inance to simply pass these costs along to consumers, find themselves squeezed by rising insurance costs.

More than half a century ago the same sorts of problems were present in the workplace as are present today in the field of product liability. Thus some authorities have proposed the enactment of a "Consumer Compensation Law," paralleling the workers' compensation system in force in most states today. Such an act would avoid the uncertainties of the "tort lottery." Injured consumers would be given swift, certain recoveries at standardized, limited rates—the consumer gaining this certainty at the cost of the occasional wind-fall recovery. The manufacturer, on the other hand, would gain predictability and limitation of losses, but would lose the possibility of "beating the rap" in court.

PATENT ABUSES

The small manufacturer also faces problems in introducing new ideas once they are developed in the laboratory. Some of these obstacles can be removed only by a simplified and modernized **patent** system. When an early patent is granted before later related discoveries are made, or when patents on minor changes in the original basic patent idea are granted almost continuously, the desire to develop new ideas diminishes. The inadequacy of our present patent system is a serious problem for small manufacturers.

It is noteworthy that an increasing number of patents have been assigned to big business by outsiders and employees in recent decades. The small busi-ness owner, for one, often lacks the funds needed to carry a patent through to successful production and marketing; it is so much easier to sell to the big com-pany for a few thousand dollars cash and a royalty on production. And employ-ees often have no choice but to assign their patents, since this has become part of many employment contracts.

The holder of a patent also has difficulty in preventing infringement of the patent rights, primarily because of the high cost of litigation. The casualty rate among patents submitted for court adjudication is very high. It was recently reported that over a thirty-month period, 72 percent of all patent suits were found invalid. The high cost of litigation and the difficulty of enforcing patent rights prompted Lewis Evans, a member of the board of trustees of the National Small Business Association, to remark that "a patent today is only worth the money that one is willing or able to put behind it."

FRANCHISING ABUSES

Not all franchising arrangements produce happy results. Some franchised businesses have suffered severe financial loss, and others have not nearly achieved the profit potential that the **franchise** promoters had led them to expect. Several factors account for the lack of success of some franchises.

One of the most apparent reasons for the unhappy results of some franchise operations is that in some localities there are more fast-food emporiums, motels, and other kinds of business than the market can absorb. As one cynic has asked, "Just how many hamburgers, pizzas, and fried chickens can the average person be expected to consume?" Thus the rapid growth of franchising has led to an oversaturated market in some industries, with the result that a number of franchisors have recently filed petitions for bankruptcy.

Uncontrolled competition in the franchising business is obviously an important cause of this condition, but it is also the result of overexpansion on the part of individual franchisors, some of whom may be more interested in the sale of franchise packaging or equipment than in the profits of their franchise holders.

Some promoters also fail to carefully screen or train their franchisees to make sure that they are capable of operating a business. The "training programs" promised by some franchisors often turn out to be nothing more than a sheaf of "canned" reading material. And in some cases prospective franchise buyers are not given sufficient information, financial and otherwise, on which to base a decision to buy or not to buy.

A particularly questionable practice employed by some franchisors is the **multilevel distributorship** or "pyramid sales" technique. Like a chain letter, franchises are sold to franchisees who may, in turn, receive commissions for selling franchises to others. The promoter's sales of franchises is thus unlimited, potentially continuing endlessly until franchisees end up trying to sell to each other.

In cases where local franchised outlets are demonstrably successful the franchise is sometimes terminated or not renewed, so that the parent company may take over the operation. The basic concept of franchising (entailing the use of *franchisees'* capital) enables the parent company to grow rapidly during the early years of its existence.[4] But at a certain point the franchising company is likely to go public and thus have increased access to outside sources of capi-

---

[4] Franchising as a method of distribution is discussed in detail in Chapter 15, pp. 238–39.

tal. Historically, with additional capital franchisors frequently try to buy back their own outlets. One problem for the franchisee arises when the parent company seeks to buy back a franchise at the lowest price. Another problem is that certain inconsequential actions, under the terms of the franchise agreement, may result in a forfeiture of the franchise—one reason for the franchisor's close scrutiny or monitoring of outlet operations. Sometimes the renewal of a franchise is refused on the grounds of supposed poor performance.

In 1971, after taking a long, hard look at these and other franchising abuses, Congress passed the Franchise Fair Practices Act. A number of states have also enacted legislation to curb franchising abuses.

But franchisees do not rely solely on legislation to protect themselves from franchising abuses, or on litigation to remedy these abuses. In the past few years an increasing number of them in particular companies or industries have organized themselves into bargaining units for the collective renegotiation of contract terms and airing of grievances. The resultant National Association of Franchised Businessmen is a bargaining and lobbying organization representing franchise holders in all industries across the country.

The bulk of the franchising companies, however, are ethical businesses who are equally concerned about undesirable franchising practices. To police the industry, a number of leading franchisors formed the International Franchise Association.

CONCERN FOR THE WELFARE OF SMALL BUSINESS

It is difficult to be dispassionate and objective about small business, whether considering it as a contributing and important segment of the economy or as an expression of free enterprise and "The American Way of Life." Because there are strong human considerations involved, various individuals and groups, either genuinely or ostensibly interested, often exhibit great concern. These include (1) the small business owners themselves; (2) their suppliers, who depend on them for existence; (3) various trade associations; (4) economists and other students of "the problems"; and (5) politicians. All are properly concerned with the welfare of small business, its future progress, and often its reciprocal support, be it economic or political. This concern manifests itself in various studies of small business's problems, in philosophic and patriotic essays, and in aid programs at all governmental levels.

ORGANIZED VOICES FOR SMALL BUSINESS

Labor unions and big business have for years been potent lobbying forces in the legislative halls of Washington and various state capitals. But until fairly recently the small business community has had no organized voice to promote and protect *its* interests.

Small business owners have been notoriously hard to organize, perhaps because of their strong individualism. Prior to the 1930s, various attempts to get them together failed. It was not until 1937 that the first successfully organized "voice" for small business—the National Small Businesss Association—came into being, followed six years later by the organization of the larger National Federation of Independent Business. Although these groups differ in organization and mode of operation, they have basically the same purposes or objectives: to inform their members of what is going on in Washington and to carry the message of the small business community back to the legislative policymakers.

SUMMING UP

The owner/manager of a small business is in trouble today—plagued by capital shortages, double-digit inflation and interest rates, excessive taxation, unreasonably high product liability insurance premiums, and the ever-increasing burden of government regulations and paperwork.

Among other external or environmental conditions with which small businesses must cope, though perhaps having a somewhat lesser impact on them than those listed above, are franchising and patent abuses and artificially high minimum-wage requirements.

A growing recognition of the importance of small business to the nation's economy and a recognition of the problems that small business owners face is bringing increasing support for them from government agencies, educational institutions, and others.

KEY WORDS

business cycle	merger
capital	minimum wage
capital gains	monetary policy (federal)
cost of capital	multilevel distributorship
depression	patent
equity capital	prime rate
F.I.C.A. taxes	product liability
fiscal policy (federal)	progressive income tax
franchise	recession
gift tax	tax credit
inflation	tight money
inheritance tax	vertical integration

1. One advantage of a study of *small* business is that the recognition of its special problems stimulates effort to solve them. Some of these have been noted in this chapter. What other solutions can you suggest? Discuss fully.

2. Since its inception, the Small Business Administration has guaranteed bank loans to small businesses unable to obtain bank financing otherwise, up to 90 percent of the loan. Do you believe that this is a desirable policy of government? Why or why not?

CASE IN
POINT

The Argent Specialties Company has long made and sold "Shine Again" polish for silver and certain other metals. Their product is good, well-accepted by homemakers and the trade. They sell it through hardware and other wholesalers to consumers, and through industrial supply houses to silver repair shops.

Recently a large manufacturer of miscellaneous household products introduced "Shine On," describing it as a new development and its performance as "sensational." Much of the wording of its advertising and labeling carries phrases that are very similar to Shine Again's. One sentence says: "Your silver will not only shine again, it will shine more and longer because of this, our newest product, and the patented applicator that is included with every bottle."

On investigation the new product is found to be very similar to Shine Again—a different color and consistency, but basically the same chemical composition and polishing performance. The "patented applicator" is not a new idea, only a standard brush-fabric combination with an attractive handle and plastic case.

Argent is concerned with the deceptive nature of the name and the competing company's claims. What legal recourse does Argent have? What are the major problems faced by small innovative firms relative to patents and product development? Can you suggest solutions to these problems?

Success
and Failure Factors

CHAPTER THREE *Business difficulties, of course, may be caused by the poor quality of management (that is, by internal factors) as well as by factors external to the firm. After reading this chapter you should be better informed and thus better able to answer the question of why a business "takes" or fails to take, why some businesses succeed and others "go by the board."*

Small businesses rarely fail for any of the reasons discussed in the preceding chapter. Making a fetish of small business, as such, serves no useful purpose. Most business is small business and most of it likely is here to stay. The poorly-operated will fail, the well-managed will succeed. There will always be elephants and lions and tigers in the economic jungle, yet through the years the balance of nature has been preserved somehow. The individual business, if its management is knowledgeable of its environment, alert, resourceful, and flexible, can adjust to the constant changes in our dynamic economy and survive.

CAUSES OF BUSINESS FAILURE

Business is a hard competitive struggle. In 1980, for example, forty-two out of every ten-thousand firms listed in the Dun & Bradstreet Reference Book closed their doors.[1] And this figure included only those business closures that resulted in loss to creditors following such actions as assignment of **bankruptcy,** foreclosure or attachment, and court-approved debt settlements initiated by the debtor. For every such business there are many others in which losses are withstood quietly by the firms' owners, or (if profits are earned) where the profit margins are inadequate.

The mortality rate among the newer, smaller enterprises is high, particularly during the first year of operation; but the odds for survival improve as the firm grows older. In retailing, one out of three new stores does not survive the first year and two out of three close their doors within six years. In wholesaling and manufacturing, one out of five concerns discontinues in the first year and two out of three close within nine years.

[1] *The Business Failure Record Through 1980* (New York: Dun & Bradstreet, 1981).

Why do these businesses die? In the opinion of the **creditors** and others who had dealt with the demised firms, ineffective **management** was cited as the underlying cause in 98 percent of the business fatalities recorded by Dun & Bradstreet in 1980. It was their opinion that more than 45 percent of these businesses should never have been started in the first place because of the incompetence of the owners. In the remaining instances, poor management was attributed to the owners' lack of experience in the business; lack of management experience or "know-how"; or unbalanced management training or experience—that is, knowledge or experience not well-rounded in sales, finance, and production.

In any discussion of the causes of **business failure,** one should distinguish between the owner's explanation and that of outside agencies, and between the apparent and the actual (underlying) causes. What may be described by the person who fails as "excessive competition" might instead be ineffectual sales effort. What may have been called "bad debts" may in reality have been careless extension of credit. And "inadequate capital" could mean anything from too expensive fixtures to too many relatives on the payroll or spending inventory capital for a Christmas trip to Florida.

The following table, prepared by the author from a study of 570 businesses that became bankrupt, summarizes the causes or occasions of failure as expressed by the owners of the bankrupt businesses and as expressed by the creditors of these businesses:

	PERCENTAGE OF ENTERPRISES AFFECTED	
CAUSE OR OCCASION OF FAILURE	OWNERS' OPINION	CREDITORS' OPINION
Business depression	68	29
Inefficient management	28	59
Insufficient capital	48	33
Bad-debt losses	30	18
Competition	40	9
Decline in value of assets	32	6
Poor business location	15	3
Excessive interest charged on borrowed money	11	2
Unfavorable changes in trading area	11	2

Unsuccessful business owners do not see themselves in the same way that others do, and they rarely attribute their failure to personal defects. The basic difficulty in small business is bad management, and few business owners will admit that they are bad managers. They generally attribute their failure to other reasons, such as poor location, excessive competition, difficulties relating to receivables and inventory, and, for whatever reason, inadequate sales.

Obviously failure means a situation where available capital is insufficient to pay all the obligations of a business. No matter how large or how small ini-

tial capital may have been, incompetent management has not only exhausted it but incurred debts beyond ability to pay. To the failing entrepreneurs the most obvious reason is lack of capital, regardless of how inefficiently they have managed what capital they had.

It is poor management, as we have stressed, that is at the root of most of the operating problems of small business. Poor management in the failed or failing firm is evidenced by conditions such as:

Inventory Imbalance

Many business failures are the result of poor judgment in buying. Some small business operators are tempted to overstock a particular item because someone offered them a good deal. Others have made quantity purchases that they could not sell or use within a reasonable period. They may not have realized it because they didn't actually see the cash going out, but it was costing them money just to hold such slow-moving items in stock.

Overextension of Credit

Business is dependent on a constant rotation or turnover of capital. If a business is to pay its own bills regularly, it must in turn receive prompt payment for the goods it sells or the services it renders. Some small businesses get into hot water because they extended unwarranted credit in their eagerness to make sales.

Excessive Overhead and Operating Costs

Some small businesses tie up too much money in fixed assets (buildings and equipment); others lack adequate expense controls and operational expenses become top-heavy.

Cash Flow Difficulties

Some of the firms in Dun & Bradstreet's 1980 file suffered from "hardening of the business arteries." Their financial circulatory system, so to speak, slowed down to a dribble or came to a complete halt as a result of one or more of the three previous conditions. In cases where a firm's need for cash is greater than its cash inflow, the firm is not able to pay its bills when they become due and therefore is technically **insolvent,** even though the value of its assets may exceed its liabilities.

Competitive Weakness

Among the contributory causes of business failure is competitive weakness, which manifests itself in a variety of ways. One is the inability of the business to overcome the lower costs of its more efficient competitors. Another is poor location, which all too often in the small business is determined to a large degree by personal, or nonbusiness, considerations; this sometimes results in the owner's locating the business originally in and subsequently refusing to move from an area from which a substantial portion of the market has departed.

Competitive weakness is also the result of the failure of some small business operators to understand the changing world about them. Environmental conditions change so rapidly that, unless they keep abreast of developments, even a good start is lost. Business management calls for constant reorientation. Those who own and operate their own businesses or who manage someone else's small business must recognize the changing economy, the new social structure, and the new forms of competition, and they must be prepared to respond accordingly. Otherwise, they will lose out in the competitive struggle.

> *Business is like a man rowing a boat upstream. He has no choice; he must go ahead or he will go back.*
>
> —Lewis E. Pierson

FACTORS IN SUCCESSFUL SMALL BUSINESS MANAGEMENT

Up to this point we have emphasized the reasons why some small enterprises fail. However, to know why some businesses fail is to know why others succeed. Business success and business failure are two sides of the same coin.

Courtesy of Small Business Administration.

In essence, a small business succeeds in direct proportion to its highly motivated owner's possession of certain essential talents of modern business operation. These include (1) alertness to change, (2) ability to adjust or to create change oneself, (3) ability to attract and hold competent workers, (4) 180° vision with respect to operating details, and (5) a knowledge of the market—one's customers and their needs.

"The purpose of the economy is to satisfy the wants of people." This phrase or its equivalent is near the opening of most economics textbooks. It says that every business function, every business institution, every person engaged in performing these functions in or for a business institution is seeking to satisfy human wants and needs. To the extent that consumer wants and needs are satisfied effectively, economically, and therefore profitably, these businesses are successful and remain in existence. If any one of them is deficient in this regard, it soon ceases as an economic institution. Such are the realities of public preferences and of competition.

That there is need for knowledge of the market and the customer is obvious. Planning in business is an absolute *must,* if "having the right goods at the right place at the right time and price" is the accepted goal of a business. Controls are indispensable; these include financial controls as well as good records. The need for adequate capital, a good location, a needed product or service is also obvious. In general, successful management of a small business requires:

1. Careful study of markets
2. Wise planning of activities
3. Vigilant control of investment, merchandise, personnel, equipment, and buildings to ensure maximum use for production

4. Adequate expense records
5. Thoughtful selection of goods
6. Strategic location with particular reference to the market, but also bearing in mind resources and transportation of goods
7. Sound policies, unalterable in general objective, but flexible and adjustable to meet obvious business expediencies
8. Strong working relationships with suppliers
9. Judiciously controlled credit
10. Customer selection and market concentration
11. Skillfully selected personnel
12. A well-planned sales promotion program

The above list represents a very general set of modern operating rules. If the operating problems and discussion of the reasons for business failure considered in the preceding section of this chapter are reviewed, it will be observed that they stem from violations of these basic guidelines.

All of these elements are present in the successful business, and always in proper *balance*. If the small business owner/manager will liken his or her firm to a motorcar, the significance of this balance can be seen more clearly. A smooth-running automobile, one that gives its driver comfortable, dependable, and economical performance mile after mile, is a well-balanced mechanism. The engine has just the right compression ratio and spark timing. The chassis has just the right strength and resiliency. The body is the right size. Wheels and tires are engineered to coordinate with engine power and speed and with road conditions.

Most poorly designed, unsatisfactory cars lack this balance, this coordination of mechanical elements and effort. An oversized engine or undersized tires will immediately cause trouble, as will insufficient battery power or a malfunctioning distributor. These facts are familiar to all of us. An automobile fails because its engineers did not provide for balanced elements and effort.

This homely parallel seeks to reemphasize the need for balanced facilities and effort in the operation of a business. Offerings to the community, to the market, must be in proportion to its needs. The money supply must be adequate to carry it safely over the early rough roads. The advertising appropriation must be one that will give the most "mileage," one where the results will justify the cost. The payroll must be paid to people who are achieving results, who are not a drag on the firm's progress. So on and on, the parallels are seemingly endless.

Also important in the effective management of a business are the personal factors. The ability to direct, to lead, even to inspire others, is obviously a human attribute, as is the ability to accept and execute assignments of responsibility from another. The ability to win and maintain confidence—as reflected in securing financial backing, credit extensions, loyal employees—is a personal characteristic of vital importance in business. Remember also that the business is a projection of management's personality. In general, individuals have what it takes or they do not, and having "it," they do a good job willfully or they fail. These points cannot be overstressed, for business success is a philosophy, a point of view, an approach that must permeate the entrepreneur's mind thoroughly if he or she is to have mastery of the enterprise.

Success is good management in action.
—William E. Holler

SUMMING UP

According to the Dun & Bradstreet Failure Index, tens of thousands of businesses "go by the board" each year. Most of these are small businesses; in fact, the smaller the business, the greater the failure rate.

Most experts agree, however, that it is because of their weakness as businesses, rather than their small size, that these undertakings fail.
In the highly competitive arena in which all businesses contend, poor judgment, careless handling of detail, or other *incompetencies in management* will very likely bring failure. The trouble usually lies in the owner/manager's limited preparation, lack of administrative experience, and failure to apply the easily understandable principles and methods of business operation which have always characterized the successful firm.

Although many reasons are cited by them for business failures, these reasons usually represent the *occasions* for the failure rather than the underlying *cause(s)*. Had the owners managed their businesses more efficiently, they would have anticipated and controlled them. Most businesses fail for a very simple, readily understandable reason: poor management. Improving the level of competency in the management of a new or small business is what the remainder of this book is all about.

KEY WORDS

bankruptcy
business failure
creditor

insolvent
management

1.   What significance do you place on the fact that most businesses that fail are *small* businesses? Is this cause for alarm? What, if anything, can or should be done to correct this situation?

2.   Which is basically a more important cause of the demise of small firms: shortage of capital or lack of managerial ability? Explain.

3.   Creditors and bankers often report that some business closures result from neglect, fraud, and disaster (such as a fire, or a personal injury or death for which the firm was held legally responsible). Might these also be considered "management" failures? Discuss fully.

EXERCISES AND
PROBLEMS

1.   Consult the latest issue of the Dun & Bradstreet *Business Failure Record* (available in your school or public library) and answer each of the following questions:

a. How might you explain the long-term fluctuations in the Dun & Brad street Failure Index?

b. Of the businesses that failed, what proportion of them had been in business three years or less? Four to five years? Six to ten years? Over ten years? What conclusions can you draw from this information?

c. In the opinion of the creditors of these firms and of other outside agencies, what percentage of these business fatalities was attributed to lack of experience in the business? Lack of management experience or "know-how"? Unbalanced management training or experience? Incompetency?

2.   Think of a business in your community that failed during the past year. Why, in your opinion and that of nearby business owners, did this business fail? (Identify the firm by name and location.)

CASE IN
POINT

> Ben and Marjorie Batten for many years had owned and operated a small restaurant at a busy intersection in the motel district of a resort city. It had grown from a simple husband-and-wife operation to a place seating fifty or so, open from early morning

until late at night and employing six waitresses and a kitchen staff. Mrs. Batten had done most of the cooking, until her health failed and they retired, selling the restaurant to Nicola and Sam Ambrosio.

The Battens had catered to the tourist trade and to business people in a few nearby stores and offices. The Ambrosios, however, operated a more "plush" place in another part of the city. They felt that, with new homes and quality motels being built within a few blocks of the new location, a luxury restaurant–lounge type operation would succeed. Consequently, they changed the outside appearance and the decor and inside furnishings, installed an attractive bar, and announced more sophisticated offerings. From breakfast for tourists, luncheon for the local trade, and a generally inexpensive family dinner place for the neighborhood, it changed to "Ambrosio's West," with prices that the expected new clientele could afford.

Their change in business concept, however, proved unsuccessful. After considerable advertising of various sorts, the Ambrosios decided to go after the family breakfast trade. Then they offered "noon lunch specials," but without success. Later they tried "All the spaghetti you can eat for $2.79," but that was not very successful either. Finally at the end of only four months they closed the business. Their other restaurant remains successful.

Another restaurant operator, of limited experience, took the location over. He kept the Ambrosio's exterior, fixtures, and decor intact, but advertised family menus, endeavoring to emulate the original Batten's. After an auspicious start, two major problems arose. First, the tourist season declined for several months and he was not well-enough established to survive the decline. Another problem was pricing, which had to be high to pay the rent still due on Ambrosio's lease, tending to scare off the family trade. After a few months' struggle, the effort to be another Batten's failed.

Our last word is that another fancy new place, with "expense account" prices, is moving in nearby. But the former Batten's Breakfast Shop has been leased and is now being refurbished by On Long Lee, who will offer Mandarin cuisine.

Was this series of events caused by each individual's unwise decisions, or by basic business conditions; or was it simply a matter of bad luck? What advice might have helped each owner, or how might they have proceeded differently with better results?

Part Two

THE MANAGEMENT PROCESS IN THE SMALLER BUSINESS

In terms of the functions that must be performed, managing a small business is no different from managing a large one. However, these functions are performed in an environment (described in the preceding chapters) that creates different demands and provides different opportunities for the owner/manager of a small business. After reading the following four chapters you should have an increased awareness of these differences as well as a greater appreciation of the "art" of managing a small business enterprise.

Basic Management Functions

CHAPTER FOUR *As noted in Chapter 3, the success of any business depends in large measure on how effectively and efficiently it is managed. While businesses may differ in size and kind, the elements of sound business management are common to all. This chapter will familiarize you with these basic management functions.*

Successful business **management** may be described as the profitable use of those factors that are necessary to conduct a business successfully. The same money, materials, machinery and other equipment, and personnel will, when managed differently, yield entirely different results. The effective utilization of assets is necessary and evident in any successful effort. In athletics, for example, one coach will have a string of team victories while another, using the same players, may suffer only losses. In engineering or construction great differences can result from the use of the same steel, bricks, and mortar by different individuals. The same canvas and paints may become an artistic masterpiece or only trash, depending on the hand that holds the brush.

These homely examples suggest that managing a business or any other type of group enterprise is primarily an *art*—although the body of knowledge underlying this art is generally referred to as **management science.** Differences in results arise partly from differences in how the common body of management knowledge is applied to individual situations, for a **manager** is essentially a *decision-maker* exercising judgment. But, equally important, a manager is also a leader who must impress subordinates with the nature and importance of the decisions he or she has made and with the ways that the goals set for the enterprise can be fulfilled. The science of management (discussed in Chapters 8 through 23) can be learned by most people, but management skill or art is more easily developed in some people than in others.

In any case, to utilize human and other resources effectively, that is, to manage a business successfully, the activities of the enterprise must be carefully planned, organized and staffed, directed or supervised, and controlled. The most basic of these **management functions** is *planning.*

PLANNING

If you don't know where you're going, any road will get you there.
—ANCIENT CHINESE PROVERB

39

Planning is the manager's **decision-making** function, requiring the ability to select from alternative courses of action. It involves determining the firm's objectives and the methods (policies or strategies) that will be used to achieve them.

It also requires preparation of a schedule that anticipates when various goals will be met. Managers must be able to forecast the social and economic climate in which they will operate and how they will use the available resources to attain their goals under various conditions.

Policies

The formulation of **policies** is an essential element in planning. Policies are standing plans or guides to action. They direct the business and control its activities to keep them in line with established objectives. To be effective they must be definite and stable, yet flexible enough to be adjusted to meet fundamental changes.

The elimination of inconsistencies by a well-regulated set of policies results in less lost effort and less working at cross-purposes. Policies enable the small business owner to conserve his or her energies and resources by directing them consistently toward an established goal. This concentration increases the owner's effectiveness and chances for success by lessening dissipation or dilution of effort. Experience can be utilized to the greatest extent, because policies show what should not be done as well as what should be done to accomplish a particular purpose.

Many business policies are stated in writing, but some are not. Written policies are more definite and can be followed more easily, but unwritten policies in the small business may be equally effective. The most important requirement is that the policies be understood and followed by all members of the firm. Customers, competitors, and suppliers should be informed of all policies that affect their dealings with the company.

It is also important that policies be strictly adhered to in practice. Under no circumstances should even a single exception be made to a policy. If the policy is too strict, change it, but *never* make an exception so long as the policy is in force.

Policies are of three types: general, major and minor. A general policy relates to the business as a whole and expresses its overall purpose and aims. It defines what the business is to accomplish and is vital to its success. Illustrations of general policies that provided the basic idea for the business itself include Henry Ford's concern for "economical transportation," J. C. Penney's belief in the "The Golden Rule," and F. W. Woolworth's initial concentration on the sale of "merchandise that can be sold profitably for ten cents." General policies should be the result of much forethought and planning but may need to be changed somewhat with time.

Major policies also relate to the business as a whole, but they are subordinate to the company's general policy. They provide guiding principles for such important companywide activities or concerns as finance and expansion, personnel and labor relations, research and development, and public relations. Other major policies deal with answers to such questions as: Shall we simplify or diversify our product line? How should we distribute our products? What geographic markets or market segments shall we serve? Shall we enter foreign markets or not? Deciding on these and other major matters of policy is probably just as vital to the success of a business as deciding on its general policy.

Minor (or departmental) policies are those affecting the operations of a particular department. They relate to such questions as: What advertising media shall we use? What kinds of credit, if any, shall we extend? Shall we provide clerk service or stress self-service? Shall we offer trading stamps? Shall we make trade-in allowances? Shall we "recommend" resale prices for our products? Shall we open the store on Sundays? Minor policies are determined by departmental executives, but they must be consistent with the overall policies of the firm.

Policies should capitalize on whatever advantages a business may have, including any special skills or knowledge the owner or firm members possess. Limited resources, however, may at times require the rejection of an otherwise desirable policy. Financial resources, for instance, are usually a major limitation for small businesses. The abilities of available personnel must also be considered.

Most successful business owners have the faculty of making prompt decisions. Since well-formulated policies guide these decisions, in one sense the decisions were all made well in advance at the time of policy formulation. In most cases the business owner tests each problem as it arises in the light of his or her policies and decides accordingly. This is one of the important advantages of having a good set of policies.

Occasionally a proprietor is required to make a hasty decision of far-reaching importance without having time to investigate all the ramifications of the question or to deliberate on the possible effects of the decision. In such a case the established policies are the safest. No matter how attractive a proposition that violates these policies may seem, the proprietor should reject it without hesitation if he or she does not have time for an investigation at least as thorough as that involved in establishing the policies in the first place.

Innovation

If managers do not stop now and then and take the long view of their operation, it will soon cease to be a dynamic, progressive business. They must evaluate their concern and consider how well it is fulfilling its original purposes. They must also look at the industry, the community, and the country. Is the management keeping pace with a changing world? What are the things that could be done differently? What are the things that could be done better?

If managers just keep on doing what they have done in the past, their organizations will become static. In fact, if the field in which they operate is a competitive one they will soon lose their place and not even hold their own. Good managers view their business as a challenge to their creativity. They should develop new ideas, combine old ideas into new ones, adapt ideas from other fields, and stimulate others in their organization to think creatively as well.

Good planning recognizes the ever-changing environment in which a concern operates, and it considers how to adjust an organization to these changing conditions. Innovation goes beyond this. It is a deliberate, creative process which consists of always looking for a better way to perform every function in the organization.

ORGANIZING AND STAFFING

Organization is the first step in the implementation of business plans and goals. This management function involves classifying and dividing the work or activities of the business into manageable units. Like planning, the **organizing** function must be performed continuously because business and economic conditions are constantly changing.

The business organization does not really materialize, however, until people "man" it. **Staffing** is finding the right person for the right job and is the next logical step after organization. In organizing, the manager establishes positions and decides which duties and responsibilities belong to each. Staffing may become a part of organizing if an established concern already has employees to fill the positions available. Nevertheless, staffing is a separate and essential function of management which requires continual attention as new employees are needed to replace those who leave the organization and is required to serve a growing or changing organization. How to hire the best possible employee for each job, and how to keep him or her an efficient and loyal worker are discussed in Chapter 11.

Structuring the Operating Organization

Even a "Mom and Pop" business needs an administrative structure to operate the business. To promote efficiency and avoid misunderstandings, each person in the business should know who is in charge of what. The number of people needed to staff the business depends, of course, on the volume of work to be done.

Basically, **administrative organization** involves two steps: (1) a division, by analysis, of the business into the functions or activities that must be performed; and (2) assignment of each function to individuals.

Work analysis.   A simple approach to organization is called **work analysis,** a listing of *all* the activities that *must* be performed if the business is to achieve its planned objectives. These should then be grouped into related activities such as **production** (or buying), **distribution** or **marketing** (or selling), and **facilitating functions,** as shown below for a retailing business.

Production (of goods or services) or buying is the major utility created by most firms; distribution or selling provides the firm's source of income; and facilitating functions (such as financing) are performed only to make the two pri-

PRODUCTION FUNCTIONS	DISTRIBUTION FUNCTIONS	FACILITATING FUNCTIONS
Purchasing:	*Sales:*	*Accounting and Finance:*
Select vendors	Sell goods	Keep records of income and expenses
Negotiate prices and discounts	Receive payment for merchandise	Prepare tax records and returns
Receive and inspect merchandise	Keep sales records	Keep equipment depreciation records
Stock Control:	Replenish and arrange stock	Raise needed capital
Record additions to and withdrawals from stock	Keep sales area clean	Invest idle funds
Ensure orderliness and good condition of stock	*Advertising and Sales Promotion:*	Maintain cash flow
Report overstocks and stock shortages	Plan advertising effort	*Credits and Collections:*
	Set up displays	Authorize credit charges against accounts
	Observe competitors' efforts	Approve credit applications
	Keep records of sales efforts and promotions	Keep record of credit transactions
	Pricing:	Verify credit standings
	Calculate markups	Send billing and delinquent letters
	Authorize markdowns	
	Mark prices on goods	

mary functions possible or more efficient and profitable. Thus, in a public accounting firm, accounting work for clients is production, but the accountants' own record keeping is a facilitating function.

Performance of the production function involves the purchase (acquisition) of the ingredients used in producing a product or service (materials or merchandise, buildings and equipment, and personnel), as well as the utilization of these **factors of production.** Thus in retailing, the assembling (purchase) of merchandise for sale at a conveniently furnished place of business is a service produced by retailers for the ultimate consumers of these products; the wholesaler performs a similar service for the retailers themselves. Facilitating functions include all activities related to the firm's financing of its buying and selling activities.

Production, distribution, and **finance** are the characteristic functions of a business enterprise, and it is around these **business functions** that the bulk of this text is organized. The science of production management is discussed in Part III (Chapters 8–12); that of marketing management, in Part IV (Chapters 13–16); and that of financial management, in Part V (Chapters 17–23).

Before you organize you ought to analyze and see what the elements of the business are.
                                                                    —GERARD SWOPE

Assignment of work.   The next step in structuring the administrative organization is to assign functions and subfunctions to members of the firm according to their respective abilities, capacities, and interests, being careful not to overload the better-qualified individuals.[1] In the company with relatively few employees, each job will naturally involve more duties than would be expected of one individual in a larger concern. In a small business there is a limit to specialization. It may be impossible to have even one person whose sole **responsibility** pertains to, say, purchasing or stock control; often, these functions may need to be performed by the same person, perhaps in addition to other functions. In any case it is important for employees to know who is responsible for what, and to whom. Figure 4-1 illustrates how the functions listed above might be divided between, say, two partners (or two employees).

If the functional responsibilities represented by the six middle boxes in Figure 4-1 are of sufficient magnitude to occupy the full time of six employees, leaving the two partners free to concentrate on the all-important sales-floor activities, the solid lines in the illustration would indicate the **line authority** or scalar relationships in the organization. Thus, the employee responsible for purchasing would report to Partner A, the employee responsible for stock control would report to Partner B, and so on. If the firm were to grow larger and each of these six employees needed one or more workers to assist him or her, then these six employees would become managers in their respective

---

[1] Work assignments, or the placement of employees in specific jobs, is a *continuing* function and is discussed further in Chapter 11, pp. 155–56.

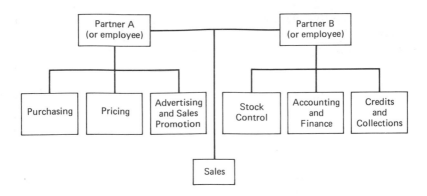

FIGURE 4-1

Division of Work and Authority in a Partnership (or a Firm with Two Employees)

departments. In a pure line organization such as that represented in Figure 4-1, each of the departmental managers or supervisors is responsible for hiring his or her own workers.

A point may be reached in the growth of an enterprise when the personnel function requires the undivided attention of one person or department. In such a case the personnel or employee relations specialist or department usually is given **staff authority** rather than line authority; that is, the personnel manager can only recommend or advise the line executives, the latter retaining final decision-making authority. Staff relationships are shown on an organization chart by broken lines, as illustrated in Figure 4-2.[2]

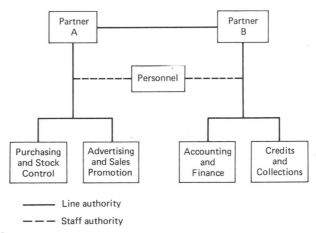

FIGURE 4-2

Line and Staff Relationships in a Small Organization

[2] This chart depicts four line departments (as opposed to the six shown in Figure 4-1), the pricing function being assumed by the two partners and purchasing and stock control being combined into a single department; all sales-floor functions are assumed by the partners.

45

Up to this point we have assumed a *functional* form of **departmentation.** This is probably the most common form in the small organization, particularly in the smaller of the small businesses. Businesses may also be organized by territories or product, as well as by function.

Delegating Authority

It would seem clear from the above discussion that personnel and organizational policies in the small business can hardly be considered separately. An organizational policy, for example, should cover the way in which responsibility and authority are distributed to different members of the firm. Decisions must be made as to the extent to which proprietors will delegate authority of various sorts to others and what authority they will retain for themselves. Proper **delegation of authority** is an important function of management.

An axiom of good organization is that responsibility and authority must always be equal. No person should ever be held responsible for a job unless he or she has the authority to do it, and no one should be given authority in a business unless he or she is held responsible for the results. Unless a policy is absolutely clear and definite on this point, it will lead to confusion and low morale.

A common weakness in many small businesses is failure to delegate sufficient authority to leave the owner free to concentrate on the more important management functions. A correct balance between delegating sufficient authority of the right type to relieve the owner of certain responsibilities, on the one hand, and maintaining sufficient control over the business, on the other hand, is the goal of good organization in the small business. In most cases the owner will want to reserve final authority over all major expenditures, the employment of persons for important positions, and final settlement of especially difficult customer or vendor complaints; the burden of final decision in all important matters relating to labor and public relations will also be the proprietor's.

Copyright 1974. Reprinted by permission of *Business Week* and Joseph Farris.

The man whose life is devoted to paperwork has lost the initiative.
He is dealing with things that are brought to his notice, having
ceased to notice anything for himself. He has been essentially
defeated by his job.

—C. NORTHCOTE PARKINSON

Division of authority and responsibility in the small business is especially important in the case of a partnership, since the acts of any partner with respect to outsiders are usually legally binding. Also, employees recognize each partner as an owner and will take orders from any partner. If no agreement has been reached among the partners as to their division of authority, conflicting orders often result.

After the jobs have been defined (in the new enterprise, in terms of actual assignments), it is necessary to prepare job *descriptions* and *specifications*. A **job description** is a list of job duties—a description of what the job incumbent does—and indicates the types of objects handled (such as machines, tools, equipment, materials, or merchandise); working conditions (if these vary widely from job to job); and the relationship of the job to other jobs in the organization. A **job specification,** on the other hand, indicates the skill, effort, aptitudes, experience, knowledge or education, and other personal requirements needed to perform the job satisfactorily.[3]

DIRECTING

Directing is the function of supervising and coordinating the activities of subordinate individuals and is the logical sequel to organization.

Coordinating

Coordination is an essential aspect of good organization. It is required because all members of an organization perform interrelated functions; therefore, what each one does in some way affects the others.

Perfect coordination is an ideal seldom, if ever, achieved. Management is always striving, however, through supervision and various control procedures, to secure the maximum coordination of all the activities of the business. Each important decision must be made in the light of its effects on all divisions of the business. Policies are important coordinating devices because they set common goals or objectives toward which various departments work. Budgets, schedules, and other types of control assist in securing coordination because they help management to plan and secure a balanced relationship between the

---

[3] The selection, training, and promotion or transfer of employees, as well as job placement, should be based largely on job descriptions and job specifications; the latter are also necessary in job evaluation. Management of the personnel function is discussed in Chapter 11.

operation of different divisions of the business. Coordination represents the culmination of effective management—nearly perfect balance between the elements of sales and production, of expansion and resources available, and of revenue and expenses plus profits.

> We are apt to forget that we are only one of a team, that in unity there is strength, and that we are strong only as long as each unit in our organization functions with precision.
> —SAMUEL TILDEN

Supervising

Supervisors deal with individuals, materials, methods, and machinery or equipment used by workers whom they supervise. It is individuals who are the most complicated, unpredictable, and difficult to handle parts of a business. Thus supervision is largely an exercise in **leadership**, accomplished by means of **communication** of ideas and instructions to subordinates, and based on an understanding of what motivates people.

Personalities, emotions, and conditions outside the business affect most workers and make many intangible elements important in achieving effective supervision. Family problems loom large with many workers. Others are upset by the details of their jobs. A good supervisor understands the importance of these personal factors in the workers' lives and is alert to the symptoms that indicate trouble is brewing. The supervisor strives for the confidence and cooperation of the workers and succeeds as a supervisor in almost direct ratio to earning this confidence and cooperation.

A supervisor must instruct, explain, train, and sometimes demonstrate what the workers are to do. In some cases an explanation is helpful, especially for anything quite new. Close observation and follow-up are needed as soon as the workers are on their own. Communicating instructions and ideas correctly and effectively takes time and skill, requiring that the supervisor (1) emphasize the use and application of the information given; (2) stir the learners to activity, get them to take part; (3) give the employees time to digest what they learn; (4) help them to see what is especially important; and (5) help them to understand the meaning of what they are learning. When the individual workers have demonstrated their ability and willingness to do the job as requested, the supervisor need only make periodic checks to see that no deviations are occurring.

When several workers are involved, some will work better together than others. The alert supervisor pairs off or groups the workers on this basis. Individual abilities, attitudes, and ambitions also differ, and the good supervisor makes the most effective use of these differences both in assigning work and in spotting men and women for promotion or other recognition. All people like praise, recognition, and treatment as individuals. Praise and encouragement stimulate and inspire workers and constitute a part of the modern positive type of leadership. When criticism or correction must be given, real tact is needed, but it is better to help the workers to help themselves in such cases early than to delay remedial action too long. This is, at times, one of the unpleasant but essential duties of a good supervisor.

Even when workers have learned to perform their prescribed or routine tasks well, in the day-to-day operations of a business special problems often arise which are new and unusual and defy classification under any of the stated policies of the concern. These problems may not be anticipated during the training of the employee and he or she will be at a loss to handle them. Sometimes a major unexpected expense is involved, an accident may occur, or a delivery may not have been made as promised. Managers must be prepared to help their subordinates deal with such situations; or they themselves may find it necessary to deal with the customer, client, machine, or material that presents the special problem.

CONTROLLING

Controlling means measuring and correcting the actions of subordinates to ensure that plans for the business are fulfilled. It involves (1) setting standards or objectives for accomplishment, (2) maintaining current operating records for comparison with standards set, and (3) acting promptly when operations deviate too much from the goals established.

The ability to control depends on some sort of feedback, as, for example, a thermostat controls temperatures that register too high or too low. Managerial control similarly operates on the feedback principle—requiring an appraisal of the *reasons* why operating results are different from those planned, and intelligent decisions as to what action is needed. For example, production control in a small factory plans a daily output of thirty units, based on anticipated sales department needs. Daily reports show actual production to be averaging only twenty-five units. Investigation discloses recurring delays because of repeated breakdowns of one machine. Review of sales estimates verifies the need for thirty units daily. Immediate action by management will prevent an increasing amount of back orders, broken promises, and lost sales. If possible, the defective machine should be repaired or replaced at once. Otherwise it would be better to slow down on sales immediately to keep sales in bounds with productive capacity than to have disappointed customers and the other likely results of failing to coordinate sales and production.

In addition to the control of production levels, techniques of control have been developed for other aspects of business operation such as inventory levels, costs, cash flow, and quality of product. These administrative controls and others are discussed elsewhere in this book.

SUMMING UP

The owner/manager or prospective operator of a small business must perform the following basic functions if the business is to be managed effectively:

 Planning, or selecting the future courses of action (goals, policies, strategies) for the business.

 Organizing and *staffing,* or dividing the work or activities of the business (production, distribution or marketing, and finance) into manageable units, and assigning these business activities to individuals qualified to perform them.

 Directing, or supervising and coordinating the activities of these subordinate individuals.

 Controlling, or measuring and correcting the actions of subordinates to ensure that plans for the business are fulfilled.

KEY WORDS

administrative organization
business function
communications
controlling
decision-making
delegation of authority
departmentation
directing
distribution
facilitating function
factor(s) of production
finance (n.)
job description
job specification
leadership

line authority
management
management function
management science
manager
marketing
organizing
planning
policies
production
responsibility
staff authority
staffing
supervisor
work analysis

DISCUSSION QUESTIONS

1. If you owned a shoe store selling men's, women's, and children's shoes in a small town of twelve thousand inhabitants, what service policies might you establish? What price policies? Explain, stating assumptions.

2. Is efficient management of the small firm always concerned primarily with profit maximization? Discuss fully.

3. We often speak of "leadership style," meaning the methods by which a leader (manager) achieves his or her administration's goals. Some leaders are quiet, unassuming, and genial, but get results equivalent to others who are quite vocal, overbearing, and domineering. Which style is "better," that is, which would you prefer? Explain.

CASE IN POINT

Two young men, Arthur Steele and John Hubbard, plan to establish a plumbing-heating-air-conditioning business. Steele is an experienced plumber and tinner, having worked with his father for many years in another community. Hubbard has some engineering training and has successfully sold supplies to the heating and air-conditioning trade. They propose to take over an old shop that was closed after its owner died and that remained closed while the estate was settled. It is in a good location and has basic equipment and plenty of room.

They believe, at this point, that they can raise enough capital to lease the shop and buy existing equipment, buy a truck and adequate new equipment, establish an inventory of parts and materials, renovate the showroom, and get a few floor samples of products for display. Hubbard is confident that several good product lines are available, and feels that the local area is not now being properly served, particularly in regard to heating and air-conditioning requirements. He is certain, he says, that they can pick up a lot of business working with contractors on new buildings. Much of this work is now being handled by representatives from cities some distance away.

As to nontechnical personnel, they will have a stenographer-clerk-office manager, and an accountant on a part-time basis. To start, they will need at least one plumber-heating man and one helper-truckdriver. Steele intends to work both in and out of the shop. Hubbard expects to make sales calls, build goodwill with contractors, and generally supervise the office.

As for capital, Steele will provide $18,000 and Hubbard $12,000. The remainder will be borrowed from the bank, with the equipment offered as security. Both men have excellent credit and financial records.

These two men plan to sit down together this evening and put their ideas about organization on paper. Not only must they be clear in their own minds as to individual rights and responsibilities, but their creditors and the bank will have some questions to ask. Briefly outline, hypothetically, the duties and responsibilities of each man. Suggest a type of organization that will satisfy all concerned.

Differences in Managing ✳ Small and Large Firms

CHAPTER FIVE *Although the functions of management are common (basic) to all types and sizes of business, the conditions under which they are performed vary considerably from a "one-man operation" to a "linear organization structure." After reading this chapter you should have an increased awareness of the inherent difficulties, as well as some unique advantages, in managing the smaller business enterprise.*

The thought has often been expressed that the art of managing a small firm is no different from that of managing a large one. However, this attitude has become less prevalent in recent years, and there is a growing conviction that the specialized big-business-oriented management training that a student receives in a school of business or the highly specific instruction a management trainee receives in a large company is not necessarily the kind of training that a person needs to be successful in small business.

THE STRATEGY OF SIZE

The small business remains small because it has functions to perform that are impossible or impractical for most large organizations. Frequently it operates in a limited market serving as supplier to local household consumers or to other firms. Some firms are small by choice, seeking to retain strong personal control. Some are small because they are specialists in a greatly limited field.

Some businesses, by their very nature, can *never* become large—the nation's many small repair shops, for example. Others start small in order to introduce a new idea or a new product or service. They may grow as the idea, product, or service grows, or they may fail. Many, however, are small-scale operations in industries where the size range, as well as the efficiency of operation, varies greatly.

In every type of business, and in every aspect of business operation, the small firm's unit costs are higher than those of its larger competitors. In manufacturing, for example, more efficient use of labor results from the large firm's ability to subdivide work for greater specialization. The specialization or simplification of work tasks, in turn, has led naturally to the development and use of machine methods. For both these reasons labor **productivity** has increased tremendously in larger firms.

In addition, the large manufacturer's enormous purchasing power makes it easier to buy and use materials more efficiently, usually through purchases according to specification and often on an extended-contract basis. Such materials may be carefully engineered to the machine processes to be performed and to requirements of the finished product, which constitutes another advantage.

In the merchandising field, chain stores often secure lower prices from their suppliers not only because of the larger volume of their purchases, but also because their organizations are more **integrated**—performing for themselves most of the functions performed for the independent retailer by the wholesaler.

In competing with large concerns, however, the small firm has at least two important factors working to its advantage: (1) closer contact with customers and employees and (2) flexibility in production, marketing, and service. These competitive advantages were repeatedly cited by 173 small business owners and executives in a survey conducted by the National Industrial Conference Board.[1] How these factors contribute to the strength of small business can be no better stated than in the words of the small business owner/managers themselves. "Basically," said one respondent to the NICB survey in regard to maintaining close contact with the community, "the smaller company has the advantage of being managed customarily by long-time residents of the community, resulting in a more intimate knowledge of the community's needs, peculiarities, and relationships. Normally such management has a large circle of friends and acquaintances that are a definite plus in the acquisition of business. There is also generally a desire on the part of inhabitants of a community to do business with a concern closely identified with that particular community." The importance of flexibility or adaptability was stressed by all respondents. In the words of one of them: "The small company generally has a closely knit organization that operates on an informal basis and, generally, has excellent **communications.** This allows a small company to react to changes and problems arising in any area and take corrective action quickly." This same idea was expressed in a different way by another respondent, who replied: "Our decisions are often made very close to the point of customer contact, and our people dealing with customers usually have more authority than those in larger corporations." One respondent spoke of the corresponding disadvantages of a big company. "It would seem apparent from our experience," he commented, "that the systems and procedures utilized in larger corporations impose a penalty in the time required for such a concern to respond to a customer's (request for information or service)."

---

[1] Sorrell M. Mathes, "Competing with the Big Fellows," *Conference Board Record* (April 1967), 13–14.

In addition to flexibility and the "personal touch," Professor Alfred Gross cites *greater motivation* as a third factor that possibly contributes to small business strength: "In small companies the top executive is often the owner or a major stockholder. He usually works harder, longer, and with more personal involvement than do executives of larger corporations."[2]

In general, the small enterprise has inherent advantages or is otherwise more appropriate under the following conditions:

1. Where a high degree of flexibility is required because of (a) frequent demand changes; (b) demand for small quantities in a wide variety of styles; or (c) rapidly developing techniques of production

2. Where manual labor and personal attention to details by the owner/manager are of dominant importance, as in most of the service trades; common examples are automobile and other repair services, and beauty and barber shops.

In discussing the strategy of size one day, the manager of a large distributor of automotive machinery told the author that he wasn't particularly concerned about the competition he was facing from other large wholesale houses. He could handle them, he said, because he was competing with them on even terms. His problem, he went on to say, was with the small service wholesaler who worked in his shirt sleeves and called his customers by their first names!

The more personal nature of small business management, however, is not an unmixed blessing; there are some inherent disadvantages as well. In contrast with professionally-managed large corporations, small owner-managed businesses are largely projections of the entrepreneurs' own ideas as to how they want to go about making their economic contribution and gaining the related satisfactions. Their policies are the way they visualize a business should be operated—in terms not only of quality, service, and price but also appearance, atmosphere, and attitudes. Thus their business philosophies become their business practices, which are extensions of their own personalities and thus of themselves.

This inseparability of the owner's personality from the owner's business reflects itself in many ways, not all of them always in the interests of the firm. The owner's knowledge of business methods may constitute the firm's knowledge of them. The owner's competence in the various functional areas will be the firm's competence. Open-mindedness to the need for change, willingness to ask for and accept advice, to take proper action, or to adjust in time of emergency are purely personal characteristics that can make or break a business. Business is indeed a personal thing and the smaller the business the more personal it is.

---

[2] Alfred Gross, "Meeting the Competition of Giants," *Harvard Business Review* (May–June 1967), 175.

THE "ONE-MAN BAND" PROBLEM

In a small business there are limited opportunities to specialize management. Thus a shortage of capable management personnel permeates most small enterprises; this, in turn, creates unique problems in providing for management in the small firm. In the beginning of a very small concern one person is likely to bear all managerial responsibilities without an understudy or assistant manager. With increased size, an opportunity to share responsibility and to specialize the management functions appears and the company is able to attract qualified personnel.

Any discussion of the versatility required of the owner/manager of a small business calls to mind the "one-man band." Those small business operators who have seen this musical phenomenon in operation will agree that they and the musician have a common problem. With a bass drum at one foot, a snare drum at the other, a cymbal on each knee, a harmonica on a frame in front of his mouth, and a guitar hung over his chest, the musician is an amazing sight. Any veteran of small business will agree that the need to coordinate and to keep things running smoothly and profitably according to plan are eclipsed only by the efforts of the musician in a one-man band who achieves harmony while following the melody outlined in the score. Both individuals are very busy operators. Yet this versatility and the ability to plan, to concentrate, and to coordinate are the measures of one-person managerial success.

Management in a small firm has considerably less latitude in its capacity to make some major errors in judgment from which the firm can recover. In a

large business, for example, the effect of a bad decision on the part of one individual is absorbed by the corporate body and the subsequent shock so distributed as to cause no serious aftereffects; but in a small business—because of its limited resources—even a single costly error in judgment can have disastrous consequences. Whereas a large organization can succeed based on decisions that are occasionally wrong, a small enterprise can fail because of even *one* wrong decision by its management!

EDUCATION FOR SMALL BUSINESS MANAGEMENT

It is the growing awareness of the "one-man band" problem that has led to the conclusion by an increasing number of business educators and consultants that the art of managing a small independent business *is* indeed different from that of managing a large corporate enterprise. The large corporation usually employs a person with special qualifications and training in the key job in each department. It has a treasurer or comptroller, a secretary, a sales manager, a production manager, and a host of **staff** specialists—along with an executive vice-president who picks their brains and hands the results to the president, who usually consults the board chairperson. On the other hand, the small marketer must wear all these hats—and some of them don't fit any too well.

Thus courses in small business operation are being offered by an increasingly larger number of colleges and universities. Additional evidence of the interest of colleges and universities in training and education for small business are the many conferences, institutes, and seminars sponsored by these institutions in recent years. Some of these, covering limited topical areas, have been attended by specific trade or industrial groups; others have been general in

Courtesy of the Small Business Administration.

nature. Many have been sponsored or encouraged by the Management Assistance Division of the Small Business Administration.

Surveys conducted by the Center for Venture Management and other organizations continue to reveal this greatly increased attention by schools of business to preparation for entrepreneurship and assistance to existing entrepreneurs, in contrast to what some have considered to be an emphasis on training for big business employment. Many of the titles of university and college courses indicate that their primary concern has been with the problems of high-level finance, mass production, mass communications within massive plants, and mass employment.

The owner/manager of a small business, with a restricted scope of activities, has definite limits as to the sophistication of the operating methods that can be employed. One objective of this book is to compensate for the failure of many other business texts to recognize the importance of small business by emphasizing some of the special skills and techniques particularly needed in the management of the smaller organization.

Self-improvement of the small, independent business owner is also the primary objective of two unique organizations that have come into existence in recent years. One is the International Council for Small Business and its U.S. affiliate, whose memberships are composed of management educators, entrepreneurs, and government executives interested in the development of research and educational programs for small business owners and managers. This group also publishes a professional journal, the *Journal of Small Business Management,* oriented exclusively to small business and the small business owner. The other organization is CIM-SAM (Council of Independent Managers, Society for the Advancement of Management), an association of independent business owners whose primary objective is to educate themselves through a sharing of experiences and with the assistance of outside management specialists.

> *It is costly wisdom that is bought by experience. . . . Learning teacheth more in one year than experience in twenty.*
>
> —ROGER ASCHAM (in *The Scholemaster*)

SUMMING UP

The owner/manager of a small business must perform competently many of the business functions that large companies hire specialists to do; he or she has to be considerably more *versatile.*

Small business management calls for a wide variety of talents far beyond those of the person performing or in charge of any single business function in a large **linear organization structure.**

The large firm has greater latitude in its capacity to absorb some major errors in managerial judgment from which it can recover; mistakes or "goofs" at one level of responsibility are readily absorbed at other levels in the management hierarchy. A small business manager cannot afford to make many bad decisions.

Small business firms, almost by definition, lack the internal resources and market size that provide competitive advantages to the larger firm. The owner/manager of a small business must adopt operating policies that adjust to these inherent deficiencies.

On the other hand, in competing with large firms the small firm has two important factors working to its advantage: (1) closer contact with customers and employees; and (2) flexibility in production, marketing, and service.

For all these reasons there is an increasing awareness on the part of college and university administrators and others of the need for training students for *small* business management.

KEY WORDS

communications
integration (of industry)
linear organization structure

productivity
staff

DISCUSSION QUESTIONS

1. In what ways can a small business compete successfully with a large business? Discuss fully.

2. Many small business owners believe that they can use the sophisticated, complex personnel records systems and methods adopted with apparent success by large corporations. In your opinion, what limitations, if any, are there for the small concern?

Jack Fratelli and his wife Teresa own a little flower shop in a suburban area. When they first opened the shop, they specialized in the usual wedding, funeral, and gift creations, and purchased their flowers from local and distant greenhouses. Later they rented a vacant lot nearby and built their own greenhouse. This arrangement being profitable, they leased more land and put up more greenhouses. In addition to various evergreens, fruit trees, and shrubs, they grew a variety of flowering plants suitable for potting for home use.

Their hard work and good judgment, combined with a good location, made their business mushroom beyond all expectations. After just three years they could afford to employ six persons—truck driver, handyman, accountant, office manager, and two gardeners. Jack spent much of his time out of the shop checking the market and soliciting business, while Teresa kept her eye on the office and greenhouses. She was not happy, however, with the responsibilities of supervision or with her job of doing so much alone.

She and Jack finally decided that an outside salesperson, one of high abilities and good contacts, was needed. After a methodical search they were happy to find and hire George Anderson, a recent arrival in the community with good florist, nursery, and landscaping sales experience in another part of the country—and with good references to prove it. He agreed to work on a drawing account of $300 per month, plus a scaled percentage or commission on all sales over $3,000 per month. This would cost Jack and Teresa 10 percent on all sales under $3,000. On sales over that amount George was to receive 5 percent on orders under $100, 7½ percent on those of $100 to $500, and 10 percent on orders over $500. This was what George said he had been accustomed to getting and it seemed reasonable to Jack and Teresa.

Now that the business has expanded even further, the customers can be separated into three types: smaller florists who buy potted items and some blooms; chain drugstores, grocery stores, garden supply shops, and builders' supply houses; and more recently, landscaping contractors, a business that George Anderson developed and cultivated himself. Sales averages for the smaller customers are very low, seldom going above $100. The chain stores buy substantial quantities; depending on the season, they can be expected to place orders of up to $1,000 a week. Much of this business can now be done by telephone, but since so much of it was due to the expansion for which George claims credit, they are to him, *his* sales and *his* commissions. However, accounts with the small, independent florists have often been neglected in the process.

The landscaping contractors now represent a serious problem as far as compensating George is concerned. He has created business up to 100 miles away. He often lands orders of several hundred dollars, and $1,000 orders are not uncommon for landscaping new apartments, schools, hospitals, and factories. And all of these commissions are George's, most of them at 10 percent, which means a sizeable monthly paycheck for him.

The business is prospering far beyond the Fratellis' early hopes—they have a large market area, a highly successful salesman, and a good income. But George's monthly income is sometimes higher than Jack's. Yet the new market and sales volume are George's creating; he has the contacts in the field, and more and more Jack has kept to the office and production parts of the firm. The couple is puzzled as to what it can do, should do, and wants to do in this situation.

What is your advice?

Special ✗

Management Concerns

CHAPTER SIX *For reasons cited in the preceding chapter, certain management processes or concerns require considerably more attention and are of critically more importance to the small business than to the large. After reading this chapter you will learn why it is particularly necessary for the owner/manager of a small firm, if the enterprise is to achieve its objectives, to (1) manage efficiently the limited time he or she can devote to the affairs of the business, (2) fulfill expected community obligations, (3) keep up with rapid environmental changes and advancements in management science, and (4) plan for succession in management and continuity of business operations.*

TIME MANAGEMENT

A major problem characteristic of small business is the limited amount of *time* of the owner/manager. Employees usually have their time managed for them by company regulations, but small business owner/managers must manage their own time. With so many essential duties to perform or supervise, and only the same amount of time available as is used by each of a number of persons in big business, the finite number of hours in a day is usually the most serious problem of the typical small business owner.

With all of its advantages, even being one's own boss has a maximum price in terms of time that can be devoted to the business and still leave enough for the enterpriser to enjoy a normal outside life. A major goal of **time management** is to keep this price for success reasonable. Some small business owners pride themselves on their unusually long hours devoted to achieving success—a modern version of the martyr complex. Good time management in most such cases could reduce these long hours from 25 to 35 percent and produce better results.

> One realizes the full importance of time only when there is little of it left. Every man's greatest capital asset is his unexpired years of productive life.
>
> —P. W. LITCHFIELD

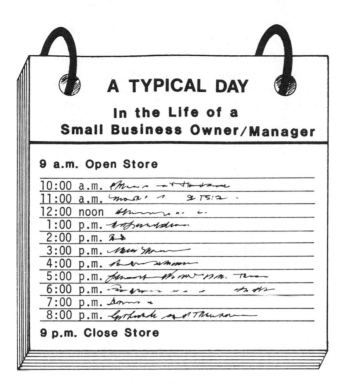

A TYPICAL DAY

**In the Life of a
Small Business Owner/Manager**

9 a.m. Open Store

10:00 a.m.	
11:00 a.m.	
12:00 noon	
1:00 p.m.	
2:00 p.m.	
3:00 p.m.	
4:00 p.m.	
5:00 p.m.	
6:00 p.m.	
7:00 p.m.	
8:00 p.m.	

9 p.m. Close Store

To manage his or her time more effectively, the entrepreneur should: (1) rank the various jobs in order of importance; (2) divide them into at least two classes based on the manager's ability to control the time when they will be performed; (3) decide which ones can best be delegated to other members of the organization; (4) determine those where time can be saved in the long run by adopting suitable procedures; and (5) select or formulate suitable aids to time economy. These five steps in time management have been listed in their order of importance and will now be discussed in that sequence.

The manager must *first* define his or her goals and set priorities. Time is limited, fixed within absolute and reasonable limits. Managerial and other duties are virtually unlimited for the small-scale beginner. Choice is essential, and ranking is the only intelligent approach. "First things first" should be the guide, but like other maxims it is often difficult to accomplish, mainly because of lack of planning. Which should come first, serving a customer when all other employees are busy or doing essential paperwork that must be completed before tomorrow? The customer's arrival could not have been predicted a few minutes earlier, but essential paperwork was known days or even months in advance. You must be the judge—it's your enterprise.

Ranking involves valuation. First to be accomplished are those mandatory duties required by law: keeping adequate records for income tax, sales tax, social security, excise, and other tax reports; filing all tax reports and making payments according to times specified for each; and maintaining any other legally mandatory records and reports.

Next are provisions necessary for protection: appropriate insurance with its necessary records and payments made on time; adequate safety provisions for the premises and property; and meeting contractual obligations for the payment of interest and principal on loans, rent, and other current operating expenses, and for merchandise and other purchases.

Nearly all the foregoing are dated obligations, most of which can be taken care of at any convenient time up to the deadline. To avoid a last-minute rush and possible penalty for tardiness they should be cared for as time permits, well in advance of the deadline. This requires planning in advance so as to be adequately prepared; much of the work should be done during slack periods, interrupting such work temporarily to take care of an emergency or immediate need—such as service to a customer when all other employees are busy—and doing a more thorough job on each activity by allowing ample time for it. A simple device to use is a tickler or reminder file or desk calendar. For every duty at least two dates are recorded, the deadline and the beginning or warning date, if ample time is to be allotted. Most entrepreneurs take these steps, but they do so mentally instead of recording the dates on a calendar or setting up a card file. The result is that frequently important duties are overlooked in the rush of day-to-day tasks. Even the tickler file will be of little value unless it is used constantly, consulted each day or often enough to ensure its effective use.

A third group of managerial duties consists of all acts necessary to maintain continuous day-to-day operations. Most of these are routine, recurring regularly: opening and closing the shop; maintaining the premises, merchandise, or machinery, and having adequate personnel; operating the enterprise by serving customers or maintaining production; and conducting such activities as advertising and communication. They should be performed in a systematic and businesslike manner but need not require the personal attention of the owner/manager except in the one-person enterprise. Most can and should be delegated to other members of the firm so as to economize the time and effort of top management. Adequate guides can be formulated, such as policies and regulations, and limits to authority clearly defined, so that only unusual or exceptional cases need be taken up personally with the manager. This is the very important **exception principle of management.** Failure to apply this principle is a major weakness of the management in many small concerns. The difficulty usually results from an unwillingness to delegate authority and uncertainty as to how it should be done. **Delegation of authority** can free managers from day-to-day tasks so that they have adequate time for planning, deliberation, and attention to the important duties that they alone can perform satisfactorily.

> As the gardener, by severe pruning, forces the sap of the tree into one or more vigorous limbs, so should you stop off your miscellaneous activity and concentrate your force on one or a few points.
>
> —RALPH WALDO EMERSON

In the one-person enterprise it is, of course, not possible to delegate duties, just as in the two- or three-person firm the owner/manager is likely to bear some responsibility for routine tasks. Time management is important, however, even for the lone operator. Routine duties are not all of equal importance, nor do they all have the same degree of urgency from a time standpoint. In a customer-service type of enterprise the shop must be open for business at regular or announced times even though some maintenance may have to be deferred. Also, in other respects serving the customer properly takes precedence over all other duties except extreme emergencies such as fire or serious misfortunes. But serving customers on the premise is usually irregular and difficult to predict. All time not required for customer service should be used most effectively for other duties in the order of their importance. These other duties include the dated ones discussed earlier, as well as daily tasks. A useful device is a daily memorandum or **order of work** that lists the important jobs to be done, if possible, during each business day. This list is prepared in advance, away from the pressure and interruptions of business hours, and is partial protection against two dangers—failure to complete essential work on time, and dissipation of available customer-free time on odd jobs that appear continuously but are less important than those on the "do today" list.

Time management involves self-discipline. We all sometimes dissipate time on such things as idle conversation, newspaper reading, or just daydreaming. Entrepreneurs must keep up with important new events that might affect their business or family life, but many spend more time than necessary in the process. Conversation also is needed to spark fresh ideas, to make new friends, and to build goodwill, but a lot of time is often wasted on unimportant exchanges of comments regarding the weather, the latest gossip, and the like. Experience shows that from one to two hours per day can often be saved from these sources alone. Of course, time-consuming habits such as these are often relaxing and enjoyable. The main point is that unless controlled they frequently use up the only time the entrepreneur has to use for deliberation and planning.

> You will never "find" time for anything. If you want time, you must make it.
>
> —Charles Bixton

COMMUNITY OBLIGATIONS

Fulfilling **community obligations** may also present problems to the small business owner/manager. A manager often finds it necessary to represent the business to many groups outside the organization. This may include having a membership in the community service club or holding office in a trade association. He or she may need to meet with government officials or representatives of unions which may represent or wish to represent the business's employees. The manager must also be the spokesperson for the business in dealing with financial institutions, other companies in the industry, suppliers, customers, and the general public. Sometimes only the manager's presence is required; at other times community leadership is expected; and on yet other occasions great tact is required in order to handle very delicate negotiations.

The owner/managers of small businesses, however, sometimes find that the contribution of either time or money becomes a relatively heavy burden. They may also discover that friends and relatives put pressure on them for jobs or perhaps for prizes for charity raffles and the like. As responsible business owners they want to participate in civic development and belong to local service clubs. Often these activities demand and consume a large amount of their time. Also, because they are well-known in the town, they may be called on quite frequently for donations toward community development. While the larger organization with sales of $200,000,000 might contribute $200 to some cause and feel virtuous about it, the owner of a small business with $400,000 in sales would probably feel ashamed to contribute a proportionate $40.

Although there is no single solution for such problems, there is a plan that, if followed tactfully and consistently, will assist in dealing with most such situations. First, the manager, in conference with specifically qualified individuals, should formulate policies covering each of these circumstances. Then the owner may truthfully say to a job-seeking relative that on the advice of the suppliers and banker the firm has adopted a policy of not employing relatives. Similarly, to the friend soliciting contributions the owner may reply that on the advice of the Chamber of Commerce (or some other group), the firm has adopted a policy of making contributions in the same relative proportion as those of large concerns in the same field on a corresponding ratio of sales volume. It is much easier to handle these situations in this way than to have to depend on direct, impulsive personal decisions.

CONTINUING MANAGEMENT EDUCATION

Change is a reality every business manager must face. The passing of each business day brings with it new pressures for possible changes in philosophy, product, program, processes, or procedures.

A craftsman depends most on his basic skills perfected through the years; many skilled laborers, such as carpenters, masons, or plumbers, find that their basic trade changes little from year to year. But business management, like many other professions, calls for constant reorientation. The business owner must recognize the changing economy, a new social structure, or the advent of competition; he or she must be prepared to respond accordingly and to make use of **continuing management education.**

There are new techniques, new materials, new products, and new equipment being introduced and being used every day. A progressive entrepreneur must actively seek information on change, both technical and social, and learn how to incorporate it in the business's plans or deal with it effectively. This

' "Gentlemen," I said then, "We're going to stick with our line of slide rules. Those electronic pocket calculators are just a fad..." '

Reprinted by permission. © 1977, NEA, Inc.

may mean independent study or attending classes so the entrepreneur can learn what is necessary to continue to operate with the best possible methods, materials, and machines available.

Many organizations, government agencies, and schools provide opportunities for managers to expand their training and education. Trade associations, for example, often publish technical bulletins or sponsor management training courses, and local Chambers of Commerce also present useful programs. High schools as well as college and university extension divisions sometimes offer courses or promote conferences for particular industries or lines of business, such as retailing or metalworking; often they also provide courses in various business functions, such as accounting, marketing, or purchasing. The federal government sponsors courses and supplies educational materials through the Small Business Administration.

Many trade and professional associations hold annual management conferences for their members in cooperation with colleges and universities. In these meetings, speakers from the academic world are intermixed with speakers from industry who have achieved notable success in some activity. Meetings take the form of seminars, panel discussions, and workshops.

Small business proprietors, however, have proven to be somewhat enigmatic to outside observers. Their business ventures are extremely risky, yet they often fail to take advantage of the aforementioned opportunities for reducing risk.

The Small Business Administration, for example, recently published documentary evidence pointing out that small firms generally fail to make use of the wealth of business data published by that agency. Another study revealed that most small businesses do not avail themselves of SBA's educational services.[1] A study of adult education, night school, and correspondence courses probably would reveal that most enrollments consist of employees who are taking regular courses under the pressure of advancement and demands by employers. Employees will study in depth a particular subject, such as salesmanship or accounting, because they want to get ahead. Unfortunately, many small business proprietors (unlike many of their employees) display a limited perception of the value of education as a means of personal achievement and success, an attitude which tends to reduce their motivation to learn.

It is hoped that the increasing pace of technological and social change and the increasing pressures of a more enlightened competition will in the future cause a relatively larger proportion of entrepreneurs to avail themselves of opportunities to improve their managerial competence in order to increase their probability of success.

It is impossible for a man to learn what he thinks he already knows.

—EPICTETUS

MANAGEMENT SUCCESSION AND BUSINESS CONTINUITY

A common weakness in businesses of all sizes is the lack of a clearly outlined provision for a line of succession to key jobs in management. In larger concerns this may be due to lack of foresight, preoccupation with current problems, unwillingness to make the necessary investment, or the incumbent's fear of being replaced. In the small firm it is due largely to the nature of the one-person operation. The manager sometimes refuses to delegate authority either for fear of subordinates' errors or for fear of losing control. This lack of provision for **management succession** is apparent in many small concerns. Although most firms promote from within unless the special skills required are not possessed by any of the employees, few small businesses have any organized program for training potential managers.

The lack of capable management to carry on the business may result in operating losses or lowered earnings for a considerable period of time following the death or retirement of the owner. Aside from this, if the business is unincorporated, it may legally come to an end and have to be sold at a forced-sale price; there also may not be adequate cash funds in the business to pay estate taxes in the event of the owner's death. Thus the owner of a small and growing business would be well-advised to both execute a will giving authority to the executors of the owner's estate to carry out provisions for the contin-

[1] Informational, educational, and other management assistance programs of the Small Business Administration are discussed in Chapter 7.

Courtesy of Small Business Administration.

uance of the business, and formulate a detailed plan for the management development of the heirs or other successors to the business.

The plan for management succession and perpetuation of the business should begin years ahead of the time the owner/manager expects to retire. Some of the key questions each business owner will need to consider are:

1. Do I have a son, son-in-law, daughter, or other relative interested in and capable of taking over?

2. If not, are any of my employees potential successors?[2]

3. How can I train potential successors so that they will be assured of successful operation of the business?

These are important questions for both the owner and the employees of the business. If a management succession plan is implemented and the business thereby perpetuated, the owner salvages a lifetime of work and a lifelong accumulation of assets (on which he or she can realize capital gains if the business is sold to the successor) and loyal employees are assured of the continuance of their jobs; if the management successor happens to be an heir, it also means the continuance of a family tradition.

SUMMING UP

Employees usually have their time managed for them by company regulations, but small business owner/managers and other employers must manage their own time. The opinion is widespread that success in small business requires long hours of hard work, and most owner/managers do put in long hours. Others, however, equally successful through adroit time management, accomplish just as much and

---

[2] Selling a business to nonfamily members of the firm or to other investors is discussed in detail in Chapter 29.

achieve the same results in more nearly normal working hours. In other cases, learning more rapid ways to perform essential tasks may be indicated. In most cases, however, the owner/manager of a small business must learn to set priorities, establish time-saving routines and policies, and delegate authority to employees.

Small business owners and the corporate managers of large firms are expected to become involved in the political and social structures of the communities in which their businesses are located. The owner/managers of small businesses, however, often find that for them the contribution of time and money can become a relatively heavy burden unless carefully controlled.

Change is a reality every owner/manager of a small business must face. To operate a business successfully he or she must not only have education, training, and/or experience in basic management and business skills, but be *adaptable to social and economic change.* Adaptability to change often requires re-education, or a continuing form of management education.

As with any other aspect of business planning, plans or provisions should be made for a line of succession to key jobs in management or for the continued operation of the business in the event of the owner/manager's untimely death, incapacity, or retirement. While the need to plan for *management succession* exists in all businesses, the loss of leadership and management skill usually is much more damaging to a small business.

KEY WORDS

community obligations
continuing management education
delegation of authority
exception principle of management

management succession
order of work
time management

DISCUSSION QUESTIONS

1. Why is a discussion of time management more appropriate in a small business text than in one concerned mainly with big business?

2. Why is it desirable for the small business manager to participate in a program of continuing management education?

A manufacturer in North Carolina had built up over the years a very nice business, netting over $500,000 a year. After his son finished college with a degree in anthropology, he came into the shop and was "trained" (the word is used loosely) for about three months, whereupon Pop retired and turned the operation over to Junior. For a year or so thereafter Pop traveled, dabbled in politics, and lived the "life of Riley," attending fraternal conventions and nocturnal wingdings. He had never had so much fun—or so he thought—in his entire life.

At about this time he dropped around to take a look at the operation and he found that it was now losing $100,000 a year. More than that, competition had caught up with it. And so, in his twilight years when he should have been taking it easy, he's doing what he should have done years ago—trying to make a manager of his son and regretting the fact that he had not encouraged him to take a degree in business administration, or at least to read and study a book on small business management.

In what other ways might Pop have avoided all this? What are some of the possible effects or results of not preparing adequately for the management or ownership succession of a small business?

* Adapted from an incident related in SBA's former *Administrative Management Course Program.*

Need for

Outside Staff Assistance

CHAPTER SEVEN *When time constraints and the wide range of duties required of a manager of a small business are considered, the need for occasional outside aid is apparent. After reading this chapter you should have an increased awareness of the wide range of counseling, educational, and data services available to small business operators when faced with specific management problems that they lack either the time or skill to handle themselves.*

Lack of managerial ability and lack of sufficient time to perform well all the functions of management have been proven to be significant weaknesses in almost all unsuccessful small businesses. Adequate planning and preparation greatly lessen these weaknesses but cannot remove them entirely as long as the enterprise remains small. Until a business becomes large enough to employ its own management specialists and staff experts it must make use of an **outside staff,** or eventually lose out in the competitive struggle.

CLARIFICATION OF TERMS AND CONCEPTS

Many specialists in big business have line rather than staff authority, but specialists in the same line functions who are not members of the firm may be utilized as outside staff. The sales manager of a large corporation, for example, is a *line executive,* a specialist in his or her function, but when sales consultants are employed they normally serve in a staff or advisory capacity. A small firm may have a person responsible for sales and still make effective use of many outside agencies to improve the performance of this function. The latter are specialists in a line function but serve in a staff or professional advisory capacity only. Only in a dire emergency would the typical independent business firm grant full, or line, authority to an outsider (such as in the case of a creditors' committee to ward off bankruptcy). Our interest in this chapter is in the kinds of assistance available from outside a firm's own organization, where the decision to use or reject such aid rests with the management of the firm.

Scope of the Outside Staff

Outside staff assistance can be obtained by the small business owner in every area or function where similar assistance is furnished to executives of our largest corporations. Some types of assistance are more appropriate than others for the small enterprise, such as a simple but sound procedure for selecting employees rather than an extensive battery of scientific personnel tests that must be administered and interpreted by experts. Some are too expensive in one form but are available in other suitable but less expensive forms, such as a costly firm of management consultants compared with a part-time small business consultant. Some render individualized services (such as a detailed market analysis of a particular company's product and its competitive position), whereas others furnish basic data of a general nature with special applications to be made by the management of each firm (such as an analysis of basic statistics and trends affecting that class of product).

There are two types of business information provided by the outside staff: (1) technical, legal, and statistical information on which management decisions may be based, such as industry sales figures and the various federal and state government census reports; and (2) "how to" or instructional information to assist the business owner in the efficient performance of various management functions such as plant layout, employee relations, and advertising layout. Most business information of interest to the small business owner is distributed by the following sources: trade associations, trade and other publications, professional management consultants, suppliers and equipment manufacturers, miscellaneous business-service practitioners and organizations, and government. These outside staff relationships are illustrated in Figure 7-1.

GOVERNMENT SOURCES OF BUSINESS INFORMATION

More than two dozen agencies of the federal government furnish information useful to the small business owner at little or no direct cost. The most important of these are the Department of Commerce and the Small Business Administration, and the services of each will be discussed in some detail. However, a few others are worthy of mention.

Federal Reserve banks, for instance, publish reports on business and economic conditions in their respective districts, including continuing series such as sales and inventory indexes and stock-sales ratios. These reports are available in local banks and in many libraries, and by direct request from the Board of Governors in Washington or the district Federal Reserve bank.

Similarly, the U.S. Department of Agriculture has a large number of periodic series and many special research publications dealing with agricultural products (both raw materials and foods ready for consumption), the status of farm families, agricultural cooperatives, farm prices, consumer preferences

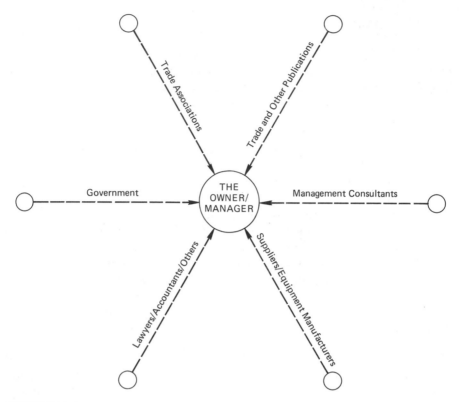

FIGURE 7-1
Sources of Outside Staff Assistance

and buying habits for foods and textiles, home economics topics, and, fairly recently, certain phases of retail food marketing.

For special studies and statistical series relating to labor, the status of wage earners' families, employment, and similar data, the Bureau of Labor Statistics of the U.S. Department of Labor publishes material that is often helpful in appraising economic conditions and in keeping abreast of developments affecting labor. The *Monthly Labor Review* is available in many libraries or by direct subscription.

The U.S. Department of Education administers the Vocational Education Amendments of 1968 in cooperation with state departments of education. Federal vocational education funds have been used in various states to sponsor management seminars, shoplifting clinics, truth-in-lending seminars for merchants, and other programs related to small business operation.

Compliance with tax laws can be overwhelming—especially to the small business owner or manager. The Internal Revenue Service publishes each year the *Tax Guide for Small Business*. IRS has also prepared a tax kit to assist the small business owner. Entitled *Mr. Businessman's Kit*, it supplies these entre-preneurs with every type of tax form they will need, and it contains many con-venience features to help them file their tax returns properly. Both the tax guide and the tax kit are available through local IRS offices. Small business owners are also encouraged to visit their local IRS office for assistance.

Ambitious enterprisers should purchase from the Superintendent of Docu-ments or obtain from their local library the latest edition of the *United States Government Organization Manual* for a fairly complete listing and description of the activities of every federal agency. Only in some such manner are they likely to become familiar with certain agencies that may be useful to them.

U.S. Department of Commerce

Prior to 1953, when the Small Business Administration was established, the U.S. Department of Commerce was the government agency most active in conducting projects of interest to independent enterprisers. It is still the busi-ness owner's department of the federal government. From time to time bibliographies or compilations of the publications of the USDC are released which may be consulted in many libraries.[1] A small business owner may re-ceive current publications in certain areas by asking that his or her name be put on the desired mailing list. The biweekly *Selected United States Govern-ment Publications* issued by the Superintendent of Documents, Washington, D.C., also lists many recent USDC publications.

Among the current publications of the USDC of likely interest to small in-dependents is the monthly *Survey of Current Business.* This periodical is the standard reference source for data on production and distribution activities of the nation's basic industries. It also contains data on the business population and its changes, the level and distribution of income, and about twenty-five hundred statistical series covering nearly every measurable factor of signifi-cance to the national economy.

The Department of Commerce maintains forty-two field offices and over six hundred local cooperative offices for the purpose of providing ready access to the reports, publications, and services of the Bureau of the Census, and also those of the Bureau of International Commerce, the Business and Defense Services Administration, the Economic Development Administration, and the Office of Business Economics. Information on certain activities of the National Bureau of Standards, Patent Office, and the Institute of Applied Technology is also available. Experienced personnel will assist in the solution of specific problems, explain the scope and meaning of regulations administered by the department, and provide practical assistance in the broad field of domestic and foreign commerce. Field offices act as official sales agents of the Superinten-

---

[1] See *United States Department of Commerce Publications: A Catalogue and Index*, Annual Supplements (Washington, D.C.: Superintendent of Documents).

dent of Documents and stock a wide range of official government publications relating to business. Each office maintains an extensive business reference library containing periodicals, directories, publications, and reports from official as well as private sources.

Through its Census Bureau, the USDC also compiles and publishes, on a periodic basis, data on a wide variety of the nation's social and economic characteristics. The Census Bureau reports of major interest to the business owner are the following:

1. The *Census of Population,* taken every ten years, presents information on age, race, sex, marital status, family status, ethnic origin, migration, education, income, occupation, employment, and other characteristics of the population. These data are universally available for states and counties, and much of the information is also broken down for cities and towns with populations of twenty-five hundred or more. Of special significance to the business owner are the trends in the level and composition of employment and income, the changing occupational pattern and age composition of the population, and the population migration pattern. These data have important marketing implications. Changing wants may be anticipated and opportunities for new enterprises, products, and services disclosed by careful analysis of census data.

2. The *Census of Manufactures* is taken every four or five years. Included in this census are data on the number of manufacturing establishments, the number of production and other employees, value added by manufacture, cost of materials, value of shipments, and recent capital expenditures for each of the nation's manufacturing industries. These data also are compiled for each of the states, and much of the information is available for counties as well. To fill the gap between census years, the Bureau of the Census conducts *Annual Surveys of Manufactures* to yield estimates for the more important industrial classifications.

3. The *Census of Business* is also taken every four or five years. This census provides information on all types of retail and wholesale trade and on selected services. Included are data on the number of establishments, gross annual sales or receipts, the number of employees, annual payroll, and the number of active proprietors of unincorporated enterprises. These data are compiled for each state and county, and for all communities with a population of twenty-five hundred or more. Their usefulness, however, is limited, though not seriously so, by the number of years that elapse between census surveys; unlike the *Census of Manufactures,* there are no interim estimates or reports.

Other recurring censuses conducted by the Bureau of the Census include the *Census of Agriculture,* the *Census of Mineral Industries,* the *Census of Governments,* and the *Census of Housing.*

In addition to the publication of the above census volumes, the Bureau of the Census cooperates with the Social Security Administration in the publication of *County Business Patterns*. This joint publication is issued quarterly, and it contains data for each major industry on the number of reporting business establishments, "covered" employment, and taxable payrolls under the Old Age, Survivors, and Disability Insurance Program (OASDI).

No really intelligent decisions that are contingent on the state of the national, state, or local economy can be made by the management of any firm, large or small, without reliable data of the type furnished only in the above-mentioned volumes. The typical owner/manager of a small business enterprise may not fully appreciate the significance of the work done by the Bureau of the Census, because ordinarily he or she does not read the various statistical reports. But trade association editors read, analyze, and make important conclusions and recommendations on the basis of them, as do university bureaus of business research and other agencies with which the owner/manager has contacts. So, indirectly, at least, the small business manager has a vital interest in the continuation of or even an increase in the frequency and coverage of these reports.

Special assistance to minority-owned businesses.   In recent years the federal government has endeavored to mobilize public and private leadership, funds, and other resources to support the development and growth of minority-owned businesses. For this purpose, the Minority Business Development Agency (MBDA) was established within the Department of Commerce in March 1969.[2]

The coordination of management and technical assistance programs at the local level is achieved by MBDA by means of its *affiliate* system. Business development organizations in selected cities with large concentrations of minority populations have been chosen to work with MBDA in assisting minority business and developing effective methods of meeting local needs. To be designated an MBDA affiliate, an organization must have an established reputation and be capable of providing a full range of management or technical assistance to existing or prospective minority-owned businesses. Among the private agencies participating in the MBDA program as affiliates are selected universities, human rights commissions, human resources divisions of Chambers of Commerce, Urban Leagues, and various ethnic economic groups. MBDA affiliates serve as the focal point for information, business and technical assistance, and follow-up services. They also sponsor workshops, seminars, and short courses in small business management. Many of them are funded by the Economic Development Administration.

In addition, the Bureau of the Census publishes a periodic *Census of Mi-*

---

[2] Only MBDA's management and technical assistance program is discussed here; the promotion of business opportunities for present or prospective minority entrepreneurs is discussed in Chapter 15, and assistance in locating sources of venture capital in Chapter 17.

nority-Owned Businesses. The basic purpose of this census, conducted in cooperation with the Minority Business Development Agency, is to fill an existing gap in economic data about minority participation in business. Information is provided on the number and kind of businesses, employment, receipts, legal form of ownership, and geographic location of businesses by black, American Indian, Mexican-American, Puerto Rican, Cuban, Chinese, and other minority-group members. This information is used as source material for measuring the impact and efficiency of SBA, MBDA, and other federal programs designed to stimulate minority participation in the national economy.

Small Business Administration

The Small Business Administration, established in July 1953, is the first permanent peacetime agency of the federal government created solely to advise, assist, and protect *all* small business enterprises. Previous agencies were limited to helping manufacturers engaged in defense or essential civilian production. Since the SBA took over from its predecessor, the Small Defense Plants Administration, the scope of government assistance to small business has been broadened to include distributors, construction contractors, retailers and service establishments, as well as manufacturers. The SBA has ten regional offices and ninety-seven branch field offices. The latter are located in larger cities in all fifty states and in Puerto Rico, Guam, and the Virgin Islands.

Three major areas of assistance to the small business owner are provided by SBA: (1) financial assistance, (2) the procurement of government contracts, and (3) management and technical assistance. It is the latter type of assistance with which we are concerned in this chapter.[3]

Staff specialists in the Small Business Administration's field offices assist with many types of management problems. Their services are available to established business owners who have a specific problem or who want authoritative information on various aspects of management, and to persons who are considering starting their own businesses. One feature of this counseling service is a system of business reference libraries, which the SBA has established in its Washington office and in each of its regional offices. These libraries contain textbooks, government and private publications dealing with business management, and business papers and other helpful publications, and are available for reference use by the small business owner.

The Small Business Administration cooperates with leading educational institutions and distributive education groups throughout the nation in sponsoring courses in administrative management, providing instruction in the basic functions of planning, organizing, staffing, directing, and controlling small business enterprises. These courses, generally taught by experienced

---

[3] Financial assistance programs and assistance in procuring government contracts are discussed in Chapters 17 and 15, respectively.

educators and successful business owners, are usually held in the evenings and run from six to eight weeks.

Also conducted by the Small Business Administration at little or no cost are workshops for *prospective* small business owners. In these *pre*business workshops, consisting of one-day sessions or a short series of evening meetings, prospective entrepreneurs are helped in examining all the aspects of operating their proposed business ventures, such as tax and other regulations, insurance requirements, and good management practices.

The SBA also sponsors the Service Corps of Retired Executives. SCORE, as it is popularly called, is a group of more than thirty-five hundred retired business executives who make their management skills and experiences available to small businesses on a voluntary, part-time basis. By pointing out weaknesses in management policies and practices and suggesting ways of correcting them, SCORE volunteers help the small business owner improve his or her chances for success. Many of them also serve as lecturers or coordinators in the above-mentioned administrative management courses and prebusiness workshops. SCORE's counseling services are available on request; such requests should be addressed to the nearest SBA field office. No fees are charged during the first ninety days. However, the business is asked to pay the volunteer's out-of-pocket expenses during this period. After ninety days, if the business desires to retain the volunteer's services, mutually satisfactory compensation arrangements may be made.

Also sponsored by the SBA is the Active Corps of Executives. ACE was organized to supplement the talents of SCORE by merging the expertise of active business owners with that of the SCORE volunteers. As with SCORE, the ACE program is designed to help small business owners who cannot afford a professional consultant.

Another of SBA's management assistance resources is the Small Business Institute (SBI) program. Contracts with over five hundred junior or community colleges and collegiate schools of business have been made by the Small Business Administration to provide student counseling services to small business owners who are having managerial problems. The SBI program both supplements and complements other management counseling services provided free of charge by the Small Business Administration, such as the SCORE and ACE programs.

Another management assistance resource of the SBA is the funding of Small Business Development Centers in various universities. The purpose of these SBDCs is to aid in the development of new, viable business ventures and to ensure their maintenance and growth after they have been properly launched. To accomplish this, the resources of the university are combined with those of the business community and various governmental agencies to study the feasibility of the new business idea or concept, and to provide management training and counseling to the prospective entrepreneur.

The SBA also publishes several series of management and technical pamphlets and booklets of value to established or prospective operators of small business concerns under the following titles:

1. *Management Aids for Small Manufacturers*
2. *Small Marketers Aids*
3. *Technical Aids for Small Manufacturers*
4. *Small Business Management Series*
5. *Starting and Managing Series*
6. *Small Business Research Series*

In addition, the SBA publishes sources of information (*Small Business Bibliographies*) on specific kinds of business or business operations in serial form, as well as a number of nonseries publications.[4]

Special assistance to minority-owned businesses.   Professional management and technical assistance is provided for minority business enterprises qualifying under Section 406 of the Equal Opportunity Act. The kinds of assistance provided under the "406 Program" range from accounting to complex engineering and electronics studies, according to the specific needs of the individual firm, and are offered without charge. At least one of the professional consultants under contract to provide "406" assistance is located in each of the SBA's ten regions.

To qualify for assistance under this program the minority enterprise must have received an SBA loan and be located in a designated high unemployment area.

NONGOVERNMENT SOURCES OF BUSINESS INFORMATION

The nongovernment agencies discussed in the following pages provide many outside staff services to small business firms. Although some of these services overlap to some extent, usually one type of agency will have advantages in a particular case.

Trade Associations

Almost every kind of business has a **trade association.** In contrast to Chambers of Commerce and other civic groups that cut across occupational or business boundaries, a trade association functions in a particular type of business or industry (such as hardware retailing, dry goods wholesaling, or bolt and nut manufacturing). They are typically membership organizations financed by

---

[4] Nonseries publications and those numbered 4 and 5 in the above list are available at nominal cost; all others are free of charge. A list of titles currently available is published periodically and may be obtained from your local SBA field office or by writing to the Small Business Administration, 1441 L Street, N.W., Washington, D.C. 20416.

dues that average a small fraction of 1 percent of the member's sales volume. In a few cases a requirement for membership is that the applicant must have been in business in the particular industry for a prescribed minimum period of time, usually one or two years.

Most of these restricted-membership organizations lend whatever aid they can to beginners, and a few have prepared kits to help newcomers get off to the right start. In addition, nearly all of them will accept subscriptions to their official journals and sell their other publications to nonmembers, though at prices higher than those charged to their own members.

Because trade associations are concerned with the needs and problems of member firms, their services are naturally designed more for the established than for the beginning enterprise. However, the prospective small business owner can profit from the accumulated experience of older firms in the industry. Among the membership services typically supplied by trade associations are the following:

1. Promoting better accounting and record keeping methods
2. Sponsoring industrywide meetings and developing leadership within the industry
3. Operating a liaison service between federal agencies, the Congress, the industry, and its individual members; some trade associations also provide liaison service for their members with state and local governments
4. Providing publicity and public relations programs for the industry
5. Fostering industrywide technical research
6. Maintaining a labor relations service within the industry designed to prevent work stoppages and promote industrial harmony
7. Issuing special information bulletins to their members; these bulletins report on current affairs affecting the industry, on government orders and legislation, and other similar matters
8. Gathering statistics for the industry
9. Publishing specialized data concerning their industries; many of these relate to such activities as promoting sales, educating the public to possible uses of the industry's products, or attracting qualified individuals into employment within the industry
10. Offering training courses to employees of member companies
11. Supplying other services to the industry such as credit-reporting services, savings on the purchase of insurance, and varied economic studies
12. Furnishing the industry with specialized technical advice that few small members, individually, would be able to afford

Most trade associations have developed uniform accounting systems, standard record forms, and standard expense classifications. A major block to greater success for some small firms, however, is their failure to follow these simplified and standardized procedures. This emphasizes a point basic to this book: Often the small independent needs help in applying the best practices to his or her own concern.

Compiling statistical data and other information for use by its members is another valuable service performed by trade associations. Uniform expense classification and accounting are essential to render such data useful for developing standard operating ratios, and for individual members effectively to compare their operations with others in their type of business. Annual surveys on the cost of doing business are also conducted by many trade associations. Progressive small independents make effective use of their associations' cost and expense surveys to check on their own operations, to locate danger spots, and to take appropriate management action promptly that might otherwise have been delayed until conditions became really serious. Data on operating results of the industry are also valuable when managerial decisions involving a new enterprise, department, or other activity must be made.

In many fields of small business, industry cost studies and operating ratios are assembled by other agencies, such as producers, university research bureaus, accounting firms, and Dun & Bradstreet, often with trade association cooperation. The trade association interprets such data, and it reports to members pertinent conclusions and often the entire survey report. This type of activity—keeping in touch with all studies and developments of concern to members, and analyzing and reporting on them in terms understandable and applicable to members—is one of the major managerial aids to small independents.

Education and training is another important trade association service. This is provided through conventions, field contacts and periodicals, and by correspondence and short courses—often in cooperation with a college or university. Increasingly, national associations have been publishing management handbooks or manuals.

Many trade organizations also assist members through store or shop visitations, and all associations welcome member visits at headquarters to discuss individual problems. Trade association executives assist and advise on proposed layouts, and some even originate layouts from information furnished by members. Aid in modernization of building, fixtures, and methods is provided by leading associations, sometimes through their own staffs or from specialists approved by headquarters. The main method for receiving individual assistance is naturally by correspondence. Large, well-established associations answer many inquiries by mailing published materials, but they endeavor to make the service as individualized as possible.

On the local level, trade groups in the larger cities also render a large number of services to members. Many locals are affiliated with the national trade associations in their respective industries, and many of the services previously cited as being performed at the national level are also carried out through the local association. Among the national associations, there seems to be a trend toward state and local managerial training conferences. Conditions differ in various cities and among the states, so trade association services are often adapted to local needs.

In recent years interindustry competition has increased to such an extent that it is often more important than competition among concerns in the same industry. This is particularly true among industries producing consumer goods and services. Movies, for example, compete with television for a share of the consumer dollar. Similarly, food competes with drugs and hardware, clothing with automobiles and jewelry, and so on. So each industry, through the cooperative efforts of trade association members, endeavors to increase, or at least retain, its share of total consumer spending. Both types of competition—interindustry and intraindustry—complement each other. Healthy competition within an industry improves its competitive position relative to other industries, but overemphasis or rivalry among firms in the same industry may not be to their combined self-interest. This means that competitors must subordinate their individual rivalries and pool their efforts at times to maintain their industry's proportionate share of the total consumer market.

Many trade association services to members require the pooling of technical information, statistics, and ideas for the benefit of the entire industry. To obtain maximum benefits from a trade association a member must give as well as take. The decay of industries in foreign countries in which individual firms closely and jealously guarded their trade secrets is mute testimony to the obsolescence of this independent approach or noncooperative attitude. In the United States the opposite point of view is evident by patent pooling and industrywide simplification and standardization programs, as well as by open membership trade association activities.

In addition to sharing information and furnishing statistical data requested by one's association, it is advisable for more small entrepreneurs to attend their trade association conventions and participate actively in discussions. Those independent owner/managers who take a week away from their business to attend a trade association convention may share in and profit by the experience of fifty others having an average of ten years' experience, or a total of five hundred years of diversified experience in their line of business. In addition, they meet people who are superior in certain activities and can learn much from them through conversation. When meetings are not in session, the owner/manager may want to visit stores or other types of business of interest in the convention city; sometimes these may be his or her own suppliers. Conventions are planned and conducted by experts to emphasize topics of current importance. Trade association officials understand the needs and problems of their members and are glad to talk about them. Many associations maintain model stores, complete libraries, and other facilities well worth study by visiting members. Time away from one's own business premises often leads to adaptation of the outside viewpoint on return from a trip.

Trade and Other Publications

For the independent enterpriser starting on a small scale, active participation or membership in a trade association may be difficult at first. However, familiarity with the trade publications in the field of business, both before launching the enterprise and continuously thereafter, is of the utmost importance.

It is well to read up on everything within reach about your business; this not only improves your knowledge, your usefulness and your fitness for more responsible work, but it invests your business with more interest, since you understand its functions, its basic principles, its place in the general scheme of things.
                                                        —DANIEL WILLARD

Trade publications constitute one of the most economical ways for small independents to keep abreast of developments in their field. This category includes the official publications of trade and professional associations that are usually available to nonmembers by subscription. Both association publications and commercial trade and business periodicals are available in many libraries, and these sources may be useful. As a minimum, however, small business owners should subscribe to at least one good trade journal in their business field and to one good general news periodical or newspaper that carries significant reports on business developments and topics affecting the class of trade or industry with which they are concerned. Retailers should also subscribe to the popular magazines read by their customers, from which they may glean trends in consumers' tastes. Failure to do so may result in a situation where customers are better informed about new styles, new merchandise, or new materials than is the merchant. In the fashion fields a number of periodicals issue retailers' editions that contain advance notices to the merchants of what their customers will soon be demanding.

Professional Management Consultants

Recently an increasing number of small business owners have come to realize the assistance they can obtain from **management consultants,** and more and more consultants are tailoring their services to the needs of small firms. This trend is likely to continue because it is the result of fundamental conditions. Management, as an activity, is becoming increasingly complex, specialized, scientific, and professionalized, and it is distinct from the unique idea or motivation characteristic of a particular business. The operator of the firm is intensely concerned with promoting the firm's basic reason for existence or the unique idea that justifies continuing the enterprise. Thus, while most owner/managers of small firms are thoroughly familiar with this aspect of the business, much more so than an outsider could be, they often lack the expert organization and communications skills to successfully manage certain aspects of the business. It is this latter need that management consultants are equipped to meet.

In many small concerns, however, problems requiring the special abilities of a consultant are intermittent and of short duration. It would not pay such firms to have management specialists continuously on their payroll any more than it would pay an individual to employ a physician full-time when the doctor's services are needed only occasionally to help prevent or remedy an illness.

What most small firms need are (1) specialized assistance when some serious difficulty is encountered, and (2) periodic checkups to detect hidden pitfalls that may be avoided if discovered in time.

There are over fifteen thousand management consultants or consulting firms in the United States. Although some limit their services to a special phase of management, such as plant layout, plant location, or communications, most of them are able to service all the needs of the average business; if they specialize at all, they specialize mainly by advising firms of only a certain type and size. Part of this results from the way consultants are usually selected—by personal recommendations of satisfied clients. Choosing the right consultant for the small enterprise should receive careful attention.

When management consultants are employed, it is of the utmost importance to cooperate with them in every possible manner, both during and after their employment. Their work consists of two major parts: (1) diagnosis of the trouble or weakness and (2) recommendations for improvement. Their recommendations are of no value unless followed. In some cases it may be necessary to have the consultant carry through certain recommendations. This need occurs when a recommendation calls for some technical job beyond the ability of the concern's own management, such as the installation of more efficient methods, a quality control system, or a new layout.

Management consultants are relatively expensive but may represent an excellent investment. A small consulting firm or an individual consultant may charge $100 per day or more, but may be needed for only a short time to remedy some trouble that would otherwise result in loss of profits far in excess of the consultant's fee.

The small business consultant is usually a limited-service type of management consultant. Such individuals are often currently employed by an educational institution or large corporation and do consulting work on the side. Progressive colleges and universities encourage their faculties to engage in a reasonable amount of private practice in their teaching specialties. Most of these academics have had exceptionally fine training and considerable practical experience. The nature of their academic positions requires them to keep abreast of the latest developments and exposes them to continuous requests for information and advice. They are obliged to observe high standards of honesty, integrity, and professional ethics. In many cases the typical independent enterpriser will find a small business consultant better suited to his or her needs, and probably less expensive, than a full-time management consultant.

Suppliers and Equipment Manufacturers

Manufacturers of cash registers, weighing and measuring scales, electronic computers, production machines, handling devices, and other equipment often render many complimentary services to the users or prospective users of their products in an effort to build and maintain goodwill. Some have established special divisions for the purpose of aiding or informing small businesss owners, such as the Department of Management Counseling Services of NCR Corp.

These manufacturers provide a variety of services. Assistance on store layout and modernization, for example, is available from companies producing floor coverings, display materials and equipment, and modern storefronts. A similar service is performed for small industrial plants by manufacturers of machine tools and materials handling equipment.

The **suppliers** from whom a business secures its merchandise, materials, and supplies are particularly valuable sources of information and assistance and will be discussed in Chapter 9.

Lawyers/Accountants/Others

Many local public utilities have specialists available for consultation on lighting, heating, and air-conditioning. Public utilities also make surveys and advise on power installations. The customer's banker can render valuable assistance on financial and credit matters. The small business owner will naturally seek the help of a lawyer on legal problems as they occur, but a lawyer can also help the owner *avoid* problems. Accountants can suggest ways to improve the business's cash position, increase its profit, and minimize its tax liability.

Other examples of outside staff assistance to small business include the services of such organizations as Dun & Bradstreet and the A. C. Nielsen Company. These firms render invaluable service in such areas as credit reporting, advertising, and market research. In addition to these are other firms specializing in plant location studies, the analysis of traffic problems, the design of control systems, or other matters of primary concern to management. Also available to the management of a small firm, on a subscription basis, are a number of business reporting services, such as those of the Bureau of National Affairs, Research Institute of America, Commerce Clearing House, Merten's and Prentice-Hall, whose reporting services keep management abreast of developments in tax laws, pension plans, profit sharing, and labor legislation and arbitration. Of particular interest to the small retailer are the subscription services that specialize in reporting fashion trends, shelf prices in chain food stores and supermarkets, or other kinds of market information.

SUMMING UP

Services of a high quality related to any function of management and to any phase of operations of the small enterprise are available from the outside. In particular, the chapter strongly endorsed the services of trade associations and trade press services, and those of the U.S. Department of Commerce and the Small Business Administration. It was also suggested that management and small business consultants, or "business doctors," may save a business life just as a physician or surgeon may save a human life. Aids and services furnished on a goodwill basis by companies with a product to sell may also be of great value in many situations.

It has often been said that the chief problem of independent business owners is their independence. Small business ownership does indeed attract an independent, self-reliant type of person—one less likely to seek advice and assistance from those of greater experience and know-how. Often the biggest problem is to get the independent to appreciate the need for outside management assistance, and then to be willing and able to take the time to profit by it.

He that won't be counselled, can't be helped.

—Benjamin Franklin

KEY WORDS

management consultants
outside staff
suppliers

trade associations
trade publications

DISCUSSION QUESTIONS

1.   What is an outside staff? Why must most small business owners rely heavily on such a staff?

2.   Cite examples of how a small business owner can use basic economic and statistical data published by government agencies in policy formulation and long-range planning.

EXERCISE

Interview the owner of a small, nonfranchised business in your community. Limit the interview to the general area of outside staff assistance. *Who* has been (is) of particular help to the owner in the management of the business? Bank? Suppliers? SBA? Others? *How* have they helped, or *how* are they helping? Identify the kinds of business *services* purchased from other firms (such as bookkeeping, legal advice, management consulting). Of what trade association, if any, is the firm a member? What kinds of services are supplied by this trade association to its members? Identify by name the person you interview, and the name and location of his or her firm.

CASE IN POINT

> Arthur Tracy's upholstering business has grown to the point that even with competent craftsmen he can no longer handle it efficiently alone. Much of his time is spent in supervising workers, maintaining an inventory of materials and supplies, and keeping records—some of them quite complex, particularly those concerning costs of materials and labor on individual jobs.
>
> From time to time he has used professional accountants, most of them small-time operators. These people have been helpful, but as Arthur's business grows they often find themselves in situations beyond their technical capacities or facilities. Arthur has also employed full-time accountants, but is not quite large enough to support a good one for long; they find the compensation inadequate or move to a larger firm, usually to one of Arthur's competitors.
>
> Arthur has been approached recently by Accountants Associated, a fairly new group made up of retired accountants from larger companies. They want to come in and take over on a contract basis, visiting the shop regularly and analyzing records and financing in general. As a newly organized accounting firm, however, the principals are unproven in regard to long-run management and the permanency of their employees.
>
> At the same time one of the local banks is installing a computer data bank, into which Arthur could feed his figures and have results

within a week, sometimes over the weekend. Arthur is a little distrustful of this modern unit since it is not well-established as yet.

Another possibility also appears on the horizon. The State Upholsterers' Guild is setting up a facility for weekly submission of operating data for upholsterers and small manufacturers to be combined, averaged, and returned for comparison. This arrangement costs $50 per month and is said to be backed by a large central city wholesaler of textiles. It is supervised by a man who was once Arthur's accountant but who left with hard feelings. Arthur is not confident that his data will be kept confidential, and, furthermore, since the figures would be broken down by county, his firm's figures might be very easily identifiable unless the membership increases.

As a consultant, how would you advise Arthur to proceed in his selection of an adequate accounting program?

Part Three

MANAGING THE PRODUCTION FUNCTION

As noted in Chapter 4, the production of goods and/or services to satisfy human wants is the major utility created by a business firm. In this context the purchase of goods for resale—merchandising—is a "service" to the consumer. The first four chapters comprising this section are concerned with the planning, acquisition, and organization of the resources needed to produce either a product or a service: physical facilities (Chapter 8), merchandise or materials (Chapters 9 and 10), and labor (Chapter 11); the concluding chapter (12) relates only to the production (manufacture) of products. After reading these chapters you should have an increased awareness of the importance of management as a factor of production.

Providing
Physical Facilities

CHAPTER EIGHT   *A building properly equipped is neces-*
sary to the conduct of any business. After reading this chapter you
should more fully appreciate the importance of a firm's management
of its capital assets.

As with any other resource in business, such as money, personnel, equipment, or materials, the building housing the enterprise can be poorly selected
or poorly utilized. The degree to which it is properly selected and used is often
a major factor in determining the amount of return on the entrepreneur's expenditure of time, effort, and money.

Most businesses, particularly merchandising and service establishments,
lease or purchase existing building space; few are in a position to design and
construct their own business houses. The same fundamentals apply in either
case, but more compromises are needed to utilize an old building effectively.

Procuring the business premises, of course, is only the first step in providing the necessary physical facilities for conducting business. The building must
also be adequately furnished, and the furnishings and equipment must be arranged or laid out to make the most effective use of the space available for the
work to be done. A good building effectively used is as valuable to an operating plant as are good home facilities for a household.

BUILDING REQUIREMENTS

Purchasing or constructing the business premises is a risky *long-run* commitment, and entrepreneurs are encouraged to rent rather than to buy or build
the first building they occupy. This counsel is particularly appropriate for
those planning to launch a manufacturing enterprise. It is usually more difficult, for instance, when a manufacturing firm ceases operations to get another
company to take over than it is to transfer ownership of a retail or service establishment. A factory's plant and equipment are specialized. When conditions make it unprofitable for one company to produce in a given plant, it is
unlikely that new owners could make the same product profitably. Conditions
making it difficult or impossible to operate a given factory profitably are likely

Courtesy of Dun & Bradstreet, Inc.

to be beyond the individual company's control. When the market for a product evaporates or shifts to other products, a manufacturer is powerless unless he or she can shift with the market—or can hedge against this by diversifying the firm's product lines. Nor are industrial plants easily adapted to other uses. They are sometimes difficult to dispose of, as abandoned plants seen in various parts of the country bear silent witness.

Another reason for leasing the building in which to house the new business is that the entrepreneur's initial capital requirements will be lower than they would otherwise be. Thus, an important consideration in selecting a site for a new business (or, often, a new site for an existing business) is the availability of rental building space.

Regardless of whether it is to be leased, purchased, or constructed from the ground up, some points to check in regard to the building are (1) suitability for its intended use, (2) accessibility, (3) internal transportation or traffic, (4) room for business expansion, and (5) external appearance.

Suitability

A building is good or bad in proportion to its suitability for the activities that must be performed. Excellent housing for one business may be next to impossible for another business. Simple protection from the elements and from burglary might be sufficient for many lines of retailing, whereas heavy construction and solid concrete floors might be required for certain manufacturing or service industries.

Accessibility

Accessibility requirements vary by kinds of business. In retailing, customer accessibility is of greatest importance, but adequate facilities for receiving merchandise and making deliveries should be provided. In manufacturing, easy receipt of **raw materials** and shipment of **finished goods** are dominant considerations. Service industries usually require accessibility for customers or clients and often also require access for delivery equipment. Accessibility to a building is hampered by steps, a narrow entrance, or any type of obstruction, such as a post. Also, receipt of goods may be difficult if there is no door to an alley or if goods must be unloaded from a heavy-traffic lane without provision for trucks; delivery through the main customer entrance is clearly undesirable.

Internal Transportation and Traffic

Closely related to external accessibility are the internal transportation and traffic facilities provided by the building. Retail stores naturally wish customer traffic to be unhindered by columns, different floor levels, irregularly shaped buildings, and similar conditions. Ease of movement within the store may be important for items like furniture, heavy appliances, or especially bulky containers. In service and manufacturing establishments the nature of the process largely determines the importance as well as the type of internal transportation facilities. A beauty parlor and a machine shop obviously have very different requirements.

The flow of materials or the movement of customers or employees is directly related to *layout;* both must be considered together. The basic purpose behind physical plant layout is to integrate personnel, materials, and equipment so as to move material as easily as possible over the shortest distance or to attract customers to the merchandise or service offered for sale. Either of these objectives can be accomplished by providing a natural sequence of operations, in a safe manner and in a pleasant atmosphere. The achievement of these objectives should result in a lower cost of operation.[1]

Room for Expansion

Will the building permit expansion or alterations that may be needed later? Is it flexible enough to be adapted to other possible uses? Potential growth and changes in the business during the term of the lease should be considered. Will the occupant want to add new departments? Where can they be housed? If the business is a service establishment and is contemplating adding retail sales later, is the building, as well as its location, suitable? Can the area

---

[1] Building layout is discussed in more detail later in this chapter.

or space be used economically? What about subleasing part of the building now to have it available later for expansion? Is extra space that can be used effectively during dull seasons available for recurring peaks of selling, storage, or processing? These are some of the many questions that should be investigated in planning the future space needs of the business, and many of them should be provided for in the lease.

External Appearance

The external appearance of the building is also important in many ways. In the capacity of an advertising medium, it should represent the character of the business, identifying it and at the same time distinguishing it from others. Some attempts to make the building represent the character of the business take extreme forms, such as the massive columns and thick marble walls, floors, and fixtures of many older bank buildings. A building of this kind may become a white elephant if the bank moves to different quarters and the building cannot be converted to other uses. However, modern architecture can achieve the desired impression of safety, stability, permanence, and dignity by less expensive means. Even the storefront may represent the character of a business, the luxurious front of the exclusive shop being contrasted to the practical, economical appearance of the popularly priced retail store.

The building, including the front, may distinguish a particular business merely by being different yet fashionable, or by attempting to visualize the nature of the business or its name. The Brown Derby, a supper club in Hollywood, is an example. For the entrepreneur entering a line of business in which such novel treatment of the appearance of the building is neither too costly nor too permanent, it may be an effective way of capturing and holding the interest of potential customers. If successful, the design may be patented and serve as the basis for granting franchises, as was the case with Clarence Saunders's unusual Piggly Wiggly storefronts, or it may be used if one decides to open additional stores of a similar nature. Often the theme of the business is carried out in the store's interior design. A luggage shop in Little Rock, Arkansas, for example, was constructed in the shape of a Pullman car. Unless watched carefully, however, these attempts to visualize the nature of the business may result in a single-purpose structure that can be adapted to other uses only at great cost.

OBTAINING THE EQUIPMENT

If procuring the premises is the first step in providing a home for the business, the second step must necessarily be furnishing that "home." For a proposed enterprise, the entrepreneur should make a complete list of the different kinds of equipment needed for the proper performance of all the activities of the business and the number of each required.

Most merchandising and service establishments require *office* equipment (such as desks and chairs, typewriters, and calculators), *sales* equipment (such as cash registers and display counters and racks), and *delivery* equipment (trucks); manufacturing and service establishments require, in addition to the above, various types of *processing* equipment. The cost of obtaining this equipment depends largely on whether the equipment is purchased or leased and on the lease or purchase terms.

Advantages of Purchasing

The current tax structure influences capital decisions in many ways. Prior to 1954 it was often better to **lease** than to own land, buildings, fixtures, equipment, or other **fixed (capital) assets** because **depreciation** rules were rigid, whereas rental costs were (and are) fully deductible as business expenses. In 1954, however, the Internal Revenue Service eased the burden of capital financing by allowing the use of the **double-declining-balance** method of depreciation, increasing the amount of depreciation taken in the early years. The Economic Recovery Tax Act of 1981 further loosened depreciation rules.[2]

The **investment tax credit** has also stimulated the purchase of capital goods by allowing a percentage of the purchase price as a credit against taxes due and not merely as a deduction from taxable income. The current allowable credit is 10 percent of the full cost of new or used equipment that qualifies for depreciation as "5-year" or "10-year" property under the **Accelerated Cost Recovery System** (ACRS).[3] On a capital asset that qualifies as "3-year" property under ACRS, the 10 percent credit is applied to 60 percent of the cost. Thus on 5-year property that costs $50,000, the allowable tax credit is $5,000; on 3-year property that costs $50,000, the allowable tax credit is $3,000.

On capital assets that do not qualify as **recovery property** under ACRS, the investment tax credit is 10 percent of the full cost of assets with a useful or **service life** of seven years or more. For assets with a five- or six-year life, the investment credit is 10 percent of two-thirds the cost; for assets with a three- or four-year life, the credit is 10 percent of one-third the cost. No investment credit is allowed if the service life of the asset is less than three years.

The investment tax credit is in addition to depreciation deductible as a business expense. The total investment credit, however, is limited to the income tax shown on the business owner's tax return, or to $25,000 plus 90 percent of the tax that is more than $25,000, whichever is less. For example, if the small business owner's income tax liability is $40,000, his or her maximum investment credit is $38,500 ($25,000 plus $13,500).

Recent changes in the tax laws have thus encouraged more business operators to purchase equipment rather than to lease it. When equipment is pur-

---

[2] Rules and methods of depreciating capital assets are discussed in detail in Chapter 20.

[3] See pp. 339–44 for a discussion of ACRS and other methods of depreciation.

chased, two forms of credit contracts are commonly negotiated: (1) the **conditional sales contract,** in which the purchaser does not receive title to the equipment until it is fully paid for, and (2) the **chattel mortgage contract,** in which the equipment becomes the property of the purchaser at the time it is delivered but the seller holds a mortgage claim against it until the amount specified in the contract is paid. To take advantage of the investment tax credit provision, however, the chattel mortgage form of contract (in which title to the equipment is passed to the purchaser immediately) should be used.

Advantages of Leasing

Although changes in the tax laws have made purchasing equipment—whether new or used—more attractive, *leasing* equipment has certain advantages not related to taxation. Not only are funds released for working capital purposes, but the lessees are exempt from the maintenance costs that they would otherwise incur. The possibilities of leasing, as opposed to outright buying, should not be overlooked.

In actual fact, leasing has so increased in recent years that it is estimated that half of all plants, stores, and offices in the United States lease at least part of the equipment used in their operations. In addition to the advantages just cited, new models of equipment are usually more readily available to the user, and under short-term contracts the leased item is removed and no longer constitutes an expense when its use is no longer required.

In considering these advantages, however, the small business owner should also recognize that the total cost of leasing over a number of years is likely to be greater than if the equipment is purchased.

ARRANGING THE LAYOUT

Layout means the arrangement of machines, fixtures, and other equipment. Good layout often depends on the nature of the building. At one extreme is the industry that almost requires a specially constructed building; at the other is the type of business for which any strategically located building is suitable.

In most retail and many service fields, trade associations have developed model layouts suited to the needs of the particular business. Consulting firms also supply helpful advice concerning layouts for all kinds of businesses.

The best layout is the one that makes the most effective use of space for the particular business. The principal factor here is not area or volume, but *location*. The same area or volume in one part of a store, for example, may be worth many times more than an equal area or volume in another part of the same store.

Layout starts with an analysis of the activities involved in operating the business, the objectives sought, and the facilities for achieving them. In manufacturing and in many service businesses, the primary objective is to facilitate productive operations. In the retail store it is to direct the flow of customer traffic for maximum sales.

Certain factors must always be considered in arrangement and layout, regardless of the type of business:

1. *Logical and optimum arrangement of equipment and merchandise with reference to production flow for manufacturing and to customer buying habits for merchandising.* Having machinery in proper sequence and conveniently located expedites the flow of material and saves factory workers much lost motion. Also, having merchandise in the right place at the right time increases sales per customer and reduces steps for salespeople.

2. *Maximum use of light, ventilation, and heat, to take full advantage of natural conditions resulting from the building construction.* Effective use of windows, doors, vents, and skylights will save eyesight, improve work and health, and reduce the costs of lighting, heating, and air-conditioning. Customers and employees will also appreciate the fact that arrangements made with these factors in mind facilitate their personal comfort.

3. *Maximum efficiency in the use of equipment.* Layout for any kind of business—merchandising, manufacturing, or service—involves the arrangement of office, processing and other equipment to secure maximum efficiency in use.

4. *Maximum facilities for a clear view of the establishment by management, worker, or customer.* Thus management can readily observe all activities of customers and employees, workers can observe customers and their movements, and customers can easily see all the firm's offerings and the location of service areas or particular groups of merchandise or other products.

To summarize, the same principles of layout apply to all types of businesses, because the following factors are always present: (1) *people*—workers, customers, management; (2) *equipment*—machinery or fixtures; (3) *goods*—materials, merchandise, supplies; and (4) *the building and its fixtures*—windows, doors, stairs, and so forth. The relative importance of these factors, however, varies from one type of business to another.

Store Layout

Space locations within a store can be used more effectively in some ways than in others. It is usually poor business to try to increase the volume of a slow-selling department by giving it one of the better locations when this requires shifting another department better able to take full advantage of the good location.

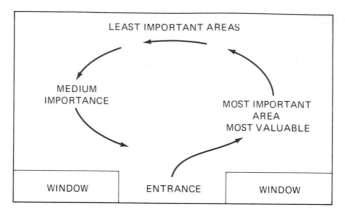

FIGURE 8-1
Diagram of Floor Space Values in a Retail Store

It is the space nearest the traffic flow, therefore offering the greatest exposure to customers, that has the greatest sales potential. Thus the value of space in a retail store decreases as one moves from the front of the store to the rear. Also, because shopping traffic tends to circulate through a store in a counterclockwise direction, the space toward the right, as one enters the store, is more valuable than the space toward the left. These differences in floor space values are illustrated in Figure 8-1.

The following are some of the more important *principles of floor space distribution* in a retail store:

1. The fastest-selling, most profitable merchandise should be placed in the locations that sell best.

2. Impulse goods should be placed in good locations at eye level.

3. Staple goods should be placed in areas of medium importance.

4. Shopping goods can be placed in the less accessible locations; people will go to them.

5. The office and other "nonsale" departments should be located in the poorer sections.

Factory Layout

Layout of the manufacturing establishment depends on the type of manufacturing process in which the factory is engaged. In general, there are three basic types of **manufacturing processes: intermittent, continuous,** and **repetitive.**

In intermittent manufacture, products are made only to customers' specifications. Since the product is nonstandard, it cannot be produced for stock;

thus it cannot be manufactured continuously. A plant engaged in this type of manufacture is called a **job shop.**

In continuous manufacture, on the other hand, one or only a few standard products are manufactured continuously to the company's own specifications in anticipation of sales. If two or more products are manufactured, they are manufactured simultaneously on separate production lines. Such a shop is commonly called a **mass-production shop.**

The repetitive type of manufacture falls between the intermittent and continuous types. In this type of manufacture, a large and diverse line of standard products is manufactured, each product being processed from time to time in lots of economic size. No single product is produced in sufficient volume to justify its manufacture on a continuous basis; yet, since it is a standard product, the processing of additional quantities or lots can be *repeated* from time to time without change in departmental or machine routing or in operation method and allowed operation time. This type of shop is known as a **miscellaneous shop.**

Obviously, the type of manufacture determines not only the kind of production equipment that is used but also the manner in which this equipment is laid out. In the intermittent and repetitive types of manufacture, for example, a *functional* (or **process**) **layout** of production equipment is required. In this type of layout there is a separate department for each process; that is, each type of operation is performed in a single department on all types of products. Hence, production equipment is of the *general-purpose* type. This type of layout is typical of most small manufacturing plants.

In continuous manufacture, on the other hand, a *line* (or **product**) **layout** of production equipment is required. In this type of layout, there is a separate department for each product; that is, all operations on a single product are performed in one department, the equipment being arranged in a line according to the most economical sequence of operations. Hence, production equipment is of the *special-purpose* type. The best-known example of this type of layout is automobile assembly.

Figure 8-2 is a schematic comparison of these basic types of layout.

The most important advantage of the functional type of layout is its *flexibility*. Different products or customers' orders can be processed on the same (general-purpose) machines. Similarly, changes in the product mix (elimination of unprofitable products and the introduction of new ones) can be made without changes in the layout. Also, since the machines are functionally independent, a breakdown in one machine does not delay operations on the other machines. Thus the flexibility of this type of layout results in a greater utilization of both machines and labor.

Another advantage is a lower capital investment in production equipment, since general-purpose machines are standard (stock) items that can be made at higher volume and sold at lower cost than special-purpose equipment. However, since general-purpose machines are less efficient than special-pur-

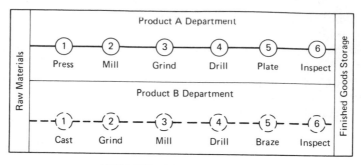

LINE LAYOUT (Layout by Product)

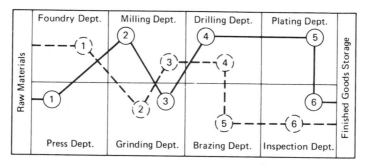

FUNCTIONAL LAYOUT (Layout by Process)

————— Product A   — — — — Product B

FIGURE 8-2

Schematic Comparison of Functional Layout and Line Layout

pose machines, unit operation costs are higher. Also, because the manufacturing requirements of the various products or job orders often conflict, there is a considerable amount of backtracking of **work-in-process;** for the same reason a flexible system of shop transportation (sporadic movement of work-in-process by lift trucks rather than the continuous movement of material by conveyor) is necessary, resulting in lengthy delays between operations and long manufacturing cycle times. The longer processing time, in turn, requires more storage space for work-in-process in addition to larger inventories. It is also difficult to estimate costs and completion times on many jobs, and detailed daily planning and scheduling of work is necessary to avoid costly congestion at certain work centers.

The functional layout is strong where the line layout is weak, and weak where the line layout is strong. The advantages and disadvantages of the latter type of layout may thus be inferred from the preceding discussion. The disadvantages of the line type of layout (principally high fixed costs and lack of flexibility) can be overcome if the volume of production is high and reasonably stable. However, this type of layout is not feasible for most small manufacturing firms.

Service Establishment Layout

The appropriate layout and building design for a service establishment depends on whether the enterprise is of the merchandising or the processing type. A merchandising type of service business includes motels, restaurants, and most personal service establishments. Customer convenience, pleasing appearance, and similar considerations are of relatively great importance in this type of service enterprise.

The processing type of service business has, on the other hand, much in common with a factory. Here various operations, such as cleaning, repairing, or altering, are performed on articles owned by the customers. In many cases the customer never sees the work being done and may not even come to the plant at all. Factors governing productive efficiency are of relatively greater importance in such cases with regard to both building and layout. The principles governing factory layout, as discussed in the preceding section, will apply to service establishments of this type.

Wholesaling Layout

Layout of the wholesale establishment is based on the primary function of the business—order filling. In general, the wholesale layout will more closely resemble that of a factory, and many good ideas can be adapted from factory layouts.

Most wholesale and warehouse activities lend themselves to a production line type of operation (or *order-pick* line pattern), as illustrated in Figure 8-3. Unlike a manufacturer who turns out goods that are identical, however, the wholesaler turns out orders of goods that are seldom alike. The wholesaler's problem is to arrange an order picking route and routine that will facilitate the handling of the unpredictable assortments without special adjustment for any of them. Therefore, both the routing and the routine should be flexible enough to meet any reasonable contingency.

An important objective in any type of work-center layout is to reduce the amount of employee "travel." A wholesale-warehouse employee ordinarily walks several miles each day in the routine of order filling. As illustrated in Figure 8-3, this mileage can be effectively lowered by (1) laying out picking aisles so that they are perpendicular to the shipping dock, and (2) storing the fast-moving (large-volume) items on pallet racks nearest the shipping dock. The aisle space between the pallet racks and shelf stock should be four to six feet, depending on the type of merchandise.

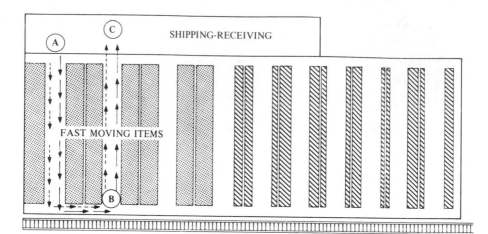

FIGURE 8-3
A Wholesale-Warehouse Layout

Order filling can also be speeded up by splitting orders into *trip routes.* For example, in the illustration the order picker travels up one side of one aisle (A), loading only one side of the trailer. Then, he (she) travels down the opposite side of the next aisle (B), loading the other side of the trailer, and finishing the trip right back at the shipping dock (C)—no dead travel time. Meanwhile, other workers follow similar picking routes, filling other splits of the order.

When preparing warehouse layouts, wholesalers should also determine the feasibility of using mechanical materials-handling equipment and other labor-saving devices. Pallets and gravity chutes frequently offer a means of simplifying materials handling under certain conditions.

SUMMING UP

A good building effectively used is as valuable to an operating plant as are good home facilities for a household. The manner in which a building is used for production or for merchandising is comparable to the importance to the homemaker of successfully placing pieces of furniture and household equipment within the home. Most businesses are successful only if the flow of materials, customers, and employees within the building is smooth, efficient, economical, and safe. Good layout will produce these results.

To be considered also is the appropriateness of the building in terms of internal and external appearance. Ideally, a retailing or service business in its external appearance reflects the character or personality of the firm. Manufacturers are becoming increasingly aware of the importance of the effects and community tolerance of their plants on the local environment. Factors of light, ventilation, and heat, plus those of facility in supervision of employees must also be kept in mind.

Business owner/managers should also weigh the advantages of leasing versus buying buildings or equipment. If the business is short of capital, leasing may be the more feasible short-run alternative.

KEY WORDS

Accelerated Cost Recovery System
capital assests
chattel mortgage contract
conditional sales contract
continuous manufacturing process
depreciation
double-declining-balance
finished goods
fixed assets
functional layout
impulse goods
intermittent manufacturing process
investment tax credit
job shop

lease
line layout
mass-oroduction shop
miscellaneous shop
process layout
product layout
raw materials
recovery property
repetitive manufacturing process
service life
shopping goods
staples goods
work-in-process

DISCUSSION QUESTIONS

1. Discuss the particular needs or general requirements for layout in (a) a retail store, (b) a restaurant, (c) a dry cleaning business, and (d) a small production plant.

2. Considering the principles of layout discussed in the text, how would you prepare a layout for an engineering firm, an insurance company, or other office-type production?

EXERCISES AND PROBLEMS

1. Calculate the investment tax credit for each of the following capital assets that qualify as recovery property under the Accelerated Cost Recovery System. (See pp. 341–44 for a detailed discussion of this system.)

    a. 3-year property costing $100,000

    b. 5-year property costing $125,000

    c. 10-year property costing $150,000

2. Calculate the investment tax credit for each of the following capital assets that do not qualify as recovery property under ACRS.

a. machine costing $120,000 with a service life of four years

b. machine costing $180,000 with a service life of six years

c. machine costing $200,000 with a service life of eight years

3. What would be the small business owner's total investment credit in exercise 1 if all three properties were purchased during the same tax year? Assume that the business owner's tax liability as shown on the tax return for that year is $23,000.

4. What would be the small business owner's total investment credit in exercise 2 if all three machines were purchased during the same tax year? Assume that the business owner's tax liability as shown on the tax return for that year is $35,000.

CASE IN POINT

Arthur Adams rents an entire building for $700 per month. His dry cleaning and laundry service occupies the first floor, but he sublets the second floor to a real estate broker who pays him $300 a month. The owner of the building has just approached Mr. Adams, offering him the building for $90,000. Mr. Adams can borrow $70,000 at 14 percent from the bank, and can spare $20,000 from the business if he needs it.

The building is in a good location and in fair condition. The area is at a standstill economically but is not declining. Taxes on the property are $1,500 per year, insurance $800. Arthur believes that upkeep should cost about $3,000–$4,000 per year. In a year or so, he had planned to ask the owner for considerable renovation, which would of course increase the rent.

Arthur is forty-five years of age and has a son in high school who, when he is graduated from college, expects to enter the business with his father. In the meantime, Arthur has been considering the establishment of branch units of his business, one to the northeast, the other in the southern part of the city. This, too, will take money. Hence, the decision of either continuing to rent or buying this building outright is related to other plans.

If Arthur Adams should buy the building, what would his annual costs be? Should he buy it or continue renting? Can you draw up a recommendation addressed to him, explaining your viewpoint and reasoning?

Purchasing
Goods and Supplies

CHAPTER NINE *Goods or supplies are necessary to the conduct of any business. The retailer and the wholesaler must have merchandise to sell, the manufacturer requires materials to fashion into finished products, and the service establishment needs supplies to function. In most businesses, it is almost as important to know how and where to buy as it is to know how and where to sell. The objective in purchasing is to obtain the best goods for the intended use at the lowest cost. Your study of this chapter will give you a clearer understanding of the fundamentals of buying for the small business.*

The art of careful buying involves six basic processes: (1) determining needs; (2) locating suitable sources of supply; (3) negotiating terms; (4) maintaining favorable relations with suppliers; (5) receiving, checking, and marking goods; and (6) following up after purchase.

DETERMINING INVENTORY NEEDS

Too often, buying in the small business is based on hunches instead of on adequate information. Often it is spasmodic rather than planned. The buyer should know the type, quality, brand, and size of supplies or goods needed and the quantities required. For the merchant this involves a study of the needs of the firm's customers. Even for the same class of trade, demand may be quite different in two locations even though they are not far apart. Alert merchants will keep abreast of fashion changes—anticipating such changes whenever possible, perhaps by reading the same magazines and seeing the same shows as their customers. Wholesalers' and trade journals are valuable aids to the small merchant in anticipating customer demand.

For the small manufacturer and service operator the intended use for materials, parts, and supplies is the important factor. The small enterpriser should watch for opportunities to use new, improved, or even less expensive materials that will do the job equally well. Trade journals, suppliers' representatives, and manufacturers' catalogs or descriptive printed matter will help the enterpriser in this task.

In determining the correct quantities to buy and when to buy them, the close relationship between purchasing and **inventory** or stores control becomes apparent. In merchandising, estimated needs minus quantity on hand (from inventory control records) equals quantity to buy. A **model stock plan** or list serves as a guide in the purchase of products (shopping or fashion goods) that must be carried in a particular combination of sizes, colors, styles, or price lines. In the replenishment of all other products carried in stock (staple goods), a **basic stock list** is followed: for each item, a basic stock list indicates the minimum quantities to be maintained, reorder points, and the quantities to be reordered at any one time.[1]

In manufacturing, estimated sales or planned production of each article is the starting point. Then a **materials or parts list** is used to determine the quantities needed for each unit. By multiplying planned production in units by the quantity of each material or part required per unit, the various quantities to purchase during the planning phase are calculated.

Purchasing for the small factory aims to maintain inventories that are balanced in terms of production needs. If only one product is made and the rate of production is fairly constant, purchasing can be simplified to a nearly routine operation. In other cases, when items needed can be obtained regularly as wanted within a predictable time limit, it may be sufficient merely to establish maximum and minimum stock limits and the economic ordering quantity. However, when deliveries are uncertain, **purchasing lead time** becomes an important consideration. So that manufacturers may receive their production materials on a proper scheduling basis it is necessary that they know how far in advance they must place their orders with a given **vendor.**

The importance of purchasing in different kinds of service establishments will vary with the following factors: (1) the percentage of total revenue obtained from the resale of merchandise, (2) the ratio of material and supply costs to labor costs, and (3) the range of qualities available from different suppliers.

Many service establishments secure almost half of their total revenue from the sale of merchandise. It is likely in such cases that materials, parts, and supplies used in conjunction with services performed will also make up an important part of the total service charge to customers. Examples include television, radio, and electrical repair shops, plumbing contractors, and some beauty parlors. In establishments of this type, purchasing is a function of major importance. In many personal service types of business, such as bookkeeping and advisory services, the cost of materials and supplies used bears such a small ratio to labor costs that the importance of the purchasing function is reduced to a minimum. Whenever the service performed on the person of the client or on the client's property is of high unit value, there may be significant quality variations in available materials and supplies that would lead to considerable

[1] See the following chapter for a complete discussion of inventory control.

differences in the quality of the resulting service. An expensive garment cleaned with a cheap solvent that is inadequate for the task is one example. By contrast, some establishments, such as sheet metal shops, work with materials that are so close to a standard that improvising or substitution is impossible or, at the least, difficult.

Important distinctions in the purchasing function exist also for small wholesalers, many of whom are also retailers. Throughout the country, but especially in small towns in the less densely populated states, small business owners in fields like groceries, meats, hardware, electrical supplies, and some others function as both wholesale and retail distributors. In such cases the wholesale division is influenced greatly by the needs and policies of the retail division in matters such as brands carried, price lines, and quantities to order.

In gauging demand, the small retailer-wholesaler may have a slight advantage over a large counterpart. Consumer demand is immediately reflected through the retail store. However, the person who is exclusively a wholesaler would anticipate this demand and have stocks on hand to fill orders for retail customers as they come in. In practice many wholesalers try to maintain continuous contact with consumer demand and trends by means of frequent visits of their representatives to retail stores. In addition to this firsthand observation, small wholesalers should use all available sources of **demand forecasting,** including the advice of their resident buying offices, reports on market trends, and tips received from manufacturers' representatives.

LOCATING AND SELECTING SUPPLIERS

Once needs or requirements have been determined, the next step is to locate suitable sources of supply. Resources available to small business owners usually are more limited than those for big companies. Often small business owners are restricted to the particular market representatives or channels of trade used by the producers from whom they want to buy. Sometimes they are limited to the immediate area in which their own business is located. Regardless of these limitations, they will nearly always have some choice between competing **suppliers.**

In selecting a supplier, a business owner should consider which one carries

the quality and variety of goods best suited to the business's needs as previously determined. Other important factors will be price for the quality desired, time required for delivery, transportation costs, and services rendered by the supplier (including willingness to sell in the quantities desired).

Types of Suppliers

Before small business owners can effectively formulate their buying policies or undertake the actual purchase of goods needed to operate their business, they must be familiar with the different types of suppliers available to them and the advantages and limitations associated with each type. Three groups of suppliers are usually recognized, and most small businesses will find that they must make some of their purchases with representatives of each group: **producers, merchant middlemen,** and **functional** (or **agent**) **middlemen.**

Producers. Manufacturers, miners, farmers, or processors of natural products all may be classed as producers. These business units may be of any size, ranging from very small to very large. Many of these suppliers, especially the larger manufacturers, have their own methods of distribution and may not be available for direct dealings with the small enterprise; their products may be purchased, but only through middlemen or representatives used by the particular manufacturer.

Merchant middlemen. Merchant middlemen constitute the chief source of supply for most small firms, especially retailers and service establishments. These are wholesalers who buy and take title to goods for resale.

Most merchant middlemen are *full-service* **wholesalers** (also called *service wholesalers*); some perform only limited services. The most common type of *limited-function* **wholesaler** is the cash-and-carry wholesaler. Some service wholesalers, however, also operate cash-and-carry departments.

Since small business owners often patronize local wholesalers, the possible savings through purchasing by the cash-and-carry method can be significant. The reason for the cash-and-carry policy is to reduce prices to retailers by lowering some of the wholesaler's operating expenses. It also enables the buyers to inspect their purchases and keep their payments up to date, and it eliminates the clerical work necessary for buying on a charge basis. However, cash-and-carry takes the buyers away from their business where they may be needed, requires more working capital than many small business owners have, and usually provides a more limited assortment of merchandise than that carried by the service wholesaler.

The service wholesaler, who is more likely to carry a broad line of goods, provides (1) the opportunity to purchase from a single source products made by hundreds of producers; (2) assurance at all times of a supply of new items made available locally through the wholesaler's constant scouting of markets; (3) quick delivery of goods as needed; (4) opportunity to buy on credit; (5) service and advice rendered through salespersons who visit the store; and (6) assurance of the wholesaler's interest in the retailer's success, because this is the only basis on which the wholesaler can continue in business.

Merchant middlemen differ in their degree of product specialization, such as general wholesalers versus drug houses, as well as in the range of services offered. The majority of merchant middlemen do not have any well-organized plan of voluntary cooperation for buyers, although many will work more closely with customers who concentrate their purchases than with those who do not.

In merchandising, small independent retailers have learned from experience that a reliable wholesaler is one of their best assets. The amount of confidence most retailers have in their wholesalers would surprise anyone not familiar with the field. This trust and confidence has been earned by the ever-increasing interest wholesalers have exhibited in the welfare and success of their retail customers.

Functional middlemen.   Small business owners may also have occasion to purchase from *functional* or *agent* middlemen. These are suppliers who do not take title to the goods they buy or sell; they serve merely as agents for the buyer or seller. Familiar examples are manufacturers' representatives and independent resident buying offices.

Independent buying offices, located in the leading manufacturing centers, are of two major types: merchandise brokers and resident buying offices.

Merchandise brokers bring buyer and seller together. No charge is made to retail clients for the broker's services, but the vendor pays a brokerage commission based on a percentage of sales. The advantages to retail clients who use a merchandise broker are that it saves them time on market trips, and they have access to goods that might not be available to them if they tried to locate this merchandise themselves. The brokers assemble a large number of lines from which the buyer makes a selection, or they may take the buyer to various wholesalers and manufacturers. The brokers also can make additional purchases when the buyer is unable to come to the market. Because the brokers' first concern is to sell the merchandise of their clients, some merchandise lines, regardless of their merit, may not be recommended by the brokers to their retail customers. Merchandise brokers usually limit themselves to one customer in a particular city, which makes it more likely that a retailer's merchandise will differ from that of his or her competitors. Merchandise brokers investigate the credit standing of retailers before accepting them as customers; thus manufacturers and wholesalers may take their orders with confidence. Some brokers place a "floor" on the size of a retailer's purchasing power before accepting the retailer as a client. Although no contracts exist between the retailer and the broker—contracts being made only between the broker and the sources of supply—brokers send market bulletins and advice to retail customers and assist them in many ways when they come to market.

Merchandise brokers represent and are compensated by manufacturers. **Resident buying offices** (or **purchasing agents,** as they are sometimes called), on the other hand, represent and are compensated by retailers and wholesalers. Resident buying offices maintain continuous contacts with a selected group of retailers on an annual fee and contract basis. In addition to buying merchandise for subscribing stores, they furnish a wealth of market information and forecasts. Many stores large enough to afford a resident buying office seem to be more interested in this market information service than in actually buying much merchandise through the office. However, when buyers from these stores go to market they work closely with the merchandise experts in their resident buying office, which saves the buyer's time as well as keeping the buyer in touch with the latest trends and best resources. The buying office is normally used as the store buyer's temporary headquarters when in the market.

There are several hundred resident buying offices in New York City, and many in other major markets, such as Chicago, St. Louis, Los Angeles, San Francisco, and Dallas. In general, each buying office serves only one client (subscribing retail store) in any community. The usual practice is to charge an annual fee of approximately 0.5 to 1 percent of the subscriber's net sales.

Apart from providing market information, most functional middlemen are not in a position to offer merchandising plans, although in some types of business they are highly respected as technical advisers regarding the uses of the product with which they deal.

Selecting One or Several Suppliers?

Retailers or service businesses holding dealerships or franchises usually are under obligation to concentrate purchases with the franchising organization. Only one supplier is used by manufacturers when a monopoly of supply exists or when the nearest supplier is traditionally the least expensive source of materials. Other businesses should decide whether to concentrate their buying with one or a few suppliers or to play the market.

A small business that is free to choose its suppliers should give preference to those who:

1. Can provide goods of the required quality, type, or model
2. Have goods available at desired prices and terms and in quantities needed
3. Are reliable—that is, goods are continuously available
4. Provide reasonable and customary protection of the buyer's interests, such as quality guarantees, right to make legitimate returns, and limited agency or similar franchise rights
5. Supply good service, not only in making deliveries but also in handling transactions and making adjustments
6. Make appropriate provisions for managerial or merchandising aids and technical assistance when needed

7. Employ suppliers' representatives of the type with whom the business owner can work and cooperate successfully

Whether to diversify or concentrate purchases will involve additional considerations, many of which are special applications of the foregoing standards. In any instance in which the owner is a shrewd buyer who enjoys trading and procurement activities, and when the owner wants various suppliers competing for the business and believes that the firm is in a position to take advantage of any variations in lines, prices, or services that different suppliers may offer, diversification would be the logical policy to follow. Diversification also enables the business to match popular lines carried by competitors, with the exception of exclusively franchised or otherwise restricted lines. Finally, it protects the small business in case any one supplier should cease business, change its lines, or change its business policies.

On the other hand, small business owners should also consider the advantages of purchasing from a single source or a limited number of suppliers. By carrying the same lines continuously, their customers are not shifted from brand to brand, nor their employees from materials of one kind to another. As a good customer of one supplier, they may receive special favors or cumulative quantity discounts, valuable advice and assistance in merchandising the goods, tips on market changes, and special considerations during times of difficulty.

Those are the advantages on each side. There are, however, disadvantages in either case. Dangers encountered in diversification include stocking too many lines, perhaps attended by difficulty in maintaining complete stocks in any one, and inability to capitalize fully on the advertising program of any one brand of merchandise or on technical advice regarding the use of certain materials or supplies.

The business owner with a close working relationship with a single supplier must acknowledge certain drawbacks to such an arrangement: inability to take advantage of unusual offers in other lines; some loss if the supplier changes policy or becomes poorly managed; and the risk that the merchandising advice, assistance, and guidance offered may become irritating or of no use. The last cited weakness is particularly likely to be present in some franchising systems. During periods of scarcity, some suppliers unfortunately use their available supplies getting new accounts instead of serving their regular customers adequately.

Cooperative Buying Groups

Some retailers have formed **cooperative buying** groups to reduce buying costs, obtain price concessions, and benefit from the market and merchandising knowledge of others.

The retailer cooperative is owned entirely by the retail merchants, operates entirely for their benefit, usually has its own warehouse, and sells exclusively to member stores. In some respects, such as in the use of patronage dividends, it resembles the consumer cooperative type of organization. The retailer usually pays dues to the organization.

If a retailer decides to affiliate with a cooperative buying group, his or her policies should be formulated to capitalize on all the advantages that such a group offers. Concentration of buying and full cooperation with the group is usually desirable, if the affiliation is one worth forming.

Merchandise Marts and Trade Shows

The majority of the purchasing for most stores, both large and small, is done on the premises. Many small retailers stock their stores by dealing with area wholesalers or their wholesaler affiliate. Where goods have a high turnover, as in the grocery, hardware, and drug fields, salespeople may call on each customer once a week. Others supplement local purchases by making wide use of wholesalers' or manufacturers' catalogs, which provide a wider choice of merchandise than is offered locally. Some manufacturers have sales representatives who call on merchants once or twice a year.

In the general merchandise fields, however, even small retailers find it desirable to "go to market" occasionally. Markets are sometimes located in a single building or **merchandise mart** where the leading vendors have displays and representatives. The Merchandise Mart in Chicago contains seven miles of display corridors with the offerings of some of America's best-known manufacturers. Atlanta's Merchandise Mart has over four hundred lines of furniture, home furnishings, and juvenile and gift wares, and has built a twenty-two story building to provide space for appliances, luggage, jewelry, and wearing apparel. The Trade Mart in Dallas has 160 showrooms for one thousand lines of furniture and accessories. Other major markets are located in San Francisco, Los Angeles, and St. Louis.

Trade shows also provide an opportunity to examine merchandise and place orders. They are held in the principal market centers at least once a year. However, they are also held by state trade associations at their annual conventions. There are usually several hundred merchandise display booths in an exhibition hall. These are rented for the duration of the convention by manufacturers, wholesalers, and manufacturers' agents. Often demonstrations are made as to how the merchandise may be used or sold. Retailers thus have an opportunity to examine new and unusual merchandise and familiarize themselves with new trends and developments in their type of store, often without traveling more than one or two hundred miles.

Importing

Many small business owners import products for domestic distribution. These **imports** include automobiles; electrical, electronic, and other mechanical articles; wearing apparel of either distinctive design or economic appeal;

gifts, novelties, and other impulse items; and foods. A few small producers import some of their raw materials or parts. Although many of these goods are purchased from importers or wholesalers, other methods are common. Some retailers have friends abroad with whom they deal directly. Many make initial contact with foreign vendors through responding to international advertising either in mass media or by direct mail. Others buy from foreign representatives present at trade fairs or exhibits. And some are solicited by foreign producers seeking distribution in different countries. The latter approach is common where franchised dealers merchandise and service products such as automobiles and sewing machines.

A small business owner importing direct may engage a **customs broker** and **freight forwarder** to handle technical details and expedite the shipment. Government agencies, such as the Bureau of International Commerce and the Small Business Administration—as well as trade associations, many banks, and others—can also assist the importer. International marketing is often complex and should not be undertaken lightly by the uninformed or inexperienced.[2]

NEGOTIATING TERMS

In negotiating prices and terms, the small buyer will do well to steer a middle course. A buyer who really is an expert on the goods purchased needs no advice, but the average person should try to be a careful buyer, to keep as well informed as possible on current prices, and to insist on fair treatment. Attempting to pose as a know-it-all, however, or developing a reputation for trying to beat down prices is likely to invite trouble. Nearly always the salesperson is better informed on qualities and prices than is the small purchaser, and some salespersons enjoy "putting it over" on the "smart" buyer. The exact quality needed for the purpose, at a fair price, should be the standard to follow.

Terms available to the small buyer are of two principal types: **cash discounts,** and **datings,** which specify the length of time before the net amount of the invoice is due. Often the trade will have its customary terms, or they will be fixed for the smaller business.[3] When opportunity for bargaining does exist, however, some small business owners are more interested in datings—that is, the length of time credit is extended—than they are in the cash discount, because **trade credit** provides a source of working capital for them. But unless a business is in dire financial straits, the cash discount is usually more important than the period of credit extension.

Cash discounts amount to important savings in most cases. The typical term "2 percent, 10 days, net 30" (or 2/10, n/30) is equivalent to an annual interest rate of 36 percent when cash discounts are taken. For example, an **invoice** dated January 1, amounting to $100 with terms of 2 percent, 10 days, net

[2] See Chapter 16 for a discussion of exporting and sources of assistance in international trade.
[3] See pp. 301–4 for a discussion of trade credit.

30 would carry a 2 percent discount of $2 if paid on the tenth. If it were paid twenty days later, on the thirtieth, the gross amount ($100) would be due. Assume it is necessary to borrow from the bank at 14 percent to discount the bill. Interest on $100 (actually only $98 would be needed) at 14 percent would be due for only 20/365, or approximately one-eighteenth, of a year to secure $2 or 2 percent of the principal. The annual rate would be 18 times 2 percent, or 36 percent. Thus by borrowing at 14 percent to discount the invoice the business owner actually makes 22 percent interest. A bill with terms of 5 percent, 10 days, net 30 (5/10, n/30) would net the owner a 76 percent return on the bank loan at 14 percent; one with terms of 3/10, n/30 would give the owner a gain of over 29 percent on a 14 percent loan.[4]

The business should be emphatic about paying bills promptly when due. Some small businesses tend to be slow in making payment even when bills are due at the net amount. A reputation for paying bills promptly is a valuable business asset.

If cash discounts are offered by vendors, the policy should provide for taking full advantage of every cash discount. If funds are inadequate for this purpose, procedures for increasing the cash flow should be formulated. These may include short-term bank loans, special sales, use of a revolving reserve fund set up by the business for such emergencies, and special efforts to collect accounts due the business.

MAINTAINING FAVORABLE RELATIONS WITH SUPPLIERS

Merely to buy goods is easy. To maintain favorable relations with vendors seems, at times, to be especially difficult for the small business owner. But it is always worth the effort. The smaller the business, the greater the importance of cultivating friendly relations with suppliers. In contrast to the big buyer, the small operator has far less to offer vendors in the way of profits. But small operators can be considerate of salespersons, prompt in paying their bills, and fair in all their dealings with suppliers.

"A business is as strong as its suppliers" is a widely accepted principle that applies whether vendors are furnishing merchandise to the retail store, raw materials to the factory, or supplies to the service establishment. "A business is as strong as its customers" is also a generally accepted principle of business. This interdependence of the business, its suppliers, and its customers emphasizes the need for extremely close working relationships among them.

RECEIVING, CHECKING, AND MARKING GOODS

Receiving, checking, and marking goods purchased are routine activities in most cases, and they are apt to be performed carelessly unless provisions are made for their proper handling. In the small business this involves recognizing

---

[4] These illustrations assume continuous discounting of invoices throughout the year.

the importance of carefully checking order quantities and the cond
merchandise or materials when received. Alert buyers have a go
nity to build a desirable reputation and to cement favorable futu.
with their suppliers by the way they handle these activities. Overages as well
as shortages should be reported promptly to the seller. Damage claims should
be made, insofar as possible, to the party responsible—either the vendor or the
transportation company. In either case they should be made promptly and
supported by adequate proof. Care in observing little details like these will
help considerably in setting the small business owner apart from the vendor's
other customers, and stamping such a person as a "business operator on the
way up."

The way goods are marked on receipt varies by type of business, the firm's
policy, and other factors. Merchants should always mark on each item or container the date it is received. Whether size, cost, selling price, vendor's identification, or other data are marked on the individual items will depend on the
needs of the business. Small manufacturers and service operators may need to
do little or no marking, except where identification of the grade and source of
materials is significant in operations control.

FOLLOW-UP AFTER PURCHASE

Follow-up relates to the history of the goods once they have been received. In
merchandising, it includes data on how the article sold, rate of turnover,
markdowns, customer complaints, returns, adjustments, and allowances. It is
an always up-to-date picture of the item from the time it entered the store
until it was finally disposed of. Small wholesalers will watch this record closely
in terms of reorders by their retail customers. In either case, retailer or wholesaler, one of these situations will develop: the article will be a "hot" item to be
reordered at once; or it will be an averge piece of merchandise; or it will be a
"buyer's mistake."

In small manufacturing and service establishments follow-up is more difficult and more frequently neglected than in merchandising. Of course, if a particular purchase turns out to be a "dud," appropriate action is taken. However, in the small firm most purchases are moderately satisfactory and too little
effort is exerted toward tracing the success of each. Small operators could well
give more consideration to follow-up activities, particularly in the purchase of
materials and supplies.

When any firm has reached the size at which purchase records beyond
those required for legal and accounting purposes are needed, a **resources file** is
indicated. In this file is kept a card for each supplier that carries a complete
record of the success of all transactions with that supplier. It also contains data
on prices, unit packages, discounts, and other purchasing information. Such
a file serves as a current history record, which is a valuable guide to reordering.

SUMMING UP

 In most businesses material costs or the costs of purchasing merchandise for resale exceed 50 percent of every dollar of sales income; how well this purchasing function is performed may well spell the difference between profit and loss. Just as the homemaker compares brands and prices at the supermarket, so also should the manager of a small business shop for the best buys.

In formulating their buying policies, small business managers have a number of critical choices to make. One of the most important of these is the selection of the supplier(s) with whom they want to do business. They have a wide range from which to choose when purchasing materials, merchandise, and supplies. Although sound arguments may be presented in favor of distributing orders among many vendors, *it is usually better policy for the small business to concentrate and work closely with one major supplier.* Purchasing from a single source is rendered particularly important because buying is so often associated with valuable assistance from the supplier in many management activities.

In many lines of business, voluntary chains and cooperative buying associations have sprung up. Such groups enable the small, independent firm to compensate for its smaller buying power.

Maintaining favorable relationships with sources of supply is a characteristic of successful buying that is particularly important in the small enterprise. "A business is as strong as its suppliers" is a widely accepted principle that applies whether vendors are furnishing merchandise to the retail store, raw materials to the factory, or supplies to the service establishment. Relationships with suppliers for most businesses are fully as important as relationships with customers and employees.

KEY WORDS

agent middleman
basic stock list
cash discount
cooperative buying
customs broker
datings
demand forecasting
follow-up
freight forwarder

full-service wholesaler
functional middleman
imports
inventory
invoice
limited-function wholesaler
materials (parts) list
merchandise broker
merchandise mart

merchant middleman
model stock plan
producer
purchasing agent
purchasing lead time
resident buying office

resources file
supplier
trade credit
trade show
vendor

DISCUSSION
QUESTIONS

1. Summarize the main points of difference or emphasis in the purchasing activities of retailers, wholesalers, manufacturers, and service establishments.

2. In most markets where purchasing managers buy merchandise, materials, or equipment, buying is most active when the market is already active enough to cause rising prices, and buying declines as prices become lower. What accounts for this phenomenon?

EXERCISES AND
PROBLEMS

1. An invoice in the amount of $1,000 dated September 1 has terms of 2/10, net 30. The bill was paid on September 15. How much should be remitted? What is the last date that the discount may be taken? When is the bill regarded as delinquent?

2. On March 20 John Doe buys $500 worth of merchandise from one of his suppliers with credit terms of 3/5, 2/10, 1/15, n/30. He returns $50 worth of merchandise on March 25. If he pays the invoice on April 4, how much must he pay?

3. An invoice in the amount of $1,000 dated July 1 has terms of 3/10, 2/20, n/30. What amount should be remitted if the invoice is paid on July 6? On July 13? On July 27?

4. What are the effective annual interest rates on the following cash discount terms: (a) 1/10, n/30; (b) 1/10, n/60; (c) 1/5, n/10; (d) 2/10, n/30; (e) 2/10, n/60; (f) 2/30, n/120; (g) 3/10, n/30. (For simplicity in calculations, assume 360 days per year.)

5. On October 1 you make a purchase of $1,000 on terms of 2/10, n/30. In order to take advantage of the discount you must borrow $500 at 14 percent for 20 days to pay the invoice on October 11. How much will you save by borrowing to take advantage of the discount?

6. Since all other activities of a business enterprise are dependent on sales, it is only logical that a sales budget must be prepared before other planning can take place (such as merchandise budgeting and control, discussed in the following chapter; and advertising and other expense budgeting, discussed in

Chapters 15 and 21). The most obvious starting point in planning is a review of past sales, particularly those in the immediately preceding year; sales trend analysis may indicate the probable upward or downward movement of sales for the coming year.

The company that hopes to make sales of a certain amount should be aware that those sales will not come all at once. Rather, it is necessary to break the total projected sales volume into appropriate periods based on seasonal patterns of customer demand. For most firms, a monthly budget period is the most convenient and workable.

Assume, for example, that a retailer's sales last year totaled $250,000 and that the firm has experienced a healthy sales growth over the past few years. The owner/manager estimates that, based on this sales trend plus a sharply increased advertising expenditure, sales can be increased by about 20 percent next year. Approximately 10 percent of its business occurs in December; 8 percent in each of the months of January, March, April, July, and August; 15 percent in September and in October; and 5 percent in each of the months of February, May, June, and November. Given this information, indicate the *planned sales* for this company for each of the months in the calendar year. (*Note:* This is the first of a sequential set of problems; the data derived in this exercise will be used in working exercise 4 in Chapter 10 and exercise 1 in Chapter 15.)

CASES IN POINT

Barry Bates is a manufacturers' agent representing eight different manufacturers; he sells various items to laundries and dry cleaners including hangers, plastic bags, and laundry or dry cleaning tickets. His items are related but noncompeting. His area is upstate New York, where the business of any one of the lines is not enough to support a full-time salesperson. Selling them together is economically profitable for his principals and for himself. He keeps busy and is making money as the business grows.

Recently he was approached by a former employer—The Fire-Stop Corporation—who has developed a new pre-alarm fire extinguisher endorsed by fire prevention authorities that is attached to the electrical system of a building. When a fire occurs, not only does an alarm sound but a harmless foamy substance is sprayed onto the area, quenching the fire. The costs of the equipment and of installation are relatively high, but justifiable in terms of increased security and reduced insurance rates.

Fire-Stop wants Barry to add this item to his line, to sell it not only to his present customers but to offices, stores, banks, and gas stations (as well as laundries and cleaners) in the towns he visits. They assure him that after the first few sales are made, local people can be trained to install and service the units. They argue that since he is in that particular town anyway, he might just as well sell a few Fire-Stop units. The commission is good—better even than that of his regular lines. He would, however, have to take a training course at the factory before selling Fire-Stop units.

Mr. Bates is tempted to give it a try. While he can keep busy developing his regular business, he feels that this added product would give him a change of pace and possibilities for added personal growth. If you were in his shoes, how would you analyze the situation? What factors would you weigh? What further facts would you need? And what is your first general advice to him?

Alex Gronewald has operated "The Leather Merchant" in Danville for many years, having succeeded to the ownership when his father died. His is probably the best established shop in the area.

For almost twenty years he has sold Tripster luggage—a medium- to high-priced line offering high quality and an adequate variety of models. Highly advertised, it is popular and profitable. And he has had sole representation of the Tripster line since twelve years ago when a competitor selling it went out of business.

Competing merchants have tried to get the line without success, and none has offered a competing line that has given Alex much competition. He prizes his sole distributorship highly and has worked closely with the salespersons and others at Tripster. No one is unhappy except his competitors.

Recently the Tripster people announced a new lower-priced line under the name of Traveller, to be sold by any merchant who cared to retail it, including, of course, Gronewald. It would be a "fighting brand" for the Tripster firm in competition with other manufacturers who recently entered low-priced lines into the market.

Alex is greatly disturbed—the new line will carry "Made by Tripster" in its advertising and on its labels. He feels that Tripster has betrayed him, and has written to the company president saying so. At the same time, two of his competitors are hedging with Tripster about not taking on the Traveller line unless they can have Tripster as well.

Another factor in Tripster's policy is its willingness to permit all who handle the new line to price it at their discretion. Heretofore, Alex has held Tripster prices firm, there being no local competition in the line. The nearest competitor offering it is located forty miles away. Neither reduces his prices except at semi-annual clearance sales as suggested by Tripster.

As he analyzes the situation, he visualizes his competitors using the "Made by Tripster" slogan to their advantage in selling the Traveller line. He can also see the loss of Tripster itself as a prestige-holding line as it, too, is bargain-priced among his competitors.

Alex has considered suggesting that he and his competitors agree on minimum prices for the Traveller line, or, if all get the Tripster line, that they agree to offer it at the same price.

The Tripster representative is in a quandary—this was a management decision made in New York. He sees Alex's viewpoint and problem and is trying to help.

What recourse(s) does Alex have? Comment fully.

Controlling Inventories

CHAPTER TEN *Inventory represents the major capital investment in merchandising, in many small manufacturing concerns, and in some types of service businesses. The firm's ability to reconvert inventory into cash at a profit is basic to its success. Even in businesses where inventory represents only a small portion of the total invested capital, it occupies a strategic position. No work can be completed without essential materials and supplies. Workers and machines remain idle, and possibly orders and customers are lost, all because the firm is out of stock on some inexpensive item. The purpose of inventory control is to utilize large investments in goods effectively and to facilitate efficient operation of the business. Your study of this chapter will help you understand some of the ways in which the owner/manager of a small business can achieve this important objective.*

Unless inventories are controlled they tend to get out of balance and result in loss to the business. An inventory may be out of balance in either direction; that is, it may be too large or too small. If it is too large relative to the demand for it, the cost of carrying the inventory will be higher than it need be. **Inventory carrying costs** include such things as interest on the inventory investment, handling costs, depreciation and obsolescence, taxes and insurance, and storage or warehousing costs. Often these costs, per year, run as high as 25 percent or more of the inventory investment. Therefore, an important objective in inventory control is to reduce the average investment in inventory by increasing the **inventory turnover.** With each increase in the number of times the material turns over during the year, there will be a proportionate *decrease* in the annual cost of carrying the inventory.

On the other hand, if the inventory is too small relative to the demand for it (that is, if inventory turnover is too fast), **stockouts** will occur, which will add to the firm's operating costs. For example, rush orders or special orders not only require special handling but almost always involve uneconomic ordering quantities. If it is an item that is needed in the factory, it may also cause costly production delays. And if it is a consumer item, then there will be dissatisfied customers and lost sales. Not only is the immediate sale lost, but an indeterminable amount of future business as well. Though stockout costs of the latter

WORK FOR...

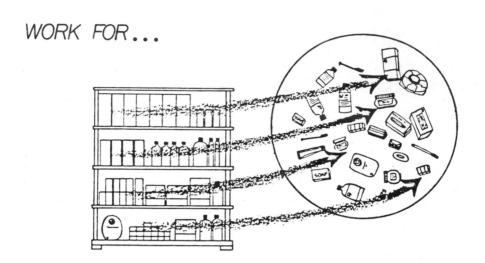

...HIGH TURNOVER
...WITHOUT EXCESSIVE STOCKOUTS

Courtesy of Small Business Administration.

type are difficult to estimate, they are nonetheless real. In any case, the business owner should estimate these stockout costs and strike a balance between these costs and the costs of carrying a larger inventory.

Thus a major purpose in business is to have the right goods at the right place at the right time. This means having adequate merchandise, materials, and supplies on call and available to meet the demands of customers, or sufficient parts and materials on hand to meet the demands of the production schedule. Also, as we have noted, inventory represents an investment of funds, an investment that can be well or poorly controlled, well or poorly guarded and guided in use. In any measure of business efficiency the degree to which the wants of customers are satisfied readily, and the degree to which capital funds are used effectively must be given proper weight.

Some system must be used if inventory control is to be even moderately efficient. An early question in establishing a system is whether value or quantity is the factor to be controlled. In merchandising especially, both dollar-control and unit-control systems are often used. Regardless of the system used, however, certain information must be fed into it. Effective inventory control requires accurate information from the using departments (sales in the case of merchandising, processing in the case of manufacturing or a service business) concerning the kind or quality of goods wanted, the quantities required of each, and the dates on which they are needed. Systems or methods used to secure the information essential for inventory control will usually operate through (1) periodic physical counts or (2) perpetual inventory records.

Any form of inventory or stores control works with the following basic data: quantities needed, amounts on hand, additions to stock through purchase or manufacture, subtractions through sales or issues, goods on order, and critical points at which action is needed. Critical points are usually expressed as **reorder points;** whenever the quantity on hand or available reaches a predetermined level, steps must be taken to replenish the inventory if it is to be kept in balance. The quantity to order at any one time is also predetermined and is an important element in the operation of many inventory control systems.

Finally, **storeskeeping**—or the physical handling and storage of merchandise, materials, and parts—must also be performed efficiently. This requires adequate facilities to store each item in such a way that it will be protected and can be located quickly as needed. If some items are carried on consignment, storeskeeping should provide for their special identification.

DOLLAR CONTROL VS. UNIT CONTROL

Inventory management may involve either **dollar control** or **unit control.** Unit control is particularly important in the control of raw materials and parts used in manufacturing, and in those manufacturing establishments that market a wide variety of products. But even in these cases, entrepreneurs may *also* be concerned with the total amount of capital they have invested in the inventory.

For example, an inventory may be well-balanced in terms of the number of units of each item within a total amount, but be dangerously out of balance with regard to the dollar value invested. This is true especially (1) at the peak of a rising price trend, (2) just before a pronounced upward swing in prices, and (3) when shortages with controlled prices are imminent. Each of these three important but unusual situations requires management policy decision and lies beyond the normal scope of inventory control, although each may influence management's concern regarding present conditions of the firm's inventory.

KEEPING TRACK OF INVENTORIES

Among the methods of securing the information needed for inventory control are (1) observation, (2) physical checks, and (3) perpetual inventory records. Observation may be sufficient in a very small business in which the variety of merchandise or other materials is not large and the sales or production demand rate is fairly constant. Usually, however, a physical check or count is necessary at intervals that vary according to the demand rate and importance of the inventory item.

For some types of inventory a perpetual inventory system is used, but such book records need to be checked or verified by a physical count at least once a year.

Perpetual Inventory Records

With a **perpetual inventory** record, the business owner/manager knows at all times the amounts of goods that are on hand. Such a record for a retailing or wholesaling establishment is illustrated in Figure 10-1. In controlling the inventory level of *finished goods* in a manufacturing establishment, a perpetual inventory record similar to that illustrated in Figure 10-1 is appropriate. However, in controlling the inventory of *raw materials* used in fabrication or the inventory of *component parts* used in assembly, it is often necessary that these materials be reserved to ensure their availability when needed; otherwise, production might be slowed down or even stopped for the lack of some essential material or part. A simple material **reserve system** is illustrated in Figure 10-2.

Balances "on order" (1) and "on hand" (2) are self-explanatory. The balance "on reserve" (3) denotes material that has been allocated to specific production orders but has not yet been withdrawn from the storeroom. The balance "available" (4) denotes material that is unassigned and hence available for allocation to subsequent production orders. Material on order may be assigned (reserved) even though it has not yet been received from the supplier(s), and unreserved material on order is considered **available stock** because (theoretically) if the reorder point has been determined properly (based on normal demand or usage rates and **replenishment lead times**) the quantity ordered will be in the storeroom before the present supply is exhausted. After each material transaction is entered on the ledger sheet, the balance on order (the quantity ordered minus the quantity received) plus the balance on hand should equal the balance on reserve (the quantity reserved minus the quantity issued) plus the balance available. Thus the **balance-of-stores ledger** provides a

Unit of Issue:	Description:				
Location:	Unit Value			Time required to obtain:	
Maximum Stock:	Minimum Stock:		Reorder Point:	Ordering Quantity:	
Date:	Quantities in terms of units of issue:				Remarks
	On order	Rec'd	Del'd	Bal. on hand	

FIGURE 10-1
Perpetual Inventory Record, as Commonly Used in Merchandising Establishments

Date	Order No.	(I) On Order			(2) Bal. on Hand	(3) On Reserve			(4) Bal. Available
		Ordered	Received	Balance		Reserved	Issued	Balance	

Description _____ Min. Quantity _____ Ordering Point _____

Code _____ Max. Quantity _____ Amount to Order _____

Unit of issue _____

FIGURE 10-2

Balance-of-Stores Ledger Sheet (or Perpetual Inventory Record) for Control of Raw Materials and Component Parts Used in Factory Production

continuous check on the accuracy of the entries made therein, in much the same way as does a double-entry bookkeeping system.

Posting to a perpetual inventory record, of course, requires other records, such as sales slips, purchase or production orders, material and finished stock delivery authorizations, and so on.

Periodic Physical Counts

Stores records must be correct in both quantities and values, and periodically it will be necessary to check the book inventory against the actual amount on hand. Each item in stock should be checked at least once a year. Some firms do this by inventorying all items at the same time, requiring that the store or shop be closed for business during the process. Other firms, however, stagger inventory checks throughout the year, thereby eliminating or at least minimizing inventory shutdown time; for this purpose a "tickler" (reminder) file is usually kept showing the dates to inventory each department.

A **physical inventory** should be taken carefully by important lines or classes of goods, and by age or length of time each item has been in stock. The inventory sheet in Figure 10-3 provides spaces for describing the merchandise, raw material, component parts, or other material; the quantity on hand; the unit of measurement (yards, pieces, dozens, gross, etc.); and the cost or price per unit.[1]

[1] Inventories are valued at cost or at "cost or market, whichever is lower"; inventory valuation methods are discussed in Chapter 20, pp. 344–47.

INVENTORY

Sheet No.		Department				Date		19				
Called by		Entered by				Extended by						
Description		√	Quantity	Unit	Price	√	Extensions					
Amount forward												

FIGURE 10-3
Inventory Sheet

SETTING THE QUANTITATIVE LIMITS

The two most important quantitative standards in the control of inventories are the ordering point and the amount to order. The ordering point is the predetermined level in the "balance on hand" column (in Figure 10-1) or the "balance available" column (in Figure 10-2); this signals the time at which the purchasing or production department (or person in charge) should be notified to order merchandise or other material or to schedule production in the specified amount. This advance notification reasonably ensures that a sufficient amount of inventory will be on hand to meet all sales or production requirements between the time the purchase (or production) order is placed and the time the material is received from the vendor or the shop. *If* the material was always ordered and received on time, and *if* it was always issued to customers or to the shop at the same rate, the *minimum quantity* on hand when an incoming shipment is received would be zero. However, this theoretical or idealized minimum cannot be depended on, and in practice a safety factor is applied in the determination of the ordering point. The amount to order when the ordering point is reached should be that quantity at which the unit cost of procurement and inventory maintenance is *least*. The theoretical *maximum quantity* on hand (or available), of course, is the sum of the minimum quantity and the ordering quantity, and the **average inventory** is the sum of the minimum quantity and one-half the ordering quantity. Thus, as diagrammed in Figure 10-4 the minimum inventory is 2 units, the maximum inventory is 12

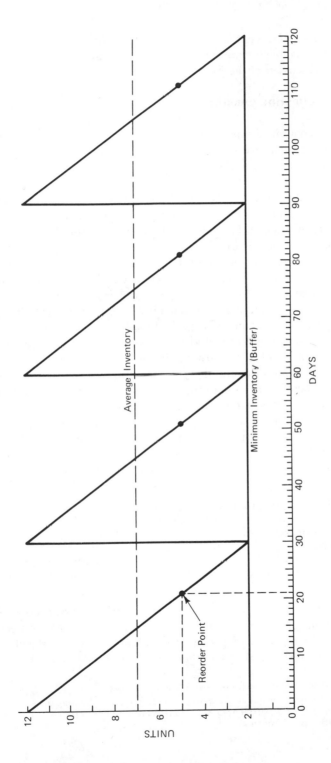

FIGURE 10-4
Idealized Inventory Behavior

units, and the average inventory is 7 units. Determination of the proper *reordering point* and *economic ordering quantity* in the **min-max system** of inventory control is discussed in the following sections.

Economic Ordering Quantities

The most economical amount of material to purchase at one time, at a given price, is that quantity at which the total cost per unit of acquiring the material is at a *minimum;* this point occurs when the unit cost of preparing the **purchase order** for that quantity is *equal* to the unit cost of carrying the material in stores.[2] That is, in determining the most economical quantity of material to order at one time, the inventory **possession costs** must be balanced with the inventory **acquisition costs.** These fundamental cost relationships are illustrated in Table 10-1 and Figure 10-5.

In the case of purchased materials, the acquisition costs are the **incremental costs** of preparing the purchase orders. These costs are determined by multiplying the **standard cost** of writing a single purchase order by the number of purchase orders that would be required each year at varying ordering quantities.[3] For example, let us assume that in the Small Business Company a total of 10,000 units of material are expected to be needed during the coming year, and that the standard cost of preparing a purchase order is $15. Obviously, the acquisition cost per unit of material (and hence the acquisition costs per year) *decreases* when the amount of material ordered at one time increases. If only 100 units are ordered the unit acquisition cost is $0.15 (i.e., $15/100) and the total acquisition cost per year is $1,500 (i.e., 10,000/100 × $15). For an order size of 200 units, both the unit acquisition cost and the annual acquisition cost would be halved ($0.075 and $750, respectively). The acquisition costs per year on purchase orders of other sizes are indicated in Table-10-1 on p. 131, where:

Q = Number of units ordered at one time
R = Annual requirements = 10,000 units
N = Number of orders written per year = R/Q
A = Acquisition (or order-writing) costs per order = $15
P = Possession costs, i.e., cost of holding one unit of inventory for one year
    = 20% of unit purchase price = $1.20 (assuming a price of $6 per unit)

Certain incremental costs are associated with the possession, as well as the acquisition, of materials. Inventory carrying (or possession) costs are comprised mainly of taxes, depreciation and obsolescence, shrinkage, insurance, and interest on the average inventory investment. Unlike unit

---

[2] Determination of economic lot sizes in *production* is discussed on p. 133.

[3] The standard cost of preparing a purchase order is determined by dividing the total operating expenses of the purchasing department (or function) by the number of purchase orders written over a representative period of time.

TABLE 10-1

Tabular Method of Determining the Most Economical Ordering Quantity

(1) ORDER SIZE (UNITS): Q	(2) NUMBER OF ORDERS PER YEAR: $N = R/Q$	(3) ACQUISITION COSTS PER YEAR: NA	(4) POSSESSION COSTS PER YEAR: $PQ/2$	(5) TOTAL COSTS PER YEAR: (3) + (4)
100	100.00	$1,500.00	$ 60.00	$1,560.00
200	50.00	750.00	120.00	870.00
300	33.33	500.00	180.00	680.00
400	25.00	375.00	240.00	615.00
500	20.00	300.00	300.00	600.00
600	16.67	250.00	360.00	610.00
700	14.29	214.35	420.00	634.35
800	12.50	187.50	480.00	667.50
900	11.11	166.65	540.00	706.65
1000	10.00	150.00	600.00	750.00
1100	9.09	136.35	660.00	796.35
1200	8.33	125.00	720.00	845.00
1300	7.69	115.35	780.00	895.05
1400	7.14	107.10	840.00	947.10

acquisition costs, the cost of holding one unit of material in inventory *increases* when the amount of material ordered at one time increases. With larger order sizes and fewer purchase orders, inventory turnover is lower and the average inventory level is higher. For example, the cost of holding one unit in inventory for one year in the Small Business Company, as noted above, is $1.20. If only 100 units are ordered at a time, the unit possession cost is $0.006 (i.e., $1/100 \times \$1.20/2$) and the total possession cost per year is $60 (i.e., $100/2 \times \$1.20$).[4] For an order size of 200 units, both the unit possession cost and the annual possession cost would be doubled ($0.012 and $120, respectively). The possession costs per year on purchase orders of other sizes are indicated in column 4 in Table 10-1.

Figure 10-5 is a graphic representation of the above tabular data. From an examination of both Table 10-1 and Figure 10-5, it is observed that the most economical amount of material to order at one time, *at a price of $6 per unit,* is that quantity (500 units) at which the annual acquisition and possession costs are equal ($300 in each case) and at which these costs when combined are at a minimum ($600).

---

[4] If the entire 100 units were held in inventory for the entire period of 1/200 year (inventory turnover period), the company's investment in each unit during this period would be the entire unit purchase cost, but since this material is used in sales or production regularly throughout the period the *average* investment is only one-half this amount.

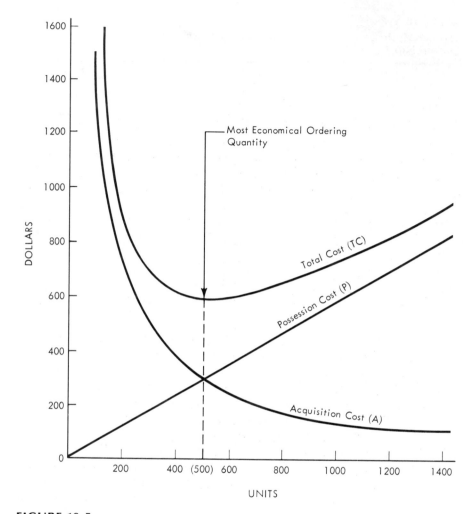

FIGURE 10-5
Graphic Representation of the Basic EOQ Formula

These fundamental cost relationships may be expressed more easily and conveniently by means of the following formula:

$$Q = \sqrt{\frac{2RA}{P}}$$

Thus,

$$Q = \sqrt{\frac{2 \times 10,000 \times 15}{1.20}} = \sqrt{\frac{300,000}{1.20}} = \sqrt{250,000} = 500$$

Quantity discounts.   The basic **economic ordering quantity** (EOQ) formula, as noted above, assumes that the purchase price per unit will be the same regardless of the number of units ordered. However, vendors often lower the unit price as the quantity ordered increases, because of the lowered unit costs of shipping and handling the order. When **quantity discounts** are offered, therefore, such savings reduce unit acquisition costs still further as the order size increases.

Suppose, for example, that the vendor offers the Small Business Company a price of $5.95 per unit if it orders 2,500 or more units at a time. Should the company take up this offer? The answer lies in a comparison of the total of all costs generated annually with orders of 500 and 2,500 units, respectively. For individual orders of 500 units at a unit price of $6, the annual costs are calculated as follows:

Purchase costs:	10,000 units × $6	= $60,000
Ordering costs:	20 orders × $15	= 300
Inventory carrying costs:	250 units × $1.20	= 300
		$60,600

For individual orders of 2,500 units at a price of $5.95, the annual costs would be higher:

Purchase costs:	10,000 units × $5.95	= $59,500
Ordering costs:	4 orders × $15	= 60
Inventory carrying costs:	1,250 units × $1.19	= 1,488
		$61,048

Therefore the company should order the smaller quantity at the higher unit price.

Lot sizes in production.   The fundamental cost relationships noted above come into play in determining the size of **production orders** as well as purchase orders. In each case, the costs of acquiring the material must be balanced against the cost of possessing it or having it in stock. Where the inventory is to be replenished by means of *manufacture,* however, the acquisition costs include the cost of machine setups in addition to the cost of writing production orders.

The basic EOQ formula is again illustrated below, with parameters assumed as follows:

R = Annual requirements = 500 units
A = Acquisition costs per order = $50
P = Possession cost, or cost of carrying one unit of inventory for one year = $5

Thus,

$$EOQ = \sqrt{\frac{2 \times 500 \times 50}{5}} = \sqrt{\frac{50,000}{5}} = \sqrt{10,000} = 100 \text{ units}$$

Reordering Points

In addition to knowing *how much* material to order, it is important also to know *when* to order. If the material is ordered too soon, the inventory is increased unnecessarily; if ordered too late the present inventory might become exhausted, thus holding up production (in the case of purchased raw materials and finished components) or failing to satisfy customer demand (in the case of finished goods).

Two important factors in determining the ordering point are the rate of consumption (or demand rate) in units, and the procurement time. In the Small Business Company, for example, the time it takes material on the above order to be delivered from the time it is requisitioned is two weeks; thus, with 10,000 units of material demanded annually by the sales or production department, the reorder point might (theoretically) be set at approximately 385 units (10,000 ÷ 26), which is the average biweekly rate of consumption. In such a case, the theoretical minimum inventory would be zero, for if the procurement time and annual consumption rate both remain unchanged, the balance of stock on hand will be depleted just as the new shipment of material is received.

Such preciseness, however, is seldom attainable. Sound management requires that a **safety stock** or **buffer inventory** be maintained for use whenever temporary exceptions to the normal or usual operating conditions occur. Furthermore, the demand for most materials is seasonal and fluctuates widely from month to month during the year. In the above illustration, if we assume a minimum safe inventory (buffer) equal to the average sales or production requirements for one week (approximately 195 units), the reordering point would be set at 580 units (the sum of the buffer inventory and the average amount of inventory consumed during the normal replenishment period).

A-B-C Control

If the small business carries stocks of different materials that vary widely in relative importance to sales or production, in price, or in other significant ways, inventories should be classified and appropriate methods of control (often called **A-B-C control**) adopted for each classification. For example, often relatively few materials make up the bulk of the dollar investment in inventories. In one company it was found that 10 percent of the items in stock accounted for 75 percent of the inventory value, and that 70 percent of the items accounted for only 5 percent of the firm's inventory investment. For control purposes these are classified as "A" and "C" items, respectively. Between these extremes were the "B" items, which accounted for 20 percent of the total number of items and 20 percent of the total inventory value. Staples—the "C" items—may be controlled by using *bin* (or *shelf*) *minimums* or a simple "last container" arrangement, or perhaps by tying up the reorder point quantities in sacks or otherwise physically separating them from the remainder of the stock. Only the "A" and "B" items need to be controlled under a stringent perpetual inventory and reserve system of the type described in the preceding pages.[5]

MERCHANDISE CONTROL SYSTEMS

Most small businesses, as we have noted, are retailing businesses. For this reason, and also because of the much greater diversity of merchandise inventories in terms of cost, stability of demand, and regularity of sale, our attention in the remainder of this chapter will focus on *merchandise* control systems.

The small retailer's biggest investment is the inventory of merchandise carried. When this can be kept at the optimum amount, profits are increased. When inventories are well-balanced at all times, the investment in merchandise is working most effectively. Among the major advantages of inventory or merchandise control in retailing is the fact that it enables the retailer to do the following: (1) balance stocks as to value, size, color, style, and price line, in proportion to sales; (2) play the winners, as well as move slow sellers; and (3) secure the best rate of stock turnover for each item. Expenses and markdowns are reduced. The store's reputation for always having new, fresh merchandise in wanted sizes and colors is one of the major long-run benefits of good merchandise control.

Information provided by a good system of merchandise control that will improve both buying and selling activities includes the following:

1. Price preferences of customers
2. Items no longer popular
3. Right quantities to buy
4. Amount of a given item sold
5. Season or time a given item sells
6. Time to stop buying seasonable goods
7. Kind and style of goods customers want
8. Time to display and promote certain items
9. Slow movers
10. Particular items for which demand is falling off
11. Best buying sources
12. Best buying prices
13. Possibilities for new lines or kinds of goods
14. Whether stock is in proper balance

A control system giving this information will eliminate guesswork and memory—both unreliable guides in inventory management.

---

[5] In retailing businesses, as a practical matter, perhaps only the "A" items need be so controlled in most cases.

Keeping Track of Inventories

For some types of merchandise, particularly the A-rated items, a perpetual inventory system similar to that illustrated in Figure 10-1 is used. The posting of sales to this stock record is made from sales slips or from stub tickets or tags that are detached from the merchandise when it is sold. Separate running records are kept of individual sizes, colors, styles, and so forth. However, this method of merchandise control is practical only for goods of high unit value and pronounced demand changes.

For most departments of an average small store, periodic stocktaking is sufficient. The following tabulation, for example, illustrates how the retailer can order sizes, colors, or styles of merchandise in proper proportion without the expense of individual record handling:

| | SIZE OR STYLE NUMBER | | | | | |
	1	2	3	4	5	TOTAL
On hand, June 1	18	26	21	16	15	96
Received during June		18	36	18		72
	18	44	57	34	15	168
On hand, July 1	6	21	24	9	3	63
Sold during June	12	23	33	25	12	105

The quantity sold is obtained by adding the number on hand at the beginning of the period and the number received, and deducting the number on hand at the end of the period. The amount needed to bring stock up to normal is estimated and the order made out. Assuming that no seasonal change in sales is anticipated, that a one-month supply is sufficient to order, and that 6 is the minimum packing for each size or style (or color), the order is estimated as follows:

| | SIZE OR STYLE NUMBER | | | | | |
	1	2	3	4	5	TOTAL
Sold during June	12	23	33	25	12	105
On hand, July 1	6	21	24	9	3	63
Needed to replenish stock	6	2	9	16	9	42
Necessary to order, July 1	6	6	12	18	12	54

Although 12 units more than are required for the next period are being purchased, the stocks will be balanced again at the time of the next check and order.

Dollar Control

Merchandise control, as in the control of other kinds of inventory, may involve either dollar control or unit control. *Dollar control* provides a means of regulating the amount of money invested in inventory to achieve the desired or expected level of sales; standards are set, operations are reported, and corrective action is taken in terms of the dollar value of the inventory concerned. The first step in the development of such a control system is the preparation of a merchandise budget, that is, the determination of the amount of money needed to replenish the inventory in such a way that a satisfactory balance is achieved between the anticipated sales and the amount of merchandise on hand. For example, assume that next month's sales of a particular class of goods (department of the store) are expected to reach $20,000, and that the retail sales value of the stock on hand is $10,000. Assume further that the optimum minimum inventory level for this class of merchandise is estimated to be equal to the average monthly sales, which in this case is $15,000. Also to be considered are the expected **retail reductions** during the month, such as markdowns, discounts given to employees, discounts or gifts of merchandise to nonprofit organizations, and stock shortages due to shoplifting and employee theft; at an assumed standard ratio of 4 percent of sales, such reduction would be expected to total $800 during the budget month. Thus the budgeted dollars *at retail* for purchases in this department during the month will be $25,800, calculated as follows:

Desired (optimum) end-of-month inventory	$15,000
+ Planned or expected sales	20,000
	$35,000
− Inventory at beginning of the month	10,000
	$25,000
+ Retail reductions	800
	$25,800

The amount of dollars that may be spent for these goods will, of course, be somewhat less than $25,800. If these goods have an average markup of 40 percent,[6] then the *cost* to the retailer will be $25,800 × 0.60, or $15,480. The latter figure is commonly referred to as the **open-to-buy.**

This merchandise control system makes the buyer responsible for converting the open-to-buy dollar amounts into specific items and quantities of goods. That is to say, the open-to-buy figure at the end of the month is not intended to be spent all at once; some open-to-buy allowances in the **buying plan** should

[6] Markups are commonly calculated on retail price (not cost); see pp. 210–12 for a discussion of markups and gross margins.

be available at all times to take advantage of special price concessions and discounts offered without notice during the month, and to purchase merchandise so as to maintain complete assortments on all lines carried.

Dollar control may include the total store inventory or any subdivisions as needed, such as price line and merchandise classification.

Unit Control

Although some form of dollar control should be used for all merchandise, *unit control* may be needed to supplement dollar control, particularly in fashion lines. In unit control, the same steps are carried out in terms of number of items of each kind of merchandise or inventory. Unit control frequently involves some form of perpetual inventory to cover in physical quantity each important variation within the line of goods concerned. The type of unit control to use depends on regularity of the relative sales of each variety, unit value of the merchandise, length of the selling season, and type of merchandise.

When each variety within a line or class of goods sells at a fairly constant rate throughout the year, a **basic stock** system with periodic physical counts is sufficient.[7] A checklist may be used with clerical assistants doing the checking. In the case of seasonal goods or goods with a short selling period, such as skates, sports equipment, or rubbers, checking should be more frequent and greater attention should be given by the buyer to prevent loss from "outs" or end-of-season overstocks. When the unit value of each item is small, unit control can be operated in terms of reserve stock or full cartons rather than of individual items.

For style goods, and other lines where balanced assortments are of great importance, the **model stock** is the usual buying guide. A model stock plan means carrying a predetermined assortment of merchandise that is in proper balance by types, sizes, and colors with the sales of the line of goods. If the model stock plan were perfect, it would include the exact quantities of the right sorts of goods in relation to the actual rate of sale. In other words, if the estimates of the model stock plan were entirely correct, the merchant would sell all the goods projected in the plan; and in doing so, this would achieve exactly the stock turnover rate for which the merchant had planned.

The most valuable area for unit control is in shopping goods and especially in fashion merchandise of fairly high unit value, such as wearing apparel, shoes, furniture, and many home furnishings and appliances. For such merchandise, unit control is obtained by keeping a daily running record of sales and stocks of each variety of each item within the line or class of goods. Two

---

[7] A basic stock list is used for staple merchandise and should indicate not only the names of the items to be carried but also the minimum quantities to be maintained, reorder points, and the quantities to be reordered at any one time. In contrast, a model stock is most applicable to fashion merchandise and is a general breakdown of the line or class of goods in terms of such factors as size, color, style, and price line.

types of systems are in general use: merchandise tag and clerk tabulation. In the former each piece of merchandise has attached to it a tag of some sort, usually perforated and ordinarily with duplicate parts. Each time an article is sold, one part of the tag is removed and either sent to the office with the sales-check or deposited in a special container by the salesclerk. Small stores often have each salesclerk record or tabulate the specific size, style, color, and other characteristics of the merchandise as each item is sold. Sometimes this information is included on the salescheck instead of being kept as a separate record. Modern cash registers furnish stubs that are often used for unit control records. In all cases a unit control clerk, who may be the proprietor in a very small store, should summarize the data at least once a day so that a perpetual inventory in units of each variety may be kept.

To the small or beginning merchant, unit control seems like an unnecessary amount of trouble. However, it is the basis of modern merchandising. To be out of a particular size, style, color, price line, or other variety of a line or class of goods is the same as for a carpenter to be out of nails or a stenographer to be without a pencil. One lacks what it takes to do the job. The merchant not only loses the sale but helps the prospective customer acquire the habit of trading with competitors. There is probably no greater error in merchandising than to be out of wanted items, even occasionally! Naturally, however, this does not mean that a retailer should stock every item asked for by customers no matter how infrequently.

Also, every store that has tried a stock control system for the first time has found that the greatest number of items in stock are rarely asked for or sold. Difficult as this is to believe, it has been found that from 20 to 25 percent of the items in a poorly controlled store produce from 75 to 80 percent of sales.

Our emphasis on unit rather than dollar control has been deliberate. The whole trend of merchandising for four decades has been toward greater unit control. Dollar control is necessary, especially for the huge organization with hundreds of merchandise departments and scores of buyers; but it is unit control that spells merchandising success or failure in the small store. If the unit control is right, dollar control will take care of itself—to the merchant's profit.

SUMMING UP

Inventories of merchandise, materials, and supplies represent one of the major assets of most businesses. Yet the peculiar thing about many small businesses is the extreme care with which actual cash is guarded and the lack of care exercised over "cash" in the form of inventories. A good rule for small business managers is to regard their suppliers as their *bankers* as far as materials and other inventories are concerned.

The inventory turnover rate (the number of times the average inventory has been sold or used up during the year) is the small business manager's best measure of how well he or she has managed purchases and inventories. The *optimum* inventory level or turnover rate occurs at that point when the combined annual costs of running out of stock and the costs of carrying or maintaining the average inventory are at a minimum.

The amount and value of stock on hand may be determined by taking a periodic physical inventory or by recording each addition to or withdrawal from stock as such transactions occur. Perpetual inventory records, however, need to be verified by occasional actual counts.

Whenever the quantity of stock on hand or available reaches a predetermined reordering point, steps must be taken to replenish the inventory if it is to be kept in balance. The (economic) quantity to order at any one time is also predetermined and is an important element in the operation of an effective inventory control system.

Good inventory control depends in part on whether the small business manager can rely on receiving shipments from suppliers within an allotted time. As noted in the preceding chapter, good vendor relationships, fair treatment of suppliers in matters of claims, and prompt payment of bills will help to make this possible. Even in the best of inventory control systems, emergencies will arise when unexpectedly depleted inventories must be replaced quickly. At such crucial times good vendor relations are of paramount importance.

KEY WORDS

A-B-C control
acquisition costs
available stock
average inventory
balance-of-stores ledger
basic stock
buffer inventory
buying plan
dollar control
economic ordering quantity
incremental cost
inventory carrying costs
inventory turnover
min-max system
model stock
open-to-buy

perpetual inventory
physical inventory
possession costs
production order
purchase order
quantity discount
reorder point
replenishment lead time
reserve system
retail reductions
safety stock
standard cost
stockouts
storeskeeping
unit control

1. Why is the total cost curve in Figure 10-4 U-shaped? Explain fully.

2. A hardware retailer wishes to establish minimum and maximum stocks for such items as screwdrivers, bolts, screws, and hammers. How should he go about it? Explain fully.

3. Summarize the main points of similarity and differentiate between the inventory control practices of merchandising and manufacturing establishments.

EXERCISES AND PROBLEMS

1. In each of the following situations, compute the inventory turnover rate:
   a. The average inventory of the ABC Company is 2,500 units. The company sold 12,500 units during the inventory accounting period.
   b. The Small Business Company sold products last year costing $625,000 to produce. It started the year with a finished goods inventory of $100,000 at cost and ended the year with $150,000 worth of inventory.
   c. The January 1 inventory for the Hawkeye Dress Shop was valued at $20,000 at retail (that is, at the prices the dresses sold for). The inventory on December 31 was valued at $15,000 at retail. Retail sales for the year were $70,000.
   d. Last year the XYZ Company sold 402 units of a particular product. The firm's beginning-of-the-month inventory figures for this product were as follows:

January	32 units	July	74 units
February	42	August	75
March	53	September	71
April	45	October	65
May	62	November	98
June	82	December	105

2. a. Prepare a form similar to that shown in Figure 10-1 on p. 126, indicating the reordering point at 50 units and the economic ordering quantity at 100 units. Then, assuming a beginning balance on hand of 60 units and none on order, record the following transactions. (*Caution:* The replenishment-order transaction has been intentionally omitted; you are to reorder when required.)

   Jan. 10 — sold 8 units
   Jan. 14 — sold 3 units
   Jan. 17 — sold 4 units

Jan. 19 — sold 10 units
Jan. 24 — received order from vendor

b. Prepare a form similar to that shown in Figure 10-2 on p. 127, indicating the reordering point at 440 units and the economic ordering quantity at 500 units. Then, assuming a beginning balance on hand of 555 units, balance on reserve at 50 units (for production order #80), and the balance available at 505 units, record the following transactions, reordering when necessary.

July 24 — 50 units of material reserved on production order #81
July 25 — material issued for production order #80
July 26 — 35 units of material condemned and disposed of as scrap
July 27 — 100 units of material reserved on production order #82
July 28 — material previously ordered received from vendor

3.   a. Calculate the economic purchasing-order quantity (in units) based on the following data:

Units sold per year = 120
Invoice cost per unit = $100
Order-writing and handling costs = $2.50
Annual cost of holding one unit in inventory = $6
Desired minimum (buffer) inventory = 2 units

b. With an order of this size, what will be the total cost per year of inventory acquisition and possession?
c. What will be the maximum inventory?
d. What will be the average inventory?
e. What should the reorder point be if the normal procurement time is nine days?
f. What quantity would you purchase at one time if the vendor reduced the unit price by $5 for quantities of twelve or more? Explain.
g. Using the basic EOQ formula given on p. 132, calculate the economic order quantity in *dollars*.

4.   Proper planning of merchandise purchasing is vital to the successful operation of a retail business. The decision to buy is based on a number of carefully made estimates, the most important of which (as noted in exercise 6 in the preceding chapter) is the sales budget. *Planned purchases* for any given month are calculated by subtracting the inventory at the beginning of the month from the sum of the planned or expected sales for that month, the estimate of retail reductions during the month, and the desired (optimum) inventory at the end of the month. Since merchandise inventories are customarily valued at retail (as well as at cost) for merchandise control purposes, as noted in the text, the planned purchases for the month are then recalculated at cost to determine the open-to-buy. The calculation procedure is illustrated on p. 137.

Now assume the following additional information for the firm whose sales budget you prepared in exercise 6 in Chapter 9:

Inventory, September 1 (at retail)	$23,500
Estimated retail reductions during the month	5,000
Desired inventory at end of the month (at retail)	27,500
September purchases of merchandise received by September 15	16,500
Merchandise on order to be received before the end of the month	8,250
Average markup on merchandise	30%

a. Calculate the firm's planned purchases at both retail and cost for the month of September.

b. Calculate the firm's open-to-buy as of September 15.

CASE IN
POINT

One of the top men's wear shops in Peoria, Illinois, was recently bought by Norman Schultz with funds he had accumulated as a professional hockey player. Established forty years before, it was known for good assortments of current styles at reasonable prices. On retiring, the former owner gave Mr. Schultz a generally good price and worked with him for three months following his retirement.

Yesterday, on a buying trip to Chicago, Norman was approached by a shirt salesman, who offered him eight dozen shirts at an attractive price. Usually priced at $36 per dozen or more to sell at $4.95, these were available at $29.50 per dozen, and thus could be sold for as low as $3.95. The styles were somewhat mixed, but generally good for this season, which is now almost half over.

An inventory of the shirts as to sizes in the assortment is presented below in numbers of shirts in each size:

	14	14^2	15	15^2	16	16^2	17	17^2	TOTAL
White, plain	6	9	3	6	3	6	3	6	42
Colors, mixed, plain	3	9	—	3	6	—	6	3	30
Novelty stripes	3	6	6	—	—	3	9	3	30
Novelty prints	9	6	3	—	6	—	3	9	36
Mod collars, mixed patterns	—	6	9	3	—	3	3	—	24
Semiformal	3	3	6	9	6	3	3	6	39
Totals	24	39	27	21	21	15	27	27	201

Shirts are in boxes of three; sleeve lengths tend to be appropriate to neck sizes, color assortments are well-balanced.

Norman was definitely interested in this opportunity. His stocks were low, particularly in the more popular sizes and styles. The former owner had left him a simple model stock plan, which he had followed for many years, that looked somewhat like this:

	14	14^2	15	15^2	16	16^2	17	17^2
Whites (%)	8	10	18	24	15	12	8	5
Colors (%)	8	12	20	24	15	10	6	5
Novelties (%)	6	12	21	22	18	10	8	3

Norman has studied the inventory of the assortment offered, has looked at the percentages recommended in the model, and now must let the shirt salesman know if he wants to buy the shirts. While he respects the former owner's judgment, he feels that the price offered is attractive and that the price he could offer his customers would bring him the business he needs. In many ways, his predecessor was an old-fashioned and conservative buyer. Norman feels that a more aggressive and youthful approach will appeal to his hockey fan customers and other admirers.

Norman Schultz must make a decision now. If you were in his situation, what would be today's decision and why? Any alternatives?

Acquiring, Training, and Motivating Employees

CHAPTER ELEVEN *We will now deal with another important factor in production: acquiring and maintaining an adequate staff. You will discover that a good, competent group of employees is the best asset your business can have. Finding and keeping good employees is not a matter of luck but rather the result of aggressive recruitment, careful selection, proper training and motivation, and thoughtful management. This chapter should make you more aware of what is required on the part of a small business owner/manager to ensure that he or she has an adequate and productive staff for the business.*

The importance of personnel as a factor of production in the smaller business cannot be denied. Every progressive business seeks some point of superiority over its competitors. The major competitive advantage of the small business over the large business may well be its closer personal contact, and therefore its more effective communication and teamwork, between the owner/manager and the employees.

Materials, equipment, machines, and other things used by business are available to all competitors at approximately equal prices. It is the firm's personnel that are unique and susceptible to the greatest individual development. The result of good **employee relations**—a loyal, efficient group of workers—cannot be copied or purchased by competitors. Furthermore, the increased worker efficiency that usually accompanies good employee relations is of greater importance in the small business than in the large concern. The larger firm is better equipped physically, having specialized machinery and mechanical aids; the small business must, therefore, rely more heavily on its personnel alone.

> *If you took away all of my steel mills and all of my money but left me my men, I'd be a millionaire again within a year.*
>
> —ANDREW CARNEGIE

The human element in the small business, however, is complicated by the close personal relationships that normally exist between the owner and the employees. It often happens that many of the employees are relatives or lifelong friends of the owner. The result may be an unwillingness by the owner to

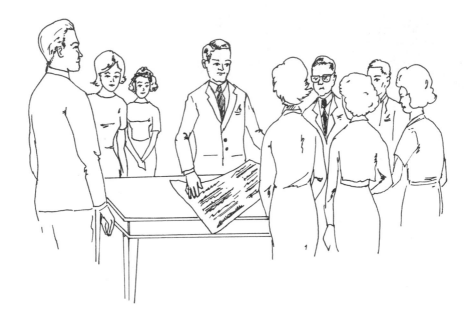

follow approved personnel practices as developed in larger organizations, either because the owner feels that they are too impersonal for the firm's small group of intimately known workers or because the owner lacks understanding of modern personnel practices and their adaptation to the needs of the small firm. Offsetting these obstacles in the small firm is the owner's greater knowledge of each of the employees and the feeling of mutual friendship that so often exists. These are *real advantages*. Actually one of the main reasons for the development of most so-called modern personnel practices has been the need of large organizations to make up for this lack of personal contact and understanding between management and employees. Yet the importance of separating business from personal and family relations in the small company should be a major incentive to using the personnel procedures discussed in the remainder of this chapter.

THE IMPORTANCE OF JOB ANALYSIS

A logical starting point in any personnel program, in both large and small firms, is **job analysis.** It is from the factual data secured in job analysis that **job descriptions** and **job specifications** are prepared. A job description, as previously defined, is simply a list of job duties or responsibilities, or a description of what the person on a particular job does and the conditions under which the work is performed; a job specification, on the other hand, indicates the skill, effort, knowledge or education, and other personal requirements needed to perform the job satisfactorily.[1] The selection, placement, training, promotion or transfer, and remuneration of employees should be based largely on job descriptions and job specifications.

RECRUITMENT AND SELECTION

The small business is usually limited geographically when recruiting employees, and it is sometimes further handicapped by the fact that the best local talent may prefer employment in larger and better-known companies. By paying wages comparable to those offered by large employers and by stressing promotion opportunities or a better chance to learn the business, the small employer can largely offset this handicap. Aggressive solicitation and selling of the company by the small business owner can further lessen some of these limitations and help to secure an adequate supply of the right type of job applicants. Owners should strive to create a public image of their plant or store as a good place to work.

Another point of special importance to the small business is to seek out and select candidates rather than to wait for employment applications. Perhaps the best sources of manpower are the friends and relatives of present (satisfied) employees. Clergymen, teachers, and the company's customers and suppliers can also be solicited for their help in locating prospective employees who possess desirable skills or personality traits. In any case, when applications for employment are received, standard employment procedures should be followed, though perhaps more informally in the small business than in the large one.

Screening Potential Employees

Several procedures may be followed in screening job applicants. The most basic of these is the application-for-employment form. Its first use is to eliminate the obviously unqualified applicants. It also serves as a guide in interviewing job candidates, another way to screen applicants. In some cases, applicants who "survive" the interviewing process may be given a test or battery of tests.

The application blank.   An application blank is a record of statements made at the time the applicant first seeks employment. In addition to name, address, and social security number, it should contain *only* information that will aid in deciding whether or not the applicant is qualified to perform the job for which he or she is applying, such as education and work experience. Recent laws and court rulings requiring **equal employment opportunity** and **affirmative action** effectively prohibit inquiries concerning an applicant's race, sex, age, religion,

[1] See p. 47.

color, ancestry, or arrest and court record.[2] These laws and court rulings make it necessary for the small business owner and other employers to take precautions concerning the content of their application form as well as the questions asked of job applicants in employment interviews. Table 11-1 summarizes the kind of questions an employer *may* or *may not* ask a prospective employee.

It should be noted, however, that information required for records, such as age, sex, and number of dependents, may be requested *after* the applicant has been hired, provided such information is not used for any subsequent discrimination, as in promotion and layoff.

Nor are the equal employment opportunity laws intended to prohibit employers from obtaining sufficient *job-related* information about applicants, as long as the questions do not elicit information that could be used for discriminatory purposes. These laws do not restrict the rights of employers to define qualifications necessary for satisfactory job performance, but they do require that inquiry or restriction of employment is permissible only if a **bona fide occupational qualification** (BFOQ) exists and that these same standards of qualifications for hiring be applied equally to all persons considered.

> Streaker Wanted—*15 seconds at business anniversary party, genteel audience. An Equal Opportunity Employer.*
>
> —*TIMES*, TRENTON, N.J.

The application blank should be tailored to fit the needs of the particular company. At a minimum, however, it should contain such basic hiring data as education and work experience. Character references (including the occupation as well as the name and address of each reference) should also be given, as well as the name and title of the applicant's immediate supervisor on each of his or her past jobs.

In addition to its uses in employee selection, the application blank provides an initial record of employment if questions of fact later arise, and it serves as part of a permanent record in which added experience and training should find a place.

The employment interview.   As a selection procedure the interview is a primary way of judging the applicant's appearance, poise, speech, and other characteristics. Also, since the objective is to hire an individual who satisfies the requirements of a particular position, the completed application blank should be studied prior to the interview, and the job descriptions and specifications likely to be needed should be at hand.

---

[2] Technically, the equal employment opportunity laws do not "prohibit" the use of such questions. However, if they are used *prior* to the actual decision to hire or not to hire they can be viewed by the courts as discriminatory; i.e., the burden of proof would be on the employer to show that the use of such a potentially discriminating question was *not* a criterion in refusing employment to the applicant. See also the section on fair employment practices, pp. 433–35, in Chapter 26.

TABLE 11-1

Pre-Employment Inquiry Guide

Subject	Permissible Inquiries	*Inquiries to be Avoided
1. NAME	"Have you worked for this company under a different name?" "Is any additional information relative to change of name, use of an assumed name or nickname necessary to enable a check on your work and educational record? If yes, explain."	Inquiries about name which would indicate applicant's lineage, ancestry, national origin, or descent. Inquiry into previous name of applicant where it has been changed by court order or otherwise. Inquiries about preferred courtesy title: Miss, Mrs, Ms.
2. MARITAL AND FAMILY STATUS	Whether applicant can meet specified work schedules or has activities, commitments or responsibilities that may hinder the meeting of work attendance requirements. Inquiries as to a duration of stay on job or anticipated absences which are made to males and females alike.	Any inquiry indicating whether an applicant is married, single, divorced, or engaged, etc. Number and age of children. Information on child-care arrangements. Any questions concerning pregnancy. Any such questions which directly or indirectly result in limitation of job opportunities.
3. AGE	Requiring proof of age in the form of a work permit or a certificate of age—if a minor. Requiring proof of age by birth certificate after being hired. Inquiry as to whether or not the applicant meets the minimum age requirements as set by law and requirement that upon hire proof of age must be submitted in the form of a birth certificate or other forms of proof of age. If age is a legal requirement, "if hired, can you furnish proof of age?," or statement that hire is subject to verification of age. Inquiry as to whether or not an applicant is younger than the employer's regular retirement age.	Requirement that applicant state age or date of birth. Requirement that applicant produce proof of age in the form of a birth certificate or baptismal record. *The Age Discrimination in Employment Act of 1967 forbids discrimination against persons between the ages of 40 and 70.*

TABLE 11-1 (*Continued*)

Subject	Permissible Inquiries	*Inquiries to be Avoided
4. HANDICAPS	For employers subject to the provisions of the Rehabilitation Act of 1973, applicants may be "invited" to indicate how and to what extent they are handicapped. The employer must indicate to applicants that: 1) compliance with the invitation is voluntary; 2) the information is being sought only to remedy discrimination or provide opportunities for the handicapped; 3) the information will be kept confidential; and 4) refusing to provide the information will not result in adverse treatment. All applicants can be asked if they are able to carry out all necessary job assignments and perform them in a safe manner.	An employer must be prepared to prove that any physical and mental requirements for a job are due to "business necessity" and the safe performance of the job. Except in cases where undue hardship can be proven, employers must make "reasonable accommodations" for the physical and mental limitations of an employee or applicant. "Reasonable accommodation" includes alteration of duties, alteration of work schedule, alteration of physical setting, and provision of aids. *The Rehabilitation Act of 1973 forbids employers from asking job applicants general questions about whether they are handicapped or asking them about the nature and severity of their handicaps.*
5. SEX	Inquiry or restriction of employment is permissible only where a **bona fide occupational qualification** exists. (This BFOQ exception is interpreted very narrowly by the courts and the EEOC.) The burden of proof rests on the employer to prove that the BFOQ does exist and that **all** members of the affected class are incapable of performing the job. Sex of applicant may be requested (preferably not on the employment application) for affirmative action purposes but may not be used as an employment criterion.	Sex of applicant. Any other inquiry which would indicate sex. Sex is **not** a BFOQ because a job involves physical labor (such as heavy lifting) beyond the capacity of **some** women nor can employment be restricted just because the job is traditionally labeled "men's work" or "women's work." Applicant's sex cannot be used as a factor for determining whether or not an applicant will be satisfied in a particular job. Questions about an applicant's height or weight, unless demonstrably necessary as requirements for the job.

6. RACE OR COLOR	General distinguishing physical characteristics such as scars, etc., to be used for identification purposes. Race may be requested (preferably not on the employment application) for affirmative action purposes but may not be used as an employment criterion.	Applicant's race. Color of applicant's skin, eyes, hair, etc., or other questions directly or indirectly indicating race or color.
7. ADDRESS OR DURATION OF RESIDENCE	Applicant's address. Inquiry into length of stay at current and previous addresses. "How long a resident of this State or city?"	Specific inquiry into foreign address which would indicate national origin. Names and relationship of persons with whom applicant resides. Whether applicant owns or rents home.
8. BIRTHPLACE	"Can you after employment submit a birth certificate or other proof of U.S. citizenship?"	Birthplace of applicant. Birthplace of applicant's parents, spouse, or other relatives. Requirement that applicant submit a birth certificate before employment. Any other inquiry into national origin.
9. RELIGION	An applicant may be advised concerning normal hours and days of work required by the job to avoid possible conflict with religious or other personal conviction. However, except in cases where undue hardship can be proven, employers and unions must make "reasonable accommodation" for religious practices of an employee or prospective employee. "Reasonable accommodation" may include voluntary substitutes, flexible scheduling, lateral transfer, change of job assignments, or the use of an alternative to payment of union dues.	Applicant's religious denomination or affiliation, church, parish, pastor, or religious holidays observed. Any inquiry to indicate or identify religious denomination or customs. Applicants may not be told that any particular religious groups are required to work on their religious holidays.
10. MILITARY RECORD	Type of education and experience in service as it relates to a particular job.	Type of discharge.

TABLE 11-1 (*Continued*)

SUBJECT	PERMISSIBLE INQUIRIES	*INQUIRIES TO BE AVOIDED
11. PHOTOGRAPH	May be required for identification after hiring.	Requirement that applicant affix a photograph to his application. Request that applicant, at his option, submit photograph. Requirement of photograph after interview but before hiring.
12. CITIZENSHIP	"Are you a citizen of the United States?" "Do you intend to remain permanently in the U.S.?" "If not a citizen, are you prevented from becoming lawfully employed because of visa or immigration status?" Statement that, if hired, applicant may be required to submit proof of citizenship.	"Of what country are you a citizen?" Whether applicant or his parents or spouse are naturalized or native-born U.S. citizens. Date when applicant or parents or spouse acquired U.S. citizenship. Requirement that applicant produce his naturalization papers. Whether applicant's parents or spouse are citizens of the U.S.
13. ANCESTRY OR NATIONAL ORIGIN	Languages applicant reads, speaks, or writes fluently. (If another language is necessary to perform the job.)	Inquiries into applicant's lineage, ancestry, national origin, descent, birthplace, or native language. National origin of applicant's parents or spouse.
14. EDUCATION	Applicant's academic, vocational, or professional education; schools attended. Inquiry into language skills such as reading, speaking, and writing foreign languages.	Any inquiry asking specifically the nationality, racial or religious affiliation of a school. Inquiry as to how foreign language ability was acquired.
15. EXPERIENCE	Applicant's work experience, including names and addresses of previous employers, dates of employment, reasons for leaving, salary history. Other countries visited.	

152

16. CONVICTION, ARREST, AND COURT RECORD	Inquiry into actual **convictions** which relate reasonably to fitness to perform a particular job. (A conviction is a court ruling where the party is found guilty as charged. An arrest is merely the apprehending or detaining of the person to answer the alleged crime.)	Any inquiry relating to arrests. Any inquiry into or request for a person's arrest, court, or conviction record if not **substantially related** to functions and responsibilities of the particular job in question.
17. RELATIVES	Names of applicants' relatives already employed by this company. Names and address of parents or guardian (if applicant is a minor).	Name or address of any relative of adult applicant.
18. NOTICE IN CASE OF EMERGENCY	Name and address of persons to be notified in case of accident or emergency.	Name and address of **relatives** to be notified in case of accident or emergency.
19. ORGANIZATIONS	Inquiry into any organizations which an applicant is a member of providing the name or character of the organizations does not reveal the race, religion, color, or ancestry of the membership. "List all professional organizations to which you belong. What offices do you hold?"	"List all organizations, clubs, societies, and lodges to which you belong." The names of organizations to which the applicant belongs if such information would indicate through character or name the race, religion, color, or ancestry of the membership.
20. REFERENCES	"By whom were you referred for a position here?" Names of persons willing to provide professional and/or character references for applicant.	Requiring the submission of a religious reference. Requesting reference from applicant's pastor.
21. CREDIT RATING	None.	Any questions concerning credit rating, charge accounts, etc. Ownership of car.
22. MISCELLANEOUS	Notice to applicants that any misstatements or omissions of material facts in the application may be cause for dismissal.	

• These inquiries should be avoided as selection criteria unless it is provable that a bona fide occupational qualification (BFOQ) is involved. A BFOQ is a qualification that is **absolutely necessary** to perform a job. Any inquiry should be avoided which, although not specifically listed above, is designed to elicit information concerning race, color, ancestry, age, sex, religion, handicap, or arrest and court record unless based upon a bona fide occupational qualification.
Source: *Personnel Journal* (Oct., 1980). Reprinted with permission of the author, Clifford M. Koen, Jr., and the publisher.

The interviewer should also have handy an interview guide; this device is like a grocery shopping list, useful in ensuring complete coverage of essential items, guarding against diversions, and assisting in directing and distributing effort.

The interview should be conducted in a suitable place, such as the office or a quiet part of the building. The applicant should first be put at ease. Often asking general questions designed to start the applicant talking and to "break the ice" is sufficient. Informality consistent with the dignity or importance of the interview is the goal usually sought. The trend in larger companies is to use two or three interviewers. Even the smaller employer may well have an applicant interviewed by different members of the organization. In addition to seeking information from the applicant, the interviewer should furnish all important information regarding the company, the job, employment conditions, pay, company policies, and similar data, as well as answer questions the applicant may ask. If employed, the newcomer should be given specific instructions and encouragement. If rejected, he or she should leave with a feeling of goodwill toward the company.

The use of tests.   Three general types of tests or examinations are often used during the selection process: psychological tests, performance tests, and the physical examination. There are numerous varieties of psychological tests, some designed to measure intelligence or the ability to learn and others to rate aptitudes, interests, attitudes, and particular personality traits. Opinions differ regarding their value to the small firm. Where used, however, they should not be administered or interpreted without expert guidance. Such guidance is available from many educational institutions, personnel institutes, and practicing psychologists.

Performance or achievement tests should be used, even in the small business, if the nature of the work for which an individual is applying permits. These need not be elaborate; often a mere tryout preliminary to actual employment is sufficient. The physical examination should be used much more generally than it is, especially when the job requires strength, good vision, hearing, ability to stand continuously, stamina, or other qualities above the average and wherever the health and safety of the public or fellow workers are involved.

In using tests to screen job applicants, however, the small business owner should take particular precautions to ensure that they are geared to the job descriptions and specifications and that they meet the Equal Employment Opportunity Commission's standards of reliability and validity.

Checking References

The wise employer does not take an application at its face value. References given should be investigated, either in person, by letter, or over the phone. Naturally the applicant will select persons who he or she thinks will give the best recommendations. Usually relatives, church officials, and politicians should be eliminated from further consideration because the very nature of their positions precludes securing useful information from them regarding the applicant.

The logical business references for an applicant to give are readily apparent to any employer: the applicant's present or former employer, banker, school officials (in the case of recent graduates), and possibly a few business acquaintances. The applicants who give references other than these may be attempting to conceal certain "unfortunate" episodes in their past experience, but they may have thoroughly justifiable reasons for doing so. Former supervisors and employers are often biased in their evaluation of an employee, and an unfortunate set of circumstances—personality conflicts, accidents, and so forth—may distort their opinions. In such cases the job applicant may justly prefer to give as references unbiased co-workers or others rather than a present or former boss. Organizations of all types and sizes have internal politics. Often publicity given to this condition in a particular organization or a knowledge of its existence by various individuals will help the prospective employer decide which recommendations should be given greatest weight. On the other hand, an employer may overlook an ex-employee's weaknesses so as not to jeopardize the latter's chances of finding other employment. Small business owners should therefore be as circumspect in judging the work references as they are in evaluating the personal references of job applicants. In doubtful cases the prospective employer should exercise judgment supported by understanding.

Employment Records

If the job applicant is hired, his or her employment application, test scores or reports, and letters of reference, along with the interviewers' notes and any pre-employment correspondence, should be placed in the newly hired employee's employment file. In addition, during the period of his or her employment, a variety of personnel reports should be completed periodically or as the need arises, reporting such things as outstanding work performance, breach of discipline, progress of employee on the job, tardiness, absence, change in work attitude, or any other phase of the employee's work activity. Placed in a permanent file of the employee, these reports may be used as a basis for promotions, counseling, and discipline, and in union negotiations of grievances.

PLACEMENT

The **placement** of employees after they are hired is also important. Many employers could use their wage dollars more efficiently than at present by capitalizing fully on the special abilities of each employee when assigning duties. The employer who would never wear an expensive pair of dress shoes when gardening is often the same person who would use a $600-a-week pharmacist to sell chewing gum or shoestrings. Since the pharmacist's time is worth $15 per hour, or 25 cents per minute, and selling costs are at least 5 percent of sales, an employee would have to sell twenty pairs of 25-cent shoestrings each minute for the store to get full value from the employee's wages.

This example indicates that low-priced items should be sold by inexpensive help or by self-service and that the higher-paid salespeople should devote their time to "big-ticket" items exclusively. A store that carries both high- and low-priced items should have low-salaried people to sell one class of merchandise and qualified specialists to sell the other if the sales staff is large enough. However, the one- or two-person business may not find this plan of labor specialization advisable. It may be that it must sell all price lines and that contacts in selling small items serve as leads for the sales of large ones.

The production shop's problems along similar lines are obvious. A competent mechanic's time should not be misspent with menial tasks, nor should the apprentice or handyman be entrusted with exacting technical work. Misspent payroll funds come directly out of profits. Profit is jeopardized whenever the wrong employee is assigned to the wrong task at the wrong wage rate. Furthermore, the job may not be properly performed, and the employee is likely to become discontented as well.

The first few days in a new position are usually the hardest. A newcomer should be introduced to the other workers, shown the location of employee facilities, informed of any regulations, and encouraged to ask for additional information as it may be needed. A good plan is to assign an older, more experienced worker to act as sponsor until the introductory period is over. The boss should personally follow up on new employees by occasional visits with them until they feel at home in the organization. Consideration and reasonable attention at this time are a good investment in employee relations.

TRAINING

Some *preliminary training* in standardized work methods is an important part of the new employee's introduction to the job. This may require a few hours, a few days, or even a few weeks or months, varying with the nature of the work and the previous training or experience of the worker. The need for *improvement training,* on the other hand, is fairly continuous in most cases; this type of training may be *remedial* or *developmental* in nature.

Remedial training seeks to correct errors or mistakes made by individual workers regardless of how long they may have been employed. It is usually based on error reports of individuals, on reports by the immediate supervisor, on periodic reports of the operations of each department, or on the amount of spoiled work, lost sales, breakdowns, schedule delays, accidents, and similar indicators of a department's inefficiency or ineffectiveness. Either group or individual training methods may be used in remedial training.

Developmental training assumes that every job can be done better, that there is always something more an employee can learn about a job, and in many cases that certain workers wish to prepare for advancement to better positions. Continuous on-the-job training is recognized as an integral part of the responsibility of every supervisor and executive. Unfortunately it is a responsibility often neglected.

Many direct benefits result from a good remedial or developmental training program. It reduces labor turnover, improves the quality of work performed, reduces accidents, facilitates the discovery of promotion-worthy employees, and tends to lower the unit costs of labor.

Since state-supported vocational training of various types covering a wide range of jobs is available at little or no cost in most communities, there is no need for small business owners to neglect employee training because they lack time or teaching experience. Nearly every state has a vocational division associated with the state department of public instruction, employing coordinators at the local level in both industrial and distributive education. The coordinators are expert teachers. Most of them are required to have at least two years of occupational experience in addition to college training.

Two types of programs conducted by the coordinators can be of direct, immediate benefit to small business owners. One, the **distributive education** program, is a cooperative program for high school seniors in which the students spend part of the school day working in a business. The students are also enrolled in regular classroom work that is directly related to the business in which they are working. The work experience phase includes a cooperative effort on the part of the business owners and coordinator to organize the experiences of the students so that real training occurs on the job as well as in the classroom.

In addition to the cooperative programs for high schools students, most coordinators are willing to organize adult courses on request from local business people. Generally, one-half of the cost of instruction will be paid by the state and federal government for such classes. The subject areas are unlimited as long as the course is valid preparation for an occupation requiring less than a college degree. In addition, many state universities and colleges employ specialists in their extension divisions to supply instructors for adult training organized by local coordinators.

TRANSFERS AND PROMOTIONS

Neither employees nor jobs are static. Jobs are continually changing, both in content and in the company's need to fill them. Employees also change; many become qualified for better jobs, while others become discontented or disillusioned in their present jobs. Adjustments to these changes are made principally by transferring or promoting workers to different jobs.

Transfers are changes in the occupation of workers not properly considered as promotions. The need for transfers arises from one of four conditions: (1) elimination of a job; (2) request for change by an employee; (3) belief by management that a worker has been misplaced; and (4) fluctuations in the need for certain kinds of jobs.

When a job is eliminated through no fault of the worker, every reasonable effort should be made to place him or her elsewhere in the organization. If this is impossible, the employer should help the worker secure a satisfactory position with some other company.

For various reasons employees sometimes ask to be shifted to another position. If the reasons given for the request are plausible, it should be granted if possible. In other cases management may take the initiative when it appears that a particular worker would be better suited to a different job. Usually a satisfactory transfer can be made in such cases if the reasons are discussed with the employee, but sometimes this is not possible. A surprisingly large number of workers resent any change in their job or duties, even when it involves a promotion, increases their income, or is otherwise to their benefit. In some cases certain locations for a desk or even a workplace in the shop acquire prestige value for employees, and those favored with such locations show resentment when moved.

A **promotion** involves assignment to a job of greater difficulty, requiring greater skill or a larger measure of responsibility, and consequently better-paid. In making promotions, merit and seniority are important factors. Only in cases where employees are approximately equal, however, should seniority control. Since merit is of primary importance, there should be some provision for the systematic evaluation of employee performance on their present jobs. Operating reports should be supplemented by periodic **merit ratings** by supervisors and others in a position to make impartial evaluations of qualities like attitude, initiative, personality, self-development, and preparation for promotion. Often promotions may be preceded by one or more trial periods in the new position.

REMUNERATION

Job analysis provides the factual data needed for the intelligent selection, placement, training, transfer, and promotion of employees; it also forms the basis for determining the relative worth or value of each job in the enterprise. The process of determining relative job worth is called **job evaluation.** The most basic determinants of what the hourly wage rate of a job should be, relative to other jobs, are the duties that must be performed, the conditions under which they are performed, and the qualifications required to perform them. Jobs are evaluated with reference to one another and to their importance to the company in terms of skill, effort, responsibility, and similar factors. To the extent that equitable wage rates are established by this procedure, job evaluation minimizes a common source of employee grievance—namely, the belief of a worker that he or she is underpaid relative to other workers.

The wage that an individual worker receives, however, is dependent only in part on the requirements of the job. It is also a function of the worker's performance on the job. Thus it is common practice in wage administration to establish a *rate range* for each job by means of job evaluation, and to determine an individual employee's wage rate *within* that range on the basis of seniority and/or merit. Merit rating (or the rating of the employee on the job rather than the job itself), as noted in the preceding section, is also used in deciding whether or not to promote an employee to a higher-paying job when that employee has reached the top of the wage scale on the present job.

Wage Payment Methods

Wages also vary with the method of wage payment. The small firm is likely to find the simpler systems of payment better suited to its needs. These are straight salary or **time wages,** straight commission or **piece rates,** and simple bonus plans, such as regular salary plus a definite reward or bonus for achievement beyond a standard or quota agreed upon in advance.

Incentive systems based on time studies or other measured output may be used effectively in the small business if restricted to jobs where such plans are appropriate and if kept simple. Benefits to be derived from such systems must be compared with the added expense entailed and with employee attitude toward the method. An **incentive wage plan** should give the worker more pay for the same amount of time worked, give management a lower labor cost (or a predetermined unit cost for purposes of pricing and budgeting), be understandable and acceptable to the worker, and be economical for management to administer.

The negative attitude of some workers toward incentive plans is sometimes difficult for the inexperienced manager to understand. Not all employees are ambitious. Many prefer their present income to prospects for a higher income if this involves changing established habits. The majority of workers are suspicious and fearful of new plans to increase output even though they will share in the larger returns.

Wage Supplements

In recent years various types of *wage supplements* have come into vogue. These supplementary forms of income—commonly referred to as **fringe benefits** (notwithstanding the fact that across the nation, in all sizes of business, they average more than 30 percent of payroll)—include such items as paid vacations, group insurance, sick leave, pensions, and profit-sharing plans.

Though such wage supplements are more common in large firms, the smaller business has found it increasingly necessary to introduce them in order to compete in labor markets. This is particularly true in the case of pension plans. For the small business, however, the most common type of wage supplement is profit sharing. These employee benefit programs will now be discussed in some detail.

Profit sharing. In many respects **profit sharing** is better suited to the small than to the large enterprise. For it to be successful, there must be a feeling of mutual trust and confidence between management and employees. The company's books must be open to inspection by those included in the profit sharing, although not indiscriminately. A basis previously agreed on for sharing the profits must be established and followed, and a satisfactory wage and salary scale must be maintained. Under no circumstances should profit sharing be used as a deferred wage-payment plan.

There are certain basic questions regarding profit sharing, especially for employees, that should be considered before adopting such a plan. Profit, which is a residual after all costs and expenses of the business have been paid, fluctuates widely, often as a result of causes external to the business, such as competition and general economic conditions. Even under favorable conditions only a few employees are likely to be in a position to actually increase or decrease the company's profits. For these reasons, profit sharing is not a form of incentive wage, except in a limited sense for the few persons in a position to affect profits materially. Profit is the reward to owner/managers for both risking their own capital and exercising good managerial ability. The owners bear losses when they occur; but those employees who share in the profits when there are any do not conversely share in the losses when they occur. And finally, it is discouraging to employees who anticipate sharing in the profits and who may even have done extra work to help the company make a profit to discover at the end of the year that there are no profits to share.

Pensions. The primary purpose of a **pension** plan is to provide a regular income to employees following their retirement from the firm. Most pension plans also provide disability benefits to the employee and death benefits to his or her surviving spouse. Retirement, disability, and death benefits may come from either an insured fund or a trust fund.

So that there may be some assurance that the fund will be adequate to the anticipated benefits, the services of an actuary are needed in the design of the plan. It is also a good idea to consult a lawyer to make sure that the plan qualifies under Section 401 of the Internal Revenue Code. A pension plan that thus qualifies has certain tax advantages for those contributing to the plan.

The pension plan is financed by regular contributions of an amount within the minimum and maximum limits prescribed by regulations of the Internal Revenue Service. Contributions by employees may or may not be required by the business seeking to establish such a plan.

The legal and actuarial costs of establishing a pension plan can be substantial. These setup costs can be avoided, however, by adopting one of the IRS-approved *prototype* plans developed by many banks, mutual funds, and insurance companies. The IRS itself has also prepared a number of model plans from which small business owners can choose in tailoring a pension program to suit their particular needs and purposes.

MORALE BUILDING

Fair and adequate pay (and fringe benefits), however, aren't all it takes to make employees happy; their jobs must also be satisfying to them. The key to employee satisfaction or good employee relations is an effective **communications** system.

Effective communications in any business organization is a two-way street. On the one hand, employees want to be advised of company rules and personnel policies, operating procedures, advertising and sales promotion campaigns, and plans for future expansion of the business; in other words, they want to know what the employer is thinking. On the other hand, the employer wants to know how well the employees understand the firm's rules, policies, programs, and plans, and particularly to learn of their gripes or complaints before they develop into full-blown grievances.

Teamwork and two-way communications in a business organization are based on the premise that there is a mutuality of interests between employer and employees. The story is told about the two stubborn mules that found themselves tied together with a halter between two bales of hay. Each mule pulled in the opposite direction until both were worn out and half-starved. Only then did they discover that by pulling together they could enjoy both stacks of hay.

Modern management also stresses **leadership** and the human element. Because the human element is a factor common to all businesses regardless of type, application of the basic principles of human relations is necessary in any business. Two standards of paramount importance in personnel management are fair treatment, and the recognition of each employee as an individual, not merely as a cog in the machine. Fair treatment is not easy to define, but its absence is quickly detected by employees. Promotions or pay raises for reasons other than merit and seniority, for example, soon become known and increase the difficulty of securing and retaining loyal, dependable, and efficient employees. **Morale** in any organization is directly related to the manner in which these and other matters of mutual concern are handled.

Recognition of good work by the manager, for example, will usually do more to encourage employees than incentives that are less personal. Criticisms of individual employees, on the other hand, should be made privately, sympathetically, and constructively.

Great care is taken by the real leader to treat all employees fairly and un-

Courtesy of Small Business Administration.

derstandingly as individual human beings. Employee suggestions are welcome; they are actively sought by alert managers, and the personal nature of the small concern can be used to advantage in getting employees to express themselves, to offer suggestions, and to call attention to opportunities for improvement. In the more progressive organizations employees are consulted on management problems, and they are furnished with management information formerly of a confidential nature. Employee–management cooperation is one way for the small business to attract and hold personnel of excellent quality.

Achieving worker participation and distributing some responsibility among as many workers as possible usually enlists support and cooperation and leads to other objectives—to make workers conscious of the importance of costs, quality, safety, and preventive maintenance. Sometimes these goals may be achieved by a challenge to the workers, such as contests or awards that are significant as recognition symbols and need have no monetary value. But they are more readily attained by a constructive approach to personnel relations which gives workers a voice in making decisions that vitally affect them in their everyday work lives. Such an approach recognizes that in every individual there is a desire for self-expression, and that as a means of increasing worker efficiency the sense of participation is valuable in itself (regardless of whether the participants receive awards).

The constructive approach to dealing with one's employees has always been deemed desirable, but it has become much more urgent or necessary in recent times. Employees who entered the work force prior to or during World War II were raised in an era in which discipline, both in the home and in the school, was firmly established, and they were trained to accept the unques-

162

tioned authority of their parents, teachers, and employers. The present generation of employees, on the other hand, has been raised in an affluent society in which a permissive atmosphere prevails, and workers today have adopted a questioning, often arrogant, attitude toward all forms of authority.

Small business owners must now rely on their leadership qualities rather than their line authority to gain the loyalty, respect, and cooperation of their employees. They must recognize that holding the confidence of their employees is much more vital to the operating efficiency of the business than maintaining doctrinaire areas of authority. They must think less in terms of management prerogatives and more in terms of the benefits to be derived from the democratic self-expression of their employees. Just as political government functions with the consent of the governed, so also must management function with the consent of the managed.

SUMMING UP

Although every business operates through its personnel, probably less has been done to utilize this valuable resource *effectively* than has been done for other factors of production. Since payroll is usually a major and often the largest item of expense in any business, the opportunities for financial improvement through better personnel relations are great. In addition, a firm's personnel is one thing competitors cannot copy or duplicate. Capital assets and goods and supplies are generally available to all business owners on approximately equal terms, but this is not true of a good group of employees. Only the workers' time can be purchased or hired; their attitudes, loyalty, cooperation, and productivity must be earned. This is the aim of good personnel management. *The many advantages small business has over big business in handling employee relations should be developed to their fullest extent.*

In recruiting and screening job applicants, small business managers should be particularly aware of the restrictions imposed on them and other employers by the equal employment opportunity laws. They should avoid asking questions in the pre-employment process that would elicit potentially prejudicial information.

Carefully selected and well-trained, an employee becomes an investment of value. Although small business managers often lack the time or teaching experience to train employees themselves, high school distributive education and other public vocational programs available in most communities can furnish practical and relevant training without cost to the business.

Good management stresses leadership and the human element. This requires that employees be given some voice in decision-making. If the results of group effort are as dependent on management as they most certainly appear to be, then we can understand why athletic contests tend to become contests between the managers of the teams. A group of mediocre performers under strong leadership often will excel over a team of excellent individuals under a poor leader. Similarly, competition in business is to a great extent a contest between managements. Products and services are indeed the weapons, and employees and facilities are important, but the contest is between the people at the top. Certainly the best team under the best coach will win.

KEY WORDS

affirmative action	job specification
bona fide occupational qualification (BFOQ)	leadership
communications	merit rating
developmental training	morale
distributive education	pension
employee relations	piece rate
equal employment opportunity	placement
fringe benefits	profit sharing
incentive wage plan	promotion
job analysis	remedial training
job description	time wages
job evaluation	transfer

DISCUSSION QUESTIONS

1. Do you think employment tests or examinations are worthwhile to the small concern? Why or why not?

2. What kind of controls result from job evaluation, formal wage structures, and incentive-wage systems?

EXERCISES AND PROBLEMS

1. Following are questions that are sometimes asked in interviews and on employment applications. Mark those that you think are lawful with an L and those that you think are unlawful with a U. Feel free to qualify any of your answers.

a. How many years of work experience do you have?

b. (To a housewife) Why do you want to return to work?

c. Are you a citizen or a resident alien of the U.S.?

d. What is your religion?

e. Who recommended you to us?

f. What schools did you attend?

g. The women in the office take turns making coffee. If you are hired, would you be willing to share this task?

h. What would you do if your husband (or wife) got transferred?

i. Do you rent or own your own home?

j. This position requires extensive travel. Are you free to do so?

k. What languages do you speak fluently?

l. Have your wages ever been attached or garnisheed?

2.   Personnel development is essential to the successful operation of a small business. Many times, business difficulties are rooted in a personnel situation that was not handled properly. The following "lie detector" points up human relations factors that the owner/manager of a small business should be particularly concerned with. Mark what you believe to be the "true" statements and check your answers against those given at the bottom of this page. (Minimum passing grade: 100%)

a. Treat all employees alike—they are first of all a group.

b. The objective of management is to keep all employees busy, wasting no time, at whatever tasks need doing.

c. The employer's first duty is to see the employee's personal viewpoint.

d. It is a fundamental truth that all employees seek increased responsibility.

e. An employee's feelings of worth are usually not closely related to his or her feelings of accomplishment.

CASES IN POINT

Sylvia Simms has been employed by her uncle, a Chicago greeting card manufacturer, for the seven years since she left college. Having become restless on her job and impatient with her uncle, she recently got his permission to represent the firm on the West Coast by opening offices in Los Angeles. The firm has had distributors and occasionally one of its own salespeople out there, but sales efforts have not been rewarding in any sense. Sylvia believes that with a company-sponsored distribution center she can do a more effective job of serving and expanding the firm's market.

All are false except statement c.

One of her first problems as she surveys the new assignment is designing a sales compensation plan. She finds that prospective salespersons differ in their preferences for straight salary vs. straight commission, and that most of them would welcome some combination of the two. Generally, newcomers seem to prefer the security of a straight salary, while veteran salespersons want the opportunity the straight commission provides to make "real" money in proportion to talent and effort. There is great variety of methods in the industry locally.

Miss Simms believes that a beginning salesperson will be well-satisfied with $15,000–$20,000 a year, but that those with experience would demand $25,000–$30,000 if they "produce." She believes that she can afford to pay each salesperson on the straight commission plan 5 percent of sales, and that, since the line is well-established, this should be sufficient. This means that a salesperson would have to sell $400,000 annually to earn $20,000 in straight commissions. If a person on straight salary sold that much, Sylvia's 5 percent requirement would be met. If more were sold, the sales-cost percentage would decline; if less, it would increase.

a. Which method of compensation should Sylvia adopt? Why?

b. Assume that her costs can (or must) be increased to 6 percent. What salary would be earned for $400,000 sales? What commission for $300,000 sales? What salary and what commission for $600,000 sales?

c. What arrangement might be made whereby the new salespersons could start with straight salary and go on straight commission later?

d. Can you suggest a combination of salary and commission that might be useful?

Fred Warren worked in men's clothing stores during his high school and college years and for two years thereafter until he entered the armed forces. In the service he achieved sergeant's stripes and made some good friends. In addition, with the help of some well-played poker hands and occasionally lucky dice, he came home with almost $20,000 cash in hand.

His captain, who had taken a liking to him and whom Fred admired greatly, persuaded him to enter the stock brokerage business in a major city. He turned out to be good at that, too. However, when a light recession hit, Fred decided to take the $50,000 he had by then accumulated and to go into the clothing business on his own, in the old home town. The store he had worked in for so long as a young man was now for sale.

With his $50,000 and the help of the local bank, he had no trouble buying the inventory and store name and getting the lease renewed at a reasonable figure. A part of his capital went into new fixtures, improved show-windows and a general "dressing up" of the store.

All of the seven employees stayed on under his ownership. In general, they were a good crew—loyal, honest, hard-working, interested. The three key people were Amanda Adams, in charge of boys' wear; Arthur Jewell, accessories and hats; and Bart Reisling, men's clothing manager. The first two were in their early forties. Bart, who was approaching sixty, had been with the store for over thirty years, knew the clientele and all of the visiting salespersons and competitors, and was related to the former owner.

The clothing line was basically conservative. Bart had a well-established following of business and professional men, for the former owner with his help had catered to that trade with great success. The younger salespersons were not allowed to sell suits, sport jackets, or topcoats—at least not to complete the sale. Thus the clothing customers, who were mostly older men, were "Bart's customers." Fred had long known of this situation, but assumed it would change as his ownership asserted itself.

Several times he talked to Bart about adding a line more appealing to younger men but the Beau Saville brand they specialized in was very dear to Bart, and he resisted adding any new line—first mildly, then strongly. He argued that the more mature customers would "get the wrong idea," that the store's reputation must be maintained, space was at a premium, and so on. Fred pointed out that more and more younger men were moving into the area, that the local college was expanding, and that a large manufacturer was planning a new branch facility just outside town.

When Fred went to the next clothiers' convention, he was attracted by a moderately sporty new line carrying the First Mate label. It was suitable for older teenagers and college men as well as for the 20-30 age group and older. It was priced in line with Fred's policies. Yet it was not "far out." Fred thought it was just what the store needed, as men's clothing was becoming more colorful for all ages and Bart's oldsters would not live forever.

However, before actually placing an order, he decided to talk it over with Bart. Bart was again vehement in his objections—considered it too great a departure from policy—wasn't priced right—was an insult to his intelligence and judgment. Fred had expected some resistance but not this much. He went on to explain plans for better space usage and new customers, but Bart refused to listen and said he wouldn't be caught selling the new line ever!

Later, the young First Mate representative came by and talked to both men, building up more enthusiasm in Fred and more animosity in Bart. The salesman suggested that a competitor in a new shopping center a few miles away was interested in First Mate. Bart's reply was, "Let him have it!" Fred's reply was, "Not if I can help it!"

How can he help it? What else can he do?

Planning and Controlling Factory Production

CHAPTER TWELVE *Manufacturers, unlike merchandisers, must first produce the products they sell. The manufacture of these products must be planned and controlled carefully. This chapter describes and illustrates how this may be done effectively in the typical small plant.*

The production function in a small manufacturing plant involves not only allocating the right amounts of resources (labor, money, and machines) to the right places (products or projects), but also having them ready at the right time. Thus the end result of all **production planning** is an output schedule. Once the production schedules are formulated, however, steps must be taken to ensure that the schedules will be adhered to; these activities or steps are known collectively as the **production control** functions.

It is the manufacturing process that determines the general pattern of production planning and control that is appropriate in a given case.[1] There are two general patterns—the *flow* type and the *order* type. Since, as noted in Chapter 8, products processed continuously on specialized equipment laid out on a production-line basis permit the smooth flow of work from one work station to another, **flow control** is appropriate in mass production plants, that is, in the **continuous manufacturing process.** As its name suggests, this type of

[1] See pp. 100–103 for a discussion of *intermittent, repetitive,* and *continuous* manufacturing processes.

production planning and control requires the maintenance of a predetermined rate of flow from each work station.

Order control, on the other hand, is appropriate for diversified production on general-purpose equipment laid out on a functional (rather than line) basis, that is, in the **intermittent** and **repetitive manufacturing processes.** Since most small plants are engaged in one or the other of these manufacturing processes, or in a combination of the two, the planning and control of **production orders** will be given top priority in this chapter.

PLANNING PRODUCTION ORDERS

When products are fabricated to the customer's specifications (as in the intermittent process), or when a standard stock item is manufactured for the first time (as in the repetitive process), a **route sheet** must be prepared showing the following information for each of the product's component parts:

1. Complete list of operations in sequence

2. Type of machine (or other equipment) on which each operation is to be performed, and/or the department in which each operation is to be performed

3. Material requirements for each operation (kind and quantity)

4. Tools, jigs, and fixtures required for each operation

5. Time allowance for each operation (time allowance per unit x the number of units on the production order + machine setup time)

An illustrative route sheet is shown in Figure 12-1.

The next step in the planning procedure is to prepare the production **schedule.** The production schedule may be likened to a timetable, indicating *when* as well as *where* the operations on each component are to be performed. The last column in Figure 12-1, for example, indicates the starting dates in the schedule for the three operations on a hypothetical product; the planned or expected completion dates may be inferred from the machine **setup** and **process time** requirements shown in the chart.

> *Existing wealth or property can be and is being redistributed by law, but new wealth can be created only by man and by the man-made machines they guide . . . and schedule.*
> —PHILIP D. REED

Operation	Type of Machine to be Used	Department No.	Tools	Material	Set-Up and Process Time	Starting Date
1 Shearing	Square Shear	10		50-42" x 72" x ¼"	5 hrs	7/19/72
2 Perforating	Roller Press	20	Die 182		55 hrs	7/19/72
3 Rolling	Plate Roll	30			4 hrs	7/31/—

FIGURE 12-1
Route and Schedule Sheet

PRODUCTION ORDER CONTROL

The preceding paragraphs describe the first phase of production-order planning and control—*plan the work* (production planning). The next task is to *work the plan* (production control). Production planning is futile unless a control system is set up so that the plans are fulfilled.

Production control functions may be broadly classified as (1) the **dispatching** of work-in-process and (2) the **follow-up** of work-in-process.

Dispatching

Route and schedule sheets (illustrated in Figure 12-1) indicate merely the general *type* of machine or manual operation required on each part and the dates on which these operations are to begin. The next step is to dispatch the work to *particular* machines; this involves the determination of the sequence in which the orders scheduled to start on a given day should be taken up for assignment to the various work stations.

In performing this function, a **dispatch rack** or machine-loading board may be effectively employed. Such a device has a section for each machine or workplace, under which there are three hooks or pockets to hold **job tickets**— one for the job in process, one for the next job ahead, and one for jobs temporarily assigned but not yet ready for work. By examining the job tickets which indicate the work ahead and in-process on a particular machine, the foreman or dispatcher can determine whether or not new work should be assigned to it.

Before the first operation (job) on a production order can be started, however, the required raw material (if the work involves machining) or component parts (if it is an assembly operation) must be on hand. The authority for releasing materials from the stockroom is called a **materials requisition.** A **materials reserve system** (as described on pp. 126–27) is also necessary for scheduling control as well as for inventory control in the intermittent or repetitive type of manufacturing process.

After an operation on a specific job has been completed, the work must be moved to the next production center. The authority for this is a **move order.** To fix responsibility for defective work, where many different "areas of responsibility" are involved in the process, it is also frequently necessary to issue **inspection orders** before the work is moved, particularly after certain critical operations. Job tickets, material requisitions, move orders, and inspection orders comprise the bulk of the large amount of paperwork required in production-order planning and control.

Follow-up or Expediting

Dispatching, as we have noted, is the function of starting production orders on schedule. *Follow-up,* on the other hand, is the function of recording the progress of work in the shop and taking remedial action in those cases where the work is behind schedule. In the latter case, the function becomes one of **expediting** or "stock chasing."

Follow-up is a particularly important production control function in custom work, for special-order customers make frequent inquiries concerning the progress of their orders and often request special services. It is, of course, also important in the repetitive processing of low-volume standardized products.

FLOW CONTROL

Where there is sufficient demand for the product, special-purpose equipment (as we noted in Chapter 8) can be set up for its continuous manufacture. In this type of manufacture the *flow* type of production planning and control is indicated; order control is not appropriate. Here, the planning function is the determination of the rate of flow of work-in-process from one work station to the next; the control function, obviously, is the initiation and maintenance of this predetermined rate of flow.

Production planning in continuous manufacture begins, as in all types of production, with an analysis of the product for determining the most economical sequence of operations, and the time allowance for each operation on each part or parts-assembly. The next step is to install the production equipment in accordance with this planned routing. Since the rate of flow to and from each work station should be as nearly equal as possible (to permit the smooth flow of work), the number of workers and machines at each work station will vary, depending on the capacity of each machine and the predetermined or standard times of the operations to be performed along the line. Thus, once a production line has been set up for continuous manufacture, route and schedule sheets (such as that illustrated in Figure 12-1) are no longer necessary. Routing is automatic because the layout of the equipment determines the direction of material flow throughout the plant. Likewise, scheduling is largely automatic because the rate of output is determined by the speed of the conveyor; as long as materials are supplied to the production line in the right amounts and at the right times, the volume of output can be readily calculated for any time period. Because of the steady flow or use of materials, balance-of-stores ledger sheets (such as that illustrated on p. 127) are not necessary; instead, a purchasing schedule is set up which is synchronized with the production schedule, thus minimizing the amount of storage space and working capital tied up in inventory.

The production control functions of dispatching and follow-up are also relatively simple. Once material is on the production line, the flow of material from one work station to the next is automatic. Dispatching in continuous manufacture, therefore, involves simply the feeding of material onto the production line in the amounts and times specified in the production plan. This is done by means of **track sheet instructions** which are transmitted to the appropriate line stations over a telautograph or other type of communications device.

The follow-up function involves simply a comparison of the *actual* rate of output with the *scheduled* rate of output over a period of time; this is in contrast with the follow-up function as performed in the intermittent and repetitive types of manufacture, wherein the progress of each order is monitored.

SUMMING UP

The production function in a manufacturing establishment involves the allocation of the right amounts of resources (labor, materials, machine time) to the right places (processing departments or line stations) at the right time.

While no two production planning and control systems are exactly alike, nevertheless the routine in one firm follows a general *pattern* which is common to the system of other firms engaged in the same type of manufacturing. The similarities and differences between these patterns of production planning and control are summarized in the table below:

Production Control Patterns Common to Firms Engaged in Intermittent, Repetitive, and Continuous Manufacturing

TYPE OF CONTROL	INTERMITTENT MANUFACTURING	REPETITIVE MANUFACTURING	CONTINUOUS MANUFACTURING
	ORDER CONTROL		FLOW CONTROL
Determining quantity to manufacture	Requirements of the sales order	Economic lot size	Requirements of the production program
Routing of work-in-process	For each production order	Largely predetermined	Predetermined
Scheduling of work-in-process	For each production order		Production schedule prepared for entire manufacturing period—broken down into weekly and daily schedules
Dispatching	Release of labor and material requisitions for each production order		Periodic release of manufacturing schedules
Follow-up	For each production order, compare with standards set for performance		Compare actual rate of output with scheduled rate of output

KEY WORDS

continuous manufacturing process
dispatching
dispatch rack
expediting
flow control
follow-up
inspection order
intermittent manufacturing process
job ticket
materials requisition
materials reserve system

move order
order control
process time
production control
production order
production planning
repetitive manufacturing process
routing (route sheet)
scheduling
setup time
track sheet instructions

1. What part does a production order play in planning and scheduling manufacturing activities?

2. What is the relationship of production planning, scheduling, and control to the following departments or activities of the firm: (a) sales, (b) engineering, (c) manufacturing, (d) personnel, (e) purchasing, and (f) inventory control?

3. How would you plan, schedule, and control production in a three- or four-person metal-working job shop? Describe the kinds of information you would need and how you would obtain and coordinate that information.

CASE IN POINT

When Eric Hansen's father retired as president of the Hansen Appliance Company last spring, Eric took over the small metal-processing and electric assembling firm. Three products comprise the product line: (1) a wall-attached kitchen can opener, (2) a vacuum dust-collecting unit attachable to hand power woodworking tools, and (3) a hand-operated soil tiller for home use. All of these items involve the use of the same compact electric motor, all are (or can be) cordless for brief periods (calling for occasional recharging), and all are sold mainly to hardware and department stores.

The wall-attached can opener, now eight years old and the first of the line, is the most popular and lowest priced of the three. The vacuum dust-collecting unit, which followed the can opener four years later, is the next most popular item, and its sales are growing steadily. The tiller is new and is also growing in sales, but is not yet a contributor to profit.

Eric has a degree in electrical engineering and has worked in the shop, but he has done most of the selling in recent years. This consists primarily of calls on wholesalers, with occasional calls on larger retailers (including chains) and on manufacturers who are adding to their lines of private brands or providing an item such as the vacuum unit as an accessory to their own products.

Eric employs sixteen people—an office-credit manager, an accountant, a clerical force of three, and the remainder in production, each product line managed by a foreman. These latter, although quite young, are very competent and devoted to the firm and its management and products. Under Eric's father's leadership, they have developed from selected vocational school graduates into good and promising minor executives. They have been granted considerable freedom of action, for the senior Mr. Hansen spent most of his time in the shop and handled them in a somewhat paternal manner. It was a tight ship, but a pleasant place to work.

However, Eric can presently see problems ahead. In the first place, he cannot both run the shop and sell outside. Second, he sees the necessity for a constant flow of new product ideas to be evaluated. Third, the company is becoming large enough to demand a better costing and general accounting system. All of these problems are coming up at once and all call for fairly prompt action.

As he sees it, he has these alternatives:

1. He can take over production management and delegate sales to manufacturers' agents or hire his own sales personnel.
2. He can hire an outside production manager. (He believes that none of the present department managers is mature enough to handle the job.)
3. He may be able to sell out to a larger firm at a nice capital gain.
4. He can phase out one of his products.
5. He can find a capable partner.

What would *you* advise him to do? Explain your reasoning fully.

Part Four

MANAGING THE DISTRIBUTION FUNCTION

After products and services are produced they must be distributed (sold) to those who want them. Distribution or selling—marketing—provides the business firm's source of income. The ultimate sale is the focal point of all business activity; without sales, all other operations (production, finance, and the like) become meaningless.

In the chapters comprising this section the basic principles involved in all successful marketing programs are examined. The important relationships between price, type of product or service, and customer wants, as well as advertising and other sales promotion methods used to achieve the firm's profit goals are carefully reviewed. From your study of this material you will learn how to delineate a business firm's market—its size, location, and important characteristics—and how to develop a strategy for marketing the firm's product or service.

Market Analysis
and Business Location

CHAPTER THIRTEEN *Before products and services can be distributed it is necessary to know where the potential customers are. Some businesses can thrive in one location but not in another. The first marketing decision by the owner/manager of a business was made when the original location for that business was selected. Your study of this chapter should give you a greater appreciation for the importance of location in the success of a small business.*

Where a business is located is usually a deciding factor in its success or failure. All too frequently in small business the matter of location is determined to a large degree by personal, or nonbusiness, considerations. This sometimes results in the business's being originally located or remaining in an area from which a substantial portion of the market has departed. In a somewhat exaggerated example, Joe's haberdashery in a ghost town seems certain to fail—but a shopping center full of haberdasheries might be an even worse location.

In deciding on a location for a business, two steps are required: (1) selecting the particular community, that is, defining the firm's market or trading area, and (2) choosing a site within that community. In terms of economic factors, selecting a geographic region and a community in that region is relatively more important for the small factory or wholesale concern than for most retail

179

and service establishments. Conversely, choosing the district and site within a particular community is usually of more importance to the retail store or service business.

Although the various types of business enterprises have many of the same market or location requirements, they also have individual requirements that need to be considered. To lessen repetition we shall first consider some basic factors to be evaluated in any of these businesses, and then discuss special needs later in the chapter.

SELECTING THE COMMUNITY

Market analysis is customary in large businesses, where it prevents many misplaced stores, shops, and plants. The thousands of dollars spent for this purpose are considered good investments. But market analysis should not be limited to large organizations. Entrepreneurs contemplating establishing a small concern should also analyze a market in order to determine (1) what a given community wants so that they can offer the right product or service, or (2) which community wants the product or service they are offering. And since communities and the wants of their inhabitants change, market analysis should be a *continuing* process. The lack of such a precautionary step is an important reason for many small business failures.

In selecting a community in which to locate a retail, wholesale, or service establishment the following factors must be evaluated: the local economic base, population and income trends, customer demographic data, and competition. While small manufacturers may also be concerned with community attitudes and living conditions, their primary objective is to choose a location at which their costs of production and distribution are at a minimum. The small business owner/manager should be sufficiently familiar with the specific requirements for his or her business to rate each of these factors in terms of the business's needs.

The Economic Base

A community's **economic base** determines to a great extent the opportunities that exist for the small business owner in a particular place. As measured by the value of farm products sold and value added by manufacture and the extractive industries, the wealth produced in or near the community has important consequences in terms of local employment, income, and population growth.

The occupational makeup of a community, for example, depends on the type of jobs its resources and location will support, and its population density depends on the number of such jobs that are available. The nature and number of jobs also influence the size and distribution of incomes earned by residents of the community.

It is the purchasing power of the community that is of utmost importance to entrepreneurs in retailing and contract construction and in the service trades. The success of these kinds of business will, in turn, provide opportunities to the local wholesalers and manufacturers who service them.

A community's economic base can be evaluated by studying available census data and other business statistics. However, one can also learn a great deal about a community by looking and listening. Some danger signals are:

1. The necessity for high school and college graduates to leave town to find suitable employment
2. The inability of other residents to find jobs locally
3. Declining retail sales and industrial production
4. An apathetic attitude toward the community on the part of local business owners, educational administrators, and other residents

Favorable signs include:

1. Chain or department store branches
2. Branch plants of large industrial firms
3. A progressive Chamber of Commerce and other civic organizations
4. Good schools and public services
5. Well-maintained business and residential premises
6. Good transportation facilities to other parts of the country
7. Construction activity accompanied by an absence of vacant buildings and unoccupied homes or houses for sale

Preference should be given to a growing community. A rare opportunity would be needed to compensate for a static population or one that shows a long-term declining trend. It is always possible that with enlightened civic leadership and other favorable conditions such as the rerouting of a major highway, a static or declining community may stage a rebirth, but it should not be counted on.

Population and Income Trends

Retailers and the owners of service establishments will want to locate where customer income is regular and assured, as well as large. Both the amounts of money paid to workers in different occupations, and the regularity and frequency of payments differ. Some communities serving farmers must expect to grant long-term credit; others do a week-to-week credit business, because their customers are paid weekly. The cash business volume of many communities fluctuates according to the paydays of establishments in which sizable groups of citizens are employed.

Population movements should also be examined by retailers and the owners of service establishments. One of the most significant trends affecting modern business is that of population moving to the suburbs. The result is that new and active shopping centers have been growing up on the outskirts of the big towns. Even smaller cities are finding it desirable to plan for more decentralized growth, with new neighborhoods being developed as entities served to a considerable degree by their own community shopping and service centers.

Demographic Characteristics

Wise business decisions can only be made if, as a first step, the market that the entrepreneur wishes to serve has been carefully defined. A suburban area made up largely of professional leaders and business executives contrasts notably with a densely populated district located on the wrong side of the tracks.

Sociologists roughly divide people into *social classes*. Social class is determined by evaluating income, occupation, and education. These differences are reflected in buying habits. It has been shown that people tend to have predictable tastes and modes of behavior which are determined to a great extent by the class to which they belong. Prospective entrepreneurs must first decide what class and type of customer they wish to serve. When this is known the community can then be evaluated in terms of **demography:** (1) **purchasing power** of the potential customers, (2) the types of residences (whether rented or owned, houses or apartments), (3) their place and kind of work, (4) their means of transportation, (5) their age, (6) their family status, and (7) their leisure activities. Conversely, once these entrepreneurs are established in a location they must always be aware of these same customer characteristics, because as communities change and customers change, the business owners must be prepared to either change their location or change the definition of the market that they wish to serve. Failure to follow one of these courses can mean reduced profits or business failure.

Competition

Whether competition is good or bad for a business depends to a great extent on the kind of business and on the owner's competence. Some establishments thrive on competition while others are destroyed by it. Many lines of business do well if located in a market or shopping center with the right type of competitors. Retail stores that handle shopping goods or general merchandise sold to customers who live in a large trading area surrounding the town generally do better when they are located in proximity to one another for the convenience of the shopper. Small wholesalers or manufacturers who are not dependent on the local market, such as dry goods wholesalers and furniture makers, also find that healthy competition attracts buyers and suppliers' representatives from out of town. In contrast to this, the small grocery wholesaler intent on serving the local market would view the presence of many alert competitors as undesirable.

Another aspect of competition is the small business owner's ability and ambition. Where an inexperienced and less ambitious individual might rate strong competition undesirable, an experienced, well-qualified, ambitious person might welcome such a situation as assurance of a healthy condition likely to make for greater permanence and stability. He or she would count on being able to get a fair share of the business.

SELECTING THE SITE

After a prospective small business owner has decided on the community in which he or she wishes to locate and understands some of the special requirements of the business, the owner is ready to select the **business site.** Site considerations will vary from one type of business to another.

In determining the best site for a retail establishment, retailers think in terms of the place that will be most accessible to the customers who need the kind and quality of goods they intend to sell. While some wholesalers may also need to consider accessibility, they are more likely to regard as important their delivery costs or the cost of the space they occupy. Manufacturers, on the other hand, consider such things as room for expansion, highway or railway access, and waste disposal. Service establishments, to a greater or lesser degree, have characteristics of both retailing and manufacturing, and their operators must evaluate accessibility, space costs, and other pertinent facts in terms of the functions they will perform.

Since the location of a business tends to be more permanent than many other aspects of business, and since a lease is often involved, a business must anticipate the future correctly and continuously adapt to the changing conditions affecting its site. Ownership of the site aggravates this problem.

THE RETAIL LOCATION

Once the store's merchandising policies are formulated and the region selected, the next step is to appraise the present and future prospects of each community under consideration. Wholesalers and manufacturers can often help, as can agencies of the federal, state, or local government, Chambers of Commerce, local banks, building and loan associations, and real estate agencies. The activities of the larger chain stores in establishing or closing branches in the town can serve as an indirect but usually reliable indicator of the community's prospects. (At the same time, however, the prospective retailer should be aware of the strong price competition that corporate chain stores *in the same line of retail trade* can provide, since they can operate on narrow profit margins.) In any case, a personal investigation should be made of the community to compare it with others as well as to select the business district and possible sites within it. High-priced merchandise, for example, requires a trading area of above-average income, a more refined or exclusive shopping district, and the presence of a suitable environment or atmosphere. The retailer should also consider whether competing stores are attractive and if they draw as customers the people who live in the community.

The Trading Area

Competition between communities is defined in terms of **trading areas.** The size of a trading area for a community or for a store depends largely on competition from stores in neighboring communities. Competition will express itself in lower prices or better quality, wider assortments or more services. In general, as communities increase in size their trading areas increase at a much greater rate than their populations.

A *trading area* may be defined as that territory within which people who trade or shop in a specific community live. In general, it may be said that the larger the community, the farther the people will come to trade there. However, the size and proximity of neighboring towns, as well as the merchandise or service provided by each community, affect the operation of this rule.

The size or extent of a community's trading area can be estimated in a number of ways, as follows:

1. Taking license numbers from parked cars and then locating the owners' addresses from the tag registration office
2. Checking newspaper circulation within a trading area
3. Sending questionnaires to people to find out where they buy
4. Securing addresses of customers from established stores in the territory, or by interviewing customers as they leave the store
5. Asking local bankers from what territory they draw depositors
6. Applying Reilly's law of retail gravitation

Reilly's law is a mathematical formula that is used to determine the breaking point between competing trade centers, that is, the point between towns where a consumer will purchase equal dollar amounts of good and services in each community. The theory behind the formula assumes that the size of a community's trading area for **shopping goods**[1] depends on two factors: (1) the population of competing towns and (2) the distance between these towns. For illustrative purposes, the formula is applied as follows to determine the

---

[1] As opposed to convenience goods, such as groceries, cigarettes, and other commodities for which people do not shop around.

point between Town A and Town B beyond which the majority of people will make the majority of their retail purchases in Town A rather than in Town B:

$$\text{Breaking point in miles from Town B} = \frac{\text{Distance between Town A and Town B}}{1 + \sqrt{\dfrac{\text{Population of Town A}}{\text{Population of Town B}}}}$$

$$= \frac{19}{1 + \sqrt{\dfrac{15,247}{32,430}}} = \frac{19}{1 + \sqrt{0.470}}$$

$$= \frac{19}{1.686} = 11.3$$

From the formula it can be seen that the size of a community's shopping goods trading area varies directly with the community's population and inversely with the square of the distance to competing communities.

There is a close relationship between the number of customers served by a trading area and the types of business that the trading area can support. The number of persons required to support a representative independent store varies greatly according to how specialized or widespread its merchandise appeal is; highly specialized stores, such as toys or sporting goods, may require one hundred times as large a population to draw from as those having an almost universal market, such as groceries or food service. Table 13-1 illustrates the relationship between population and kind of establishment for selected kinds of retailing in the nation as a whole. Similar ratios can be calculated for particular geographic areas (locations) and for other kinds of business.

Ratios of the type discussed above for the retailer's trading area, when compared with similar ratios for similar stores around the country and in other trading areas, provide a strong indication as to how well (or poorly) the store might do in the area. Any state or city, however, may deviate considerably from the national average.

TABLE 13-1
Population Required for Selected Kinds of Retailing

Restaurant	1,008	Jewelry Store	10,985
Gasoline service station	1,786	Florist	11,624
Grocery store	1,894	Hardware store	11,876
Cocktail lounge or beer parlor	3,788	Retail Bakery	13,731
Drugstore	4,674	Radio & television store	14,647
Women's ready-to-wear	5,492	Household appliance store	21,125
Shoe store	7,087	Department store	24,411
Furniture store	7,323	Tobacco store	109,850

SOURCE: *1979 County Business Patterns: U.S. Summary*, data adjusted to include establishments with no employees, and 1979 estimate of population, U.S. Bureau of the Census.

In using ratios such as these it should also be remembered that different kinds of stores vary considerably in drawing power or trading area; ladies' fashion apparel may attract customers from several miles away, whereas a drugstore or grocery may be limited to its immediate neighborhood. The composition of different communities may also cause deviations from the average; where most families are large and have many children, food expenditures as well as children's wear expenditures are likely to be well above average; in a district containing an unusually high proportion of sports enthusiasts, sales in this line may be substantially above average.

Another approach in market analysis is to utilize an index of sales potential, such as the per capita consumption for a particular line of goods, or perhaps an index of consumer purchasing power. There is probably no better source of information regarding markets than *Sales Management* magazine's "Buying Power Index," published annually. This publication contains a wealth of information helpful in setting sales quotas, planning distribution, locating warehouses, and studying sales potential. It includes information on population and income for every state by county and city, including per capita and per household incomes. Retail sales estimates are also made for every state by county and city. This information is combined and weighted to produce a buying power index to be used in predicting sales in a particular locality.

Business Districts

Every community has a downtown or central business district and some neighborhood shopping areas. Large cities may have several large outlying shopping centers. In addition, there are highway and interceptor locations to consider. Each type of business district is discussed below in some detail. But first, a few concepts warrant explanation.

Locations and stores may be generative or suscipient. A **generative location** is one to which the consumers are directly attracted from their place of residence; to shop there is the principal reason the consumers have left their residences. Such a location is selected expressly to be easily accessible to the greatest proportion of persons away from home for the primary purpose of shopping.

A **suscipient location** is one to which the consumers are impulsively or coincidentally attracted while away from their place of residence for any primary purpose other than shopping. It takes or receives rather than generates business.

Downtown locations. Downtown locations may be on the main street or on side streets. Until recently every city had its **"100 percent block"** or hard-core area where the heaviest concentration of shopper traffic was present—including branches of the national variety chains. This traffic was generated by the extensive advertising and pulling power of the leading department stores. The decline in the relative importance of downtown in many cities has caused many variety chains and some department stores to abandon these former 100 percent districts. The department stores that remain, however, are still the chief generators of pedestrian shopper traffic.

In the **central business district** are located a large collection of stores carrying shopping and **specialty goods.** In addition to the department and variety stores are departmentalized specialty stores, such as furniture, wearing apparel, shoes, and jewelry. There are also a number of **convenience goods** retailers such as drugstores and cigar stores.

In large cities the central shopping district may be a composite of several districts, usually adjacent to one another and each noted for a particular price range or kind of goods, such as the general department and specialty store district, women's department and specialty store district, women's apparel district, men's clothing district, and others. Each central business district will have one or more streets parallel to the main street and several at right angles to it. The latter are the secondary retail areas. Most of the centrally located, smaller retail stores and some service establishments will be found here.

Leading out from the central district will be "string" streets connecting this district with various sources of customer traffic. Some of these streets are main traffic arteries. Specialized districts with stores and shops catering to automobile traffic grow up along these traffic lanes, frequently for many blocks outward from the central business district.

Although declining in relative importance for most lines of retailing and services, downtown has become increasingly important as a center for administrative, financial, and professional services. It still has the major hotels and convention facilities, libraries and other cultural attractions, bus terminals, financial institutions, and office buildings. Many new office buildings and apartments have been erected downtown in recent years. Downtown stores cater principally to three major types of customers: (1) downtown working people (engaged in clerical and professional occupations), who have characteristic buying habits and practices; (2) apartment house occupants, who tend toward higher style and less casual wear; and (3) regional shoppers or occasional visitors.

Stores and service establishments located in the large downtown office and apartment buildings are typically small-scale independents. Many that locate on the street level, either on side streets or the main street, are also small independents. The best locations tend to intercept pedestrian traffic from large buildings, attracted to the department store districts; the same kind and size of store located between the large building and the department stores will do much better than if located at an equal distance from the building but in a direction *away* from the department stores.

Downtown has enjoyed over a century of retail supremacy. In many cities it still has the largest assortment of offerings in merchandise and in professional services, as well as being the hub of financial, administrative, and cultural establishments. Although plagued with traffic congestion, parking problems, high occupancy expense and taxation, antiquated buildings, and slum areas, it is not dead yet. It may stage a comeback, slow and expensive, but ultimate. For department stores with suburban branches, the parent store downtown is often important—although Wanamaker's in New York and other leading firms have closed their downtown stores.

Federally and locally supported urban renewal programs are bringing new hope and new opportunity to many big-city shopping areas. Sometimes this has meant the razing of existing buildings and redevelopment with new buildings, malls, and courts. Other communities have emphasized redevelopment and rehabilitation by private investors and have added parking ramps and malls.

Shoppers must be able to find adequate parking facilities. If the ramps are occupied by the cars of people who work in the central business district or by those seeking only entertainment, they are not available to shoppers. The shopper who has free parking available in outlying shopping centers close to home may choose to shop there instead. Reimbursement for parking expenses is one way of attracting customers to downtown shopping districts, but established stores in many cities have been reluctant to do so.

In very large cities, such as New York and Chicago, access to downtown has been over 90 percent by public transportation for many decades. In almost all other large cities, however, public transit is woefully inadequate. It *may* be revived through generous public subsidy. Until there is some evidence of a real improvement in public transportation, the prospective small business owner would be well advised to think twice before selecting a downtown location.

Neighborhood shopping areas.   Large cities are divided into districts and then into neighborhoods. The districts are often centered on a school or hospital and may have physical boundaries such as a river, railroad tracks, or arterial highways. Each of these sections is likely to develop its own well-balanced business district. This includes a combination of shopping and specialty goods as found in the central business district, but the stores are not as large and the variety of specialty goods is more limited. There will be a large proportion of convenience goods stores, including groceries.

The districts are in turn subdivided into neighborhoods, each with its own shopping facilities but with a smaller assortment of stores. The emphasis here is on service establishments and convenience goods.

A district or neighborhood of a city in many ways assumes the characteristics of a town of comparable size. The number, type, and size of stores in a particular group, whether in a city district or in a town, reflects the size of the trading area that it serves. Thus the cluster of stores found in a city neighborhood that might be defined as having a population of one hundred thousand would be comparable to that found in a town of the same size. As pointed out previously in the discussion of trading areas, the size and composition of the grouping also depends on the proximity and size of other shopping areas. Superior and aggressive merchandising methods extend the size of the trading area, allowing it to support more stores with greater profit potential.

Outlying shopping centers. Individual **shopping centers** differ in (1) degree of integration, (2) layout and facilities, (3) size, and (4) sponsorship and control.

Earlier shopping centers were mere clusters of stores and service establishments, each independently owned and operated. These are the familiar strip centers that often lack even a name for the center. Parking, if provided at all, consists of space in front of each store and barely out of the main flow of automobile traffic. Not all of the land is necessarily owned by one person, although sometimes it is.

The newer strip centers provide off-street parking. Stores and parking run parallel to the traffic artery and sometimes on both sides of it. Some are L-shaped around a corner location. In these centers the first group of stores to appear is usually on land owned by one person or a small group. Later other developments often take place adjacent to the first center but on property owned by different people. Such centers share a common parking space and often have a name for the entire center, but they do less group promoting than the controlled centers. Often tenant selection is neither planned nor controlled.

Although there are many other shapes and layout arrangements that shopping centers have taken, nowadays the trend in the larger ones is toward the mall type. The mall may simply be an area reserved for pedestrian shoppers with all stores having access and visibility along its sides; many provide amenities such as greenery, flowers, protection from the elements, and even year-round air-conditioning. Parking is outside the stores that surround the mall, on two, three, or four sides. Mall centers usually have two department stores with numerous independent and chain units between them on both sides of the mall.

Shopping centers may be of the community or regional type. **Community shopping centers** have from twenty to forty stores with ample assortments of shopping and convenience goods and services to serve the entire community or the part of town in which they are located. **Regional shopping centers** have from forty to over one hundred stores and draw shoppers from well beyond the city limits.

Community and regional centers are planned, usually controlled, and operated as an integrated going concern. Tenants have leases that stipulate a minimum monthly rental plus a certain percentage of sales, often also above a stated minimum. Many tenants like this arrangement. The center management strives to have minimum guarantees sufficient to cover fixed financing and, usually, maintenance expense. The center advertises and promotes as a unit even though individual stores may also do their own advertising.

It is the control aspect of many shopping centers that is most controversial. Control refers to tenant selection and certain provisions in the leaseholds. The degree of control varies from one type of shopping center sponsor to another. Most large planned centers have been sponsored by industrial real estate promoters. Many have been promoted by department stores, and a few by supermarkets, discount houses, and corporate chains.

Many controlled centers sponsored by real estate promoters and department stores exclude discount houses and sometimes supermarkets. The latter have reacted by sponsoring their own centers. Often such centers give the sponsor an exclusive for a certain type of business. Since both supermarkets and discount houses are generative of shopper traffic, they tend to attract smaller stores, both independent and chain, that capitalize on the presence of these shoppers. The character of shoppers may differ, however. Those attracted by the supermarket are usually interested in convenience goods; those drawn by the discount house usually behave more like department store bargain hunters. Although there may be exceptions, centers sponsored by department stores, supermarkets, and discount houses are less likely to feel the impact of the financier's demands in tenant selection than those sponsored by real estate promoters. Their established financial rating and contacts are probable explanations.

Real estate promoters who sponsor large shopping centers require generous financing, available chiefly from insurance companies and similar institutional lenders. These financiers insist on well-established, financially strong, big name tenants. This usually means national corporate chains and the dominant local department store. With the power to make or break a center still in the planning stage, these two types of retailers are often able to dictate their own terms by demanding very low rent, exclusive repesentation for their types of retailing, and restrictions on the type of merchandise that other tenant stores may carry.

Two major difficulties arise for controlled shopping centers: excessive competition from other centers, and interceptor highway enterprises.

One danger of too close control is the stimulation of competing centers that may exceed the local market potential; that competing centers may be launched by supermarkets and discount houses has already been mentioned. Normal free enterprise competition could also lead to the launching of more shopping centers than warranted by demand. In either case, operation of competitive forces will determine the outcome, but with results weighted against the center and those tenants that sought a monopoly through their attempts to obtain exclusives. Probably more serious for most shopping centers, and of special interest to small business owners, is the expansion in the number of highway retail and service establishments.

Highway or wayside locations. Car ownership and the use of cars have expanded tremendously in recent years, providing a new pattern of living and shopping. Many workers drive fifty miles each way daily in car pools. Women are doing more taxiing of family members and more shopping by car. Earlier distinctions between urban and rural people are becoming blurred, and highway business extends beyond city limits.

Although independents pioneered highway retailing, chains and department stores have joined the movement. Solo locations are common, especially for department stores, furniture and floor coverings retailers, supermarkets, and discount houses.

Highway stores are free of architectural and merchandising restrictions, price restraints and coercion for group efforts found in integrated shopping centers. They can often capitalize on traffic drawn by the shopping centers, either as interceptors or as spillover recipients.

Also, **scrabbled merchandising** is typical of many highway locations. Restaurants, for example, carry a wide range of nonfoods; discount houses carry foods; supermarkets carry more nonfoods than usual.

The expansion of drive-in businesses of all kinds is also noteworthy. On arterial highways and string streets mere off-street parking may be sufficient for the typical retail store and service establishment, but newer types of business enterprises are based strictly on drive-in service where patrons do not need to leave their cars. These include theaters, banks, dairy products stands, snack bars, and batteries of vending machines accessible from the driver's seat, as well as conveyor systems for dispensing foods and refreshments.

For many independent enterprisers the multibillion-dollar recreation market offers numerous opportunities for highway drive-ins, motels, and many types of business located in or en route to recreational areas. The market in transient regions has expanded greatly in recent years and appears likely to continue expanding with increases in the amount of leisure time available to workers and their families.

Basic Factors in Site Selection

Probably in no other type of business is the building site as important a factor in determining the success of a business as it is in retailing. Some studies have found poor location to be among the chief causes of retail failures. In selecting a business district within a community, or on its fringes, the following factors are usually of maximum importance: (1) rent-paying capacity of the business, (2) terms of the lease, (3) type of merchandise to be carried or services rendered, (4) clientele desired, (5) anticipated volume, (6) accessibility of the store to prospective customers, (7) customer parking facilities, (8) the rent-advertising relationship, (9) proximity to other businesses, (10) restrictive ordinances, and (11) history of the site.

Rent-paying capacity. Usually the rent-paying capacity of a business will be a major factor in site selection. Certain businesses, such as drugstores, men's and women's apparel stores, jewelry stores, and department stores, can afford to locate in a high-rent area. Others, such as furniture and furnishings, appliance, and food stores, must stay in the low-rent districts. The following table lists important characteristics of stores suitable to each district:

HIGH-RENT DISTRICT	LOW-RENT DISTRICT
1. High value of merchandise in proportion to bulk	1. Low value of merchandise in proportion to bulk
2. Window display highly important	2. Large amount of floor space for interior display
3. High rate of turnover	3. Low rate of turnover
4. Appeal to transient trade	4. Established clientele

Terms of the lease. Most retailers rent rather than construct the store building. Of major importance to the small retailer is that the building be suitable to his or her type of business or that it could be made so, preferably at the landlord's expense.

Two types of lease agreements are used in retailing—the flat rate and the percentage lease. The **flat-rate lease** is an annual rental of a definite amount payable monthly in advance as stipulated in the lease. The **percentage lease** usually guarantees the landlord a minimum monthly rental, with additional payments at some percentage of sales agreed on by both parties. Leases may be secured for periods ranging from one to ten years or more.

The lease usually provides for many other important points, such as any remodeling to be done, who is to pay for it, liabilities and duties assumed by each party, and permission or authority for the tenant to erect certain external signs or make alterations to the premises in the future if needed. A lease is an important legal document, and the small business owner should always seek competent legal counsel before entering into a formal lease agreement.

Type of merchandise carried. In general, convenience goods stores locate wherever a sufficient number of potential customers have quick and easy access to the store. This may be on streets of heavy transient traffic, in outlying shopping centers, in well-populated neighborhoods, in industrial or other business areas, as well as in the downtown shopping center. Usually, however, only the large-volume convenience stores able to justify the high rents demanded for such sites are located in the larger shopping centers. Small food stores, notions and variety stores, small drugstores, and similar enterprises will do better outside the larger shopping centers and closer to the homes of their customers.

Shopping goods and specialty stores require a location in one of the shopping districts. This may be the central area or one of the suburban or outlying shopping districts or centers.

Class of trade desired. In most communities, certain districts are more exclusive than others in terms of income level or occupational status. Population patterns are also important, as business subdistricts often cater to special groups such as business executives and office workers, transients (hotel guests), students, and various racial or ethnic groups.

Anticipated sales volume.   Usually only large-volume stores, one for each line of merchandise, can profitably locate in the central shopping district. The small-volume stores may find it preferable to locate in one of the secondary districts.

Accessibility of the store.   Because a retail store depends for profits on a sufficient number of customers coming into it, customer accessibility is an all-important consideration. For small retailers accessibility is mainly a question of the ease with which their customers can reach the store. A site with the heaviest volume of pedestrian traffic would be ideal except that the rent might be beyond their means. Accessibility to pedestrian traffic for other sites will be influenced by distance from the traffic generators, terrain, dangerous street crossings or other hazards, or similar factors. The nature of the entrance may be important if it is even slightly above sidewalk level or if the store has an off-the-street location, such as an upper floor.

By means of careful **traffic analysis** it is possible to determine the approximate sales volume of each pedestrian passing a given location. In making traffic counts, the analyst should select a few half-hour periods during the normally busy hours of the day, with men and women recorded separately. To estimate the probable number of pedestrians who would enter a given kind of store, sample counts may be made of the proportionate number of them that enter stores of the same kind in similar business districts.

The mode of transportation used by customers is also an important consideration. When most customers come to the store in their own cars, a site several blocks from the shopping center that has ample parking space is often more accessible than a downtown store. Corner locations with entrances on each street have similar advantages for pedestrian traffic.

The accessibility of a site is sometimes related to the sequence of shopping stops. For example, food stores located on the right-hand side of an artery leading away from a major shopping district are more accessible because grocery customers usually shop on the way home, whereas a laundry or dry cleaner located on the right-hand side going into town is more accessible because customers prefer to unload the wash or cleaning before continuing to town.

Customer parking facilities.   Accessibility should also be considered in terms of parking facilities. Sometimes provision is made for customer parking on the premises itself, as in wayside locations and some neighborhood shopping areas. Ground parking facilities are, of course, an integral part of the modern shopping center. Downtown stores must rely on nearby parking ramps or on street parking.

In evaluating the adequacy of customer parking facilities for a particular site, consideration should be given to peak traffic hour conditions.

The rent–advertising relationship.　Some merchants utilize shopping traffic where they find it; others try to attract shoppers to their stores by means of newspaper, TV, or radio advertising. Rent and advertising expenses are often so closely related in the retail business that their relationships should be clearly understood.

Rent is payment for the opportunity to make a profit by selling merchandise. The highest rents are paid for locations having the greatest volume of profitable shopper traffic. Competition for these locations tends to keep the rent up to the maximum that can be paid for their most effective use by the most efficient entrepreneurs. A profitable business may be operated in these so-called 100 percent locations without expenditure for external advertising. For example, for years variety chains have followed the policy of selecting sites in the line of customer shopping traffic built up and maintained by the larger department stores.

Some specialty stores—such as those selling apparel, furniture, or food products—also locate near the large department stores. But in contrast to variety stores, they often find it pays to advertise: first, because they carry shopping goods that are suitable to advertising; second, because their central location makes possible effective use of the low-cost-per-reader mass media like newspapers; and third, because they can often "ride the tail" of department store advertising. Shoppers coming to the center anyway will often respond to these advertisements, though they might not make a special trip in response solely to the smaller store's advertisement.

Other specialty stores locate several blocks from the major shopping district, and they pay lower rent for these locations but require higher advertising expenditures. Although the returns per dollar of advertising expenditure alone may be less for these fringe stores, the combined effect of low rent and moderate advertising may be very profitable. Thus it is the rent–advertising combination that is the largest item of expense in retail stores except for wages and salaries.

Proximity to other businesses.　A retail store, like an individual, should keep the right company. It is well-known that certain kinds of stores do well when located close to each other. Customers who patronize stores of one type in such a group are the best prospects for others in the same **retail affinity** class. Studies of these natural clusterings of stores have shown the following:

1. Men's and women's apparel and variety stores are commonly located near department stores
2. Restaurants, barber and beauty shops, and candy and jewelry stores are often found near theaters
3. Flowers shops are usually grouped with shoe stores and women's clothing stores
4. Paint, home furnishings, and furniture stores are generally in proximity
5. Launderettes and groceries are also usually found in proximity

Customers are people with habit patterns and buying needs that are often associated with other activities, as the above list illustrates. Proximity to offices of professional men or women may also be desirable, especially in outlying shopping centers; people having appointments with doctors, dentists, optometrists, and so on quite often will become shoppers if stores are conveniently accessible.

In contrast to complementary or related store groupings, certain kinds of stores do better if *not* located close together. For the exclusive sale of convenience goods, unless the customer traffic is unusually heavy, stores of the same kind should not locate close to competitors. An apparent exception to this generalization arises where an alert independent in the drug, variety, or similar line finds advantageous a location adjacent to a chain store in the same line. The spillover traffic attracted to the chain may provide sufficient business for the independent. By making merchandise offerings that fit in with those of the chain, the independent may secure additional volume. This means that some of the chain's customers who normally buy standardized popular styles or colors will be attracted by similar goods in novel designs, unusual colors, or other variations. Good examples of this are party novelties, popular-priced gift items, unusual but low-priced toys, and seasonal greeting cards.

The small independent's natural tendency is to want to avoid competing stores. The foregoing discussion should demonstrate that locations close to the right kind of competitors are sometimes desirable.

Restrictive ordinances.   Sometimes unusual restrictive ordinances may be encountered that would make an otherwise ideal site less desirable than another; these restrictions might include limitations on the hours of the day when trucks are permitted to load or unload. **Zoning regulations** are of importance when individuals attempt to open a store in an area restricted against their kind of business, or, in some instances, against any kind of business. In many cities licensing is used to enforce zoning restrictions. Licenses will be granted to operate a given type of business only in areas where zoning regulations permit this type of business. For example, a retail store will not be licensed to operate in a district zoned exclusively for residences. Similarly, a dry cleaning *store* may get a license to operate in a retail shopping district but a dry cleaning *plant* using certain dangerous fluids will be licensed to operate only in the industrial district.

History of the site.   At least the *recent* history of each site under consideration should be known by the retailer before he or she makes a final selection. Although most Americans no longer believe in haunted houses, experienced merchants know that **"hoodoo" locations** do exist. These are sites that have been occupied by a succession of retail failures. Naturally there are logical reasons why the site has not been a successful one at certain times in the past, but there are also the dangers that prospective customers have formed a habit of avoiding the location or that the next prospective renter will overestimate his or her ability to succeed where predecessors have failed.

LOCATION REQUIREMENTS IN OTHER TYPES OF BUSINESS

Service Businesses

A service establishment will have many of the same location requirements as a retail store; to the extent it engages in retail trade, it will be affected by the same considerations. However, the kind of service business to be established will probably have more bearing on the requirements for a good location than in most other types of business.

A personal or professional service where clients call at the place of business should be as accessible as possible. This may mean an office location in the financial district or a shop location in one of the better retail districts. If the customer does not visit the business, then the site may be selected in terms primarily of rent, space requirements, and owner's convenience.

An interesting characteristic of most service businesses is that a reputation for extra high quality of workmanship will attract customers in spite of a poor location to a far greater extent than is true of other kinds of business. However, since this is an exception, and since it comes about only after the reputation is earned, the beginner should seek the best location in which to build such a reputation.

Some kinds of service businesses require both a factory-type location where the work is performed and a retail site for customer contact. For example, a laundry or dry cleaning firm may do a large amount of cash-and-carry business.

Policies relating to the market or type of clientele desired will influence the choice of town and area within a town whenever (1) a special type of customer constitutes the market, such as office workers or factory workers; (2) the service is one for which there is widespread demand; or (3) existing competition deviates appreciably from normal.

Drive-ins are important in many service fields where the customer brings the article to the shop. These include many types of repair shops and laundry and cleaning establishments.

Wholesaling

The market for most small wholesalers consists of retailers within the wholesaler's own community or within a trading radius of less than ten miles. In this respect the typical small wholesaler emphasizes the same community location factors as do retailers. The small wholesaler is primarily interested in a community with stability of income, diversified industry in the trading area, prosperous retail stores, and lack of competition from other wholesalers in nearby communities.

In selecting a site within the community wholesalers have special needs and problems. Within the wholesale district space may be limited; plants may need to be multistory because of high ground rents; warehousing costs, which usually constitute a major item of expense, may be high; and traffic may be congested. Largely because of these conditions it is improbable that in the established wholesale district of a city small operators will be able to secure the efficient street-level type of plant they need.

There has been a growing trend recently for small wholesalers and a few large concerns that have built new plants to choose sites near the edge of town. The chief advantages are lower rent and ample space, the latter making possible the construction of the most efficient type of ground-floor warehouse with transportation access on all sides. More rapid transportation and good highways, less traffic congestion, and new types of construction that provide better light and ventilation all have contributed to this trend.

Manufacturing

Regardless of the kind of manufacturing enterprise, the entrepreneur should consider each of the following basic factors in determining the region, state, or community in which to operate a plant:

1. Nearness to market(s), including market trends
2. Nearness to suppliers
3. Labor supply and cost
4. Power supply and cost
5. State and local regulations and taxes

6. Transportation services and costs

By locating closer to its customers, the small manufacturing firm can provide them with quicker service. By locating closer to its sources of supply, the small plant will receive quicker deliveries of raw materials and component parts. In addition, in each case, there is a lowering of freight cost. The manufacturer pays the cost of transporting the materials and other supplies it buys (freight in) as well as the cost of transporting the finished goods it sells (freight out).

Most freight rates, however, are closely correlated with the value of the commodity that is shipped. Because of the value added by manufacture, these rates are considerably higher for completely processed products (finished goods) than for raw materials and parts; that is, they can "bear" a higher tariff. For this reason, *most* manufacturers find it more economical to locate closer to their market than to their sources of supply. Industry in general tends to seek its market. The ideal, of course, occurs when the areas in which the plant's customers and suppliers are located overlap or coincide. Usually, however, they do not.

Another important factor in plant location, and particularly in smaller firms where there has been little or no development in automated processing, is labor supply and cost. Area wage rates vary considerably, and often this is the factor that tips the scale in favor of one community over another. Seasonal factors are also an important consideration in both the supply and the cost of labor, and the small manufacturer should be aware of the activity and characteristics of prospective neighboring industries.

Although their requirements may vary considerably, all manufacturing enterprises need power to operate production machines. Therefore, the supply and cost of power is another common factor affecting plant location. However, with the recent development of electric power grids in many of the relatively less populated parts of the country, this factor has become less important.

State and local industrial regulations and taxes should also be considered in choosing the community in which to establish a manufacturing plant. A favorable attitude toward industry increasingly is being stressed by industrialists seeking plant locations, particularly since they usually have a choice of several communities that are more or less equally desirable from other points of view. The local attitude toward industry is reflected, in part at least, by the industrial regulations and taxes it imposes. Tax costs may also vary widely.

It is obvious that a community may rate high on some factors and low on others. Also, many of the factors interact and cannot be considered in isolation. Ignoring personal and other intangible considerations, the decision rule is this: *Select that location at which the combined cost of production and distribution is at a minimum.*

After the community is selected, the next step is to select the site on which to construct the plant. This site may be within the corporate limits of the community, or it may be a suburban location. Among the factors considered in making this decision are the following:

1. Land (and assessment) values
2. Property taxes
3. Room for expansion and for employee parking
4. Contour of the ground, or shape of the plot
5. Disposal of waste
6. Utilities and public improvements, such as water, sewer, gas, and electric connections; paving, gutters, and sidewalks; and street lighting
7. Building restrictions or codes (zoning)
8. Railway or highway access

SUMMING UP

Wherever there are people there are unfilled needs. The challenge to the small business manager (or to those contemplating starting a business) is to determine what these needs are and how they may best be satisfied. This knowledge is acquired through market research and analysis. Because people move about and needs change, market research and analysis is a continuing process for the small business manager.

Market analysis and business location go together like love and marriage, or, to borrow another expression, they are two sides of the same coin. The location requirements for any business are determined by the type of goods or service to be sold and the market that is sought; this market must be clearly defined, and the business appropriately located.

There are two aspects to consider in locating a business establishment: (1) choosing a particular community, and (2) selecting a site within that community. The choice of a community is influenced by such factors as competition, the economic characteristics of the town, its demographic characteristics, and (in the case of retail establishments) the size of the trading area or (in the case of manufacturing) transportation services and the balance of costs in shipping raw materials and finished products. Wholesalers locate where their retailer-customers are. Location requirements for the service firm are similar to those of the retailer.

For merchandising establishments, the appropriate site within the community or its environs—whether a downtown, neighborhood, shopping center, or highway location is determined by the type of goods sold, the class of customers desired, and the anticipated volume. Retailers must also consider accessibility and convenience for the customer in relation to the rent they will pay, the amount they will advertise, the prices they will charge, and the nature of their business. For manufacturing establishments, pertinent site factors include land values, property taxes, room for expansion, room for employee parking, waste disposal, and railway trackage or highway access. All businesses, of course, are subject to local zoning regulations.

KEY WORDS

business site	purchasing power
central business district	regional shopping center
community shopping center	Reilly's law
convenience goods	retail affinities
demography	scrabbled merchandising
economic base	shopping center
flat-rate lease	shopping goods
generative location	specialty goods
"hoodoo" location	suscipient location
market	trading area
100 percent block	traffic analysis
percentage lease	zoning regulations

DISCUSSION QUESTIONS

1. How do you account for the decentralization of shopping areas? Do you expect this trend to continue? Why or why not?

2. Discuss each of the following statements:

a. "Most people will go out of their way for 'good' service; therefore, store location is not too important."

b. "An area with high unemployment and irregular income is not a good location for any type of store."

c. "It is ordinarily desirable to locate as far from your competitors as possible."

EXERCISES AND PROBLEMS

1. Walk through the central business district of your community (or your neighborhood shopping center, as your instructor may direct) and note (a) the kinds of stores that have recently opened or expanded, and (b) the kinds of stores that have recently gone out of business. What kinds of business are growing, and what kinds are declining? What accounts for these trends, in your opinion?

2. Assume you contemplate opening a retail store in your community. A downtown site is available at an annual rental cost of $12,000. Also available is a site of approximately equal floor space in one of the neighborhood shopping centers, which can be leased for $10,000 a year. Because of the heavier concentration of shopping traffic in the downtown district, you would expect sales next year of approximately $300,000—about 50 percent higher than your projected sales level at the outlying location.

a. Considering only the difference in rental expense, which location would you prefer? Explain.

b. What other *financial* factors would you consider that might cause you to choose a location other than the one you selected above? Explain fully.

3. Using the formula on p. 185, calculate the breaking point in miles between Dension, Iowa, and Carroll, Iowa, beyond which most customers will buy most of their goods and services in Denison (pop. 4,930) rather than Carroll, a larger community located 27 miles away (pop. 7,682).

Frank Gilbert operates a short-order restaurant (open 6:00 A.M. to 10:00 P.M.) on Elm Street, where he has been for 10 years. His sales have averaged $65,000 per year. His largest volume is in the morning (early) and at lunchtime (drawn from route men—bread, milk, etc.—and nearby business establishments). He feels that his volume could be increased significantly if the seating capacity of the restaurant could be expanded. This is impossible in the present building; however, three blocks to the west of his present location there is a space available which would make the expansion possible. This new store is within three hundred feet of a high school. Parking is also available on a basis similar to his current location. What should be considered before deciding on such a move?

In 1979, with $15,000 of his savings and a $25,000 loan, Mr. Robert Duval opened his own beauty salon in a well-established section of Denver. Prior to opening Robert's Salon, Mr. Duval had 15 years' experience as a beautician and manager of beauty shops. His most recent job had been manager of a large beauty shop that was part of a national chain.

When he opened Robert's Salon, Mr. Duval decided to establish a discount price salon. In order to keep prices low, he decided to pay a direct commission for each type of service the operator performs on a customer instead of paying each operator a regular salary. Also, because of the high volume, the general policy of Robert's Salon is to assign the first available operator to an arriving customer. This keeps each operator from developing a clientele which would follow her or him if she or he leaves Robert's Salon. Paying a straight commission also allows Mr. Duval to keep a large number of beauticians at the salon during slow periods without paying salaries while the operators are idle. The operators appear satisfied with this system and Mr. Duval's labor turnover is no worse than that of his competitors.

The salon is open more hours during the week than most other shops and the variety of services is limited to the major areas of operation which can be accomplished in a relatively short period of time. Elaborate time-consuming services are not offered.

The salon is located in a shopping mall that contains a variety of stores, including a large grocery supermarket, in a middle-income area containing a broad economic and age mix. The area is well-serviced by public transportation. Currently Mr. Duval advertises in the major city newspaper, a small local newspaper, a local advertising paper, and the Yellow Pages of the telephone book.

The shop has been quite successful since it opened. In 1979 with gross sales of $70,000, Mr. Duval realized a net profit of $10,000 before his owner's draw of $5,000. In 1980 his gross sales were $90,000 with a net profit of $18,000 before a draw of the entire $18,000. In 1981 his gross sales were $95,000 with a net profit of $17,500 before a draw of $12,000.

Late in 1981 Mr. Duval contracted to lease an additional shop for $400 a month in a "bedroom" suburb of Denver. This expansion accounted for $4,000 of Duval's 1981 expenses. This shop, approximately fifteen miles from his first shop, is located in a small new shopping center containing a furniture store, a radio-TV store, four other small retail stores, two restaurants, and two specialty food stores. The center is scheduled to open in February 1982.

An analysis of census and city planning office data indicates that the income level of this suburban area is the same or a little higher than that of the area in which the present shop is located. The age level in the suburb is a little younger and the average number of children is greater. There are some new apartments that have just been opened in the area but the bulk of the residents own their own homes. Public transportation in the area is very poor but most families have two cars.

A student team from the local university has conducted a survey of the customers of the present shop. The results of this survey are summarized on p. 203.

What predictions can be made for success in his present shop? What guidelines might be here for the proposed new shop?

1. Why do you use this particular shop?	Convenience	27.5%
	Price	37.0
	Fast service	17.6
	Specific operator	15.8
	Other	2.1
2. What age group are you in?	15–25	8.8%
	26–35	13.2
	36–45	25.7
	46–55	30.2
	56 and up	22.1
3. How many miles away do you live?	1 to 1.5 on the average	
4. How many miles away do you work?	4 to 4.5 on the average	
5. What is your family income bracket?	$ 0–10,000	41.2%
	10,000–15,000	29.4
	15,000–20,000	17.6
	20,000–25,000	6.6
	25,000–35,000	1.5
	35,000 and up	3.7
6. What is the primary salon service you use?	Shampoo set	50.0%
	Haircut	31.9
	Permanent	8.9
	Tint	3.9
	Other	5.3
7. Do you live in an apartment or a house?	Apartment	19.1%
	House	80.9
8. What is your marital status?	married	72.8%
	single	7.4
	widowed	11.8
	divorced	8.0
9. What is your occupation?	Housewife	26.9%
	Unskilled	16.7
	Skilled	2.5
	Semi-prof	46.2
	Professional	7.7
10. What is your husband's occupation?	Retired	21.0%
	Unskilled	15.1
	Skilled	23.8
	Semi-prof	25.4
	Professional	14.7
11. How many children do you have?	1.6 on the average	
12. Do you use other stores in this shopping center?	Yes	74.3%
	No	25.7
13. How did you find out about Robert's?	Friend	47.0%
	Noticed while in center	32.2
	Major newspaper	.7
	Minor newspaper	8.7
	Advertising paper	5.6
	Yellow Pages	5.8

Pricing Methods
and Strategies

CHAPTER FOURTEEN *After establishing the market potential for a given product or service, the small business manager's next task is to determine how his or her firm can obtain an adequate share of that market. Setting the "right" price for the product or service is one way of expanding sales, although not necessarily the best way and certainly not the only way. In this chapter you will learn the strategic part pricing plays in marketing.*

Once a business owner has acquired and stocked merchandise, materials, or supplies, he or she adds value to these goods. For example, manufacturers process materials; the service establishment uses supplies in the performance of a requested service; wholesalers, having shopped a wide variety of markets, make the goods they buy available under conditions where these goods can be examined and then purchased in smaller quantities; and retailers assemble an assortment of goods in sizes and quality suitable to their particular customers, and present them for sale along with information as to care and use. Each of these entrepreneurs hopes to make a profit on the function performed.[1] How much additional value has the entrepreneur added to the goods? How much will customers be willing to pay? What price level will bring maximum profits? Will selling a small volume at a high price be more profitable than selling a large volume at a low price?

Formulating price policies and setting the price is one of the most important aspects of management. Whether maximum profit will be attained by raising or lowering prices depends on a wide variety of conditions. Business owners must know their costs, understand buyer motivation, and evaluate the competition.

ECONOMICS OF PRICING

Price reflects the cost of goods (or services) sold, administrative and selling expenses, and, hopefully, some profit. If the seller is a manufacturer, the **cost of goods sold** is represented by the costs of manufacture. If the seller is a wholesaler or a retailer, the cost of goods sold is the amount paid for the goods originally. The difference between cost of goods sold and selling price is called

---

[1] These constitute what we have previously defined as production functions.

How Much?

Courtesy of Small Business Administration.

markup or **gross margin.** Gross margin includes marketing or distribution costs, such as rent, wages, administration, and advertising, plus an allowance for profit.

Correct pricing policies depend on many factors in addition to costs. Among these other considerations are (1) the nature of the product or service, (2) company policy, (3) competition, (4) business conditions, and (5) market strategy.

Nature of the Product or Service

The quantity sold of either salt or sable coats will be little affected by raising or lowering the price. The **demand** for these products is inelastic. However, the demand for color television sets or for ice cream is very responsive to a change in price and can be stimulated by advertising. These latter products have a demand that is both elastic and expansible. Whether the article is of great or small monetary value does not, in itself, determine the nature of demand; rather, it is how much and for what reason the article is needed or desired. The nature of the product will determine the elasticity or the expansibility of demand. **Elasticity of demand** refers to the change in dollar value of sales that accompanies price changes. If a lower price alone increases total revenue, demand is elastic; if it decreases total revenue (even though the number of units sold increases), it is inelastic; if a price change does not change total revenue, the elasticity is unitary. Different products and services also vary in the amount advertising increases sales. This property is known as **expansibility of demand** or **advertisability.** An article that sells only slightly better when well-advertised has a low coefficient of expansibility; one that sells much better has a high coefficient. In most cases both price reductions and advertising will be used simultaneously, but in amounts proportionate to the product's relative elasticity and expansibility.

Demand elasticity and the most profitable price that the small business proprietor can set on a particular product can be illustrated by applying the traditional **marginal-income/cost** analysis taught in introductory economics courses. In Table 14-1 it is assumed that the product has some degree of elasticity, and that production and/or distribution takes place on a decreasing cost basis. Thus the business proprietor estimates that 10,000 units of the product, costing $4 each, could be sold at a price of $10. The proprietor further estimates that for each $1 decrease in price, sales would be increased by 2,500 units, and that for each increase in sales of this amount (2,500 units), the unit cost of the product would decrease by $0.20. On the basis of these estimates, Table 14-1 indicates a most profitable price of $8 per unit. Note that at the lower price of $7, although sales income is further increased, profit is lower.[2]

TABLE 14-1
Demand Elasticity and the Most Profitable Price

Price	$10.00	$9.00	$8.00	$7.00	$6.00
Volume (units)	10,000	12,500	15,000	17,500	20,000
Cost per unit	$4.00	$3.80	$3.60	$3.40	$3.20
Sales income	$100,000	$112,500	$120,000	$122,500	$120,000
Cost of goods sold	40,000	47,500	54,000	59,500	64,000
Profit	$ 60,000	$ 65,000	$ 66,000	$ 63,000	$ 56,000

Company Price Policy

Company price policy will normally be influenced by factors like location, size or position in the industry, customer services rendered, and the owner's preference for a particular market or price reputation. Some business owners seek a particular class of trade and consequently follow a price policy intended to appeal to that group. Or a business owner may set out to establish a reputation for having either the lowest or the highest prices in the field. In such cases the price level is the starting point; expenses, location, organization, and policies other than pricing must be adjusted to conform.

Competition

The price at competitive business establishments will guide price policies within certain limits. Sellers must recognize the nature of their competition. If the product offered by a competitor is similar to theirs, a competitive price

[2] Expansibility of demand for a product at a *given* price by means of advertising is similarly illustrated in the following chapter.

must be set. The value of a product at the time of sale, however, includes—among other things—the service that accompanies it, the location of the selling establishment, and any unique features of the product that set it apart. Also, whether a seller must place a competitive price on a product depends on the policy of the firm, the elasticity of demand, and many of the other factors here discussed. It should be remembered that, in a competitive situation, the demand for a product that is considered to be inelastic becomes elastic for the individual business. For example, although the demand for bread is inelastic, if one store lowers the price on bread it can increase its own bread sales greatly.

Business Conditions

Manufacturers' and retailers' prices fluctuate less readily than do wholesalers' prices. The latter are most responsive to changing economic conditions, since wholesalers deal in large quantities on a narrow margin and their markets are well-organized. Manufacturers' prices fluctuate less frequently because of the general attempt to stabilize or maintain prices on differentiated products. A retailer does not respond readily to economic change since, at this level of distribution, (1) customary or convenient prices are common; (2) many of the goods are "price-lined"; (3) it is impractical to re-mark goods frequently; (4) it is not convenient to make changes in fractional amounts; and (5) the wider operating margins are usually adequate to absorb minor variations in the retailer's cost of goods over a short period of time. When fluctuations in retail price do occur, however, they are more violent.

Business owners must decide whether their prices will reflect the cost of goods they have on hand, or whether their prices will be based on replacement costs that may be either higher or lower. Within the limits set by the level of distribution in question, if general economic conditions are good and the economy is expanding, sellers may be inclined to increase their share of the wealth by raising prices. Often at such times labor and other costs are also increasing, and the seller will probably want to pass this added expense on to the buyer. During periods of economic stress sellers are likely to ignore margins, for their greatest concern at such times is to retain their share of the market and, hence, price cuts may be taken which reflect more than merely the decrease in costs.

Market Strategy

Market strategy may involve deciding whether to seek a large volume at a low markup, or a low volume at a high markup. It may also involve **loss leader** pricing; this is the pricing of some merchandise close to or below cost to attract to the premises customers who may make other purchases.[3] Another con-

---

[3] Some states have *unfair practice* laws intended to prevent selling at a price below the cost of doing business, or *antiloss leader* laws requiring a price no less than landed cost plus 6 percent. For a further discussion of these laws, see pp. 426.

sideration in market strategy is whether the item being sold is a long-run or a short-run item. For example, high-fashion items (midi-skirts) or fads (hula hoops) have a limited market or may have sales appeal for a short period of time. The optimum selling price is one that will net the most dollars (after allowing for applicable selling costs) during the time the product is on the market. Sometimes, also, a new product is introduced at a price that is higher than that justified by the cost of producing it (**prestige pricing**), in order to establish it as a prestige product.

PRICING BY RETAILERS

The prices placed on goods to be sold in a retail establishment will be affected by many of the same economic considerations that are basic to all pricing decisions, company policy, the nature of competition, business conditions, and the type of product and resulting demand factors, as well as the business's freedom to price as it chooses.

Company Policy

A store's pricing policies should respond to the general policies of the company. A store that wishes to provide extra services or handle unique and distinctive goods will likely charge higher prices. A store that provides a bargain basement atmosphere will plan for a high volume with a low profit margin. Most stores fall somewhere between these extremes, using normal markups which reflect differences in the quality of the goods being sold.

Competition

Retailers need to recognize that their competition comes not only from similar stores in their own community but also from specialty and department stores in neighboring towns and from catalog sales. The price of goods depends not only on the quality or character of the goods themselves but also on their degree of availability and the services that accompany them. Retailers must evaluate their own and their competitors' prices in these terms. Customers are quick to decide whether or not they are getting their money's worth.

Nature of the Product

The elasticity of the demand, how goods are shopped for, and their special characteristics are important factors in the determination of the right price.

Staple convenience goods.   For staple **convenience goods,** which are fairly well standardized items available in a large number of stores, either customary prices or the going market price is used. These are usually the lowest prices at which such merchandise can be handled profitably. A serious danger in cutting prices on such items is that all competitors will quickly reduce their prices and no permanent increase in volume or traffic will result.

Another pitfall is to price convenience items in amounts that make it inconvenient for customers to pay for them. For example, because of inflationary pressures it has become necessary for many retailers to increase the price of "five cent" candy bars and packages of gum. Those retailers who increased the price by only a penny or two found that their sales of these items had dropped. Market analysts concluded that customers do not like to dig out several coins for a small purchase—they would sooner pay a dime as six or seven cents.

Shopping goods.   **Shopping goods** are nonstandardized items that change frequently in both quality and style. **Price lining,** that is, establishing a small number of prices within each merchandise classification, is a common method of price-structuring these items. Knowing the price at which goods will sell, the retailers can purchase their stock with these retail prices in mind.

Fashion and novelty goods.   Although most **fashion goods** and seasonal items are subject to price lining, they show the additional influence of the time factor in relation to pricing. Store policy will determine whether fashion merchandise is first offered at the very beginning of the season, or somewhat later after the risk element and retail prices have been reduced. Initial fashion offerings should be priced high enough to allow for the greater amounts of risk, as well as for the larger **markdowns** as the **fashion cycle** develops and price becomes competitive.

A store catering to the middle or upper middle class but not to the fashion leaders in a community would price merchandise relatively high early in the season, expecting to take markdowns as the fashion cycle progresses and before the more popular-priced stores enter into competition. Initial prices would be somewhat higher than those in volume or promotional stores, but substantially lower than prices in fashion leader stores. Markdowns to be allowed for in the initial price would be normal for fashion (not high-fashion) goods and would be similar for different styles, because the fashion acceptance of all styles carried would be assured before this type of store begins promotions. By contrast, the high-fashion store will offer some styles that may not receive public acceptance. These will be difficult to sell at any price, often even well below cost. Consequently, the accepted fashion lines must bear the loss of less successful lines. Also, even predicting what percentage of styles offered at the very beginning of the fashion cycle will eventually become fashionable is far more difficult than estimating markdowns for the more conservative store.

Novelties or specialties usually carry a relatively high markup. Also, they may often be selected with price strategy in mind. Since novelties are likely to have a short selling season, prices may be high at first but often must be lowered as the novelty demand wears off. As with seasonal or fashion items, drastic markdowns may be needed to close out stocks as the demand drops toward zero. Careful daily watching of sales prices is important with goods of this type.

Pricing Freedom

Retail prices on some merchandise is set by the manufacturer by means of national advertising or price agreements. Such prices can be enforced by exclusive or selective distribution or by depending on **fair trade laws.** Retailers who charge less than a minimum price may find that the line of goods is no longer available to them. Because the fair trade laws of some states have been challenged in many courts,[4] some manufacturers still seek to control retail price by selling on **consignment,** cutting retailers' margins, or refusing to pay cooperative advertising allowances if prices are not maintained. When vendors suggest retail prices or quote prices in national advertising, small retailers usually conform to them unless the store policy is to cut prices.

Laws in existence also forbid a store to have two different prices on the same item at the same time. For example, when new supplies have arrived for which the store has had to pay more or less than previously, and if the store desires to change its prices accordingly, the prices on identical merchandise already on the shelves must be re-marked to match.

Setting the Price

Although retailers have some of their prices set for them by competitors' prices, manufacturers' or wholesalers' recommendations, and the existence of accepted or expected prices, they must still determine prices for many or most of the items they sell. In general, a retailer's selling price must cover the cost of goods (or **landed cost**), selling and other operating expenses, and a margin for profit.

Markup. The difference between the cost of goods sold and selling price, as previously noted, is called *markup* or *gross margin.* Markup may be calculated for each item of merchandise, or the term may denote the average markup on all goods. It may be expressed in dollars and cents or as a percentage. When expressed as a percentage, the calculation may be based either on cost or on the retail price. Most retailers, however, state markup as a percentage of retail price. For example, if goods cost $0.50 and sell for $1 most retailers will call this a markup of $0.50 or 50 percent; if the goods cost $1.02 and sell for $1.50, the markup is expressed as $0.48 or 32 percent.

The calculation of markup as a percentage of cost makes it difficult to analyze one's business over a period of time. It is the percentage of what the retailer sells the firm's goods for (*gross profit*) that is more meaningful, for that

---

[4] See pp. 426–27 for a discussion of resale price maintenance.

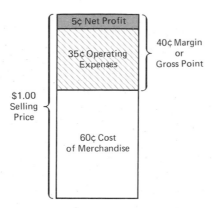

$1.00
Selling
Price

5¢ Net Profit

35¢ Operating
Expenses

40¢ Margin
or
Gross Point

60¢ Cost
of Merchandise

FIGURE 14-1
Components of Selling Price

tells the retailer how much of the sales dollar can be used to pay bills, and how much will be left over for income (*net profit*). These components of the selling price are diagrammed in Figure 14-1.

Knowing the cost of goods and the average amount of markup needed to operate profitably, the retailer may use the following formula to determine the price to charge for an item:

$$\text{Retail price} = \frac{\text{Cost}}{100 - \text{Markup on retail}} \times 100$$

For example, if a retailer receives a gross of T-shirts for a total cost of $172.80, and wishes to provide for a gross margin of 36 percent (estimated expenses of 26 percent plus target profit of 10 percent), desired income from the sale of this merchandise would be calculated as follows:

$$\frac{\$172.80}{100 - 36} \times 100 = \$270$$

Dividing this figure ($270) by 144 (a gross) yields a unit price of $1.88. However, the retailer would probably mark the T-shirts to the level of the next highest established price line, such as $1.89, or perhaps $1.98 or $2.00. A special promotion or other situation might require a price of less than this, but in such a case the retailer should recognize that these goods are marked below the average markup and attempt to compensate for this somewhere else.

Some retailers, particularly those of an older generation, follow the practice of expressing markup as a percentage of the cost. In this case, the calculation of retail price may be made by first converting the desired markup from a percentage of retail price to a percentage of cost. A convenient way of doing this is to use a markup table, such as that illustrated in Table 14-2. This conversion may also be made by using the following formula:

$$\text{Markup on cost} = \frac{\text{Markup on retail}}{100 - \text{Markup on retail}} \times 100$$

TABLE 14-2
Markup Table

MARKUP AS PERCENTAGE OF SELLING PRICE	MARKUP AS PERCENTAGE OF COST	MARKUP AS PERCENTAGE OF SELLING PRICE	MARKUP AS PERCENTAGE OF COST
5%	5.26%	28%	38.89%
6	6.38	29	40.85
7	7.53	30	42.86
8	8.70	31	44.93
9	9.89	32	47.06
10	11.11	33	49.25
11	12.36	34	51.52
12	13.64	35	53.85
13	14.94	36	56.25
14	16.28	37	58.73
15	17.65	38	61.29
16	19.05	39	63.93
17	20.48	40	66.67
18	21.95	41	69.49
19	23.46	42	72.41
20	25.00	43	75.44
21	26.58	44	78.57
22	28.21	45	81.82
23	29.87	46	85.19
24	31.58	47	88.68
25	33.33	48	92.31
26	35.14	49	96.08
27	36.99	50	100.00

The derived percentage, whether read from a markup table or calculated by applying the above formula, is then multiplied by the cost of the article. This markup is then added to the cost of goods to arrive at the correct selling price.

For example, if the retailer wishes to price the T-shirts by this method (and in the absence of a markup table), markup on cost would be computed as follows:

$$\frac{36}{100 - 36} \times 100 = 56.25\%$$

$$.5625 \times \$172.80 = \$97.20$$

Adding this markup ($97.20) to the cost of the goods ($172.80 per gross) yields $270.00, or a unit price of $1.88 (or $270/144).

Markon.   For many goods the initial price the retailer sets must be high enough to allow for **retail reductions** such as stock shortages, markdowns, and discounts to employees, in addition to the cost of goods, operating expenses, and a margin of profit. The difference between the cost of goods and the first price placed on the goods is called the **initial markup** or **markon.** Some goods require a higher markon than do others because of the need for larger allowances for reduction. Examples of goods that require high initial markups are (1) high-fashion goods, which have a limited or unpredictable market; (2) seasonal and novelty items, because they seldom can be economically held over to another year; (3) goods easily damaged or soiled, such as delicate lingerie or white gloves; and (4) easily pilfered goods, such as pens or perfume.

To arrive at the initial retail price, a markon or initial markup percentage is figured as a percentage of the initial retail price. However, the markdowns, shortages, employees' discounts, expenses, and profits are customarily figured as percentages of net sales. Adjusting for this shift in the basis of percentages, the formula for deriving a markon percentage is:

$$\text{Markon (\%)} = \frac{\text{Gross margin (\%)} + \text{Retail reductions (\%)}}{\text{Net sales (100\%)} + \text{Retail reductions (\%)}}$$

For example, for a retailer with operating expenses of 30 percent, a desired profit of 4 percent, and anticipated reductions of 6 percent, the markon percentage would be computed as follows:

$$\frac{34\% + 6\%}{100\% + 6\%} = \frac{40\%}{106\%} = 37.7\%$$

Thus when reductions are expected, to obtain a gross margin of 34 percent an initial markup (markon) of approximately 38 percent is needed. Once the average markon percentage for this class of goods is determined, it is applied to the cost of the goods in the same manner as a markup percentage is used to arrive at a selling price.

Although retailers are not ordinarily able to price each item to cover its landed cost, expenses, retail reductions, and a fair margin of profit exactly, they should always consider these factors and aim to average the results of a line or class of goods, or at least a department, to achieve this goal. In the case of nonstandard goods, the small retailers' intimate knowledge of their customers will often enable them to select different styles for two or more retail prices from a lot of goods that all cost the same, or they may find it possible and necessary to sell for the same price lots of goods having different landed costs. These are both cases of averaging to achieve the desired gross margin.

PRICING BY WHOLESALERS

In general, wholesale as well as retail prices are based on the markup or gross margin necessary to handle each line of goods profitably. Competition tends to keep margins small on staples, but larger margins are needed on lines affected by fashion or other influences resulting in large markdowns.

Most of the same forces affect the prices and profits of wholesalers as operate at other levels of distribution, but some of them affect wholesalers in a distinctive way. For the customers of wholesalers, price is usually the determining factor in the buying decision. Price competition is more direct and more intense for wholesaling than other levels of distribution. A wholesaler has many rivals, including the manufacturers who sell direct, the functional middlemen, and other wholesalers in the same or broader lines. Wholesalers' markets are well-organized and are very sensitive to supply and demand factors. Since dealers buy and sell in large quantities a slight change in the price they pay involves substantial dollar amounts. Wholesale prices fluctuate much more than do retail prices or manufacturers' prices because wholesalers operate on narrower margins and are less able to absorb increases in cost, even over a short period of time.

Even small wholesalers are likely to follow the varying price policy—that is, quoting different prices on the same merchandise to different buyers depending on bargaining ability, size of order, and similar factors which can be substantiated under the legal requirements. Even under the one-price policy, actual prices may vary according to the services extended, such as credit and delivery. Usually a uniform discount schedule can be used, or a price schedule prepared for each grouping of services. Under the varying price policy it is desirable for the wholesaler's salespersons to have maximum and minimum prices for each product, and some incentive to sell at or near the maximum price whenever justifiable.

PRICING BY THE SERVICE ESTABLISHMENT

The variety of businesses classified as service establishments is enormous and among them the methods of determining price will differ greatly, but certain concepts should be useful in the wise pricing of all services whatever their character. Every service performed should contribute to the profit of the firm and bear its share of the expenses. Every service establishment should have a bookkeeping system which accurately records operating expenses and the cost of all materials used in providing the service. The manager must understand the distinction between direct costs (labor, materials, etc.) and **indirect costs** (rent, utilities, etc.) and have some suitable way of allocating the indirect costs to the cost per unit of service.

Sometimes there are special conditions in some areas of service that place limits on this approach to pricing, such as **guild pricing** used by barber and beauty shops, prevailing price schedules used by competing firms, or limitations placed by franchise agreements. When prices are fixed, the manager's challenge is to control costs and increase operating efficiency for maximum profits.

In the broad class of services, including personal service establishments and common repair or reconditioning plants, there will usually be several establishments of each kind with currently accepted prices for the basic or more standardized services.[5] Pricing in these fields often starts from fairly stable prices for a few of the usual services provided by each kind of business. For example, in dry cleaning plants a lady's plain dress and a man's business suit are commonly used as standards. Appliance and other repair services may take the typical cleaning and tuning-up job for a popular model of car, refrigerator, television set, or boat motor, as the case may be, for the basic price. In barber shops a haircut is the same price whether it is an easy or a complicated job. From these basic service prices a price schedule can be set up for other important and fairly standard services. Special jobs are priced according to the amount of labor required. In all cases adequate allowance must be made for wide variations in the amount of materials and supplies needed.

When prices are not based on well-known community standards the **multiplier method of pricing** may be used to fairly allocate indirect costs. It is particularly useful when the amount of service varies from customer to customer, and if the labor cost is the most significant item and the hourly wages do not vary greatly among the productive laborers. The multiplier is determined by dividing annual labor costs into annual total sales. A new firm may need to use estimates of costs and sales during a trial-run period; adjustments can be made when actual figures are available.

Three figures are then multiplied to determine the price to charge for a particular job: (1) the worker's hourly pay, (2) time on the job, and (3) the multiplier. For example, if a welding and metalworking shop had annual sales of $50,000 and total productive labor costs of $20,000, and the average worker were paid $6 per hour, the multiplier and the price to be charged for a job that took 4 hours would be figured as follows:

$$\frac{\$50,000}{\$20,000} = 2.5$$

$$\$6 \times 4 \times 2.5 = \$60$$

---

[5] In some states minimum prices that may be legally charged for many kinds of personal services are set by state boards.

To this amount would be added the costs of material required for the particular job.

Because the multiplier is based on operating figures it must be kept up to date and reflect actual conditions.

Many small repair shops in the automobile, television, appliance, and similar fields find that customers like **flat-rate pricing.** It can be used on 80 to 90 percent of the jobs that come to the average shop. Company agencies will ordinarily use the **list prices** suggested by the manufacturers they represent. Others may use published lists, or subscribe to a price-reporting service like those used by plumbing and heating contractors.

When price lists are published an average wage rate is the basis for the flat rate recommended for each service. The flat rate is figured by multiplying the standard time to do the job by the average wage rate times a multiplier. If the local wage rate is very different from that used in a published list, flat-rate prices must be recalculated by substituting the local wage rate in the formula, but using the same multiplier as used in calculating the given list prices. The assumption is that a particular service industry will have similar indirect-cost-to-sales ratios throughout the area.

Sometimes a small operator in applying wage rates to an industry formula for setting prices will use hourly rates that are too low. For example, a list may give the standard time for a particular job as 4½ hours, the multiplier as 2, and the average hourly rate as $5. Thus the standard flat-rate price would be $45 plus cost of materials used. A small operator may figure the price for the job as follows: 4½ x 2 x $4 (his or her hourly rate in dollars) = a flat price of $36. If his or her labor at $4 per hour is fully as efficient as the average $5 per hour worker, he or she will be in the clear. The standard time is usually based on efficient labor skilled in the particular kind of work being priced.

PRICING FOR THE SMALL FACTORY

In manufacturing the price of each product, in general, is closely related to its cost of production. When only one product is made, unit cost is easily calculated by dividing processing costs plus total costs of materials and parts for a given period by the number of units of product made during the same period. Then, to determine a minimum sales price, distribution or selling costs per unit plus a fair margin of profit must be added to unit production costs. A higher price than this minimum may be charged if there is a lack of competition, a demand greater than the company is able at present to supply, or the desire to create a prestige reputation. In setting a price above the calculated minimum there is always the danger of inviting competition. Usually it is better for the small business to figure a fair profit in the minimum calculation and to price at that point.

When two or more products are manufactured, cost accounting becomes necessary in order to arrive at the approximately correct minimum price for each product. Expenses are divided into two groups, fixed or overhead, and variable or direct; the sum of these two is the total unit cost. As volume increases, **fixed** or **overhead costs** remain approximately the same in total amount but decrease per unit. **Variable** or **direct costs** increase in almost direct proportion to increased volume but remain fairly constant per unit of output. Consequently, the cost of production can be decreased, per unit, in proportion to the relative importance of overhead or fixed costs. When additional products of a different nature can absorb some of this overhead, the effect is similar to that of manufacturing one product in greater volume.[6] When certain variable costs, such as that of raw materials, are small or even decrease with increased volume, as they may in the utilization of waste or by-products, actual additional costs of production for the by-product may be relatively very low. Finally, when several products are made in the same factory, the determination of unit costs becomes somewhat arbitrary, and standards for pricing should be shifted from so-called cost of production to other factors like competition, nature of demand for the product, and company pricing policy.

In pricing to meet competition the first question to decide is what competition the firm plans to meet. If a company has successfully differentiated its product, the pressure to meet direct price competition is greatly reduced. If there are products that nearly meet the same need as the company's product and are popular in the marketing area, competitive prices are necessary.

Another factor especially important for small manufacturers to consider is the way competitors are likely to react to their prices. If pricing is keenly competitive and price changes take place frequently, it may be risky for the small business to take the lead in offering lower prices. At one extreme is a policy of **administered prices,** by which the leaders set their prices and stay with them for considerable periods of time. At the other extreme is the policy of meeting all price reductions and keeping prices at the lowest possible point. Between these extremes will be found the policies followed by the majority of companies.

Manufacturers, like retailers, must understand the nature of their product and its elasticity of demand. It is well to remember that price is only one way in which manufacturers can expand their market and should be emphasized only when it is more effective than advertising, personal selling, packaging, and changes in the quality level of the product. Frequently, experimentation with customer response to different possible prices may be necessary to determine the relative importance of the price factor. In this experimentation competitors' actions should be noticed and care taken to avoid starting a price war.

Very often some pricing must be done before actual production takes place. This involves the necessity of estimating costs fairly accurately, because

---

[6] See p. 359 for a discussion of the incremental cost (or marginal income) approach to pricing.

the price set will influence volume of sales; this in turn will react on unit cost of production. Thus it is desirable to determine for each product the break-even point, beyond which further price reductions should not be made under existing conditions. It means that point at which the extra revenue obtained from increased volume just equals additional production plus marketing costs.[7]

Another condition likely to be encountered by the small manufacturer is that involving **differential pricing.** It may be desirable when the company's products are sold through two different types of outlets. For example, a small factory may contract to sell approximately half of its output to one large distributing organization, such as a mail-order house, chain store, or department store. Since these large firms perform the wholesaling functions and selling to them usually involves a low selling cost per unit of product, a low price can be quoted on this part of the plant's output. Pricing the rest of the product will follow the principles already discussed, except that in calculating costs of production allowance must be made for the fact that a large share of indirect or overhead expenses has already been absorbed by the sale of the large order. It is considered a violation of the Robinson-Patman Act to price the product to the large buyer so low that it does not include a proportionate share of overhead costs. A second consideration in such cases will be the effect of this dual distribution on the price necessary to induce individual dealers to handle the product. For the small manufacturer this may not be serious because the large distributor will probably resell the product under its own **private brand** name. It is only when the product is offered by the large distributor in easily identifiable form and in direct competition with individual outlets that pricing to the latter becomes a serious problem.

Another consideration in pricing by the manufacturer relates to the use of list prices from which discounts are granted, as compared to quoting direct net prices each time a sale is under consideration. The use of list prices has at least three advantages: (1) it suggests the retail price to the dealer; (2) it is often useful to the dealer in selling to the final consumer; and (3) it permits more flexibility in making price changes and quoting different prices to different buyers. A closely related question is the extent to which individual salespersons are to be given authority to determine prices at which the company's product will be sold.

Small factories located in market centers for their type of product often find it desirable to use wholesale price lines. When the goods produced are sold through retail stores that use price lines, as is the case with many articles of popular women's wear, this method of pricing is used. If manufacturers thus have their prices determined for them within narrow limits, their problem is the profitable manufacture of goods to sell at these price lines.

---

[7] See p. 217.

SUMMING UP

Pricing is a very important aspect of management. Business owners are in business to make a profit. For them or their hired managers to set the right price which will result in the greatest profit, they must know their costs and their prices must reflect these costs. Wise business managers also recognize that the more efficiently they are able to operate their business, and the better their costs are controlled, the larger their profit margin will be. Many other considerations, however, affect their pricing decisions besides the cost of their goods or services and their operating expenses; these considerations include the nature of the product or service, the amount of competition, company policy, business conditions, and market strategy.

Not all goods can be priced for profit, but the *aggregate* price charged on all good should yield a profit. Also, in some cases the *volume* of sales of certain items may provide substantial dollar profits even when the percentage markup on these items is low.

The small business manager must also weigh the role to be played by price in relation to other factors in the marketing mix, such as advertising and other forms of sales promotion (discussed in the following chapter), quality or distinction of the product or service, and (for the manufacturer) styling and packaging.

In general, price is the most dangerous of the marketing instruments for the small business to use aggressively. This should not discourage carefully directed experimentation in pricing, but there is a need for careful study and understanding before changing prices or price policies.

KEY WORDS

administered prices
advertisability
consignment sale
convenience goods
cost of goods sold
demand
differential pricing
direct costs
elasticity of demand
expansibility of demand

fair trade laws
fashion cycle
fashion goods
fixed costs
flat-rate pricing
gross margin
guild pricing
indirect costs
initial markup
landed cost

list price

loss leader

marginal-income/cost

markdown

markon

markup

multiplier method of pricing

overhead costs

prestige pricing

price lining

private brand

retail reductions

shopping goods

variable costs

DISCUSSION QUESTIONS

1. Assume that you are setting prices on merchandise carried in a college bookstore. On which items would you use a standard or average markup? Higher-than-average markup? Lower-than-average markup?

2. If you were starting an entirely new kind of business, explain how you would endeavor to determine the most profitable prices to charge.

3. Name as many products and services as you can think of in which consumers rely chiefly on price as a guide to quality. Suggest probable reasons in each case.

EXERCISES AND PROBLEMS*

1. The Hawkeye Shoe Store is now selling for $30 a pair shoes it purchased for $18 a pair. The owner thinks that if the selling price were reduced slightly, more sales and more profits might be made since the operating expenses would not increase. The store has sold an average of 50 pairs daily. What percentage increase in the number of shoes sold will be necessary to achieve the same amount of gross profit if the selling price is reduced by 10 percent?

2. A merchant estimates that sales next year will be $100,000 and that operating expenses will be $20,000. What will be the amount of his or her gross margin if the merchant expects to have a net profit of 5 percent on sales? What is the gross margin (markup) percentage?

3. A manufacturer sells his/her product for $150 a unit. What is the price to the consumer if the wholesaler takes a markup of 20 percent and the retailer take a markup of 50 percent?

4. A manufacturer distributes his/her products through wholesalers and

---

° *Note:* Base all markup calculations in these exercises on selling price, unless otherwise instructed.

retailers. The retail selling price is $300 a unit, and the manufacturing cost is $120. The retail markup is 40 percent, and the wholesale markup is 20 percent.

     a. What is the cost to the wholesaler?

     b. What is the cost to the retailer?

     c. What markup did the manufacturer take?

5. What percentage markup on cost is equivalent to:

     a. a 20 percent markup on selling price?

     b. a 60 percent markup on selling price?

6. What percentage markup on selling price is equivalent to:

     a. a 100 percent markup on cost?

     b. a 200 percent markup on cost?

7. What price should you charge for an item that costs you $60, if your selling expenses are 35 percent and you seek a profit of 5 percent?

8. The Hawkeye Manufacturing Company is attempting to set a price on an item so that the retail price (the price to the final consumer) will be $25, taking into account the traditional markups of 20 percent at wholesale and 30 percent at retail. At what price should the manufacturer sell the item?

9. What would be the manufacturer's selling price if he/she grants trade discounts of 35 percent to retailers and 20 percent to wholesalers off a list price of $100 per unit?

10. The price structure of an industry gives a 40 percent markup to retailers and 20 percent to wholesalers. The retail price is $100 and the manufacturer's factory cost is $24.

     a. What is the wholesale price?

     b. What is the manufacturer's price?

     c. What is the manufacturer's gross margin in dollars?

     d. What is the manufacturer's gross margin percentage?

     e. What is the retailer's percentage markup on cost?

     f. What is the wholesaler's percentage markup on cost?

11. Considering the cost factors and profit goal in exercise 7 above, what price should you originally charge for the item if you anticipate shoplifting losses, late-season markdowns, and other reductions amounting to approximately 8 percent of sales?

12. Dresses in a women's clothing store are priced at $19.95, $24.95, $29.95, $34.95, and $39.95. The dress department data are: expenses, 31.5 percent; profit, 8 percent; and retail reductions, 10 percent. Landed cost of two dozen dresses just received is $400. At what initial retail price should they be offered?

13. The owner of a portrait studio incurred the following operating costs last year:

Rent	$ 1,800
Insurance	400
Utilities	700
Labor	2,000
Owner's salary	9,000
Advertising	500
Depreciation	1,000
Interest	600
Photographic supplies	1,500
	$17,500

Fixed costs are recovered by charging customers a sitting charge. In pricing his/her pictures, the proprietor adds a markup of 20 percent on picture frames, film, paper, and other photographic supplies to the sitting charge. The studio is open eight hours a day, five days a week, except for a two-week vacation period in the summer. On a typical day, the studio averages five sittings. What should the sitting charge be if the owner of this portrait studio wishes to earn a 25 percent return on his/her investment of time and money?

CASES IN POINT

The sporting goods store of Harris and Harris is operated by William and Edwin Harris in a fairly remote college town. It started ten years ago when the two brothers became campus representatives for a wholesaler in the nearest large city. The business has grown with the local college and with the expansion of other educational facilities in the area. New golf courses and athletic activities connected with new industrial plants within the 50-mile radius they serve have also helped in their growth.

Generally, the two young men have prospered, although frequently in the early days they agreed that they were better athletes than businessmen. They have kept the firm's business evenly balanced, not having entered any particular branch of athletics. Rather, they have responded to demand as it has developed. In fact, most of their business has come to them, although they do make sales calls and do the usual goodwill-building things such as holding contests and giving awards to student athletes.

Recently they have seen some serious competition developing, as mail-order houses, department stores, discounters, and others in larger cities some distance away are advertising, by direct mail and by newspaper, TV and radio, in their markets. Some of the items advertised are loss leaders, the brothers believe. Others are closeouts, some apparently rejects or seconds. The brothers know that these competitors are trying to get customers into their stores so that while there they will buy not only sporting goods, but home appliances, automotive accessories, and other offerings.

Will and Ed are worried but not discouraged. They feel that there must be some way of combating this invasion of their market. Their profits have been satisfactory. They have a markup varying from 33⅓ to 50 percent of the sales price, often as suggested by the manufacturer. Now they fear they will have to reduce prices on certain highly competitive items. If they do this, they might have to raise prices on other goods. The trouble is that they do not know what their price-cutting competitors will do next. Nor do they know which items or supplies bring in the most profit during any given period.

Something must be done, although not necessarily abruptly or all at once. How would you go about establishing a policy that will ensure the permanence of their business over a reasonable period in the future?

George Hunter had discovered an unusual fabric-filament that because it is light-, water-, and air-tight, as well as sturdy, provides a suitable material for swimming pool equipment and outdoors gear of all kinds. His first product is an inflatable sleeping bag that can also be used as a raft for swimming pools. It is sturdy, attractive, and better than many now on the market. Furthermore, in case of a fabric rip, it is easily repaired with a household iron.

His first problem is how to price his product. In quantities of 1,000, his costs are $2.45 per unit. In lots of 5,000, $2.28. If he could sell 10,000, he could get down nearer $2 each, possibly less as he goes into larger-scale production. If he sold them to distributors, he would ask $3.95 each in quantities of one dozen, according to present market plans. His distributors could then resell to retailers for $5.50, and the retailers in turn for $7.95 up to $9.95.

The question arises: These are normal pricings; couldn't he enter the market faster at a lower price, say $2.10, which could give all concerned a similar profit percentage and probably greater sales volume? His banker has suggested that, since his product is unique, he charge a premium price to begin, so that he can recover his development and starting costs earlier. How would *you* respond to this question?

Advertising
and Sales Promotion

CHAPTER FIFTEEN   *As market research and analysis is at one end of the marketing spectrum, so is* selling *at the other. Selling is nothing more than getting the word to the potential customer. This may be done by personal contact, window and interior displays, and by advertising. In this chapter you will learn the strategic part advertising and other forms of sales promotion play in marketing.*

Perhaps the best definition of **sales promotion** is the *effective coordination of all marketing activities having to do with the performance of the selling function.* The effectiveness of the coordination of time, effort, and money to achieve the efficient use of the sales dollar is the measure of success in sales promotion. Sales promotion is of vital importance to the business; but it must not be overemphasized to the neglect of the other functions, and it must be long-range as well as short-range in its viewpoint and approach, and be "tuned in" on the buying motives of the firm's customers. Good sales promotion is carefully planned and directed toward specific goals. Adequate records of promotion costs and sales volume should be maintained.

Sales promotion may be direct or indirect. Direct methods, in all types of business, include advertising and personal selling, and in recent years the franchising method of distribution has gained in popularity; other forms of direct sales promotion, applicable in retailing, include window and interior displays and special sales events. Indirect sales promotional devices, on the other hand, are represented by customer services, favorable customer relations, and good public relations; these pave the way for the increased effectiveness of the direct methods. To be continuously successful, sales promotion must be based on customer satisfaction, good customer relations, and sound sales policies. Only when customer relations are the best will advertising and other direct sales promotional efforts be completely successful.

CUSTOMERS' BUYING MOTIVES

The effectiveness of any form of sales promotion depends on a knowledge and understanding of customers' **buying motives.**

People want many things, and nearly everyone wants the same basic things, although in varying degrees, to satisfy his or her personal needs. The presence of many individuals with similar preferences in the same community makes it a good or a poor market for specific goods and services, depending on what a firm has to offer.

Buying motives generally include the following consumer needs:

Comfort—the desire for physical or mental ease and well-being
Convenience—the desire for a minimum of effort, for saving of time and energy
Security—the desire to know that the future is provided for and personal welfare assured
Prestige—the desire to be recognized as personally outstanding or a member of a desirable group
Health—the desire to feel and look physically fit
Economy—the desire to secure full value for each penny spent, to save money

It is the goal of the business community to help consumers satisfy these needs.

But groups and communities differ. Certainly a traditionally low-paid group would respond to any offering stressing *economy;* they might forego the *convenience* and *comfort* of certain services to achieve this economy. Others will buy exotic and similarly unusual goods to secure *prestige,* which may be more important to them than economy. These preferences will differ among people of different incomes and ages and sexes. If, for example, the good or the service contemplated offers *health* or *security* with economy as well, then the small business operator will find ample business volume in communities containing many older people living on limited incomes.

There are many other reasons why people buy things, including the desire to gain and hold the affection of others, the desire to belong to the crowd, the desire for recreation and amusement, and so on. Those that have been listed above, however, are the more common ones. If customers' buying motives or their relative strengths are unknown, advertising and other sales efforts will be wasted in almost all cases.

Running a business without advertising is like winking at a pretty girl in the dark—you know what you're doing but she doesn't.

—STEUART HENDERSON BRITT

ADVERTISING

Advertising includes those activities by which oral and visual messages are directed to the public for the purpose of informing and influencing them either to buy or act favorably toward the subject featured. Profit-minded entrepreneurs use advertising because it is a quick and convincing way to increase sales.

Since advertising is a message directed to a particular group of people, a basic principle for the entrepreneur to follow is to know his or her market.

Careful selection of the logical prospects for a particular advertisement should be one of the first steps in planning. The message or theme and its form of presentation in copy, illustration, and layout, as well as the appropriate media to use, all depend primarily on the particular group to be reached by each advertisement. A great deal of advertising would be much more effective if the business owner first made certain that the objective of the advertisement is sound.

Probably the greatest single waste in advertising results from the careless preparation of many advertisements and sales campaigns. Recognition of this fact has led an increasing number of business owners to take steps to test and measure the effectiveness of their advertising. Keeping adequate records of all advertisements and relevant conditions at the time each is released is important. Some retailers make a practice of asking each new customer how he or she happened to come to the shop. An analysis of these results as a basis for planning future advertising increases the number of successes and reduces errors.

Frequently it is possible for the small business owner to pretest advertisements before they are released on a large scale. This may be done by using a less expensive, more easily controlled medium like a display, handbills, or direct mail to test the effectiveness of various elements of the advertisement before completing it in final form for use in such media as newspapers. Another plan, sometimes called **elements research,** is an adaptation of split-run testing as used by national advertisers. If the element to be tested is the headline, one-half of a sample mailing will receive the circular with one headline and the other half with another. On the next mailing the heads will be reversed. Results of each mailing will be carefully recorded, either by inquiries received or by calls in the store if a retailer is working the test. Comparison will show which headline is more effective. Copy, illustration, or the theme to use may be tested in a similar manner.

Advertising can be typified, according to primary purpose or objective, as **institutional** (selling the business) and **direct action** (selling the product or service the business has to offer). Both are necessary, although small business owners will usually devote most of their limited advertising funds to the promotional or direct action type. Selling the business and selling the goods are in many respects similar. Some business owners will wish to promote many aspects of the business, while others will emphasize only one or a few. Some of the business attributes that advertising may sell are services, integrity, brands carried, courtesy, business success, credit terms, prestige, location, size, price, quality, and fashion policies.

> *The business that considers itself immune to the necessity for advertising sooner or later finds itself immune to business.*
> —DERBY BROWN

Market Analysis

The first step in advertising (or in any other form of sales promotion) is to learn as much as possible about the **market** to which the advertisement will be directed. The business owner can begin by considering these questions:

1. Who are my potential customers?
2. How many are there?
3. Where are they located?
4. Where do they now buy the things or services I want to sell them?
5. Can I offer them anything they are not getting now? If so, what?
6. How can I convince them they should do business with me?

Business owners should never cease to survey or study their customers. Neighborhoods and customers change habits. If a customer drifts away, the business owner should try at once to find out why.

Consumers may not realize a need for certain products until "educated" by advertising. This is nearly always true of new products for which extensive pioneering advertising may be required. This explains in part why advertising expense may be higher during the first few years. However, if customers do not want a product or service, advertising alone cannot *make* them buy.

The Advertising Budget

Determining the right amount to spend for advertising is important because this expense is a major one. For the small business it is especially important that limited funds be used to the best possible advantage. Once the **advertising budget** is drawn up, a more intelligent campaign can be planned, involving the determination of items to promote, prospects to seek, media to use, and frequency of releases.

For most types of retailing and some service trades, industry **expense ratios** provide valuable guides in determining *how much* to spend for advertising and other forms of sales promotion. However, it should be cautioned that these are guides, not absolute standards. Firms starting from scratch, for example, will most likely find it necessary to spend somewhat more than the average for their industry. Manufacturers, on the other hand, have no standard ratios to serve as guides; nevertheless, they must make some estimate as to how much the sales of their product can be increased profitably through advertising.

The following illustrations demonstrate how the right advertising expenditure can be determined for any firm. Table 15-1, for example, shows the ef-

TABLE 15-1

Effect of Advertising on Profits

	CURRENT YEAR		PROJECTED	
Sales	$250,000	100.0%	$300,000	100.0%
Less Cost of goods sold	175,000	70.0	210,000	70.0
Gross margin	$ 75,000	30.0	$ 90,000	30.0
Less Expenses:				
Fixed	40,000	16.0	40,000	13.3
Variable:				
Advertising	4,000	1.6	8,000	2.7
Other	21,000	8.4	25,200	8.4
Total expenses	$ 65,000	26.0	$ 73,200	24.4
Net profit	$ 10,000	4.0	$ 16,800	5.6

fect that doubling the modest amount a firm currently spends on advertising can have on its profit, with an assumed increase in sales resulting therefrom of 20 percent. The projections in the table also assume that variable expenses other than advertising (such as part-time or seasonal employees, delivery costs, packaging costs, etc.) will increase at the same rate as sales.

Table 15-1 demonstrates that increased advertising *can* increase profits; not only has profit increased by 68 percent, but the projected net profit ratio has increased from 4.0 to 5.6 percent of sales. But this is true only *up to a point,* as sales become increasingly harder to come by. Since a basic premise in business is that a firm should invest every dollar that will pay for itself and increase profits, the key question for the small business owner/manager is: How much *at the very most* can I profitably invest in advertising?

As you learned in the preceding chapter, **marginal-income/cost** analysis can be helpful in arriving at an answer to this question. To determine the most profitable advertising expenditure for any business, one must analyze the marginal (extra, or hard-to-come-by) sales that can be generated as a result of an incremental increase in advertising costs.

Thus, in Table 15-2 (a continuation of Table 15-1) it is assumed that with a further increase of $2,500 in advertising expense, sales can be increased by another 5 percent; similarly, by increasing advertising expenditures by another $2,500, sales will further increase by 4 percent, and a third $2,500 advertising increment will increase sales still further by another 3 percent. As in Table 15-1, it is also assumed that variable expenses other than advertising will increase at the same rate as sales. Based on these assumptions, it is clear that $13,000 would be the optimum advertising expenditure for this firm's product. While the demand for this product could be further expanded (sales increasing from $327,600 to $337,428, and the gross margin from $98,280 to $101,228), additional advertising effort would actually lower the level of profits.

TABLE 15-2

Determining the Optimum Advertising Expenditure

Sales	$315,000	$327,600	$337,428
Less Cost of goods sold	220,500	229,320	236,200
Gross margin	$ 94,500	$ 98,280	$101,228
Less Expenses:			
Fixed	40,000	40,000	40,000
Variable:			
Advertising	10,500	13,000	15,500
Other	26,460	27,518	28,344
Total expenses	$ 76,960	$ 80,518	$ 83,844
Net profit	$ 17,540	$ 17,762	$ 17,384

In budgeting advertising expense it is important to recognize that advertising has a *cumulative* effect. Response is slow at first but increases with time. Sporadic splurges rarely pay. It is much better to advertise regularly and continuously on a small scale than to use large and expensive advertisements infrequently.

Advertising Media

Deciding *where* to invest the money budgeted for advertising depends on many factors. In appraising **advertising media** or comparing them in terms of effectiveness, the prospective advertiser should consider the following:

1. *Cost per contact*—How much will it actually cost to reach a prospective customer?

2. *Frequency*—How frequent are these contacts or message deliveries? In this business, is a single powerful advertisement preferable to a series of constant small reminders, or vice versa?

3. *Impact*—Does the medium in question offer full opportunities for appealing to the appropriate senses, such as sight and hearing in presenting design, color, or sound?

4. *Selectivity*—To what degree can the message be restricted to those people who are known to be the most logical prospects?

Newspapers and radio or television offer broad geographical coverage of the general public; direct mail is the most selective. The radio and television commercial may reach many thousands, only a few of whom are possible customers. An expensive direct-mail piece may reach only a limited number, yet the cost per contact may be the same or even lower. The extent to which the prospective customer can be identified beforehand will influence the choice of

YOUR PROMOTION BUDGET IS AN INVESTMENT

Courtesy of Small Business Administration.

media. If unidentifiable, newspaper, radio, or television advertising may reach potential customers; if identifiable, the expensive direct-mail piece might be the best investment. These considerations are a few of the fundamental decisions concerning advertising media. An advertising media comparison chart is provided in Table 15-3.

Wholesalers and manufacturers, in contrast to retailers and service establishments, do relatively little advertising. Most of the sales of wholesalers are obtained by means of personal selling; the small factory will direct whatever advertising it does either to consumers or to dealers or business users (other manufacturers) of its products.

When selling consumer products only in the local markets, whether through local dealers or directly, small manufacturers may use newspaper, radio or television, outdoor signs, and direct-mail advertising effectively; when selling through dealers or to other businesses, they will use principally direct mail and trade publications read by their prospects. However, in the latter case, spot radio and television announcements may be an effective way to get a new product off to a good start, to draw attention to other media used, and to gain dealer acceptance and distribution for the product because it is being supported by consumer advertising.

WINDOW AND INTERIOR DISPLAYS

Most authorities agree that window displays provide an effective sales promotion medium. Showing the merchandise or product in three dimensions in all its true color and beauty is a strong point in window displays. Not only is window display space the most valuable sales-generating space in the store, but goods on display help to make up the face of the store that impresses traffic.

Displays should be tied in with national advertising whenever possible. This may be accomplished in many ways, such as by timing displays to ap-

TABLE 15-3
Advertising Media Comparison Chart

MEDIUM	MARKET COVERAGE	TYPE OF AUDIENCE	PARTICULAR SUITABILITY	MAJOR ADVANTAGE	MAJOR DISADVANTAGE
Daily newspaper	Single community or entire metro area; zoned editions sometimes available	General; tends more toward men, older age group, slightly higher income and education	All general retailers	Wide circulation	Nonselective audience
Weekly newspaper	Single community usually; sometimes a metro area	General; usually residents of a small community	Retailers who service a strictly local market	Local identification	Limited readership
Shopper	Most households in a single community; chain shoppers can cover a metro area	Consumer households	Neighborhood retailers and service businesses	Consumer orientation	A giveaway and not always read
Telephone directories	Geographic area or occupational field served by the directory	Active shoppers for goods or services	Services, retailers of brand name items, highly specialized retailers	Users are in the market for goods or services	Limited to active shoppers
Direct mail	Controlled by the advertiser	Controlled by the advertiser through use of demographic lists	New and expanding businesses; those using coupon returns or catalogs	Personalized approach to an audience of good prospects	High cost per message

231

TABLE 15-3 (Cont.)
Advertising Media Comparison Chart

MEDIUM	MARKET COVERAGE	TYPE OF AUDIENCE	PARTICULAR SUITABILITY	MAJOR ADVANTAGE	MAJOR DISADVANTAGE
Radio	Definable market area surrounding the station's location	Selected audiences provided by stations with distinct programming formats	Businesses catering to identifiable groups; teens, commuters, housewives	Market selectivity, wide market coverage	Must be bought consistently to be of value
Television	Definable market area surrounding the station's location	Varies with the time of day; tends toward younger age group, less print-oriented	Sellers of products or services with wide appeal	Dramatic impact, wide market coverage	High cost of time and production
Transit	Urban or metro community served by transit system; may be limited to a few transit routes	Transit riders, especially wage earners and shoppers; pedestrians	Businesses along transit routes; especially those appealing to wage earners	Repetition and length of exposure	Limited audience
Outdoor	Entire metro area or single neighborhood	General; especially auto drivers	Amusements, tourist businesses, brand name retailers	Dominant size, frequency of exposure	Clutter of many signs reduces effectiveness of each one
Local magazine	Entire metro area or region; zoned editions sometimes available	General; tends toward better educated, more affluent	Restaurants, entertainments, specialty shops, mail-order business	Delivery of a loyal, special-interest audience	Limited audience

SOURCE: "Advertising Small Business," Vol. 15, No. 2, 1981 (*Small Business Reporter*, Bank of America).

pear during national campaigns, by including pages from the national media, or by using placards stating "As advertised in *Vogue*," and the like. Seasonal displays are usually effective, offer opportunities for originality and related item selling, and help to build the store's reputation for merchandising alertness.

Interior displays are also effective in promoting sales. In recent years they have become increasingly important as the trend toward self-service in retailing continues, particularly in convenience stores.

Interior displays should always have price cards and usually informative signs. For **impulse goods** and **convenience goods,** mass displays are very effective, especially the jumbled type with nothing for the customer to knock down when selecting articles from the display. Grocers have found that the effectiveness of mass displays is noticeably increased by the addition of advertising placards calling attention to featured goods and giving the price. If the offering is a special-price feature and there is a time or quantity-per-customer limit, this information should also be given.

As a rule, the display cards and other dealer merchandising aids offered by manufacturers and distributors should be utilized, because they provide authentic sales information about the goods and provide space for pricing. Such dealer aids represent extensive and often expensive study to discover the appeal that will be most effective in presenting a product to the public, and they contain tested catch lines that are bound to help sell the goods.

SPECIAL SALES EVENTS

For the retailer, timeliness, advertising the right merchandise, and selecting the best advertising theme are particularly important in planning special sales promotions.

Timing

The distinguishing feature of successful sales promotion is its *timeliness,* either when planned in advance for certain days or seasons or when capitalizing on some unexpected development. Merchants have available to them calendars of suggested promotional events, usually prepared several months in advance by the trade association in the field, which give all important dates likely to be useful in staging promotions. Most of these are published in trade journals and in dealer material released by wholesalers.

Timing the release of fashion advertising should be related to the store's position in the **merchandise acceptance curve** or **fashion cycle.** Fashion leaders in the community advertise heavily at the very beginning of the selling season; those catering to the middle class advertise just before the peak of the selling

SALES MUST BE WELL TIMED

Courtesy of Small Business Administration.

period; and stores in the economy group put out their ads just after the selling crest has been passed.

For **staple goods** and special sales events, stores serving lower- and average-income groups should time their advertising to fit in with the paydays and shopping habits of their customers; those catering to the upper-income brackets will be more concerned with tax dates and special customer preferences.

Sometimes the nature of the business provides opportunity for timely promotions of seasonal merchandise. Feed dealers, for example, time their promotions with the planting, cultivation, or marketing of customers' (farmers') products; auto accessory stores time their promotions to the weather and the vacation use of the family car.

Selecting the Merchandise to Promote

Selecting the right merchandise to advertise is of great importance to the retailer because only about 15 to 20 percent of all goods carried is suitable for external advertising. Not only should goods selected produce enough sales of the advertised articles to cover the direct cost of advertising, but they should also attract to the store customers who will buy unadvertised merchandise. In other words, advertising should attract shopping traffic of regular customers rather than bargain hunters or specific item buyers exclusively.

Selecting items to advertise may be done in many ways. Preference should be given to goods representative of the store's character and with an established appeal. Customer **want slips,** sales records, and the results of past advertising promotions may help in selecting the products to advertise. For new items customer response to display is considered the best guide. Opinions of **buyers** and salespeople are useful guides if time will not permit test displays before advertising.

Choosing a Theme

To help in choosing the theme to be used in advertising, buyers should state the features about each article that caused them to buy it for the store. Current practice is to require each buyer at the time he or she purchases new merchandise to secure from the vendor the sizzle or selling story for each article. Salespeople should also be able to give valuable suggestions as to what features of the merchandise would be most attractive and interesting to customers. The question "What advertisable features does the merchandise have?" should be asked before it is purchased by the store's buyers.

Naturally, certain merchandise suggests its own theme, such as fashion rightness, authenticity, or economy. Experience has shown, however, that such obvious points of appeal as durability, strength, economy, or assumed use of the article may differ widely from the *real* reasons why customers buy particular merchandise. National and state holidays, and important promotions in the community such as Mardi Gras and Days of the Forty-Niners also offer profitable advertising themes.

The range of themes or ideas useful in building sales promotions is unlimited. Each issue of the trade journals contains suggestions and stimulating ideas from nearly every field of retailing. Often ideas developed by large city stores can be used to advantage by the small store, such as having customer juries select one hundred perfect gifts for Christmas from the store's offerings.

Coordinating the Event

To be effective, the sales effort should be coordinated with other aspects of the total business operation. A useful approach to planning sales promotions is to follow a checklist to provide for all details and proper timing. Important points to be included are the following:

1. Opening and closing dates
2. Name of promotion and any explanations needed
3. Merchandise to be featured
4. Complete plans for advertising and window and interior displays, including coordination of media and use of all appropriate devices —signs, price cards, window streamers, banners, special layout, and display
5. Organization plans—including staff meetings, employee incentives, and provisions for extra help or special training.

A SUCCESSFUL SALES EVENT MUST BE TOTALLY COORDINATED

Courtesy of Small Business Administration.

The retailer should keep records of each promotion and consult these records in planning future events. Contrary to popular belief, previously successful promotions of a seasonal or recurring nature are more likely to be effective when repeated than are entirely new ones. Each new promotion is an experiment that may or may not prove successful. Since the customers of one store do not change greatly from year to year, an event that has proved its appeal to the customers once is very likely to succeed several times more. Of course details may be changed, but the basic idea of the promotion will remain the same. This should not discourage careful experimentation, but it should be a warning against seeking change merely to be different.

PERSONAL SELLING AND CUSTOMER RELATIONS

Although the trend in retailing has been toward self-service, personal selling remains an important means of promoting the sale of most products. This is certainly true in the sale of **shopping goods** and **fashion goods,** such as clothing, footwear, jewelry, and similar items; and of course in businesses other than retailing, personal selling is of paramount importance. In most businesses still, "Mr. Whipple" is indispensable.

The small businessperson's challenge may be aptly summarized in the often quoted definition of good salesmanship: "Selling goods that won't come back to customers who will." Improving the quality of personal selling seems to be a never-ending process. Perhaps it could go without saying that the salesperson should be knowledgeable of the merchandise, helpful to the customer, well-groomed and neatly dressed, and above all courteous regardless of any aggravation the customer may provoke. How attentive a salesperson should be will depend on the customer. Some customers prefer to look before being waited on, while others prefer immediate attention from the clerk; the salesperson should make this judgment on an individual basis.

Surveys made by trade associations, schools of retailing, and others dealing with customer likes and dislikes and effective selling have consistently shown the importance of the salesperson and the quality of his or her training. Small business owners can secure help in sales training from representatives of their suppliers and from the local distributive education program if there is one in the community.

Salesmanship consists of transferring a conviction by a seller to a buyer.

—PAUL G. HOFFMAN

To be continuously successful, however, sales promotion must be based on good **customer relations.** Policies with reference to returns and allowances, telephone and mail orders, delivery, check cashing, special orders, complaints and adjustments, layaways (if a retailer), small orders (if a wholesaler or manufacturer), and a variety of other customer services provide an important means of building and maintaining good customer relations. The services demanded or expected of the business firm will be determined by such factors as customers' shopping or buying habits, class of trade, competition, and the nature of the merchandise (delivery for furniture and heavy appliances, for instance).

Other ways to secure good customer relations include the following: courteous treatment of customers in personal selling, over the telephone, or in correspondence; strict adherence to the company's product or merchandise guarantees; service of the product after sale, when required; care and courtesy in handling customer accounts; provision of services desired by customers, such as parking facilities; prompt answering of all inquiries; and scrupulous observance of delivery dates and other promises.

It is sometimes difficult for employees to realize that to the patron or customer, they, the employees, *are* the store, the company, the firm. In the customer's mind, and in reality, the employees are delegated by management to represent the firm. Thus their behavior, representing the company as the customer sees it, can be constructive or destructive to the goals of the business.

Although customer satisfaction is the basis for the continued success of all business, casual observation of a large number of companies will show that this fundamental is often neglected. A large part of goodwill, that intangible asset that may be worth thousands of dollars to some firms, is the result of maintaining favorable customer relations. In big business goodwill usually grows with the company or brand name; in the small business personal attributes of the owner are of relatively greater importance. How to establish good customer relations should be planned as carefully as any other major objective of the business.

An initial step is to define the company's customers and to recognize their likes and dislikes. Modern management provides routines and channels

TRITE BUT TRUE: CUSTOMERS COME FIRST.

Courtesy North American Precis Syndicate, Inc.

through which information regarding customer attitudes is continuously obtained. Some of these will be impersonal, such as **consumer surveys** and periodic analyses of returned goods and of customer complaints. In addition, the business proprietor as well as salespeople and other employees have personal customer contacts that provide a means of judging customer attitudes. Why do we as customers continue to patronize a given plumber, insurance agent, barber, or clothing salesperson? It is because these people know what we like and what we need. They make our buying easier and they give us a feeling of confidence and of security. They have dignified us by setting us apart from the crowd. The keeping of sales records and service records, and their constant analysis and use as guides to the offering of further service to the individual customer, is the secret weapon of many successful small businesses in sales promotion. The satisfied customer of long standing is the most valuable possession any business can have.

> *A big corporation is more or less blamed for being big; it is only big because it gives service. If it doesn't give service, it gets small faster than it grew big.*
>
> —WILLIAM S. KNUDSEN

FRANCHISING AND OTHER METHODS OF DISTRIBUTION

Franchising, as we noted in Chapter 1, is a system for selectively distributing goods or services through outlets *owned by the franchisee.* The franchising or licensing technique is selected over other means of distribution by firms that lack ready capital and other resources to market its own product or service. By licensing prospective entrepreneurs to perform the marketing function for it, the franchising company is able to achieve rapid expansion at relatively low cost, a substantial part of the investment being contributed by the franchise holder.

Another advantage of franchising to the franchisor is that an owner of a business (the franchisee) is likely to be more diligent and to strive harder for success than the hired manager of a company-owned outlet. The franchisor is also assured of faster community acceptance because of the local management-ownership.

Manufacturers of **consumer goods** who have not resorted to franchising usually sell through independent wholesalers and/or retailers, although in recent years an increasing number of them have established their own marketing outlets. Manufacturers of **industrial** (or business) **goods,** on the other hand, often employ the services of **manufacturers' agents** or **selling agents.** Such manufacturers have found that their success in this relationship is dependent on good communications between principal and agents. Although the contacts, talents, and aggressiveness of these agents are important, it is the manufacturer who has the responsibility for keeping them informed about new products, price changes, and changes in policy. In fact, the small factory owner must regard them as the company's sales force, truly members of the marketing organization, even though their services are shared with other manufacturers. From another viewpoint it may be recognized that with numerous principals to represent, the agents or other middlemen will give most attention to those principals who encourage them most and to those products with which they are most familiar.

GOVERNMENT ASSISTANCE PROGRAMS

The Small Business Administration assists small firms that want to obtain government prime contracts and related subcontracts in two important ways. Under its **joint determination,** or **"set aside" program,** certain government procurement orders may be earmarked for competitive bidding exclusively by small firms. Under its **production pool** arrangement, several small firms may merge their facilities to bid on orders too large or complicated for any one of the firms to handle alone; an inventory or register of the capabilities of small manufacturers (and other types of small firms) is maintained for this purpose.

SBA works closely with the largest contract-awarding government agencies, such as the Department of Defense, General Services Administration, and National Aeronautics and Space Agency. Under regulations established by these agencies, prime contractors must give small concerns an adequate opportunity to compete for their subcontracts. SBA maintains close contact with prime contractors and refers qualified small firms to them. In the case of minority enterprises, SBA assists *directly* in the procurement of subcontracts. Under section 8(a) of the Small Business Act the SBA has authority to negotiate procurement contracts from other federal agencies on a noncompetitive basis and to award subcontracts for the performance of these contracts to minority-owned businesses.

PUBLIC RELATIONS—AN INDIRECT FORM OF SALES PROMOTION

Public relations are those attitudes toward the public that are expressed in business behavior. Since every business by its very nature deals with the public, every business has a public relations program, whether or not it knows it.

A business may create **goodwill** or ill will in the community. Some small businesses create a favorable image through their sponsorship of youth projects or Little League baseball teams and the free use of window space for announcements and displays of community projects or events. How the general public regards an enterprise may also depend on the courtesy of its truckdrivers on city streets, the support given to a charity campaign, or whether the refuse of the business is properly disposed of. These and similar matters may determine whether a resident of a community will ever become a customer of the business.

Reports in the local newspaper or on the radio concerning the owners and employees of the business are another way in which the public image of the firm may be enhanced (and its sales possibly increased). Many local broadcasting stations have hometown news periods during which the activities of small business owners and their employees are reported. A company picnic for employees, the promotion of John Doe from salesman to buyer for the store,

Reprinted by permission of King Features Syndicate, Inc.

240

the election of the business proprietor to office in a community organization—these and similar items should be reported by the small business operator to the local paper or radio station. But they must be items of real news value even though the reason for giving them publicity is to keep the name of the business before the public in a favorable light.

SUMMING UP

 Effective advertising and other means of promoting sales depend on a knowledge and understanding of customers' *buying motives.*

 Direct forms of sales promotion include advertising, window and interior displays, special sales events, and personal selling. Franchising and other forms of distribution are also important.

 Sales of a business may be *indirectly* promoted by means of publicity and good public relations and by customer services and satisfactory customer relations.

 Any effort to increase sales, however, is more effective when relations between the business and its customers are favorable. For example, much of the effectiveness of advertising or other special promotions can be destroyed by poor salesmanship or other undesirable employee performance.

KEY WORDS

advertising
advertising budget
advertising media
buyer
buying motives
consumer goods
consumer survey
convenience goods
customer relations
direct action advertising
elements research
expense ratios
fashion cycle
fashion goods
franchising
goodwill

impulse goods
industrial goods
institutional advertising
joint determination program
manufacturers' agent
marginal-income/cost
market
merchandise acceptance curve
production pool
public relations
sales promotion
selling agent
"set aside" program
shopping goods
staple goods
want slips

DISCUSSION QUESTIONS

1. If the standard expense for advertising in your chosen line of business were 4 percent, would you be justified in spending 6 percent during your first year in business? In spending 10 percent? 25 percent? Explain.

2. If a retail store has to dispose quickly of a limited quantity of some item of outer wearing apparel representing good value, what medium (media) would be best to use? Why?

3. Ed advertised several slow-selling items over the radio and in the newspaper. Many people asked about these items, but none bought them. What errors are apparent here? What should Ed do, and why?

EXERCISES AND PROBLEMS

1. The retail store whose sales and merchandise budgets you prepared in exercises 9-6 and 10-4 expects sales next year of approximately $300,000. Its projected advertising expense ratio is 2⅔ percent. Of its total advertising expenditures in the past, an average of 65 percent was spent on local newspaper advertising. The remainder was distributed as follows: local radio and television spot announcements, 20 percent; window displays, 10 percent; direct mail, 4 percent; and outdoor media, 1 percent.

    a. How much does the retailer expect to spend next year for each type of advertising?

    b. How much should the retailer budget each month for each type of advertising expenditure? (Refer to exercise 9-6 for the store's seasonal pattern of sales.)

2. Regardless of the level of advertising expenditures, some small firms fail to make full use of their advertising potential. In the following "lie detector," mark what you believe to be the "true" statements and check your answers against those given at the bottom of p. 244.

    a. Increased sales will not always justify the cost of advertising.

    b. The cost of direct-mail advertising is high relative to the additional sales it generates.

    c. Direct-mail advertising is an effective method for introducing new products.

    d. The value of a particular location for outdoor advertising depends only on the traffic flowing by it.

    e. The advertisement itself, rather than its position in the newspaper, determines the number of people who will read it.

    f. Window displays are especially effective for advertising shopping goods.

g. In an advertisement it is important to stress equally all satisfactions or needs a product fills.

h. The use of photographic illustrations can lend authenticity to an advertisement.

i. The extra cost of color in advertising is always justified because of its high attention value.

j. Many radio and television commercials try to tell too much in the time provided.

k. The number of people reached by an advertisement is usually more important than audience characteristics.

l. For most consumers, psychological satisfactions are more important than physical ones.

3. Cite newspaper advertisements prepared by three different small businesses in your community. Rate them as "good" or "bad" (or "mediocre") and give reasons for your evaluation. Identify and attach the ads to your written report.

4. For some kind of small business of particular interest to you, list four or five unusual ideas to promote sales. (For example, in New York City a gasoline service station encourages repeat business by presenting gifts to customers on their birthdays.) Indicate the kind of business that you think could make effective use of each of the ideas suggested.

CASES IN POINT

While Bernice Brevoort, widow and former schoolteacher, was ill one spring and needed some added income, she remembered an unusual candy her mother used to make. After locating the recipe and experimenting a few times, she packaged some and took it to a friend's gift shop. It became very popular, and eventually she took over a section of the shop for her candy business. Later she arranged to sell it on consignment through other friends in various spots and after a few errors developed seven dependable outlets. Selling on consignment permitted her to replace older stock.

Her candy was high-priced, but was of exceptional quality and came in a variety of appealing flavors. She called her package "Bonny's Bon Bon Assortment" originally, but later put it out in smaller packages of single flavors. In the meantime her manufacturing and sales facilities had required considerable expansion. Yet she was making money at an increasing rate.

One day the president of the largest local department store asked her if she would mind coming to see him; so in a few days she did so. He surprised her by suggesting that her candy was good enough to carry the store name, and that he was willing to place a substantial order under those conditions. This order was several times the monthly sales of any of her outlets, and almost as much as her total sales had been until recently. But the payment offered per pound was considerably lower than she was being paid by her retailers at this point. However, the order would not be on consignment.

About this same time a drugstore chain, locally represented but with its main offices elsewhere, sent a representative to see Bernice. He complimented her on her success, then said he was authorized to place an order for a year's supply at about the same price and amount per month as the department store offer. In this case, however, the "Bonny's Bon Bons" label was to remain; when questioned, the representative indicated that it would be sold in the drugstores, often as a "special," at a price considerably lower than Bernice's other outlets had been getting.

Bernice is now considerably upset and confused, but nevertheless excited. Jokingly, she says, "All I can expect now is to be asked into a conglomerate." Yet it is satisfying and challenging to be so in demand. Her health is now excellent, and she is only approaching middle age, so could operate the business whichever way she decides. However, she has some misgivings about making any move that would cause her to depart from the pattern which has become so successful thus far.

How would you approach a solution to the problem facing Bernice Brevoort? What factors and people are involved in each decision, and what situations might arise, favorable and unfavorable, as a result? Assume prices and amounts based on conversations with stores, if it will help to make the problem clearer.

a) True	e) False	i) False
b) False	f) True	j) True
c) True	g) False	k) False
d) False	h) True	l) True

244

Helen Sparks, retired teacher, active in one of the local church organizations, came to Alliance Appliances, Inc., seeking a used dishwasher for use in one of the interchurch centers. This center was interdenominational and offered teenagers and other groups a place to gather for social affairs. Cooking, serving, and most of the maintenance work was done by teams of volunteers from the different churches, at times assigned to them and for which they were responsible. Equipment was owned jointly by the churches. Mrs. Sparks had recommended trying a dishwashing unit and had authority to buy—but to pay no more than $100 for the appliance, installed. She hoped to find a good used one, and had bought other appliances in this store. She was approached by Jay Russell, a salesman.

Jay Russell's employer, Ray Dawson, was out of town when Mrs. Sparks came in. Jay's first thought was of a large dishwasher that had been taken in trade over a year ago, but which they had been unable to sell because it was so large and because it was a very old model. Yet despite its age it looked good, for it had not been mistreated in use. It would probably serve Mrs. Sparks's purpose. The major problem, if it did break down, would be finding replacement parts. Jay felt that if used with care, it should last two years at least.

As they discussed the group's need, the amount of money available, and the machine, Jay explained that it was of a good brand name, "a good big unit" that had been carefully used, and that it should last "a long time" if used with care. He did not say how old it was, but did give the name of the well-to-do family who had owned it. As Jay was about to close the sale, Mrs. Sparks said, "Well, I think I'll take it, but would you mind waiting until tomorrow, when Mr. Dawson comes back, so that I can talk with him?" Jay agreed to this and Mrs. Sparks left the store.

The next morning, when Mr. Dawson did return, Jay's first remark was, "Well, I think I sold the old Crescent unit at last. Some woman came in, wanted a cheap machine for some church group. Mrs. Sparks, of Maple Street, she said."

Mr. Dawson was greatly dismayed, although he did not say anything to Jay. He was worried about the possible consequences of selling this particular unit to this particular group. Mrs. Sparks, whom he knew rather well, would not return again until after lunch. In the meantime, he must decide how to handle the situation.

What worries might Mr. Dawson have in this situation? What should Mr. Dawson do, and how should he go about any changes he might wish to make?

A few years ago, three young men—one a chemist, one a salesman, and the third an accountant—learned of a formula for a liquid fertilizer having unique characteristics. A 5/10/5 formula (5 percent nitrogen, 10 percent phosphoric acid, 5 percent potash), the fertilizer also contained certain trace elements more or less standard for garden and lawn use. It was considered suitable for greenhouses, for home gardens, and for truck gardens, and found some acceptance among growers of tobacco and tomatoes, who used it in the starting of small plants. It was also valuable for house plants during the winter. It was not difficult to handle, it had no odor, and it went to work at once. The cost of manufacture was negligible, and the chemicals were easily available. At the time, the idea of liquid fertilizer was relatively new, and there was no competition in the field except for the standard, dry, bulky fertilizers and a few dry-chemical fertilizers which could be mixed with water to make a liquid similar to that offered by this group.

The men proceeded to arrange to package the liquid in bottles, jugs, and drums for consumer, farm, and greenhouse use, allowing adequate discounts for dealers, yet making its price (cost) to users about the same as the conventional products. It was advertised as Gro-Green in local newspapers, and the men themselves did the selling, to get the feel of the market as well as to reduce expenses.

Considerable sales resistance was encountered in contacts with both household consumers and with flower shops, hardware stores, and feed stores. It was thought at one time that wholesalers might be employed to take the line, but wholesalers did not accept it readily because it had no record of sales. After a number of hardware merchants, feed-and-seed stores, and nursery outlets had purchased small quantities of the product in the various sizes, second calls were made in an effort to see how the product was moving and to see if any reorders were available. The partners in the manufacturing company found that it had not moved, that either through lack of effort on the part of the salespeople in the places where it was available, or perhaps through an obstacle in the minds of possible users, it was not being readily accepted.

Feeling that the product needed something to go along with it to make a combination deal or to make it appear easier to use from the consumer's standpoint, an arrangement was made with a company making a product called the Hozer, which when attached to a garden hose drew the liquid from an attached bottle. They tried also to sell it as a package with garden seeds, but this called for an investment in seeds or practically giving the product away to the seed company.

An effort toward cooperative advertising was made, whereby the Gro-Green Company would pay merchants 50 percent of local newspaper advertising costs up to a maximum of 10 percent of their orders. Since most orders were in two- and three-dozen lots of various sizes, seldom amounting to more than $50, the advertising allowance was seldom more than $5. An effort to acquaint the public with the product was made by taking a booth at the local Home and Garden Show, which occurred in the early spring in a larger city nearby. This got some reaction, but it was not lasting. These men also considered sale or licensing of the formula to some larger concern under a better-known name. Yet the product could easily be duplicated through analysis.

After almost two years of effort and expense, these young men threw in the towel and closed out their business. Less than a year later, a major manufacturer of garden supplies put a liquid fertilizer on the market, and after a slow start it succeeded. Currently there are several brands on the market, and makers of farm and garden equipment are doing well in marketing products for the application of liquid fertilizers of various types, some in combination with weed killers or insecticides.

Why did this enterprise fail? List basic reasons and explain each briefly.

The Pot Plant is a manufacturer of plastic pottery that distributes its products in the Los Angeles area. The company was originally formed in 1972 by Ramon Camacho and Luis Torres as partners. Mr. Camacho, a man of 40, started manufacturing decorative clay pots in Mexico in 1965. Mr. Torres is no longer with the firm and has been replaced as a partner by Jose Castillo.

The current line consists of thirty-four different sizes and colors of pots ranging from 4 inches to 16 inches in height. The finish on the pots is such that they are competitive with Mexican-made clay pots that may be purchased locally or across the border. The pots are sold wholesale to local nurseries, dime stores, Navy exchanges, and gift shops at prices ranging from $1.50 to $10 per pot. Retailers double these prices.

Mr. Camacho, the senior partner, and Mr. Castillo do the majority of selling, which consists of calling on local shops. Their time is limited since Mr. Camacho also supervises the manufacturing and Mr. Castillo handles the purchasing of materials. In addition to a labor force that varies from 10 to 15 semi-skilled employees, they also have an office manager, Mrs. del Rio, who handles all bookkeeping, secretarial work, and telephone order taking.

The manufacturing process requires the use of expensive aluminum and latex molds and is highly efficient. Because of the fire hazard involved in the use of the resins, they were forced to close their original plant in October 1974. They reopened in January 1975 in a new location with facilities that were acceptable to the local fire department and to OSHA. In order to finance this move, they received a $40,000 SBA-guaranteed loan from a local bank.

The current facility is used at only 60 percent of capacity. The move resulted in losing most of their workers, so new ones had to be hired and trained. Currently the work force is efficient, although low productivity at the beginning of the year did increase costs. Mr. Camacho feels that their current sales are about 90 percent of what they need to reach their break-even point at year end.

Since their move, the company's product has become well-accepted locally, and local branches of national retail stores are beginning to carry their line. Several managers of these branches have indicated to the partners that their companies might be interested in carrying Pot Plant's line on a national basis.

The company does no advertising and the only promotional expense is an attractive one-page color display of their line accompanied by the price list. These two pages are given to retailers when Mr. Camacho or Mr. Castillo calls. More and more orders are being taken over the telephone from retailers who have seen the products on display.

The partners realize that the company has great potential for growth; they both realize also that if they are to expand they must give careful thought to their entire marketing approach. In effect, they are now at a major decision point in the company's life. They must think about distribution channels, national and local, about advertising policies and media, and about salespersons and compensation plans; and they must also consider the effect of their decisions on their financial and production resources.

Outline a basic marketing approach and justify it in terms of costs and probable results.

Exporting

CHAPTER SIXTEEN *After reading this chapter you will have a greater appreciation for the export market as a source of business opportunities. However, because exporting activities cross national, political, and cultural borders they present problems not found in domestic marketing. These also will be examined, as will the strategies and methods available or suggested for solving them.*

Increasingly, the marketplace is becoming worldwide. One obvious reason for this is the rapid development of instantaneous communications. An even more important reason is the breakdown in national **tariff** barriers and the development of multinational trading areas, such as the European Common Market and the Latin American Free Trade Zone. These developments are of utmost importance to small business firms engaged in either importing or exporting activities; our focus in this chapter, however, is on **exports** and the export environment.[1]

A business enterprise engaged in exporting is likely to be a manufacturer or other producer, or a technical or professional service firm. The Bureau of International Commerce estimates that in the United States three out of five companies currently engaged in export trade have fewer than 100 employees. Thus it is seen that exporting is not the exclusive territory or turf of large corporations, as it is often assumed to be; *any* company, regardless of size, with a product or service that will appeal to some segment of the population abroad can compete successfully in the huge and expanding international market.[2]

In terms of the value of exports the Bureau of International Commerce estimates further that the small business share of the U.S. total falls somewhere between five and ten percent. This, however, is considerably less than the comparable shares accruing to small Japanese and West European exporters. In Japan, for example, small firms account for approximately 40 percent of that nation's exports. The question arises: Why isn't the small business community in the U.S. getting a bigger piece of the action? According to a survey by the National Federation of Independent Business, the main reason is lack of knowledge of potential overseas markets and the procedures involved in doing business abroad. The author of this book suggests an additional reason: the

[1] Importing is discussed on pp. 114–15.
[2] It is estimated that 95 percent of the world's population and two-thirds of its purchasing power are outside the U.S.

More exports needed to balance foreign oil purchases.

Courtesy of Center for Industrial Research and Service, Iowa State University.

more dominant (and effective) role of government in foreign trade in most other industrialized countries.

In recent years the United States has been suffering chronic **balance-of-payments** difficulties. The long-range implications and adverse effects on our way of life if severe trade deficits continue cannot be overly stressed. Yet if there is to be a large increase in U.S. exports to improve the balance-of-payments, it is going to have to come from *small* companies, for large firms have been enthusiastically exporting for years. Because of its overall importance in the U.S. economy in terms of employment and **gross national product** (as noted in the introductory chapter), increasing small business exports can make positive contributions to some of the nation's most important economic problems by decreasing unemployment, strengthening and stabilizing the dollar, and decreasing imported inflation.

DISTRIBUTION CHANNELS

Several avenues of distribution are available to the small business that wishes to sell its product(s) overseas. The business may (1) set up its own export department, including foreign distributorships; (2) license (franchise) the manufacture of its product to a foreign producer; (3) employ **export agents** or **commission houses;** or (4) sell to **export firms.**

The latter two methods of distribution are usually the simplest and most feasible for most small firms. *Export agencies* assume responsibility for proper packaging, insurance, marking, and meeting all legal requirements; arranging transportation and credit; billing; and collecting payments on invoices. *Export firms*, on the other hand, buy outright the products of domestic producers and then resell them in foreign markets; thus they assume all the risks as well as the headaches associated with **foreign trade.**

MERCHANDISING TO FOREIGN MARKETS

Regardless of the method of distribution, the small U.S. exporter needs to understand the subtleties of merchandising to foreign markets. As used here, merchandising refers to adapting the individual products to each market, primarily with regard to their functional design.

While it would be an endless task to detail all features about every product for all countries, a few suggestions as to what to investigate are in order. For mechanical and electrical goods, the sources and kinds of power available are important: American 110-volt electrical goods are unsuited to countries where 220-volt current is standard. Electrically powered products are obviously unsuited to regions where electric current is not available, or where it is too expensive or unreliable. Similarly, gasoline-powered products are unsuited in areas where gasoline is difficult to obtain or too expensive.

Availability of repair and maintenance service as well as of repair parts and supplies is important for most mechanical products. If proper installation and instructions on use and care are relevant, they should be provided. In many countries potential customers may not be able to read or understand even simple printed instructions. Tools required for repair and maintenance may not be available. What we take for granted in industrialized countries may be nonexistent elsewhere. Even many industralized countries have not yet adopted international standards for such common necessities as bolts, nuts, and screws.

The personal characteristics of the foreign user or consumer of the product may also be important. Does this individual have the strength, intelligence, or adaptability to use the product? Will normal hazards be recognized or cautions observed? Will beliefs or even prejudices prevent or hamper proper use? Wide differences in beliefs, superstitions, and prejudices exist in many parts of the world. Although these may at times seem silly to an exporter, and actually run counter to well-founded scientific knowledge, they cannot safely be disregarded. Similar conditions still exist in many technically advanced nations, not excluding the United States.

For satisfactory consumer use certain products depend on local factors such as character of the water supply, climate, and temperature. At one time European furniture was found to be unable to survive overheated stuffy American apartments. Pumps and other products may function efficiently with soft water, but poorly with hard water, and hardly at all with sea or heavily saline water. Additional conditions that may hamper a product's proper functioning include humidity, sand, dust or other air pollution, extreme temperatures, terrain, and many others. Relevant ones for each product should be investigated.

GOVERNMENT ASSISTANCE PROGRAMS

For those small manufacturers interested in exporting their products, the federal government provides assistance in numerous ways, primarily by means of (1) various publications and programs relating to international marketing, (2) the export financing programs of the Export-Import Bank, and (3) cooperation with private insurers on offering **credit insurance** to exporters.

Foreign Trade Publications

Among the periodicals and other publications of the federal government that are related to international marketing is the monthly *Foreign Trade Report* prepared by the Bureau of the Census. This report provides statistics on a country-by-country basis on the amounts and kinds of goods and services purchased from American firms. Other publications available from the Bureau of International Commerce include:

1. *Commerce America*—a biweekly devoted in part to developments in world trade, changes in trade regulations, and trade opportunities
2. *Overseas Business Reports* (by country)—an annual analysis of trade regulations in over one hundred countries (as well as information about starting businesses in those countries)
3. *Trade Lists* (by country)—a list of names and addresses of principal manufacturers, wholesalers, and distributors' agents, by commodity groups
4. *World Traders Data Report*—a report of credit information on specific foreign customers
5. Series of pamphlets on preparing shipments to specific countries, summarizing import regulations, rules for labeling and marking, and customs procedures

Also available from the Bureau of International Commerce for those small businesses wishing to enter world markets for the first time is an excellent handbook, *A Basic Guide to Exporting.*

Foreign Trade Programs

The federal government, through the Bureau of International Commerce, assists the small exporter in a number of other ways by:

1. Maintaining the *Foreign Traders Index,* an automated file of information on American firms that are active in, or interested in, international trade (or investment); commercial officers in American embassies and consulates refer to this index when answering inquiries from prospective foreign purchasers, and small firms seeking to find overseas buyers for their products or services should request to be registered in this index

2. Providing an *Agent/Distributor Service* to assist American firms in finding overseas agents to handle their products in a specific country

3. Providing an *Export Mailing List Service* for American firms that already have agents abroad; State Department commercial officers refer to these mailing lists to find local sources of American products for interested overseas customers

4. Organizing or sponsoring overseas **trade missions** and **trade fairs**

5. Maintaining permanent **trade centers** in Beirut, Frankfurt, London, Mexico City, Milan, Moscow, Osaka, Paris, Seoul, Singapore, Sydney, Stockholm, Taipei, Tokyo, Vienna, Warsaw, and other central marketing areas where the sales potential for American products or services is high

6. Sponsoring a **piggyback service** for those firms desiring to export on a cooperative basis

The Bureau of International Commerce has also signed an agreement of cooperation with the Small Business Administration in support of foreign trade for smaller businesses, by which the SBA makes and guarantees short-term (working capital) loans to cover such costs as the following:

1. Professional foreign marketing advice and services

2. Foreign business travel

3. Ocean freight and insurance of merchandise shipped abroad

4. Shopping foreign markets

5. Participating in U.S. trade center shows

6. Exhibiting at international trade fairs

7. Foreign advertising and other promotional materials

The Export-Import Bank

The Export-Import Bank of the United States, familiarly known as *Eximbank,* is actively engaged in financing American foreign trade. Recognizing that credit availability is as important a competitive tool as price, quality, or service, Eximbank is determined that no American exporter will lose a sale for lack of credit, if the sale is sound. If credit facilities for American exporters are at least as good as those made available to exporters in other countries by their governments, then they are free to compete in world markets solely on the basis of their products, their prices, their salesmanship, and their services. To this end Eximbank offers a number of export financing programs, including:

1. Making **direct** or **participation loans** to borrowers outside the United States for purchases of American goods and services, or guaranteeing loans made to the purchasers of American goods and services by U.S. and foreign banks

2. Lending to U.S. commercial banks up to 100 percent of the bank's export-debt obligations; in addition to such loans, Eximbank may purchase (discount), on a case-by-case basis, the underlying export-debt obligation

3. Guaranteeing repayment of export-debt obligations acquired by U.S. banking institutions from American exporters. (It is becoming increasingly essential for American exporters to grant appropriate credit terms on their sales in world markets in order to meet the financing offered by their foreign competitors; thus the purpose of this program is to encourage and assist greater participation by commercial banks in the support of American exporters who must provide credit terms on their sales.)[3]

Export Credit Insurance

Eximbank also cooperates with the Foreign Credit Insurance Association in offering export credit insurance to American exporters. The Foreign Credit Insurance Association (FCIA) is a consortium of fifty stock and mutual insurance companies. Backed by the resources and experience of its member companies, as well as the resources of Eximbank, FCIA endeavors to match competitive terms quoted by foreign suppliers who have long operated under their government-supported insurance and financing programs. Not only is a policyholder insured against loss resulting from failure of its foreign customers to pay their bills for commercial or political reasons, but also the policyholder is normally able to arrange favorable financing of export receivables because of the security and collateral afforded by the insurance.

Several types of FCIA credit insurance policies are available to exporters, including a "Small Business Policy." For businesses that are new to export trade and for exporters having a modest sales volume, this policy provides comprehensive coverage up to 90 percent for short- and medium-term sales. Eligibility is limited to businesses with average annual export sales over the preceding three years of not more than $200,000. The policy may remain in force for a period not to exceed two years or until the exporter has insured $500,000 aggregate contract value of exports, whichever occurs first. A deductible clause may be required, and the exporter may request the FCIA in-

[3] For detailed information concerning any of these programs and how to apply for loans and financial guarantees, write to Export-Import Bank of the U.S., 811 Vermont Ave. N.W., Washington, D.C. 20571.

surer to obtain data to show the creditworthiness of buyers in lieu of obtaining this information from the exporter's own sources.[4]

RECOMMENDATIONS FOR CHANGES IN GOVERNMENT POLICY

The above programs notwithstanding, governments in most other countries of the world play a more dominant role in foreign trade than does the United States. To help expand the market for the products and services of American small businesses, the following changes in U.S. government policy seem worthy of consideration.

A pool of funds should be established to support small, new-to-market companies that want to attend trade shows or fairs. U.S. firms that participate in international trade shows are aware of the difference in financial support other nations give their participants. Some pay for all expenses of their participating companies (equipment, transportation, travel/living expenses of sales representatives, and show participation fees) plus an incentive paid directly to the company. U.S. firms, in contrast, must pay all their own costs except the return freight on unsold products. Most small businesses in this country find these costs too high to allow them to participate in these shows, and are envious (if not resentful) of the export sales encouragement given to their foreign competitors by their governments.

A cooperative marketing program should be created for manufacturers and service industries, similar to the agricultural commodities promotion programs established through Public Law 480. Industry associations and state development organizations should be able to establish nonprofit international market development subsidiaries with matching funds from the Department of Commerce. In emulation of the highly successful efforts on behalf of agricultural exporters, these subsidiaries would use these funds to establish offices in various countries to supply marketing assistance to small companies.

METRIC CONVERSION

When President Ford signed the Metric Conversion Act in December 1975, for the first time the United States established a national policy to encourage conversion to the **metric system** of weights and measures. This legislation, however, did not make conversion to the metric system compulsory; it merely established a Metric Board to coordinate those industries that choose to convert.

---

[4] For premium rates and for further information concerning small business export credit insurance, write to the FCIA home office, One World Trade Center, New York, N.Y. 10048; or to one of its regional offices located in Atlanta, Chicago, Cleveland, Houston, Los Angeles, Milwaukee, San Francisco, and Washington, D.C.

Some businesspersons and groups maintain that Congress should mandate full conversion to the metric system, pointing out that the U.S. has been losing sales in nations where there is a clear choice between metric and nonmetric equipment. It has been estimated, for example, that the United States could earn an additional $15 billion a year in export business if its products were made to metric standards. The United States is the only major country in the world that has not yet fully converted to the metric system.

There is no doubt, in the opinion of many people, that worldwide standards are desirable. At present there is confusion in foreign trade with the United States still on the English system of weights and measures and most of its foreign customers or suppliers on the metric system.[5] There is also, for the American exporter, the expense of duplicating products for metric markets.

SUMMING UP

One way a small business can promote its sales is to expand the market for its products or services to the rest of the world. At the present time, increasing exports by small businesses can make positive contributions to some of the nation's most pressing economic problems by decreasing unemployment, strengthening and stabilizing the dollar, and decreasing imported inflation.

The financing programs of the U.S. Export-Import Bank and the publications and programs of the federally-sponsored Bureau of International Commerce are particularly helpful to those small business owners and managers who wish to export their products and services. Export credit insurance is also readily available under certain conditions.

In addition to reviewing current government assistance programs in foreign trade, the text suggests how export trade by smaller businesses in the U.S. can be effectively increased by certain changes in government policy, such as trade show subsidies, and cooperative marketing programs for manufacturers and service industries similar to those already existing in the agricultural sector.

Full conversion to the metric system of weights and measures is also important, in the opinion of many people, if the United States is to regain a favorable **balance-of-trade** in world markets.

---

[5] The common term, *English* system, is now a misnomer inasmuch as the British as well as the Canadians have adopted the metric system; a more appropriate term would be the *American* system.

balance-of-payments
balance-of-trade
commission houses
credit insurance
direct loans
export agents
export firms
exports
foreign trade

gross national product
metric system
participation loans
piggyback service
tariff
trade centers
trade fairs
trade missions

**DISCUSSION
QUESTIONS**

1. Do you agree or disagree with the following reasons commonly given by some small companies for *not* exporting their products or services? Comment fully.

a. A firm must be large to export successfully.

b. Payment by foreign buyers is uncertain.

c. U.S. products and services are unsuitable for foreign markets.

d. American-made products are too expensive for foreign markets.

e. Export start-up costs are too high.

f. Unfamiliarity with foreign exchange leads to financial difficulties.

g. Language barriers hinder export marketing operations.

2. Recently an anti-metric group, Americans for Customary Weights and Measures, has sprung up in the United States. Do you believe that the American public should be coerced to start counting in meters? What valid reasons can you think of for *not* mandating conversion to the metric system?

Part Five

MANAGING
THE FIRM'S FINANCES

One of the most important functional areas of small business management is managing the firm's finances. This area presents a problem for many small businesses, however, because the managerial strengths of the owners usually lie in the areas of production and marketing rather than in paperwork and financial details. Their ventures often fail because they lack the basic financial management skills needed to guide the business. These skills include determining the need for and ability to raise capital; forecasting, directing, and controlling the business's cash flows; planning and analyzing the business's financial condition and direction; and making wise investment decisions. Developing these skills is important to the small business owner who manages his or her own business. It is to this cause that this section of the book is directed. By studying the following seven chapters you will learn the basics of financial management.

Raising Capital

CHAPTER SEVENTEEN *It is trite but true that "it takes money to make money." None of the production and marketing activities described in the nine preceding chapters can be performed without adequate financing. The purpose of this chapter is to familiarize you with the types of financing available and their sources.*

Money, either in hand or in the form of **credit,** is the key to a profitable enterprise. Although there is no one best way to finance a business under all conditions, great care should be exercised in determining the amount of money needed to operate the business effectively, the ways in which the **capital** will be used, and the sources from which the funds are to be secured.

ESTIMATING CAPITAL NEEDS

It is important that the entrepreneur be realistic and not under- or overestimate his or her capital requirements. If too much capital is raised, capital costs will be unnecessarily high; if too little is raised, the business may be short of funds at a time when it is difficult to raise more on favorable terms. Usually, however, a business requires *more* money than the entrepreneur expects because of unexpected expenses that almost always crop up.

It is also wise to anticipate the business's needs and arrange for the funds in advance, rather than wait until a period of cash stringency occurs. If a realistic forecast, *including an allowance for contingencies,* indicates an amount greater than that needed immediately, the entrepreneur can frequently obtain a bank **line of credit** against which he or she can draw.

If the small business owner/manager demonstrates that the funds sought n be used profitably at reasonable risk, he or she can usually raise the money needed. Whether the money is used for starting a new business, expanding an existing one, or just making the periodic outlays that are required of all active businesses, the entrepreneur should be able to answer the following questions:

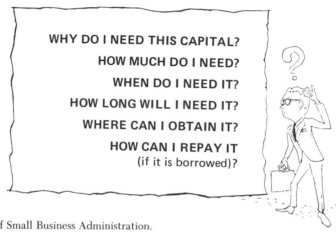

WHY DO I NEED THIS CAPITAL?

HOW MUCH DO I NEED?

WHEN DO I NEED IT?

HOW LONG WILL I NEED IT?

WHERE CAN I OBTAIN IT?

HOW CAN I REPAY IT
(if it is borrowed)?

Courtesy of Small Business Administration.

KINDS OF CAPITAL

In raising funds to launch a new business or to keep an established one going, however, it is not merely the *amount* of money required that is important but the *kind* of money as well.

There are two basic kinds of capital. Deciding on the type to use depends on the uses to which the capital is put and on the liquidity requirements of the firm's assets. Assets that will be retained for a long time, such as land and buildings, machinery, furniture and fixtures, and other equipment, are classed as **fixed capital. Working,** or **circulating, capital,** on the other hand, includes the firm's cash reserves and all assets that can be readily converted into cash, such as inventories and accounts receivable. Working capital is used to buy materials or merchandise and to pay off current obligations such as rent and wages.

The relative requirements of fixed and working capital will vary. The ratio of working capital to total assets of the retail store, for example, will differ from that of the service business, and that of a factory will be different still.

Capital can also be classified according to the sources from which it is obtained. **Equity capital** is that invested in the business with no legal obligation to return the principal, or to pay interest on it, to another party. It is owner-ship capital, although in the small family-sponsored enterprise the ownership aspect is often relinquished or donated by the contributor (frequently a parent or close relative of the proprietor).

On the other hand, **borrowed capital,** often called **debt capital,** implies the obligation to return the principal together with some interest or other com-pensation for the use of the funds. In the small business this distinction be-tween equity and borrowed capital is often blurred. Investigators have found that loans made to entrepreneurs by relatives or close friends sometimes re-semble investment in the enterprise; no definite time for repayment is set, and interest charges are deferred until some indefinite future date when the busi-ness can afford such payments. In most cases, however, funds borrowed to supplement owner' equity capital, even when obtained from relatives and friends, are secured with the intention that both principal and interest will eventually be repaid.

Debt and equity funds, of course, may be used to finance either fixed or current assets; thus the above classifications are not mutually exclusive. In the case of debt capital, the use to which the borrowed money is put should pro-vide the means with which to repay it. Thus, **short-term loans** are generally repaid from the liquidation of current assets, and **long-term loans** are usually repaid from the firm's earnings.

> *Teacher to boy:* "I admire your reasoning, David, but 'It takes money to make money' is not the golden rule."
>
> —JANIK
> *The Wall Street Journal*

DEBT VS. EQUITY CAPITAL

A major decision faced by the entrepreneur is whether the firm should be fi-nanced through debt capital or equity capital. Is it better to seek **loans** from private or government agencies, or to share the ownership and profits with those who can provide the necessary capital?

Since equity capital does not have to be repaid, it is much safer than debt for a new or small company. Nor does it entail fixed interest charges. However, the tendency in recent years is toward debt rather than equity financing. To those small business owners who can obtain capital on reasonable terms within approved ratios to their own equity, this situation may have advantages. They can deduct interest paid as a valid business expense in computing their tax lia-bilities, enlarge the funds under their control, retain control over their enter-prises, and take advantage of conditions causing people to be more willing to lend rather than to invest savings.

When the earnings made possible by borrowed funds exceed the cost of the debt, the firm has high **financial** *leverage* and the use of debt capital is more attractive to the entrepreneur. Assume, for example, that the profit potential of an additional $10,000 invested in the business is $2,000 per year. By investing this entire amount himself (herself), the entrepreneur would thus obtain a 20 percent return on his (her) investment. If, on the other hand, only half this amount was invested and the rest borrowed at 8 percent, the $400 tax-deductible interest expense would reduce the entrepreneur's profit by a like amount; however, since the entrepreneur invested only $5,000, the yield on this investment would be 32 percent ($1,600/$5,000). Similarly, by investing only $2,500 of his or her own money, and borrowing the difference of $7,500 at the same rate of interest, the entrepreneur's yield on investment would be further increased to 56 percent ($1,400/$2,500). If the firm is a taxable entity or corporation, leverage in each of these instances would be even higher because of the effective double tax on the entrepreneur's dividend income.[1]

Financial leverage is further enhanced in times of inflation, which makes possible the repayment of debt capital with depreciated dollars. It should be noted, however, that leverage works in reverse during times of deflation, or when earnings fall below the cost of borrowed capital.

Entrepreneurs should be reminded, also, that debt capital (unlike equity capital) must be repaid. If they cannot pay their debts, they may be forced to yield temporary control of the business to creditors or even to liquidate the venture through bankruptcy proceedings.

Not only is there a greater risk of failure through bankruptcy but when the entrepreneurs' equity is too "thin," they will find it increasingly difficult to borrow the additional funds needed in times of growth and expansion; they may have reached their borrowing limit. Creditors are naturally concerned about the entrepreneur's investment of his or her own money in the business; they feel that the entrepreneur should stand to lose something, too, if things go wrong, Many authorities feel that the owner's equity in the assets of the business should be no less than 25 percent, and in some types of business even more. Where the business is incorporated, the Internal Revenue Service has been successful in challenging the taxpayer's equity ratio only in cases when it was less than one-third of the firm's total capital. The latter is also the guideline used by the Small Business Administration in its business loan program, though it has relaxed this standard on occasion. There are generally accepted guides in each line of business as to the proper ratio of long- and short-term loans to owner equity. Small business owners may secure advice on the standard ratios for their business from their banker, accountant, or trade association. In general, however, it would appear that the desired equity of the owner(s) in the business will vary from one-fourth to two-thirds of the firm's total capital investment.

---

[1] The double-tax disadvantage is discussed in Chapter 25, p. 413.

SOURCES OF FUNDS

Small business owners have a number of sources they can tap for funds. The sources from which they obtain funds will depend to a large extent on the manner in which they intend to use the funds.

The business is generally faced with three types of financial need—initial capital, working capital once the firm is in operation, and expansion capital. Initial capital includes that necessary to get the business started and enough to keep it going until returns from operations provide sufficient funds to meet normal recurring expenses. That is, initial capital includes the beginning operating or working capital. As the volume of business increases, as it ordinarily does during the early months of operation, the amount of working capital needed tends to increase until the normal level of operations is reached. Whether this additional capital is provided for initially, or is obtained from profits or from other sources after the business has been operating depends on the conditions in each enterprise.

Other than the capital that may be freed or conserved through more adroit management of a going concern, additional funds may be obtained from the following sources:

1. The owner and his or her associates, including family and friends, who may or may not become partners or shareholders in the venture

2. Partners and shareholders of a corporation

3. Representatives of banks or other established lending institutions whose business includes making loans to business organizations

4. The Small Business Administration financial assistance program

5. SBA-licensed small business investment companies

6. Members of the trade, including suppliers of materials such as manufacturers and wholesalers; and, in some instances, customers who prepay their contracts

7. Other businesses, local capitalists, **sales finance companies, factors,** and miscellaneous other sources

Borrowing from Friends and Relatives

It is generally necessary when getting started in business for individuals to invest their own savings. Though it is considered poor business practice to do so, it may also be necessary to borrow from friends and relatives in many cases. Yet business and family or social relationships should not be mixed if the most desirable results are to be obtained.

Securing funds from friends and relatives, whether for a new enterprise or an existing one, builds a highly personal financial relationship that conflicts

Courtesy of Small Business Administration.

with both independence and business. The business owners whose backing requires them to weigh personal considerations constantly are in weak positions when they make decisions for the business itself. Furthermore, these financial associates frequently feel impelled to assert their proprietary interests by offering advice or even by insisting that certain business actions be taken, and their recommendations may not be in harmony with the wishes and objectives of the proprietor.

A *business* loan should be a *business* transaction, not a favor. One's friends and relatives may be more easily convinced of the possibilities involved in investing, but they are seldom in a position to pass sound business judgment.

Forming a Small Business Corporation

The entrepreneur can make his or her business more attractive to investors by qualifying as a **small business corporation,** as defined in Section 1244 of the Internal Revenue Code. This section of the code offers a large tax inducement to investors in a small business. In computing income tax liability, the law permits losses from investments in 1244 stock to be deducted from *ordinary* income, while gains are treated at the capital gains rate. For example, individuals in the 50 percent income tax bracket who invest in **Section 1244 stock** limit their *maximum* loss to 50 percent of their investment after taxes; on the other hand, since the profits earned by the company are taxed as capital gains, these investors will retain 80 percent of their share of the profits after taxes.

As defined in the code, a 1244 company is a corporation with less than $1,000,000 in capital and paid-in surplus. The stated purpose of Section 1244 is to "encourage the flow of new funds into small business."

266

Commercial Banks and Other Lending Institutions

Commercial banks are a primary source of funds for small business, and for debt rather than equity capital. Some banks have personal loan departments and many more make small loans to individuals in a manner similar to business loans. Actually, a great many small loans made to individuals as personal loans are used for small business financing. Some banks have established small business loan departments and others delegate the financing of small enterprises to particular officers.

An undetermined, but probably substantial, amount of **semiterm loans** made by banks on a sixty- to ninety-day basis are subject to virtually continuous renewal under favorable circumstances. As a business proves to be successful both the amount and duration of such loans tend to increase.

Although short-term loans for less than a year predominate, many banks make long-term loans ranging from one to ten years with an average maturity of about five years. About four-fifths of the latter term loans are **collateral loans,** that is, they are secured by assets having a value well in excess of the amount of the loan.

Term loans that are unsecured are called **character loans.** Although they tend to be for shorter periods and smaller amounts than collateral loans, so much depends on the individual borrower that exceptions to this generalization are easy to find. A person with proved managerial ability, an excellent reputation, and a good business proposition may receive a character loan for several thousand dollars on a long-term favorable-interest basis in the same bank where another, less well-known individual must put up collateral worth $500 to secure a short-term loan of $200 at the bank's maximum rate of interest.

Loan prerequisites. The following standards are considered important by bankers and other lenders when making loans to small business persons:

LOAN PREREQUISITES

1. **YOUR PERSONAL AND BUSINESS REPUTATION**

2. **ADEQUATE RECORDS**

3. **PRODUCTIVE NATURE OF THE LOAN**

4. **SUITABLE SECURITY**

Courtesy of Small Business Administration.

In making decisions regarding loan applications, the banker needs reliable facts. Usually the balance sheet and profit-and-loss statement will be requested for a going concern or, in the case of a new venture, a prospectus stating estimated sales, expenses, and anticipated profits and cash flows. The use to which funds obtained will be put is a major consideration.

Since collateral is so often required to obtain bank loans, the small businessperson should understand the nature of assets considered to be good collateral. These are usually **quick assets** or property that can be converted readily into its money value. Other things that the entrepreneur often pays good money for may be poor collateral for bank loans. Among these would be items such as the following:

1. Specially made machines, equipment, fixtures, or built-in construction not salable to others in the same or similar trades—examples: canning, wrapping, labeling, or processing machines; store or restaurant fixtures built to fit particular spaces; wall decorations and floor designs

2. Stationery, signs, wrapping paper, souvenirs, or other items carrying the name of the concern for which they were purchased and therefore salable to others at only a fraction of their cost, if at all

3. Style merchandise or other goods likely to become outmoded; supplies of materials used in a declining industry or to meet a passing need—examples: cast-iron items that are being replaced by aluminum, and kerosene lamps and equipment.

4. Partly finished products, such as mechanical parts and materials intended for particular assemblies, and even completed assemblies for which a market has ceased to exist—examples: metal parts made to specifications for one buyer.

The loan contract. The loan contract sets forth the basic conditions of the loan and includes all provisions that the lender feels are necessary to ensure payment:

1. Length of loan period and schedule for repaying in installments

2. Interest and other charges

3. Provision that the entire balance of the loan be made due and payable immediately if any default is made in repayment

4. Any warranties that may be necessary

5. Requirements to maintain working capital at the proper level

6. Restrictions on other borrowing during the life of the loan

7. Description of assets, if any, pledged to secure the loan, and the terms under which they are pledged

8. Restrictions on the payment of salaries and dividends or distribution of earnings during the life of the loan

The SBA Financial Assistance Program

Under Section 7(a) of the Small Business Act of 1953, as amended, SBA is empowered

> to make loans to enable small-business concerns to finance plant construction, conversion, or expansion, including the acquisition of land, . . . equipment, facilities, machinery, supplies, or materials; or to supply such concerns with working capital to be used in the manufacture of articles, equipment, supplies, or materials for war, defense, or civilian production or as may be necessary to insure a well-balanced national economy.

The SBA has legislative authority to make loans *directly* or to *participate* in a loan with a private lending institution up to a maximum of $500,000 in any one situation. At times, however, the agency places a lower limit on its portion of the loan in order to conserve its funds. In any case, in a **participation loan,** the bank is expected to provide at least 25 percent of the loan.

The SBA may also *guarantee* bank loans up to 90 percent or $500,000 of the loan, whichever is less. The bulk of SBA's financing of small business (approximately 90 percent of it) is of this type.

However, the Small Business Administration is prohibited under the act from making any of the above types of business loans unless private financing is not available on reasonable terms. On any share of an immediate participation loan, or on a **guarantee loan,** the bank's interest rate may not exceed a maximum ceiling set by SBA from time to time. The interest rate charged by SBA on its direct loans is set by Congress and also changes from time to time but is considerably lower—approximately only two-thirds as high as the bank's ceiling. Loans made to finance business start-ups or business expansion have a maximum term of ten years, except when construction of facilities is involved; in the latter case, the maximum term of the loan is twenty years.

In addition to business loans, the SBA makes certain types of **disaster loans,** unrestricted in amount, for as long as thirty years. Under one type of lending program the SBA helps small businesses restore or replace property damaged by floods, hurricanes, earthquakes, or other natural disasters. Under a second type of lending program these businesses would also be helped to overcome economic injuries suffered as a result of such disasters. SBA loans of the latter type are for the purposes of stocking normal inventories and paying financial obligations which the small business owner would have been able to meet had he or she not lost revenue because of the disaster. To receive either type of loan the firm must be located in an area officially declared as a disaster area by the President or the Secretary of Agriculture. The damage or injury must also have been substantial. Both physical disaster and **economic injury loans** may be made by SBA entirely on its own, or in participation with a bank or other lending institution.

Another type of economic injury loan is designed to assist the small firm

269

that is forced to relocate because of federally aided urban renewal and high-way construction programs. Loans of this type may also be made by SBA directly or jointly.

The maximum rate of interest on an SBA disaster loan or on its share of a joint loan is set annually by statutory formula. No specific figure is set as the maximum rate of interest on the bank's share of such loans, but it must be within reasonable limits.

Since 1964 the SBA has been making **economic opportunity loans,** in addition to regular business loans and disaster loans. The purpose of these loans is to help low-income people who have the potential to successfully operate a business but who cannot qualify for SBA's regular business loans. Such persons can borrow up to $150,000 for up to ten years (fifteen years, if construction of facilities is involved). The interest rate is the same as for regular business loans. However, in considering economic opportunity (EO) loans, SBA relaxes traditional credit standards and places greater emphasis on the character and ability of the individual. In late 1972 the benefits of the SBA economic opportunity loan program were extended to honorably discharged veterans of the Vietnam War.

The SBA also helps small business concerns *indirectly* in the acquisition of land, construction, conversion or expansion of buildings, and the purchase of machinery and equipment through loans to state and local development companies. These development companies are formed for the express purpose of promoting and assisting the growth and development of small businesses in the state or local area by supplying them with needed long-term loans and equity capital.

In August 1971 a new program was launched to provide SBA-guaranteed lines of credit to small building contractors. The line of credit is available at any bank that has entered into an agreement with SBA to participate in the program. The amount of the line of credit cannot exceed a reasonable estimate of the contractors' current cash requirements needed to finance the work that they have the capacity to perform and which they can reasonably be expected to generate under firm contracts. Guarantees are limited to $500,000 or 90 percent of the line of credit, whichever is less. The line of credit is in force for one year, but sixty days before it is due to expire it is reviewed for possible extension for another year. This program removes a major handicap to small building contractors, since they often have difficulty in obtaining government and other contracts because of inadequate financing for the early part of the work. It also encourages large building contractors to subcontract a larger share of their work to small firms.

Small Business Investment Companies

Another way in which the Small Business Administration assists in the financing of small business is through the licensing and regulation of privately owned **small business investment companies,** or SBICs as they are commonly called, which was made possible by the Small Business Investment Act of 1958. The purpose of the act was to meet the needs of small business for long-term debt funds and equity capital which the Congress felt were not being adequately met by other lending institutions. Section 102 of the act reads as follows:

> It is declared to be the policy of the Congress and the purpose of this Act to improve and stimulate the national economy in general and the small business segment thereof in particular by establishing a program to stimulate and supplement the flow of private equity capital and long-term loan funds which small business concerns need for the sound financing of their business operations and for their growth, expansion and modernization, and which are not available in adequate supply: *Provided,* however, that this policy shall be carried out in such manner as to insure the maximum participation of private financing sources. . . .

In addition to the making of long-term loans, an SBIC may finance a small firm by purchasing its **capital stock** or **debt securities,** or by purchasing **debentures** which are convertible into stock of the business. However, it is limited by law to a maximum investment in any single firm to 20 percent of the SBIC's combined capital and surplus. If a small firm needs more money than one SBIC is permitted to provide, several SBICs may join in the financing. Loans and debt securities must have a maturity of not less than five years. Loans may have terms for as long as fifteen years, and there is no maximum maturity provision on debt securities, except as may be imposed as a policy of the individual SBIC.

A small business investment company may issue its long-term subordinated debentures to SBA in an amount equal to three times its private capital, but not more than $35 million. Under certain circumstances in which an SBIC is specializing in **venture capital** financing, the maximum loan available from SBA is $10 million. Such loans may be subordinated with up to fifteen-year terms. No SBIC will be licensed by SBA, however, unless it has a combined private capital and surplus of at least $150,000.

Trade Credit

Trade financing is essentially a method of buying materials, merchandise, or equipment on credit. Equipment manufacturers and dealers know that the average small business owner is not financially able to pay cash for expensive installations and may have difficulty in securing local loans for this purpose. All major companies have financing plans to stimulate the sale of their equipment. Usually a down-payment of from 20 to 30 percent is required, the remainder to be paid in monthly installments over a period of one to two years or more.

Trade credit from suppliers for the purchase of materials, merchandise, and supplies is the most common and most widely used type of financing in the small enterprise. It often provides a major part of the small business owner's working capital needs, especially in the retail fields.[2]

Internal Sources of Funds

The average going small business in need of working capital, or funds for expansion or some special purpose should analyze its own resources carefully before seeking outside financing. Inventories, for example, are a frequent source of idle funds. Usually from 20 to over 50 percent of the merchandise and materials on hand in the average small business is in excess of needs, and often some of the surplus items are currently being reordered. When surplus stocks have been identified, these should be disposed of as quickly and as economically as possible.

Also, when credit is extended by a small business in need of funds, it is very likely that too much capital has been tied up in slow or doubtful accounts. A vigorous campaign to collect all past-due accounts and the adoption of careful credit control for future operations is necessary in such cases. In some cases it might be advisable to explore the possibilities of shifting to a cash basis.

A small business may also have idle assets in the form of fixtures, equipment, and other odds and ends that could be sold without affecting business operations adversely. Excess space may be rented or subleased, or the firm's telephone or display facilities may be leased to secure extra income, if this does not encroach on regular business activities.

Some of the larger sources of capital from within the average small business are likely to be available through more effective expense control. Three aspects are of special importance: (1) owner withdrawals should be consistent with the needs of the business and can often be cut drastically when capital is needed; (2) certain operations performed in traditional ways may be shifted to less expensive methods, such as from personal service to self-service; and especially (3) closer control over payroll, rent, publicity, and other major expenses may be possible. This does not necessarily mean reduction of the dollar expenditures but, rather, securing maximum profitable returns from every expenditure. These procedures also greatly strengthen the firm's borrowing position if outside financing is still needed.

Miscellaneous Sources of Funds

Other sources of credit to the small business owner include commercial credit companies that make loans on manufacturers' or wholesalers' accounts receivable, sales finance companies that specialize in buying dealers' installment account paper at a discount, and others.

Under a recently enacted federal law, the Farmers Home Administration (an agency of the U.S. Department of Agriculture) is authorized to make

[2] Trade credit is discussed in detail in Chapter 18, pp. 301–4.

guaranteed loans for the purpose of acquiring, establishing, or operating a small business in rural areas outside metropolitan areas of fifty thousand people or less. The FHA loan program is similar to that of the SBA guaranteed loan program, except that FHA establishes no limit or ceiling on individual loans.

The U.S. Department of the Interior contributes to the development of minority enterprise through its Bureau of Indian Affairs. In July 1970 the bureau initiated the Indian Business Development Fund to assist Indians with the financing necessary to start or expand small businesses. The fund provides grants to serve as cash equity for those Indians having less than sufficient equity to qualify them for small business loans from either public or private sources. Most Indians have found it difficult to take advantage of even the 90 percent loan guarantee program of the Small Business Administration because most private lending institutions have required a 100 percent guarantee for Indian loans.

Another source of funds is the Economic Development Administration of the U.S. Department of Commerce. To promote economic redevelopment in areas of substantial unemployment or low median family incomes, small firms located in these areas may receive long-term loans (up to twenty-five years) from the EDA at an interest rate considerably lower than current market rates.

The Economic Development Administration also participates with the Ford Foundation and other private groups in the funding of a national program to assist minority contractors in the contruction industry—the Minority Contractors Assistance Project (MCAP). Lack of capital and inability to meet bonding requirements are major reasons why minority contractors have had difficulty in competing for construction jobs. Usually they have been limited to small projects not requiring large seed capital. MCAP was launched in 1971 to help overcome this difficulty by providing interim construction financing and bonding assistance to minority contractors.

SUMMING UP

The **capital structure** of any business requires a mix of *debt* and *equity* financing. Equity must be provided from the personal assets of individual owners or business partners (or from the retained earnings from the business) or by the issuance of corporate stock. For closely-held corporations with a proven record of success, small business investment companies (SBICs) and other venture capitalists are often viable sources of additional equity funds.

When the earnings made possible by borrowed funds exceed the cost of the debt, the firm has high financial leverage and the small business owner/manager would find it preferable to raise debt capital rather than equity capital. However, a business firm's debt/equity ratio can become dangerously "thin."

Business financing requires both *long-term* funds (for the acquisition of capital assets) and *short-term* funds (for inventory and operating expenses, and for the financing of receivables). Trade credit and commercial bank loans are the primary sources of short-term or *working capital*. Sources of long-term or *fixed capital* include small business investment companies (usually in the form of convertible debentures) and commercial banks (often with SBA loan guarantees); retained earnings, however, provide the major source of long-term funds for the small business.

KEY WORDS

borrowed capital	financial leverage
capital	fixed capital
capital stock	guarantee loan
capital structure	line of credit
character loan	loan
circulating capital	long-term loan
collateral loan	participation loan
commercial bank	quick assets
credit (n.)	sales finance company
debentures	Section 1244 stock
debt capital	semiterm loan
debt securities	short-term loan
disaster loan	small business corporation
economic injury loan	small business investment company
economic opportunity loan	trade credit
equity capital	venture capital
factor	working capital

DISCUSSION QUESTIONS

1.   Some entrepreneurs insist on 100 percent ownership of their businesses. Do you agree with them? Why or why not?

2.   More often than not, entrepreneurs underestimate their capital needs. Comment fully on the statement: "The smaller the capital, the greater the risk."

3. In what ways do the problems of financing a small factory differ from those of financing a small store?

4. In what ways do the problems of financing a small service establishment differ from those of financing either a small store or a factory?

EXERCISE

André Preneur is considering the purchase of a small office building for $500,-000, in which he would house his travel-service business and lease the remaining space to professionals and to other businesses. He has estimated a range of values for the building's net rental earnings before interest and taxes. However, André is really wondering how his return on invested capital would change if he financed part of the purchase price with a 10 percent bank loan. Therefore, he has requested that you complete the following analysis. (Assume a 40 percent tax rate.) What conclusions can you draw from this analysis?

EARNINGS BEFORE INTEREST AND TAXES (EBIT)	$100,000	$75,000	$50,000	$40,000
1. Assuming $500,000 investment with no borrowing:				
EBIT	$100,000	$75,000	$50,000	$40,000
Tax	40,000	_____	_____	_____
Net income after tax	$ 60,000	$_____	$_____	$_____
After-tax return	12%	____%	____%	____%
2. Assuming $300,000 investment with a $200,000 loan:				
EBIT	$100,000	$75,000	$50,000	$40,000
Interest	20,000	_____	_____	_____
Earnings before tax	$ 80,000	$_____	$_____	$_____
Tax	$ 32,000	_____	_____	_____
Net income after tax	$_____	$_____	$_____	$_____
After-tax return	____%	____%	____%	____%
3. Assuming $100,000 investment with a $400,000 loan:				
EBIT	$100,000	$75,000	$50,000	$40,000
Interest	_____	_____	_____	_____
Earnings before tax	$_____	$_____	$_____	$_____
Tax	_____	_____	_____	_____
Net income after tax	$_____	$_____	$_____	$_____
After-tax return	____%	____%	____%	____%

The Ramos Produce Company is located in the heart of the wholesale produce district of El Paso, Texas. It was founded in 1925 by Jorge Ramos, father of the present owner. Within a few years it became a successful business. By 1970 it had twelve full-time employees including John Ramos, the present owner. Jorge owned the land and the buildings and the company owned a 40-foot semi-truck that was used to haul produce from as far as 200 miles away. The company enjoyed an excellent credit rating and had every promise of continued success.

Unfortunately when Jorge died three years ago the company found itself in a difficult position. Since Jorge had little insurance, most of the capital was expended in taxes and estate settlement costs. The property is now owned by John's mother who leases it to the company well below current market rates. However, the property cannot be used as collateral by the company.

Due to the lack of working capital the company is no longer listed in the industry blue book, which contains a rating of each wholesaler based on payment record, trading practices, and net worth, and is commonly used as a basis for securing credit. Therefore, the firm must now pay cash for all its purchases. This in turn has reduced its volume of total purchases and has forced the firm to buy higher priced small-lot purchases of some items needed to provide a full line of produce. As a result, profits from sales have been reduced to about $175,000 per year. Monthly sales during the three summer months are about $25,000, while the other nine months average about $10–12,000 each. The monthly break-even point is about $13,000 with the current four to five employees.

Last year John arranged a bank loan of $30,000 for working capital. The repayment schedule is based on the fluctuating nature of the business. The loan calls for payments of $250 per month in the three winter months, $850 per month in the three summer months (the peak season), and $550 per month the rest of the year. In projecting his need for cash for working capital, John did not allow for the effects of inflation. Thus, the loan still leaves the company in a short cash position.

Approximately 25 percent of the firm's sales are made to restaurants that pay cash. The remainder of the sales are made to markets that take from 15 to 90 days to pay, with an average of 45 days. Comparable dealers in the area tend to have an average of about 25 days on their accounts receivable.

Deliveries are made to about 90 percent of the customers in a company stake truck while the other 10 percent of sales is picked up by local customers. The large semi-truck, with a market value of $6,000, has been idle for almost two years.

The company has also made an advance of $6,000 to a cherry tomato farm owned by John, which produces one crop per year. Although it is common in the area for very large wholesalers to make such advances to small farmers, it is rather unusual for this small a company to do so.

Although the company can probably continue to operate at its current level, John Ramos realizes it can be much more profitable with additional working capital. His problem is to determine the best sources for this working capital.

What sort of presentation should be made to the bank or other sources of capital? How might John otherwise alleviate his short cash position?

Credit
and Collections

CHAPTER EIGHTEEN   *Credit is a powerful sales-facili-
tating tool. By extending credit, business establishments allow a customer the use of the firm's money for a certain period of time. This
amounts to an interest-free loan that saves the customer the cost of
borrowing. But it increases costs for the firm. These range from the
cost of credit investigations and bad-debt losses to the cost of the additional funding the business needs to carry its accounts receivable.
The purpose of this chapter is to provide you with a basic knowledge of the principles of consumer and mercantile credit and how
a small firm's credit-and-collections program can be effectively
managed.*

The use of **credit** in business has often been described as representing
"man's faith in man." Since the beginning of time, provision for the postpone-
ment of payment by seller to buyer has characterized business transactions between responsible parties. Certainly, if in these times all business or domestic
transactions were handled on a strictly cash (or **C.O.D.**) basis, the wheels of
business would be slowed down appreciably.

Credit may be identified as either **consumer credit** or **trade credit.** Consumer credit is extended to the final consumer for the purpose of facilitating
the sale of consumption goods (and services). Trade credit, on the other hand,
is credit that is extended by one business firm to another to facilitate the sale of
commercial or production goods; it is often called **commercial credit** or **mercantile credit.**

In determining their capital requirements most businesses include the
need for funds representing goods sold but not paid for. The money represented in the cost of the goods may be regarded as being loaned to the buyer.
Because the use of capital must be compensated for and because of the record
keeping involved in the maintenance of credit accounts, the handling of credit
relationships by the seller represents a business expense. As with any other
tool, device, or method whereby business is facilitated or expedited, the credit
function must be carefully controlled if its use is to be a profitable one for the
business.

ADVANTAGES AND DISADVANTAGES OF EXTENDING CREDIT

The business owner should weigh the advantages and disadvantages of granting credit. Generally speaking, the following reasons explain and summarize why small businesses have employed credit in their efforts to attract, accommodate, and retain customers:

1. Sales are increased. Experience shows that, in retailing, credit-granting firms are more profitable and do a larger volume of business than do strictly cash stores.

2. A more personal relationship can be maintained with credit customers, who feel a bond with the firm.

3. Credit customers are likely to be more regular than cash customers, who tend to go where bargains are greatest.

4. Credit customers are more likely to be interested in quality and service than in price.

5. Goodwill is built up and maintained more easily.

6. Goods can be exchanged and adjustments made with greater ease. If necessary, goods can also be sent out on approval.

7. Credit applications and charge files contain customer information that is useful in planning inventories and special sales promotions.

Some disadvantages of extending credit are:

1. Capital is tied up in merchandise bought by charge customers.

2. If the firm has borrowed the extra money required when credit is granted, the interest must be added to the cost of goods sold.

3. Some losses from **bad debts** and customers with fraudulent intentions are bound to occur.

4. Some credit customers pay slowly because they overestimate their ability to pay in the future.

5. Credit customers are more likely to abuse the privileges of returning goods and having goods sent out on approval.

6. Credit increases operating and overhead costs by adding the expenses of investigation and bookkeeping entailed in keeping accounts, sending out statements, and collecting payments.

For some businesses the financing aspect—that is, the lending factor—may be the uppermost consideration in the extension of credit. Retailers may not be able to pay until a part of the shipment is sold and paid for. Wholesalers may be unable to pay until their retailer clientele have paid them. Manufacturers are quite often unable to pay until the materials or parts purchased are assembled into the finished product, sold, and paid for. Thus we have a situation where creditor is dependent on creditor and debtor on debtor—a basic interdependence of business.

CONSUMER CREDIT

In most countries a substantial amount of credit business is done at the retail level as a service to customers. In the United States, however, it has become a dominant characteristic of retail merchandising to the point that almost all retail businesses (even the variety stores, which a few years ago would never have thought of extending credit!) are now offering credit as a means of attracting trade.

How much consumer credit business is to be accepted or even encouraged will depend on particular circumstances in each case. First, the local situation is important. While it is not always necessary for a retail store to follow competitors' policies, if credit is extended by all other stores in the same line of business in the community, customers will probably expect it or an alternative benefit for paying cash.

Second, and of probably even greater importance, is the class of trade desired and what they expect in the way of credit. The fact that people in the upper-income bracket do not *need* credit is no assurance they will buy for cash. Rural customers may be in the habit of buying on credit, but when agricultural conditions are favorable they might prefer to pay cash. The retailer may find that even customers who think they want credit because of habit, convenience, or financial need will discover the desirability of buying for cash when the right inducements are offered.

The final determinant will be the retailer's financial resources. Credit extension of any amount requires more capital and involves greater risks for the smaller retailer than most other activities. Total costs of open-account credit extension are likely to be from 3 to well over 5 percent of credit sales.

Types of Consumer Credit

Consumer credit may be classified by the characteristics of the credit instruments used or the methods of payment. Many consumers, for example, purchase goods on ordinary *charge accounts*, the payments being due when the bill is sent to the customer. Some consumers, however, because of unusually large purchases or perhaps the irregularity of their purchases, may find it difficult to pay their bills all at once; hence they may elect to buy some items on the *installment plan* (or some variation of it, such as the *lay-away* sale or *budget* plan), or to open a *revolving credit* account.

Charge accounts.   Ordinary or regular **charge accounts** are usually thirty-day accounts for retail customers. Purchases made during a month appear on the following month's statement, and the balance is due within thirty days from the date of the statement. If the number of charge accounts is small, bills are usually mailed at the end of each month. Where the number of such accounts is large some retailers group them alphabetically and bill in cycles throughout the month, each customer receiving his or her statement on approximately the same date each month; this procedure is known as **cycle billing. Interest** is not charged if the account is paid within the **billing period.**

Installment credit.   When durable (and hence repossessable) goods of high unit value are sold on credit, they are often paid for by the customer in installments. In selling such goods on the **installment plan** (often called **closed-end credit**) the merchant usually adds a service or **carrying charge** to the cash price to recover bookkeeping costs and the costs of repossessing some of the merchandise and selling it secondhand. The customer pays for part or all of the added installment credit expense, whereas **open-account** costs[1] are levied against cash and charge customers alike.

When merchandise is sold on the installment plan the customer is usually required to make a **down-payment,** since customers who already have a substantial investment in the merchandise are less likely to default in their payments. The customer may also receive credit in the form of a **trade-in allowance.** The remainder of the price, plus the carrying charge, is then paid in

---

[1] *Open-account costs* are markups on costs to all customers to cover costs of extending credit, collecting outstanding debts, bookkeeping, and the like.

equal weekly or monthly installments, over one or more years; however, the length of the credit period should not exceed the useful life of the merchandise.

Installment selling provides a protection for the seller not available in open accounts. To protect the seller, two forms of legal devices are usual in extending installment credit: the conditional sales contract and the chattel mortgage. The **conditional sales contract** states that the title remains with the seller until the full price agreed on has been paid, even though the goods have been sold and delivered to the purchaser. In case of failure to make payments, it is easy from a legal standpoint for the seller to repossess the goods. This device is very convenient from the seller's point of view. Under the **chattel mortgage,** title passes to the buyer at the time of sale, but the buyer either transfers it back to the seller on the condition that he or she will get it back when all the provisions of the mortgage have been fulfilled, or gives the mortgagee a first lien on the goods.

Open-end or revolving credit terms.   A **revolving credit** or **open-end credit** plan has the convenience of an ordinary charge account plus the privileges of installment payment. Customers are assigned a fixed credit limit and must pay a specified percentage of the outstanding balance monthly. Interest is charged on the unpaid balance at the end of the month.

The maximum allowable interest rate varies from state to state; many states allow 1½ percent per month (or 18 percent per year), while others permit a maximum of only 1 percent or 1¼ percent per month (i.e., 12 percent or 15 percent per year). Sometimes the individual store assesses a rate that varies with the amount of the unpaid balance; for example, 1½ percent per month on balances up to $500 and 1 percent on any amount over $500. Many retailers also assess an arbitrary fifty cent or seventy-five cent charge (allowable by law) on any unpaid balance below a certain amount, say $10 or $25. As a rule, interest is not charged on purchases made during the current month, in effect giving the revolving charge account customer the same thirty-day period to pay for his or her purchases as the ordinary charge account customer. Similarly, by paying the bill in full within each monthly billing period, the customer can avoid a finance charge altogether; in this way, the revolving charge account operates exactly the same way as a regular charge account.

Regulation of Consumer Credit Terms

A survey by the Federal Reserve Board early in July 1969 revealed that there was considerable confusion among consumers about the interest rates they paid on their credit purchases, particularly on installment plans and revolving open-end charge accounts. Shortly thereafter the **Truth-in-Lending Law** went into effect. The stated purpose of this law, known officially as the Consumer Credit Protection Act, is "to assure a meaningful disclosure of credit terms so that the consumer will be able to compare more readily the various credit terms available to him and to avoid the uninformed use of credit."

The key word in the above statement is *disclosure.* The Truth-in-Lending Law is a *disclosure* law and does not set maximum interest rates.[2] It simply requires that the finance charge, expressed in both dollars and the annual percentage rate, be disclosed in writing before credit is extended to the consumer and in periodic statements on unpaid balances. The term **finance charge** is defined in the act to include not only interest but other fees involved in granting credit, such as carrying charges and the cost of appraisal or investigation reports. Costs that would be paid even if the goods were sold for cash, such as taxes and registration or title fees, are excluded. In effect, the finance charge is defined as the **cost of credit.**

To implement the Truth-in-Lending Law (administered by the Federal Trade Commission), the Federal Reserve Board has issued **Regulation Z,** which states the detailed disclosure rules that apply to the two common types of consumer credit, open-end or revolving charge accounts, and closed-end or installment contracts. Where revolving charge accounts are maintained by the creditor, the following information must be disclosed to the consumer *before* his or her account is opened.

1. Conditions under which a finance charge may be made and the period within which, if payment is made, there is no finance charge

2. The method of determining the balance on which a finance charge may be imposed

3. How the finance charge is calculated

4. The periodic rates used and the range of balances to which each rate applies, as well as the corresponding **annual percentage rate (APR)** calculated to the nearest quarter of a percent (0.25%)

5. How additional charges for new purchases are calculated

6. A description of any lien the creditor may acquire on the customer's property, such as the right to repossess a car, household appliance, or similar purchased commodity

7. The minimum periodic payment required

Periodic statements must also be mailed to the customer on all accounts with a balance of more than one dollar. Figure 18-1 is one of several formats prepared by the Federal Reserve Board which will permit a creditor to comply with the disclosure requirements of Regulation Z. In general, periodic statements on revolving charge accounts—as noted in the illustration—must contain the following information:

[2] Regulation of interest rates, as such, is left to the states. Fewer than half the states, however, have usury laws.

Any Store U.S.A.

MAIN STREET—ANY CITY, U.S.A.

(Customer's name here)

AMT. PAID $ _____

TO INSURE PROPER CREDIT RETURN THIS PORTION WITH YOUR PAYMENT

PREVIOUS BALANCE	FINANCE CHARGE 50 CENT MINIMUM	PAYMENTS	CREDITS	PURCHASES	NEW BALANCE	MINIMUM PAYMENT
	▲					

FINANCE CHARGE IS COMPUTED BY A "PERIODIC RATE" OF   % PER MONTH (OR A MINIMUM CHARGE OF 50 CENTS FOR BALANCES UNDER $) WHICH IS AN **ANNUAL PERCENTAGE RATE** OF   % APPLIED TO THE PREVIOUS BALANCE WITHOUT DEDUCTING CURRENT PAYMENTS AND/OR CREDITS APPEARING ON THIS STATEMENT.

NOTICE

PLEASE SEE ACCOMPANYING STATEMENT(S) FOR IMPORTANT INFORMATION.

PAYMENTS, CREDITS OR CHARGES, RECEIVED AFTER THE DATE SHOWN ABOVE THE ARROW, WHICH IS THE CLOSING DATE OF THIS BILLING CYCLE, WILL APPEAR ON YOUR NEXT STATEMENT. TO AVOID ADDITIONAL FINANCE CHARGES PAY THE "NEW BALANCE" BEFORE THIS DATE NEXT MONTH.

ANY STORE, U.S.A.   MAIN STREET, ANY CITY, U.S.A.

FIGURE 18-1

Typical Open-End Charge Account Statement

1. The previous (or unpaid) balance at the beginning of the billing period

2. The amount and date of each purchase or credit extension, and an accompanying statement or brief description of each item bought (if not previously given to the customer)

3. Customer payments, and credits such as rebates, adjustments, and returns

4. The finance charge expressed in dollars and cents, as well as in terms of the annual percentage rate

5. The periodic rates used in calculating the finance charge, and the range of balances, if any, to which they apply[3]

---

[3] In Figure 18-1, the finance charge is determined by a single periodic rate, with a minimum charge of fifty cents applicable to balances under a specified amount.

6. The closing date of the billing cycle, and the unpaid balance as of that date (i.e., the new balance)

Similar disclosure requirements are imposed on installment contracts. As noted in the typical retail installment contract in Figure 18-2, the following information must be disclosed to the customer:

Seller's Name: ______________________ Contract #______

____

RETAIL INSTALLMENT CONTRACT AND SECURITY AGREEMENT

The undersigned (herein called Purchaser, whether one or more) purchases from ______________(seller) and grants to ______________ a security interest in, subject to the terms and conditions hereof, the following described property.

QUANTITY	DESCRIPTION	AMOUNT	
Description of Trade-in:			
	Sales Tax		
	Total		

PURCHASER'S NAME______________

PURCHASER'S ADDRESS______________

CITY__________ STATE__________ ZIP__________

1. CASH PRICE $______
2. LESS: CASH DOWN PAYMENT $______
3. TRADE-IN ______
4. TOTAL DOWN PAYMENT ______ $______
5. UNPAID BALANCE OF CASH PRICE $______
6. OTHER CHARGES:

   ______________ $______

   ______________ ______
7. AMOUNT FINANCED $______
8. FINANCE CHARGE $______
9. TOTAL OF PAYMENTS $______
10. DEFERRED PAYMENT PRICE (1+6+8) $______
11. ANNUAL PERCENTAGE RATE ______%

Insurance Agreement

The purchase of insurance coverage is voluntary and not required for credit. (Type of Ins.) insurance coverage is available at a cost of $__________ for the term of credit.

I desire insurance coverage

Signed______________ Date__________

I do not desire insurance coverage

Signed______________ Date__________

Purchaser hereby agrees to pay to______________ ______________ at their offices shown above the "TOTAL OF PAYMENTS" shown above in ______ monthly installments of $______(final payment to be $______) the first installment being payable ______ 19____, and all subsequent installments on the same day of each consecutive month until paid in full. The finance charge applies from (Date)

Signed______________

Notice to Buyer: You are entitled to a copy of the contract you sign. You have the right to pay in advance the unpaid balance of this contract and obtain a partial refund of the finance charge based on the "Actuarial Method." [Any other method of computation may be so identified, for example, "Rule of 78's," "Sum of the Digits," etc.]

FIGURE 18-2
Typical Retail Installment Contract

1. The cash price (exclusive of trade-in allowance)

2. The down-payment in cash, and trade-in allowance (if any)

3. The unpaid balance of cash price (cash price less trade-in allowance and cash down-payment)

4. Charges not related to the extension of credit, such as taxes, registration, or title fees

5. The total amount financed (sum of lines 5 and 6)

6. The finance charge expressed both in dollars and cents and as an annual percentage rate (lines 8 and 11 in the illustration)

7. The deferred payment price (cash price + finance charge + other charges as noted in line 6)

8. The date on which the finance charge will begin to take effect (if this is different from the date of sale)

9. The amounts and due dates of installment payments, and the total of payments

10. The amount that will be charged for default or delinquency of payment, and the method of calculating this charge

11. A description of the security (if any) held by the creditor

12. The penalty charge, if any, for prepayment of principal, and the method of computing this charge

Where the installment contract involves merchandise to be installed in the home, and where the retailer or contractor retains a lien on the home as part of the sales contract, the Truth-in-Lending Law grants customers the **right of recission,** that is, the right to change one's mind and cancel the contract, if this right is exercised in writing within three business days following (1) the date of sale, or (2) the date the required disclosures were made, whichever is later. The law also requires that two copies of a "Notice of the Right of Recission" form be given to the customer at the time he or she receives the credit-term disclosure information, or prior thereto.

Severe penalties are imposed on those creditors who inadvertently fail to disclose credit information, who willfully disregard the law, or who mistakenly overstate a finance charge that they do not rectify within fifteen days after discovering the error.

The Truth-in-Lending Law also regulates the advertising of credit terms. By the terms of this legislation, a retailer is prohibited from advertising that an installment plan or a specific down-payment or amount of credit can be arranged unless the retailer *usually* arranges terms of that type. In addition, no advertisement may allude to a specific credit term, such as "No Money Down" or "36 Months to Pay," unless *all other* related terms are also spelled out, particularly the finance charge, expressed not merely in dollars and cents but as an annual percentage rate.

The Arithmetic of Selling on Credit

So that small business owners and managers may comply with requirements of the Truth-in-Lending Law, it behooves them to learn the arithmetic of selling on credit.

Installment sales and finance charges.   Let's say, for example, that a housewife trades in an old refrigerator for a new one costing $600 (the cash price), receiving a trade-in allowance of $60 and making a down-payment of 10 percent on the net amount of the sale; to this the merchant adds a carrying charge equal to 10 percent of the cash sales price. The unpaid balance, then, on the date of the sale is $546 ($600 − $60 − $54 + $60). The customer contracts to pay this amount over the course of a year in twelve equal installments, that is, at $45.50 per month.

Note that the customer actually borrows $546 when she buys the refrigerator on the installment plan. The procedure is similar to borrowing $546 from the storeowner and paying interest on this debt. She pays $60 (the carrying charge) for the use of $546 for one year, even though she won't have its full use for the entire year. Because she is slowly repaying her loan, she has the use of $500.50 (the unpaid balance) during the second month, $455.00 during the third month, and so on, as observed in the following table:

UNPAID BALANCE:	BEGINNING OF:
$ 546.00	Month 1
500.50	Month 2
455.00	Month 3
409.50	Month 4
364.00	Month 5
318.50	Month 6
273.00	Month 7
227.50	Month 8
182.00	Month 9
136.50	Month 10
91.00	Month 11
45.50	Month 12
$3,549.00	78

This is a very expensive way for the customer to buy merchandise. Because many consumers are unaware of the high interest rates they are really paying when interest is computed on the *original* balance, as in installment purchases, the Truth-in-Lending Law (as we noted in the preceding section) requires stores and other creditors to tell the customer in writing the *actual* interest rate they are paying.

What rate of interest did the housewife actually pay on her installment purchase of the refrigerator? One way to calculate it is to add up the twelve sums in the above table ($3,549) and divide by 12 to determine the average sum of money she had use of during the year ($295.75). Since it cost her $60 (the finance charge) to obtain this credit, she actually paid 20.3 percent interest ($60 divided by $295.75).

But this, of course, is a long and tedious computation. An easier way to calculate the average unpaid balance (over any period of time) is to add the beginning and ending balances, and then divide by 2, as follows:

$$\frac{\$546.00 + \$45.50}{2} = \$295.75$$

Dividing this average debt into the carrying charge, as before, yields the same result as before (20.3 percent).

Note that this percentage rate coincides with the annual percentage rate, since the payments were spread over a period of one year. This conforms to the requirements of the Truth-in-Lending Law stating that creditors must be informed of the *annual* interest rate they are being charged. (See line 11, Figure 18-2, p. 285). Where payments are spread over shorter or longer periods of time, the percentage rate as derived above will need to be adjusted accordingly.

Calculating partial refunds of finance charges.   The typical installment contract gives the creditor the right to pay in advance the unpaid balance of the contract and thereby obtain a partial **rebate (refund)** of the finance charge. Any method of computing the refund may be used, so long as the customer is informed as to how the calculation is made. The method used by most retailers is the **sum-of-the-digits** method.

Assume, for example, that the housewife paid off the balance of her account shortly after she made her sixth monthly payment. Without being advised to the contrary in advance, she might reasonably expect a refund equal to one-half the carrying charge, or $30. However, her refund will be somewhat less than that under the sum-of-the-digits method commonly employed. The calculation procedure is as follows:

First, add the values of each of the total number of installment payments to be made (in this case, 1, 2, 3, . . . , 12 to get 78); this is the sum-of-the-digits. Use each of these individual values as the numerator of a fraction whose denominator is the sum-of-the-digits (thus 1/78, 2/78, . . . , 12/78). These fractions are then used in reverse order in determining the portion of the finance charge to be retained by the creditor (and thus the amount of the rebate to the customer), the fraction 12/78 being used in calculating the amount kept by the creditor if the customer makes full payment shortly after the first installment, an *additional* 11/78 if payment is made after the second installment, etc. Thus, by paying off the balance due on her contract shortly after having made her sixth monthly payment, she would be entitled to a rebate of 21/78 of $60, or $16.15. The fractional rebate of 21/78 is calculated by first cumulating the creditor's monthly portions (12/78 + 11/78 + 10/78 +9/78 + 8/78 + 7/78 = 57/78), and then subtracting this cumulated portion from the total (78/78).

Determining the sum-of-the-digits can also be a long and tedious computation. To save time or to compute the sum-of-the digits for installment contracts longer than one year in duration, the following formula may be used:

$$\text{Sum-of-the-digits} = N \frac{(N + 1)}{2}$$

where N = the number of months the contract will last.
Thus, 12 × (12 + 1)/2 = 78. In practice, retailers selling by the installment method use tables (such as the one following) that give rebate fractions at a glance.

INSTALLMENT PERIOD	FINANCE CHARGE	CUMULATIVE FINANCE CHARGE	CUSTOMER REBATE
1	12/78	12/78	66/78
2	11/78	23/78	55/78
3	10/78	33/78	45/78
4	9/78	42/78	36/78
5	8/78	50/78	28/78
6	7/78	57/78	21/78
7	6/78	63/78	15/78
8	5/78	68/78	10/78
9	4/78	72/78	6/78
10	3/78	75/78	3/78
11	2/78	77/78	1/78
12	1/78	78/78	0/78

Interest rates on revolving or open-end charge accounts. On revolving charge accounts, interest may be calculated by the retailer on (1) the previous balance, (2) the adjusted balance, or (3) the average daily balance. Thus, the amount of interest charged a customer can vary, even if the annual percentage rate is the same.

Let's assume, for example, that Jane Doe's balance on her September statement from the ABC Department Store was $209.28. During the month she made two purchases, one for $25.95 on September 5 and another for $35.95 on September 15, and made a payment on account of $100 on September 20. The retailer's annual percentage rate (APR) is 18 percent (the maximum allowed by law in most states), or 1½ percent per month. Under the *previous balance method* (the method specified in Figure 18-1 on p. 284), the finance charge on Jane Doe's October statement would be $3.14: $209.28 (previous balance) × 1½ percent (monthly interest rate) = $3.14.

If the retailer used the *adjusted balance method,* she will be assessed interest only on what is left after her $100 payment: (previous balance of $209.28 — payments during the month amounting to $100) × 1½ percent = $1.64.

Since she owed $209.28 for 20 days, $109.28 for 10 days ($209.28 less her $100 payment on September 20), $25.95 for 25 days (for a purchase made on September 5), and $35.95 for 15 days (for a purchase made on September 15), her average daily balance on account in September was $215.55, calculated as follows:

$$
\begin{array}{lll}
20/30 \times \$209.28 = & \$139.52 \\
10/30 \times 109.28 = & 36.427 \\
25/30 \times 25.95 = & 21.625 \\
15/30 \times 35.95 = & \underline{17.975} \\
& \$215.55
\end{array}
$$

Thus, the finance charge on her October statement under the *average daily balance method* would be $215.55 × 1½ percent, or $3.23.

Using a Controlled Credit System

Properly controlled, credit can increase sales and bring the merchant steady customers; handled in a slipshod manner, it can cause an overinvestment in accounts receivable, large bad-debt losses, and perhaps eventual failure of the business. A sound credit system is one in which (1) credit applicants are thoroughly investigated; (2) limits are placed on the amount of credit extended; (3) charge accounts are systematically monitored or controlled; and (4) delinquent accounts are followed up promptly.

The credit application and investigation. The consumer credit application should include the following information: (1) full name; (2) home address; (3) if less than two years at that address, previous place of residence; (4) business affiliation and address; (5) names of personal references; (6) trade references (other accounts); (7) assets and outstanding debts; and (8) the name of the applicant's local bank. It should not, of course, contain information of a discriminatory nature. Figure 18-3 shows a model credit application form for use in open-end, unsecured credit transactions; it was developed by the Federal Reserve Board, the agency responsible for administering the Equal Credit Opportunity Act. The small business owner may, of course, delete any information request printed on the model form or rearrange its format to suit the business's own needs and preferences. Also, the board's regulations expressly permit the addition of any of the following information requests:

1. An inquiry about the names in which an applicant has previously received credit

2. A request to designate a courtesy title (such as Ms.)

3. An inquiry about an applicant's permanent residence and immigration status

CREDIT APPLICATION
IMPORTANT: Read these Directions before completing this Application.

Check Appropriate Box

☐ If you are applying for an individual account in your own name and are relying on your own income or assets and not the income or assets of another person as the basis for repayment of the credit requested, complete only Sections A and D.

☐ If you are applying for a joint account or an account that you and another person will use, complete all Sections, providing information in B about the joint applicant or user.

☐ If you are applying for an individual account, but are relying on income from alimony, child support, or separate maintenance or on the income or assets of another person as the basis for repayment of the credit requested, complete all Sections to the extent possible, providing information in B about the person on whose alimony, support, or maintenance payments or income or assets you are relying.

SECTION A—INFORMATION REGARDING APPLICANT

Full Name (Last, First, Middle): .... Birthdate: / /

Present Street Address: .... Years there:

City: .... State: .... Zip: .... Telephone: ....

Social Security No.: .... Driver's License No.: ....

Previous Street Address: .... Years there:

City: .... State: .... Zip: ....

Present Employer: .... Years there: .... Telephone: ....

Position or title: .... Name of supervisor: ....

Employer's Address: ....

Previous Employer: .... Years there:

Previous Employer's Address: ....

Present net salary or commission: $ .... per .... , No. Dependents: .... Ages: ....

Alimony, child support, or separate maintenance income need not be revealed if you do not wish to have it considered as a basis for repaying this obligation.

Alimony, child support, separate maintenance received under: court order ☐ written agreement ☐ oral understanding ☐

Other income: $ .... per .... , Source(s) of other income: ....

Is any income listed in this Section likely to be reduced in the next two years?
☐ Yes (Explain in detail on a separate sheet.) No ☐

Have you ever received credit from us? .... When? .... Office: ....

Checking Account No.: .... Institution and Branch: ....

Savings Account No.: .... Institution and Branch: ....

Name of nearest relative not living with you: .... Telephone: ....

Relationship: .... Address: ....

SECTION B—INFORMATION REGARDING JOINT APPLICANT, USER, OR OTHER PARTY (Use separate sheets if necessary.)

Full Name (Last, First, Middle): .... Birthdate: / /

Relationship to Applicant (if any): ....

Present Street Address: .... Years there:

City: .... State: .... Zip: .... Telephone: ....

Social Security No.: .... Driver's License No.: ....

Present Employer: .... Years there: .... Telephone: ....

Position or title: .... Name of supervisor: ....

Employer's Address: ....

Previous Employer: .... Years there:

Previous Employer's Address: ....

Present net salary or commission: $ .... per .... , No. Dependents: .... Ages: ....

Alimony, child support, or separate maintenance income need not be revealed if you do not wish to have it considered as a basis for repaying this obligation.

Alimony, child support, separate maintenance received under: court order ☐ written agreement ☐ oral understanding ☐

Other income: $ .... per .... , Source(s) of other income: ....

Is any income listed in this Section likely to be reduced in the next two years?
☐ Yes (Explain in detail on a separate sheet.) ☐ No

Checking Account No.: .... Institution and Branch: ....

Savings Account No.: .... Institution and Branch: ....

Name of nearest relative not living with Joint Applicant, User, or Other Party: .... Telephone: ....

Relationship: .... Address: ....

SECTION C—MARITAL STATUS
(Do not complete if this is an application for an individual account.)

Applicant: ☐ Married ☐ Separated ☐ Unmarried (including single, divorced, and widowed)
Other Party: ☐ Married ☐ Separated ☐ Unmarried (including single, divorced, and widowed)

SOURCE: Federal Reserve Board.

FIGURE 18-3
Model Credit Application

SECTION D—ASSET AND DEBT INFORMATION (If Section B has been completed, this Section should be completed giving information about both the Applicant and Joint Applicant, User, or Other Person. Please mark Applicant-related information with an "A." If Section B was not completed, only give information about the Applicant in this Section.)

ASSETS OWNED (Use separate sheet if necessary.)

Description of Assets	Value	Subject to Debt? Yes/No	Name(s) of Owner(s)
Cash	$		
Automobiles (Make, Model, Year)			
Cash Value of Life Insurance (Issuer, Face Value)			
Real Estate (Location, Date Acquired)			
Marketable Securities (Issuer, Type, No. of Shares)			
Other (List)			
Total Assets	$		

OUTSTANDING DEBTS (Include charge accounts, instalment contracts, credit cards, rent, mortgages, etc. Use separate sheet if necessary.)

Creditor	Type of Debt or Acct. No.	Name in Which Acct. Carried	Original Debt	Present Balance	Monthly Payments	Past Due? Yes/No
1. (Landlord or Mortgage Holder)	☐ Rent Payment ☐ Mortgage		$ (Omit rent)	$ (Omit rent)	$	
2.						
3.						
4.						
5.						
6.						
Total Debts			$	$	$	

(Credit References)   Date Paid

1. $

2.

Are you a co-maker, endorser, or guarantor on any loan or contract?	Yes ☐ No ☐	If "yes" for whom?	To whom?

Are there any unsatisfied judgments against you?	Yes ☐ No ☐	Amount $	If "yes" to whom owed?

Have you been declared bankrupt in the last 14 years?	Yes ☐ No ☐	If "yes" where?	Year

Other Obligations—(E.g., liability to pay alimony, child support, separate maintenance. Use separate sheet if necessary.)

Everything that I have stated in this application is correct to the best of my knowledge. I understand that you will retain this application whether or not it is approved. You are authorized to check my credit and employment history and to answer questions about your credit experience with me.

Applicant's Signature   Date   Other Signature (Where Applicable)   Date

FIGURE 18-3
Model Credit Application (cont.)

The next step should be to obtain credit information on the applicant from the local **credit bureau** or, if there is none in the community, from other stores and businesses, the applicant's place of employment, and his or her bank and neighbors.

Aided by information provided on the application blank and by credit references, the merchant can get some clues to the applicant's ability and willingness to pay his or her debts—the sole criterion for extending credit; the applicant's ability to pay is obviously dependent on his or her *capital* resources and *capacity* to manage them well, whereas willingness to pay is a matter of *character*. These factors—capital, capacity, and character—are commonly referred to as the three Cs of credit.

In deciding to whom to extend credit, the small business owner must comply with provisions of the federal Equal Credit Opportunity Act. This act guarantees **equal credit opportunity** to all applicants for credit; it prohibits credit discrimination on the basis of race, color, religion, national origin, age (provided that a person has the capacity to enter into a binding contract), sex, marital status, or because all or part of a person's income derives from any public assistance program. The act also stipulates that wives can open their own accounts and must be given credit ratings separate from those of their husbands; this right was granted, in part, to ensure that credit histories will be available to women who become divorced or widowed. A wife, however, is liable for all debts taken on *jointly* with her husband, even if she is later divorced or widowed. Another provision of the federal law is that any person who is refused credit must be told the reasons why, if the small business owner or other lender is so requested.

Setting a credit limit.   The amount of credit granted to customers should be based largely on their income and will vary, of course, with the type of store. A credit limit is usually set so that customers will not buy beyond their capacity and by doing so jeopardize their credit record. To let a customer know that his or her account has been accepted, the store should write a friendly letter telling how pleased it is to count the applicant as a regular customer and also restate the conditions under which credit is granted.

Establishing terms of payment.   As a safeguard against bad-debt losses, the merchant should have a definite understanding with the customer as to the credit terms. The merchant may stipulate that payments are to be weekly, monthly, or on paydays. The time for which credit is extended on open accounts is frequently one month for salaried workers and weekly for wage earners, especially in food and other convenience goods stores. Usually payment by the tenth of the month for the previous month's account is customary on regular open accounts.

Monitoring or controlling the account.   From the day the account is opened, the merchant should watch it carefully to see that the customer upholds his or her part of the agreement.[4] If credit is on a monthly basis, some merchants permit no further charges on an account if it is not paid by the end of the month in which payment is due. Others insist on giving personal approval for additional purchases on such accounts.

The control of credit involves adequate records and prompt collections. The important provisions are an individual record for each customer, a filing system to keep the records straight, and a follow-up file to take care of delinquent accounts. The credit limit is often placed on each account record. It is important to observe the customers' habits—to know how much they owe and how they pay.

Follow-up of delinquent accounts.   Prompt follow-up is likely to show delinquent accounts to be the result of (1) oversight on the part of the customer, (2) temporary financial difficulty, or (3) unwillingness to pay. In the first case, a reminder by the merchant will usually result in prompt payment. In the second case, if the retailer understands the customer's difficulty a mutually agreeable payment plan can be arranged. The third situation may be the result of customer dissatisfaction that could be settled agreeably if understood and acted on promptly, or it may represent the typical "deadbeat" charge customer. When the dealer has determined the reason why each account is delinquent, the appropriate action to take is usually apparent. Aggressive collection procedures should be instituted if necessary, but should be delayed in favor of remedial action whenever possible.

> *Creditors have better memories than debtors.*
> —JAMES HOWELL

Credit Bureaus and the Fair Credit Reporting Act

Credit bureaus are service agencies organized to gather, compile, and distribute information concerning the resources, debts, and financial responsibility of individual consumers. They serve banks, insurance companies, small-loan companies, oil company and other national credit-card firms, local merchants, credit unions, and some professional people. They can compile a dossier on anyone who has ever purchased goods on credit—which includes almost everyone of adult age. A credit bureau's report on a consumer's credit application plays a major role in determining whether or not the retailer will grant credit to this consumer.

In recent years, however, there have been an increasing number of complaints against credit bureaus, centering on errors that have caused some consumers to lose their good **credit rating.** To protect consumers against the use of erroneous data in the files of credit bureaus, Congress in 1971 passed the Fair Credit Reporting Act. Under this law, if the consumer's application for credit

---

[4] A commonly used technique for monitoring and following up slow accounts, known as the aging of accounts receivable, is described on pp. 296–97 and in Figure 18-4.

(or for a job, loan, or an insurance policy) is rejected because of an unfavorable credit report, he or she must be told so by the retailer (or other business owner) who turned the application down. Rejected applicants have the right to review the credit bureau's file on them, and to request a reinvestigation of any item that they question. If the item is found to be inaccurate or can no longer be verified, it must be deleted from the file. In the event that the reinvestigation does not resolve the question—as, for example, when applicants have lost the receipt for a bill paid in cash, or when they are withholding payment for defective merchandise until the defect is corrected—they may have placed in the file a brief statement giving their side of the argument. Rejected credit applicants also have the right to be told the names of those who have received credit reports about them within the past six months, who then must be notified by the credit bureau of any corrections, additions, or deletions in the applicants' dossiers. The credit bureau is not permitted to charge the rejected applicants for these services so long as the review of their credit file is requested within thirty days from the time they were denied the credit.

The new law also requires credit bureaus to delete from credit files adverse information that is more than seven years old, except bankruptcy information, which may be reported for as long as fourteen years. However, no time limits are placed on the information in credit reports on those who apply for a loan or a life insurance policy of $50,000 or more or on those who apply for a job with an annual salary of $20,000 or more.

Retailers and other credit granters as well as credit agencies or bureaus also have certain obligations under the law. As noted above, a business owner who turns down a credit applicant because of a credit bureau report containing adverse information must give the consumer the name and address of the credit bureau supplying the report. But sometimes retailers contact credit references directly, so that a credit report from a credit bureau is not involved in their decision. In such a case, if someone is turned down for credit the retailer must inform that person (at the time the credit application is rejected) that he or she has the right to request in writing within sixty days the nature of the information on which the credit decision was based. Although the law does not require retailers to disclose the source of the information against the applicant, they must supply the consumer sufficient facts with which the accuracy of the information can be refuted or challenged.

Under certain circumstances a business may be regarded as a consumer-reporting agency under the law and thus be subject to the same strict requirements as those imposed on credit bureaus. There is nothing in the law, for example, that would restrict retailers from providing their own ledger experience about a consumer to the credit bureau of which they are a member as long as that information is accurate; this type of exchange is obviously basic to the operation of a cooperative credit-rating system and is not itself a credit report. But suppose that the retailer granted credit to a customer despite a slightly unfavorable report on that customer by another retailer in town. Suppose, further, that the local finance company calls the first retailer to inquire about the customer and the retailer relays the information given by the second retailer. In this instance the first retailer would be regarded as a credit-reporting agency in the eyes of the law. Thus if the finance company rejects the customer's loan application and is thereby obliged to give the retailer's name and address to the rejected applicant, the retailer would be subject to the same requirements of the law as any other credit-reporting agency. Retailers and other business owners would be well advised to leave credit reporting to the credit bureau and give out only *their own* factual ledger experience about consumers.

Another requirement of the Fair Credit Reporting Act with which the small business owner should be familiar is that any store that discounts consumer installment contracts through a bank or finance company must give the name and address of the third party to the indebted consumer. The bank or finance company, if it denies the loan, must then notify the consumer as required by the act.

Collections

For the small business that extends credit, the ability to collect accounts may spell the difference between the success or failure of the firm. Although credit business can be very profitable, too many slow accounts will probably cause the firm to suffer losses and prevent making a profit because

1. The older an account becomes, the harder it is to collect

2. Attempting to collect the money due takes time away from other duties

3. Former good customers avoid the firm because it is embarrassing to meet the one to whom they owe money

4. Slow accounts tie up funds needed to operate other divisions of the business; as a result, the firm's own credit suffers and the firm is not able to take advantage of cash discounts

Experience shows that unless those firms that extend credit are continually alert to the danger of slow accounts, the owners may find themselves in a hopeless situation before they realize that something is wrong. Two basic methods are commonly used to measure the trend toward slow accounts: (1) comparing charge sales to collections, and (2) comparing charge sales to the amount owed by customers. When retailers' charge sales during a week amount to more than their collections on charge sales, it may mean either that their charge business is increasing or that their collections were poor. There should be a close relationship between collections and charge sales. The danger sign is when collections lag behind charges week after week.

To minimize losses on bad debts, an **aging of accounts receivable** should be made by the small business owner at least once a month—using a form such as that illustrated in Figure 18-4. Such an analysis focuses attention on those accounts that have become past due. The longer an account is carried on the

ANALYSIS OF ACCOUNTS RECEIVABLE

Name and Address	Month ending October 19____					
	Under 30 Days	30–60 Days	60–90 Days	Over 90 Days	Total	Remarks
John Smith 123 A Ave.	$143				$143	
Jane Jones 456 1st St.	75	$ 225			300	
William Brown 901 Kenmore				$190	190	Account in hands of collection agency
Harold Black 465 Clinton	227				227	
Glen Brown 787 Adams		81	$176		257	Will pay ½ this month, ½ next
Totals	$18,900	$ 3,024	$ 2,106	$ 1,260	$25,200	

FIGURE 18-4

Accounts Receivable Aging Schedule

books, the less likely it will be collected. It has been estimated, for example, that there is only a 45 percent probability of collecting accounts that have been on the firm's books for as long as a year. Thus, in estimating the bad-debt expense at the end of the fiscal year, the small business owner should write off more than half of these accounts.

Bad-debt losses normally are deductible from income before taxation. The

KEEP ACCOUNTS OUT OF

THE DEEP FREEZE

The older it gets, the tougher it becomes to collect

Courtesy of Small Business Administration.

full amount of the debt may be written off if it logically can be assumed uncollectible, or a part of it if collection appears to be only partially possible. Naturally, debts written off but later collected are considered income.

Once an account becomes past due, there are two objectives to accomplish: getting the money, and retaining the patronage and goodwill of the customer. Prompt follow-up after the due date is desirable, whether by letter, telephone, or personal call. Telephone conversation or personal contact permits ready adjustment of the caller's approach to the debtor's reaction. The collection letter calls for most careful preparation. It must be brief, worded tactfully and pleasantly, employ the positive approach (avoiding such words as "can't," "refuse," "unfavorable," "unsatisfactory"), and possess other qualities that will help collect the bill yet maintain the customer's goodwill.

The cost of collections.   The question often arises as to who must eventually "pay" for credit—for the use of funds involved, for collection procedures, for the risks involved, and for losses. Some authors in the field of credit feel that the credit department should support itself, and indeed this is true where credit extension is limited to that of the installment type. In the typical retail store the regular thirty-day charge account comprises a large percentage of the credit volume. The major portion of credit department work (and therefore, expense) is caused by those accounts not paid within the thirty-day period.

These expenses must be reflected either in increased prices or in losses to the merchant; if it be in increased prices, the burden is on the good paying customer. It has been suggested that merchants add a surcharge to consumer credit purchases, but the regulations of the Fair Credit Billing Act provide that such a surcharge would constitute a *finance charge* and would therefore be subject to provisions of the Truth-in-Lending Law which requires disclosure of effective annual interest rates. A surcharge of (say) 5 percent, if computed at an annual rate, would work out higher than most state laws allow. However, the Fair Credit Billing Act does allow merchants to offer a *discount* of up to 5 percent to cash-paying customers; discounts greater than this amount are interpreted as a finance charge to credit customers.[5]

Resolution of customer billing disputes.   The Fair Credit Billing Act also protects credit customers against **billing errors** and charges for shoddy or unsatisfactory merchandise. Under the law customers have sixty days to notify the merchant of a contested billing. The merchant must correct or challenge the alleged error within ninety days or forfeit the amount in dispute. Furthermore, while a dispute is in progress the creditor cannot cancel a customer's account or file an adverse report on the customer's credit rating. The law also allows the customer to demand a refund of previous installments in cases

---

[5] Cash discount provisions of the Fair Credit Billing Act apply only to *consumer* credit transactions (not trade credit).

where he or she can reasonably demonstrate that the purchased goods were never delivered, were damaged, or were fraudulently represented in the sale.

Financing Credit Sales

Banks and **sales finance companies** help retailers finance their credit sales by purchasing retailers' installment contracts and unpaid open accounts. Whether or not these accounts or contracts are purchased at face value or are discounted depends on the lending institution, the nature of the contract, the customer, and local practice.

Conditional sales contracts are generally sold to the bank or sales finance company for the face value of the unpaid balance, plus the going rate of interest for such a transaction in that community at that time, plus additional collectable charges such as **credit life-and-disability insurance.** The debtor signs a security agreement promising to pay the secured party (bank or loan company) a net amount each week or month until the unpaid balance and other charges are paid. Sales finance companies usually buy these contracts **without recourse** if the debtor is a reasonably good credit risk. Under such an agreement the retailer is free of further responsibility. Banks usually buy contracts **with recourse,** so that if the debtor does not pay, the retailer is liable to the bank. However, often the bank charges a lower rate of interest than does the sales finance company.

Sales finance companies are more likely than banks to purchase accounts receivable. Unpaid accounts are solicited and purchased (usually at a discount) from doctors, retailers, and others. The sales finance company advances a certain percentage of the amount due on the account to the entrepreneur and holds another percentage in escrow as a **deferred payment reserve** that serves to increase the security of the advances made by the loan company. The loan company, then, through collection letters attempts to collect the account. Advances to the retailer by a bank range from 75 to 90 percent of the face amount of accounts receivable. The bank usually requires the retailer to be personally responsible for entire payment of the accounts.

Although we have discussed elsewhere the use of banks in business financing, it should be recognized here again that (1) credit granters may find a bank loan necessary, as noted, to finance their lending at times; also (2) the customer may find the bank a more convenient or agreeable creditor than the establishment from which he or she is making the purchase; and (3) the seller and buyer may go to the bank together to solve the buyer's financing plan.

As noted earlier, under terms of the Fair Credit Billing Act a consumer can withhold payment for unsatisfactory goods and services. This new law also makes credit-card companies, factors, and other third parties just as liable for customer satisfaction as is the original seller; thus it eliminates the **holder-in-due-course** doctrine under which a third party was not held responsible for any commitments the dealer might have made, such as the correction of a defect in the merchandise or an adjustment of some kind. Under the latter doctrine, though the consumer had no recourse against the third party, the third party could sue the consumer for collection of the debt. Consumer advocates had criticized this doctrine and finally succeeded in having it abolished in 1974 with passage of the Fair Credit Billing Act.

Subscribing to a Credit-Card Service

Sometimes, instead of the customer applying for credit, the local credit bureau takes the initiative and issues **credit cards** (charge plates) to a selected number of individuals who have already established good credit records. A group of stores may form an association with an agreement to extend credit to all customers to whom a charge plate is issued. Cooperating stores all accept this plate as evidence of credit approval.

The credit card, as developed originally by the oil companies, hotels, and others, has become a popular means of extending consumer credit, with advantages for both buyer and seller. The individual operator of a service station, for example, has the benefit of professional screening of applications at the headquarters of his supplier, who also assumes liability for loss unless formal warning has been issued to the contrary. The consumer has the advantage of being able to charge at any of the affiliated establishments.

Credit-card service of this type is also available to other sellers of consumer goods or services. The American Express card, the Hilton Carte Blanche, and the Diner's Club card, for example, are used by stores and restaurants of all kinds all over the world and thus have been particularly helpful to travelers. For this service the card-issuing agency levies a charge on the subscribing business establishments amounting to approximately 6 percent of the amount of sale.

In recent years banks also have entered the consumer credit market. Originally introduced locally in New York City, bank credit cards are now available in most communities throughout the country. The largest bank credit-card plans are Master Card and Visa. In these plans the bank makes a credit investigation of an applicant for consumer credit, whether the application is made at the store or the bank. If approved, an embossed plate is issued that henceforth becomes identification and authorization when used for charge purposes in any cooperating store up to the floor limit. If a customer wants to charge more than the floor limit the merchant telephones the bank and secures the information needed immediately. Sales checks are furnished by the bank, and retailers record each charge transaction on these, insert the plate in a stamping machine, and usually secure the customer's signature if the purchase is made in person. Each day copies of the charge-sales checks are deposited with the bank, which then credits the merchant's account with the total amount less service charges. Service charges are usually 5 percent for open accounts and 6 percent for two- or three-payment budget accounts up to ninety days.

The bank does the recording and once a month sends a single statement to each customer accompanied by copies of all charge-sales checks from all cooperating stores. The account is due and payable to the bank within ten days after billing. It is a nonrecourse plan, since the bank assumes full responsibility for approving credit applications and making collections.

Credit-card plans are variously viewed as an effort to aid small merchants to meet the credit promotion competition of large department stores, to separate financing from merchandising, and to furnish additional revenue for banks. The subscribing retailer (or service business operator) gains the advantages of receiving immediate cash on an increased sales volume without the need to (1) investigate the customer's credit, (2) set up a credit bookkeeping system, (3) bill customers, (4) dun slow-paying accounts, (5) incur bad debts, (6) take time that could be more profitably devoted to merchandising, (7) tie up the retailer's own capital, or (8) incur possible ill will or loss of sales by refusing credit.

Until recently, some credit-card companies included a provision in their contracts with retailers that prohibited them from offering a discount to cash-paying customers. Under the provisions of the Fair Credit Billing Act, merchants can no longer be restrained from offering **cash discounts.** The law allows cash discounts to retail and other customers up to a maximum of 5 percent, or approximately the amount of the service charge imposed on merchants for credit-card transactions. Retailers who offer cash discounts must advertise this option to customers by signs placed near cash registers; and the discount must be available to *all* cash customers, not merely to credit-card holders.

TRADE CREDIT

Trade credit is that usually extended by a manufacturer to a wholesaler, distributor, or retailer; or by a wholesaler to a retailer; or by a manufacturer or distributor to an industrial consumer. It may be less of a lending or financing device than a means of simplifying payment. A frequent buyer finds it quite convenient to postpone payment until a number of purchases and deliveries have been made, usually over a period of a month. In this way, when each party adds the figures on his or her copies of the **invoices,** including any returns, they should agree, and the obligation is settled by the buyer with one check.

The Credit Application and Investigation

A credit application form for mercantile or trade use should include the following information:

1. Name of firm (or proprietor if unincorporated)
2. Street address and telephone number
3. Kind of business
4. Number of years in operation
5. Other firms who have granted this firm credit
6. Banking connections
7. Other financial references
8. Personal credit data on owners or management—previous connections, home ownership, and so on
9. Amounts of credit and terms desired

Information on new or prospective customers may be obtained from other creditors, and from banks and other financial references, either personally or by correspondence. The financial standing of many business firms is rated by credit-reporting agencies like Dun & Bradstreet and the smaller business may find it worthwhile to subscribe to this service. Trade credit bureaus maintained by associations of credit managers for the exchange of ledger experience, as well as those operated by many trade associations are also useful sources of information.

The rating books published by Dun & Bradstreet and by other credit-reporting organizations usually indicate, by symbol, the listee's general credit standing, current capital resources, and paying habits and method, supplemented by any pertinent special information. Such special items include evidence of continued unethical or troublesome practices, excessive returns of merchandise, chronic complaints without justification, disregarding of sales contract terms such as deduction of discounts not earned, or unreasonable requests for service. All such data are accumulated from field investigations conducted by the mercantile credit agency.

Trade Credit Terms

If a prospect seems to be a good risk, credit is extended and an account is opened for that firm. Terms must be decided on at the beginning. Slow accounts are just as dangerous in a manufacturing or wholesaling concern as they are in a retail or service business. Not only do they tie up working capital, but if they are not collected over a period of time they will slow down production.

In most trades, cash discounts are offered for payment within a certain length of time; otherwise the total amount must be paid. Such terms are stated "2/10, net 30," which means that a 2 percent discount is allowed if payment is made within ten days and that in any event the total amount must be paid within thirty days. Some businesses buy in small quantities, and frequently. In such cases the manufacturer may extend M.O.M. or E.O.M. terms. Under **M.O.M.** (*middle of month*) terms, all purchases bought before the middle of the month are billed as of the fifteenth; if a discount such as "2/10, net 30" is allowed, it can be taken through the twenty-fifth of the month. For example, an invoice dated March 3, terms 2/10, net 30 M.O.M., could be discounted at 2 percent if paid on or before March 25, the net amount of the invoice being due April 15. An invoice dated March 16, with the same terms, could be discounted up to April 25 or paid net May 15. **E.O.M.** (*end of month*) terms are similar to M.O.M. except that all purchases are billed as of the end of the month instead of the middle, and discount periods as well as due dates are based on that date. Other terms often used are: **R.O.G.** (*receipt of goods*), which means that the discount period starts only after the goods have been received; **extra dating,** which indicates that the discount period is extended for so many days after the regular allowed term; and **season dating,** which is another form of extra dating but for a much longer period of time, because buyers are reluctant to pay immediately for goods purchased as much as seven or eight months in advance of demand.

A misuse of credit insofar as cash discounts are concerned may occur when some firms remit the amount of the bill less the cash discount even though the discount period has passed and, in some cases, the net period as well. Permitting such a practice would certainly be unfair to the prompt-paying customer. Sometimes the remittance must be accepted, but no further credit should be extended. The amount of the discount may be added to the next bill, or the check may be returned with a note reminding the debtor that the discount was not to be taken and asking him or her please to remit the proper amount. Laxness in enforcing terms will only bring loss to the company.

Manufacturers and wholesalers often find it desirable to relate credit terms to the size of the order. This procedure has a dual purpose. By this limitation of credit to orders above a minimum quantity, customers are encouraged to place orders of sufficient size for economical handling; furthermore, encouraging the larger orders favors the better-established firms and thus tends to reduce the risk of granting credit.

Credit Insurance

Unlike consumer credit, trade credit is insurable. **Credit insurance** is a guarantee of accounts receivable as additional security for loans to business concerns. Coverage is limited to manufacturers, jobbers, or wholesalers that sell on credit to firms which have one of the stipulated mercantile credit ratings.

The insurance policy provides protection against all forms of debtor insolvency, and it guarantees the payment of all past-due accounts filed with the insurance company within ninety days after due date in accordance with the provisions of the policy. The policyholder, however, is required to bear a small percentage of the covered loss.

SUMMING UP

Although credit carelessly handled can ruin any small business, carefully controlled credit has two major advantages. In many cases business gravitates to the credit-granting firm; the mere availability of credit is sufficient to attract and hold many customers who would not trade with the firm if credit were not extended. Furthermore, information furnished by the credit customers' records can be used by management in planning advertising and special sales promotions.

However, because of the large sums of money tied up in accounts receivable and the inevitability of some bad-debt losses, credit applicants should be thoroughly investigated. Credit histories are available from local credit bureaus on individuals and from Dun & Bradstreet on business firms. Experience shows that using these services greatly reduces losses resulting from credit extension.

In screening consumer credit applicants and administering the firm's credit-and-collections program, small business managers should be particularly aware of the restrictions imposed on them by the Equal Credit Opportunity Law and the Fair Billing Law and by the Consumer Protection (or Truth-in-Lending) Act.

Certain principles governing credit extension have been well-established and should be observed. One is that the length of the credit period should not exceed the useful life of the merchandise or product. Another is that the longer an account is overdue, the harder it is to collect.

The credit-card plans offered by banks, oil companies, and other organizations appear to be ideal opportunities for small retailers and service establishments to secure the advantages of doing business on credit while avoiding many of the disadvantages.

aging of accounts receivable
annual percentage rate (APR)
bad debts
billing errors
billing period
carrying charge
cash discount
charge account
chattel mortgage
closed-end credit
C.O.D.
commercial credit
conditional sales contract
consumer credit
cost of credit
credit (n.)
credit bureau
credit card
credit insurance
credit life-and-disability insurance
credit rating
cycle billing
deferred payment reserve
down-payment
E.O.M.

equal credit opportunity
extra dating
finance charge
holder-in-due-course
installment plan
interest
invoice
mercantile credit
M.O.M.
open account
open end credit
rebate (refund)
Regulation Z
revolving credit
right of recission
R.O.G.
sales finance company
season dating
sum-of-the-digits
trade credit
trade-in allowance
Truth-in-Lending Law
without recourse
with recourse

DISCUSSION QUESTIONS

1. Since most surveys show that credit-granting stores are more profitable than stores selling only for cash, how do you explain the success of some cash-and-carry retailers?

2. Sam's small department store did 50 percent of its volume on open-account credit, 15 percent on installment, and 35 percent in cash. An increasing proportion of customers were young families in their early twenties. Sam had complete records on all credit sales since 1962. Sales had increased rapidly from 1962 to 1978, then declined each year thereafter, falling to its lowest level in 1982. Sam suspected that credit plans recently being promoted aggressively by several of his larger competitors were responsible for his failure to progress. What recommendations would you make to Sam in handling this problem?

3. *Without regard to legal considerations,* which method would you prefer in incorporating the cost of credit in the prices you set on your product or service—a surcharge on credit purchases or a discount on cash purchases? Discuss fully.

EXERCISES AND PROBLEMS

1. Assume that Jane Doe bought a $350 microwave oven for $400 on the installment plan. She made a $67 down-payment and promised to pay the balance in eighteen equal monthly installments.

    a. What is the carrying charge on this purchase?

    b. What is the amount of the periodic payment?

    c. What is the actual rate of interest she is paying on this installment purchase during the eighteen months of her contract?

    d. What is the annual rate of interest she is paying, calculated (as required by law) to the nearest quarter of a percent (0.25%)?

2. Shortly after she made her sixth payment on account, Jane Doe (in problem 1) decided that she would like to pay off the balance of her account.

    a. What rebate of carrying charge would she be entitled to?

    b. How much would be needed to pay off her debt?

3. A customer's balance in his/her last monthly statement was $500. During the ensuing month the customer made purchases totaling $200 and a payment on account of $300. The store assesses a finance charge of 1 percent on the previous balance less payments on account during the current month (i.e., on the "adjusted" balance).

    a. What will be the finance charge on the customer's next statement?

    b. What will be the customer's new balance on this statement?

4. In problem 3 (above), what would be the finance charge on the customer's next statement if the firm used the previous balance method of calculation? What would be the finance charge under the average daily balance method, assuming that the purchases were made on the 10th and 15th of the month (for $75 and $125, respectively), and the payment on account was made on the 20th of the month?

5. Assume that accounts receivable for the Hawkeye Company were $100,-

000 at the end of the year. Of this sum, $70,000 was current (less than 30 days old); $16,000 was from 30 to 60 days old; $10,000 was 60 to 90 days old; $3,000 was between 6 and 12 months old; and the balance was more than one year past due. Based on the company's past credit experience, its collection probabilities are as follows:

AGE OF ACCOUNT	PROBABILITY OF COLLECTING
Less than 30 days	99.8%
1–2 months	99.0
2–3 months	95.0
3–6 months	80.0
6–12 months	50.0
Over 1 year	25.0

Calculate the company's anticipated bad-debt losses.

6. The Small Business Co. had charge sales in December amounting to $750 a week for a 6-day week, or $125 per day. Every Monday morning the owner/manager adds up the charge sales for the preceding week and runs through his customers' accounts with his small adding machine to determine (1) the total charge sales for the preceding week, and (2) the current total of his accounts receivable. These amounts for the month of January are recorded in the first two columns of the following table.

DATE	LAST WEEK'S SALES	AMOUNT DUE TODAY	NO. OF DAYS' BUSINESS ON THE BOOKS*
Jan. 3	$700	$1,300	10.4
10	650	1,400	
17	800	1,550	
24	750	1,625	
31	600	1,700	

* Amount due today divided by average charge sales per day last month.

    a. Complete the above table.

    b. On the basis of the credit sales trend, what conclusions can you draw about this firm's business?

7. A trade customer's invoice dated September 1 has terms of 2/10 E.O.M. What is the last date that the customer can take the discount?

8. An invoice dated October 1 has terms of 2/10, n/30 R.O.G. The merchandise was received by the customer on October 15. What is the last date that the discount may be taken? When is the bill regarded as delinquent?

In the past five years, John Spangler's old crossroads gas station at Cox Corners has become an important auto service center. Now under the operation of John's son David, the Spanglers sell the gasoline and oils of a small regional oil company. In addition to oil, fuel, tires, and batteries, they now install mufflers, brakes, and other replacement parts. Despite discount-house tire and major oil-company competition, their business grows because of their location, their reputation, and their low prices.

Most of the business has been on a cash basis, except for their local oil company's credit-card trade.

Currently, transient customers and those who buy gas and oil elsewhere are increasingly requesting credit. The transient customers, particularly, now present Visa, Master Card, American Express, and even major oil-company cards for credit. These visitors insist that many such businesses across the country honor almost any such cards. David Spangler and his father are concerned with this development. They are anxious to expand their business in any way possible, hoping to add a motel-restaurant eventually. Friends suggest that they take on a different line of gasoline. However, the brand is very well-known locally and is responsible for some of their best trade; more than that, the oil company owns the land on which their business is located. They have a lease for the next 18 years, but the oil company also owns a plot almost next door. The mutual but unwritten agreement between the two parties, who are old friends, is that the Spanglers will handle this line alone and that the oil company will not permit a competitor nearby. Yet the problem of credit remains if the Spanglers are to achieve their full potential.

Here is a firm that wants to extend credit along modern lines. The older Spangler suggests simply that they extend their own line of credit. David replies that this would serve local people only, and would involve difficult clerical work. The father then suggests American Express. Only recently, also, the local bank approached them about Master Card. At the moment they are puzzled and a little confused.

What would you do? (Any bank will be willing to provide factual data on most such arrangements.)

Accounting Records
and Financial Statements

CHAPTER NINETEEN *Accounting has been described as a means whereby business owners and managers can "figure out where they have been, where they are going, and possibly how to get where they want to go." Some knowledge of accounting is required for almost every operating aspect of business. Inventory and cost control, and certainly pricing cannot possibly exist, nor can credit, without adequate accounting records. Effective employment of resources is impossible without them. Historically, accounting records were needed solely for the profitable management of the business. But with the increasing insistence on accuracy of records on the part of the Internal Revenue Service and the Social Security Administration, the keeping of complete records is assuming a new importance. From your reading of this chapter you will learn how to keep books, set up internal financial controls, and measure the financial performance of a business.*

IMPORTANCE OF FINANCIAL RECORDS

A businessman's judgment is no better than his information.
—Robert Patterson Lamont

Any experienced entrepreneur knows that it is just common sense to keep an accurate, written record of every business transaction. The individual who has no oil pressure gauge on his or her automobile would have no way of knowing whether the motor was being properly lubricated until a knock in the motor or the mechanical failure of some moving part showed that it was not. Similarly, the lack of proper **accounting** and record keeping in the business concern makes it impossible for managers to know how their enterprise is functioning, and in the majority of cases the first indication that something is wrong comes too late. Failure is already upon them.

Others also will want to know how you are scoring in business. During recent years, a great deal of emphasis has been placed on the need for complete records in the small business. Tax laws and the proliferation of government

Courtesy of Small Business Administration.

regulations of all sorts have encouraged better record keeping, because those affected must keep sufficiently detailed records to prepare the required reports. In addition, when they have to borrow funds from banks, managers in small business have come to recognize the need for information only available from good records. The creditor will invariably ask for the most recent balance sheet of the business and sometimes for a copy of the profit-and-loss statement of last year's operations.

The importance of maintaining adequate, up-to-date financial records is underlined by the fact that surveys have repeatedly shown that a large percentage of all small businesses that fail have been operated with merely a single-entry memorandum record of transactions or, in some cases, with no records whatsoever except possibly check stubs. Conversely, the managers of successful concerns have placed complete and accurate records on their list of "musts" for efficient management.

An adequate financial record keeping system will either provide the required information or assist the small firm operator in obtaining answers to such basic questions as the following:

1. What was my income last year? What were my expenses?

2. How do the income and expense trends in my firm compare with those in similar businesses? How do they compare with my own operations during previous years? Does the present trend of my sales justify an increase or decrease in any of these items, such as advertising?

3. In what ways can I cut down or eliminate some of my last year's expenses?

4. What are my assets, liabilities, and net worth? How much money do I actually have invested in my business, and what rate of profit am I earning on my investment? What is my rate of profit after taxes?

5. Am I carrying too large or too small an inventory?

6. What is the current value of my building, delivery equipment, and other fixed assets after deduction of depreciation allowances?

7. How much cash business do I have? How much credit business?

8. How much do my charge customers owe me now? How much of this is overdue, and how long overdue? When does the remainder fall due? Am I extending too much credit or could I stand some more accounts? How much did I lose last year from bad debts?

9. How much ready cash do I have with which to meet my obligations? Will my income during the next thirty, sixty, or ninety days be sufficient to take care of obligations I have assumed?

THE ACCOUNTING EQUATION

Assets are anything of value that the business *owns,* such as cash on hand or in the bank, merchandise, **accounts** (and **notes**) **receivable,** and building, land, and equipment. **Liabilities,** on the other hand, represent the claims of creditors against the assets of the business, such as **accounts** (and **notes**) **payable** and accrued wages and taxes; in other words, what the business *owes.* The difference between what the business owns (assets) and what it owes (liabilities) is the **net worth** of the business, or the **owner's equity** or **capital** in the business. From these definitions it follows that assets must always equal liabilities plus net worth. This is known as the **accounting equation** and is the framework on which the firm's basic financial records are set up.

·From the accounting equation it is seen that any increase (or decrease) in assets must result in a corresponding increase (or decrease) in liabilities or net worth; this is so because in every business transaction there is an exchange of

ASSETS ≡ LIABILITIES ✚ OWNER'S EQUITY

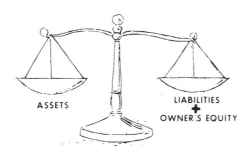

Courtesy of Small Business Administration.

one thing for another. This gives rise to the concept of **double-entry book-keeping,** in which every transaction is recorded as a **debit** entry in one **account** and as a **credit** entry in another.

Assets (on the left side of the accounting equation) typically have a *debit* balance. Liabilities and net worth (on the right side of the accounting equation) normally have *credit* balances. Any account, of course, may be debited or credited depending on whether the account is increased or decreased in value by the transaction. (A check **disbursement,** for example, would decrease the cash asset account, requiring a credit entry to that account.) At any point in time the net worth (or capital) account represents the original investment in the business plus or minus any accumulated losses or reinvested profits; thus expenses (representing a decrease in capital) are normally *debited,* and income accounts (representing an increase in capital) are normally *credited.*

BASIC ACCOUNTING RECORDS

For tax purposes and for the maintenance of an adequate system of financial control, there must be a written record of *every* business transaction. A record keeping system for a small business should include at least the following records:

1. *Cash Receipts Journal*—a detailed, daily listing of all incoming cash from sales, collections on account, and other sources. (Retailers and other types of business with a considerable number of over-the-counter cash transactions should also prepare a *daily cash report* as a supplement to, or perhaps in lieu of, a Cash Receipts Journal.)

2. *Cash Disbursements Journal*—a detailed, daily listing of all outgoing cash. (This journal is maintained in addition to the information provided by the stubs of the business owner's checkbook.)

3. *General Journal*—a detailed, daily listing of all other (noncash) financial transactions, such as credit sales and purchases, **depreciation** or **amortization,** and **adjusting** and **closing entries.**

4. *General Ledger*—to which are posted, monthly or quarterly, the individual or summary entries from the above journals. (This ledger provides the basis for the firm's financial statements.)

Journals, or **books of original entry** as they are sometimes called, record the basic types of financial transactions occurring in every business enterprise. In smaller businesses they are often combined into *one* book or journal, as shown in Figure 19-1.

In addition to a **general ledger,** the typical small entrepreneur may also find it desirable to maintain the following specialized or **subsidiary ledgers:**

1. *Accounts Receivable Ledger*—in which is recorded each customer's credit purchases and payments on account; sometimes called a **customers' ledger.**

2. *Payroll Ledger*—in which is recorded each employee's wages and withholdings therefrom. The maintenance of this ledger provides a convenient basis for the preparation of federal, state, and local tax reports. (This ledger also provides a record of hours worked and overtime earnings, for purposes of complying with provisions of the Fair Labor Standards Act.)[1]

The record keeping system described below is based on the **accrual** method of accounting and assumes that (1) *all* receipts will be deposited in the bank each business day, (2) a **petty cash fund** will be used for all cash paid out other than by check, and (3) *all* purchases by the firm will be made on credit with a cash-discount option.

Under the recommended accrual method of accounting, revenues and expenses are recorded in the company's books not on the basis of when the cash is received or paid out, but on the basis of when the revenue is earned or the expense incurred. A credit sale, for example, is entered in the books as income even though the customer will not pay for the goods until a later date; it is not the actual receipt of payment but the right to receive it that governs. The firm's own credit purchases and tax and wage accruals are similar examples on the other side of the coin. Where inventories play an important part in accounting for the firm's income, the Internal Revenue Service *requires* that the accrual method be used. Only in pure service establishments is the **cash** basis of accounting permissible under IRS rules. But even in these few instances the cash method is not recommended, because it often disguises the true financial condition of the company at any point in time.

In making the entries in Figures 19-2 through 19-6, and preparing instructional footnotes thereto, it is further assumed that subsidiary ledgers are kept for accounts receivable and wage payments because it is felt (by the author) that these records are most convenient and useful both for tax compliance and for managerial control purposes. In situations where such subsidiary records are not maintained, the alternative method of recording these transactions will be explained. In any case, the basic elements of the record keeping system herein described are applicable to any type and size of business, and the illustrations can be easily modified to fit the needs of individual firms.

Accounting for Cash Receipts

All cash receipts should be deposited daily, after a record has been made of the sources of this income in the Cash Receipts Journal, illustrated in Figure

---

[1] Tax and other governmental regulations affecting the operation of a business are discussed in Chapters 26 and 27.

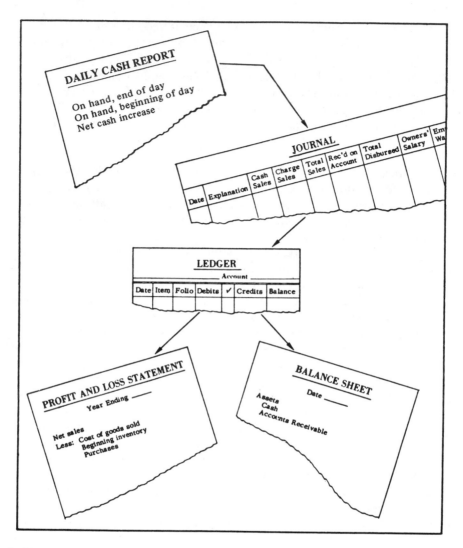

FIGURE 19-1
Basic Accounting Records

19-2. This will be the only cash receipts record in wholesaling, manufacturing, and other establishments whose customer-remittances are received largely through the mail.

However, where large amounts of cash are handled over the counter, as in retail stores and some service establishments, a *cash control system* is also needed. Such a system is illustrated in Figure 19-3. A major purpose of the **daily cash report** (in addition to its bookkeeping function) is to reconcile the amount of cash actually received with the amount that was rung up on the

Date 19__	Description and/or Account	Post	Cash Deposited (Dr.)	Sales (Cr.)	Sales Taxes (Cr.)	Accounts Receivable† (Cr.)	Other Income‡ (Cr.) Account	Other Income‡ (Cr.) Amount
Aug. 1	Daily Cash Report		700.00	662.00	20.00	15.00	Repairs	4.00
1	" " "						Misc. exp.	(1.00)
3	John Smith		8.24			8.24		
15	Joseph Brown		100.00				Rent	100.00
MONTHLY TOTALS*			16,164.80	15,160.60	459.40	364.80		180.00

* Post to respective accounts in the General Ledger (except for "Other Income").

† Post individually to customer accounts in the Accounts Receivable Ledger.

‡ Rent for concessions, service charges, interest, dividends, sale of stock, and other miscellaneous forms of income; post individually to accounts in the General Ledger.

FIGURE 19-2
Cash Receipts Journal

cash register or noted on sales slips. For example, line 5 (in Figure 19-3) represents the cash that was taken in during the day from all sources—sales, sales taxes, collections on account, and miscellaneous other sources. It is the cash that must be accounted for over and above the amount that was on hand at the beginning of the day. Line 6, on the other hand, represents the total amount of cash that was rung up on the cash register (or written up on sales slips if a cash register was not used). If the amount to be deposited (line 5) and the total cash rung up (line 6) do not agree, the difference is entered as a "cash shortage" (line 7) or as a "cash overage" (line 8).

If the firm has more than one cash register or till, a daily cash report should be prepared for each one. The individual reports are then combined into one overall summary for convenience in handling.

```
                              (Front)
                    Date Aug. 1      19___

 1. Cash on Hand, End of Day .........................   $   755.00
 2. Cash on Hand, Beginning of Day ...................   -    65.00
 3. Net Cash Increase  ...............................   $   691.00
 4. Petty Cash Slips .................................   +    10.00
 5. Total Cash To Be Accounted For  ..................   $   700.00
    REGISTER READINGS:
            Cash Sales* ..................   $   662.00
            Sales Taxes* .................       20.00
            Received on Account (see back)†..       15.00
            Misc. Receipts (see back)‡ ......        4.00
 6. Total Cash Rung Up and Deposited* .................       701.00
 7. Shortage (line 6 — line 5)§  .....................   $     1.00
 8. Overage (line 5 — line 6)§ .......................   $
```

```
                              (Back)
                     RECEIVED ON ACCOUNT
                        (List separately)

 ...Glenn Brown..........................................   $     8.00
 ...Harold Black.........................................         7.00
 ..........................................
 ..........................................
 ..........................................
                               TOTAL                      $    15.00

                    MISCELLANEOUS RECEIPTS
                        (List separately)

 ...Repair Services......................................   $     4.00
 ..........................................
 ..........................................
 ..........................................
                               TOTAL                      $     4.00
```

* Post to Cash Receipts Journal.
† Post total amount in Accounts Receivable column in Cash Receipts Journal;
  post to individual customer accounts in the Accounts Receivable Ledger.
‡ Post individual amounts in Cash Receipts Journal.
§ Overages posted as "Miscellaneous Income" in Other Income column of
  the Cash Receipts Journal; shortages posted in the same column as
  "Miscellaneous Expense," using red ink or by circling the entry.

FIGURE 19-3
Daily Cash Report

316

In retailing and other establishments with many over-the-counter cash transactions, the petty cash fund is usually combined with the **change fund** retained in the cash register. (The change fund is the amount kept on hand each day for purposes of making change.) Thus the cash on hand at the beginning of the day plus the petty cash slips in the register or till is a fixed amount. When the amount of cash on hand for making change reaches a predetermined low level, a reimbursement check is drawn to replenish the petty cash fund.

At the close of each day's business, the summary figures for the cash deposit, sales, sales taxes, and the individual amounts for the miscellaneous income accounts are entered in the Cash Receipts Journal (Figure 19-2). If an Accounts Receivable Ledger is kept (as the author recommends for firms doing a credit business), the summary figure for Accounts Receivable is also entered in the journal, and the individual accounts are posted to customer accounts in the subsidiary ledger. (If a subsidiary ledger is not kept for accounts receivable, the individual customer accounts are listed in the journal—from which they will be posted to the General Ledger at the end of the month.)

Miscellaneous receipts itemized on the back side of the daily cash report must be similarly listed in the "Other Income" account column of the Cash Receipts Journal. Cash overages and cash shortages are also entered here—cash over as a credit ("Miscellaneous Income") and cash under as a debit ("Miscellaneous Expense"). When a debit entry is made in a credit column (as in the example in Figure 19-2), or a credit entry in a debit column, that entry is circled or written in red; when the columns are totaled, these entries will be subtracted instead of added.

In addition to over-the-counter cash receipts, as described in the above paragraphs, receipts received in the mail should also be recorded each day in the Cash Receipts Journal. For example, on August 3 (see Figure 19-2), John Smith remitted a check for $8.24 in payment of merchandise he purchased on open account on July 10, and on August 15 Joseph Brown mailed his monthly $100 check for leased space in the store.

At the end of the month, each column in the journal is totaled, and the totals are checked. The total in the "Cash Deposited" column (or cash debit) should equal the sum of the totals in the remaining columns (the income credit accounts). These monthly totals (except for the "Other Income" entries) are then posted to their respective accounts in the General Ledger. The "Other Income" entries are summarized so as to give a single figure for each type of account appearing in the column, and the balance of cash shortages and cash overages are summarized as "Miscellaneous Expense" or "Miscellaneous Income." Credits to customer accounts are posted individually in the Accounts Receivable Ledger (or to the General Ledger if a subsidiary ledger is not kept).

Accounting for Cash Payments

One of the best methods of accounting for cash disbursements and receipts in modern business is to deposit to a checking account in the bank all money taken in and to write a check for each and every expenditure, except for very small items (costing, say, $2 or less) like postage, window cleaning, or express charges. The bank helps to keep the firm's records, because cancelled checks furnish a complete record of each disbursement.

The matter of small cash disbursements is easily taken care of through the petty cash fund. A small fund of from $10 to $50, depending on the need, is set aside to cover minor expenses. Each time an expenditure is made, a petty cash form is filled out for the amount of the expenditure in order to provide information for charging it to the proper expense account. When the fund is exhausted, a reimbursement check is drawn on the checking account, with the expense accounts being charged as indicated on the petty cash forms.

In addition to a checking account, the small business owner should keep a Cash Disbursements Journal. This journal brings together on one page the information recorded on the stubs of the checkbook. This provides a better permanent record and makes the information easier to work with, for purposes of expense classification and control.

The Cash Disbursements Journal shown in Figure 19-4 has a minimum number of columns. It is quite possible, for instance, that additional columns will be needed for payroll deductions such as employee contributions to company pension plans, and group medical and life insurance plans. Also, separate columns should be provided for the major cash **overhead** expenses typical for the particular kind of business, such as rent, utilities, insurance, taxes, and delivery expenses.

As in the case of accounts receivable, a subsidiary ledger may be kept for payroll deductions. If a Payroll Ledger is kept, the individual business owner may prefer to have just one column in the Cash Disbursements Journal for payroll deductions and enter the details of the deductions in the Payroll Ledger. An illustration of one page from this type of subsidiary ledger is shown in Figure 19-5.

Owners' salaries should not be recorded in the same way as employees' wages *unless* the firm is incorporated and the principals pay themselves salaries. If the firm is organized as a proprietorship, a proprietor's salary account is set up in the General Ledger (as an **operating expense**); if there are two or more partners, such an account will be set up for each partner.

At the end of the month, each column in the Cash Disbursements Journal is totaled, and the totals are checked. The total in the "Checks Disbursed" (*credit*) column should equal the sum of the totals in the remaining (*debit*) columns. These monthly totals (except for the "Other Disbursements" entries) are then posted to their respective accounts in the General Ledger. Entries in the

Date 19__	Payee	Check Number	Post	Check Amount (Cr.)	Accounts Payable† (Dr.)	Gross Pay (Dr.)	Social Security	Federal Income Taxes	State Income Taxes	Other‡	Other Operating Expenses§ (Dr.)	Account	Amount
							Wages and Salaries					**Other Disbursements‖**	
							Deductions (Cr.)						
Aug. 1	Nash Wholesale Co.			2450.00	2500.00							Cash Discount	50.00
3	Jeanne Jennings			162.31		192.00	11.23	15.30	3.16				
3	Ray Boone			92.15		108.00	6.32	8.50	1.03				
15	Petty cash			25.00							25.00		
MONTHLY TOTALS*				13,805.63	9212.40	1200.00	70.20	95.20	16.76		350.44	✕	75.00

* Post to respective accounts in the General Ledger (except for Other Disbursements).
† Post individually to employee accounts in the Payroll Ledger.
‡ Provide separate columns, as needed, for other deductions.
§ Provide separate columns for major cash operating (overhead) expenses typical for your kind of business.
‖ Asset acquisitions, loan repayments, income taxes, remission of withheld employee taxes, financial expenses, and other nonoperating expenditures.

FIGURE 19-4
Cash Disbursements Journal

Name: _Jeannie Jennings_
Address: _824 Summit Ave._
Iowa City 52240

Soc. Sec. No. _999-99-9999_
Date of Birth: _10/1/35_
No. of Exemptions _0 (single)_ Wage Rate _$4.80/hr._

Pay Period Ending	Hours Worked							Total Reg. Hours	Overtime	Earnings			Deductions				Net Pay
	S	M	T	W	Th	F	S			Regular Rate	Overtime Rate	Total	Social Security	Fed. Income Tax	State Income Tax	Other	
8/3/-		8	8	8	8	4	4	40		192.00		192.00	11.23	15.30	3.16		162.31
8/10/-		4	8	8	8	4	4	36		172.80		172.80	10.10	13.77	2.84		146.09
Quarterly Totals												120000	70.20	95.20	16.76		9212.40

FIGURE 19-5
Payroll Ledger

"Other Disbursements" column are summarized so as to give a single figure for each type of account appearing in the column.

Accounting for Other Financial Transactions

All other financial transactions of the business, in which there is no immediate exchange of cash, are recorded in the General Journal. Credit sales and purchases represent the most common type of transaction recorded in this journal. (See entries of July 10, August 1, and August 17 in Figure 19-6.) Bad debts are also written off in this journal. For example, on August 5 the bank returned a $20 check for which there were insufficient funds in the customer's account. If payment is later made on this check, the entries in Figure 19-6 will be reversed. Equipment depreciation and other adjusting entries, such as accruals and **deferred expenses,** are also made in this journal.

The General Journal is also used in making closing entries in the income and expense accounts at the end of the accounting period. These accounts are transferred to a summary profit-and-loss account—a credit balance indicating a profit, and a debit balance a loss. The profit-and-loss account, in turn, is closed out by transferring the profit or loss to the retained earnings account. If the firm is incorporated and a dividend is later declared, the retained earnings account will be debited, and the cash account credited.

Posting to the Ledger Accounts

The journals, or books of original entry, provide a record of the firm's financial transactions in chronological order. The purpose of **posting** the journal entries to the General Ledger and to the subsidiary **ledgers** is to *group* the transactions into asset, liability, capital, income, and expense accounts for convenience in preparing the firm's financial statements. Separate sheets are provided in the ledgers for each account. An example of a standard General Ledger account sheet is shown in Figure 19-7; a typical customer's subsidiary ledger account is illustrated in Figure 19-8.

Journal entries are posted to the ledgers at the end of each accounting period, usually monthly or quarterly. Checkmarks ($\sqrt{}$) are made beside the dollar figures in the journal to indicate that the particular transaction has been posted. As each entry is made in the ledger, the journal page from which the entry came is recorded and the account balance brought up to date.

At any time, the balance in the **control** (or summary) **accounts** in the General Ledger (accounts receivable and the various payroll accounts) should equal the sum of the balances of all the individual accounts in the subsidiary ledgers. A **trial balance** should also be taken to verify the equality of the debit and credit sides of the General Ledger. After the accounts are in balance, the firm's **financial statements** are prepared.

Date 19__	Account/Explanation	Post	Debit	Credit
July 10	John Smith		8.24	
	James Jones		25.75	
	Sales			33.00
	Sales Taxes			.99
	To record sales on open acct.			
Aug. 1	Purchases		2500.00	
	Nash Wholesale Co.			2500.00
	To record credit purchase			
Aug. 5	Bad Debts		20.00	
	Cash			20.00
	Bank charge for ISF check			
Aug. 17	Furniture and Fixtures		225.00	
	City Office Supply Co.			225.00
	To record purchase of desk			
Dec. 31	Depreciation		143.00	
	Reserve for Depreciation			143.00
	To allocate monthly equipment overhead			
Dec. 31	Profit and Loss		11,108.00	
	Retained Earnings			11,108.00
	To close P. and L. account			

FIGURE 19-6
General Journal

Account: _Cash_				Number: _100_	
Date 19__	Description	Transactions Posted Debit	Credit	Balance Debit	Credit
	Balance brought forward			5025.00	
Aug. 31	From Cash Receipts Journal	16164.80		21189.80	

FIGURE 19-7
General Ledger Sheet

Customer: _John Smith_				
Address: _705 Court St._				
Date 19__	Description	Debit	Credit	Balance
	Balance brought forward			8.24
Aug. 3	Received on account		8.24	—

FIGURE 19-8
Accounts Receivable Ledger Sheet

The two basic financial statements are the **balance sheet** and the **profit-and-loss statement.** The latter, as the name implies, is a summary of business transactions that have taken place during the **calendar** or **fiscal year** (or month, or quarter, or any other **accounting period**) resulting in either a profit or a loss; it is sometimes called an *income* or *operating* statement. It is like a motion picture of business operations during the period covered by the report; careful analysis of the profit-and-loss statement will reveal what has happened and will indicate why the business is now where it is. The balance sheet is the statement that shows exactly where the business stands; it can be thought of as a snapshot of the business as it stood on the last day of the accounting period. The balance sheet shows where the business is; the profit-and-loss statement shows how it got there. Used wisely, these two statements will give a good indication of what may be expected in the future.

The profit-and-loss statement summarizes the business transactions as follows:

INCOME STATEMENT
THE SMALL BUSINESS COMPANY
January 1, 198___ to December 31, 198___

Gross sales	$210,000
Less: Sales returns and allowances	10,000
Sales	200,000
Less: Cost of goods sold	140,000
Gross margin	60,000
Less: Expenses (itemized)	40,000
Net profit	$ 20,000

The financial records make readily available all these amounts except the **cost of goods sold,** which is easily computed from inventory records as follows:

Inventory, beginning of period	$ 44,000
Plus: Purchases of goods during period	132,000
Goods available for sale during period	$176,000
Less: Inventory on hand, end of period	36,000
Cost of goods sold	$140,000

The above illustrates the procedure for calculating the cost of goods sold in a merchandising business. Methods of computing the cost of goods sold in other types of business enterprises are summarized in Table 19-1.

From the balance sheet (illustrated on the following page), the owner can see how much cash there is in the cash register and in the bank, how much inventory is on hand, how much the customers owe the firm, the value of the equipment, how much is owed to creditors, and the net worth, the last being the difference between what is owned and what is owed.

This is called a balance sheet because the total assets balance with, or are equal to, the total liabilities and net worth. It is closely related to the profit-and-loss statement, in that almost every entry made in the financial records affects both statements. An addition to cash in the balance sheet is usually an addition to an income account in the profit-and-loss statement. A deduction

TABLE 19-1
Computing the Cost of Goods Sold in Various Types of Business

I. *Merchandising and Retail/Service Establishments*
  Merchandise inventory, beginning of period
  + Purchases
  − Merchandise inventory, end of period
  = Cost of goods sold
II. *Manufacturing Establishments*
  Raw materials inventory, beginning of period
  + Purchases
  − Raw materials inventory, end of period
  = Raw materials used
  + Direct labor
  + Factory overhead (indirect labor; supplies; factory utilities; machine and plant depreciation, repairs, and maintenance)
  = Manufacturing costs incurred
  + Work-in-process inventory, beginning of period
  − Work-in-process inventory, end of period
  = Cost of manufacturing
  + Finished goods inventory, beginning of period
  − Finished goods inventory, end of period
  = Cost of goods sold

BALANCE SHEET

The Small Business Company
December 31, 198___

ASSETS

Current Assets

Cash on Hand	$ 6,000	
Cash in Bank	32,000	
Accounts Receivable	26,000	
Inventory	36,000	$100,000

Fixed Assets

Equipment	$ 12,000	
Building	120,000	132,000

Total Assets $232,000

LIABILITIES AND NET WORTH

Current Liabilities

Accounts Payable	$15,000	
Notes Payable	5,000	$ 20,000

Fixed Liabilities

Long-Term Bank Loan	$20,000	
Mortgage Payable	80,000	100,000

Net Worth 112,000

Total Liabilities and Net Worth $232,000

from cash in the balance sheet is usually charged to some expense account or to the cost of goods sold in the profit-and-loss statement. And when the two statements are drawn up at the close of the accounting period, the amount of **net profit** or **net loss** for the period as shown in the profit and loss statement is exactly the sum that is needed to effect a balance between the capital account plus liabilities and the total assets as shown on the balance sheet.

Assets and liabilities are classified on the balance sheet as *current* or *fixed.* **Current assets** include cash and assets that can be converted into cash within a short time (one year or less); similarly, **current liabilities** are debts that will be paid within a year. All other assets and liabilities are regarded as **fixed.** Net worth, as noted, is the equity of the owner or owners in the assets.

Financial statements are interpreted (analyzed) by calculating certain *ratios.* Ratios show the relationship between two items. When car owners, for example, talk about miles-per-gallon, and miles-per-hour, they are dealing in ratios. They are tools with which we measure performance and are used in the analysis of financial statements because a business owner (or the prospective buyer of the business) might be misled by a comparison of dollar figures alone. It is likely, for example, that increased sales volume would produce a greater dollar profit from one accounting period to the next, although profit in relation to sales might be down by a rather large percentage.

Financial ratios can be used in the determination of policies for future operation of the business in two ways. First, business owners may find it helpful to compare their firm's ratios for the period under scrutiny with similar ratios for previous periods. Such a comparison can often help to pinpoint conditions in their business that merit attention. If profits are declining, they can quickly check the firm's financial ratios and ascertain possible reasons for the decline.

Second, business owners can compare the ratios for their business with the standard ratios in their industry. Standard ratios are averages of the results achieved by thousands of firms in the same line of business. Such ratios are compiled and published annually by trade associations in many lines of business and by organizations such as Dun & Bradstreet and Robert Morris Associates.

In interpreting the differences between the firm's ratios and the standard ratios, however, the business owner (or prospective purchaser) should weigh the effects of seasonal fluctuations in both the firm and the industry as a whole. In addition, the owner or the prospective purchaser should recognize and use standard ratios for firms of similar size and geographic location. Also, standard ratios are meaningful only if they are based on standard cost classifications and accounting systems.

There are four types of ratios that may be used in examining the financial health of a business enterprise: (1) **profit ratios,** which measure the firm's earnings in relation to sales and investment; (2) **liquidity ratios,** which indicate the firm's ability to pay its bills as they become due; (3) **turnover ratios,** which

TABLE 19-2

Computing Ratios Measuring a Firm's Financial Health

I. Profit Ratios	Numerator	Denominator
Gross Margin Ratio	Gross Margin	Net Sales
Net Profit Ratio	Net Profit	Net Sales
	or	
	Net Profit	Average Tangible Net Worth
II. Liquidity Ratios		
Current Ratio	Current Assets	Current Liabilities
Acid-Test Ratio	Current Assets − Inventories	Current Liabilities
III. Turnover Ratios		
Working Capital Turnover	Net Sales	Current Assets − Current Liabilities
Investment Capital Turnover	Fixed Assets	Tangible Net Worth
Inventory Turnover	Cost of Goods Sold	Average Inventory at Cost
	or	
	Net Sales	Average Inventory at Retail
Receivables Turnover:		
Average daily credit sales	Net Sales on Account	365
Average collection period	Accounts Receivable + Notes Receivable	Average Daily Credit Sales
IV. Leverage Ratios		
Debt-Equity Ratio	Current Liabilities + Fixed Liabilities	Tangible Net Worth
Fixed Debt Load	Fixed Liabilities	Fixed Assets

measure how effectively the firm uses its resources (assets) to generate sales or profit; and (4) **leverage ratios,** which measure the firm's debt load.

Using the financial statements illustrated above, we will now proceed to calculate and interpret some of the more important financial ratios of each type. The calculating procedures are summarized in Table 19-2.

Profit Ratios

Two common measures of a firm's profitability are the ratios of **gross margin** and net profit to **net sales** as shown on the profit-and-loss statement—30 percent and 10 percent, respectively, in our example.

The gross margin, as we noted in our discussion of pricing in Chapter 14, is the difference between the purchase price (or cost of manufacture) and the selling price of the product.

A high gross margin ratio, relative to ratios of other firms in the industry, may indicate purchases at low prices, sales at high prices, or both. A low ratio, on the other hand, may indicate either inadequate markups, high merchandise costs as a result of poor buying judgment and heavy inventory write-downs, or a deliberate merchandising policy of selling at low prices to obtain a large sales volume.

The bottom-line figure on the profit-and-loss statement, of course, is the ultimate yardstick in measuring profitability. Net profit, however, should be interpreted in the light of the amount of capital invested *as well as* sales volume. A low ratio on a large sales volume, for example, may mean a good profit; likewise, the same ratio is more satisfactory when sales volume is the same but investment is less.

The rate of profit on the owner's investment is regarded by many as the final criterion of profitability. Business owners can determine the amount that their investment is earning for them by dividing the business's net profit (as shown on its profit-and-loss statement) by its average tangible net worth as shown on its balance sheets at the beginning and at the end of the period. (**Tangible net worth** is the worth of the business minus **intangible assets** such as goodwill, trademarks, patents, franchises, copyrights, etc. Intangible assets are excluded from ratio calculations because it is difficult to estimate their worth until they are actually sold.) If we assume that there was no change in net worth during the period, the firm in our example earned a healthy 17.9 percent on the owner's investment in the business ($20,000 ÷ $112,000). This is a considerably higher rate of return than could have been earned had the owner invested in corporate or government bonds, purchased savings certificates, or invested in many other ways. The higher rate of return compensates the business owner for his or her risks and provides the owner with sufficient incentive. This, after all, is why the entrepreneur went into business.

Liquidity Ratios

The most commonly used measure of a firm's liquidity is the **current ratio,** which is the ratio between current assets and current liabilities. In other words, does the business have enough customers' accounts coming due to enable it, when accounts receivable are added to the cash and to the income that the firm will realize from sales during the next few weeks, to pay all the accounts that will fall due to creditors within the same period? Dividing total current assets by current liabilities will provide a current ratio that can be compared with the standard ratio or with former ratios of the business. In the balance sheet given, this ratio is $100,000 ÷ $20,000, or 5-to-1. A current ratio of not less than 2-to-1 is generally considered satisfactory. It is important to note, however, that the current ratio is affected by seasonal fluctuations. The high 5-to-1 ratio in the case given, for example, may reflect a carryover of inventory from one season to the next.

Because they may deteriorate or become obsolete and be subject to **write-offs** or write-downs, some business owners do not include inventories in computing the current ratio. Also, the conversion of merchandise inventory into cash takes more time than is true for other current assets. This more conservative ratio is called the **acid-test ratio.** In the example, it is $64,000 ÷ $20,000, or 3.2-to-1.[2]

Courtesy of Small Business Administration.

---

[2] The importance of liquidity as an objective in sound financial management is further discussed in Chapter 22, pp. 372–76.

Turnover Ratios

A related measure of the liquidity of a business is the *turnover of working capital.* **Working capital** is the excess of current assets over current liabilities. It is working capital that allows the business owner to meet the weekly payroll, pay the monthly utility bills, and make regular payments on suppliers' invoices. As we noted, current assets normally should be no less than twice as large in amount as current liabilities; this is equivalent to saying that working capital should be about equal to current liabilities. Thus the turnover of working capital, measured by dividing working capital at the end of the accounting period ($80,000) into the net sales during that period ($200,000), is closely related to the current ratio. In evaluating the adequacy of a 2-to-1 current ratio in a given case, the business owner should give consideration to the number of times the working capital turns over. With a fast turnover, a low current ratio might suffice. If the turnover is slow, the slow turn should be compensated for by a higher current ratio. Each ratio must be considered in relation to the other.

It is important for the small business owner to measure the turnover of **investment capital** as well as working capital. This figure is obtained by dividing the fixed assets (such as land and buildings, furniture and fixtures, and machines and other equipment) by the tangible net worth. Doing this for the data given, we derive a ratio of $132,000 ÷ $112,000, or 1.2-to-1. To guard against purchasing too many fixed assets, the small business owner should try to keep this ratio at not much more than 1-to-1. In other words, the owner should have enough capital invested in the business to pay for most, if not all, of the fixed assets. By this standard, the above ratio is too high. If fixed assets are high relative to net worth, earnings may not be sufficient to meet maturing installments on the long-term debt, and the small business owner may be compelled to seek new capital. Excessive fixed costs (overhead) is a contributory cause of many small business failures.

Courtesy of Small Business Administration.

Inventory turnover is another important measurement for the prospective purchaser of a business to make. This is done by dividing the **average inventory** (one half the sum of the **beginning** and **ending inventories**) into the cost of goods sold over a given period.[3] (Thus, $140,000 ÷ $40,000 = 3.5-to-1.) Ordinarily, the business owner should strive for as high an inventory turnover as possible without excessive stockouts. With a fast turnover, inventory levels will be lower; hence, inventory carrying costs, and losses from depreciation and changes in style, will also be lower. Excessive inventories also contribute to many small business failures.

The net sales-to-receivables ratio is also helpful in small business management. When a firm's sales are predominantly credit sales, the ratio may be used to estimate the **average collection period.** Net sales is first divided by 365 to derive the average daily credit sales. In our example, this would be $200,000 ÷ 365, or $548. The average daily credit sales figure is then divided into the total of the notes and accounts receivable to determine the average number of days the firm's working capital is tied up in credit sales. In our example, the average collection period is 47.4 days ($26,000 ÷ $548).

This analysis will disclose important trends and danger signals. An increase in the ratio signals a potential working capital shortage; if a business is to pay its own bills regularly and make a profit, it must in turn receive prompt payment for the goods it sells or the services it renders. In general, the average collection period should not exceed the net maturity indicated by selling terms by more than 10 to 15 days.

Leverage Ratios

A business, of course, needs to borrow money to make money, but how much debt can it safely incur? In other words, what should be the ratio of total

---

[3] In merchandising establishments, inventory turnover is also commonly computed by dividing the average inventory *at retail* into *net sales;* the result is the same, however, as noted in the following calculations: average inventory at cost converted into average inventory at retail = $40,000/0.7 = $57,000; and $200,000/$57,000 = 3.5.

debt to net worth? Because equity capital does not have to be repaid, it is much safer to use than debt capital. Dividing, in our example, the sum of the firm's current and fixed liabilities ($120,000) by its tangible net worth ($112,-000) yields a ratio of 107 percent. When this relationship exceeds 100 percent, the equity of creditors in the assets of the business exceeds that of the owners. Commercial banks, the Small Business Administration, and other authorities feel that this ratio should be no greater than 75 percent of the owner's equity and in some types of business perhaps even less.

Another measure of debt load is the ratio of fixed liabilities to fixed assets; $100,000 divided by $132,000, or 76 percent, in our example. In general, this relationship should not exceed 100 percent.

PRINCIPLES OF INTERNAL CONTROL

To prevent errors and to safeguard the assets of the business, the financial record keeping system should provide for a variety of internal checks and balances. Following are some of the more important principles of internal control:

1. All cash receipts should be deposited in the bank each day.

2. All disbursements should be supported by documents evidencing receipt and approval.

3. Except for minor petty cash items, all disbursements should be made by prenumbered check, preferably one processed through a check protector.

4. Petty cash should be on a replacement only basis and kept at a minimum balance.

5. Monthly **bank reconciliations** should be made by someone other than the person writing the checks or recording the disbursements.

6. Credits and allowances to customers' accounts should be carefully supervised and approved.

7. Subsidiary ledgers (such as accounts receivable and employees' earnings) should be balanced to the control accounts.

8. A complete physical inventory of all merchandise, materials, or supplies under the owner's supervision should be taken at least once a year. (Inventory control was discussed in detail in Chapter 10.)

COMPUTERIZED ACCOUNTING AND OTHER RECORD KEEPING

With the advent of minicomputers and the availability of time-sharing facilities and computer-processing services, the automation of bookkeeping and other records has become practical for many small businesses. Business minicomputers, loaded with standard programs needed to do general- and subsidiary-ledger accounting, including the computation of payrolls and the preparation of financial statements, are available in "turn-key" systems, which can be purchased for as little as $25,000 or rented for a few hundred dollars a month. All that the small business owner needs to do to take advantage of such a fully operational **computerized accounting** system is to train someone to push the buttons; maintenance of the computer and the computer programs is provided by the manufacturer from whom the system is purchased or rented.

In addition to recording financial transactions and preparing financial statements, minicomputers can be programmed to analyze costs, keep track of inventories, update customer accounts and prepare billings, analyze sales, and prepare payrolls. They free the small business owner from much of the drudgery of manual record keeping.

For smaller businesses with an insufficient number of financial transactions to justify the purchase or rental of a minicomputer, time-sharing facilities and computer-processing services can be obtained at a cost considerably less than the cost of hiring a bookkeeper.

SUMMING UP

Financial records are necessary to determine profit or loss, return on investment, owner's equity, assets, liabilities, and other pertinent facts. By means of ratio analysis of the items in a firm's financial statements, the financial condition and operating effectiveness of the business can be measured and evaluated. Information obtained from accounting records furnishes the basis for managerial decisions ranging in scope and importance from policy formation or revision down to day-to-day decisions regarding routine operations.

Financial and related records are also required for tax and regulatory purposes. Often federal or state laws require that certain records be kept and that reports based on these records be made. Penalties are imposed for failure to comply with these statutes.

KEY WORDS

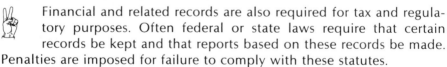

account	adjusting entry
accounting (bookkeeping)	amortization
accounting equation	assets
accounting period	average collection period
accounts payable	average inventory
accounts receivable	balance sheet
accrual	bank reconciliation
acid-test ratio	beginning inventory

book of original entry
calendar year
capital
cash
change fund
closing entry
computerized accounting
control account
cost of goods sold
credit
current assets
current liabilities
current ratio
customers' ledger
daily cash report
debit
deferred expense
depreciation
disbursement
double-entry bookkeeping
ending inventory
expenses
financial ratios
financial statements
fiscal year
fixed assets
fixed liabilities
general ledger

gross margin
intangible assets
inventory turnover
investment capital
journal
ledger
leverage ratios
liabilities
liquidity ratios
net profit (loss)
net sales
net worth
notes payable
notes receivable
operating expenses
overhead
owner's equity
petty cash fund
posting
profit-and-loss statement
profit ratios
subsidiary ledger
T-account
tangible net worth
trial balance
turnover ratios
working capital
write-off

DISCUSSION QUESTIONS

1. Certain records are necessitated by the requirements or provisions of various federal and state laws. Would such records be unnecessary if these laws were repealed? Explain and discuss.

2. What would you regard as the major weaknesses in the record keeping systems of many small businesses?

EXERCISES AND PROBLEMS*

1. On January 1, 19XX, André Preneur opened his new general merchandise store, with capital totaling $75,000. The sources and uses of this capital are indicated by the following transactions:

* Problems 1 through 4 must be completed in sequence and provide necessary input for solutions to certain exercises in later chapters.

a. Withdrew $20,000 of his personal savings to provide an initial cash fund for his venture.

b. Store fixtures and equipment worth $50,000 purchased with $5,000 cash and a 15 percent note due in five years for the balance; the equipment has a ten-year life, with an estimated salvage value of $5,000 at the end of ten years.

c. Borrowing the remaining $10,000 needed to start the business from various relatives and friends, giving them 15 percent promissory notes payable in five years.

d. Purchased a delivery truck for $7,000 cash; the truck has a five-year life, with an estimated trade-in value of $2,000 at the end of five years.

e. Purchased $40,625 of merchandise on account.

f. Paid annual insurance premium of $200.

g. Paid one-month's advance rent of $1,250.

Using a form similar to Figure 19-6 (p. 322), prepare journal entries for the above transactions. Then post these entries to their respective **T-accounts** (ruled off as required on separate sheets of paper).

2. During the year, André's firm engaged in the following transactions:*

h. Sales during the year were $260,000, of which $100,000 were cash sales.

i. Collections on accounts receivable were $75,000, and $10,000 of the merchandise that the charge customers had bought was returned.

j. Purchases on account during the year amounted to $169,000.

k. Employees' wages and salaries paid during the year amounted to $19,-600.

l. André withdrew $10,000 cash during the year for his living expenses. (Consider this as the proprietor's salary.)

m. Paid interest on the notes amounting to $8,250.

n. Incurred the following cash expenses:

Rent	$15,000
Advertising	4,000
Miscellaneous	3,900

o. Paid $130,000 on account to merchandise suppliers.

Prepare journal entries for the above transactions and post the entries to the T-accounts.

3. At the end of the year, the company owed its employees $400. There were no other accrued expenses.

Prepare adjusting entries for insurance and the accrued wages and post the entries to the T-accounts. (Omit entries for depreciation at this time; methods of depreciating fixed assets will be discussed in Chapter 20.)

* Excluding sales tax collections, employees' income tax withholdings, and employer's payroll taxes; these transactions will be discussed in Chapter 27.

4. Take a trial balance of the open accounts.

5. Prepare a statement of profit-and-loss from the following information: net sales, $300,000; net profit, $12,000; proprietor's salary, $27,000; employees' wages, $43,200; inventory on hand at beginning of the year, $90,000; inventory on hand at end of the year, $110,000; merchandise purchases, $200,000; rent and occupancy expense, $15,400; and other expense, $22,400.

6. Prepare a balance sheet for the firm in problem 5 from the following additional information: cash on hand or in the bank, $10,000; furniture and fixtures, $10,000; mortgage, $65,000; accrued taxes, $12,500; notes payable within one year, $15,625; notes payable due more than one year hence, $27,500; accounts payable, $34,375; accounts receivable, $30,000; building, $100,000; land, $8,000; and delivery equipment, $7,000.

7. With reference to the financial statements prepared in problems 5 and 6, compute the following and indicate the significance of each ratio to the management of a small business:

    a. Current ratio
    b. Acid-test ratio
    c. Fixed assets to tangible net worth
    d. Debt/equity ratio (total debt to tangible net worth)
    e. Gross margin ratio
    f. Net profit to net sales
    g. Net profit to tangible net worth
    h. Net sales to working capital
    i. Cost of goods sold to average inventory
    j. Net sales to average inventory at retail
    k. Average collection period
    l. Fixed liabilities to fixed assets

CASE IN
POINT

John Proctor, experienced accountant with a CPA firm, found himself specializing in costing problems, particularly those of smaller metalworking plants. With the larger firms it was a matter of aiding them in improved methods they knew they needed and wanted, but the typical small firm had little or no idea as to the breakdown of costs on past or present contracts nor an interest in such costing. This lack of knowledge was often expensive in bidding for new work; sometimes the question of profit on a contract could not be answered until long after the work was completed. Many of these small firms got as few as 5 percent of the jobs they bid on, and as low bidder on the jobs they did get they often took a loss.

After working with many such operators, John concluded that their need for accounting systems—for cost accounting particularly—was often greater than their need for operating expertise: the best technician could not make money on unprofitable sales. In talking with Karl Schmidt, the depressed owner of Premier Stampings one day, the suggestion was made by John that he become a partner, with the understanding that he would keep the books and eventually do some selling, while Mr. Schmidt ran the shop. After considerable discussion, they decided to give it a try. A contract was drawn up, the firm was incorporated, and John Proctor invested a very reasonable $16,000 for a half-interest.

After a six months' study of past costs and their composition as to processes and materials involved, John developed a process-costing formula for the firm. They went slowly with the new idea at first, lost a job or two, but made money on those they got. John found in his talks with potential customers (and even with some competitors) that they preferred to deal with a firm which knew its costs. Too often, they had found themselves signing a contract with a firm that suddenly found itself financially embarrassed because of a series of losing contracts. This meant delays, and sometimes even advance payments by the buyer to get the work completed.

The business has doubled and tripled over the past four years. The annual volume now approaches $500,000; Mr. Schmidt and John can confidently anticipate, in good years, combined personal income of around 10 percent of sales.

They are receiving more and more invitations to bid, and their customers are increasingly loyal. They are less and less dependent on a few customers for whom they were often almost forced to price themselves out of existence.

The above case provides examples of benefits resulting from sound business practices. Can you suggest, as you review the firm's various outside business relationships, other benefits which might accrue as a result of its improved costing methods?

338

Depreciation
and Inventory Valuation

CHAPTER TWENTY *In calculating a business's taxable income (or that of the proprietor or business partner) each year the accountant may deduct as a depreciation expense a reasonable allowance for the wear and tear, or obsolescence, of the firm's capital assets, and the amortization of certain intangible assets. Valuing the items in a firm's inventory is also a major factor in the measurement of taxable income. The adoption of sound depreciation and inventory valuation policies, the subject of this chapter, is of prime importance to the manager of a small business.*

DEPRECIATING CAPITAL ASSETS

Regardless of the type of business operated, the owner needs a certain amount of equipment as well as a place of doing business. In many cases the owner will need to purchase or lease new equipment each year in order to keep up with competitors and with the trends in this type of business. Often this equipment will be rather expensive and its use will raise operating expenses, but if it brings in enough additional business at a gross margin greater than the increase in expenses, it will prove to be a good investment.

If the equipment is purchased rather than leased or if the business premises are owned by the firm, it will need to be *depreciated*. **Depreciation** in an accounting sense is simply allocating the cost of an asset by charging a portion of this cost to each year of its estimated service life or cost recovery period. Depreciation is an expense of the business, just as much as rent, utilities, or salaries.

Traditional Methods

The most common methods of depreciating assets put into service before 1981 are (1) the **straight-line** method, (2) the **double-declining-balance** method, and (3) the **sum-of-the-years'-digits** method.

With the straight-line method the cost of the asset, less its **salvage value,** is allocated in equal installments over the estimated **service life** of the asset. Thus, as noted in column 1 of Table 20-1, a $10,000 machine would be depre-

TABLE 20-1

Comparison of Depreciation Methods

I. ANNUAL WRITE-OFFS

	(1)	(2)		(3)	(4)
YEAR	STRAIGHT-LINE	DOUBLE-DECLINING-BALANCE	REMAINING VALUE	SUM-OF-THE-YEARS'-DIGITS	ACRS
1	$2,000	$4,000	$6,000	$3,333	$1,500
2	2,000	2,400	3,600	2,667	2,200
3	2,000	1,440	2,160	2,000	2,100
4	2,000	864	1,296	1,333	2,100
5	2,000	518	778	667	2,100

II. BOOK VALUE OF THE ASSET

YEAR	STRAIGHT-LINE	DOUBLE-DECLINING-BALANCE	SUM-OF-THE-YEARS'-DIGITS	ACRS
0	$10,000	$10,000	$10,000	$10,000
1	8,000	6,000	6,667	8,500
2	6,000	3,600	4,000	6,300
3	4,000	2,160	2,000	4,200
4	2,000	1,296	667	2,100
5	0	778	0	0

ciated at the rate of $2,000 (or 20 percent) per year over a five-year period, assuming no salvage value at the end of this period.

Using the double-declining-balance method of depreciation the cost of the asset is allocated over the five-year period of its estimated service life by *doubling* the straight-line percentage rate and applying this doubled percentage to the undepreciated balance existing at the start of each year. Thus over a five-year period of amortization, as noted in column 2 of Table 20-1, the asset would be depreciated at an annual rate of 40 percent on its current **book value** (undepreciated balance); no salvage value is used in calculating the annual **write-offs.** Note, however, that the remaining, or undepreciated, book value approaches but never reaches zero.[1] In practice, therefore, the entrepreneur should switch to straight-line depreciation near the end of the asset's service life (allowable by the Internal Revenue Service on equipment acquired when new); in our example, the asset might be depreciated by $1,080 for each of the final two years (the remaining value at the end of the third year, $2,160, divided by 2).

---

[1] Where the asset has a salvage value, the remaining (or book) value at the end of its depreciable life under the double-declining-balance method approximates this value but may be slightly higher or lower.

Under the sum-of-the-years'-digits method the cost of the asset, less its salvage value, is spread over the estimated service life of the asset by deducting each year that fraction of the asset's net value, determined in the following manner. First, add the values of the number of years of life of the asset (for example, add 1, 2, 3, 4, and 5 to get 15), and use each of these values as the numerator of fractions whose denominator is the sum-of-the-years'-digits (thus 1/15, 2/15, 3/15, 4/15, 5/15). The fractions are then used in reverse order, the first year's depreciation being 5/15ths of the asset's value, the second year 4/15ths, and so on. Multiplying the cost of the asset by the fraction for any specific year results in the value of the depreciation for that year, as observed in column 3 of Table 20-1.

Both this method and the double-declining-balance method are used whenever quick recovery of the investment is desirable. **Accelerated depreciation** is particularly desirable when the asset has a high rate of **obsolescence** and its market value consequently decreases rapidly.

Accelerated Cost Recovery System

In an effort to spur new capital investment Congress in 1981 loosened depreciation rules considerably by introducing a new method of accelerated depreciation in the Economic Recovery Tax Act. For tax purposes this method, known as the **Accelerated Cost Recovery System** (ACRS), *must* be used in depreciating the cost of new or used **tangible assets** placed in service after 1980. On property placed in service before 1981, the business owner must continue to use the same method of depreciation that he or she used in the past.[2]

The Accelerated Cost Recovery System differs from the traditional methods of accelerated depreciation in one important respect: The period of time over which an asset must be depreciated, that is, its **cost recovery period,** is much less than the asset's useful or service life. Under ACRS, tangible property that is placed in service after 1980 is depreciated over a 3-year, 5-year, 10-year, or 15-year recovery period, depending on the type of property it is.[3] The depreciation percentages for 3-, 5-, and 10-year **recovery property** are given in the table below:

3-year property (**personal property** with a short useful life, such as automobiles and delivery trucks)

1st year	25%
2nd year	38%
3rd year	37%

---

[2] The method of calculating depreciation used for tax purposes may be different from that used in the firm's regular books or accounting records.

[3] For detailed listings of eligible property under each of these classifications as well as for more detailed information on the new tax law, consult *IRS Publication 534.*

5-year property (personal property that is not 3-year property, including office furniture and fixtures and most equipment)

1st year	15%
2nd year	22%
3rd through 5th year	21%

10-year property (certain **real property**, such as mobile homes and other manufactured structures)

1st year	8%
2nd year	14%
3rd year	12%
4th through 6th year	10%
7th through 10th year	9%

The above percentages are applied to the landed cost of the property regardless of its salvage value and *regardless of when the property was placed in service during the tax year.*

The differences between ACRS and other methods of accelerated depreciation are illustrated in Table 20-1. As observed in column 4, the depreciation deduction is considerably less under this method for the first year of the asset's cost recovery period and considerably more for the later years.

The yearly depreciation percentages for *15-year property* (all real property, such as buildings, not designated as 10-year property) depends on *when* the property was placed in service during the tax year, as illustrated in the following table:

Month Placed in Service

YEAR	1	2	3	4	5	6	7	8	9	10	11	12
1	12%	11%	10%	9%	8%	7%	6%	5%	4%	3%	2%	1%
2	10	10	11	11	11	11	11	11	11	11	11	12
3	9	9	9	9	10	10	10	10	10	10	10	10
4	8	8	8	8	8	8	9	9	9	9	9	9
5	7	7	7	7	7	7	8	8	8	8	8	8
6	6	6	6	6	7	7	7	7	7	7	7	7
7	6	6	6	6	6	6	6	6	6	6	6	6
8	6	6	6	6	6	6	6	6	6	6	6	6
9	6	6	6	6	5	6	5	5	5	6	6	6
10	5	6	5	6	5	5	5	5	5	5	6	5
11	5	5	5	5	5	5	5	5	5	5	5	5
12	5	5	5	5	5	5	5	5	5	5	5	5
13	5	5	5	5	5	5	5	5	5	5	5	5
14	5	5	5	5	5	5	5	5	5	5	5	5
15	5	5	5	5	5	5	5	5	5	5	5	5
16	—	—	1	1	2	2	2	3	4	4	4	5

Suppose, for example, that the small business owner constructed a $350,000 building which was placed in service on August 14 and that the firm is a calendar year taxpayer. Since August is the ninth month of the tax year, its ACRS deduction for the first year is 5 percent (as read from the above table) of $350,-000, or $17,500. For the second year of the cost recovery period, the depreciation is calculated at 11 percent of $350,000, or $38,500; for the third year, 10 percent of $350,000, or $35,000; and so on. This new IRS rule on building depreciation differs from that in effect prior to enactment of the Economic Recovery Tax Act in that building owners, under the old rule, were allowed to depreciate their properties on a straight-line basis only and then over much longer periods of amortization.

Regardless of the method of depreciation that is used, of course, the total amount of deductible depreciation expense at the end of the recovery period cannot exceed the cost of the asset. Thus when more such expense is deducted in the earlier years, less can be deducted in the later years. Yet from a tax point of view it may be more desirable for the small business owner to spread this expense more evenly throughout the recovery period. For this reason the new tax law allows use of *straight-line* depreciation for 3-, 5-, 10-, and 15-year properties and, if desired, over specified *longer* periods of capital recovery. The property owner can choose from among three different alternate recovery periods for each class of property, as follows:

3-year property	3, 5, or 12 years
5-year property	5, 12, or 25 years
10-year property	10, 25, or 35 years
15-year property	15, 35, or 45 years

Under the straight-line ACRS method for *3-, 5-, or 10-year property*, the small business owner must calculate depreciation using the *same* recovery period for *all* property in the same class that is placed in service in the same tax year. For example, if in a given tax year two items of 5-year property are placed in service, and the business owner elects to use a 12-year recovery period, depreciation of *both* items must be calculated on a stright-line basis over the 12-year period.

Under the straight-line ACRS method for *15-year property*, on the other hand, the small business owner's choice of a recovery period is made on a *property-by-property* basis, and the first year's depreciation deduction must be *prorated* for the number of months the property is in use. Thus, in our previous example of a $350,000 building placed in service on August 14, the first year's depreciation (assuming a cost recovery period of 35 years) is 4/12ths of $10,-000, or $3,333; deductible depreciation allowed at the end of the recovery period (occurring during the 36th year) would be 8/12ths of $10,000, or $6,667.

Not all tangible property is eligible for depreciation under the ACRS method. Personal property acquired after 1980 is excluded if (1) the business owner or a party related to the business owner owned or used the property in 1980, (2) the business owner leased the property to anyone who owned or used the property in 1980, or (3) the business owner acquired the property from its 1980 owner, but the person who is actually using the property does not change. Real property acquired after 1980 is excluded if (1) the business owner or a party related to the business owner owned the property during 1980, (2) the business owner leases the property back to its 1980 owner or a party related to its 1980 owner, or (3) the business owner acquired the property in certain **nontaxable exchanges.** If any of these conditions applies, some other method of calculating depreciation deductions must be used.[4]

Tax law permits the depreciation of **intangible assets** as well as tangible assets, provided that the asset in question has a useful (service) life that can be determined and if the useful life is more than one year. Patents and copyrights, for example, may be depreciated since their useful life is granted by the government. Similarly, covenants not to compete (for an agreed number of years by the buyer and seller of a business) are depreciable. Goodwill, on the other hand, may not be depreciated because its useful life cannot be determined. Depreciable intangible assets, however, *must* be amortized by the straight-line method.

Depreciation Accounting

In accounting for depreciation, accounts must be set up for *each* depreciable asset, each showing the cost basis of the asset. Depreciation expense is calculated separately for each property; and rather than crediting the asset account itself the expense is recorded in a separate **accumulated depreciation** account, known in accounting terminology as a **contra account.**

DETERMINING INVENTORY VALUES

The method by which **inventories** are *valued* on the firm's books, like the methods used in depreciating the firm's assets, affects the amount of profit and, hence, the amount of taxes paid. For this reason it is important to give careful consideration to the valuation method selected. Once the small business owner/manager has decided on a particular method, he or she cannot switch to a different procedure without approval of the Internal Revenue Service.

In addition to consistency in inventory valuation methods from year to year, the IRS requires that different inventory items be identified so that proper values can be applied to the quantities shown in the inventory records. There are two common bases for valuing inventories, either of which is permissible under IRS regulations: cost, or **"cost or market, whichever is lower."**

If a cost-or-market inventory is used, the **market value** of each item is compared with the cost of the item, and the lower of the two is applied to that

---

[4] IRS-specified amortization periods are much longer under the traditional straight-line, double-declining-balance, and sum-of-the-years'-digits methods.

item. Market price is determined by current quotations; the cost price is commonly determined by either the **average-cost** method (weighted to reflect the number of units purchased or manufactured at different prices or costs), the **first-in, first-out** (or **FIFO**) method, or the **last-in, first-out** (or **LIFO**) method.[5]

Under the FIFO method, it is assumed that the *first* items purchased were the first ones sold, the remaining items being the last purchased. Under the LIFO method, it is assumed that the *last* items purchased were the first ones sold, the remaining items being those purchased at an earlier point in time. It is obvious that in a rising cost market the FIFO method tends to overstate profits (and taxes), whereas when prices are falling it tends to minimize profits (and taxes); the opposite is true under LIFO. During periods of steady prices, there would of course be no gain from either method. Under the average-cost method of inventory valuation, the effect of rising or falling prices lies somewhere between FIFO and LIFO.

The differences in these methods of costing closing inventories may be illustrated by the following example. Assume that a firm had an inventory of 1,000 units of a particular item at the beginning of the taxable year. Of these units, 500 were purchased at $10 each in the earlier part of the preceding year, and 500 were purchased later in that year at $12 per unit. During the taxable year the firm purchased an additional 1,500 units, consisting of orders of 500 units each in March, June, and September at $14, $15, and $16 per unit, respectively. By the end of the taxable year, the firm had sold 1,200 units, leaving a closing inventory of 1,300 units. Calculations of the **cost of goods sold** under each of the preceding methods are shown in Table 20-2.

Cost methods of inventory valuation, it should be noted, do not provide for automatic depreciation in inventory value, and retailers particularly have found that these methods often result in overstating the value of their inventories. Shoplifting, late-season markdowns, and employee discounts, for example, are problems peculiar to retailing, and the task of recording inventory values for hundreds of items in terms both of cost (for determining the cost of goods sold in the profit-and-loss statement) and retail values (for determining the amount of sales income) would be monumental. As a result, the **retail method of inventory valuation** (illustrated in Table 20-3) has come into popular use and has been approved by the IRS for use by merchandising establishments in approximating the value of a closing inventory at the lower of cost or market.

Note that the beginning inventory and all subsequent purchases are recorded at both cost and retail prices. Freight and express charges are added to the cost column, and net markups are added to the retail column. The resultant column totals are the cost and retail prices of goods available for sale during the period. The *cost* value of this merchandise is then deducted from the

---

[5] Where the LIFO method is used, however, IRS regulations require that the inventory be valued at *cost* regardless of its market value.

TABLE 20-2
Comparison of Inventory Valuation Methods

	FIFO	LIFO	AVERAGE COST
Beginning inventory:			
500 units @ $10	$ 5,000	$ 5,000	
500 units @ $12	6,000	6,000	
(1,000 units @ $11)			$11,000
	$11,000	$11,000	$11,000
+ Purchases:			
500 units @ $14	7,000	7,000	
500 units @ $15	7,500	7,500	
500 units @ $16	8,000	8,000	
(1,500 units @ $15)			22,500
= Cost of goods available for sale	$33,500	$33,500	$33,500
− Ending inventory:			
(300 units @ $14) + (500 units @ $15)			
+ 500 units @ $16	19,700		
(300 units @ $14) + (500 units @ $12)			
+ (500 units @ $10)		15,200	
1,300 units @ $13.40°			17,420
= Cost of goods sold	$13,800	$18,300	$16,080

° Average cost for the five 500-unit orders is calculated as follows: ($10 + $12 + $14 + $15 + $16) ÷ 5 = $13.40

retail value to get the markup in dollars. Dividing the markup in dollars by the *retail* value of the merchandise available for sale and multiplying by 100 will result in the markup as a percentage.

The next step is to add markdowns, discounts to employees, and shortages in dollars to net sales in dollars for the period. This sum, representing the retail price of the goods sold or otherwise disposed of, is then deducted from the total retail price of the goods available for sale to give the *retail* price of goods still on the shelves. The *cost* price of these goods is the objective. The retail price is multiplied by the cost complement of the markup percentage (100 minus percentage markup) to give the final figure for this ending inventory at cost.

Cost of goods sold is easily calculated by deducting the inventory at cost from the cost of goods available for sale. The explanation is that, from the total cost of goods available for sale, the cost of goods still on the shelves has been deducted, the resulting figure being the cost of goods sold or disposed of.

It will be noted that the markup percentage (37 percent) was calculated without including markdowns, discounts, and (estimated) shortages, but these were added to sales as recorded to get the total value at retail of goods disposed of. Therefore the calculated cost value of the closing inventory is less

TABLE 20-3

The Retail Method of Inventory Valuation

	COST	RETAIL
Beginning inventory	$27,000	$ 45,000
Purchases	49,400	76,000
Add: Freight and express (cost column only)	460	
Add: Net additional markups (retail column only)		1,000
Goods available for sale (at cost and at retail)	$76,860	$122,000
Markup (retail minus cost) = $45,140		
Markup of $45,140 divided by merchandise at retail of $122,000 = 37% markup		
Net sales	$50,000	
Add: Markdowns, discounts to employees, and shortages	3,000	
Goods sold or disposed of (at retail)		53,000
Retail value of goods on the shelves (ending inventory)		$ 69,000
Cost percentage (100% minus 37%)		0.63
Ending inventory at cost	43,470	
Cost of goods sold (cost of goods available for sale minus inventory at cost)	$33,390	

than actual cost, and this is proper because some of the goods were marked down. If, however, the price trend has been upward and additional markups (rather than markdowns) have been taken, these *would* be included in calculating the markup percentage, and the calculated cost would more closely approximate actual cost.

Implicit in the retail method is the assumption that the relationship between cost and retail price in the ending inventory is the same as in the goods available for sale. Since markups vary somewhat from one type of merchandise to another, this method of inventory valuation should be used by *departments* or by fairly homogeneous *merchandise classifications*, not on a storewide basis.

SUMMING UP

Depreciation is an expense deduction that allows a business firm to recover the cost of certain intangible assets and its investment in buildings, equipment, and other fixed assets (except land). For tax purposes, the Accelerated Cost Recovery System must be used in depreciating new or used *tangible* assets placed in service after 1980. On tangible property placed in service before 1981, the business owner must use the same method of depreciating the asset that was used in the past. On tangible property that does not qualify for depreciation under ACRS, either the straight-line, double-declining-balance, or the sum-of-the-years'-digits method must be used.

Intangible assets that have a determinable useful life of more than one year (such as patents, copyrights, and covenants not to compete) may also be depreciated, but only on a straight-line basis; such property does not qualify for treatment under ACRS.

The small business manager should also weigh the tax consequences of different methods of valuing inventories. Inventories may be valued at cost or at "cost or market, whichever is lower." Costs may be averaged, or determined by the first-in, first-out (FIFO) or last-in, first-out (LIFO) method. An accepted procedure for determining the lower of cost or market in merchandising businesses is the retail method. Once the inventory valuation method is selected, it cannot be changed in later years except by approval of the Internal Revenue Service.

KEY WORDS

Accelerated Cost Recovery System (ACRS)
accelerated depreciation
accumulated depreciation
average-cost (inventory valuation)
book value
contra account
cost of goods sold
cost or market, whichever is lower
cost recovery period
depreciation
double-declining-balance method of depreciation
first-in, first-out (FIFO)
intangible assets
inventory

last-in, first-out (LIFO)
market value
nontaxable exchange
obsolescence
personal property
real property
retail method of inventory valuation
salvage value
service life
straight-line method of depreciation
sum-of-the-years'-digits method of depreciation
tangible assets
write-off

DISCUSSION QUESTIONS

1.   Is it always wise to write off the cost of plant and equipment as rapidly as the law allows? Why or why not?

2.   If you were starting a business today, which method of inventory valuation would you choose? How would you justify your choice? Remember, whatever method you pick, you're stuck with it; it cannot be changed in later years.

EXERCISES AND PROBLEMS

1. Assume that a $11,000 machine (not qualifying for depreciation under ACRS) has an expected useful life of ten years and an estimated salvage value of $1,000. Calculate the annual depreciation write-offs under each of the following methods.*
   a. Straight-line
   b. Double-declining-balance
   c. Sum-of-the-years'-digits

2. Calculate the annual ACRS depreciation write-offs for each of the following properties, assuming that the higher permissible level of depreciation is not taken.
   a. 3-year property costing $10,000
   b. 5-year property costing $20,000
   c. 10-year property costing $30,000

3. Calculate the annual ACRS depreciation write-offs for a 15-year property costing $300,000 and placed in service on July 15, under each of the following methods:
   a. regular ACRS method
   b. alternate ACRS method with a 15-year recovery period

4. The first item in an inventory cost $100, the second cost $200, and the third cost $300. Assume that two of these units were sold. Calculate the cost of goods sold and the value of the ending inventory under each of the following methods:
   a. Average-cost
   b. FIFO
   c. LIFO

5. A merchandising firm had a beginning inventory of $100,000 at retail and during the taxable year made purchases at a total cost of $30,000; the initial markup (markon) on these goods was 40 percent. During the year sales netted $110,000 after markdowns, employee discounts and stock shortages amounting to $10,000. Calculate the cost of goods sold under the retail method of inventory valuation. (*Note:* A review of pricing methods in Chapter 14 will be helpful in completing this exercise.)

6. Referring to exercise 1 (b) and 1 (d) on p. 336 in Chapter 19:
   a. Prepare adjusting entries in André Preneur's journal for the depreciation expense on his delivery truck and store fixtures. Assume that he used the straight-line method of depreciation in both cases.
   b. Post these adjusting entries to their respective T-accounts.**

---

* Round calculations to nearest dollar
** The next exercises in this "continuing" problem are exercises 2 through 8 on p. 458.

Profit Planning
and Cost Control

CHAPTER TWENTY-ONE *Will Rogers once said that business is just a matter of dollars and sense. "If you don't make a few dollars, there's no sense being in it." This chapter discusses and illustrates various means of evaluating the profit potential of a business. In addition it endeavors to show how profits can be increased by keeping expenses down.*

Profit is the motivating force in business. A business is successful only to the degree that it makes a profit; that is, to the degree that it continues to serve its customers so satisfactorily that they continue to support it as an enterprise. Profit may be described as that which is left over for the business owner after the goods are paid for and the bills are met. It is the business owner's "payoff," the pot of gold at the end of the rainbow.

Profits, however, should not be left to chance; they should be *planned* for, not hoped for.

> *Profit is the ignition system of our economic engine.*
> —Charles Sawyer

DEMAND FORECASTING

An essential element in profit planning and cost control is the sales forecast. The **demand forecast** is particularly important in the budgeting of operating expenses, labor and material needs, and other costs that vary with volume.

The most common forecasting procedure is to assume, first, that sales in the industry in which a firm operates will grow at approximately the same percentage rate as in the past, or that sales will grow in proportion to the **gross national product** (GNP), taking into account the ups and downs of the **business cycle** (**secular trend** analysis); and then to estimate the firm's share of the potential market, based in part on what it has been in the past but also on planned changes in the firm's advertising and sales promotion strategies. On the basis of these two estimates, **pro forma financial statements** can then be prepared for the ensuing one or more years. (*Pro forma* is a Latin term meaning "for the sake of form" and is used to describe financial statements based on assumed or anticipated facts.) However, pro forma financial statements are no better than the estimates on which they are based.

There are many ways in which small business owners can improve the accuracy of demand forecasting. By subscribing to the trade journals in their field, they can keep better informed of future conditions likely to affect the demand for their products. There are numerous forecasting services available, one or more of which should be helpful. It is possible to cooperate with business neighbors in subscribing to some of these services and thus to reduce their cost to each. Attending meetings of trade associations, at which trends in the industry are frequently discussed by representatives of large companies that spend a great deal of money on their forecasting research, should be helpful to the small entrepreneur. Monthly reports of the Federal Reserve Banks for each district report major trends that can be used to forecast demand. Many state universities publish a monthly bulletin analyzing economic and business conditions within a state, often undertaking to forecast demand and supply conditions likely to have a bearing on the sales plans of local business owners. The charge for these bulletins, when there is any, is seldom much more than the cost of printing and mailing. Small business owners should write to the college of business or bureau of business research at the state university to have their names placed on the mailing list for monthly bulletins and other useful publications. In many industrial fields, the U.S. Department of Commerce publishes monthly analyses and forecasts of conditions. This material, too, is either free or so inexpensive that no small business owner can afford to neglect using it.

BREAK-EVEN ANALYSIS

Although two firms may have the same (actual or projected) production and sales income volume, one firm may be more or less profitable than the other because of differences in their cost structure. A valuable tool in evaluating the effects of cost structure on profitability is **break-even analysis.**

Break-even analysis is simply the determination of the cost-volume-profit relationship. Cost and profit vary with the volume of sales. By separating that portion of total cost that varies in proportion to the volume of sales (**variable cost**) from that portion that exists regardless of the volume of sales (**fixed cost**), the relationship between cost, profit, and sales can be expressed graphically on what is known as a break-even chart as shown in Figure 21-1.

The break-even chart is a square with a 45-degree sales income line drawn from the lower left to the upper right of the chart. The cost scale (in dollars) on which the total cost line is plotted is located on the vertical axis; the volume scale, which is identical to the cost scale, is located on the horizontal axis. The point at which the total cost line intersects the sales income line is called the **break-even point.** It is the point at which cost is equal to income, hence profit is equal to zero. The area between the total cost and sales income lines above the break-even point is the *profit area;* below the break-even point is the *loss area.* The break-even chart in Figure 21-1 is based on the following data assumed for the Small Business Company:

Total sales income for the period		$75,000
Total cost at that sales volume:		
Fixed cost	$20,000	
Variable cost	45,000	65,000
Profit		$10,000

The total cost line in Figure 21-1 was drawn by first plotting two points: fixed cost of $20,000 at zero sales volume; and total cost of $65,000 at $75,000 sales volume. (The difference between these two figures, of course, is the variable cost at the indicated volume; in this case, $65,000 minus $20,000, or $45,000.) These points were then connected and the line extrapolated to the edge of the chart on the right. By inspection of the chart it can be seen that the break-even point is $50,000.

A break-even chart can be prepared from past cost records at various capacity levels. As noted above, a twofold classification of costs is used. *Fixed cost* is that part of total cost that does not change as volume changes. These are the costs that are necessary to maintain the essential skeleton of the business organization; hence, they are costs that are incurred even if the firm is temporarily shut down for lack of business (zero capacity). Examples of fixed cost are rent, depreciation, salary of the owner/manager(s), property taxes, and interest on **funded debt.** *Variable cost* is that part of total cost that varies in

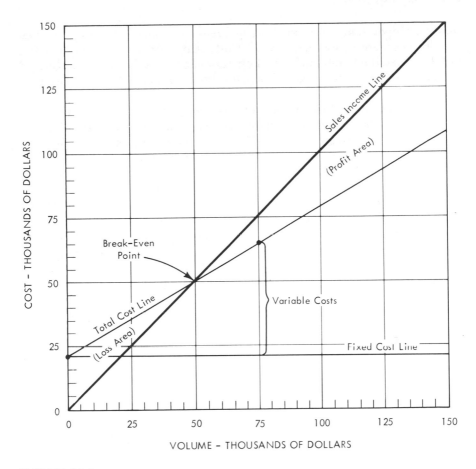

FIGURE 21-1
*Break-even Chart Illustrating Effect of Production
Volume on Rate of Profit or Loss*

direct proportion to volume, such as materials, direct wages, and interest on **floating debt.**[1]

In relation to volume, there is in addition a "gray area" between the fixed and variable cost behavior patterns; that is, some costs increase with increases in volume but not in direct proportion. These are called **semivariable costs.** For example, when a firm first opens for business (or reopens its doors after a temporary shutdown) it must hire clerks and supervisors and incur other expenses which bear little relation to the initial volume of business; that is, they are **standby costs** that represent the difference in costs between shutdown and

[1] Funded debt represents long-term funds borrowed for capital expenditure purposes; floating debt, in contrast, represents short-term funds borrowed to pay for materials, labor, and other needs that fluctuate with the volume of business.

minimum operation.[2] For purposes of break-even analysis, however, these standby costs are considered "fixed." Costs that vary with volume in a step fashion *above* the minimum level of operation, on the other hand, such as advertising and the wage costs of part-time or seasonal help, are considered "variable."

The significance of the break-even chart for purposes of profit planning is that it clearly shows that above the break-even point the company is able to make increasingly greater profits. Thus above the level of sales at which the company breaks even its rate of profit increases faster than the rate of increase in sales. Conversely, the company suffers increasingly greater losses with decreases in sales. The break-even chart graphically illustrates to the small business owner/manager the importance of maintaining a high level of production and sales for the minimization of losses or the maximization of profits.

As a practical matter, of course, it is not necessary for small business owners to draw a picture in order to determine their break-even sales point or the profit they could expect to make at a particular sales volume. For the break-even chart, after all, is merely a graphic representation of the profit equation:

$$P = S - (FC + VC) \tag{1}$$

where

> P = Profit (or loss)
> S = Sales income (or service-trade receipts)
> FC = Fixed cost (at minimum operating level, defined as zero capacity)
> VC = Variable cost

Since variable cost is that part of total cost that varies in proportion to the volume of sales, it is necessary to substitute the expression pS for the expression VC in the above equation. Thus:

$$P = S - (FC + pS) \tag{2}$$

where

> p = Variable cost per dollar of sales, expressed as a ratio.

Applying equation (2) to the problem data on p. 352, we first derive p as follows:

$$p = \frac{45}{75} = 0.6$$

Then, to compute the break-even point (where profit P is equal to 0):

$$P = S - FC - 0.6S$$
$$0 = S - 20 - 0.6S$$
$$20 = 0.4S$$
$$S = \$50 \text{ (thousand)}$$

[2] In a factory, similar standby costs are incurred between the one-shift capacity of the plant and minimum second-shift operation.

Similarly, to compute the company's expected profit at $100,000 sales volume:

$$P = S - FC - 0.6S$$
$$= 100 - 20 - 0.6(100)$$
$$= 100 - 80$$
$$= \$20 \text{ (thousand)}$$

Or the company's loss at $25,000 sales volume:

$$P = S - FC - 0.6S$$
$$= 25 - 20 - 0.6(25)$$
$$= 25 - 35$$
$$= -\$10 \text{ (thousand)}$$

Each of the above calculated results can also be read from the chart in Figure 21-1.

At a sales volume of $75,000, the company's rate of profit on sales is 10/75 = 13⅓ percent. At a sales volume of $100,000, the rate of profit rises to 20 percent (20/100). Similar computations can be made in the loss area. To repeat, as the break-even chart in Figure 21-1 graphically illustrates: *above the break-even point, increasingly greater profits are earned as sales volume increases; below the break-even level, increasingly greater losses are incurred as sales volume decreases.*

In addition to determining the effect on profit (or loss) of increases (or decreases) in production and sales, break-even analysis enables the small business owner/manager to determine changes in break-even volume and rate of profit resulting from (a) a change in cost (for example, a cost-reduction program, or a wage or tax increase); or (b) a change in price or product mix (under conditions of assumed product demand).[3] All that is necessary is to plug in the assumed cost and income data and solve the preceding profit equation.

Another significant fact shown by the break-even chart is that the break-even point and the rate of profit or loss is directly affected by the *proportion of fixed to total cost.* For example, let us assume that in the Small Business Company a major change in equipment will add $10,000 to fixed costs (raising them to $30,000) but will reduce direct labor costs by an estimated 37½ percent. At the current sales level of $75,000, at which direct labor costs are assumed to total $20,000, this would be a reduction in labor cost amounting to $7,500 (thus reducing variable costs to $37,500). The effect of this change in the company's cost structure is graphically illustrated in Figure 21-2—the solid line depicting total cost before the change in equipment, and the broken line depicting total cost after the change in equipment.

[3] For decision-making in the area of pricing policy, another (and perhaps even simpler) approach is marginal-income analysis, discussed in the following section.

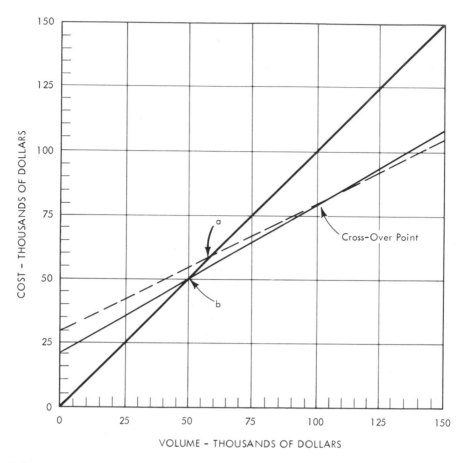

FIGURE 21-2
Break-even Chart Illustrating Effect of Fixed and
Variable Cost Proportions on Rate of Profit or Loss

It is observed that in the latter case the break-even point will be at a higher level of sales; $60,000 instead of $50,000. (The "before" and "after" break-even points are designated on the chart as *b* and *a*, respectively.) However, the rate of profit or loss at sales above or below the break-even point will also be higher.

At the current ($75,000) level of sales, total cost would be higher, and profit lower, if the change in equipment were made. But at what point in sales would the investment result in a larger profit? In other words, when would the investment begin to pay off? This also can be determined by inspection of the break-even chart in Figure 21-2. Profit is equal, of course, at the point where the two cost lines intersect. This **crossover point** occurs at a sales volume of

$100,000. Beyond this volume, the rate of profit would be greater with the new labor-saving equipment than it would be without it.

The crossover point can also be calculated. Since profits are equal at this point, this is done by equating the "before" and "after" profit equations and solving for S, as follows.[4]

$$S - 20 - 0.6S = S - 30 - 0.5S$$
$$0.4S - 20 = 0.5S - 30$$
$$10 = 0.1S$$
$$S = \$100 \text{ (thousand)}$$

In making the investment decision, the small business owner would compare this volume with the company's short- and long-run sales forecasts.

INCREMENTAL COSTS AND MARGINAL INCOME

We shall now try a slightly different method of evaluating the profit potential of the business. The significance of this new approach can best be appreciated by first posing a problem, one not uncommon among small manufacturers. Let us assume that the Small Business Company (whose cost structure was defined above) is operating at only half capacity. It is primarily a job shop, more than half of its usual output consisting of products manufactured to customers' specifications. The company receives orders from two customers, as follows:

	ORDER A	ORDER B
Number of units to be delivered	250	200
Price customer is willing to pay for each unit	$5.00	$6.25
Estimated variable cost per unit	$3.00	$3.50
Estimated total cost per unit	$6.50	$8.00

In order to meet the customers' delivery specifications, it would be necessary to start both orders in production immediately. However, though the plant is operating at only half capacity, there is insufficient machine time available to process the orders simultaneously. Therefore the owner/manager can accept only one of the orders. Of course, he need not accept either. What should he do? What would you advise him to do?

If your advice to him is to reject both orders, your decision would be typical of the decision that most small business owners would make (and have made) in a similar situation. But it would be a wrong decision, as the following analysis attests:

[4] The new variable cost ratio, $p = 37,500/75,000 = 0.5$.

	ORDER A	ORDER B
1. Price per unit	$5.00	6.25
2. Volume in units	250	200
3. Variable cost per unit	$3.00	$3.50
4. *Added* income	$1,250	$1,250
(line 1 × line 2)		
5. *Added* variable cost	$750	$700
(line 2 × line 3)		
6. *Added* **profit-volume income**	$500	$550
(line 4 − line 5)		
7. Programmed cost (see p. 359)	0	0
8. *Added* profit contribution	$500	$550
(line 6 − line 7)		

As the figures indicate, the company's profit would be $50 higher if order B is accepted rather than order A—or, if the company is presently operating in the loss area, its loss would be $50 less. And if neither order is accepted, the company would have foregone an opportunity to increase its profit (or decrease its loss) by as much as $550.

The important point for the reader of this book to bear in mind is that, for purposes of managerial decision-making, it is the **incremental cost** associated with a particular plan or alternative course of action that is important, not the conventional cost-accounting concept of average or total cost. For example, if variable cost varies in amount with the volume of business but is always the same percentage of the business done (within a wide range of volume, as noted in our discussion of break-even analysis), while fixed cost is the same regardless of the volume of business, then the difference between 100 percent (as representing the business done) and the variable cost proportion may be called the **contribution margin** (or *contribution to fixed cost and profit*). In other words, if variable cost is 60 percent or $0.60 out of each dollar of business, there must be $0.40 out of each dollar of business applicable to fixed cost until it is offset, and thereafter, to profit. Thus in choosing between order A and order B, the small business owner should compare only the added income and costs associated with each order to determine the *net effect* on profit.[5] To use the accountants' concept of average cost, involving the allocation of fixed overhead cost, would be misleading.

Incremental costs, however, may be fixed as well as variable in nature. Under the conditions as assumed for the Small Business Company (that is, under conditions of unused capacity), the building, machinery, and supervisory staff already exist; the fixed costs associated with these factors remain the same *regardless of the course of action taken.* Hence, for purposes of manage-

[5] The terms *incremental costs* and *marginal income* are used interchangeably. Incremental costs are also often referred to as "out-of-pocket" or "differential" costs.

ment decision-making they are **passive costs** and can be disregarded. However, if one of the orders required special tooling which could be used only on that job, the added cost is regarded as a fixed **programmed cost** which would be charged against the income produced by that order. On the other hand, if the plant was already working at full capacity, and the company decided to process both orders at overtime, the overtime labor cost of each order would be a programmed cost of a variable nature. For purposes of **marginal-income** analysis, therefore, we find it convenient to differentiate between fixed costs, variable costs, and programmed costs (which may be fixed or variable), and to consider as pertinent only the latter two classifications of cost.

This type of analysis has many practical applications in small business. Its usefulness can be further demonstrated by considering other management plans or programs under similar conditions, that is, when a plant has a large amount of excess capacity. One way in which production and sales volume might be increased is to lower the price. Let us assume, for example, that in addition to its job work, the Small Business Company manufactures widgets and a variety of other low-volume standard products. Last year, the company sold 20,000 widgets at $6 each. The *variable* cost per unit to produce them was $3. The owner/manager estimates that an additional 5,000 could be sold if the price were reduced to $5.60. If such a pricing policy were followed, what would be the added **profit contribution?** Using the same analytical framework as above, we find that the company's profit would be increased (or its loss decreased) by $5,000:

1. Price per unit	$5.60
2. Volume in units	25,000
3. Variable cost per unit (unchanged)	$3.00
4. *Added* income (line 1 × line 2 − $120,000 original volume)	$20,000
5. *Added* variable cost (line 2 × line 3 − $60,000 variable cost at original volume)	$15,000
6. *Added* **profit-volume income** (line 4 − line 5)	$5,000
7. Programmed cost	0
8. *Added* profit contribution (line 6 − line 7)	$5,000

Another way in which a small business might use its excess capacity is to add a new product to its line. Let us assume that, according to a market study, the Small Business Company could expect to sell an estimated 10,000 units of a new product during the coming year at a price of $5 per unit, with a special advertising and sales promotion effort costing $10,000. The new product can be produced on existing equipment, and direct labor and direct material costs would total an estimated $3 per unit. If the company diversified its product line, what would be the added profit contribution? Proceeding as before, it is seen that there would be a $10,000 contribution to fixed cost and profit:

1. Price per unit	$5.00
2. Volume in units	10,000
3. Variable cost per unit	$3.00
4. *Added* income (line 1 × line 2)	$50,000
5. *Added* variable cost (line 2 × line 3)	$30,000
6. *Added* profit-volume income (line 4 − line 5)	$20,000
7. Programmed cost	$10,000
8. *Added* profit contribution (line 6 − line 7)	$10,000

Another familiar example of the incremental-cost or marginal-income approach to small business management decision making is the "make-or-buy" decision. If the company is currently purchasing an item, and it has excess machine capacity of a type used in its manufacture, the company may well consider manufacturing the item itself. On the traditional full-costing basis the company probably cannot manufacture the product as efficiently as the manufacturer from whom it had been buying the item, but so long as the company's out-of-pocket (or variable) cost is less than the purchase price it has been paying, the company's profit situation will be improved.

EXPENSE BUDGETING

Just as business firms in a given industry may differ in terms of their cost structure, so also may they differ in terms of their operating efficiency. Many small businesses can increase their profit margins by more careful planning and control of their **operating expenses.**[6]

An **expense budget** is a control device used by management to predetermine what each major class of expenses should be for the period of time covered, and to aid executives in conducting the business in line with these expenses as planned. Expense budgeting, like cash budgeting and capital budgeting, is a valuable management aid.

In modern business, control is always exercised in relation to some goal. There must be a desired objective, certain standards set or predetermined, current reports or records for comparison with these standards, and prompt executive action to keep in line with planned figures. These goals or standards may be time or output standards, or they may relate to production, inventory and employment levels, or other operating aspects of the business; but our attention here will be confined to business expenses. To repeat for emphasis, control requires predetermined standards, current comparable reports, and prompt, intelligent executive action.

As applied to the expense budget, the objective may be to achieve a certain volume of business at minimum cost or to expand volume rapidly even

[6] Operating expenses include all costs of doing business *except* the cost of goods sold; includes only selling, general, and administrative expenses.

EXPENSES

SALARIES & WAGES	$ 16,500
UTILITIES	2,200
DEPRECIATION	2,600
INTEREST	200
INSURANCE	350
ADMINISTRATIVE EXPENSE	15,000
SUPPLIES	400
BAD DEBT EXPENSE	300
ADVERTISING	1,150
STATE & LOCAL TAXES	1,300
TOTAL EXPENSES	$40,000

though the cost of doing so will be high temporarily. In either case, standards will be set in terms of anticipated expenses appropriate to the objective planned; operating reports that show at frequent intervals what expenses have been actually incurred will permit comparison with planned figures. Appropriate action taken in time will prevent an unsatisfactory condition from continuing.

An expense budget is a "must" for every business. In launching a new enterprise, it is the basis for deciding whether the venture should be undertaken, or for satisfying the banker that the enterpriser has a good proposition for a loan. To the established business it means the difference between success and failure. It should be made in terms of an accepted expense classification for the particular business field and in line with available data from other successful firms.

Expense Classification

By adopting the standard expense classification in the particular line of business in which they are engaged, small business owners will be able to use current **operating ratios** and expense data published by their particular trade association, Dun & Bradstreet, and other reporting agencies as a continuing guide to the success of their operations. If they select their own expense accounts, definitions, or classifications, they will have no assurance that these are comparable to published data. For example, does the expense for advertising include only payment to newspapers and other media, or also payroll, donations, and other such items? Are the same items included in the delivery, credit, or other expenses for customer services that other business owners in that type of business include? Discrepancies in expense classifications such as the few suggested here will render comparisons with average data for the industry worthless.

For the small owner-operated business it is also important that *imputed* as well as *actual* costs be included in the standard expense accounts. Examples of actual expenses are payments made for utility services, labor, interest on loans, and, if the building is not owned by the proprietor, rent. Imputed expenses are those that would be charged for property or services of the proprietor if secured from someone else; they include interest on the proprietor's own capital invested in the business, rent for the premises the proprietor owns that are used for business purposes, and a fair salary for the proprietor's own services as manager of the business.

With an accurate, complete record of the expense items that make up the totals in standard expense accounts, an operator can immediately tell whether one item that is too high can be cut down in future operations. Suppose one of the accounts is lower than standard. Ordinarily, the operator would experience a certain amount of satisfaction over this, but it should be examined anyway. Perhaps something is wrong. If this was an advertising account, the operator might have brought in a larger sales volume and a correspondingly higher profit if more had been spent for advertising. In studying expense control it is well to know how much can wisely be spent to increase sales volume and where adjustments, up or down, can be made to increase net profit in the long run.

Operating Ratios

Operating ratios are used in expense control; profit and each item of expense in the profit-and-loss statement are expressed as a percentage of sales income, as follows:

		PERCENTAGE
Net sales	$200,000	100%
Less: Cost of goods sold	140,000	70%
Gross margin	$ 60,000	30%
Less: Expenses (itemized)	40,000	20%
Net profit	$ 20,000	10%

An excessive operating cost (compared with past cost experience in the firm or with the experience of other firms of the same size in the industry) may be caused by carelessness; a below-normal expenditure may indicate neglect of a particularly vital activity that would improve if properly financed. Frequently if the same amount of money is intelligently spent on one activity, and not misspent on another, improvements in volume and profit promptly appear.

The number of sources of published standard operating ratios runs into the hundreds. The expense items for which standard ratios are developed, of course, vary from one line of business to another, and within each industry there are differences among firms on the basis of size, geographic location, credit policies, and other factors.

Standard operating ratios for various types of business are available from trade associations and from a number of nontrade sources. The two principal booklets dealing with summary ratios in retailing are *Expenses in Retail Business*, published by NCR Corporation, and the *Barometer of Small Business*, published by the Accounting Corporation of America; the latter publication also includes data on many types of service establishments. Other sources are Dun & Bradstreet and Robert Morris Associates, publishing standard operating ratios in wholesaling and manufacturing as well as in retailing.[7]

Even though the standard expense ratios are based on the profit-and-loss statements of a group of similar businesses of similar size, the ratios for a particular firm may vary considerably from the standard ratios because of differences in operating conditions. Some of the reasons for variations from one firm to another in particular ratios are discussed below.

Total operating expense ratio.   A higher-than-average total operating expense ratio does not necessarily reflect any unfavorable conditions in the firm. If it is accompanied by a high gross margin ratio[8] and a satisfactory net profit ratio, it may simply reflect the character and policy of the firm. For example, sales based on additional service to customers or clients may yield extra gross margin to cover the extra expense involved and to provide a satisfactory net profit.

Nevertheless, a firm with a total expense ratio much higher than that for similar firms is quite likely to be unprofitable. The typical unprofitable firm has a high total expense ratio for its kind of business. This may be due to small sales volume as compared with the profitable firm, and not necessarily because it pays higher wage rates or higher insurance rates. More frequently, however, a higher-than-average total operating expense ratio in an unprofitable firm indicates low efficiency; that is, poor management in controlling expenses.

Net profit ratio.   The net profit ratio reflects the net results of the operation of the firm. This ratio indicates the effectiveness of the management of the firm and measures the efficiency of its operation. The net profit ratio is in-

---

[7] Many of these sources also publish other types of financial ratios, such as liquidity ratios, turnover ratios, and leverage or debt ratios; see pp. 327–33.

[8] The gross margin ratio is discussed on p. 329.

fluenced by many factors. A profitable firm is usually the result of efficient management which, on the one hand, succeeds in maintaining a satisfactory dollar gross margin—from purchases at low cost and from sales at prices that are neither too high nor too low—and, on the other hand, succeeds in keeping all expenses under control.[9]

Proprietor's wage ratio.   Since many small business owners do not make a distinction between money that is withdrawn for their wages and that which is a withdrawal of profits, a proprietor's wage ratio that varies from the average may have no significance. A higher-than-average ratio may indicate either that the firm earns large profits or that excessive wages are being paid to the owner. It is important that excessive portions of capital not be withdrawn, for this limits future growth.

A low owner's wage ratio accompanied by small withdrawals of profits and a satisfactory net profit ratio indicates that the entrepreneur is building up capital by leaving the profits in the business. On the other hand, a low wage ratio accompanied by a low net profit ratio indicates that the owner is getting a small total return on his or her investment in the business.

Employees' wage ratio.   A relatively high employees' wage ratio is ordinarily an unfavorable sign. A high wage ratio may be the result of inefficient use of help, or the employment of too many sales clerks or production workers for the volume being obtained, or it may be the result of other factors. Like a high gross margin ratio, however, a high wage ratio may be the result of a carefully thought-out management policy. It may, for example, indicate the firm's policy of attracting the better (more productive) workers in the local labor force by paying wages higher than the going rate.

A low employees' wage ratio is usually evidence of efficient management, especially if it is accompanied by a low total operating expense ratio and a satisfactory net profit ratio. It may mean, however, that the firm is not employing enough workers for the given production or sales volume, or that it is not employing the right kind of workers because of a relatively low wage structure.

Rent (or occupancy) expense ratio.   A high rent or **occupancy expense** ratio may be the result of the business premises being larger than necessary to handle the present sales or production volume. For a retailer, however, a high rent ratio may mean that a favorable location has been obtained that makes it possible to obtain sales without high expenditures for advertising which might otherwise be necessary.[10]

A low rent or occupancy expense ratio may mean that the owner has been able to secure the building premises at a low rental or purchase price. Or it

---

[9] A firm's profit should also be measured in relation to the owner's investment; see the discussion of profit ratios on pp. 328–30.

[10] For a discussion of the rent-advertising relationship, see p. 194.

may mean that the building is too small for the volume of business. A mutual comparison can be made with a rent-to-gross-margin ratio.

Advertising expense ratio.   An advertising expense ratio that is in line with a standard ratio may not necessarily be favorable. The advertising may have been successful in increasing dollar sales volume, so that the added dollar advertising expense represents no greater percentage of sales than normal. But, if the added sales volume consists mainly of staples or low-margin goods, the advertising may not be profitable. To be profitable, advertising must result in added dollar gross margin more than sufficient to cover the added dollar advertising and other expenses. That is, the advertising should sell goods carrying high gross margin rates as well as staples.

On the other hand, a low advertising expense ratio, which is accompanied by low sales and net profits, may possibly mean that one of the causes of the unfavorable results is insufficient advertising.

Delivery expense ratio.   Unless the proportions of delivered sales to total sales are known, no worthwhile comparisons of delivery expense ratios can be made. A firm that delivers two-thirds of its sales will almost necessarily have a higher delivery expense ratio than a firm with only one-third delivered sales, and any difference between the ratios of such firms will be of no significance. Only when a firm has approximately the same proportion of delivered sales as that of the group with which it is being compared can significant comparisons be made. A high ratio will then indicate inefficiency in the delivery operation, ane a low ratio the opposite.

Bad-debt loss ratio.   One of the factors to be considered in analyzing the bad-debt loss ratio is the proportion of credit sales to total sales. Just as in the case of the delivery expense ratio, a more worthwhile comparison can be made if the proportion of a firm's credit sales is approximately the same as that of the group of firms with which it is being compared.

A low bad-debt ratio is usually evidence of a credit-and-collection policy that has been carefully planned and strictly enforced. Or it may be an indication that too much caution is being used in the development of credit sales. A high ratio usually indicates laxness in extending credit and in making collections.

Other expense ratios.   Higher than standard ratios for any of the other expense items on the profit and loss statement usually indicate an opportunity for expense reduction. More often than not the costs of supplies and utilities (heat, light, power, and water), and particularly miscellaneous expenses, may be higher than average because of carelessness in cost control. Depreciation of equipment, on the other hand, being a noncash expense, may be high because of the methods of computing depreciation.

All money invested in a business, whether in fixtures, equipment, stock, or in operating expenses, is expected to yield a profit to the investor. Because of the risks incurred in going into business for one's self, this capital should yield a higher rate of return than could be obtained from investment in government or corporate securities having a guaranteed rate of interest. But this requires careful management by the entrepreneur.

A firm's profit may be increased through more effective *profit planning* and/or more effective *cost control.* In this chapter, two methods of determining profit goals or evaluating the profit potential of a small business were examined—break-even analysis and marginal-income analysis. Interrelated cost control techniques that were discussed included expense budgeting and ratio analysis. These methods are not difficult to apply in a small business. Those small firm operators who learn them and apply them in the conduct of their businesses will be well-repaid for their efforts by the greater profits that will ultimately result.

KEY WORDS

break-even analysis	occupancy expense
break-even point	operating expenses
business cycle	operating ratios
contribution margin	passive cost
crossover point	profit
demand forecast	profit contribution
expense budget	profit-volume income
fixed cost	pro forma financial statement
floating debt	programmed cost
funded debt	secular trend
gross national product	semivariable cost
incremental cost	standby cost
marginal-income analysis	variable cost

DISCUSSION QUESTIONS

1. How might the topics discusssed in this chapter be of use to a person (a) in appraising a business for possible purchase? (b) in justifying a new business?

2. Outline some of the ways in which (a) a small-scale retailer can reduce operating costs without hurting the business. Do the same for (b) a wholesaler and (c) a small manufacturer.

EXERCISES AND PROBLEMS

1. For each of the following, mark (F) for fixed cost and (V) for variable cost:
   a. Interest on funded debt
   b. Part-time help
   c. Full-time salaried help
   d. Property taxes
   e. Rent
   f. Depreciation
   g. Cost of goods sold
   h. Insurance
   i. Interest on floating debt
   j. Materials and supplies
   k. Production workers on incentive
   l. Seasonal help
   m. Bad debts
   n. Utilities
   o. Administrative expense
   p. Delivery expense

2. Fill in the blanks below:

SALES	VARIABLE EXPENSES	FIXED EXPENSES	TOTAL COSTS	NET PROFIT	CONTRIBUTION MARGIN RATIO
$1,000	$700	___	$1,000	___	___
$1,500	___	$300	___	___	.30
___	$500	___	$ 800	$1,200	___
$2,000	___	$300	___	$ 200	___

3. Following is the cost structure of the Hawkeye Company, as derived from last year's profit-and-loss statement:

Sales		$96,000
Fixed costs	$20,000	
Variable costs	64,000	84,000
Profit		$12,000

a. On an arithmetic grid (cross-section paper), plot and identify both the sales line and the total cost line.

b. Determine each of the following (both by inspection of the break-even chart and by calculation):

    1) Variable cost per dollar of sales

    2) Break-even point

    3) Profit (or loss) at $50,000 sales volume

    4) Profit at $80,000 sales volume

    5) Profit at $100,000 sales volume

    6) Profit at $120,000 sales volume

c. Calculate the rate of profit (on sales) at each of the following sales levels:

    1) $80,000

    2) $100,000

    3) $120,000

4. Assume that you have purchased a small establishment in your line of business. Last year's sales were 100,000 units, which had been acquired (manufactured in your shop, or purchased for resale) at a cost of $200,000. Monthly occupancy expense (rent, light, heat, insurance, etc.) is $1,000. Sales and administrative costs (mostly salaries) totaled $23,000 last year, and equipment depreciated at the rate of $1,000 per year.

    a. How many units of product must you sell to break even if you plan to set the price at $5 per unit?

    b. What would your profit be at a sales volume of 20,000 units?

    c. Suppose that the unit acquisition cost increased to $3, but the selling price remained the same to keep it competitive. What effect will this have on the volume of business you must do to break even?

5. Assume that the fixed costs in your business are $200,000 for the year. The variable costs are 60 percent of sales, and sales are expected to reach $750,000.

    a. Calculate the volume of sales you would need to break even.

    b. Calculate your expected profit.

    c. If sales were forecast at only $400,000, should you shut down operations? Why or why not?

CASES IN POINT

Alonzo Billings operates a small printing plant in a medium-sized midwestern city. His wife, father-in-law, one salesman, and one press operator are the entire staff, except for a number of housewives living nearby who are on call to come in and help with sorting, assembling, addressing, and stuffing of direct mail and similar jobs when needed. Mr. Billings also does much of the selling. This is an old, well-established, and reasonably prosperous firm. They handle all kinds of small printing jobs and have not specialized in serving any particular industry such as banking, retailing, or manufacturers, or in performing any particular kind of work such as stationery, brochures, direct mail, or business forms.

Much work brought in by salespeople is on a bidding basis. Sometimes Mr. Billings is forced to accept jobs (to hold a customer or keep the plant busy) that he must do at a price that does not permit him to produce the quality of work he really prefers in his shop. There is, of course, much repeat business, jobs which come from old customers and with which the employees are all familiar—to the point that the type may remain set up for years with little alteration from order to order. This is not often very profitable work, but it is, he feels, desirable for the firm because it is dependable. It also builds and holds goodwill, he believes.

Mr. Billings knows that he does not get all the business of all of his present customers. He also knows that there are potential customers in the community who give him no business at all, simply because neither he nor his salesman have had time to call on them.

He also knows that he can do some kinds of printing better than others. Furthermore, various new printing processes are competing for some of his business. Business is good, but not improving. Recently he said, "How can I develop a plan or program that will get me the kind of business I do best at a profit?"

At a printers' convention seminar a few weeks ago, he heard a panel discussion concerning "Planning for Profit." The general theme was that by classifying customers' past records as to types of jobs done for them, and then classifying these types of jobs as to profitability, it is possible to concentrate on quality business at a profit. This sounds good, but Mr. Billings' father-in-law is afraid it would offend many customers, would take too long, and would be an expensive experiment for such a well-known firm as theirs. Furthermore, Mr. Billings' salesman, also an older man, wants no interference with his established routine and familiar contacts. Mr. Billings knows, too, that any such change in policy might call for new equipment.

Assume that you are Mr. Billings and that you have decided to go ahead, at least in a small way. Draw up a pattern for analysis of work done, in terms of what you think you want to achieve.

For twenty-seven years Gerkensmeier's, under the control of Emil Gerkensmeier, who started the business, made quality ice cream in Phoenix. Gerkensmeier, who learned ice cream making at Kansas

State University where he majored in agriculture, says he developed his flavors one at a time, each getting a personalized touch. He made his ice cream only 10 gallons at a time and taste-tested every batch.

Now 68 years old and a widower, Gerkensmeier sold his business to Bill and Ruth Harris six months ago for $50,000 with the understanding that he would train the Harrises. After three months, Gerkensmeier decided that he still wanted to stay active in the business so a partnership was formed. Emil put in $10,000 and was placed in charge of quality control. Alonso Yturbi, age 23, put in $10,000 and was put in charge of production. Ruth Harris, age 33, serves the customers at the counter, supervises several part-time workers, and attempts to keep some very sketchy records. Bill, age 35, with a degree in civil engineering, is in essence the general manager. He also works part-time as a highly paid consultant in the construction industry, thus permitting the Harrises to live modestly without drawing any funds from the business.

The quality of the ice cream is so superior to that of any competitors that retail sales and sales demand from six retailers have far outstripped the present capacity. The superior quality has been written up in the food column of the local newspaper. Currently about 20 different flavors are produced, all having wide acceptance. Advertising has been done on a rather casual basis in local papers at various times.

Practically no records were kept by Gerkensmeier. A review of his city sales tax forms and personal income tax forms (those he kept) indicates a steady sales volume of about $100,000 a year in the last few years, with a profit of about $12,000 a year. Naturally, the summer months' sales were about 50 percent higher than the rest of the year.

Unfortunately since the Harrises have taken over the business, the record keeping has not improved. They are aware of the need for good records for decision-making, and Ruth is willing to keep a set of books, but she doesn't know where to start. They have collected various records for the month of May that could serve as a starting point for a cost control system, a cash flow forecast, and a profit-and-loss statement. The data are summarized on p. 371.

The owners feel that these expenses are fairly typical of their monthly operation costs and that the maximum retail sales at the store for any given month are about 3,600 gallons. The Harrises have continued Gerkensmeier's policy of paying cash for everything and selling on net 30 days, resulting in no accounts payable and no meaningful accounts receivable.

Data for month of May

Gallons produced	6,500	
Sold wholesale	3,600 gallons	$4,500
Sold retail	2,900 gallons	$4,500

Inventory remained constant at 50 gallons

Cost of ice cream materials	$4,000
Cost of ice cream related supplies	900
Cost of store supplies	200
Wages—retail store	500
Maintenance	100
Advertising	60
Delivery	100
Utilities	190
Loan payments	700
Draw–Gerkensmeier	100
Draw–Yturbi	400

At the present time a conservative estimate is that wholesale sales could triple if additional capacity were available. The firm can purchase a second ice cream maker and related equipment, including a freezer, for $10,000; this would effectively double capacity and increase production labor costs only about 10 percent. Materials and supplies would, of course, double. The Harrises have accumulated about $5,000 additional savings and feel that the remainder can be generated out of cash flow in a few months. If the new equipment is purchased it may be paid for over a six-month period.

The lease on the building has four more years to run. Currently, about half of the building is used for retail sales and one quarter for production. The remaining space is basically unused.

To date the relationship among all the partners is excellent. The Harrises, of course, are anxious to devote full time to the business and draw a good income from its operation. Furthermore, in casual conversation, the Harrises have mentioned that eventually they would like to franchise retail outlets, first in Phoenix and eventually over a larger area.

Under what conditions should the Harrises expand the business?

Cash Flows
and Capital Expenditures

CHAPTER TWENTY-TWO *The manager of a small business must not only anticipate* short-run *cash shortages or surpluses, but make* long-term *commitments of funds for additions to or replacement of the firm's fixed or capital assets. The discussion of the concepts of cash flow and cash cycle in this chapter will help you in your understanding of the movement of cash into and out of the business. You will also gain a greater understanding of the techniques used in evaluating proposed capital expenditures.*

For the established concern, careful financial planning is a continuing necessity. A shortage of funds in the present is often the result of the unwise use of funds in the past. In particular the firm should (1) avoid excessive investment in fixed assets, (2) maintain receivables and net working capital in proper proportion to sales, and (3) avoid excessive inventories. There is no financial difficulty of any firm, regardless of size, that cannot be traced to the violation of one or more of these three basic principles of financial management. Proper financial planning requires the budgeting of both short- and long-term funds (*cash* budgeting and *capital* budgeting).

IMPORTANCE OF CASH FLOW

In addition to profit, a basic objective of any business is **liquidity.** From Day 1, and continuously thereafter, the small business owner/manager must be deeply concerned with the **cash flow** (money and checks) into and out of the business; how he or she manages this cash is critical to the firm's survival and growth.

The first inflow of money into the business consisted of the owner's own investment, supplemented in most cases by other investors' funds and/or a loan from the bank or other capital source. The firm's first outflow of money, obviously, went into its physical facilities or fixed assets—building, equipment, furniture and fixtures—and for certain other start-up expenses, including most importantly an inventory of merchandise or raw materials. The sale of the company's inventory of products, in turn, creates the largest inflow of cash into the business. The time lapse between the purchase of goods and materials

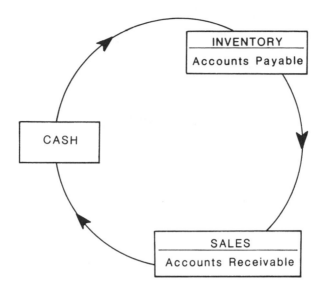

and the collection of accounts receivable for the merchandise or finished products sold is known as the **cash cycle.** The length of this cycle varies from one firm to another, but in any case the cash flows are *continuous,* for physical assets will always need to be replaced and the firm will always need inventory for sale.

The *balancing* of these cash flows in a **cash budget** is a major responsibility of the small business owner/manager. If, at any time, the cash outflow is greater than the cash inflow, then the firm will not be able to pay its bills when they become due and will therefore be technically **insolvent.**[1] Failure to pay its bills on time seriously affects the firm's credit rating and its ability to obtain the additional capital that every growing company will need at some point. Nor will the firm be able to take advantage of cash discounts on its purchases; thus its cost of sales will be increased, and its gross margins reduced. On the other hand, the firm's earning power is also adversely affected if the cash balance is excessive, for idle funds earn no profit.

It is clear from the above discussion that liquidity and profit are *interdependent* objectives. The achievement of these twin objectives requires that the funds on hand be used in the most effective manner[2] and that future needs for funds be carefully planned.

In some businesses, such as grocery stores, drugstores, restaurants, and bars and cocktail lounges, there is little seasonal fluctuation in sales. Automobile dealers, in contrast, have big ups and downs—typically, high in spring and low in winter. Apparel stores also have substantial seasonal variations in sales

---

[1] It might not be bankrupt in the sense that its liabilities exceed its assets, but neither is it paying its bills; thus bankruptcy proceedings *could* be initiated against the firm. See pp. 348–49 for a discussion of the bankruptcy laws.

[2] Expense budgeting and control was discussed in Chapter 21.

income. Operating expenses for the typical business, on the other hand, vary considerably less from one month or season to another than do sales, because many of these costs are fixed or uncontrollable. There are times in most businesses when cash inflow will exceed cash outflow, and other times when cash operating expenses exceed cash income. The challenge to small business owners, as noted, is to balance these cash flows and preserve the firm's liquidity. Lack of liquidity can drive a business to the wall just as easily as can insolvency.

It seems incredible to some that a business firm with growing sales and rising profits can become bankrupt—but it happens, particularly in times of tight credit. The dilemma of a very successful, expanding company requiring increasing amounts of additional cash is a common occurrence. Cash needs always exceed cash sources in a growth situation. In many cases successful companies find themselves short of cash because a large part of their increasing production is sold on credit, and goods or materials will not be paid for immediately. For a while, the more they sell, the more their supply of money on hand diminishes. Without sound planning, this situation eventually leads to a crisis. Cash budgeting points up the problem in advance and permits a course of action *before* it becomes critical.

The first step in the preparation of a cash budget is to make a **sales forecast** broken down by months to reflect seasonal fluctuations, as illustrated in the following table:

MONTH	SALES FORECAST	WAGES AND SALARIES
November	$26,000	$1,600
December	28,000	1,600
January	14,000	1,200
February	12,000	1,200
March	11,000	1,200
April	17,000	1,200
May	18,000	1,200
June	16,000	1,200
July	15,000	1,200
August	15,000	1,200
September	19,000	1,200
October	24,000	1,600

Cash flow into the firm's treasury, however, will be affected by the amount of cash business and by the average collection period on credit sales, as well as by seasonal sales variations. For example, let us assume that 40 percent of the projected sales are cash transactions. Let us further assume that of the credit sales, 60 percent is collected the first month following the sale, and the remaining 40 percent is collected in the second month following the sale. In such a case, the cash budget in Table 22-1 will show only 40 percent of the monthly sales estimate coming into the business, plus collections on accounts receivable for credit sales made during the preceding two months. Thus, for the month of January collections on accounts receivable are estimated as follows:

Step 1.	(a)	60 percent of December sales	$16,800
	(b)	60 percent of November sales	15,600
Step 2.		60 percent of (a)	$10,080
	+	40 percent of (b)	6,240
			$16,320

The next step in the preparation of a cash budget is to make an estimate of how the cash flows *out* of the business. The major single expenditure will be for the replenishment of inventory. If the profit margin on sales averages 25 percent, for example, then the average cost of the merchandise purchased for resale is 75 percent. If it is further assumed that (1) inventory is purchased each month to cover the next month's sales, and that (2) all merchandise purchases are paid for during the month of purchase, then the estimated cash outlay for merchandise purchased in January would be 75 percent times the expected February sales of $12,000, or $9,000.

375

TABLE 22-1
Cash Budget, or Cash Flow Statement

LINE		JANUARY	FEBRUARY	MARCH
1	Cash balance— start of month (line 8)	$ 5,000	$ 5,000	$ 5,000
2	Expected cash sales	5,600	4,800	4,400
3	Expected collections on accounts receivable	16,320	11,760	7,680
4	Other cash income	—	—	—
5 (2+3+4)	Total receipts	$21,920	$16,560	$12,080
6 (1+5)	Beginning cash balance plus receipts	$26,920	$21,560	$17,080
7	Cash operating expenses (total)	11,230	10,440	14,920
8	Minimum cash balance	5,000	5,000	5,000
9 (6-7-8)	Cash available for loan payments or investment	$10,690	$ 6,120	($ 2,840)
10	Loan payments			
11	Cumulative investment (or borrowing)	$10,690°	$16,810	$13,970

° Zero at end of preceding month.

The next largest cash outlay in a merchandising establishment is for wages and salaries—also estimated in the above table. The operating expenses for the hypothetical firm whose cash budget is illustrated in Table 22-1 are expected to total $11,230 in the month of January (line 7), as follows:

Merchandise inventory	$ 9,000
Wages and salaries	1,200
Occupancy expense	750 (fixed)
Other operating expenses	280 (computed at 2 percent of sales)
	$11,230

The reader is reminded that this total represents *cash* operating expenses only; not included are charges for depreciation or amortization, bad-debt write-offs, and other noncash expenses.

Cash in excess of the minimum acceptable balance each month (line 9), if not used to repay loans previously incurred (line 10), is placed in short-term investments so that funds will be available during months when cash payments exceed cash income.

INVESTMENT DECISION CRITERIA

In cash budgeting we were concerned with the net working capital position of the business, or its *short-term* needs for funds. Sooner or later, however, the small business will be faced with the problem of deciding whether or not a *long-term* commitment of a large sum of money should be made to replace equipment or buy new equipment. Such long-term commitments are called **capital expenditures** to distinguish them from short-term or operational expenditures made to increase inventory, hire more labor, or repair equipment.

Suppose, for example, that the firm is considering buying some equipment to speed up some operation. Among the questions that must be answered in deciding the desirability of a proposed capital expenditure are the following: Could the money the equipment will cost be used more profitably elsewhere? Will the expenditures strain the firm's cash position? Will the equipment's cost be offset by economies it will bring, or by the profits of expanded capacity it will make possible?

Several **capital budgeting** procedures are available to small business owners to help them find answers to these questions. In this section we will discuss some of the more important capital investment decision criteria.

The Present-Value Criterion

The **present-value** method in capital budgeting measures the net difference in cash inflows and outflows in terms of *discounted* dollars. Its significance as an investment criterion can best be illustrated by first balancing the *non*discounted cash flows in a given situation. Let us assume, for example, that the small business owner is faced with the problem of selecting one of two machines to perform an important operation in the business. Machine A costs less to buy and install but is less efficient than Machine B; the annual costs of operating the machines (to achieve the desired output) are $5,000 and $4,500, respectively. Both machines are expected to have a useful or economic life of eight years. The higher initial cost of Machine B is reflected in a higher salvage value at the end of this period—$5,000, as compared with $3,000 for Machine A.

The average annual cost of Machine A, therefore, may be calculated as follows:

$$\frac{(\$15,000 - \$3,000) + (8 \times \$5,000)}{8} = \frac{\$52,000}{8} = \$6,500$$

The average annual cost of Machine B, on the other hand, is:

$$\frac{(\$20,000 - \$5,000) + (8 \times \$4,500)}{8} = \frac{\$51,000}{8} = \$6,375$$

Based on these calculations, the small business owner would select Machine B over Machine A. However, this method of analysis ignores the important fact that a dollar *today* is worth *more* than a dollar at some future date.

Would it have made any difference, in the above case, if the costs had been discounted? At what rate should the cost figures be discounted? The **cost of capital** is defined as the minimum cost, expressed as a rate per annum, that would induce bankers or other investors to place their funds at the company's disposal. This rate, of course, varies with time and circumstances, and from one firm to another.

Let us assume, in this case, that the firm's cost of capital is 10 percent per year. At this rate a dollar of cash on hand today "costs" only $0.909 if it is not paid out until one year hence [($1.00)/(1.10)^1], and only $0.826 if it is not paid out until two years hence [($1.00)/(1.10)^2], etc. To put it another way (in terms of cash *inflow*), the prospect of getting a dollar today is worth more than the prospect of getting that dollar one year hence. Table 22-2 gives the present values for single future payments or credits at various interest rates.

Discounting all *operating* costs to the present in the above example at the assumed 10 percent rate, we find that these costs total $26,670 over an eight-year period for Machine A:

1st year operating cost	=	$5,000	×	0.909	=	$ 4,545
2nd year operating cost	=	$5,000	×	.826	=	4,130
3rd year operating cost	=	$5,000	×	.751	=	3,755
4th year operating cost	=	$5,000	×	.683	=	3,415
5th year operating cost	=	$5,000	×	.621	=	3,105
6th year operating cost	=	$5,000	×	.564	=	2,820
7th year operating cost	=	$5,000	×	.513	=	2,565
8th year operating cost	=	$5,000	×	.467	=	2,335
				5,334		$26,670

The reader will note that since the cash outlay to be discounted each year is the *same,* the above calculation could have been more easily made by multiplying the $5,000 annual cost by the *sum* of the discount factors: $5,000 × 5.334 = $26,670.

The present value of the initial installed cost of Machine A, of course, is $15,000. Adding this capital cost to the $26,670 in total operating costs for the expected eight-year life of the machine yields a gross cost figure of $41,670. From this amount is subtracted the present value of the salvage value ($3,000 × 0.467), or $1,400. The net discounted cost of the investment in Machine A is, therefore, $40,270.

Comparable costs for Machine B are as follows:

Installed cost	$20,000
Total operating costs—8 years ($4,500 × 5.334)	24,003
	$44,003
Less present value of the salvage value ($5,000 × 0.467)	2,335
Total costs	$41,668

TABLE 22-2

Present Value of $1.00 to Be Received at the End of Indicated Year

YEAR	5%	6%	7%	8%	9%	10%	11%	12%	13%	14%	15%	16%	17%	18%	19%	20%
1	$0.952	$0.943	$0.935	$0.926	$0.917	$0.909	$0.901	$0.893	$0.885	$0.877	$0.870	$0.862	$0.855	$0.847	$0.840	$0.833
2	.907	.890	.873	.857	.842	.826	.812	.797	.783	.769	.756	.743	.731	.718	.706	.694
3	.864	.840	.816	.794	.772	.751	.731	.712	.693	.675	.658	.641	.624	.609	.593	.579
4	.823	.792	.763	.735	.708	.683	.659	.636	.613	.592	.572	.552	.534	.516	.499	.482
5	.784	.747	.713	.681	.650	.621	.593	.567	.543	.519	.497	.476	.456	.437	.419	.402
6	.746	.705	.666	.630	.596	.564	.535	.507	.480	.456	.432	.410	.390	.370	.352	.335
7	.711	.665	.623	.583	.547	.513	.482	.452	.425	.400	.376	.354	.333	.314	.296	.279
8	.677	.627	.582	.540	.502	.467	.434	.404	.376	.351	.327	.305	.285	.266	.249	.233
9	.645	.592	.544	.500	.460	.424	.391	.361	.333	.308	.284	.263	.243	.225	.209	.194
10	.614	.558	.508	.463	.422	.386	.352	.322	.295	.270	.247	.227	.208	.191	.176	.161
11	.585	.527	.475	.429	.388	.350	.317	.287	.261	.237	.215	.195	.178	.162	.148	.135
12	.557	.497	.444	.397	.356	.319	.286	.257	.231	.208	.187	.168	.152	.137	.124	.112
13	.530	.469	.415	.368	.326	.290	.258	.229	.204	.182	.163	.145	.130	.116	.104	.093
14	.505	.442	.388	.340	.299	.263	.232	.205	.181	.160	.141	.125	.111	.099	.088	.078
15	.481	.417	.362	.315	.275	.239	.209	.183	.160	.140	.123	.108	.095	.084	.074	.065
16	.458	.394	.339	.292	.252	.218	.188	.163	.142	.123	.107	.093	.081	.071	.062	.054
17	.436	.371	.317	.270	.231	.198	.170	.146	.125	.108	.094	.080	.069	.060	.052	.045
18	.416	.350	.296	.250	.212	.180	.153	.130	.111	.095	.081	.069	.059	.051	.044	.038
19	.396	.331	.277	.232	.194	.164	.138	.116	.098	.083	.070	.060	.051	.043	.037	.031
20	.377	.312	.258	.215	.178	.149	.124	.104	.087	.073	.061	.051	.043	.037	.031	.026

Machines A and B, it is noted, have the same expected useful life (eight years). However, in many machine selection problems the serviceable or economic life of the machines may vary; in such cases it is necessary to calculate the costs on a comparable *average-annual-cost* basis. Where the cost and salvage values are not discounted (as in the earlier illustration), this is done by spreading the costs evenly over the years of the machine's expected useful life. Where the costs and salvage values are discounted (as in the latter illustration), the **equivalent annual cost** is calculated by dividing the total costs by the present-value factor of the annuity—in this instance, 5.334, or $7,550 for Machine A and $7,812 for Machine B. Using the present-value criterion, therefore, the business owner would select Machine A over Machine B—a conclusion *opposite* to that arrived at when the cost of capital was ignored. By giving consideration to the fact that money has a time value, the present-value method of capital budgeting is more accurate.

It is also noted that, since the output needs of the firm are the same regardless of which machine is selected, the two machines in our example differed only with respect to their initial and operating *costs*. In other words, the income flow generated by the machines' production was the same in either case and hence was not a significant factor in our analysis. To complete our discussion of this method of capital budgeting, let us now apply the present-value criterion to an investment proposal in which a *current* outlay of $10,000 is expected to produce a cash inflow of $2,100 per year for the next eight years. Assuming an average annual cost of capital of 10 percent, the present value of the eight expected cash inflows would be computed as follows: $2,100 × 5.334 = $11,201. Since the present value of the income flow is $1,201 greater than the present value of the cash outlay, the decision to make the investment would be a profitable one.

The Payback-Period Criterion

In situations where the small business owner is interested in knowing how soon a proposed investment may be expected to pay for itself, the **payback-period** method of capital budgeting should be used. As in the machine selection problem illustrated earlier, the payback period can be computed using either discounted or nondiscounted dollars. Because it is more accurate to do so, however, particularly where the investment proposal involves a long projected life, the author recommends that cash flows be discounted in making *all* capital budgeting decisions.

In illustrating the payback-period criterion, and for comparison purposes, let us use the above example of a $10,000 outlay that is expected to yield eight annual cash inflows of $2,100 each. Assuming a 10 percent discount rate, the **discounted payback period** for the investment proposal would be computed as follows:

YEAR	ACTUAL CASH INFLOW	PRESENT VALUE OF $1 (FROM TABLE 22-2)	PRESENT VALUE OF ANNUAL CASH INFLOW	ACCUMULATED CAPITAL RECOVERY
1	$2,100	0.909	$1,908.90	$ 1,908.90
2	2,100	.826	1,734.60	3,643.50
3	2,100	.751	1,577.10	5,220.60
4	2,100	.683	1,434.30	6,654.90
5	2,100	.621	1,304.10	7,959.00
6	2,100	.564	1,184.40	9,143.40
7	2,100	.513	1,077.30	10,220.70

From the above calculation it is seen that the cash outlay or investment is completely recovered before the end of the seventh year. The discounted payback period is approximately 6.8 years.[3]

The discounted payback-period criterion may be applied by the small business owner in either of two ways: (1) by comparing the lengths of the payback periods of several competing investment proposals, or (2) by establishing a standard minimum payback period and approving only those investment proposals that have payback periods shorter than the standard.

The Rate-of-Return Criterion

Another way of evaluating a proposed capital expenditure is to compute the expected **return on investment.** Determining the rate of return for an investment proposal entails finding the percentage discount rate that exactly equates the present value of the cash inflows expected during the life of the asset with the capital outlay required to produce the inflows. Again, let us use our example of a proposed $10,000 initial outlay which is expected to yield cash inflows of $2,100 for each of the next eight years. By means of Table 22-2, the present value of the eight cash inflows, at different assumed rates of interest, can be determined as follows:

YEAR	ACTUAL CASH INFLOW	PRESENT VALUE OF THE CASH INFLOW @ 13%	@ 14%
1	$2,100	$ 1,858.50	$1,841.70
2	2,100	1,644.30	1,614.90
3	2,100	1,455.30	1,417.50
4	2,100	1,287.30	1,243.20
5	2,100	1,140.30	1,089.90
6	2,100	1,008.00	957.60
7	2,100	892.50	840.00
8	2,100	789.60	737.10
		$10,075.80	$9,741.90

[3] In contrast, if the cash flows were not discounted, the payback would be calculated at $10,000/$2,100, or 4.8 years.

From an examination of the above table it is obvious that the projected rate of return on the investment proposal is greater than 13 percent and less than 14 percent. Since the amount, $10,000, lies 23 percent of the way between $10,076 and $9,742, the rate of return can be interpolated at 13.23 percent.[4]

In selecting one investment proposal over another (assuming that they are competing for the same funds), small business owners will select that alternative that yields the higher rate of return on their investment.

SUMMING UP

A firm's investment in current assets is generally determined by its *cash flow* and *cash cycle*. The amount of cash in the cash cycle represents the dollar amount of the firm's investment in inventory and accounts receivable. The longer the cycle, the greater the investment in these items. The greater the variability and uncertainty in the cash flow, the greater the cash balance the firm must hold to protect its liquidity. A valuable tool in planning and controlling the liquidity of a business is the *cash budget*.

A cash budget is a forecast of the timing and amounts of the future cash flows into and out of the business. It reveals when *short-term* borrowing may be necessary, how much borrowing may be necessary, and when funds will be available to pay off the loans.

Capital budgeting, on the other hand, provides a means of evaluating *long-term* investment proposals. In this chapter, three methods of measuring investment worth were examined: present value, cash payback period, and return on investment.

KEY WORDS

capital budgeting
capital expenditures
cash budget
cash cycle
cash flow
cost of capital
discounted payback period

equivalent annual cost
insolvent
liquidity
payback-period
present-value
return on investment
sales forecast

---

[4] Calculated as follows: 13 percent + 76/(10,076-9,742). *Note:* 76 = the difference (excess) between the $10,076 total at 13% and the original $10,000 investment.

DISCUSSION QUESTIONS

1. What is the purpose of preparing a cash flow statement? How does a cash flow statement differ from other types of financial statements, such as the balance sheet and income statement?

2. Under what conditions, if any, might you deem it appropriate to average annual cost (nondiscounted) as an investment criterion?

EXERCISES AND PROBLEMS

1. Given the data used in preparing Figure 22-1 on p. 376, continue the illustration by preparing a cash flow statement for the second quarter of the year.

2. Following are the cost data on two similar machines:

MACHINE	PURCHASE PRICE	ANNUAL OPERATING COST	SALVAGE VALUE	SERVICE LIFE
A	$25,000	$5,000	$6,000	6 years
B	$40,000	$4,000	$8,000	8 years

Which of these machines would you purchase:
a. on the basis of the average annual cost, nondiscounted dollars?
b. on the basis of the equivalent annual cost, discounted at 10 percent?

3. Assume that as a small business owner or manager you have an opportunity to make an investment of $5,000, which will be paid back in six annual installments of $1,400 each.

a. What would be the payback period on this investment on the basis of nondiscounted dollars?

b. What would be the payback period if recovery of the investment is discounted at 10 percent?

4. Let us again assume you are the business owner or manager in the preceding exercise. Your criterion for this type of investment is that it return at least 17 percent interest. On that basis, should you make the investment? Why or why not?

Insurance
and Risk Management

CHAPTER TWENTY-THREE *In any business it is possible to have the results of years of hard work lost by a single fire, theft, or accident, or by the death or disability of the owner or a key employee. In this chapter we'll examine some of the ways in which a small business manager can deal with risks of this kind.*

As risk is a part of one's personal life, so is it a part of one's business. Some risks are *reducible,* such as reducing the risk of accident by driving carefully or reducing the risk of theft by more vigilant security measures. Some risks can be *transferred,* such as the purchase of fire insurance on one's home or store building. Although few risks can be eliminated completely, there are ways to lessen the possible losses caused by risk.

INSURANCE PLANNING

Knowing *what kind* of **insurance** to carry and *how much* to purchase is an important aspect of insurance planning. In making these determinations, the small business owner should consider (1) the size of the potential loss, (2) its probability, and (3) the resources that would be available to meet the loss should it occur. If, for example, the loss would likely force the business into bankruptcy or cause it serious financial impairment, then obviously the risk should be insured, even though the probability that such a loss will occur is remote.

Contrary to popular belief, a high probability that a loss will occur does not indicate that the risk should be insured. In fact, the contrary is true: The greater the probability of occurrence, the less appropriate is the purchase of insurance for dealing with the risk. First, losses that occur with relative frequency are *predictable* and are typically *small* losses that can be assumed by the business without too much financial difficulty; they are often budgeted as "normal" costs of doing business and thus are included in the prices paid by customers. Some common examples are shoplifting and bad-debt losses. Second, where the probability of loss is high, a more effective method of managing or controlling the risk is to *reduce* it by adopting appropriate precautionary measures.

Also, there should be a reasonable relationship between the cost of insurance and the value that accrues to the insured firm. For example, the additional premium required to increase **deductible coverage** in many types of insurance is quite high in relation to the added protection.[1]

Insurance planning begins with a consideration of the insurable risks faced by the business enterprise. In general, the following business risks should be covered by insurance:

1. Loss or damage or property including merchandise, supplies, fixtures, and buildings

2. Loss of income resulting from interruption of business due to fire or other damage to the firm's operating assets

3. Personal injury to customers, employees, and the general public (including product liability)

4. Loss to the business from the death or disability of key employees or the owner

These insurable risks of the small business will be discussed in detail in the following section of this chapter.

with **INSURANCE** you trade . .

Large, Uncertain Loss   *for*   **Small, Known Cost**

After listing the insurable risks and the types of insurance available to cover them, small business owners must then consider how much of a loss they can afford to bear themselves, the possible losses that they would prefer to transfer, and the insurance company's fee for assuming part of this risk. The cost of the various kinds of insurance must be matched against the possible loss and the ability of the small business owner to bear the cost.

---

[1] The annual premium on a $150 deductible collision policy is approximately $35 more than on one with a $100 deductible; thus the policyholder in effect is paying $35 more for a possible gain of only $50.

It is not possible here to cite exact figures as to insurance costs because individual business insurance rates depend on so many factors—such as the firm's location, type of business, property value, the building's construction, and average inventory level. The small business owner should seek cost estimates from at least two reliable insurance agents and should carefully evaluate them before buying any coverage. The feasibility of package insurance policies at discounted rates should also be explored.

Loss or Damage of Property

The entrepreneur usually owns considerable property. For many, the building in which the business is housed represents the greatest investment. Even when the place of business is rented or leased, the small business owner's investment in furnishings and inventory is substantial. In addition to fire insurance, these investments should be protected against other perils such as smoke, windstorm and hail, riot, civil disorder, explosion, and damage by aircraft or motor vehicles. The latter forms of risk insurance—or **extended coverage**—can be added to the basic fire insurance policy at little additional cost. Vandalism and malicious mischief coverages can also be added. If the business owns or operates a steam boiler, steam boiler insurance should also be added, for the explosion coverage of the extended coverage discussed above does not include explosion of a steam boiler.

By accepting a **coinsurance** clause in a policy, the small business owner can get a substantial reduction in premiums. Under the provisions of such a clause, the insured agrees to maintain insurance equal to some specified percentage of the property's **actual cash value** or its **replacement cost.** (Replacement cost is the cost of replacing a property of like kind and quality at present-day prices; actual cash value is the replacement cost of the property *less depreciation.*) In this sense, coinsurance works like a quantity discount. If, at the time of a loss, the insured has failed to maintain the specified percentage, he or she cannot collect the full amount of the loss, even if the loss is small. Payment is made under the coinsurance provision on the basis of the following formula:

$$\frac{\text{Amount of insurance carried}}{\text{Amount the insured agreed to carry}} \times \text{Amount of loss} = \text{Amount paid}$$

Thus if the insured owns a building with an actual cash value (i.e., a depreciated value) of $100,000 and insured it with an 80 percent coinsurance provision, he or she must have coverage equal to 80 percent of the actual cash value at the time of the loss in order to collect the full depreciated value of the property at the time of the loss. Suppose that a $10,000 loss occurs immediately after the policy is taken out and that the value of the building is determined to be $100,000:

$$\frac{\text{Amount carried}}{\text{Amount required}} \times \text{Amount of loss} = \frac{\$80,000}{\$80,000} \times \$10,000 = \$10,000$$

Now suppose that the loss does not occur for three years, and that during the period the actual cash value of the property has increased to, say, $125,000. Loss payment would be made on the following basis:

$$\frac{\text{Amount carried}}{\text{Amount required}} \times \text{Amount of loss} = \frac{\$80,000}{\$100,000} \times \$10,000 = \$8,000$$

This example illustrates an important point: The coinsurance requirement is applied at the time of the loss, and the amount of insurance that is required to comply is based on the value of the property at the time of the loss. Furthermore, *the burden of maintaining the proper amount of insurance is placed on the insured individual.*

It may be noted that in the above illustration the business owner agreed to insure the building on the basis of its actual cash value (i.e., its replacement cost less depreciation). If the building had been insured on the basis of its full replacement value and if a deficiency in the coinsurance percentage exists, the owner would be able to collect for only a part of the cost of restoring the property; if the deficiency is great enough, the owner may collect even less than the depreciated value of the damaged property.

A word of warning to the small business owner is warranted here. Building costs—which determine replacement costs—have approximately doubled in the past two decades. Thus older business buildings are likely to be more underinsured than those of more recent vintage. But because of inflation many new buildings have also rapidly slipped below 80 percent coverage. Small business owners should check frequently to see that their place of business is not underinsured. The increase in its replacement cost can be estimated by means of an *appraisal kit* that their insurance company will supply on request. These kits provide multipliers applied to the original cost of the building, based on its age and the geographical area in which it is located.

The *contents* of the building should be insured against at least the same perils as the building. Retailers, particularly, may find it desirable to purchase a special glass-insurance policy that covers all risk to plate-glass windows, glass signs, glass doors, showcases, and countertops. In addition, there should be insurance coverages on various forms of dishonesty. Employers should acquire a **fidelity bond** on employees who have access to large sums of money. Protection against the dishonesty of customers and transgressors such as theft, burglary, and robbery coverage, may also be desirable.

Burglary insurance covers losses only if there are visible marks of the burglar's forced entry. Robbery insurance, on the other hand, protects the insured against loss of property, money, or securities by force, trickery, or threat of violence on *or off* the business premises; thus it would cover hijacking, for example, and other losses not covered by burglary insurance. Perhaps the best policy to cover the dishonesty exposure is the comprehensive dishonesty, disappearance, and destruction policy; this comprehensive policy, written especially for the small business owner, provides economical protection against all the forms of dishonesty mentioned above, in addition to counterfeit currency and forgery.

Some small businesses may have difficulty in obtaining property insurance coverages at reasonable rates, particularly if they are located in deteriorated urban core or high-risk areas; in some sections—known as **red-circle zones**—property insurance is not available at *any* cost through normal channels. Small business owners in these areas may get help through the **FAIR plan** or through the Federal Crime Insurance Program.

The FAIR plan.   FAIR is an acronym for Fair Access to Insurance Requirements. Under this plan, the insurance companies operating in a particular state enter into a pooling arrangement whereby they share risks in high-risk areas and agree to pay their proportionate share toward the full sum of an approved claim. FAIR plans have been introduced in twenty-six states, and in Puerto Rico and the District of Columbia. The plan works as follows: A small business owner (or homeowner) unable to get property insurance through ordinary channels obtains an application from the FAIR plan headquarters or from an insurance agent, broker, or company. The owner fills out the form and returns it. An inspection of the property is made, and if the property meets minimum insurance requirements, a policy is issued on payment of a premium.

Even if certain dangerous conditions do exist, the property may be declared eligible for coverage, but at an increased rate until these hazards are eliminated. If the property is found to be uninsurable because of excessive hazards, the inspector points out these deficiencies and the owner may have them repaired and request another inspection. The principal deficiencies generally are faulty wiring, faulty heating units, generally dilapidated conditions that make property subject to trespass by derelicts, or poor housekeeping, (e.g., accumulations of rubbish). Protection offered through FAIR plans includes fire and extended coverage, covering (as noted above) riots, civil disorders, and other perils.

In only one of the FAIR plan states, however, does the FAIR plan include protection against crime losses—one of the most important problems of small business located in deteriorated urban core areas! To fill this void, the Federal Crime Insurance Program was launched by the U.S. Department of Housing and Urban Development on August 1, 1971.

Federal Crime Insurance Program.   In some urban core areas, privately underwritten crime insurance is totally unavailable, or available only at prohibitive premium rates. As long as crime and civil disorder continue to flourish in these areas, the responsibility for providing insurance coverage against these hazards would seem to rest with the government. The private-insurance sector just does not have the resources to provide protection against hazards stemming from social revolution—at least, not at prices that homeowners and business owners can afford to pay. That the federal government was ready and willing to assume this responsibility was evidenced by the enactment by Congress in 1971 of an amendment to Title XII of the National Housing Act. Under the provisions of this amendment, the Department of Housing and Urban Development (renamed in 1981 the Emergency Management Agency) is directed to review the types of crime insurance available in each of the states either through the normal insurance market or through a state FAIR plan. Crime insurance as defined in the amendment means insurance against burglary and robbery, and it includes broad-form business and personal theft insurance but not automobile insurance.

In any state where such insurance is not provided at affordable rates, the Emergency Management Agency (EMA) is authorized to make it available through the facilities of the federal government. The conditions of such insurance, including the setting of rates and determination of insurability, are at the direction of EMA and may vary from state to state or from locality to locality. EMA is also empowered to utilize insurance companies as fiscal agents to market the coverage and to service the insured business (or homeowner), thus making available to this program the expertise and experience of the private carriers. By 1982 federal crime insurance was available in the urban core areas of twenty-six states, the District of Columbia, Puerto Rico, and the Virgin Islands. All licensed insurance agents in each of these areas are eligible to take applications for insurance.

It is interesting to note that one of the conditions required for this insurance is that the business owner install adequate safeguards and security measures.

Estimating the cost of merchandise or other inventories lost by fire or theft. In making insurance claims on merchandise or other inventories lost by fire or theft, a helpful method of estimating the loss is the gross profit method. This method is based on the cost-of-goods-sold section of the income statement. Three steps are required in the procedure:

1. Determine the cost of merchandise available for sale in the same manner as in the preparation of an income statement
2. Convert the net sales figure (up to the time of the loss) to cost of goods sold; this is done by multiplying net sales by the difference between 100 percent and the typical (average) gross margin rate
3. Subtract the cost of goods sold (as derived in step 2) from the cost of the merchandise available for sale (as derived in step 1) to yield the estimated ending inventory

The procedure may best be illustrated by referring to the income statement on pp. 324–25. Thus:

Inventory at beginning of accounting period	$ 44,000
+ Purchases up to time of the fire or theft	79,200
= Cost of merchandise available for sale	$123,200
− Cost of goods sold up to time of the fire or theft ($120,000 × .70)	84,000
= Estimated merchandise inventory at time of the fire or theft	$ 39,200

The gross margin rate used in step 2 may be the actual rate for the preceding year adjusted for any recent changes in markup.[2] Of course, complete records of the business must be produced when making insurance claims.

Consequential Loss

Although losses resulting from property theft or damage may be fully compensated, the small business may also suffer indirect or **consequential losses.** A fire, for example, may be so damaging that business operations, if not halted completely, can be continued only by moving to a temporary location at considerable expense. Business-interruption insurance can be purchased to cover (1) the fixed costs that would continue if the business were forced to cease operations temporarily, such as taxes or lease payments, interest, depreciation, utilities, and salaries of key employees, as well as the estimated profits that would be lost during the period of the shutdown; and (2) the extra expenses incurred in moving into temporary quarters.

Legal Liability

As noted previously, the most basic principle in determining the kind and amount of insurance that a small business owner should carry is that the probability that a loss may occur is less important than the possible size of the loss. On the basis of this principle it would appear that legal liability is potentially the greatest risk that a small business owner (or anyone else, for that matter) faces. The maximum loss that can occur to the business property is obviously limited by the value of that property. But in the case of the liability exposure there is no fixed loss limit, and a judgment against the small business owner in a bodily injury or property damage suit may be far greater than the value of the property itself. The size of damage-suit awards has risen sharply in recent years, and today liability coverage up to $1 million is no longer considered high or unreasonable. Adequate liability insurance is, therefore, *essential* to small business owners; without it, a single judgment against them might well

---

[2] As derived from the income statement on p. 324, the gross margin rate in this example is $60,000/$200,000 = 30 percent, no recent changes in markup being assumed.

put their back to the wall financially, or even put them out of business entirely.

In general, there are three types of liability exposure: (1) employer's liability and workers' compensation, (2) liability to nonemployees, and (3) automobile liability.

Employer's liability and workers' compensation. Under common law as well as under workers' compensation laws an employer is liable for injuries to employees at work caused by the employer's failure to (1) provide safe tools and working conditions, (2) hire competent fellow employees, or (3) warn employees of an existing danger. In every state an employer must insure against potential **workers' compensation** claims; however, employee coverage and the extent of the employer's liability vary from state to state.

Third-party liability. **Third-party liability** is liability for any kind of bodily injury to nonemployees except that caused by automobiles. In some cases this liability may even extend to trespassers. In addition, a small business owner may be legally liable for bodily injuries sustained by customers, pedestrians, deliverymen, trespassers, and other outsiders even in cases where the owner exercised reasonable care.

Automobile liability. Cars and trucks are a serious source of liability. Most business firms own at least one vehicle. Even if they do not, under the doctrine of agency they could be held vicariously liable for injuries and property damage caused by those employees who were operating their own or someone else's car in the course of their employment.[3] Of course, in this case the firm would have some coverage under the employee's own liability policy *if he or she had one,* but even under these circumstances, the limits of the employee's liability might be grossly inadequate. If there are many employees it would be impractical to check their individual liability coverages. In businesses where it is customary or sometimes convenient for employees to operate their own car while on company business—as in the case of many road and route salespersons—the employer is well-advised to acquire nonownership **automobile liability** insurance.

Death or Disability of Key Management Personnel

More so than in a larger business the death or disability of a key individual in the organization (or the loss of such a person to another firm) can cause serious loss to the small enterprise. If one person in the organization makes a significant contribution to the success of the business, which is often the case in the small firm, that person's death may be tantamount to the death of the business itself. Disability can be even more serious if the disabled key individual

---

[3] The legal doctrine of agency is discussed in Chapter 24, pp. 402–3.

happens to be an employee rather than the owner/manager, for then the business not only would lose the services of the disabled employee but might be obligated to continue paying this employee's salary. Risks of this kind can be minimized by acquiring life and disability insurance on the key individual, (**key-employee insurance**) payable to the company, in some amount that would permit the business to make the adjustment in the event such services are lost.

Special Multiperil Program

A recent innovation in the insurance industry is a package policy approach for commercial risks similar to homeowners' policies covering personal risks. This is the **special multiperil policy,** or **SMP program.** Under this policy the small business owner can purchase *one* insurance policy to cover all the risks that formerly required separate underwriting agreements. Of the business risks described in the preceding pages, the only ones that cannot be included in a package policy are workers' compensation and company-owned automobiles.

By combining most of the business owner's usual coverages into one package, policy-writing and -handling costs are reduced and these savings are reflected in reduced premium rates. This package discount can save the small firm as much as 25 percent of its insurance cost. But more significantly, the package concept enables small business owners to view their insurance problem as a *single* problem, rather than as many individual problems; thus they are more likely to avoid overlapping coverage and to tailor their insurance program to cover only the important risk exposures—those that would be too great for them to bear alone.

LOSS REDUCTION OR PREVENTION

Risk management is a much broader concept than just insurance buying. If business owners have a fire in their store or shop, insurance can replace their damaged property, reimburse them for business interruption expenses, and even restore their lost profits; but there are *hidden* losses that they can never recover. They can never recover the loss of customer goodwill, nor the value of skilled employees who have gone elsewhere to work, nor the loss of momentum and continuity in the business. An adequate insurance program is only a part, not the ultimate goal, of risk management.

It also important for small business owners to realize that after a fire, theft, or other kind of loss they must use all reasonable means to protect their property or run the risk of having their insurance coverage canceled. Even if their insurance is not canceled, their premium rates may rise if they have not taken steps to reduce the risk or to prevent the recurrence of a casualty. Risk management involves risk *reduction* as well as risk *transference.*

The Fire Peril

The small business owner can use a wide variety of protective devices and can adopt innumerable precautionary measures to reduce business risks. The peril of fire, for example, can be minimized by installing automatic sprinklers, or by providing an adequate supply of fire extinguishers and instructing employees how to use them. Brick, concrete, and other types of fire-resistant materials can also be used in construction, as well as fire walls and doors.

The Crime Peril

One of the most serious threats to business property today is the *crime* peril—burglary, robbery, and theft. This is readily apparent to most of us as we go about our daily lives: the sign at the service station that says only checks or credit will be accepted after dark; and the sign at the store counter that says we are being monitored on closed-circuit television. A recent study of crime against small businesses estimated the total cost of such crime at over $10 billion annually. This figure represents the reported property loss resulting from crime *on the premises* only; it does not include losses in the distribution and transportation of goods. Law officials agree, moreover, that *reported* crime is only the top of the iceberg; business owners often fail to report thefts.

Burglary and robbery. Small stores are prime targets of the burglar and the robber. Among the protective devices that the small business owner can use to reduce perils of this kind are silent central-station burglary alarm systems and pin-tumbler cylinder and dead-bolt locks. Bank deposits, of course, should be made daily during daylight hours; if an armored-car service is not utilized, a different route to the bank should be taken each day and deposits should be made at different times of the day. Periodically during the day, excess cash should be removed from the cash register and placed in the safe. The safe itself should be visible from the street (not hidden in the back of the store) and should be bolted to the building structure. Overnight indoor security lighting is also desirable, and perhaps outdoor lighting as well.

Employee dishonesty. In addition to, and perhaps more serious than, the crimes from outside the walls of the business are the crimes from *inside*—from the business owner's own employees. Except for fidelity bonds which might be taken out on employees who have access to large sums of money, this type of loss is generally uninsured and most of it isn't even discovered. It has been estimated that in some stores, inventory shrinkage resulting from employee pilferage and other dishonest acts of employees is greater than that caused by shoplifting. The business owner can prevent employee theft, or at least make it more difficult, by adopting effective accounting and inventory control procedures. Among the safeguards that the owner can employ are: (1) the use of outside auditors; (2) countersignature of all checks; (3) the *immediate* deposit of all incoming checks, as well as their duplication; (4) bank statement reconciliation by employees other than those who make the deposits; and (5) *joint* access to safe-deposit boxes. Professional shoppers can also be employed to check for violations of the store's cash register and refund procedures. But the most obvious and most important safeguard is careful screening and selection of personnel.

Business owners must also contend with dishonest customers as well as dishonest employees. They face two kinds of perils from customers: shoplifting and bad-check passers.

Shoplifting. According to statistics compiled by the National Retail Merchants Association, shoplifting has increased by more than 300 percent across the nation in the last decade. On the average, retail merchants are losing approximately 3 percent of their merchandise—which, incidentally, is just about the profit margin for some stores. Thus, for every $150 of merchandise stolen, a store must sell $5,000 worth to make up the loss. Eventually, of course, the paying customer picks up the tab. It has been estimated, for example, that shoplifting costs each American household $400 a year.

Shoplifters come from every economic and social class. Some shoplifters are kleptomaniacs—those constitutionally unable to resist stealing; others are either professional or amateur shoplifters. Professional shoplifters often work in pairs. One creates a commotion to distract employees while the other takes the merchandise and leaves. At least one employee in every selling area should remain on duty to supervise customers regardless of any disturbance and should be prepared to take appropriate action if shoplifting is detected. Amateur shoplifters, on the other hand, usually work alone. They tend to lack finesse and may display signs of nervousness visible to experienced supervisors. Many of them are children.

Most shoplifting losses are uninsured because (1) much of it is undiscovered, and (2) many store owners are reluctant to prosecute shoplifters. It is much easier for retailers to pass along shoplifting losses to customers as part of their costs. This is a dubious policy, however, for it will not discourage shoplifting activity and may even encourage it. Merchants should also be reminded that shoplifters often steal handbags and packages from customers as well.

Shoplifting losses can be reduced by unrelenting prosecution. Even an antishoplifting sign prominently displayed in the store will help, by reminding the would-be offender of the consequences of such a practice. Many states have passed shoplifting laws which make it easier to apprehend shoplifters, by allowing store employees to detain a customer who has been *observed* concealing merchandise on his or her person; in these states, it is no longer necessary to apprehend the customer off the store premises with the goods in his or her possession. Shoplifting losses can likewise be minimized by hiring extra clerks, or perhaps off-duty policemen, during the peak hours. Wide aisles, clear vision, and alert employees are also helpful in defending against this common merchandising problem. Various protective devices may also be utilized, such as two-way and convex wall mirrors and closed-circuit television. Such devices as these, as well as the precautionary measures outlined above, make sure that "customers" do not always get what they want!

Bad-check losses. Bad checks pose another problem for many small business owners. Here, also, protective steps can be taken to minimize losses. Checks, for example, should not be accepted for amounts in excess of the amount of purchase. Nor should postdated, illegibly written, or two-party checks be accepted. Accept only personalized checks (no counter checks), designate only certain employees to accept them, and deposit them promptly. Proper identification should be requested before accepting checks from strangers, preferably an automobile operator's license; if the license does not have the operator's photograph affixed to it in addition to his signature, then a second form of identification should be requested.

SUMMING UP

Every business faces risks. Fire or other peril, for example, may destroy the building or its contents. In addition to the loss of the property itself are the indirect losses suffered (including reduced profits) when business operations are halted or temporarily suspended because of such a casualty. Dishonest employees, customers, and others may steal from the firm. The firm may also become liable to others for bodily injury or property damage. And premature death or disability of the owner, a partner, or a key employee may cause serious loss to the business. Most of these risks, however, are insurable (transferable).

Risk management for the small firm begins with a consideration of the need for protecting itself against these risks. In this connection, it is the magnitude of the potential loss rather than the probability of its occurrence that is more important.

An adequate insurance program is only a part, not the ultimate goal, of risk management. The owner/manager of a business should also take precautionary measures to guard against the occurrence of business losses, or at least to minimize (reduce) the severity of these losses.

It must always be borne in mind that there are certain business risks that are a part of free enterprise itself, and that these risks cannot be transferred to or assumed by someone else; these include the risk of failure, or inadequate return.

actual cash value
automobile liability
coinsurance
consequential loss
deductible coverage
extended coverage
FAIR plan
fidelity bond
insurance

key-employee insurance
red circle zone
replacement cost
risk management
special multiperil policy
(SMP program)
third-party liability
workers' compensation

DISCUSSION
QUESTIONS

1. On which measure of value (replacement cost or actual cash value) would you be more likely to insure property losses due to fire? Losses due to theft? Explain your reasoning fully.

2. Other than insurance, what measures can you suggest for reducing the risk of business losses resulting from the death or disability of the small business owner or of a key employee? Resulting from third-party liability? Shoplifting (other than those suggested in the text)? Employee theft (other than those suggested in the text)?

3. What are some of the noninsurable risks of operating a business enterprise?

EXERCISES AND
PROBLEMS

1. From the information in the following table indicate for each of the examples *a* through *g* how much of the loss will be paid by the insurance company:

	VALUE OF PROPERTY	COINSURANCE CLAUSE	FACE OF POLICY	AMOUNT OF LOSS
a.	$10,000	80%	$9,000	$9,000
b.	10,000	90	8,000	9,000
c.	10,000	80	8,000	8,000
d.	10,000	80	8,000	5,000
e.	10,000	80	8,000	9,000
f.	10,000	80	6,000	6,000
g.	10,000	80	7,000	8,000

2. The Hawkeye Company suffered a fire on August 9 that completely destroyed its merchandise inventory. The following data were obtained from the store's records:

Inventory, Jan. 1	$40,000
Purchases, Jan. 1–Aug. 9	25,000
Purchase returns and allowances, Jan. 1–Aug. 9	1,500
Sales, Jan. 1–Aug. 9	50,000
Sales returns and allowances, Jan. 1–Aug. 9	500
Average gross margin	40%

Estimate the cost of the merchandise destroyed in the fire.

3. The Acorn Company was burglarized on the night of June 4. The next morning an inventory was taken, and it was found that $250,000 worth of merchandise (cost value) was on hand. For insurance purposes, estimate the cost of the merchandise stolen. The following data were obtained from the store's records:

Beginning inventory, Jan. 1	$225,000
Purchases, Jan. 1–June 3	200,000
Sales, Jan. 1–June 3	300,000
Average gross profit	45%

CASE IN POINT

Alfred Cummins and Roy Page have operated a farm supply store near Green Creek for several years. They are experienced businessmen, both in their early thirties. Al is a born mechanic, and Roy an excellent manager. Both have many friends in the rural area around Green Creek. Their business consists of stock feed and farm seeds, hand garden tools, and more recently a line of powered garden equipment such as tractors and mowers. In connection with the last line they have an increasingly busy repair shop. They also rent garden equipment to the public.

A new development has taken place recently. Green Creek is in a semimountainous area, with enough snow in winter to encourage skiers. In fact, a ski run is being set up almost next door to their business and will no doubt attract skiers from major cities nearby. The owners of the run are friends and neighbors of Cummins and Page, and have suggested that the men contract to operate the ski lift and to rent snowmobiles to the public—in other words, to handle these mechanical aspects of the lift's operation. The wooded 80-acre area adjacent to the ski lift is large enough to permit snowmobile use.

The two men are fascinated by the whole idea. It should be a profitable and exciting year-round business. At a bridge party the other night, however, a neighbor, a lawyer who works in the city nearby, asked Al, "How much more insurance would that call for?" Al answered, "We already have standard liability insurance for the store and shop. What else would we need?" The lawyer replied, "You may have enough, or you may have been very lucky up till now. Better check into it."

Check into it. List the kinds of insurance that might be required.

Part Six

THE LEGAL ENVIRONMENT

Certain general principles of law, important legal instruments, and government regulations that have special significance for small business owners and managers are considered in the following four chapters. An understanding of these principles, instruments, and regulations should help owners and/or managers to carry on their activities without either breaking the law or sacrificing the rights and benefits to which they are legally entitled. It should also help them to recognize when legal counsel is needed.

Types of
Legal Business Transactions

CHAPTER TWENTY-FOUR *This chapter discusses the types of legal transactions in which the owner/manager of a small business is likely to be involved. It will increase your understanding of the law of agency and the rules of law as they apply to contracts, bills of sale, and negotiable instruments.*

Business law, or **commercial law** as it is sometimes called, is that body of law concerned primarily with the exchange or buying and selling of goods and services. Business transactions as discussed in this chapter are regulated by the **Uniform Commercial Code (UCC),** applicable in all states.

CONTRACTS

Almost every business act is based on agreements or promises, most of which are contracts. Mutual confidence among the various parties involved in business activities is so basic to modern society that it is difficult to conceive of the continued existence of civilization in the absence of contractual relations. A **contract** is an agreement between two or more competent parties to do, or not to do, some lawful act for a stated consideration. Although a contract is an agreement, or a meeting of minds, not all agreements are contracts. The essentials of a valid (i.e., legally enforceable) contract are:

1. *agreement,* an offer that must be accepted as offered
2. *true consent,* not under duress
3. *competent parties*
4. *some lawful objective*
5. *consideration,* the value of which is not material

It is important that if the person being offered the contract in any way manifests his or her acceptance, that person may be legally required to accept the contract; it is the law that decides whether the contract exists, not the subjective intent. The offer may be made either orally or in writing. And there is of course an entire branch of law built around whether the contract is offered and accepted. The small businessperson should consult an attorney in all matters dealing with contracts.

All persons are considered competent to enter into contracts except minors (in most states, persons under the age of 18), insane persons or idiots, inebriates, convicts, and enemy aliens. Minors, insane persons and idiots, and inebriates are termed *natural incompetents* because they are inherently unable to act for themselves. Convicts and enemy aliens, on the other hand, are termed *legal incompetents* because the law denies them the right to contract.

Contracts must also have lawful objectives. It is imperative that they not be criminal, tortious (performing some private wrong), or opposed to public policy. Examples of such laws are usurious contracts, gambling and wagering contracts, and agreements that are injurious to the peace, health, good order, and morals of the people. (The discussion in Chapter 26 will detail how legislation tending to prevent restraint of trade, price fixing, and unfair business practices has made many previously valid contracts illegal.)

The term **consideration,** in the law of contracts, does not mean that there must be an exchange of something having monetary value. Rather it indicates the doing of something or promising to do something that one is not otherwise legally obliged to do in return for the promise of another. Promises based on a past consideration have only moral enforceability, and the promisor must be under legal contract to make his or her word legally binding. It is essential to have all important contracts in writing, and according to the law in many states certain contracts *must* be in writing. This is especially true of contracts not to be performed within one year and of those involving the sale of real estate. A written contract is usually desirable, even if not required by state law, whenever common sense indicates a possibility that certain provisions, or even the contract itself, may later be questioned or forgotten.

AGENCY

Agency implies a business relationship between two parties that involves a third party. An agent may be appointed to assume entire charge of a principal's business or to transact only certain types of business. It is best when dealing with an agent to insist on proof of the agent's authority, or to have some evidence from the principal as to the delegated authority. The agent must "exercise good faith and the requisite degree of prudence, skill, and diligence," and is not allowed to act for himself or herself or for another person with a conflicting interest. Persons usually deal with the agent as though they were dealing with the company or person (**principal**) the agent represents. Since agents are usually appointed by definite agreements or contracts, the law of contracts applies to agency.

Small business owners and managers have many dealings with agents and may have occasion to appoint their own agents or to serve as agents for some principal. The purchase of insurance, many real estate transactions (whether for lease or for purchase), and the procurement of equipment, materials, or merchandise often involves dealing through agents. Small manufacturers may prefer to sell through agents rather than through their own sales force. Even small-scale retailers may secure special or exclusive agency rights for certain prestige merchandise (franchising). A very important consideration whenever agency is involved is to ascertain and clearly define the authority delegated to the agent by his or her principal and the agent's duties or responsibilities.

SALES

Small business owners and managers are also concerned with the sale of either **real property** or **personal property.** Property in this sense is the right that a person owns in something, whether land, material, or merchandise. Ownership may be transferred by gift or inheritance as well as by purchase and sale. Among the important provisions of the Uniform Commercial Code is the clear distinction between a sale and a contract to sell. Other points of law relating to sales covered in the code are the time title passes, identification of the goods, and the right or power of the seller to transfer title. Certain sales must be evidenced by a written **bill of sale.** If the goods are not delivered immediately, evidence of sale in writing is required when the amount involved is above some stated minimum.

There are so many variations of sales and payment plans that complete coverage would be impractical here. However, one question that arises frequently enough to deserve comment is the protection of the seller in case full payment is not made at or before time of delivery of the goods. For example, a retailer may buy merchandise on credit, sell the entire lot for cash to one or a few customers, and fail to pay the wholesaler or other suppliers. To protect the latter the **bulk sales provisions** of the Uniform Commercial Code require advance notice (usually delivered in person or by registered mail) to each creditor before sale of the stock of goods; if advance notice is not given, the creditors can bring action against the goods even though they have passed into the hands of a third party. And even if notice has been given, the sale may nevertheless be voided if the intent of the transfer is to hinder, delay, or defraud creditors.

Entrepreneurs and small business managers contemplating doing any installment selling should ascertain the laws of their own state and of any states in which they have debtors with regard to permissible interest rates. Most states have **usury** laws specifying the maximum rate of interest that can be exacted. All states have a legal rate of interest, to be used when an agreement says there is to be payment of interest but does not specify the rate. Penalties for charging illegal interest are very heavy, and it is important to know just what can be charged and under what sorts of agreements. Small business owners and managers must also make certain that they comply with the disclosure requirements of the Truth-in-Lending Law, discussed in Chapter 18.

A point that frequently causes confusion relates to the obligation of a business to sell goods or services to any person who may offer the full purchase price. A few broad classes of business enterprises, such as public utilities, common carriers, and hotels, are required to serve all persons alike who meet publicly announced requirements and are not obnoxious or otherwise objectionable to other patrons. Merchants are not in this class. They can refuse to sell to any person regardless of the latter's readiness to pay the full purchase price in cash. Manufacturers and other sellers not in the public service groups may also refuse to sell to any prospective purchaser at their discretion. Title II of the Civil Rights Act of 1964 prohibits discrimination or segregation in any "place of public accommodation" on the grounds of race, color, religion, or national origin. Business establishments which are explicitly covered by this provision of the act are hotels and motels, eating establishments, gasoline stations, and places of entertainment.

NEGOTIABLE INSTRUMENTS

Business transactions have been carried on to an increasing extent by means of **negotiable instruments** instead of money. Both serve as **media of exchange;** both facilitate trade and pass freely from person to person in business transactions. Money, or **legal tender,** is universally acceptable and is required by law to be accepted in this country as adequate settlement of financial claims. Although the same legal compulsion does not exist for negotiable instruments, custom, convenience, and confidence have all contributed to their widespread use. The common check and the bank draft are good illustrations.

According to the Uniform Commercial Code, any instrument must satisfy the following requirements if it is to be negotiable:

1. It must be in writing and signed by the maker or drawer.

2. It must contain an unconditional promise or order to pay a sum certain in money.

3. It must be payable on demand or at a fixed rate or determinable future time.

4. It must be payable "to order" or "to bearer."

5. Where the instrument is addressed to a drawee, that person must be named or otherwise indicated therein with reasonable certainty.

Negotiable instruments may be divided into two classes: (1) promissory notes and (2) bills of exchange.

A **promissory note** is simply a written promise by one person to pay a sum of money to another person. It may or may not be secured by some form of collateral. A note secured by a mortgage on real or personal property is called a **mortgage note.** If given in exchange for merchandise, it is called a **conditional-sale note;** such a note stipulates that title to the merchandise remains with the seller until the note is paid. When persons who sign a note agree that they will permit judgment to be taken against them without a trial if they fail to pay the note, it is called a **judgment note.** A **certificate of deposit** is a promissory note given by a bank, and a **bond** is simply a long-term promissory note. Other varieties could be cited, but these are the most common.

In contrast with a promissory note, a **bill of exchange** is an order by one person on a second person to pay a sum of money to a third person. If the order is drawn on a bank and if it is payable on demand, it is a **check.** If it is drawn by a bank on itself it is called a **cashier's check.** And if it is drawn by one bank on another bank it is known as a **bank draft.** A **traveler's check** is a special kind of cashier's check.

A check (such as those mentioned above) is a bill of exchange unconditionally payable on demand. The bank will ordinarily make payment unless (1) the person who made out the check lacks sufficient funds and has not made prior arrangements for an overdraft; (2) the drawer has stopped payment on the check; or (3) the bank has reason to believe the person presenting the check has no legal right to do so.

Another kind of bill of exchange that is of some importance to the small businessperson is the **trade acceptance.** It differs from a check in two ways: (1) It is usually payable at some specified future date, and (2) payment on the note is conditional on its acceptance by the person on whom it is drawn. It is sent by a seller to a purchaser with the understanding that if the latter approves the goods purchased, he or she will accept the draft. It is often used in selling goods on credit. The seller draws a draft on the buyer, often a retailer, for the exact amount of the invoice. This must be accepted before the goods are delivered to the buyer. Thus a promise to pay is created. The seller or drawer of the draft can often discount this trade acceptance at a bank and thus receive payment before the due date of the invoice while at the same time granting credit to his or her customers. Although drafts are sometimes accepted by a bank, by arrangement and for a fee, **bankers' acceptances** are far less common in domestic commerce than is the trade acceptance (such as the bank arranging to pay for the purchases in the above example).

Checks, trade acceptances, and other bills of exchange, as well as promissory notes, should be presented for payment when due or as soon as possible. Even though they may be legally valid claims for a reasonable time after maturity, practical considerations of security and custom dictate prompt presentation for payment. Special cases deserve special consideration and usually require competent legal counsel.

Almost all business transactions are based on voluntary agreements between firms or between a firm and its customers or other individuals. Not all agreements, however, are contracts, that is, not all give rise to legal obligations.

 Special rules of law govern the most important kind of commercial contract—the sale of goods and services.

 Most business transactions that take place are carried out by means of checks and other types of negotiable instruments. A negotiable instrument resembles an ordinary contract to pay a sum of money, but differs in that the obligation may be transferred from one person to another. Instruments to settle financial claims must meet other requirements as well.

Agency, in contrast with contracts and negotiable instruments, is a legal relationship in which one person or organization (called the agent) acts on behalf of another (called the principal). Discussed in this chapter were agency relationships other than those implied in partnerships and corporate forms of business organization, which will be discussed in the following chapter.

KEY
WORDS

agency	contract
bank draft	judgment note
banker's acceptance	legal tender
bill of exchange	medium of exchange
bill of sale	mortgage note
bond	negotiable instruments
bulk sales provisions, UCC	personal property
business law	principal
cashier's check	promissory note
certificate of deposit	real property
check	trade acceptance
commercial law	traveler's check
conditional-sale note	Uniform Commercial Code (UCC)
consideration	usury

1. A writes B that he will sell men's shirts in lots of 3 to 5 dozen at $100 per dozen. B replies that he will buy 4 dozen. Has a contract been negotiated? Why or why not?

2. A pays B $200 for a thirty-day option to lease space in the latter's office building. Thirty days later, A asks for and is granted a ten-day extension. Five days after granting the extension, however, B changes his mind and withdraws his offer to A. Can B legally revoke the offer? Why or why not?

3. A writes B a letter agreeing to pay the latter the sum of $2,400 for services to be rendered during the coming year, payable at the rate of $200 a month beginning January 1, 1983. Is the letter a negotiable instrument? Why or why not?

4. A signed a sixty-day note agreeing to pay the bearer the sum of $500 with interest "at the current bank rate." Is the note negotiable? Why or why not?

5. A signed a demand note agreeing to pay the bearer, in exchange for services rendered, "merchandise worth $300." Is the note negotiable? Why or why not?

CASES IN
POINT*

Earl M. Jorgensen Co. v. Mark Construction Inc. (540 P.2d 978, Hawaii, 1975)

In preparing its bid for a highway building project, D requested several suppliers of sectional steel plate to submit quotations for 3,-468 linear feet of steel plate. P's quotation was the lowest and D used it in its bid for the highway project. After D was awarded the highway project, P requested D to issue a purchase order for the steel. D sent P a proper purchase order. Later a dispute arose, and D claimed that its purchase order was the only offer; therefore, the terms of the purchase order control.

Issue: Was P's quote an offer that was accepted by D when it issued the purchase order, or was the purchase order the offer that P accepted by shipping the steel?

* Adapted from *Fundamentals of Business Law*, 3rd ed. (Englewood Cliffs, N.J.: Prentice-Hall, Inc., 1982), pp. 83, 101, 428, and 238, respectively; courtesy of the authors, Robert N. Corley, Eric M. Holmes, and Wilbur J. Robert. Reprinted by permission of Prentice-Hall, Inc., Englewood Cliffs, NJ 07632.

Tigrett v. *Heritage Building Co.* (533 S.W.2d 65, Texas, 1976)

P was employed by D company and was injured on her job. D promised P that she would be paid the same benefits as those provided under the state's Workers' Compensation Act, although the company did not participate in the compensation program. Companies that chose not to participate were subject to tort suits by injured employees. D paid compensation for some time but then discontinued payments. P brought suit to enforce the promise, but D contended that the promise was not enforceable and that P's only remedy was in tort.

Issue: Is there consideration to support D's promise to pay an amount equal to workers' compensation?

Meerdink v. *Krieger* (550 P.2d 42, Wash. App., 1976)

Ps wanted to buy an apartment house for $80,000 to $90,000. Since they were inexperienced in real estate transactions, they told their agent, Mr. Bunger, an employee of D, a real estate firm, that they were totally dependent on his advice. Bunger and D did not tell Ps that they were also the agents for Johnson, a builder of apartment houses. Nonetheless, D encouraged Ps to sign a contract with Johnson to build a new apartment for $120,000. Ps sued for damages on learning of D's "dual agency" status.

Issue: Is D liable?

Central States, Southeast & Southwest Areas, Health and Welfare Fund v. *Pitman* (338 N.E. 2d 793, Illinois, 1978)

D, an employer, gave P (a pension fund company) a note stating that P promised to pay D "all current contributions as they become due under the collective bargaining agreement . . . in addition to the sum of $15,606.44 with interest."

Issue: Does the note contain an unconditional promise to pay a certain sum?

Legal Forms of Business Organization

CHAPTER TWENTY-FIVE *The law of agency governs relationships between partners or between a corporation and those with whom it transacts business. As an impersonal entity, the corporation has no choice but to operate through the medium of agents, and partnerships owe their existence largely to the fact that each partner may act as an agent for the others in transacting business. The differences between corporations, partnerships, and sole ownership of a business, and the factors controlling the selection of a legal structure are discussed in this chapter.*

In deciding which form of ownership organization to adopt, several factors should be considered. Among the most important of these considerations are the following:

1. A need for additional funds may sometimes be met better by forming a partnership or corporation than by borrowing. However, this means sharing profits as well as risks and losses.

2. A need for certain managerial abilities or experience may be met by taking in one or more partners possessing the requisite qualities. However, the additional abilities are secured at the expense of sharing authority and placing some restrictions on one's independence.

3. The choice of organization form to use may be influenced by the desire to achieve such objectives as limiting liability, distributing the risks involved, and taking advantage of the tax structure. Federal and state income tax laws, for example, may make one form of organization superior to others for some small businesses. And sometimes one form of organization is given advantages by particular laws or regulations, such as those limiting the power of a corporation to engage in certain activities open to the proprietorship or partnership.

As the best form of legal organization to use, the final decision will probably be a compromise based on weighing the relative importance of certain needs or objectives against the limitations of each form. The pros and cons of the three basic types of ownership structure—the proprietorship, the partnership, and the corporation—are discussed in the paragraphs that follow.[1]

THE PROPRIETORSHIP

The simplest and most common form of ownership structure is the **proprietorship**—a business owned and controlled by one person. There are no registration requirements or legal fees unless the business is operated under a trade or assumed name. The proprietor has perfect freedom of operation; when business decisions are made or when actions are taken it is not necessary to get the consent of anyone else in the organization. Similarly, all profits are the property of the owner and need not be shared with anyone else.

There are, however, certain disadvantages in the one-owner organization. Limited personal assets, for example, do not encourage lenders and cannot always provide the capital needed to meet the needs of the business. But perhaps the biggest disadvantage is the proprietor's personal liability for business debts; in case of business failure, the owner's home, automobile, stocks, cash, and other personal assets may be seized by creditors to satisfy the debts of the business.

THE GENERAL PARTNERSHIP

A **partnership** is formed when two or more persons share in the ownership of the business. When the partners also share in the management or control of the business, it is referred to in legal terms as a **general partnership.** As in the case of the proprietorship, no registration or filing fees are required unless the business is conducted under a trade or assumed name; otherwise, a partnership can be created by a mere handshake. The most obvious advantage of this form of organization over the proprietorship form is that added capital is made available by combining the assets of the partners, and money is usually easier to borrow because the partners share debts. Similarly, the personal abilities of the partners are complemented, and they may succeed together when neither could alone.

However, each partner by law is *equally* responsible for *all* the debts of the partnership, regardless of the amount of capital contributed and regardless of any agreement among them to the contrary. Also, any one partner can bind the entire partnership in a business arrangement, even if it is contrary to the wishes or judgment of the majority.

The general partnership has other disadvantages as well, such as the termination of the business by the death or withdrawal of any one of the partners

---

[1] The significant differences in these organization forms are summarized in Table 25-1 on p. 416.

and the inability of a partner to sell or assign his or her interest in the partnership without the consent of all the other partners. However, both these conditions or eventualities can be circumvented by appropriate provisions in a written partnership agreement.

Although not legally required in order to form a general partnership, such an agreement is nonetheless advisable, even among relatives and close friends. At a minimum it should specify the following:

1. Duration of the partnership

2. Administrative responsibilities and authority of each of the partners

3. Withdrawals and salaries of the partners

4. Provision for the arbitration of policy disputes among the partners

5. Provision for the withdrawal of partners or the admission of additional partners

6. Amount of capital invested by each partner

7. Division of profit or loss (regardless of the amount of capital invested, general partners must share profit or loss equally unless there is an agreement among the partners to the contrary)

8. Distribution of assets in the event of dissolution (as in the case of profits or losses, this distribution must be on an equal basis unless otherwise agreed upon in writing)

9. Settlements in the event of death or disability of a partner. This might include a **buy-sell agreement** funded with business life insurance in amounts equal to the interest of each partner; thus the surviving partner(s) would be assured of full title to the business, and the deceased partner's estate would be assured of receiving the full value of his or her share of the business. In the absence of such an agreement, the business might well be forced into liquidation to satisfy demands of the deceased partner's estate.

The partners may also agree to share liability for the debts of the business on other than an equal basis. However, such an agreement (as noted above) would have validity only among the partners themselves; creditors would not be bound by it.

THE LIMITED PARTNERSHIP

The disadvantages of unlimited personal liability for the debts of a partnership can be circumvented by forming a **limited partnership.** Such a partnership has one or more partners whose loss is *limited* to their individual investment in the business; however, there must be at least one general partner in a limited partnership. The name of a limited partner cannot be used in the company name unless the firm name identifies the person as a limited partner. Nor can a limited partner engage in the management of the business in any way. Unlike the general partnership, a limited partnership agreement must be *publicly* recorded.

THE CONVENTIONAL CORPORATION

The **corporation** is an association of stockholders created under law and regarded as a **legal entity** or artificial "person" by courts. Because it is a creation of the law, it is impersonal and exists without reference to the particular individuals who may share its ownership and direct its activities.

State laws govern the provisions under which its **charter,** or authorization to operate as a business entity, is granted. The statutory requirements generally include (1) registering the corporate name and the **articles of incorporation,** (2) payment of a filing fee, and (3) payment of an organization tax, usually varying with the firm's **capitalization.** Registration, filing fees, and organization taxes are required in each of the states in which the corporation does business.

The chief advantages of the corporation are (1) continuity in existence, (2) easy transferability of ownership interests, and (3) **limited liability** of stockholders. The corporation is long-lived, being able to continue in existence up to the time limit granted in its charter, and may even be granted in perpetuity, whereas other forms of organization may cease abruptly with the death of the proprietor or a partner. Ownership in a corporation is easily transferred merely by sale or exchange of stock; permission of other stockholders is not required. And legal liability of owners or stockholders for suits for personal injury or other activities connected with operating the business is limited to the amount of funds invested in the business.

The corporate form of business organization is also more attractive for raising equity capital. This is so because capital can be more readily obtained from many more sources and because of the legal limited liability of corporate stockholders.

A corporation has certain disadvantages, however. Its activities are limited to those specifically granted in its charter. Similarly, its geographical area of operations is limited to the state granting its charter until permission is secured from each of the other states in which it desires to operate; this means that additional filing fees must be paid and additional legal requirements observed. The corporation must make numerous reports for taxation and other purposes in *each* state in which it does business; not only has federal and state regulation of corporations been increasing for some time, but the paperwork required increases greatly as the corporation grows in size. But the most undesirable feature of the corporate form of organization is the fact that **dividends** are not deductible in arriving at the company's net income, and the individual shareholders pay income tax on the dividends they receive in excess of $200; thus, profits from a corporation are taxed *twice*—once at corporate tax rates and again at personal tax rates when the profits are distributed to the owners.

The **double-tax** disadvantage of the corporation, however, may be minimized by the owners in four ways: (1) by paying themselves salaries and fringe benefits as managers of the business, (2) by making leasing arrangements with the corporate entity, (3) by capitalizing with debt equity as well as with ownership equity, and (4) by retaining earnings to finance company growth.

One of the most important practical features for small companies is the extent to which the owners can obtain income in the form of salary or in some other manner that represents a deduction for corporate tax purposes. If all corporate income could be paid out to stockholder-operators in this fashion, corporation taxes would not be a factor for closely-held companies in which the shareholders are active. The most immediate way to narrow the effect of the artificial tax discrimination against corporations is by compensating the owners from company income. A similar method is to rent or lease plant and equipment to the corporation, thus permitting tax-free repayment (to the corporation) of money to the shareholders. If salaries, rentals, stock options, and pensions to the shareholders are validly deductible items for the corporation, the double tax resulting from dividend payments is reduced to that extent.

The payment of salaries to shareholders who are also officers of the corporation is an obvious device to minimize corporation income tax, and it has been abused by some taxpayers by inflated and fictitious claims. The taxing authorities are alert to this kind of tax evasion, and with the courts they have worked out various standards of a general character as a guide in testing the validity of different forms of compensation. Under the general tests, deductions for officers' salaries and bonuses are allowable if the compensation is comparable to that received by other individuals with similar responsibilities in the same industry.

An additional way of getting money out of the corporation is for the owner to capitalize with debt equity as well as ownership equity. If the interests of the owner are represented to as great an extent as is possible by bonds of the corporation rather than by **capital stock,** the tax liability of the business can be significantly reduced. The effect is the same as drawing out a salary; the interest would be a taxable item to the owner, of course, but it would be a deduction by the corporation.

Thus the ultimate feasibility of the corporate form for small, closely-owned organizations depends on the extent to which the shareholders may benefit from corporate income in ways other than through dividend payments. Aside from salaries or other compensations from current income, the chief benefit to shareholders arises from appreciation in the value of their stock and its eventual sale. The appreciation in value depends in almost all cases on the growth of the company, financed largely through the retention of corporate earnings. On sale of the stock, enhanced in value by **retained earnings,** the shareholder pays only a capital gains tax. **Capital gains,** for most shareholders, are taxed at rates approximately equal to *one-fourth* the applicable rate for ordinary income.

THE TAX-OPTION CORPORATION

The **tax-option corporation,** also known popularly as a **Subchapter S corporation** (after the subchapter of the Internal Revenue Code that created it) or a "Small Business Corporation" (as it is termed in the code itself), is a corporation that pays no income tax—that is, the stockholders elect to report the corporate income on their individual income tax returns. Thus the most undesirable feature of the corporate form of organization—the double tax on dividends—is avoided.

To exercise this tax option, however, the corporation must have no more than twenty-five stockholders, none of whom can be a corporation, and all of whom must give their consent. A second requirement is that no more than 20 percent of the corporate income can be derived from investments (dividends, interest, rent, capital gains, etc.). The law also stipulates that more than 20 percent of the corporate income must be derived from business operations within the United States.

The corporation must elect to be taxed under Subchapter S during the first month of its fiscal year or during the month immediately preceding its next fiscal year. Once made, the election remains in effect for all subsequent years unless (1) it is revoked by one or more of the shareholders, (2) a new person becomes a shareholder and affirmatively refuses to consent to the election, or (3) the corporation ceases to qualify.

Subchapter S was enacted by Congress so that smaller businesses could "select a form of business organization desired, without the necessity of taking into account major differences in tax consequences." As noted, it eliminates the double tax on distributed corporate income. At the same time it provides the small business owner with the benefits associated with the conventional corporation. In addition to limited liability, these benefits include:

1. Favorable tax treatment of fringe benefits to shareholder-employees. Since the corporation is a separate legal entity, shareholders may become employees of their own businesses. Although under the terms of the Keogh Act business proprietors and partners are allowed to participate in the tax-sheltered pension plans of their companies, the degree of their participation is considerably more limited than it is in the case of corporate employees.[2] Furthermore, shareholder-employees may participate in other types of tax-sheltered fringe benefit programs not available to business organizations, such as premiums on group life insurance policies, reimbursement for medical and dental expenses, and unemployment and workers' compensation premiums.

2. Income splitting, or the ability of the owners of a family business to transfer stock shares in the corporation to their children. This has the effect of diverting some of their income to their children's lower tax brackets.

3. Deferral of income to different tax years. This ability to time the year in which the corporation's income will be taxable to the shareholder can be of considerable value, particularly if a shareholder's outside income is subject to significant fluctuations from one year to the next.

"Every coin has two sides," the saying goes, and it is significant to note that approximately 80 percent of all eligible small business corporations have *not* elected to exercise their option of being taxed as partnerships. To the principals of many small corporations, the tax advantages of Subchapter S are more apparent than real. For example, the maximum tax rate on corporate income (46 percent) is lower than the maximum rate on personal income (reduced recently from 70 to 50 percent); furthermore, the double tax on corporate income is not assessed until that income is distributed to the shareholders. Therefore, for many small companies whose growth is financed in large measure by *retained* earnings, the effective tax rate on total earnings may in fact be *lower* for the conventional corporation than for the tax-option corporation. In addition, when and if the owners decide to sell their stock in the future, income from the sale of the stock will be taxed at the long-term capital gains rate.

In assessing the tax consequences of electing Subchapter S status in individual cases, much, of course, depends on the level of the corporation's earnings and the corporate owners' personal income tax brackets. In any case, the principals should weigh the disadvantage of the double tax against the income-

---

[2] See pp. 450–51 for a discussion of the Keogh (or Self-Employed Individuals Tax Retirement) Act.

TABLE 25-1

Comparison of Legal Forms of Business Organization

	PROPRIETORSHIP	GENERAL PARTNERSHIP	CORPORATION
Ease and cost of organization	Simplest way to go into business; no registration or filing fee	No registration or filing fee	Requires charter and payment of filing fee and organization tax
Managerial control	Owner has perfect freedom; makes his/her own decisions	Shared with partners; one partner can bind all others in a business arrangement	Concentrated in a board of directors and in the corporate officers
Business continuity	Firm dissolved at death of proprietor	Firm can be dissolved at death or withdrawal of any one of the partners	Continuous existence; does not dissolve when one owner (stockholder) dies or sells his/her stock
Liability for business debts	Unlimited personal liability	Each partner equally liable for all debts of partnership	Limited to amount invested in the business
Transferability of ownership interest	Free to sell at any time	Consent of all partners required	Free to sell stock shares at any time
Attractiveness for raising capital	Least attractive, because of the disadvantages cited above	Limited attractiveness, because of the disadvantages cited above	Most attractive, because of the advantages cited above
Taxation	Profits taxed only as personal income	Profits taxed only as personal income	Business profits taxed at corporate tax rates, with dividends again taxed at personal rates[*]

[*] A corporation with no more than twenty-five stockholders may elect to be taxed as a partnership under Subchapter S of the Internal Revenue Code.

splitting and other tax benefits of the conventional corporate form noted in the preceding section.

It should also be pointed out that Subchapter S is a *federal* tax option and that the "Small Business Corporation" is still subject to a tax on its income at the state level; only a few states have imitated the federal law.

In addition to the tax consequences just cited, a potentially more serious source of difficulty is the provision in the law that any *one* shareholder may terminate the election of Subchapter S by his or her own action, for whatever reason(s), regardless of the desires of other shareholders. In such an event undistributed income already taxed to the shareholders may be locked into the corporation, since the shareholders must pay an additional tax on the *same* dollars when received later as dividend distributions. This would result in a considerably higher effective tax rate on accumulated (undistributed) earnings than would normally be the case if the tax option had not been elected in the first place.

Since taxes, especially federal income taxes, have become a major business and personal expense, the form of organization may be the deciding factor between profit or loss to an enterpriser. In addition, the tax structure has become so complicated and subject to so many changes that it is difficult to make a wise choice of legal structure. In all but very simple cases, expert legal or accounting advice should be obtained.

Often tax savings are possible, or penalties may be avoided, by an alertness to changes in the tax laws, such as longer **carry-backs** or **carry-forwards** of losses, accelerated depreciation allowances, and **tax credits.** In this regard, also, the employment of legal or accounting counsel is helpful.

SUMMING UP

The basic forms of ownership organization differ in terms of (1) organizational requirements and costs, (2) financial liability of the owners, (3) transfer of equities, (4) management control, and (5) continuity of the business.

A sixth factor is the complexity of the income tax structure; this is often the dominant factor in selecting the best form of ownership organization to use at a particular time. Legal and accounting counsel are often desirable in making the right decision.

The legal ownership forms also vary in their attractiveness for raising capital. Because of the limited liability of shareholders, and the transferability of interest, the corporate form is particularly attractive to investors. The limited partnership form of organization also attracts investors, but the equity shares of the limited partners are less liquid and less marketable than stock shares in a publicly held company.

articles of incorporation
buy-sell agreement
capital gains
capital stock
capitalization (of a corporation)
carry-back
carry-forward
charter
corporation
dividend

double-tax
general partnership
legal entity
limited liability
limited partnership
partnership
proprietorship
retained earnings
tax credit
tax-option (Subchapter S) corporation

DISCUSSION QUESTIONS

1. Explain how the law of agency governs relationships between business partners.

2. Under what circumstances might the shareholder-officers of a conventional corporation desire to increase the salaries they pay to themselves? Under what circumstances might they find it preferable to decrease their salaries?

EXERCISES AND PROBLEMS

1. Jack White is the proprietor of his own business, which last year netted him $49,775. His federal personal income tax liability on this business income, after personal exemptions for him and his wife and with personal deductions not in excess of the zero bracket amount, amounted to $14,484 (read from tax table on p. 419); he and his wife had no other income and filed a joint tax return. How much would Jack have paid in taxes if his business had been incorporated and he paid himself an annual salary of $15,000, leaving everything else in the business? (See p. 448 for the corporate income tax schedule.)

2. Bill Brown and Bob Black invested $40,000 and $60,000, respectively, in their partnership business and agreed to share profits and losses in proportion to their investments.

    a. After showing a loss the first two years, the firm netted a modest profit of $15,000 during the third year. How much of this partnership income should Brown receive? Black?

If line 34 (taxable income) is—		And you are—			
At least	But less than	Single	Married filing jointly *	Married filing separately	Head of a household
		Your tax is—			
13,500	13,550	2,194	1,723	2,611	2,095
13,550	13,600	2,207	1,734	2,627	2,107
13,600	13,650	2,219	1,744	2,643	2,119
13,650	13,700	2,232	1,755	2,659	2,131
13,700	13,750	2,245	1,765	2,675	2,143
13,750	13,800	2,258	1,775	2,690	2,155
13,800	13,850	2,271	1,786	2,706	2,167
13,850	13,900	2,284	1,796	2,722	2,178
13,900	13,950	2,296	1,806	2,738	2,190
13,950	14,000	2,309	1,817	2,754	2,202
14,000					
14,000	14,050	2,322	1,827	2,769	2,214
14,050	14,100	2,335	1,837	2,785	2,226
14,100	14,150	2,348	1,848	2,801	2,238
14,150	14,200	2,361	1,858	2,817	2,250
14,200	14,250	2,373	1,869	2,833	2,261
14,250	14,300	2,386	1,879	2,848	2,273
14,300	14,350	2,399	1,889	2,864	2,285
14,350	14,400	2,412	1,900	2,880	2,297
14,400	14,450	2,425	1,910	2,896	2,309
14,450	14,500	2,438	1,920	2,912	2,321
14,500	14,550	2,450	1,931	2,927	2,332
14,550	14,600	2,463	1,941	2,943	2,344
14,600	14,650	2,476	1,952	2,959	2,356
14,650	14,700	2,489	1,962	2,975	2,368
14,700	14,750	2,502	1,972	2,991	2,380
14,750	14,800	2,515	1,983	3,006	2,392
14,800	14,850	2,528	1,993	3,022	2,404
14,850	14,900	2,540	2,003	3,038	2,415
14,900	14,950	2,553	2,014	3,054	2,427
14,950	15,000	2,566	2,024	3,071	2,439
15,000					
15,000	15,050	2,580	2,034	3,089	2,451
15,050	15,100	2,595	2,045	3,107	2,464
15,100	15,150	2,609	2,055	3,126	2,477
15,150	15,200	2,624	2,066	3,144	2,490
15,200	15,250	2,639	2,076	3,162	2,503

49,000					
49,000	49,050	17,312	14,121	20,168	16,093
49,050	49,100	17,339	14,146	20,198	16,119
49,100	49,150	17,366	14,170	20,227	16,146
49,150	49,200	17,393	14,194	20,256	16,173
49,200	49,250	17,420	14,218	20,285	16,199
49,250	49,300	17,447	14,242	20,314	16,226
49,300	49,350	17,475	14,267	20,343	16,253
49,350	49,400	17,502	14,291	20,372	16,279
49,400	49,450	17,529	14,315	20,402	16,306
49,450	49,500	17,556	14,339	20,431	16,333
49,500	49,550	17,583	14,363	20,460	16,359
49,550	49,600	17,610	14,388	20,489	16,386
49,600	49,650	17,637	14,412	20,518	16,413
49,650	49,700	17,665	14,436	20,547	16,439
49,700	49,750	17,692	14,460	20,576	16,466
49,750	49,800	17,719	14,484	20,605	16,493
49,800	49,850	17,746	14,509	20,635	16,519
49,850	49,900	17,773	14,533	20,664	16,546
49,900	49,950	17,800	14,557	20,693	16,573
49,950	50,000	17,828	14,581	20,722	16,599

b. Though the firm grew and prospered for a while, it suffered a series of operating losses recently and last year the firm failed, its liabilities exceeding its assets by $50,000. For how much of this debt is Brown legally responsible? Black?

c. In addition to his share of the assets of the business, Black had $40,000 of other property at the time the business went bankrupt; but Brown had personal assets of only $10,000. What amount of property other than the partnership property might be required of each partner to pay the debts of the partnership?

3. Three partners invested $10,000, $15,000, and $25,000, respectively, in a partnership. The partnership agreement provides that each partner is to receive 10 percent on his investment, with the remainder of the profits to be divided equally. Last year the firm netted a profit of $65,000. What is the total amount that each partner should receive of this profit?

4. A corporation's before-tax income last year amounted to $100,000.
a. How much did the corporation pay in federal income taxes? (See p. 448 for corporate income tax rates.)
b. The board of directors of the corporation decides to distribute all of the after-tax income as dividends to its shareholders. Of the 5,000 shares of stock outstanding, John Jones owns 750 shares. What amount of dividends will he receive?
c. John Jones is in the 40 percent income tax bracket. How much personal income tax must he pay on this dividend income? (*Note:* The dividend exclusion amounts to $200 and he owns no other stock.)
d. What is the effective tax rate on John Jones's share of the corporation's earnings?

5. The above corporation in which John Jones owns stock decides to go out of business. The balance sheet of the company shows assets of $1 million and liabilities of $250,000. The assets are converted into $900,000 cash. How much should John Jones receive from the dissolution?

CASES IN
POINT*

Delaney v. Fidelity Lease Limited (526 S.W.2d 543, Texas, 1975)
A limited partnership was formed with a corporation as the general partner. The limited partners were officers and directors of the corporation. P, a creditor of the limited partnership, sought to collect a partnership debt individually from the limited partners. The law provides that a limited partner who takes part in the control of a business is liable as a general partner.
Issue: Can the personal liability that attaches to a limited partner when he or she takes part in control of the business be evaded by acting through a corporation?

* Selected from *Fundamentals of Business Law*, 3rd ed. (Englewood Cliffs, N.J.: Prentice-Hall, Inc., 1982), pp. 469, 470, 479, 481, 484–85, 488, 494, and 510 respectively; courtesy of the authors, Robert N. Corley, Eric M. Holmes, and Wilbur J. Robert. Reprinted by permission of Prentice-Hall, Inc., Englewood Cliffs, NJ 07632.

Trans-Am Builders, Inc. v. *Woods Mill Ltd.* (210 S.E.2d 866, Georgia, 1974)

Ds were limited partners in a real estate venture. After the business got into financial difficulty, the limited partners had two meetings with the general partners to discuss the problems of the venture. In addition, one limited partner visited the construction site and "obnoxiously" complained of the way the work was being conducted.

Issue: Do these actions constitute taking part in the control of the business enough to make the limited partners liable as general partners?

Johnson v. *Plastex Company* (500 So.2d 596, Oklahoma, 1972)

P, a seller of goods, sued D, an alleged partner, for the balance due on merchandise shipped to the partnership. When P extended credit, it did not know that D was a partner. The credit was extended to the partnership without the seller's even knowing the names of the partners.

Issue: Is D liable as a partner?

Montana Farm Service Co. v. *Marquart* (578 P.2d 315, Montana, 1978)

D and X entered into a written agreement with P, whereby D and X were authorized to sell tires, batteries, and accessories to be delivered to them by P. D claims that the agreement was blank when he signed it. X substantiated D's claim and testified that he, X, was the sole owner of the venture engaged as a selling agent for P. D and X made no attempt to pay for any of the merchandise delivered to them. P sued D for the account.

Issue: Did a partnership exist between D and X, making D liable to P for the merchandise delivered?

Aronovitz v. *Stein Properties* (322 So.2d 74, Fla. App., 1975)

A partnership known as Stein Properties brought suit in its firm name against a trustee on a deposit receipt contract. The partnership had not complied with the state's fictitious name statute. The defendant moved to dismiss the suit, contending that the partnership could not sue because of its failure to comply with the state statute.

Issue: Will the suit be dismissed?

Waggen v. *Gerde et ux.* (36 Wash. 2d 563, 1950)

P sued Ds, his partners, for the reasonable value of services rendered. The parties were partners in the ownership and operation of a fishing vessel. P had perfected a new type of net for catching sharks and contended that he was entitled to compensation for the time and effort expended in constructing the shark nets. P had informed his partners that he was busy getting the nets ready and that it would "be lots of work to fix" them. P did not inform Ds of what the work actually entailed or that he expected any compensation for it.

Issue: Is P entitled to compensation?

Holloway v. *Smith et al.* (197 Va. 334, 1955)

S and B were partners in the automobile business under the name of Greenwood Sales and Service. B borrowed $6,000 from P and gave a partnership note in return. B borrowed the money to make his initial capital contribution to the partnership.

Issue: Is the partnership liable on the note?

Smith v. *Director, Corp. & Securities Bureau* (261 So.2d 228, Miss., 1978)

P, a construction corporation, filed a suit against D to enforce a construction lien. P was a Tennessee corporation that was not licensed to do business in Mississippi, where the suit was filed, but it had paid Mississippi's contractor's privilege tax. D moved to dismiss the suit, contending that an unlicensed foreign corporation could not file suit in the state courts of Mississippi.

Issue: Is P entitled to file suit?

Government Regulation
of Business

CHAPTER TWENTY-SIX *Business is part of a social process, and the business community, as with any other group that must work in harmony for the public good, has need for rules and regulations concerning the conduct of its members. One type of control consists of those rules and regulations adopted voluntarily by businesspeople as codes of ethics or standards of conduct for and among themselves. Other controls on business activities consist of those established by a legislative or other public authority and administered or enforced by courts and various government bureaus and commissions. It is the latter type of business regulations with which we are primarily concerned in this chapter; after reading it you should have a fuller understanding of some of the more important non-tax laws that impose restraints on the operation of a business enterprise.*

All branches of government from the local community up through the federal government regulate the manner in which business may be conducted. Some of the more important statutes and ordinances regulating business practices are discussed in the following paragraphs. Except for the antitrust laws, these regulations apply to businesses of all sizes, large and small. In general their purpose is to restrict anticompetitive and antisocial acts.

COMPETITION

In most areas of business that are not natural **monopolies,** competition is considered to be desirable. However, unregulated business has repeatedly shown tendencies to seek monopoly powers in varying degrees. Our antitrust laws, both federal and state, have been enacted to protect business itself against those tendencies. The Sherman Antitrust Act of 1890 was passed by Congress after the states had tried unsuccessfully to check the growing monopolies of that time. Although not completely successful, it did make possible the dissolution of many monopolistic **trusts** in sugar, whisky, oil, and other industries.

A new approach was taken with the passage of the Clayton Act and the

Federal Trade Commission Act in 1914. Emphasis was now placed on preventing the growth of monopolies by "cleaning up competition," or restricting practices that would lead to monopoly, such as price fixing and **exclusive dealing** and **tie-in contracts**.[1] In 1938 the Wheeler-Lea Act extended the coverage of the Clayton Act, especially with reference to misrepresentations in advertising. Administrative powers are vested in the Federal Trade Commission (FTC), which is charged with keeping competition both free and fair. Over the years the Commission has built up a long list of unfair trade practices, such as price cutting for the purpose of eliminating competition, misbranding, secret rebates, use of misleading names, and false and misleading advertising.

Two FTC units are of particular interest to the small business owner. One is the Division of Trade Practice Conferences, which reduces to writing (after due notice and public hearing) rules that interpret the laws enforced by the Commission as they apply to particular industries. The second is the Division of Discriminatory Practices, which investigates complaints of unfair practice and also will consult with small business owners regarding applicability of laws administered by the FTC to their own problems.

Although both the Sherman and Clayton Acts are federal laws and therefore apply only to **interstate commerce,** most states have enacted similar legislation to regulate **intrastate commerce.** In addition, the decisions of the FTC regarding unfair methods of competition have set the pattern both for state courts and for practices approved by the various trade associations. Final authority for approving trade practices, however, rests with the Commission. Many of the trade prohibitions are prescribed only after extensive hearings and conferences between the Commission and trade representatives. Although

---

[1] A tie-in contract is one in which a buyer is obligated to buy products or services he or she does not want in order to obtain those the buyer does want. An exclusive-dealing contract is one in which a seller obligates a buyer to refrain from the purchase of competitors' products.

benefits to the small business owner resulting from the work of the FTC would be difficult to assess directly, there is no doubt that they have been substantial.

PRICE REGULATIONS

In a truly competitive market, price acts as the regulator adjusting supply to demand. Attempts to manipulate prices in various ways have existed since the beginning of our price economy. In this country, there are four broad areas of regulation: price fixing, price discrimination, price cutting, and resale-price maintenance.

Price Fixing

Price fixing, under court interpretations of the federal antitrust laws, includes agreements among competitors engaged in interstate commerce to stabilize prices or to hold competitive prices in a fixed relationship to each other. The term is not limited to the fixing of uniform prices. Also illegal are many indirect methods of price fixing, such as agreements to maintain uniform discounts, markups, and delivery charges.

However, many states do not have antitrust laws, and in such states, as long as a small business is not engaged in interstate commerce, price fixing is not only legal but widely practiced. The setting of uniform prices or rates is particularly common among local service establishments, such as barber and beauty shops, dry cleaning establishments, and automobile repair shops.

Price Discrimination

In 1936 the Robinson-Patman amendment to the Clayton Act declared personal **price discrimination** to be illegal. Differences in the price of goods of like grade and quality to different buyers in competition are declared to be illegal unless justified by differences in costs of manufacture, selling, or handling. However, a seller is permitted to discriminate in price between buyers in order to meet the lower prices of competitors in regional markets.

The authors of the Robinson-Patman Act recognized that there are many ways in which a seller can discriminate in price other than varying the invoice price, and these also were declared to be illegal. Specifically mentioned in the act are the following: (1) allowances for advertising and sales promotion that are in excess of a fair payment for services actually rendered by the buyer and that are not made on proportionately equal terms to all competing customers; and (2) brokerage fees collected from the seller when the broker was also acting with the buyer as principal.

The burden of proof that price (and service) differentials are economically justified rests with the seller, and the buyer who knowingly accepts such illegal price discrimination is made equally liable with the seller. The reason for making the buyer liable to prosecution for accepting a discriminatory price is the fact that many buyers for large chain stores and mail-order houses had formerly bargained for low prices that sometimes exceeded the economies resulting from their large orders.

Price Cutting

Excessive **price cutting** when used solely for the purpose of eliminating competition has quite generally been considered to be an unfair method of competition used especially by large concerns to drive small competitors out of business. If permitted, it is normally followed by a high monopoly price once effective competition is driven from the market. The temporary benefits to consumers resulting from lower prices are lost during the subsequent period of high prices.

Most states have passed laws to prohibit below-cost selling that restrains the trade of competitors. These so-called anti-**loss leader** laws define cost as invoice cost plus a fair share of the expenses of doing business. Especially in merchandising, where a large variety of articles are handled, this is so indefinite and it is so impractical to determine the cost of individual items that these laws have been ineffective. A partial solution has been to interpret "cost of doing business" arbitrarily as some fixed markup over invoice cost—say, 6 percent.

Since anti-loss leader laws have proved to be unenforceable in practice, the necessary policing is usually done by each trade group rather than by state law enforcement officers. However, the trade groups themselves have been lax in enforcement, and loss leader merchandising is common.

Resale-Price Maintenance

Beginning with California in 1931, forty-five states enacted **fair trade** statutes that legalized **resale-price maintenance** contracts for trademarked articles or merchandise identifiable as to producer. These laws permitted vertical contracts between manufacturer and wholesaler or retailer stipulating either the price at which the identifiable article was to be sold or the minimum price below which it could not be sold. A provision that a single contract between a manufacturer or his duly authorized wholesale agent and one retailer in a state became binding on all other dealers in the state (known as the nonsigner provision) was used up to 1951. By 1937 the majority of the states had passed resale-price maintenance laws, and the federal government made the practice generally legal in interstate commerce by passing the Miller-Tydings Act.

In the late 1940s, opposition began to mount against fair trade regulations. The courts were less friendly toward such legislation, and in May 1951 in the *Schwegmann* decision the United States Supreme Court decided that the nonsigner provision was not intended in the Miller-Tydings Act, thus releasing most retailers from the need to observe fair trade prices. Pressure was immediately put on Congress, with the result that the Supreme Court decision was nullified by passage of the McGuire Act as an amendment to the Federal Trade Commission Act, making it an unfair practice for any retailer to cut an established resale price even though he was not a party to the fair trade agreement. The Commission was empowered and directed to enforce the act, an ironic situation in view of its other duties and its opposition to fair trade laws.

Then, in state after state, courts began to rule against fair trade laws, and when the large companies (such as General Electric and Sunbeam) which had attempted to enforce them stopped their efforts, fair trade was dead in seventeen of the forty-five states. The consumers had all along been opposed to fair trade and were willing to overlook its provisions. Also, retailers had refused to abide by its provisions, claiming the laws restricted their freedom to operate and resulted in artificially high prices. Finally, the manufacturers themselves became convinced that high fair trade prices actually worked against their best interests because they often restricted volume production. The development of the discount house became possible with this new attitude toward fair trade.

Retailing history in the United States has demonstrated that innovations will appear and expand in *soft spots,* that is, areas where current retailing and marketing practices fail to meet widespread demands. Legislative efforts to block such American ingenuity have consistently failed since late in the last century; and current attempts to use fair trade regulations as a crutch for incompetent management appear to bear out this long-time trend. Among the popular devices used in recent years to bypass fair trade regulations are inflated trade-ins, non-fair traded articles given free with each purchase at fair-trade prices, sales tickets made out at fair trade prices accompanied by an unrecorded cash refund, and so on. No company or governmental agency can possibly detect and control all of these evasions; and even if they had virtually unlimited financial resources, the time factor alone would make enforcement impossible to achieve.

The author's discussion in this section has been a deliberate attempt to warn the conscientious independent enterpriser against the long-run hazards of seeking security in fair trade regulation or other legal devices in lieu of competent management. Efforts by business owners to guarantee their profits by various laws and legal props have not been successful for any length of time. Especially in the dynamic, free enterprise economy of the U.S., efforts of this sort appear to be less desirable than rendering a genuine public service through efficient management conducted in the interest of consumers. In the long run any legal restrictive measures that place the interests of special groups above the public interest may cause reaction unfavorable to the very groups seeking protection.

MERCHANDISE REGULATIONS

So far as the product itself is concerned, the most important regulations are those relating to health, safety, labeling, warranties, company and brand names, patents, and trademarks.

Food, Drugs, and Cosmetics

Laws designed to protect the health of the consumer have been enacted by federal, state, and local governments. The Pure Food and Drug Act was passed by Congress in 1906, making it illegal to ship injurious, falsely labeled, or adulterated foods or drugs in interstate commerce. This law was revised in 1938 by the Food, Drug, and Cosmetic Act to include cosmetics (except soap) and certain curative devices or appliances. It also provided for testing before certain drugs that might cause sickness or death are put on the market. More complete disclosure of habit-forming ingredients as well as others that might be injurious to certain types of individuals is required. Like its predecessor, the 1938 law deals mostly with adulteration and misbranding, and with information that must be given on the label. The small business owner manufacturing or handling foods, drugs, therapeutic devices, or cosmetics should study and observe in detail the provisions of this law, even though he or she may not be engaged in interstate commerce. A 1953 amendment authorizes inspectors to enter any establishment where food, drugs, or cosmetic items are held and to inspect the establishment and materials and equipment therein.

A recent addition to the food and drug regulations concerns food additives. Under this legislation, manufacturers must certify to the Food and Drug Administration that the additives are harmless in the intended use. This is done by submitting certain required data, considerably detailed, in an application to the Department of Health and Human Services; the applicant is then advised by that body as to what can be used, in what amounts, labeling requirements, and so forth. Similar regulations apply for food coloratives and lipstick color components.

All states and most cities have legislation and regulations dealing with the processing and handling of food for the public. Many have laws governing drugs and similar merchandise. Pharmacy is recognized in every state as a profession to be practiced only by qualified pharmacists, but the detailed regulations are not uniform in all states. Either the manufacture or the sale of certain other products—such as eyeglasses and similar optical goods—is frequently regulated by state law or local ordinances.

Product Safety and Liability

The Food and Drug Administration also has the power, under the Child Protection and Toy Safety Act of 1969, to ban potentially harmful toys. A provision of this act requires retailers to refund the purchase price of a condemned toy. The store owner, in turn, can seek reimbursement from the manufacturer.

Another example of Congress's concern for product safety is the Flammable Fabrics Act. This statute, administered by the Federal Trade Commission, prohibits the interstate marketing of wearing apparel or fabrics that are "so highly flammable as to be dangerous when worn." The act requires that five specimens of the fabric be tested in their original state; in addition, in the absence of proof that a fire-retarding finish has been added, five specimens must be tested after dry cleaning or washing.

Since the publication of Ralph Nader's *Unsafe at Any Speed*, federal government attention has also been focused on automobile safety, and in recent years time limits have been imposed for the incorporation in new-car design of a variety of safety features prescribed by the National Highway Traffic Safety Administration.

Consumer advocates have directed their attention to the safety of other products as well. Coupled with the increased tendency of judges and juries to make large monetary rewards in civil suits and for a greater number of causes, the result has been an escalation in the costs of **product liability** insurance. Manufacturers of industrial machinery, sporting goods, drugs, chemicals, and lawnmowers have been particularly hard hit, as have the retailers and other distributors of these products who, under the law, are adjudged equally responsible.

Product Warranties

Product warranties are regulated by the Magnuson-Moss Warranty Act. This law sets minimum standards for what a **warranty** must contain. To promise a *full* warranty to the purchaser, for example, the marketer must offer to repair the product "within a reasonable time and without charge," and to replace it or give a full refund if "after a reasonable number of attempts" at repairing it the product does not work. Any warranty that does not meet these standards must be "conspicuously" promoted as a *limited* warranty. Though this legislation, like the safety legislation discussed above, is aimed directly at the manufacturers (most of whom are of large size), it is obviously of great concern and import to the merchandisers of these products (most of whom are small retail establishments).

Product Labeling

According to the Federal Wool Product Labeling Act, all articles made of wool, except floor coverings, must be labeled as to the percentages of virgin wool and of reprocessed and reused wool content. If any fiber other than wool is present in excess of 5 percent, its percentage must also be given on the label. It is illegal for the retailer or other business owner dealing in such products to remove or deface the label containing this information.

In a similar manner, the Federal Fur Products Labeling Act outlaws the deceptive labeling of fur. Fur products must be guaranteed to consist of the type of fur indicated on the label. A retailer may replace a label provided he or she complies with all labeling requirements and maintains a complete record of the substitution for at least three years.

Both the wool and fur labeling acts are administered by the Federal Trade Commission. In connection with the fur act, the Commission has issued a register of animal names, known as the "Fur Products Name Guide," for use in properly describing furs and fur products.

Company and Brand Names

The company or firm name identifies the particular enterprise and may consist of all or part of the names of the owners or an assumed name. Sometimes proprietors use their first or last name only, or both, and partnerships frequently use the last name of each partner, as the Smith-Jones Company. Sole proprietors can ordinarily use their full name for a business without restrictions unless another firm in the same market and kind of business has this name well-established and confusion would result if a newcomer were to use the same name. If an assumed or coined name is used, and usually when only the first or last name of a proprietor or partner is used, it is necessary to file with the county clerk the company name and full name of each owner. This is primarily to protect others who may deal with the concern and to have on record essential information as to who actually owns the business. For a corporation the name under which it will operate as well as the names of the incorporators is part of the application for a charter.

A **brand** (trade) name is used to identify a product or the line of products sponsored by one firm. It is a form of **trademark.** Often it is simply the company name; for example, Maytag washing machines or G.E. toasters. It may also be a name coined or appropriated for product-identification use by one firm; for example, Dodge Charger or Ajax cleaning products. Though brand names are most often used by manufacturers, they are also frequently used by distributors; for example, Sears-Roebuck Coldspot refrigerators or A&P's Sultana canned goods.

Trademarks and Patents

A brand name, as noted above, is only one type of trademark. Sometimes a product or the company itself is more readily recognized by means of a symbol or emblem rather than a name. Some of the more familiar trademarks of this type are Exxon's tiger, MGM's lion, and Prudential's Rock of Gibraltar. Other symbols or emblems used as trademarks consist of unique arrangements of lines and/or colors, such as Chrysler's five-pointed star and Ford's blue oval. Package design may also be trademarked. Even the way the company name is written is a form of trademark. A point of major importance for the small business owner is to avoid any attempt to copy or imitate a company name or trademark already in use that might expose him or her to charges of unfair competition.

A trademark must have been used in interstate commerce before an application for registration can be filed with the Patent Office. Since July 1947, provisions of the federal Lanham Act replace those of the Trade-Mark Act of 1905. Under the Lanham Act, registration of trademarks on the Principal Register is essential to secure future protection. Also, a trademark need no longer be physically affixed to the merchandise; protection is thus given to well-advertised trademarks for such products as brands of gasoline and to service marks of service establishments. In addition to federal registration, many states have passed laws concerning the protection of trademarks used in intrastate commerce. A small firm would be well-advised to employ a competent attorney in all trademark matters.

Securing a **patent** is also a highly complex procedure and should be handled by an attorney trained in this specialized field. A patent gives an inventor the right to exclude all others from making, using, or selling his or her invention for a period of seventeen years, and it is granted only after there has been a determination of utility and a search to determine its novelty. No patent is granted on a mere suggestion or idea; the invention must be described and illustrated in detail. The patent law affords no protection prior to the actual issue of a patent, although it is common practice to serve notice of application by stating that a patent has been applied for.

OTHER CONSUMER PROTECTION LAWS

Consumer Credit

Significant consumer credit legislation has been passed in recent years. To protect consumers against the use of erroneous information in the files of credit bureaus, as well as the misuse of credit bureau reports, Congress in 1971 enacted the Fair Credit Reporting Act. Congress also passed in 1969 the Truth-in-Lending Law to protect consumers against the uninformed use of credit; and in 1974 the Fair Credit Billing Act to protect credit customers against billing errors and charges for shoddy or unsatisfactory merchandise. More recently Congress enacted the Equal Credit Opportunity Act, prohibiting credit discrimination on the basis of race, color, religion, national origin, age, sex, or marital status. **Equal credit opportunity, truth-in-lending** and fair billing regulations, enforced by the Federal Trade Commission, were discussed in detail in Chapter 18. In addition, many states have established maximum rates that can be charged for the financing of consumer credit.

Advertising

Federal regulation of advertising is administered by the Federal Trade Commission as part of its responsibility for the maintenance of fair competition. In general, false and misleading advertising is condemned. This includes the use of deceptive and misleading names and expressions such as "Cylk" or "artificial silk." Many names formerly used to describe lower-quality furs in such a way as to suggest the expensive article have also been banned. The Wheeler-Lea amendment to the Federal Trade Commission Act gives the Commission power to regulate advertising to meet the labeling requirements of the Food, Drug, and Cosmetic Act. It also gives the Commission authority for the first time to prohibit advertising that is injurious to the *public* even though it may not directly affect competition, such as the ban on cigarette commercials on radio and television. The FTC also enforces the Truth-in-Lending regulations relating to the advertising of credit terms (discussed in Chapter 18). Many states also have laws regulating false and misleading advertising.

In 1953, the Commission reversed its earlier position toward use of the word "free" in advertising and accepted its usage where the "conditions, obligations or other prerequisites to the receipt and retention of the 'free' articles" are clearly explained.

ENVIRONMENTAL PROTECTION

The Environmental Protection Agency was created by Congress in 1970 to help protect and improve the quality of the nation's environment, with particular reference to the prevention of air and water pollution, noise abatement, atomic radiation, and the control of solid waste disposal. While the EPA is primarily concerned with requiring the installation of expensive pollution-control equipment in large industrial plants, it is also concerned with the improper or excessive use of pesticides and fertilizers, the careless discarding of trash and junk, and other practices or conditions prevalent in some smaller businesses.

LABOR LEGISLATION

Federal and state labor legislation may be divided into four broad groups: (1) settlement of labor disputes; (2) fair employment practices; (3) regulation of wages, hours, and working conditions; and (4) protective legislation for women and children.

Settlement of Labor Disputes

The National Labor Relations Act (Wagner Act) of 1935 was the first important law concerned with labor disputes and is administered by the National Labor Relations Board. It provides that employees shall have "the right to self-organization, to form, join, or assist labor organizations, to bargain collectively through representatives of their own choosing, and to engage in concerted activities, for the purpose of collective bargaining or other mutual aid or protection." According to the act, certain practices on the part of an employer are considered to be unfair, including the following: (1) interfering with, restraining, or coercing of employees in the exercise of their guaranteed rights; (2) dominating or interfering with the formation or administration of any labor organization; (3) encouraging or discouraging membership in any labor organization by discrimination in regard to hiring, tenure, or conditions of employment; (4) discharging or otherwise discriminating against an employee for filing charges or giving testimony under the act; and (5) refusing to bargain collectively with representatives of employees.

The Wagner Act was unmistakably one-sided legislation; it assumed that only the employer could "sin." By 1947 many unions had become such towers of strength that they often abused their powers from the public viewpoint. As a result the Taft-Hartley Act was passed whereby unions as well as employers could be held responsible for unfair labor practices; in particular, it outlawed the **closed shop, secondary boycotts, jurisdictional strikes,** and **featherbedding."**

However, due to Supreme Court interpretation and the complexity of the issues, a number of the Congressional goals were not fully realized. Organized labor continued to grow in strength, and in 1959 the Landrum-Griffin Act was passed to protect the rights of individual members from the autocratic use of union power. In addition, the unfair labor practice provisions in the Taft-Hartley Act were strengthened.

Labor experts expect differences of opinion to arise between representatives of labor and management when negotiating a new contract. As a consequence, they are required to bargain in good faith in an attempt to reach an understanding. Furthermore, disputes will arise over the interpretation of an existing contract, and most agreements, to meet this contingency, provide for a grievance procedure culminating in **arbitration.**

One of the most important decisions in the field of labor law in the past twenty-five years concerns the question of agreements to arbitrate. Prior to 1957, state contract law controlled **collective bargaining** agreements, and neither an agreement to arbitrate nor an arbitrator's award were enforceable in court. In *Textile Workers Union* v. *Lincoln Mills,* the Supreme Court decided that agreements to arbitrate could be enforced under the Taft-Hartley Act and that federal law, rather than state law, would control. And in subsequent decisions, the Supreme Court decided that courts could not, generally speaking, tamper with the decision of an arbitrator. These decisions are extremely important because of the emphasis placed on arbitration rather than court maneuvering in labor disputes.

Fair Employment Practices

The most recent development in labor legislation has been the attack against various forms of discrimination practiced by some employers and unions. Most states have enacted fair employment practice (FEP) laws, and

Congress in 1964 passed the Civil Rights Act. Title VII of the federal act, as amended by the Equal Employment Opportunity Act of 1972, prohibits discrimination in any aspect of employment on the basis of race, color, sex, religion, and national origin. More recently, in 1975, Congress passed the Age Discrimination Act. The scope of the **equal employment opportunity** laws has been expanded by court decisions to prohibit discrimination against persons with handicaps or health problems and those with arrest or court records.[2]

In general, the state FEP laws provide that complaints of discrimination be brought before an administrative agency which could, after investigation, attempt conciliation. If conciliation should fail, the administrative agency or commission would make a subsequent formal decision which could be enforced in a state court. Until the point of failure at the conciliation level all information is confidential; if a formal decision is made, it becomes a matter of public record.

The federal law differs in one important respect from the state laws. The federal commission can only conciliate the differences between the complainant and the employer (or union); that is, its members cannot make a binding decision. However, if the employer (or union) refuses to comply with the judgment of the commission, the commission can bring a suit in a federal district court.

The federal law pertains to firms and unions functioning in interstate commerce, but states with FEP legislation are entitled to priority of jurisdiction for sixty days. Other salient features of the federal law are:

1. Segregated locals and the exclusion of blacks from unions is forbidden.
2. Professionally developed tests used for hiring and promotion are permitted. This provision has received much adverse comment because tests tend to discriminate against those people with poor economic and educational backgrounds. Based on the 1971 Supreme Court decision in *Griggs* v. *Duke Power Co.*, an employer violates the federal law if the test used is not geared to the job description and if its reliability and validity is not checked.
3. A full-time agency, the Equal Employment Opportunity Commission (EEOC), was established to consider complaints[3] and conduct technical studies. Most of the state commissions are staffed by part-time members.
4. Unions and employers must provide apprentice-training opportunities for minorities. Rapid technological change tends to wipe out the unskilled and semiskilled jobs which are held mainly by minorities. The federal law is intended to help minorities move into the skilled job categories. The controversial Philadelphia Plan, for example, where the construction in-

---

[2] For a further discussion of these laws and court rulings, see the section entitled "Screening Potential Employees," pp. 147-54, and accompanying Table 11-1, *supra*.

[3] As noted above, however, decisions of the EEOC are not binding.

dustry was required to give priority to black applicants for employment, has upgraded the black construction worker in that area.

Regulation of Wages, Hours, and Working Conditions

The Fair Labor Standards Act of 1938 provides for **minimum wages** for the employees of most firms engaged in interstate commerce. The minimum hourly wage for employees covered by this act is set by Congress from time to time. The act also requires employers to compensate employees at time-and-a-half for hours worked in excess of forty per week. It is noted that the law does *not* specify maximum working hours; the intent is merely to keep working hours from rising much above the forty-per-week norm by making the over-time hours relatively expensive to the employer.

It is also important for small business owners to note that under certain terms of an agreement with their employees' representatives they may be exempted from the overtime provision of the act. For example, the parties may agree that up to a limit of 1,040 working hours in a twenty-six-week period there will be no overtime penalty; provided, however, that the employees work no more than twelve hours per day or fifty-six hours per week. This is an important provision of the law for those firms in highly seasonal industries. The law also waives the overtime provision for employers who sign labor agreements in which they guarantee the number of working hours per year (within a range of 1,840 to 2,240 hours).

Not all firms engaged in interstate commerce, nor all employees of such firms are covered by the federal Fair Labor Standards Act. Those not covered include the employees of retail stores and service establishments with an annual gross volume of sales or receipts less than a specified minimum; outside sales personnel; and executive, administrative, and professional personnel.

However, small business owners who accept government supply contracts must comply with provisions of the 1936 Walsh-Healy Act. Unlike the Fair Labor Standards Act, in which the minimum wage is fixed by the terms of the law for all covered establishments and employees, the Walsh-Healy Act requires that firms with government supply contracts in excess of a specified dollar amount must pay "prevailing wage rates"; thus the minimum wage varies from industry to industry and from locality to locality. The Walsh-Healy Act further provides for payment of time-and-a-half for hours worked in excess of eight per day or forty per week, whichever yields the higher compensation.

Those small businesses that are not covered by the federal Fair Labor Standards Act will most likely be subject to the same minimum wage requirements in their respective states. Most states have also enacted time-off-for-voting laws; these statutes generally provide for *paid* time, particularly in cases where there is insufficient time for employees to vote before or after work.

The various states have also attempted to regulate working conditions.

Most of the state regulations deal with industrial safety and health. At the federal level, employee safety and health is regulated by provisions of the Occupational Safety and Health Act of 1970 (OSHA).

The federal law requires employers to provide employees with a workplace that is free of hazardous conditions, such as exposure to toxic materials or other physically harmful agents. In retail and service establishments, according to OSHA, the most repeated violations are improperly marked or unmarked exits, fire extinguishers not mounted and/or not easy to spot when needed, and fall-hazard debris in storerooms.

Federal safety inspections of the business premises may be made at any time and without advance notice. Firms found in violation of OSHA's safety and health standards may receive severe fines and other penalties, including forced closure of the firm until the conditions cited are corrected.

OSHA has proved to be the single greatest hurdle ever placed before small business owners by the federal government. In common with their larger competitors, small business owners have these particular problems with OSHA: (1) an excessive amount of time is required to keep up with new standards and interpretations plus ongoing record keeping; (2) corrective information for alleged violations is usually not readily available; and (3) the cost of compliance is sometimes prohibitive. Obviously these problems are aggravated by the small business owner's limited resources in terms of time and money.

Protective Legislation for Women and Children

The federal Fair Labor Standards Act limits the employment of children in the following ways:

1. Children between sixteen and eighteen years of age may not be employed in occupations defined as "hazardous" by the Department of Labor.

2. A child under sixteen years of age is not permitted to work *unless* (a) he or she is employed by a parent or guardian in an industry other than mining and manufacturing or one defined as being "hazardous"; and (b) he or she is at least fourteen years of age and has a temporary permit to work issued by the Department of Labor.

These limitations, of course, apply only to those firms engaged in interstate commerce. However, *all* of the states also have enacted child labor laws which, with only slight variations, impose the same limitations on firms engaged in intrastate commerce.

Protective legislation for women employees is of three types: (1) laws requiring special working conditions, (2) **equal-pay-for-equal work** laws, and (3) equal opportunity laws. Laws of the first type have been enacted at the state level only. In general they require the provision of special facilities and the regulation of night work and industrial home work.

In 1963 Congress passed the Equal Pay Act (an amendment to the Fair Labor Standards Act), which requires employers "to pay equal wages within an establishment to men and women doing equal work on jobs requiring equal skill, effort, and responsibility which are performed under similar working conditions." Wage differentials between classified male–female jobs are permissible only if there are demonstrable differences in job content. Similar legislation has been enacted in the various states.

Also, under the federal Civil Rights Act of 1964 and comparable state enactments, merit increases and promotions cannot be denied on the basis of sex alone.

RESTRICTIONS AND PERMITS

Some state laws restrict business activity (1) by permitting only licensed practitioners to engage in particular occupations, such as pharmacy, barber shop or beauty parlor operation, and public accounting, and (2) by requiring the maintenance of prescribed standards in equipment and processes for protection of the health and safety of employees and the public. However, in general, most regulation of this sort is local, defined by city ordinance and enforced under the community's **police power.**

A **license** is a **permit** granted by the governmental power to a person or company to pursue some business. Licensing is used both to regulate business and as a source of revenue for the government granting the license. For example, plumbers, electricians, pawnbrokers, and auctioneers, as well as dance halls, taxi companies, hotels, amusement places, and food service and drinking places are usually licensed and frequently inspected or supervised to see that regulations for protection of the public health, safety, and morals are observed. Other businesses, such as retail stores, may not be required to have a license but are subject to regulations necessary to reduce fire hazards. On both state and local levels, license requirements and regulatory taxes have been expanding.

In many cities licensing is used to enforce **zoning regulations.** Licenses will be granted to operate a given type of business only in areas where zoning regulations permit this type of business. For example, a retail store will not be licensed to operate in a district zoned exclusively for residences. Similarly, a dry cleaning *store* may get a license to operate in a retail shopping district but the dry cleaning *plant* using certain dangerous fluids will be licensed to operate only in the industrial district.

Licensing is also used to restrict competition, as when itinerant vendors selling from temporary quarters, on the sidewalk, or from house to house are required to pay a relatively heavy license fee. Some regulation of this class of merchant is considered desirable to protect the public from "con artists" and fly-by-night peddlers. It is often difficult to draw the line between licensing for necessary customer protection and that designed to lessen competition for the local merchants. For example, **Green River ordinances** that prohibit all house-to-house solicitation except by personal invitation of the householder obviously not only protect local merchants from competition with outside sellers but also relieve families from annoying interruptions and from some swindle schemes. Another viewpoint, however, is that such ordinances place serious limitations on aggressive selling, especially the launching of new products and other innovations, which can often be done most effectively through such personal contact.

BANKRUPTCY AND COURT-APPROVED DEBT SETTLEMENTS

As noted in Chapter 3, many new business ventures end in failure, particularly during the first few years of operation. So also many business firms—successful or not—have customers who are unable to pay their debts. In either case, small business owners should be familiar with the options available to them under federal and state **bankruptcy** laws.

A bankrupt is a person (including a fictitious "person," or corporation) who has been declared by a court of law as being unable to pay his or her debts. Bankruptcy proceedings may be initiated by the debtor (**voluntary bankruptcy**), or by one or more creditors (**involuntary bankruptcy**). In either case there is a hearing on the petition, and if the judge or court-appointed **referee** declares the debtor bankrupt, the debtor's property is placed in the hands of a **receiver** for liquidation. The proceeds from the sale of the property are then used to pay, first, secured claims (such as a mortgage), and then wage claims. Remaining proceeds (after the payment of taxes) are then divided among the unsecured creditors on a pro rata basis according to the amounts of their claims. For example, if a bankrupt owed $50,000 and the sale of his or her property netted $25,000 after all costs and prior claims were paid, each creditor would receive one-half the amount owed him or her, or 50 cents on the dollar. The bankrupt is *discharged* from further liability for existing debts.

There is, of course, a stigma attached to being declared a bankrupt—whether the debtor is a dependently employed consumer or a small business owner—and bankruptcy proceedings should be initiated only as a last resort. Thus Section XI of the federal Bankruptcy Act provides for *compositions* and *extensions* wherein the debtor is called a *debtor* and not a bankrupt. An **exten-**

sion is a court-approved plan, proposed by the debtor, wherein the debtor is allowed to delay payment of his or her debts for a stipulated period of time, thus providing the debtor with an opportunity to meet his (her) financial obligations in full out of future earnings. If full cash settlement out of future earnings appears unlikely, or if this imposes an unreasonable burden on the debtor, then a **composition** may be approved by the court, wherein the creditors accept the debtor's plan for a pro rata cash settlement as payment in full.

Either an extension or a composition under Section XI of the Bankruptcy Act must be initiated by the debtor. If the plan is accepted by at least half of the creditors to whom at least half of the debts are owed, the plan becomes binding on all the creditors. In this way, a business owner avoids the stigma of a legal bankruptcy and the owner's business (which might someday become viable) is not forced into liquidation. However, the court usually appoints a receiver to manage the business until such time as the extension or composition settlement is consummated.

SUMMING UP

The regulation of business by government through laws, licenses, and taxation is probably as old as business and government. Law constitutes the organized body of rules of conduct enforceable by government agencies. The small business owner/manager must deal with two important levels of legal authority (federal and state) as well as many minor levels (city, county, and other political subdivisions).

Laws have various objectives. Those concerning competition, trade practices, and public welfare are most *restrictive* in nature; in general the aim is to prohibit anticompetitive and antisocial acts. In contrast with these are other laws that are *permissive* in nature, such as permits to do business in particular lines of endeavor, and tax laws (discussed in the next chapter) which *require* particular acts and are mandatory for all concerned.

As the reading of this chapter suggests, government regulations are numerous and complex and as noted previously (in Chapter 2) they constitute one of the greatest hazards to the small independent enterpriser. Severe penalties are imposed for even unintentional violations. Ignorance of the law is not accepted as an excuse, and even licensed attorneys are not always sure of certain provisions and their interpretations by the courts.

GOOSEMYER

by parker and wilder

arbitration
bankruptcy
brand
closed shop
collective bargaining
composition (of creditors)
equal credit opportunity
equal employment opportunity
equal-pay-for-equal-work
exclusive dealing contract
extension (of credit)
fair trade
featherbedding
Green River ordinances
interstate commerce
intrastate commerce
involuntary bankruptcy
jurisdictional strike
license
loss leader

minimum wage
monopoly
patent
permits
police power
price cutting
price discrimination
price fixing
product liability
receiver(ship)
referee (in bankruptcy)
resale-price maintenance
secondary boycott
tie-in contract
trademark
trust
truth-in-lending
voluntary bankruptcy
warranty
zoning regulations

DISCUSSION QUESTIONS

1. If business is based on mutual trust and confidence, then why do we need so many laws regulating business?

2. What nongovernmental agencies are active in enforcing laws related to business? In imposing restrictions on unfair competition or unethical practices? Describe the nature of these activities.

EXERCISES AND PROBLEMS

1. The Small Business Co. sells its product to all customers at $5 each in lots of 1 to 10, at $4.75 each in lots of 11 to 25, and at $4.40 each in lots of more than 25.

a. Is this fair and legal?

b. A large chain store has offered to purchase the product in lots of 500 at $3.50 each. Would this be a lawful business transaction? Discuss fully.

2. Which of the following responses to typical on-the-job situations are lawful, and which are not?* (A review of the author's discussion of pre-employment interviews on pp. 147–54 will be helpful here.)

a. A supervisor hires a younger worker to replace an old timer slowing down on the job.

b. A mail room supervisor discharges an employee after she has suffered an epileptic seizure on the job.

c. Disturbed because Hispanic employees chatter constantly in Spanish, the supervisor orders all workers to speak only English.

d. A black employee frequently breaks work rules. He is formally reprimanded on each occasion and the supervisor scrupulously documents every infraction with a detailed, written file memo. The worker is subsequently discharged for these violations.

e. A woman, claiming a need to care for a child at home, declines overtime work. After several such refusals, she is terminated.

f. A black, non-degreed clerk who has done good work applies for a promotion to accountant. The job calls for an accounting degree. You reject the request.

3. Take one side, and then the other, in the following debate.

Resolved: Bankruptcy is a desirable legal provision for both failing businesses and their creditors.

CASE IN
POINT

> Doris Munson recently developed a means of making sweet potato chips, and has applied for a copyright on the name "Sweetaters." She expects them to serve as a snack, especially attractive to children, but also for adults, good with beverages. She has secured adequate financial backing through the Small Business Administration. A marketing consultant has been called in, and a program involving several possibilities has been laid out for consideration.
>
> Packaging will be in transparent plastic bags appropriately printed. For distance shipping, she favors tins carrying the same label and descriptions. She will also have special cartons for shelf display in stores, and some in-store banners for use particularly at times of introduction into a new store or community. She will also

---

* Mini-quiz used in a Dun & Bradstreet seminar on equal employment opportunity; used with permission of Dun & Bradstreet.

advertise to the public in newspapers and over radio and TV. She will sell through wholesalers to retail stores.

Her consultant suggests also that, since her plant will be located in a store near a shopping center and school, she establish a small retail store of her own there, to keep "in touch with the consumer" and adjust her product and programs as she sees fit. Also, she might wish to offer related food or grocery items in the store to build up her offerings and to compare them with her own product. Later she may wish to open other stores of her own.

This program, though obviously ambitious, will proceed one step at a time, probably slowly. Mrs. Munson and her business, which will probably become a corporation eventually, must bear in mind various federal, state, and local laws affecting a business of this type. She has asked her lawyer for a list of these and an explanation of the reasons why she will need to adhere to them. Can you prepare such a list?

Taxes and
Economic Security Legislation

CHAPTER TWENTY-SEVEN *Business organizations and their employees are subject to a wide variety of taxes, imposed by government for income as well as for regulatory and social welfare purposes. Federal and state laws require that certain records be kept and that periodic reports based on these records be prepared. Penalties are imposed for failure to comply. The purpose of this chapter is to summarize the employer's obligations under these laws.*

> In this world, nothing is certain but death and taxes.
> —BENJAMIN FRANKLIN

In addition to government regulation of business for the "common good," the small business owner or manager is confronted with a multitude of tax regulations. At the federal level, the ones that loom most important for any type of business are (1) payroll taxes assessed to fund **economic security** or **social insurance** legislation, and (2) the **income tax.** In addition to these, certain types of businesses will encounter special taxes, including manufacturers' and retailers' excise taxes, admissions taxes, and taxes on specific products such as tobacco and liquor. Also, a corporation often pays taxes other than those of a proprietorship or partnership, such as an **accumulated earnings tax.**

Some of the taxes that may be expected in most states are income taxes, sales taxes, and **workers' compensation** and unemployment taxes. A corporation will usually have to pay a **capital stock tax,** as well as a "foreign" tax if it operates in states other than the one in which it is incorporated. At the county or city level, most businesses will also be required to pay real and personal **property taxes.**

> The art of taxation consists in so plucking the goose so as to obtain the most feathers with the least hissing.
> —J. B. COLBERT
> French statesman, 1619–1683

ECONOMIC SECURITY LEGISLATION

Economic security legislation is designed to minimize losses to employee income resulting from industrial accidents, occupational diseases, and involuntary unemployment, and to provide workers with hospital and medical care and at least a minimal income after retirement.[1]

Unemployment Taxes

Unemployment benefits are provided by legislation at both the state and federal levels. Under the Federal Unemployment Tax Act (FUTA), all states have been encouraged to enact unemployment compensation laws funded by **unemployment taxes.** The act provides that if a state law is enacted which meets certain requirements, the state can retain approximately 85 percent of the tax levied on employers. The permissible upper limit of the tax in 1982 was 3.4 percent of each employee's annual wages up to $6,000 (of which 2.7 percent is the state's share). The tax must be paid by any firm that employs one or more persons in each of twenty days in a year, each day being in a different week, or has a payroll of at least $1,500 in a calendar quarter.

Most states, however, have a **merit-rating** or **experience-rating** system which provides that employers who have maintained a low labor turnover rate may pay a progressively lower tax. Also, the Social Security Act permits a state to use a tax base that is higher than $6,000 per year, and some states have taken advantage of this provision of the law.

Social Security Taxes

Public pensions for most workers who have reached retirement age are provided by legislation at the federal level only. Under terms of the Federal Insurance Contributions Act (FICA), old age, survivors, and disability insurance is financed by a tax, in equal amounts on both the employer and the employee, on income earned by the employee in a calendar year up to a specified maximum; the tax on this amount of income for the self-employed is approximately 40 percent higher than the tax that he or she would pay as either an employer or an employee.

In addition to the payment of taxes for old age, survivors, and disability insurance (OASDI) benefits, the Federal Insurance Contributions Act established a separate **payroll tax** to finance the federal government's program of hospital and medical insurance for people sixty-five years of age and older. Contributions to this Medicare program go into a separate trust fund, and the contribution rate (currently 0.9 percent) applies to employers, employees, and the self-employed alike.

The combined tax rate for OASDI and Medicare in 1982 was 6.7 percent for both employers and employees, and 9.35 percent for those who are self-employed; the maximum amount of income subject to this tax for taxable year 1982 was $31,800. Increases in both the tax rates and the tax base can be ex-

---

[1] Protection of workers from income loss resulting from industrial accidents and occupational diseases is afforded by the various state workers' compensation laws, discussed on p. 391.

pected in the future as an increasingly larger proportion of the population becomes eligible for these benefits. Following is the **social security tax** schedule
for 1983 and subsequent years:

CALENDAR YEAR	TAXABLE WAGE	TAX RATE (%)			MAXIMUM TAX ON EMPLOYEES' WAGES
		EMPLOYER	EMPLOYEE	SELF-EMPLOYED	
1983	$33,900	6.70	6.70	9.35	$2,271.30
1984	36,000	6.70	6.70	9.35	2,412.00
1985	38,100	7.05	7.05	9.90	2,686.05
1986	40,200	7.15	7.15	10.00	2,874.30
1987	42,600	7.15	7.15	10.00	3,045.90

To the small business owner this counsel is offered concerning his or her
obligations under the federal social security program: *Whether or not you hire
anyone, and even if you are an employee yourself, you must pay a social security tax and make an annual report.* You file and pay your self-employment tax
with your federal income tax, using Schedule C in Form 1040. This must be
done even if you have no income tax liability. If you are self-employed as well
as an employee in someone else's business, consider your wages as an employee
first; if, in 1982, for example, you were paid at least $31,800 in a covered oc-
cupation from which social security taxes were deducted, then you have
earned your maximum credit in that year and you do not report and pay on
your self-employment income. If you received $30,000 in wages and earned
$1,000 in self-employment income, you must pay tax and report on the $1,000
of self-employment income. (Self-employed persons with net earnings of less
than $400 during the taxable year need not report this income nor pay a **self-
employment tax.**)

You must also have a social security account number. If you had previously received one as a salaried employee, use the same number in making
your report as a self-employed person; if it has been lost, apply for a duplicate
of the old number. (This is not to be confused with your identification number
as an employer.[2] In a nutshell, you have two roles to play: as an employer who
is taxed for your employees' welfare; and as a self-employed person who is
taxed for your own welfare.)

For social security purposes payroll records must show the following: the
employee's name; his or her occupation, address, and social security number;[3]
the amount of each payment to this employee (including any amount with-

[2] Every employer of one or more persons in covered employment must have an identification
number. Application for such a number is made by filing form SS-4 with the nearest office of
the Social Security Administration. The assigned identification number must appear on all social security records, correspondence, and tax returns.

[3] A new employee who has not been previously assigned a social security number should be
asked to apply for one, using form SS-5.

held); the date of each payment; the period of employment covered by each payment; and the amount of social security tax deducted from the wages paid. If the employee's tax is deducted at any time other than when the wages are paid, the date of deduction must be recorded. If all or any part of the wage payment is not taxable, the reason must be included in your records.[4]

If your type of business involves tips, such as in a restaurant, employees receiving cash tips of $20 or more in a month must report these tips to you before the tenth day of the following month. You then deduct (withhold) the employee's social security and income tax on this amount from the wages due that employee. However, you are required to match only the social security taxes deducted from the employee's *wages;* you need not match the employee's tax liability on the amount earned in tips.

From each payment of wages the employees' share is deducted up to the maximum tax to be collected during the taxable year. (See tax schedule on p. 454–56.) Four times a year these deductions are reported and payment is made for them together with the employer's matching share to the district director of the Internal Revenue Service. Each employee must be given a receipt for his or her payment. It is also necessary for the nonfarm self-employed to estimate their personal social security contributions (in their capacity as individual taxpayers and beneficiaries) and pay the estimated taxes in advance in quarterly installments.

FEDERAL INCOME TAXES

The federal income tax laws make it necessary for employers to keep records sufficient to show not only their own tax liability but that of each of their employees. So far as the employers' own tax liability is concerned, they should maintain accurate and complete depreciation records. Records should also be maintained in such form as to permit them to claim allowable deductions for such things as research and development work, bad-debt losses, gifts to charitable institutions, and contributions to pension and profit-sharing plans. If they keep their records in good shape throughout the year and prepare a standard profit-and-loss statement at the end of the year, it will be a simple matter to copy the figures from the profit-and-loss statement onto their income tax return.

The kind of income tax return the firm must file with the Internal Revenue Service depends on the firm's legal form of organization. Those individuals who are in business for themselves under a sole proprietorship and have an annual gross income from this source amounting to $400 or more must file an "Individual Income Tax Return" (form 1040), reporting their business income and expenses on Schedule C of that form.

If the firm is a partnership it files form 1065. (Only the signature of one of the partners is required.) The "Partnership Income Tax Return" is filed for in-

---

[4] Some income may be subject to income taxes but not to social security taxes, and vice versa.

formation purposes only, since the partnership is not taxable as an entity. Its purpose is merely to report the business income that should be included on the partners' individual tax returns.

Individual proprietors and partners are required to put their federal income tax and self-employment tax liability on a "pay-as-you-go" basis. They do this by filing a "Declaration of Estimated Tax" (form 1040 ES) on April 15th of each year, based on expected income and exemptions. Payments on the estimate are made over a period of nine months, the first payment being due on April 15. Additional payments become due on June 15, September 15, and January 15. At the time of each payment, adjustments to the estimate can be made.

A corporation, unlike a partnership, is a legal entity endowed with the rights and responsibilities of a person, and hence pays a tax just like any other "person." Its income is reported on form 1120 ("Corporation Income Tax Return"). The corporate entity pays a tax of 15 percent on the first $25,000 of taxable income, 20 percent on the next $25,000, 30 percent on the third $25,-000 increment, 40 percent on the fourth $25,000, and 46 percent on all taxable income in excess of $100,000.

As noted in Chapter 25, certain corporations can elect to be taxed as though they were partnerships (thereby avoiding the double tax on dividends). Their manner of reporting income is similar to that of partnerships, previously discussed, and the "Small Business Corporation Income Tax Return" (form 1120 S) is also for information purposes only, reporting the corporate income that must be included on the stockholders' individual tax returns.

Income tax returns may be prepared on a calendar or fiscal-year basis. If the tax liability of the business is calculated on a calendar-year basis, the tax return must be filed with the Internal Revenue Service no later than April 15th of each year. Most businesses, however, find it more convenient to report their income on a fiscal-year cycle; in this case, the tax return of the firm (or its proprietor or partners) is due on the fifteenth day of the fourth month following the end of the taxable year.

Withholding of Employees' Taxes

In addition to his or her responsibilities as a taxpayer, the small business owner must also serve as a tax collector. The information of the greatest importance that the employer's records should show in connection with the **withholding tax** is: (1) number of persons employed during the year, (2) amount of wages paid to each person subject to withholding, (3) periods of employment of each person, and (4) amounts and dates of wage and salary payments and withholding tax deductions therefrom. The amount of the "pay-as-you-go" tax the employer is required to withhold from the wages of each employee depends on the employee's wage level, the number of exemptions claimed by the employee on his withholding exemption certificate (form W-4), the employee's marital status, and the length of the payroll period.

The law provides two methods by which the employer may determine the amount of tax to be withheld: (1) the *percentage method,* and (2) the *wage-bracket method.* Under the percentage method, the employer must first ascertain the amount of taxable wages earned by the employee during the payroll period. This is done by subtracting from the gross wages the value of the withholding exemptions claimed by the employee. The employer's next step in the procedure is to apply the appropriate tax percentage to the amount of the employee's taxable wages. This percentage is based on a sliding scale, varying with both the amount of the taxable wage and marital status of the employee. IRS percentage tables are available for weekly, biweekly, monthly, semimonthly, and other payroll periods. However, the detailed computations required under this method are tedious and time-consuming, and most employers find it more convenient to use the wage-bracket withholding tables which give approximately the same results.

The employer is not permitted to grant withholding exemptions unless the employee has listed the number of his or her exemptions on form W-4. These exemption certificates are valid until amended by the employee; however, before December 1 of each year the employer is required to *ask* the employees to file new certificates if there have been changes in the number of dependents they had previously claimed.

The total amount of income taxes withheld are reported on form 941 each calendar quarter. This report also shows the amount of social security taxes withheld (as previously discussed).

When the fourth quarterly report is filed (at the end of the calendar year), the employer must also file the district director's copy of each employee's withholding statement (form W-2), showing the total amount of tax withheld during the year. Two copies of form W-2 must also be given to each employee on or before January 31 of each year. In addition, the employer is required to file a statement reconciling the amounts withheld as shown on the quarterly statements with the amounts shown on the annual statements. This reconciliation is filed on form W-3.

Remitting Withheld Taxes

Taxes collected for the government (withheld from employees) must be deposited periodically with the district Federal Reserve Bank or with a commercial bank that is authorized to accept tax deposits, using IRS form 501. How often this must be done depends on the individual business owner's tax liability. If the owner withheld less than $500 in taxes during any month of a calendar quarter, as reported on form 941, the amount collected during that month is not due until the last day of the month following the close of the quarter. If the amount of tax withheld during any month is $500 or more (up to $3,000), the business owner must deposit this sum within fifteen days after the close of such month except for the last month of a quarter. If the business owner withheld a total of more than $3,000 in taxes for any month of a calendar quarter, he or she must make semimonthly deposits—within three banking days after the seventh, fifteenth, twenty-second, and last day of each month of the quarter.

Information Returns

The employer must also file annual **information returns,** that is, reports of income payments that are taxable to others. IRS's purpose here, obviously, is to match reported income payments with the reports of income received on individual income tax returns.

There are two types of information returns. One is the reporting of payments made in the course of trade or business totaling $600 or more during the calendar year, such as wages, royalties, rent, interest, and fees for attorneys, public accountants, business consultants, and other outside staff personnel. This report is made on form 1099. The other type of information return is the reporting of dividend payments to stockholders, or interest payments (or credits) by savings and insurance institutions to depositors or policyholders totaling $10 or more during the calendar year. This report is also made on form 1099. Copies of these reports must be sent to the persons whose incomes are reported.

The Self-Employed Individuals Tax Retirement Act

It was noted in Chapter 25 that in the corporate form of organization small business owners, for federal income tax purposes, can deduct their contributions to pension and profit-sharing plans in which they as well as their employees participate. Prior to the enactment of the Self-Employed Individuals Tax Retirement Act in 1962, small business proprietors or partners were not permitted to participate in such tax-favored plans because they were not employees. The effect of this act is to make sole proprietors and partners employees for purposes of employee pension and profit-sharing plans; a sole proprietor is treated as his or her own employer, and a partnership is treated as the employer of each partner who has earned income.

The major provisions of this law are as follows:

1. A plan providing benefits to a self-employed individual must be a definite written program and arrangement setting forth all required provisions to qualify at the time the plan is established. Even though the self-employed individual happens to be the only person covered by the plan initially, the plan must still include all the provisions relating to the participation of employees who may become eligible in the future.

2. A plan in which the owner-employee participates must also provide benefits for all full-time employees who have worked for the company for three or more years.

3. The maximum annual contribution that may be made to a plan for the benefit of an owner-employee is $15,000 or 15 percent of his or her earned income for the year, whichever is smaller. For tax purposes, the owner-employee may deduct his or her *entire* contribution (up to the stated maximum).

4. If an owner-employee is covered by the plan, his employees' rights under the plan must be nonforfeitable at the time the contributions are made for their benefit.

5. Distributions under the plan are not permitted until the participant reaches age fifty-nine years and six months, is disabled, or dies, and must commence no later than age seventy years and six months.

Several methods of funding are authorized under certain conditions and the law should be checked carefully on these.

The extent to which contributions and deductions are limited may be illustrated by an example: During the year, let us assume that Mr. Doe has net earnings of $80,000 from his small retail store. He may contribute as much as $12,000 toward his retirement plan (15 percent of $80,000); if he does, he will be entitled to a deduction of $12,000 from his taxable earnings base. Now let us suppose that during the following year, Mr. Doe's earnings increase to $110,000; in this case, his contribution is limited to $15,000 and his **tax shelter** may not exceed this amount.

The Individual Retirement Account (IRA)

Under the Self-Employed Individuals Tax Retirement Act, or **Keogh plan** as it is more commonly known, self-employed persons can make tax-sheltered payments into a pension plan on their own behalf *only* if they also contribute on behalf of their employees. The Economic Recovery Tax Act of 1981, however, provides that any person, whether he or she is self-employed or works for someone else, can establish an Individual Retirement Account (called an **IRA**) and make tax-deferred deposits up to $2,000 a year, or $2,250 for a married couple filing a joint return; for a married couple filing separate returns, *each* may contribute up to $2,000. Thus a self-employed person can now maintain *both* a Keogh plan and an IRA.

FEDERAL EXCISE TAXES

Some business enterprises will find it necessary to keep records of the sales of certain items that are subject to federal **excise taxes.** Where a business is liable for such taxes, quarterly returns on form 720 must be filed, similar to those required in the case of social security and income taxes withheld from employees.

In regard to the computation of the tax on an article, the amount of the federal excise tax is not considered to be a part of the sales price of the article before tax. In other words, if the price the retailer wants to get for himself is $2 and the federal tax is 10 percent, the sale price will be $2.20. The Revenue Act provides that any retailer who represents to his customers that he is absorbing the tax (not charging it to them) shall be liable to penalty. Thus if a seller does not charge the tax to his customers as a separate amount, he must not make any written or oral statements that will cause any person to believe that the price of the article does not include the tax.

When a state or community retail **sales tax** is imposed on an article subject to the federal excise tax and billed as a separate item, it may be excluded from the taxable price. Thus in our previous example, a 5 percent state or local tax would raise the price to the consumer to $2.30, not to $2.31—as it would if the 10 percent tax were figured on the retail price including the state sales tax. Whenever such a state or local sales tax is excluded from the taxable sales price of the article, the merchant must retain a copy of the invoice or other record of sale rendered to the purchaser that will prove to the IRS district director that the retail sales tax so excluded was stated as a separate item.

A retailer may be allowed a tax credit or refund of a tax paid on an article when the price on which the tax is based is later readjusted as a result of return or repossession of the article, or by a bona fide discount, rebate, or allowance. The allowable credit or refund is limited to the overpayment of the tax when calculated on the adjusted price. For example, if a $2 article subject to the 10 percent federal excise tax is sold for $2.20 and later a discount or allowance of $1 is made (plus $0.10 excise tax), the retailer is allowed a credit for the $0.10 tax that was refunded.

If in a business the owner is liable for the collection of excise taxes, it will be necessary for the owner to make provision in the firm's accounting system for an adequate record of taxable sales or of the actual amount of tax collected from customers so that the firm's records will be in order for inspection by federal officials at any time.

STATE AND LOCAL SALES TAXES

The sales tax is another type of tax about which a business owner will need to secure information. Various states and cities levy such taxes, with the rate varying from place to place. Owners should contact the state or local revenue office for information that will acquaint them with the applicable law; having done so, they can adapt their records to the requirements.

If such taxes were levied on all sales, they would present no appreciable difficulty. But in almost all of the states or localities having retail sales taxes there are specific exemptions, either on a certain class (or classes) of merchandise or on a particular group of customers. In most states the applicable road tax on gasoline does not apply to fuel used by farmers in their tractors. In many instances cigars, cigarettes, and tobacco are exempt from the sales tax because a specific tax already has been levied on them. Because of such exemptions, in keeping business records a manager will need to devise some type of control to distinguish tax-exempt sales that will be deducted from the total sales at the end of the taxable period.

In most cases there will be certain other items that may be deducted from gross sales after tax-exempt sales have been subtracted. Some of these are:

1. Cash discounts to customers and refunds for returned goods
2. Bad debts charged off
3. Finance and interest charges
4. Allowances on trade-ins
5. Freight and transportation charges

Small business owners should be sure to study carefully the deductions allowed by the particular state and/or city in which their business is located in order to prevent the overpayment of sales taxes.

SUMMING UP

Payroll records are necessary in meeting the requirements of federal and state social security legislation. Such legislation is designed to minimize losses of employee income resulting from industrial accidents, occupational diseases, and involuntary unemployment, and to provide workers with hospital and medical care and at least a minimal income after retirement.

In addition to workers' compensation, unemployment, and other types of social security taxes, the owner/manager of a business is confronted with a multitude of other taxes. Most important of these for businesses of any kind is the income tax. Retailers and operators of service establishments must also cope with the maze of sales-tax collections and regulations.

The obligations of the small business firm extend beyond paying its own taxes. The firm must also act as an agent for the government in administering the tax program for its employees, particularly in the withholding and remitting of their income and social security taxes.

Penalties are imposed on the business for failure to fulfill its tax-paying and tax-collecting obligations or failure to fulfill them on time. The tax calendar in Table 27-1 summarizes the numerous federal tax-reporting requirements and will help the small business owner/manager to avoid these penalties.

TABLE 27-1

Tax Calendar/Check List

IF YOU:	YOU MAY BE LIABLE FOR:	USE FORM:	DUE ON OR BEFORE[*]
Do business as a:			
Corporation	Income tax	1120	15th day of 3rd month after close of tax year
	Estimated tax	503	15th day of 4th, 6th, 9th and 12th months of year
Subchapter S corporation	Income tax	1120S	15th day of 3rd month after close of tax year
Partnership	Information return	1065	15th day of 4th month after close of tax year
Sole proprietor or partner	Income tax	1040	15th day of 4th month after close of tax year
	Estimated tax	1040ES	15th day of 4th, 6th and 9th months of, and 15th day of 1st month after close of tax year
	Self-employment	Sch. SE	Date Form 1040 is due
Employ:			
One or more persons	Income tax withholding	941 / W-3	4/30, 7/31, 10/31, and 1/31 / Last day of February
	FICA taxes	W-2 / W-2P	1/31 / 1/31
	Quarter-monthly, monthly, or quarterly deposits of withholding and FICA taxes	501	Various dates depending on extent of cumulative liability for unpaid taxes

Item	Tax description	Form	Due date
	FUTA taxes	940	1/31
	Quarterly deposits of actual FUTA liability	508	4/30, 7/31, 10/31, and 1/31, but only if cumulative undeposited liability exceeds $100
Furnish facilities for:			
Local and toll telephone and teletypewriter exchange services	Excise tax on facilities and services	720	5/3-, 8/31, 11/30, and 2/28
Transportation of persons by air Transportation of property by air	Semimonthly or monthly deposits of tax	504	Various dates depending on extent of cumulative liability for unpaid taxes
Issue:			
Foreign insurance policies	Excise tax	720	4/30, 7/31, 10/31, and 1/31
Made payments during the past calendar year of:			
$10 or more of certain dividends, interest, or original issue discount	Annual information returns	1099 1087	1/31 (furnished to income recipients)
$600 or more of certain other fixed or determinable income	Summary and transmittal U.S. information returns	1096	Last day of February
Manufacture, Produce, or Import:			
Coal (Produce only) Heavy duty trucks, trailers, or automobiles Parts and accessories for trucks Petroleum products Tires and tubes	Manufacturers excise taxes	720	4/30, 7/31, 10/31, and 1/31
Fishing equipment, bows and arrows, and parts and accessories for bows and arrows Firearms, shells and cartridges	Semimonthly or monthly deposits of tax	504	Various dates depending on extent of cumulative liability for unpaid taxes

TABLE 27-1
Tax Calendar/Check List (cont.)

If You:	You May Be Liable For:	Use Form:	Due On or Before*
Operate a:			
Truck, truck-tractor, or bus on public highways	Highway use tax	2290	Last day of month after month the vehicle is first used; annually on 8/31
Pool, lottery (including punch boards), or otherwise accept wagers	Occupational tax	11-C	First engaging in wagering, annually on 7/1
	Wagering tax	730	Last day of month after month wagers are placed
	Income tax withholding on certain gambling winnings	941 W-2G W-3G	4/30, 7/31, 10/31, and 1/31 1/31 Last day of February
Sell at retail:			
Noncommercial aviation fuels	Excise tax	720	4/30, 7/31, 10/31, and 1/31
Diesel and special motor fuels	Semimonthly or monthly deposits of tax	504	Various dates depending on extent of cumulative liability for unpaid taxes
Use:			
Fuel in commercial transportation on inland waterways	Excise tax	720	4/30, 7/31, 10/31, and 1/31

* Due dates that fall on a Saturday, Sunday, or legal holiday are postponed until the next day that is not a Saturday, Sunday, or legal holiday.

If you engage in certain other activities, you may be liable for occupational, excise, and/or stamp taxes. These may apply if you
—import or manufacture firearms (licensed manufacturer or individual "making")
—sell or transfer (or otherwise dispose of) firearms under the National Firearms Act
—manufacture beer, distilled spirits, wine, nonbeverage products subject to drawback, wines, or stills or condensers for use in distilling alcohol or alcoholic products
—manufacture cigars, cigarettes, cigarette papers, or tubes
—operate a brewery
—sell distilled spirits, wines, or beer at wholesale or retail
    For information on these taxes, write to the Director, Bureau of Alcohol, Tobacco and Firearms, Washington, D.C. 20226.

Often tax savings are possible, or penalties may be avoided, by an alertness to changes in taxes and regulations, such as longer carry-backs or carry-forwards of losses, accelerated depreciation, modifications of the IRS code on retained earnings penalties, and modifications in state and local tax regulations. It is recommended that small business owner/managers subscribe to a good tax-reporting service, such as that provided by Prentice-Hall, and have their attorney or accountant keep them posted on all significant developments.

KEY WORDS

accumulated earnings tax	payroll taxes
capital stock tax	property taxes
economic security	sales tax
excise tax	self-employment taxes
experience-rating	social insurance
income tax	social security taxes
information returns	tax shelter
IRA	unemployment taxes
Keogh plan	withholding tax
merit-rating	workers' compensation

DISCUSSION QUESTIONS

1. Is it ethical for the owner or manager of a small business (or a business of any size, for that matter) to take advantage of the "loopholes" in tax laws? Why or why not?

2. Is it proper that a small business (or a business of any size, for that matter) be required to serve as a government tax collector? Why or why not?

3. In recent years the top corporate tax rate has been reduced from 48 percent on income in excess of $50,000 to 46 percent on income in excess of $100,000. To what extent has this eased the tax burden on small corporations? Should the corporate tax structure be made even more progressive, in your judgment?

EXERCISES AND PROBLEMS

1. After working from January through August 1982 at a salary of $1,000 per month in a covered occupation, Tom Jones became a partner in a business from which his share of profits for the balance of the year was $7,000. What were his total social security taxes for the year?

2. Refer to exercise 2 on p. 336 and assume that the amounts given in transactions *h* and *i* do not include a 3 percent state sales tax.

a. Prepare journal entries for the sales tax transactions *only*.

b. Prepare the journal entry for the remittance of the sales taxes to the government.

c. Post the above journal entries to their respective T-accounts.

d. What effect do these transactions have on André Preneur's income statement?

3. Again refer to exercise 2 on p. 336 and assume that the payroll tax rates cited in the text are still in effect.

a. Total gross wages paid, as noted in transaction *k*, amounted to $19,600 during the year. Assume that $2,000 is withheld for federal income taxes from the wages of the firm's three employees, all of whom earned the same wage. Record the journal entries for the withholding of the employees' social security and income taxes.

b. Record the journal entries for the employer's tax obligations on the employees' wages.

c. Record the payment of the tax obligations in (b).

d. Record the journal entries for the employer's obligation on the $400 of accrued wages. (See exercise 3 on p. 336.)

e. Post the above journal entries to their respective T-accounts.

4. The firm was experiencing a cash flow problem, and to meet its continuing obligations André borrowed $15,000 from the bank on a 90-day note. Prepare the journal entries for this transaction and post to the general ledger.

5. Take a pre-closing trial balance of the open accounts.

6. From the trial balance prepared in exercise 5, prepare André's income statement. (The inventory on hand at the end of the year was valued at $47,-125.)

7. Close out the income and expense accounts and post the closing entries to their respective T-accounts; then take a post-closing trial balance.

8. From the post-closing trial balance prepared in exercise 7, prepare André's balance sheet on the anniversary of his first year in business.

Part Seven

LOOKING BACK
AND LOOKING AHEAD

The preceding chapter concludes our discussion of basic manage-
ment and business functions, and the management process in the
smaller business. This, the final, section of the book now takes a look
back to the time the owner/manager first planned the business oper-
ation (a sort of review of what you have learned to this point), as
well as a look ahead to the time when the owner/manager retires
and reaps the ultimate reward of a well-planned and well-managed
entrepreneurial effort.

Starting
a Business

CHAPTER TWENTY-EIGHT *The concepts covered in Chapters 8 through 27 provide essential knowledge for the person thinking of starting a business as well as for the person managing a new or small, ongoing business; only the focus or orientation is different. Using these concepts, and by means of text cross-referencing (to avoid needless replication), this chapter presents a step-by-step plan for the organization and operation of a proposed business enterprise.*

Every proposed new business venture, long before its "Grand Opening," must first be put to the test of the marketplace. The *marketing plan* describes how the product or service will be sold, to whom, at what price, and in what quantities. It also describes how the sale will be made: through distributors, retailers, door-to-door, mail order, or direct sale on the business premises.

The marketing plan, having described the market niche and size, provides the information necessary to prepare both an *organization and staffing plan* and a *financial plan* for the proposed business. The organization and staffing plan specifies how the personal and material resources needed to produce and sell the firm's products or services are to be acquired or organized. Given these resources and the necessary funding, the financial plan indicates whether the projected sales can be made at a price providing a reasonable margin of earnings to the aspiring **entrepreneur.**

THE MARKETING PLAN

Before a new enterprise can be launched with reasonable prospects for success, a genuine business opportunity must be discovered and its possibilities appraised. Too often an idea plus some ambition are mistaken for a business opportunity; or maybe a vacant store is so interpreted. Many ventures fail because they never should have been started; there is no justification for their existence. A "genuine" business opportunity exists only when there is a need for the proposed product or service in sufficient volume and at a high enough price to operate at a profit. Often a demand will have to be stimulated or developed; this is especially true when the budding entrepreneur has some-

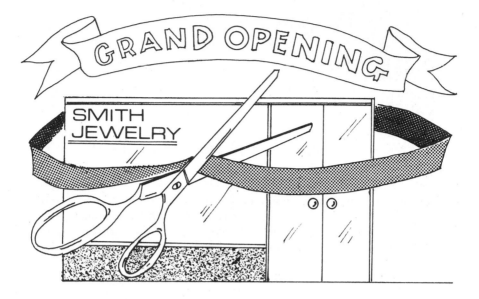

thing new to offer. The first steps in preparing your **business plan,** therefore, are as follows:

> *Step 1.* Determine the *market feasibility* for the product or service you plan to offer.
> *Step 2.* Describe your *marketing strategy.*

Business opportunities may be uncovered in a variety of ways. Most common is the situation in which an expanding market justifies the establishment of additional businesses of the same type. Another situation creating a favorable opportunity for a new business of an existing kind arises when the market is not being adequately served because of the inefficient management of existing concerns. A third type of business opportunity arises from the introduction of a new product or service that meets the needs of the market that the prospective entrepreneur proposes to serve.

Market Feasibility

As we noted in Chapter 13, choosing the right location for a business can be a major factor in its success or failure. A good location may allow a mediocre business to survive, but a bad location may spell failure for the finest of businesses. There are certain basic things to consider in selecting a location regardless of the kind of business being contemplated, and these are noted in that chapter. These considerations, however, must be weighted according to the needs of the particular enterprise and the entrepreneur's intentions.

When you selected your location, you made your first marketing decision.

This required that you know (1) your product or service, (2) its users (potential customers), and (3) your competitors. Following is a checklist of considerations that you should include in your marketing plan, based on your review of the material in Chapter 13.

Know your product or service

1. What will your product or service *do?* In what situations can it be used (applications)? What problems will it solve?

2. What is *unique* about your product or service? What particular features or advantages does it have? Is it patented or patentable (or can it be copyrighted)?

3. If your product or service is based on an entirely new idea, what is your *development cost?*

4. If it is a generic product or service, what has been the *sales trend* in your defined market area over the past five to ten years? How does this trend compare with the trend of population (potential users of the product or service) in the area over the same period? Do these trends indicate a growing market of sufficient magnitude to absorb the addition of another competitive, potentially profitable marketing unit in the area?

Know your customers

1. Who are the potential users of your product or service? (What is your *customer profile?*)

2. *How many* of them are there in your market area? What was the *growth trend* in this segment of the population in your market area over the past five to ten years?

3. What are their *buying motives?* Thrift? Service? Quality? Others? (See pp. 224–25.)

4. *How often* would they buy your product or service? *How much* would they buy? *When* would they buy? (Is it a seasonal item?)

5. If your product or service is based on an entirely new idea and has industrial uses or applications, have you attempted to secure *actual contracts or commitments* from potential customers? From whom and for how much?

Know your competition

1. *Who* are your competitors? *How many* of them are there? What are their respective *market shares?*

2. How many competitive establishments *opened up* last year in your area? Went *out of business* in the last few years?

3. Do you believe that the market is not being adequately served because of the *inefficiencies* or the *shortsighted management* of existing firms? If so, how do you know or why do you think that they are inefficiently managed? Why do you think *you* would be more efficient in the management of your business? What *sources of appraisal* did you use that are entirely independent of your own opinions?

4. How much of the total market do you expect to capture the first year? second year? third year? Use a form similar to the following in making your projections:

PRODUCT, SERVICE, OR MERCHANDISE CLASSIFICATION	FIRST YEAR	SECOND YEAR	THIRD YEAR
_____	$ _____	$ _____	$ _____
_____	_____	_____	_____
_____	_____	_____	_____
Totals	$ _____	$ _____	$ _____

5. After completing the above table, convert the annual sales projections for each service, product, or merchandise classification into monthly or quarterly (seasonal) estimates. (You will find this useful later in estimating your cash flow requirements.)

The development of a sales forecast is crucial to the planning of any business. With a sales forecast in hand, all the costs of the business can also be forecast based on knowledge of how the product or service is supplied (the organization and staffing plan) and how the sales are generated (the marketing plan). Based on the income and costs generated by the sales forecast, a financial plan can then be prepared.

Marketing Strategy

Having established your market potential, the next step in preparing your business plan is to describe how you expect to lure customers to your place of business.

"Red" Motley, the famous authority on selling, once said, "Nothing happens until something is sold." If marketing is a key element in successful business enterprise, then certainly selling is the key element of marketing. Selling is nothing more than "getting the word" to the potential customer. This may be done by advertising, personal contact, or sales promotion. All are concerned with communications.

An advertising and sales promotion program is not the only way, however, by which you can attract customers and expand your market. Other marketing factors (or instruments, as they are commonly called by marketers) include quality or distinctiveness of the product (or service), packaging, customer services, credit extension, and pricing policies, and these also should be specified in your business plan. Marketing strategies are discussed in Chapters 14, 15, and 18; for those interested in export markets, a review of Chapter 16 is also advised.

Following are some of the major types of policies that require your attention in planning the marketing operations of your business:

Product policies (for prospective merchandising and manufacturing enterprises)

1. Will you cater to custom designs or special orders, or will you concentrate on standard goods? Will you offer private brands or labels?

2. Will you offer a wide or a limited range of products or merchandise?

3. Will you dovetail your offerings into gaps left by competitors, or will you seek to meet the same customer wants?

4. What quality level will you offer? Will you offer warranties or guarantees (if a manufacturer)?

5. Briefly state your policy on each of the following:
   a. Returned goods
   b. Complaints and adjustments
   c. Handling of small orders (if a wholesaler or manufacturer)

Pricing policies

1. How will you plan your price structure to compete effectively in the segment of the market you are trying to reach?

2. To which customers will you offer discounts or rebates, and on what basis?

Customer service policies

1. What free customer services will you offer (e.g., parking)?

2. What related customer services will you offer for a fee, such as repairs, installations, and so forth?

Credit policies

1. State your policy regarding credit. Do you intend to use a credit-card service? Why or why not?

2. What credit terms will you offer?

Advertising and sales promotion policies

1. How much do you intend to spend for advertising and other forms of sales promotion (as a percentage of sales)?

2. What advertising media do you plan to use, and why?

3. Describe the different features of your business that would be appropriate for special promotions timed to your customers' needs and interests.

Distribution policies (for prospective manufacturers)

1. Will you sell directly through your own sales organization or indirectly through middlemen? Describe the channel of distribution you intend to use. Why did you decide to distribute your product in this way?

2. If you intend to distribute your product through middlemen, list your principal distributors, agents, and/or manufacturer's representatives and indicate the commissions and/or markups you intend to offer them.

THE ORGANIZATION AND STAFFING PLAN

As noted previously, the organization and staffing plan specifies how the material and human resources needed to produce and sell the firm's product or service are to be acquired and organized. This part of the overall plan for the launching of your business requires the performance of the following steps:

Step 3. Acquire and lay out the necessary *physical facilities.*
Step 4. Procure an opening inventory and project your seasonal *inventory needs* for the next three to five years.
Step 5. Acquire the necessary personnel and set up the *administrative organization.*
Step 6. Choose the *legal form of organization.*
Step 7. Review the *risks* to which the firm's material and human resources will be exposed *and how you plan to cope with them.*

Physical Facilities

The business plan should include a description of the land, building(s), and equipment that will be employed in carrying on the business, with lease terms if applicable and with photos and maps. The checklist below and a review of Chapter 8, pp. 339–44 in Chapter 20, and pp. 376–82 in Chapter 22 will help you in preparing this part of your business plan.

The building
1. Describe the special or ideal requirements for your business in terms of each of the following factors:
    a. Function (suitability for its intended use)
    b. Customer accessibility
    c. Physical layout and internal traffic
    d. Current space needs and room for expansion
    e. External appearance
2. Will you build, rent, or buy your business premises?
3. What are the terms of the mortgage or lease, including (a) the downpayment, and (b) the monthly payment or amortization cost?
4. If you rent or lease your business premises, what will be your costs (if any) of remodeling or redecorating?
5. What will be your cost, if any, of purchasing and installing an outdoor sign (if not included in the cost of constructing your building)?

The equipment. List, in a manner similar to the following, the different kinds of equipment required for the proper performance of all the activities of your business and its estimated cost to you:

			IF PURCHASED ON INSTALLMENT		
			---	---	MONTHLY RENTAL OR DEPRECIATION COST†
TYPE OF EQUIPMENT	NUMBER NEEDED	TOTAL COST	DOWN-PAYMENT	MONTHLY PAYMENT	
Office					
_____	_____	$____	$_____	$_____	$_____
_____	_____	____	_____	_____	_____
_____	_____	____	_____	_____	_____
_____	_____	____	_____	_____	_____
Sales					
_____	_____	$____	$_____	$_____	$_____
_____	_____	____	_____	_____	_____
_____	_____	____	_____	_____	_____
_____	_____	____	_____	_____	_____
Delivery					
_____	_____	$____	$_____	$_____	$_____
_____	_____	____	_____	_____	_____
Processing*					
_____	_____	$____	$_____	$_____	$_____
_____	_____	____	_____	_____	_____
_____	_____	____	_____	_____	_____
_____	_____	____	_____	_____	_____

* For manufacturing establishments, the type of equipment needed is gleaned from master route sheets prepared for each kind of product or customer's order; the number of machines required depends not only on projected sales and production (in units) but also on product processing times (as also recorded on master route sheets. These master production plans are also useful in designing the plant layout (see section immediately following), in estimating your materials requirements (see pp. 467‑68, *infra*), and in estimating direct labor requirements (see pp. 469–71, *infra*). Attach copies of all master route sheets (see Chapter 12).

† Methods of depreciating equipment are discussed on pp. 339–44.

The layout

1. Make a scaled layout drawing for your proposed business.

2. How much will it cost you to lay out and install your equipment in this manner?

Purchasing and Inventory Requirements

As noted in Chapters 9 and 10 (which you should review before completing this part of your business plan), inventory represents the major capital investment in merchandising, in many small manufacturing concerns, and in some service establishments. In addition to goods purchased for resale and materials used in manufacture or construction or in the rendering of a service, supplies are needed for the maintenance of the firm's physical assets and for the performance of various office, clerical, and administrative functions.

In meeting part or all of the new retail firm's inventory requirements, the enterpriser will have a choice among (1) making some formal buying arrangement with a major supplier or franchisor, (2) participating in a cooperative buying group, or (3) remaining unaffiliated. If you expect to be an unaffiliated retailer, or if you contemplate a business other than retailing, you then must select carefully the suppliers with whom you wish to do business. When you select a supplier, you should be concerned not only with the quality of goods and prices and terms, but also with his or her ability to deliver as promised and the services he or she is willing to provide. Supplier services should include willingness to make good on any unsatisfactory merchandise or services and counsel in letting the buyer know of changes in the market affecting the quality or price of the merchandise or materials that he or she handles.

In any case your business plan should include the names of your principal suppliers and/or franchisors. The following cost projections should also be cited, based on the sales estimates you made on p. 464:[1]

NAME OF ITEM*	NAME/LOCATION OF SUPPLIER	OPENING INVENTORY	FIRST YEAR	SECOND YEAR	THIRD YEAR
_____	_____	$_____	$_____	$_____	$_____
_____	_____	_____	_____	_____	_____
_____	_____	_____	_____	_____	_____
_____	_____	_____	_____	_____	_____
Totals		$_____	$_____	$_____	$_____

* Group these items into classifications appropriate for your type of business; for example, merchandise for resale, raw materials, purchased components, office supplies, maintenance supplies, and so on.

As a general rule you should have enough stock on hand before you open your door for business to last you for a one-turnover period. For example, in a retailing business with a first-year sales projection of $300,000 and an assumed standard inventory turnover of three times a year (or once every four months), your opening inventory at retail sales value would be $100,000 ($300,000 ÷ 3). Assuming a gross margin ratio of 32 percent, your opening inventory would cost you $68,000 ($100,000 × 0.68).

After completing the above table, your next step is to convert the annual cost projections for each material or merchandise classification into monthly or quarterly (seasonal) purchasing budgets; this will also help you later in estimating your cash flow requirements.

[1] For manufacturing enterprises this requires, for raw materials and purchased components, the conversion of the sales estimates for each product into a production budget (in units) and the conversion of the latter into a materials budget (also in units); the materials budget is then "costed" to arrive at the annual and monthly purchases budget.

The Administrative Organization

As noted in the text on pp. 42–47, the setting up of an operating structure requires (1) an analysis of the functions or activities that must be performed by the business, and (2) the assignment of each function to particular individuals. Effective administrative organization and management also requires (3) that job descriptions and specifications be prepared after the jobs have been defined; as noted in Chapter 11, the selection, placement, training, promotion or transfer, and remuneration of your employees should be based largely on these descriptions and specifications.

Work analysis

1. On a sheet of paper list in detail all the work that must be performed in the operation of your business.

2. Then group these duties or tasks into related groups or functions, such as selling, buying, housekeeping, record keeping, handling finances, manufacturing, receiving goods, stockkeeping, and so on.

3. Next place each functional group under one of the three basic divisions of any business enterprise, following the organization of this text: production functions (as described in Part III), distribution functions (as described in Part IV), and finance and other facilitating functions (as described in Part V).

Work assignments

1. Start with the management duties of greatest importance and assign them to each active manager, whether co-owner or not, according to his or her ability and liking. Keep the number of major responsibilities assigned to each manager small and keep them balanced among these executives. Be sure to have one co-owner or reliable executive responsible for each basic division. In the very small firm this may mean distribution of duties between husband and wife or among husband, wife, and one helper.

2. Next consider how many employees in addition to the management group you will have. Then assign the remaining duties or subfunctions to each person so as to have a balance of work assignments, with each worker doing what he or she is best fitted for and every duty, no matter how small, definitely assigned to one person. Often it will be necessary to assign some minor duties to each manager.

3. Now record your final personnel organization in a form similar to that illustrated below. If you have only a few individuals, list their names first, followed by the functions for which they are responsible. If you have a large number of employees, list the functions first, each followed by the name of the person responsible for it. Then be sure that every member of the firm understands and accepts his or her assigned duties.

PRODUCTION (OR BUYING)	DISTRIBUTION (OR SELLING)	FACILITATING FUNCTIONS

Job descriptions and specifications.   Your next step is to prepare job descriptions and specifications, and then to make a job evaluation.

1. Job descriptions translate each job analysis into specifications for the appropriate worker in terms of skills, effort, responsibilities, experience, knowledge, and physical and personal qualities. Do this for *each* job for which you plan to employ a full- or part-time worker. (Attach job descriptions and specifications.)

2. Job evaluation determines the relative importance of each job to the firm in terms of what can be paid and what it will be necessary to pay in the local market. It sets the wage or salary range for each job. The range between beginner or starting pay and the highest pay for each job should allow for normal wage increases but still be in line with the relative importance of the job. For each job, determine the lowest and highest pay for your business under current conditions.

Projected wage and salary costs

1. Based on the results of your job evaluation and your estimate of personnel requirements, estimate your wage and salary costs (including fringe benefits) for the next three to five years. Use a form similar to the following in making your projections:

FUNCTIONAL CLASSIFICATION	FIRST YEAR	SECOND YEAR	THIRD YEAR
Production (or buying)°	$_____	$_____	$_____
_____	_____	_____	_____
_____	_____	_____	_____
Selling	_____	_____	_____
Delivery (distribution)	_____	_____	_____
Office salaries	_____	_____	_____
Owner's salary or "draw"	_____	_____	_____
Other administrative salaries	_____	_____	_____

° For manufacturing establishments, differentiate among (1) direct labor costs, (2) indirect labor costs, and (3) foreperson's salaries.

2. To assist you in preparing the budget and in estimating the cash flow requirements, the above cost projections should then be converted into monthly or quarterly (seasonal) estimates.

The Legal Form of Organization

In addition to the administrative or operating organization, consideration must also be given in your business plan to the legal or *ownership* organization.

1. After reviewing Chapter 25 in the text, state your decision regarding the legal form of organization you plan to use. Remember, it can be changed later but it should be selected carefully now. (Consider the tax implications of your choice.)

2. If you plan to form either a corporation or a partnership for your business, prepare and attach to your business plan the wording for either (a) your Articles of Incorporation and By-Laws, or (b) your Partnership Agreement.

3. Organization requirements and fees:

a. If you will be trading in your name, no registration or filing fee is required of the proprietorship or partnership. If, however, you plan to conduct your business under a trade or assumed name, a filing fee may be required in some states.

b. If you plan to conduct your business as a corporation, the statutory requirements generally include (i) registering the name and articles of incorporation, (ii) the payment of a filing fee, and (iii) the payment of an organization tax usually based on the amount of the corporation's authorized capital. These requirements apply in *all* states in which the corporation is expected to do business.

Thus your business plan should include a list of the fees and taxes you will pay (if any) when registering your business.

4. Regardless of the legal form of organization you select, some *kinds* of businesses must be licensed by the state and/or local governmental authority. (See pp. 437–38.) Thus your business plan should also include a list of the kinds of licenses required in your business (if any) and their annual costs.

Evaluating Insurable Business Risks

As noted in the text, you should no more try to start a business without proper insurance coverage than you would attempt to operate a home without a home protection policy. Determination of the proper kind and amount of insurance to carry requires that you estimate the potential size of each kind of loss to which your firm will be exposed, as well as the ability to your firm to stand the loss if it does occur. This involves *ranking* the risks in some order of priority, such as the following:

Critical—Those risks involving possible losses that could result in bankruptcy of the firm. It is *essential* that these risks be covered.

Important—Those risks involving possible losses that would not result in bankruptcy but that would require the firm to borrow to continue operations. It is strongly *recommended* that these risks be covered to the degree affordable.

Unimportant—Those risks involving possible losses that would not require the firm to borrow but that could be met out of existing assets without imposing a strain on the finances of the firm and that could be treated as operating expenses. Coverage for these risks can be purchased if desired and affordable.

After ranking the various business risks described in the text in Chapter 23, and after discussing your rankings with an independent insurance agent, indicate those for which you plan to carry insurance and how much coverage you will have.

THE FINANCIAL PLAN

The steps necessary in preparing the financial plan for your business may be grouped into two categories: those related to *capital requirements and sources*, and those related to the preparation and analysis of *pro forma financial statements*.

Capital Requirements and Sources

Which of you, intending to build a tower, sitteth not down first, and counteth the cost, whether he have sufficient to finish it?
—LUKE 14:28

The short- and long-term capital needs off a business should be determined as accurately as possible *before* the business gets off the ground. Most new entrepreneurs will require more money than they can put into the business themselves. They then must look to other sources of funds and decide how much of this needed capital is to be in the form of debt, and how much in equity shares.

Step 8. Estimate the *initial capital requirements* for your business.

These costs are of two types: (1) those incurred in planning and establishing, or setting up, the business, and (2) those incurred in operating the new business until income from the business is sufficient to cover regular monthly expenses.

A form similar to Schedule I, below, can be used in estimating your business set-up costs:

Schedule I

SETUP COSTS

Cost of opening stock (average markup at _____%, and estimated turnover of _____ times per year)*	$_____
Furniture, fixtures, and equipment (cash purchases + down-payments)	_____
Installment payments on equipment purchases for a one-turnover period (see equipment schedule on p. 467)	_____
Installation and layout costs of fixtures and equipment	_____
Decorating and remodeling	_____
Outside sign	_____
Deposits (utilities, telephone, sales tax certificate)	_____
License(s)	_____
Accounting and legal fees	_____
Office and other supplies (including postage) for a one-turnover period†	_____
Prepaid operating expenses:	
One month's advance rent	_____
Annual insurance premium	_____
Other _____	
Minimum cash balance (for contingencies)	_____
Total	$_____

* Sufficient to cover cost of merchandise (or raw materials) sold (or used) during a one-turnover period. For example, if your estimated annual sales volume is $100,000 and if the common or expected rate of turnover in your business is four times (once every three months), then the sales value of your opening inventory need be no greater than $100,000 ÷ 4, or $25,000. If the average markup in your enterprise (based on selling price) is 40%, then the cost of this inventory to you would be .60 × $25,000, or $15,000.
† If yours is a service-type enterprise with little or no merchandising activity, estimate these payments and costs over a period of time recommended by your trade or professional association or by your banker.

In addition to the *costs of setting up* the business, your initial capital should be sufficient to cover the *cash operating expenses for a one-turnover period* once the business is launched—a time period long enough to permit funds to start coming back in from customers' payments. In making the latter estimate your first step is to estimate your *average* monthly cash operating expenses for the first year of business operation, using a form similar to Schedule II, below. Standard operating ratios for your kind and size of business (discussed on pp. 362–65) applied to your projected sales figure (p. 464) can be used as "benchmarks" against which to compare your own cost estimates. These expense estimates need not correspond closely, but any large deviation from the average ratio for your line of business should be fully explained or justified.

After completing this schedule, you can then multiply the "total" figure for the average month by the number of months representing the stock turn-

Schedule II

FIRST-YEAR AVERAGE MONTHLY CASH
OPERATING EXPENSES*

Employees' wages and salaries	$_____
Employee benefits	_____
Owner's salary†	_____
Rent	_____
Utilities and telephone	_____
Insurance	_____
Accounting and legal fees	_____
Advertising	_____
Repairs and maintenance	_____
Office supplies and postage	_____
Interest expense	_____
Taxes (other than income) and licenses	_____
Miscellaneous expenses	_____
_____	_____
_____	_____
_____	_____
Total	$_____

* Does not include cost of goods purchased, manufactured, or constructed, nor depreciation, bad debts, and other noncash items. Labor and overhead costs that can be allocated to factory or construction activities are included in "cost of sales."
† Sufficient to cover personal and family living expenses, as a minimum.

over period typical for your kind of business. (If yours is a service-type enterprise, with little or no merchandising activity, multiply by a factor recommended by your trade association or by your banker.)

A common tendency among new entrepreneurs is to minimize their requirements to the point that they often do not have enough capital to work with. Pressure on the beginners' usually limited funds is so great that they are not likely to reserve enough working capital. Some lack cash reserves to meet unexpected expenses during the first year, while others do not anticipate all their expenses and find that their capital is gone before they have adequately established their businesses. Thus great care should be exercised to include all expenses and needs for capital, including taxes and other less obvious requirements. (See Chapter 27 for a discussion of employers' tax obligations.) If you are to err in estimating your need for capital, it is better to err on the high side; as it is expressed in the insurance industry: "It is better to have it and not need it, than to need it and not have it."

Step 9. List the *sources of funds* you plan to use and the amount of start-up capital you expect from each, as follows:

Sources	Amount
Debt capital	
	$_____
	_____
	_____
Equity capital	
	_____
	_____
Total	$_____

You will find a review of Chapter 17 helpful in your understanding of the sources and uses of capital.

Experience shows that difficulties in financing often arise from a few common causes, such as lack of knowledge of available sources of funds, inability to present a convincing case to possible investors, and failure to plan and prepare in advance for likely needs. Long before their programmed date for hanging up an "Open for Business" sign, prospective enterprisers should become acquainted with a banker or two and with other influential people in their community who are potential sources of funds and sound advice. It would also be helpful to have an established consumer credit rating. Before starting a career as a business operator, prospective entrepreneurs will find it wise, perhaps essential, to create records of their financial responsibility as a part of their business history. This may be done in several ways—by maintaining a solvent checking account, for example, or by negotiating a few small loans when larger-than-usual expenditures are being considered. Even the record of small but regular deposits in a savings account may help when the need for financing arises.

Step 10. Prepare an *opening balance sheet* for your business, based on your estimate of initial capital requirements, assuming that you will be successful in obtaining the capital you need from each of the above-named sources.

Pro Forma Financial Statements

The next step in financial planning is to forecast your income, costs, and profit, based on the planning you have done in the preceding steps. Typically, these projections are expressed in the form of income, or profit-and-loss, statements. (Income and other financial statements are discussed in the text on pp. 324–27 and 372–76.)

Step 11. Prepare *pro forma income statements* for the first three to five years of business operation.[2]

[2] The Small Business Administration requires three-year financial projections; venture capitalists and many other funding sources generally require projections over a longer period of time, often five years.

Operating expenses in income statements are often classified as *fixed,* such as owner's salary, rent, utilities and telephone, insurance, interest, licenses, taxes (other than income), and depreciation; and *variable* (or *controllable*), such as employees' wages and salaries, employee benefits, accounting and legal fees, office supplies and postage, repairs and maintenance, advertising, and bad debts. As noted in Chapter 21, this cost classification is essential for profit planning and cost control. Operating expenses may also be grouped on a *functional* basis, for example by selling expense and general and administrative expense, no distinction being made between costs that are fixed and those that are variable. The prospective business owner should adopt the standard expense classification for his or her particular kind of business.

Step 12. Estimate the *monthly (or other seasonal) cash flows* for each of the first three to five years of business operation.

Use a form similar to that illustrated on p. 376 in making these estimates. Such a *cash budget* shows what receipts are expected from customers and any other sources and what expenditures are to be made. Its purpose is to allow you to *anticipate* the need for funds so that you will not be caught short of cash, particularly during periods of seasonal buildup; in other words, to enable you to anticipate your need for short-term borrowings from the bank.

Step 13. Prepare *pro forma balance sheets* for the first three to five years of business operation.
Step 14. Compute *financial ratios* for each year of projection in your financial statements to evaluate the short- and long-term potential of your planned business enterprise. (See pp. 327–33 for a discussion of financial ratios.)

SUMMING UP

The purpose of drawing up a business plan is to force the prospective entrepreneur to perform a thorough, well-thought-out analysis of his or her business proposal. Such an analysis will indicate if the proposed business venture is feasible or not, and if not, why.

A business plan considers a wide range of topics and data inputs. As in the format for this text, these can be grouped into three major categories: (1) marketing, (2) organization and management, and (3) financial. Every proposal for a new business venture must first be put to the test of the marketplace. After the prospective entrepreneur is satisfied that his or her business concept can be made economically viable, the plan for the organization and management (or staffing) of the business is prepared. The final step in the procedure is to prepare the financial plan, in which income and costs are projected for at least a three-year period.

KEY WORDS

business plan   entrepreneur

DISCUSSION QUESTIONS

1. Some entrepreneurs, including some successful ones, started their businesses on a shoestring. Discuss the thesis that people should go into business for themselves when circumstances are right even though their finances are below those considered desirable or necessary.

2. For a particular business, cite some ways in which start-up and operating costs might be reduced without jeopardizing the business's potential for success.

EXERCISES AND PROBLEMS

1. Numerous studies suggest that there are certain personality characteristics that successful small businessmen and businesswomen seem to have in common. The questionnaire below will help you decide if you are the "entrepreneurial type."
Answer each of the following questions with a simple "Yes" or "No."*

  a. Would it annoy you as an employee if your fellow workers insisted that you take it easy?

  b. Would you be concerned if your supervisor or employer was careless and inefficient in his or her work?

  c. Do you frequently get ideas as to how products or work methods could be improved?

  d. Do you like to experiment with new ideas or devices?

  e. Would you prefer to be introduced to people as a local business owner rather than as an executive of a well-known corporation?

  f. Do you study the odds in your favor before taking a chance or risk on some matter of importance?

g. In the past have you been willing to sacrifice and wait for something you really wanted?

h. If you were offered a choice between a guaranteed income of $20,000 a year for twenty-five years (or until you reached the age of seventy) with compulsory retirement at that time, and an uncertain income for life that might vary from enough for bare living essentials to well over $50,000 a year depending on your own efforts, would you choose the potentially larger but uncertain income?

i. If you want to do something of importance but learn that you will need two years of additional training and other preparation, would you make the necessary effort and wait until you are adequately prepared?

j. Do you feel less certain that you could hold a job under unfavorable economic conditions than that you could manage to hold onto customers of a business of your own under similar conditions?

k. Is it unimportant to you to limit your working time to an average workweek unless you are paid at a higher rate for overtime?

l. Would you prefer to meet the competition of other firms seeking your customers rather than the competition of fellow employees seeking promotion?

m. Does it annoy you to have an idea for some improvement but to be unable to put your idea to a test?

n. Does it annoy you to leave a job or project before you have a chance to complete it?

o. Do you prefer to do all the work on an undertaking so as to get all the credit for yourself rather than to let others help you if they will share in the rewards?

p. Does it annoy you to work under close supervision and pressure to get work out on time?

q. Do you like to participate in undertakings intended to improve your community?

r. Do you manage your own or your family's finances so as to live within your income with some saving?

s. Are you willing to borrow money when you think you can gain by doing so?

t. Are you willing to take a large risk for even greater gains when the odds are only slightly in your favor?

u. Is it easy for you to make important decisions promptly?

v. Do you do things you think should be done without waiting for someone to urge you to do them?

w. Do you keep records of your income and expenditures?

x. Do you have a strong desire to be independent?

---

* If you answered "Yes" to most of the questions in exercise 1, you would probably be happier being in business for yourself than working for someone else. If questions f, g, i, r, s, t, u, w, and x were answered "Yes," you should have an excellent chance to make a financial success of your business.

2. After a careful market analysis, a prospective business owner forecasts sales of $250,000 during the first year of operation of his general merchandise store. A suitable building is available for rent at $1,250 per month with a satisfactory lease and renewal option. The bulk of his investment would go into inventory, and he estimates that he could turn over this inventory four times a year. The standard gross margin ratio in this line of retail trade is 35 percent. Store fixtures and equipment worth $50,000 may be purchased with a 10 percent cash down-payment and a 15 percent note due in five years for the balance. He also needs a delivery truck; a used one in good condition is available for $7,000 cash. Preopening expenses (insurance premiums and one month's rent in advance) are estimated at $1,450. Annual operating expenses (rent, salaries, utilities, interest on funded debt, etc.) are estimated at $62,500. However, to meet unanticipated expenses and expenses during times of peak merchandise needs, the prospective business owner wishes to set up a reserve for contingencies (minimum cash balance) amounting to $5,300. How much initial capital is required to get this business off the ground?

3. After posting the opening journal entries described in exercise 1 on pp. 335–36, prepare André Preneur's opening balance sheet for his business.

CASES IN
POINT

Three People—Three Opportunities

Jerry Hausman was graduated from a prestigious university in the East seven years ago. Since then he has been employed as cashier's assistant in the bank where his father is a senior officer. Jerry appears to be successful as a fledgling banker. He had worked in the bank in various capacities during summer vacations when a student in high school and college. His family assumes that he will make banking a career. Jerry, however, is becoming restless; as a result of contacts made at the bank, several ideas have occurred to him.

One possibility is a partnership with Sam Snively, a successful local golf pro, in establishing a chain of pro shops, some already existing and some to be opened in selected country clubs. This arrangement would, according to the pro, be welcomed by pro shop owners and club members, for it should increase and standardize the shops' offerings and reduce some of the problems of management. Assistance of some manufacturers of golf equipment is assured in the areas of inventory selection and control, and in management methods generally. Investment requirements would be substantial.

George Hawkins is an accomplished craftsman in woodworking, and has operated successfully as a cabinetmaker for many years. His work has earned him an excellent reputation in the area, and many fine homes, restaurants, and offices show his handiwork.

George was approached recently by a younger man, Joe Ward, a recent arrival in the community and a competitor, who has found the mobile-home industry a good means of income—requiring built-in baths, kitchens, dinettes, and so forth. Joe has been able to develop enough standardization and other cost-cutting methods to merit the approval of the firms employing him. He believes that the industry has a glowing future and wants George to join him, forming a team to service mobile-homemakers and eventually to manufacture complete mobile-home units.

George has enough money saved to afford the risks involved, and the younger man is convinced he could get bank support for financing the cabinetmaking venture or even the manufacturing firm. He is very enthusiastic about the prospects.

Josephine Jones is an accomplished typist-secretary-stenographer employed by a large, long-established real estate firm in a medium-sized city. She makes an unusually good salary and is highly respected by her employers and by the real estate community. Her prospects of holding her current position with the firm appear to be excellent, with normal salary increases from time to time as before. She is unmarried at thirty-eight and is the sole support of her aging father and mother and an invalid brother.

"Joe" feels that she is not saving enough money, and for a year or more has been alert to some opportunity for larger income. She recently heard that a large stenographic-duplicating service is for sale due to the owner's death six months ago. The firm had always been very successful, but has suffered recently for lack of direction and, to some degree, lack of modern equipment. The staff is made up largely of older, quite mature workers. The price asked is reasonable in terms of past performance.

Sources of business for Joe would be smaller real estate firms and other offices too small to have their own staffs and equipment, and occasionally larger firms at their peak periods of business. She has talked with a banker who will lend her a small amount without collateral—or more, if required, through a home mortgage.

These three cases, taken from observation, represent typical problems faced by persons contemplating entrance into business for themselves. Information given is not sufficient to permit a suggested decision in any case; additional information is required.

1. What further information would you seek in each case?
2. Under what conditions should each person go ahead?
3. What possible major strength or weakness does each situation reveal?

At a regional restaurant association meeting in a small college community in the northern part of the state, Jim Herndon was fascinated by a new restaurant he visited. Specializing in home-type foods, its appeals were quality and quantity at a low price of volume operation. The decor was simple, fixtures inexpensive, and there was much self-service. Only beer was served in addition to the regular menu.

Jim has been working in restaurants, full- or part-time, for over six years. Most recently his employer, an older man, has come to depend on Jim for pricing of meals, kitchen supervision, and some buying of provisions. The restaurant is well-located downtown in a city of 150,000 and enjoys a brisk and profitable breakfast and luncheon trade but a declining evening business. It is conservative, medium-priced, homelike in atmosphere, and has been successful for many years, with a loyal following of patrons. But Jim has recently been getting the urge to strike out on his own.

Jim feels that locations away from the center of town are more likely to succeed in the coming years. He feels particularly that students, young marrieds, and others seeking just good food in an informal, inexpensive atmosphere are a good market.

As to location, there are three possibilities: (1) near the growing new junior college in a relatively undeveloped area; (2) in a well-established shopping center in a middle-income area; and (3) outside town, near a thruway intersection, where various new businesses are emerging. There are no eating facilities near the college campus, not even dormitories. In the shopping center, at least one deluxe restaurant lounge failed two years ago. The thruway spot offers the best choice as to markets, in Jim's opinion.

Financing may be difficult but not impossible. Jim has about $8,000 saved, his family is well-known, and his personal business record is good. He also has in mind to take in an older man with more money as a partner; or, he feels he can possibly interest a franchising operation in his idea, if he can find one that seems to fit into his own thinking as to the kind of restaurant he wants to operate. As a last resort, of course, he may be able to buy out his present employer in a few years.

The problem here is to select a proper location for the type of restaurant Jim has in mind.

1. What would an ideal location be? How would you evaluate any location?
2. Establish standards for the location's selection and evaluate each possibility in A, B, and C ratings, with A being the most favorable and C being the least favorable.

Jerry Simpson, out of school four years, is finishing his second year as assistant local branch manager for the Citizens Bank in Fairport, whose center is in Memphis. He has been quite successful, is respected and admired by bank officials and customers alike, and is regarded as good promotional material. In fact, he has been unofficially told to be ready to move up. The trouble is that moving up means moving out of Fairport, probably to take over a new branch—this procedure being company policy—but Jerry does not want to leave Fairport.

Recently he has given some thought to entering the insurance business in Fairport. A school friend of his recently joined the Allstate Insurance Company as salesman. Stationed at a strategic point in a large Sears store, the well-advertised line of varied types of insurance, sponsored by a prestigious firm, brings many inquiries. Some of these call for follow-up or personal calls. The friend was hired on a part-salary, part-commission basis, but has progressed to a point where the commissions provide his major source of income, and a good one at that.

Another friend has been successful in insurance for years, earlier with Prudential, later with National Life. He is, like the Allstate man, restricted to selling that particular company's policies, which are limited to life insurance. But these old-line companies pay well to start and offer comprehensive training and assistance from their offices, a main branch of each being located nearby. Leads are provided and direct-mail services are available. The program is well-controlled under supervisors in their branch offices. Pay rates for an experienced insurance agent are based on commissions of 40 to 60 percent of the first year's premiums, with a 5 to 10 percent commission on renewals. This man is also doing well, making considerably more than Jerry is now.

Recently Jerry investigated a third of the many possible insurance marketing opportunities. Jake Morris, an old friend of his father, is an independent agent-broker who represents about twenty different insurance companies—some large, some small, providing all types of coverage. He describes himself as a "counselor" and suggests to his clients whichever company, in his expert opinion, seems to do the job as he sees it. They pay varying straight commissions, and Mr. Morris makes good money and enjoys his independent status greatly.

Naturally, Jerry cannot by any means expect to step out and readily compete with a man who has taken years to build his clients' confidence. However, Mr. Morris is getting older and says he will retire within the next five to ten years. He has hinted to Jerry that there is a job there, a going business to be bought eventually. Right now it seems that Mr. Morris would expect about $20,000 in cash for a part-ownership. Income to Jerry would be a little more than that paid him by the bank.

It is possible, of course, for Jerry to open his own office and contract with his own companies, starting from scratch to build up his own clientele and business. And there are many companies not represented or not properly represented in Fairport.

What would you advise Jerry to do?

Selling (or Buying)
a Business

CHAPTER TWENTY-NINE *For those of you entrepreneurs or prospective entrepreneurs who are considering the sale or purchase of an existing business, this chapter provides the essential background needed to establish its value to you. (These values will differ because of differing perspectives.) After a sales/purchase price is negotiated, the terms of payment and other facets of the deal need to be agreed on and these factors are discussed in the chapter from opposing points of view.*

It is inevitable that someday—through death, disability, or retirement—you will no longer manage the business you started. Before that day arrives, however, it is important that you look ahead and do some long-range planning for the disposition and perpetuation of the business. Your business can be seriously harmed, for example, if an heir or an employee has not been adequately trained to take over for you or if, in the event of your untimely death, estate taxes deplete the firm's cash reserves. The sale of your business can also provide you with an additional source of retirement income.[1]

In general there are three options available to you as you plan for a change in the ownership of your business:

1. You may transfer ownership to another family member.

2. You may sell out to one or more of your employees (or partners) or to some other individual(s) outside your family.

3. You may merge with another company.

All three have important legal and tax considerations, which we will discuss in the following paragraphs. In any case, however, a price for the business will need to be negotiated by the buyer and seller. Both parties will be anxious to receive full value in the exchange.

---

[1] In addition to social security and income from a Keogh and/or Individual Retirement Account (see p. 489).

SETTING THE PRICE

Setting the sales or purchase price for a going business involves two different sets of valuations: (1) valuation of the firm's **tangible net assets** (tangible net worth) and (2) valuation of the firm's expected future earnings (or **goodwill**).

Valuation of Tangible Assets

Three terms are frequently used to express the value of a tangible asset:

1. *Book value*—what it cost or is worth to the present owner from an accounting viewpoint; the amount shown on the books as representing its value as a part of the firm's worth

2. *Replacement value*—what it would cost to go into the current market and buy the same materials, merchandise, or machinery; relative availability and desirability of newer items must be considered here

3. *Liquidation value*—how much the seller could get for this business, or any part of it, if it were suddenly thrown on the market to be bid on by sophisticated buyers

The differences in these three approaches to the determination of value are obvious and sobering. Certainly, in terms of asset valuation, **book value** may not hold up in the marketplace. Buildings and equipment, for example, may be depreciated below their **market value;** on the other hand, land may have appreciated above its original cost. Also, specialized equipment, obsolete inventories, or bad debts will rapidly depreciate book value, especially if earnings are down.

Nor is **replacement value** a reliable figure because of opportunities to buy in the used-equipment market. It is significant to the prospective entrepreneur (and the seller) as a measure of value only in the sense that starting a new firm may be an alternative means of getting into the business.

In short, **liquidation value** is the most realistic approach in determining the value of tangible assets to the prospective buyer of a business; it is also reasonable for the prospective buyer to assume that this value represents the floor below which the seller would be unwilling to sell. Only after the values of the following physical assets have been determined can serious bargaining begin:

1. Cost of the inventory at wholesale, adjusted for slow-moving or obsolete items

2. Cost of the equipment less depreciation

3. Supplies

4. Accounts receivable less bad debts

5. Market value of the building

However, a *going* business is much more than the sum of its physical assets. While the cost of reproducing or liquidating these assets can be closely determined, the cost of duplicating the firm's experience, management, technical know-how, and reputation—its **intangible assets**—is not so easily determined. These intangible factors will be reflected in the firm's past and expected future earnings, as measured by its *goodwill*, to which we will now give our attention.

Valuation of Goodwill

Goodwill is a value in excess of the tangible net assets of the business resulting from the firm's superior past and future earning power. Contributing to the superior earning power of the business—or its goodwill—may be other intangible assets, such as patents and copyrights; their dollar value as listed on the firm's balance sheet should be ignored in any determination of the amount that the prospective business buyer should pay for goodwill. In fact some intangible "assets," such as a franchise for a preferred merchandise line, may have been obtained without cost and so would not be listed on a balance sheet; yet they may have real value to the prospective purchaser if the supplier agrees to continue delivering to the new owner.

The amount paid for goodwill will reflect itself in the excess of selling price over the objectively appraised value of goods, equipment, and supplies after liabilities are deducted. Actually it will be the price, above cold appraisal of the balance of assets as against liabilities, paid by the new owner for the former owner's constructive efforts in developing the business to its present condition.

> *Goodwill is the one and only asset that competition cannot undersell or destroy.*
>
> —Marshall Field

The amount to pay for goodwill is calculated by capitalizing, at an assumed rate of interest, those earnings in *excess* of the "normal" return in that type and size of business. For example, suppose that the liquidation or market value of the firm's tangible net assets (i.e., its tangible net worth) is the same as the book value shown in our illustrative balance sheet on p. 326 ($112,000) and that the normal before-tax rate of return on the owner's investment in this business is 15 percent, or $16,800 per year. Assume further that the actual profit during the past few years[2] has averaged $41,800, *exclusive of the present owner's salary* (which may have been over- or understated).

From the latter figure should be deducted a reasonable salary for the owner/manager—what he or she might earn by managing this type of business for someone else. If we assume a going rate annual salary of $20,000, then the excess profits to be capitalized—that is, the amount of profit based on goodwill—is $5,000 ($41,800 minus $20,000 salary minus a normal profit of $16,-800).

The **capitalization rate** is negotiated by the buyer and the seller of the business. Theoretically, a capitalization rate is selected that is appropriate to the risk. The more certain the prospective buyers are that the estimated annual earnings will be realized, the more they will pay for the firm's goodwill. The less certain they are—the higher they perceive their risk to be—the less they will pay. In general, the amount paid for goodwill will depend on the following:

1. How long it would take the new owner to set up a similar business and at what expense and risk

2. The added amount of income possible through buying a going business as against starting an entirely new one

3. The relative prices for goodwill asked for other businesses of similar type with similar advantages

4. The extent to which the former owner agrees by contract to remain out of the same business within a competitive area

To return to our example, if we assume a 25 percent rate of return on estimated earnings attributable to goodwill, then the calculated value to the prospective buyer of the firm's intangible assets is $5,000 ÷ 0.25, or $20,000. This relationship is also commonly expressed as a ratio or multiplier of "four times (excess) earnings." Expressed in a different way, in light of his or her analysis of these figures, the prospective buyer of the business would expect to recover the amount invested in goodwill in no more than four years.

Putting the two figures together, the prospective buyer arrives at an **offering price** of $132,000 for the business—net tangible assets of $112,000 at liqui-

---

[2] After adjustments for the overstating of book profits due to bad debts, inventory shrinkage, and underdepreciation.

dation value plus goodwill valued at $20,000. The calculation procedure is summarized below in tabular form:[3]

1. Adjusted value of tangible net worth		$112,000
2. Earning power at 15%	$16,800	
3. Reasonable salary for the owner/manager	20,000	
	$36,800	
4. Average annual net earnings before subtracting owner's salary	41,800	
5. Extra earning power of the business (line 4 − lines 2 and 3)	$ 5,000	
6. Value of intangibles, using 4-year profit figure for moderately well-established firm (4 × line 5)		20,000
7. Offering price (line 1 + line 6)		$132,000

If, in the above example, the average annual net earnings of the business before subtracting the owner's salary (line 4) was only $36,800 (or less), the seller would receive no value for goodwill because the business, even though it may have existed for a considerable time, is not earning as much as the buyer could earn through outside investment and effort. In that case the buyer's price would be determined by capitalizing the average annual profit (net earnings after deducting all expenses including the owner's salary) by the normal or expected rate of **return on investment** in this business. The calculations are as follows:

$$\$36,800 - \$20,000 = \$\ 16,800 = \text{profit}$$
$$\$16,800 \div \ 0.15 \quad = \$112,000 = \text{buyer's price}$$

It is apparent from the above discussion that the valuation of goodwill is a highly subjective thing, and it is here that the seller and buyer will have difficulty in arriving at a consensus.

STRIKING A DEAL

Since most small businesses are family businesses, it is likely that retiring business owners will want to transfer their business assets to their offspring. If there are no active heirs and if there are no partners,[4] they often find that the best way to perpetuate the business is by selling it to one or more key employees. In the latter case a **buy-sell agreement** should be consummated *well in advance* of the business owner's planned date of retirement. In general the buy-sell agreement should include:

[3] "How to Buy or Sell a Business," Vol. 15, Nov. 2, 1982 (*Small Business Reporter,* Bank of America), p. 9.
[4] Partnership agreements, as noted in Chapter 25, should provide for settlements in the event of the death, disability, or withdrawal (retirement) of any one of the partners. The fundamentals of the buy-sell agreement among partners are the same as those described below for the sale of a business to employees.

1. A commitment by the employee(s) to buy, and the proprietor to sell, the latter's interest in the business on a prearranged date

2. The purchase price (or a formula for determining such a price) to be paid to the seller

3. The terms of sale

In **community property** states it is important that the spouse be a party to this agreement; also all parties should be protected by the cross-purchase of insurance in case of death or disability before the agreement has been fulfilled.

The Installment Sale

After agreeing to the purchase price (if the sale is imminent), or to the formula for determining it (if the sale is to be consummated in the future), the parties must next agree to the terms of the sale. Few buyers, however, will be sufficiently affluent to pay cash "on the barrelhead," and even if they could it might not be in their best interests to do so because of tax considerations. Nor is a lump-sum payment likely to be an advantageous arrangement for the seller from a tax point of view, unless he or she intends to reinvest the proceeds in another business. In most cases, therefore, an **installment sale** (purchase) will be most practical.

By means of a cash-flow projection[5], the buyer is assured in an installment purchase that the business can be paid for out of earnings, and the seller is assured that his or her investment in the business will be returned on a tax-deferred basis. To qualify as an installment sale with its attendant tax advantages, however, the buyer's initial payment in the first year cannot exceed 30 percent of the total selling price.

But heirs and employees often cannot raise enough money for even a modest down-payment on the business. In such a case the seller may plan a course of action to make the business more affordable for the prospective purchaser. One such plan is the process known as **thinning the assets.** The seller can make the asset base more manageable for the new owner in one or more of the following ways:

1. By separating real estate ownership from business ownership so that the new owner leases rather than purchases the building assets; in this way, the buyer is assisted in his or her financing and the seller receives a steady rental income

2. By similarly leasing equipment, and perhaps furniture and fixtures

3. By selling off excess inventories (if any) in an orderly fashion

4. By factoring accounts receivable, or by carrying the old ones

---

[5] As described and illustrated in Chapter 22, pp. 372–76.

Tax-Free Reorganizations

The term **reorganization** is described in the Internal Revenue Code as a **merger** or **acquisition** in which the seller corporation transfers its stock or assets to the buyer corporation. Such a merger or acquisition is a **tax-free exchange** to the buyer corporation as long as the acquired business continues to operate (though not necessarily in its present legal form), and payment in the **voting stock** of the buyer corporation is tax-free as long as the seller continues to hold that stock. Any cash or debt securities received by the seller in the exchange is considered to be a dividend and thus is taxed as ordinary income to the seller.

The Internal Revenue Code recognizes three types of tax-free reorganizations:

A-type consolidation or merger. A **statutory merger** occurs when the buyer corporation continues in existence and the seller corporation loses its identity by its absorption into the buyer corporation. In a **consolidation,** both corporations are fused into a new third corporation. This is the most common type of reorganization for small family businesses because it provides the parties greater flexibility in arranging the terms of the business sale or purchase. In either a consolidation or a statutory merger, the tax-free status of the stock received by the seller is maintained as long as it comprises at least 50 percent of the total sales (purchase) price.

B-type stock acquisition. In this type of reorganization there is a stock-for-stock exchange, the seller corporation exchanging at least 80 percent of its voting stock for voting stock of the buyer corporation.

C-type asset acquisition. In this type of reorganization there is a stock-for-assets exchange, the seller corporation exchanging all of its assets for voting stock in the buyer corporation.

SUMMING UP

Of the more important factors to consider in evaluating a business, the firm's profitability, financial health, and tangible assets can be appraised objectively and quite accurately if sufficient care is exercised. The *intangible* factors (as reflected in goodwill) are more difficult to appraise accurately, yet they are real and often are of great importance in determining the real value of a going business.

Once the price or value of the business has been agreed on, other factors in structuring a deal are less troublesome. Both parties, for example, often find it mutually advantageous to buy/sell on an *installment plan,* or to plan a *tax-free corporate reorganization.*

Because of the complex tax and legal aspects of buying and selling a business, however, both parties should obtain legal assistance in drawing up an ownership-succession plan.

KEY WORDS

acquisition
book value
buy-sell agreement
capitalization rate
community property
consolidation
goodwill
installment sale
intangible assets
liquidation value
market value

merger
offering price
reorganization
replacement value
return on investment
statutory merger
tangible net assets
tax-free exchange
thinning the assets
voting stock

DISCUSSION QUESTIONS

1. In analyzing the financial records of the business you have been thinking about buying, you discover that although the firm has excellent current and "quick asset" ratios by industry standards (i.e., its current assets are equal to or exceed its current liabilities), it is short of cash and hasn't been paying its bills on time. How would you account for this? What influence might it have on your decision to buy or not to buy this business?

2. Which is more important in appraising a business, profitability or return on investment? Explain.

3. Should a person ever consider purchasing a presently unsuccessful business (i.e., one with relatively low profits, or none at all)? Explain.

EXERCISES AND PROBLEMS

1. To consider the importance of accurate financial records and what they can mean to the owner or prospective buyer of a business, take a look at the financial statements on p. 492. In your evaluation of the business, you discover that the following are not reflected in the balance sheet:

- The customers' ledger shows accounts receivable of $20,000. According to a credit analysis, however, $5,000 of this amount cannot be collected.
- The inventory records show $120,000 in merchandise on hand. But $15,000 worth of merchandise is damaged and another $15,000 worth is old and shopworn. In order to move these goods, you'll have to mark them down 50 percent.
- Delivery equipment shows a book value of $25,000. But if you attempted to sell or trade these vehicles, the most you could hope to get is $20,000.
- The depreciated (book) value of the building is $200,000, but the market value is approximately $175,000.

a. Incorporate these conditions into a revised balance sheet that more accurately reflects the assets and capital structure of the business.

b. Relate briefly how they have affected (i) the owner's share of the business (i.e., the owner's equity or net worth), and (ii) the profit picture.

Profit-and-Loss Statement

Net sales		$200,000
Cost of goods sold:		
Inventory on hand, beginning of year	$ 80,000	
Merchandise purchases during year	180,000	
Goods available for sale during year	$260,000	
Inventory on hand, end of year	120,000	140,000
Gross margin		$ 60,000
Expenses:		
Proprietor's salary	$ 10,000	
Employees' wages	16,000	
Rent and occupancy expense	2,000	
Other expense	12,000	40,000
Net profit		$ 20,000

Balance Sheet

ASSETS			LIABILITIES AND NET WORTH		
Current assets:			Current liabilities:		
Cash on hand or in bank	$ 60,000		Accounts payable	$ 55,000	
Accounts receivable	20,000		Notes payable	25,000	
Merchandise inventory	120,000	$200,000	Taxes accrued	20,000	$100,000
Fixed assets:			Fixed liabilities:		
Furniture and fixtures	$ 50,000		Mortgage	$100,000	
Land	25,000		Notes payable	60,000	160,000
Building	200,000		Net worth		240,000
Delivery equipment	25,000	300,000	Total liabilities and		
			net worth		$500,000
Total assets		$500,000			

2. Assume that the losses indicated in exercise 1 are written off (amortized) over a period of five years. Assume further that

- The revised profit figure for the operating statement (as thus calculated) represents the average earnings of the firm over the past few years.
- The average annual salary for the owner/manager of a firm of this kind and size is $10,000.
- The standard ratio of net profit to net worth in a firm of this size in the industry is 10 percent.
- The firm is a moderately well-established one.*

Now, using the revised balance sheet you prepared in exercise 1, calculate the price that you might offer for the business should you decide to buy it. Show your calculations, using the step-by-step procedure illustrated on p. 488 in the text.

3. A prospective entrepreneur looking to buy a small retail men's store received offers to sell from three different businesses, A, B, and C. Given the following data, which of the businesses would be the best buy for him or her? Explain your reasoning.

		BUSINESS		
		A	B	C
Current net asset value		$50,000	$95,000	$60,000
Recent profit history	1978	4,500	10,000	9,100
	1979	5,000	10,500	9,600
	1980	5,500	11,500	8,600
	1981	4,500	12,000	8,100
	1982	5,500	11,000	9,600
Asking price		$50,000	$100,000	$75,000

* Use a multiplier of 4 for a moderately well-established firm.

Joe and Mary Farran, aged thirty-six and thirty-three respectively, have two children, a boy eight and a girl five. They live in a city of 45,000. Both are employed—Joe as an assistant bank cashier, Mary as secretary in a high school. Their combined income totals $25,000 per year. When not in school, the children are cared for by Mary's father (a retired teacher) and mother, who live nearby. Mary takes over this responsibility during her vacations. Joe's father (a retired railroad man) and mother live in another part of the state.

Through his banking connections, Joe has learned that a successful neighborhood grocery (Fairview Food Store) is for sale in his neighborhood, an older, established part of town having a high income level. The business has long been operated by the same owner and his wife, who are now retiring and will leave the area. They own the building and are willing to rent it at a rate which seems reasonable when compared with downtown rentals.

The store did a total business of $220,000 last year, and net profits have averaged 9.5 percent of sales. The merchandise inventory, appraised at $15,000, appears to be fresh stock. Fixtures, old but acceptable, are appraised at $6,500. Outstanding customer credit accounts total about $5,000. Other expenses will include licenses, insurance, equipment, utilities, maintenance items, and so on, in standard proportions.

Joe and Mary, according to their estimates, will need about $20,000 to get title to the inventory and equipment and to use as starting expenses for such items as advance rent, insurance, advertising costs, and credit extension. Personnel expenses have been limited by the present owners to wages to an older man who is also caretaker and provides emergency delivery and stock pickup services. A high school student sometimes helps on Saturdays.

Should Joe and Mary buy this business? What factors should they consider before making a decision to take over or not take over this business.

Affable Clifford Stubbs of Iowa City, Iowa, sold his home and used his life savings to purchase a thriving neighborhood meat market located in a rented building on the triangular point of a busy intersection. The store had operated in this location for more than forty years. The store is well-managed and popular. Business has been excellent, with customers coming from all over town to buy his prime cuts of meat. Now, one year after he purchased the market, all parking on the streets bordering his store has been made unlawful. Mr. Stubbs has decided to sell out his current stock and put his fixtures and equipment up for sale at an 80 percent loss to himself. How might this financial disaster have been avoided? What alternatives other than closing his store might have been considered?

McCook Window Co. v. *Hardwood Door Corp.* (202 N.E.2d 36, Ill., 1964)*

Ketchum sold his plant, which manufactures window frames, to Cheatham. As part of the sales contract, Ketchum agreed to refrain from manufacturing or selling window frames within a 150-mile radius of Cheatham's plant for as long as Cheatham was engaged in that business. Thereafter, Ketchum does manufacture window frames, and Cheatham sues for an injunction.

Issue: Will the injunction be granted?

* From *Fundamentals of Business Law*, 3rd ed. (Englewood Cliffs, N.J.: Prentice-Hall, Inc., 1982), p. 133 courtesy of the authors, Robert N. Corley, Eric M. Holmes, and Wilbur J. Robert. Reprinted by permission of Prentice-Hall, Inc., Englewood Cliffs, NJ 07632.

Glossary:
The Language of Business

A-B-C control. Classification of the items in an inventory in decreasing order of annual dollar volume; this array is then split into three classes, called A, B, and C. Class A contains the items with the highest annual dollar volume and receives the most attention; Class B receives less attention; and Class C is controlled routinely

Accelerated Cost Recovery System. A method of *accelerated depreciation* in which the overall period of write-off is less than the asset's expected service life.

accelerated depreciation. Any method of calculating *depreciation* in which equipment *write-offs* become progressively smaller, as in the *double-declining balance* method and the *sum-of-the-year's-digits* method; or when the period of depreciation is less than the asset's expected *service life*, as in the *Accelerated Cost Recovery System.*

account. A record of the financial transactions relating to a single asset, liability, item of income or expense, or to net worth, and showing the date of each, expressed in *debits* and *credits* and showing the current balance.

accountability. The concept that, since *responsibility* is an obligation owed, it cannot be delegated.

accounting. The art of classifying, recording, and summarizing business transactions, and interpreting the results.

accounting equation. *Assets = liabilities + owner's equity.*

accounting period. The period of time for which an operating statement is customarily prepared, usually the *calendar year* or a *fiscal year.*

account payable. A *current liability*, generally on *open account,* for unpaid purchases of goods and services.

account receivable. Money owed a business enterprise for goods and services purchased on *open account; a current asset.*

accrual. Income reported in the operating statement in the period it was earned (regardless of when it is collected), and expenses reported in the period when they occur (regardless of when the cash disbursement is made).

accumulated depreciation. A *contra account* that shows the sum of depreciation charges on a particular fixed asset.

accumulated earnings tax. See *excess profits tax.*

acid-test ratio. *Quick assets* divided by *current liabilities.*

acquisition.   A *merger* in which the seller corporation continues to operate and maintain its identity. Contrast with *statutory merger.*

acquisition costs.   In inventory control, machine setup costs (in manufacturing) and order-writing costs.

ACRS.   Acronym for *Accelerated Cost Recovery System.*

actual cash value.   In insurance, *replacement cost* less *depreciation.*

adjusting entry.   An entry made at the end of an accounting period to record accumulated *depreciation, accruals,* and other non-cash transactions.

administered price.   A price set by a producer with the intent of allowing that price to determine the quantity purchased in the market, rather than adjusting the price to market demand; a common practice in the marketing of *producers' goods.*

administrative organization.   The operating structure or *departmentation* of the business enterprise, as opposed to its *legal organization* or structure; also called *operating organization.*

advertisability.   See *expansibility of demand.*

advertising.   Any paid form of public announcement calling attention to a firm's products or services or to the business itself. See also *interior advertising.*

advertising budget.   An estimate of the probable seasonalized advertising expenses for a specified period, and the allocation of these expenses to various advertising media.

advertising media.   The means of effecting or conveying an advertising message, such as printing (newspapers, billboards, etc.) and broadcasting (radio and television).

affirmative action.   An employment policy aimed at increasing the proportion of minority groups in the firm's labor force; referred to by some opponents as "reverse discrimination."

agency.   A legal relationship in which one person or firm represents another person or firm in a business transaction with third parties.

agent middleman.   A person or firm who negotiates purchases or sales between producers and retailers, such as *merchandise brokers, manufacturers' agents, purchasing agents,* and *selling agents;* a functional middleman.

aging of accounts receivable.   Classification of accounts according to the length of time they have been on the books.

amortization.   (1) *Depreciation* of a tangible asset. (2) The gradual reduction of a debt by periodic payments sufficient to meet current interest and liquidate the debt at maturity.

annual percentage rate.   The *carrying charge* or the cost of a loan over a full year, expressed as a percentage.

antitrust legislation.   Legislation directed against *monopoly* and *restraint of trade.*

APR.   Acronym for *annual percentage rate.*

arbitration.   Settling employer-employee disputes through impartial third parties who are given the power to make a decision binding on both sides.

articles of incorporation.   A document filed with a state government authority by persons forming a *corporation*, specifying the terms and conditions under which the corporation is to operate.

assets.   Anything of value that the business owns.

authority.   The power to carry out assignments. Contrast *line authority* and *staff authority*.

automobile liability.   Legal liability for bodily injury to employees or non-employees, and for property damage, caused by automobiles.

available stock.   The sum of stock on hand and stock on order less unfilled consumption demand. See also *reserve system of stock control*.

average collection period.   The ratio of (1) the total receivables to (2) the average daily credit sales.

average-cost inventory valuation.   Valuing inventory by multiplying the stock on hand by an average cost determined by taking the weighted average of the unit cost of the *beginning inventory* and the unit costs of those units produced or bought during the accounting period.

average inventory.   One-half the sum of the beginning and ending inventories.

bad debt.   An account or amount owed that has been determined legally uncollectable.

balance of payments.   A statement of international transactions of all kinds (including and not limited to trading) which give rise to money payments between countries; see also *foreign exchange*. Contrast with *balance of trade*.

balance-of-stores ledger.   See *perpetual inventory*.

balance of trade.   A statement of the value of exports and imports to and from a particular country; such foreign trade transactions usually constitute the largest component of the *balance of payments*.

balance sheet.   A financial statement which shows, on any particular day, the firm's *assets*, its debts (*liabilities*), and the amount of *equity* or investment in the business.

bank draft.   A *check* drawn by one bank on another bank.

banker's acceptance.   A *bill of exchange* drawn on a bank and accepted by the bank.

bank reconciliation.   Accounting for the difference between the book balance of a firm's Cash in Bank account and the bank's monthly statement; takes into consideration the amount of checks issued that have not cleared, deposits that have not yet been recorded by the bank, and possible errors by the bank or firm.

bankruptcy.   A filing of a legal petition against an *insolvent* business by its *creditors* under the bankruptcy laws.

basic stock list. Used by the retailer for *staple goods* continuously maintained in stock; indicates not only the names of the items to be carried but also the minimum quantities to be maintained, *reorder points,* and the quantities to be reordered at any one time. Contrast with *model stock plan.*

beginning inventory. The cost of inventory at the beginning of the accounting period; sometimes called the *opening inventory.*

BFOQ. Acronym for *bona fide occupational qualification.*

billing error. A mistake on the debtor's monthly statement as defined by the Fair Credit Billing Act, e.g., a charge for an item not purchased or for which the customer did not accept delivery, and a charge not properly listed on the statement or which was entered on a date different from the purchase date.

billing period. The period of time for which purchases on account are billed.

bill of exchange. An unconditional written order to pay a specified sum of money to the order of a payee or bearer on demand or on a specified date; also called a *draft.*

bill of materials. A list of the raw materials and/or finished components required for the fabrication or assembly of one unit of product.

bill of sale. A legal document attesting to the sale of *personal property.*

bona fide occupational qualification. A qualification that is absolutely necessary to perform a job.

bonds. Interest-bearing certificates of debt. See also *debentures* and *convertible bonds.*

book inventory. See *perpetual inventory.*

bookkeeping. See *accounting.*

book of original entry. See *journal.*

book value. The valuation at which assets are carried in the ledgers or books of account, e.g., cost less *accumulated depreciation.*

borrowed capital. See *debt capital.*

brand. A name, sign or symbol used to identify the products of one seller and differentiate them from those of competitors. See also *product differentiation, trade name,* and *trademark.*

break-even analysis. Determination of the cost-volume-profit relationship in a given business enterprise.

break-even point. The volume point at which the business operation breaks even between a profit or a loss.

budget. A statement of plans and expected results expressed in numerical terms (dollars, units of product, costs, profit, etc.).

buffer inventory. See *safety stock.*

bulk sales acts. Statutes to prevent dishonest merchants from defrauding their creditors by selling their entire stock in bulk without having paid for it.

burden.   See *overhead.*

business cycle.   A recurring succession of fluctuations in economic activity, varying from periods of *prosperity* to periods of *depression.*

business failure.   A business closure which resulted in loss to creditors, or an operating firm in which the profit margin is nonexistent or inadequate.

business firm.   A *proprietorship, partnership, corporation,* or other organization engaged in the production or distribution of goods or services or in related financial transactions.

business function.   A characteristic activity of any business enterprise: the *production* of goods or services; the *distribution* or marketing of goods or services; and the *finance(ing)* of these basic activities. Contrast with *management function.*

business insurance.   Insurance on the life of the entrepreneur or a "key" employee, the policy being payable to the employing company.

business law.   That body of law concerned with the exchange or buying and selling of goods and services.

business plan.   A document that describes a business enterprise or a proposed new business and is distributed to potential investors; describes the venture's market feasibility and strategy, its organization and management, and its financial prospects.

business site.   The space of ground occupied or about to be occupied by the building which houses the business operation.

buyer.   A department head of a retail store, responsible for the store's purchasing function.

buying motives.   Those motives which induce a person to buy a certain type or class of product, as opposed to the selection of *brands* within a class.

buying plan.   A breakdown of the retailer's *open-to-buy* figure to indicate the number of units to purchase in different merchandise classifications or for various selling departments.

buying power.   See *purchasing power.*

buy-sell agreement.   An agreement between the seller and buyer of a business specifying the purchase price and terms of sale.

calendar year.   A year ending on the last day of December.

capital.   The amount invested in a business; may be in the form of *debt* or *equity.*

capital assets.   Assets of a permanent nature required for the conduct of the business, which will not normally be converted into cash during the ensuing fiscal year, such as buildings, equipment, furniture and fixtures, and land; same as *fixed assets.*

capital budgeting.   The process of choosing investment projects for the business enterprise.

capital expenditures.   Expenditures for *capital assets.*

capital gain (or loss).   The gain (or loss) realized from the sale or disposition of a *capital asset.*

capitalization of a corporation.   Total amount of the *securities* issued by a corporation.

capitalization rate.   The appropriate earnings rate to apply to the net income of a business to establish its value.

capital stock.   The shares of ownership of a *corporation.*

capital stock tax.   A tax on the stock of a corporation at its *par value.*

capital structure.   The total of long-term (fixed) liabilities and equity capital.

carry-back or carry-forward.   Provisions in income tax law permitting operating losses or capital losses to be carried back or carried forward to preceding or following years to offset the other year's profits or capital gains.

carrying charge.   The amount of charges added to the price of merchandise to compensate for deferred payment; an *interest* charge.

cash.   Currency (paper money), specie (metal coins), and any item (such as a check) for which a bank will immediately credit for deposit or make payment in currency or specie.

cash budget.   A statement or *budget* of expected cash receipts and disbursements.

cash cycle.   The period of time that elapses between the purchase of goods and materials and the collection of accounts receivable for the merchandise or finished products sold.

cash discount.   A reduction in price allowed the buyer for prompt payment.

cash flow.   The difference between cash receipts and disbursements for a given period.

cashier's check.   A *check* drawn by a bank on itself.

central business district.   An area characterized by heavy traffic flow and a high concentration of retail businesses, offices, theaters and hotels, and hence, an area of very high land values.

certificate of deposit.   A *promissory note* given by a bank.

change fund.   The amount of money kept on hand in the cash register(s) for purposes of making change.

channels of distribution.   The route taken by the title to a product in its passage from the *producer* to the *ultimate consumer* or business user. See also *middlemen.*

character loan.   An *unsecured loan,* made on the signature of the borrower and his or her ability to repay the obligation.

charge account.   An *account receivable.*

charter.   A license issued by a state government agency granting a *corporation* the right to do business under terms and conditions specified in its *articles of incorporation.*

chattel mortgage.   A conveyance of *personal property* as security for a loan.

check.   A *bill of exchange* drawn on a bank by a depositor and payable on demand.

circulating capital.   Same as *working capital.*

closed-end credit.   Goods purchased (sold) on the *installment plan.* Contrast with *open-end credit.*

closed shop.   A place of employment where only union members may be employed.

closing entry.   An entry made at the end of an accounting period which "closes out" an income or expense account into a summary profit-and-loss account, which in turn is "closed out" to the retained earnings or proprietorship account.

closing inventory.   See *ending inventory.*

C.O.D.   A designation on a sales invoice requiring payment of cash on delivery.

coinsurance.   A clause in fire insurance policies which requires the insured to maintain insurance equal to some specified percentage of the property's *replacement cost* or its *actual cash value.*

collateral loan.   A loan secured by the pledge of specific property.

collection period.   The average number of days to collect an *account receivable.* See *average collection period.*

collective bargaining.   Negotiation between employer and employees on wages, hours, and working conditions.

commercial bank.   A bank that specializes in demand deposits and short-term business loans.

commercial credit.   See *trade credit.*

commercial law.   See *business law.*

commission house.   A firm that sells the personal property of another firm on a commission basis.

communications.   The imparting of information from one person to another in a way that is understandable to the person receiving it.

community obligations.   Involvement of the business owner or manager in the political and social structure of the community through volunteer service.

community property.   In states where such laws exist, husband and wife are each entitled to one-half of their total earnings during the marriage.

community shopping center.   A *shopping center* serving an entire community or the part of town in which it is located.

composition of creditors.   An agreement of all the creditors with one another and with the debtor to accept a specified percentage of their claims in full settlement, thereby avoiding the expense and delay of legal proceedings.

computerized accounting.   See *data processing.*

conditional sales contract.   Agreement under which the title does not pass to the buyer until the buyer has completed payments on goods purchased under the *installment plan.*

consequential loss.   The indirect or business-interruption loss resulting from property damage.

consideration.   The inducement that leads a person to enter into a *contract.*

consignment sale.   Where one party (the consignor) sends goods to another party (the consignee) for sale, title remaining with the consignor until the goods are sold by the consignee.

consolidation.   The merging of two corporations into a new third corporation (or of three corporations into a new fourth corporation, etc.). See also *merger.*

constant dollars.   Dollars of constant *purchasing power;* calculated by dividing the current price of a product or service by a *price index.*

consumer credit.   Credit used by individuals or families for the satisfaction of their own wants. Contrast with *trade credit.*

consumer goods.   Goods used directly in satisfying a human want. Contrast with *producers' goods.*

consumer survey.   Indicates the preference for certain stores or shops and reasons for patronage and for shifting trade from one business establishment to another.

continuing management education.   Education that is continuously necessary for one to keep on "top" of one's job in a world of rapid change.

continuous manufacturing process.   Standard products manufactured continuously to the company's own specifications in anticipation of sales; commonly known as *mass production.* Contrast with *intermittent manufacturing process* and *repetitive manufacturing process.*

contra account.   An offset account that is used to establish the value of another account, such as the account for *accumulated depreciation.*

contract.   A legally enforceable agreement between competent parties, based on *consideration,* to do or refrain from doing some lawful act.

contribution margin.   The excess of sales income over the *direct costs* of production; sometimes called the "contribution to fixed cost and profit."

control account.   An account in the *general ledger* used to carry the total of account balances in a *subsidiary ledger.*

controllable cost.   See *variable cost.*

controlling.   The *management* function of measuring and correcting the actions of subordinates to ensure that plans for the business are fulfilled.

convenience goods.   Good for which people do not "shop around" or make comparisons between the prices and qualities offered by different sellers.

convertible bonds.   Bonds which may be converted into stock at the option of the bondholder.

cooperative buying.   Consolidation of purchase orders of a number of affiliated firms.

copyright.   The exclusive legal right to reproduce, publish, and sell the matter and form of a literary, musical, or artistic work.

corporation.   A *legal entity* authorized by a state to operate a business under the entity's *charter* or *articles of incorporation*.

cost of capital.   The average rate of *interest* per year the business must pay for its *equities;* the minimum cost that would induce bankers or other investors to place their funds at the company's disposal.

cost of credit.   Same as *finance charge* or *carrying charge;* also, the *interest* on funds borrowed.

cost of goods sold.   Determined for any accounting period by subtracting the ending inventory from the sum of the beginning inventory and the costs of goods purchased or manufactured during the period.

cost or market, whichever is lower.   Valuing inventory on the basis of cost or market price per unit, whichever is lower. The cost price is commonly determined by *FIFO, LIFO,* or the *average-cost* method.

cost recovery period.   The period of time over which an asset must be depreciated or written off for *ACRS* tax purposes, regardless of its expected *service life*.

covenant not to compete.   An agreement that the seller of a business will not compete with the buyer of that business for a specified time period.

credit.   As a noun, (1) the ability or right to buy or borrow in return for a promise to pay later; (2) an entry on the right-hand side of an *account*. As a verb, to make an entry on the right-hand side of an *account*.

credit bureau.   An organization that collects, maintains, and provides credit information to members or subscribers.

credit card.   A card authorizing credit purchases.

credit insurance.   Insurance protecting a creditor from losses caused by the insolvency of debtors.

credit life-and-disability insurance.   Insurance payable to a bank, finance company, or other purchaser of a *conditional sales contract* to protect it against the untimely death or disability of the debtor.

credit line.   See *line of credit*.

creditor.   One to whom money is owed.

credit rating.   An estimate as to the amount of credit that can be extended to an applicant for credit.

crossover point.   In *break-even analysis*, the volume point beyond which the firm's rate of profit would be greater with a proposed investment than it would be without it.

current asset.   An asset which can readily be converted into cash in the normal operation of the business within one year. Contrast with *fixed asset*.

current liability.   A debt that is to be paid within the ensuing fiscal year; a *short-term* liability.

current ratio.   *Current assets* divided by *current liabilities*.

customer relations.   The firm's activities relating to the enhancement of customer satisfaction and *goodwill.*

customers' ledger.   The *subsidiary ledger* in which *accounts receivable* for individual customers are recorded.

customs broker.   An *agent middleman* who represents the importer in a foreign trade transaction.

cycle billing.   The mailing of *invoices* at stipulated staggered intervals during the *billing period,* usually on a last-name alphabetical basis.

daily cash report.   Used to reconcile the amount of cash actually received with the amount "rung up" on the cash register(s) or recorded on sales slips.

data processing.   A general term designating the (manual or electronic) processing of numerical data for the purpose of converting it to some desired form; see also *information system.* Contrast with *word processing.*

datings.   The time limits governing pay for purchases.

debentures.   Bonded indebtedness for which no security has been pledged.

debit.   As a noun, an entry on the left-hand side of an *account.* As a verb, to make an entry on the left-hand side of an *account.*

debt capital.   Borrowed, or loan, capital invested in the business that must be repaid to the *creditors.*

debt securities.   See *bonds;* contrast with *debentures.*

debtor.   One who owes money to another.

decision making.   The selection from among alternatives of a rational course of action.

deductible coverage.   A provision in an insurance policy that only the loss in excess of a stated minimum amount is covered.

deferred expense.   A *prepaid expense,* such as for rent and insurance.

deferred payment reserve.   A deferred or "delayed" *credit,* the withheld payment being held in *escrow.*

delegation of authority.   The vesting of *decision-making* discretion in a subordinate. See also *authority.*

demand.   The amount of a product or service that buyers are willing to buy at a given price in a given market at a given time. See also *elasticity of demand.*

demand forecasting.   See *demand* and *forecast.*

demand loan.   A loan which is due whenever the lender asks for payment. Contrast with *term loan.*

demography.   The statistical study of human populations, especially with reference to size and density, distribution, composition, income, and vital statistics.

departmentation.   The grouping of activities in a business organization; may be on a functional, territorial, or product basis, or on any combination of these criteria.

depreciation. The allocation of the cost of an asset which will be used over a long period of time by charging a portion of the cost to each year of the asset's *service life* or *cost recovery period.*

depression. The period of a *business cycle* when production and employment are lowest.

developmental training. Training concerned with the attainment of proficiency in job performance or with the advancement (promotion) of employees to higher-rated jobs.

differential pricing. Charging different prices for the same product to different manufacturer's outlets, reflecting differences in the number of wholesaling functions performed (and thus differences in the manufacturer's distribution costs).

direct action advertising. Advertising for the primary purpose of selling the product or service the business has to offer. Contrast with *institutional advertising.*

direct costs. Same as *variable costs.*

directing. The *management* function of supervising and coordinating the activities of subordinates.

direct loan. A non-*participation* loan.

disaster loan. A long-term direct or participation loan by the SBA to help a small business restore or replace property damaged by a natural disaster.

disbursement. A payment of funds towards the full or partial settlement of a debt; an *expenditure.* Contrast with *expense.*

discounted payback period. The time that elapses before cash inflows from an investment equal the *present value* of the cash outflows.

dispatching. The starting of *production orders* on schedule, requiring the selecting and sequencing of available jobs to be run at individual work stations and the assignment of these jobs to particular workers.

dispatch rack. A mechanical device for *dispatching* work to individual machines and operators.

distribution. Those business activities involved in the flow of goods and/or services from production to consumption: market research, personal selling, advertising and sales promotion, pricing, and (for the manufacturer) packaging and the selection of *distribution channels;* essentially selling activities. A primary *business function.* Synonymous with *marketing.*

distribution channels. See *channels of distribution.*

distributive education. A federal- and state-supported program of education for workers in distributive (marketing) occupations at the high school level which combines classwork and on-the-job experience.

distributor. See *wholesaler.*

dividend. The earnings or profit of a *corporation* distributed to a stockholder, paid at a certain amount for each share of stock held by the stockholder.

dollar control.   In inventory control, the determination of the proper inventory level in terms of the dollar value of the inventory. Contrast with *unit control.*

double-declining-balance depreciation.   Spreading the initial cost of a capital asset over its estimated service life by doubling the *straight-line* rate and applying this doubled percentage to the undepreciated balance at the beginning of each year; no *salvage value* is used in the calculation.

double entry.   The system of recording financial transactions that maintains the equality of the *accounting equation,* each entry requiring both a *debit* and a *credit.*

double tax.   Same income (corporate profits) taxed at both the corporate tax rate (when earned) and the personal tax rate (when distributed as dividends).

down payment.   The initial cash received by the vendor for part payment of a purchase.

draft.   A *bill of exchange.*

earnings statement.   See *profit-and-loss statement.*

economic base.   The wealth produced in or near a community that provides employment and income to the local population.

economic injury loan.   A short-term direct or participation loan by the SBA to help a small business overcome economic injury (i.e., *consequential loss*) suffered by it as a result of a natural disaster.

economic opportunity loan.   A long-term direct loan by the SBA to help low-income persons with the potential to successfully operate a business, but who cannot qualify for SBA's regular business loans.

economic ordering quantity.   The optimum ordering quantity, reflecting the balance of ordering costs (*acquisition costs*) and the costs of carrying the inventory (*possession costs*); it is the order quantity at which these costs are equal and the total of these costs is at a minimum.

economic security.   See *social insurance.*

elasticity of demand.   Sensitivity to price change; the measurement of a small relative change in price accompanied by a proportionate smaller, equal, or larger relative change in the quantity of the product or service demanded.

electronic data processing.   See *data processing.*

elements research.   Split-run testing to determine effectiveness of headlines, copy, illustrations, color, and other "elements" in an advertising message.

employee relations.   The employer's activities in dealing with employees as individuals.

ending inventory.   The cost of inventory at the end of the accounting period; sometimes called the *closing inventory.*

entrepreneur.   One who organizes, manages, and assumes the risks of a business firm or *venture.*

E.O.M. dating. The cash discount and net credit periods begin on the first day of the following month rather than on the invoice date.

equal credit opportunity. Non-discrimination in the extension of credit to a firm's customers for reason of sex or family status.

equal employment opportunity. Non-discrimination in the hiring or advancement of employees for reasons of race, sex, age, religion, national origin, and physical handicap; also termed *fair employment practices.*

equal pay for equal work. State and federal laws which permit wage differentials between classified male-female jobs only if there are demonstrable differences in job content.

equities. *Liabilities* plus *owners' equity.*

equity capital. Capital invested in the business by the owner(s).

equivalent annual cost. In *capital budgeting,* the average annual cost derived by dividing the total discounted costs of acquiring, installing, and using an asset over the period of its service life (less the *present value* of its *salvage value*) by the sum of the annual discount factors.

escrow. A fund or deposit to be delivered to the grantee only upon the fulfillment of a condition.

estate tax. A federal or state tax levied on the right of transfer of property from the deceased to his or her heirs or legatees; same as *inheritance tax.*

exception principle. Management *control* of the business by concentrating on the exceptions, or outstanding variations, from the standard or expected result.

excess profits tax. A tax levied on corporations for the unreasonable accumulation of earnings (surplus) to avoid taxes on corporate dividends; also known as the *accumulated earnings tax* or the *undistributed profits tax.*

excise tax. A tax levied on the manufacture, sale, or consumption of a product.

exclusive dealing. A contract in which the seller obligates the buyer to refrain from the purchase of competitors' products; also called *forced-line selling.*

expansibility of demand. Sensitivity to advertising, i.e., the extent to which advertising will increase the sale of a product; also called *advertisability.*

expediting. The "rushing" or "chasing" of production or purchase orders which are behind schedule or which are needed in less than the normal *lead time;* sometimes called *stockchasing.*

expenditure. See *disbursement.*

expense budget. A *budget* of *operating expenses.*

expense ratios. Relationships between sales income and particular items of expense for the period covered by the operating statement; a major category of *operating ratios.*

expenses. The cost of assets used up to produce income; see *operating expenses.*

experience rating.   In unemployment compensation insurance, the variation in the premium rate for the abnormal or subnormal risk experience of the employer; also called **merit rating.**

export agent.   A *commission house* that assumes responsibility for the packaging and insuring of exported goods, arranging transportation and credit, billing and collecting payments on invoices, and for meeting all legal requirements. Contrast with *export firm.*

export firm.   A firm that buys outright the products of domestic producers and then resells them to foreign countries. Contrast with *export agent.*

exports.   Goods sold to customers in foreign countries.

extended coverage.   Coverages that may be added to the standard fire insurance policy for loss due to such causes as windstorm and hail, smoke, civil disorder, and explosion other than that of a steam boiler.

extensions (of credit).   Court-approved plans, proposed by the debtor, wherein the debtor is allowed additional time in which to pay his or her debts.

extra dating.   The cash discount and net credit periods are extended for so many days after the regular allowed terms.

facilitating function.   Any *business function* related to the firm's financing of its primary buying and selling activities.

factor.   A firm that finances the *accounts receivable* of other firms by purchasing these accounts at a discount *without recourse.*

factors of production.   The ingredients or resources used by a business enterprise in producing a product or service, e.g., land, labor, machines, materials, and *management.*

FAIR.   An acronym for Fair Access to Insurance Requirements, insurance companies entering into a pooling arrangement whereby they share risks in high-risk areas and pay proportionate shares toward the full sum of an insurance claim.

fair employment practices.   See *equal employment opportunity.*

fair trade laws.   Laws enacted by many states allowing manufacturers of branded products to set minimum resale prices at the wholesale and/or retail level, i.e., laws permitting *resale price maintenance* agreements.

fashion cycle.   Refers to the spreading and rising customer demand for fashion merchandise after their introduction to the market, followed by a peak period of demand and eventual decline in demand.

fashion goods.   Goods whose primary appeal rests on frequently changing design or appearance; same as *specialty goods.*

featherbedding.   Requiring an employer under a union rule to hire more employees than are needed.

FICA taxes.   Acronym for Federal Insurance Contributions Act; see *social security taxes.*

fidelity bond.   A bond covering the risk of loss due to employee larceny or embezzlement.

FIFO.   See *first-in-first-out inventory valuation.*

finance.   As a noun, the obtaining of funds or *capital;* as a verb, to raise or provide funds or capital.

finance charge.   The cost of extending credit to a customer; same as *carrying charge.*

finance company.   See *sales finance company.*

financial leverage.   The extent to which earnings made possible by borrowed funds exceed the cost of the debt.

financial ratios.   The relationships in amount and size between two or more items in a *financial statement.*

financial statement.   A report summarizing the financial condition or financial results of a business on date or for any period. The two principal financial statements are the *balance sheet* and the *profit-and-loss statement.*

finished goods.   Manufactured products ready for sale.

first in, first out inventory valuation.   Assumes that the first units purchased or produced were the first ones sold, the remaining units being the last purchased or produced.

fiscal policy (federal).   Modifying the *business cycle* by means of comprehensive budget planning (tax revenues and spending programs), in contrast to *monetary policy.*

fiscal year.   Any accounting period of twelve successive months ending with the last day of any months other than December; see *calendar year.*

fixed assets.   See *capital assets.*

fixed capital.   Long-term *capital* invested in the business.

fixed cost.   An expense that does not vary with the volume of business in the short run, such as insurance and depreciation of equipment.

fixed debt.   Same as *funded debt.*

fixed liability.   An obligation of the business which will not be paid during the ensuing fiscal year; a *long-term* liability.

flat-rate lease.   A *lease* of business property providing that the rental will be a fixed sum per period of time.

flat-rate pricing.   Charging the same price for the same service task to all customers (regardless of differences in labor time and cost), based on "average" conditions. Contrast with *multiplier pricing.*

floating debt.   Short-term funds borrowed for materials, labor, and other needs which fluctuate with the volume of business. Contrast with *funded debt.*

flow control.   Maintenance of a predetermined rate of flow from one work station to another on a production line.

follow-up.   The monitoring of job progress to see that operations are performed on schedule or that purchased material or products will be received on schedule. See also *expediting.*

forced-line selling.   Same as *exclusive dealing.*

forecast.   An estimate of the firm's future sales, or the probability of occurrence of future business and economic conditions.

foreign exchange.   The process by which the *balances of payment* between countries are settled.

foreign trade.   Trade between business firms located in different countries.

franchise.   A right or privilege granted or sold to use a name or to sell proprietary products or services. See also *license.*

franchising.   The distribution of goods or services through outlets owned by the franchisee.

free enterprise.   An economic system which permits private ownership of the means and fruits of production; also called *private enterprise.*

freight forwarder.   A firm that consolidates less-than-carload shipments from several manufacturers or distributors into carload lots.

fringe benefits.   An employment benefit granted by an employer that involves a money cost without affecting basic wage rates, such as paid vacations, group insurance, sick leave, pensions, and profit-sharing plans.

full-service wholesaler.   A *merchant middleman* who performs the full range of wholesaling functions, such as the storage and physical handling of merchandise in large quantities and the resale and delivery of these goods in smaller quantities to retailers or business users.

functional layout.   Layout of equipment by process, each process or type of operation being performed in a single department on all types of product. See also *line layout.*

functional middleman.   Same as *agent middleman.*

funded debt.   Long-term funds borrowed for capital expenditure purposes. Contrast with *floating debt.*

FUTA.   Acronym for Federal Unemployment Tax Act. See *unemployment taxes.*

general ledger.   The ledger containing the financial-statement accounts, some of which may be *control accounts.* See also *subsidiary ledger.*

general partner.   A partner liable for all the debts of the *partnership.* Contrast with *limited partner.*

generative location.   A location to which consumers are directly attracted from their place of residence for the purpose of shopping. Contrast with *suscipient location.*

gift tax.   A tax on the transfer of property by gift; primarily a supplement to the *inheritance tax,* aimed at preventing evasion of death taxes.

goodwill.   (1) The favor or advantage in the way of custom that a business has acquired beyond the mere value of what it sells. (2) That *intangible asset* which enables a business to earn a profit in excess of the normal rate of profit earned by other businesses of the same kind.

Green River ordinances.   Municipal ordinances regulating or forbidding house-to-house selling.

gross margin.   The difference between *cost of goods sold* and *net sales*, commonly expressed as a percentage of net sales; also called *gross profit*.

gross national product.   The value of a country's total output of goods and services in a given period of time.

gross profit.   Same as *gross margin*.

gross sales.   Total sales before deducting *returns and allowances*.

guarantee loan.   A loan guaranteed by a third party.

guild pricing.   Fixed charge for performing a given service by all members of a trade group, such as beauty and barber shops.

holder in due course.   A third party who receives a **negotiable instrument** before maturity in good faith without knowledge of defects or infirmities, and who gives value for the instrument.

"hoodoo" location.   A site that has been occupied by a succession of business failures.

horizontal integration.   A union or *merger* under one ownership of two or more firms engaged in the same processes or stages of production and distribution. Contrast with *vertical integration*.

imports.   Goods purchased from a foreign supplier.

impulse goods.   Goods purchased without advance planning and because the buyer was induced to buy at first sight.

incentive wage.   A system under which employees receive wages in proportion to their productivity, usually with *time wages* guaranteed.

income statement.   See *profit-and-loss statement*.

income tax.   A tax imposed by the federal government and most of the states on the income of an individual or business firm.

incremental cost (or income).   The cost of producing, selling, preparing, storing, etc., one more unit (or the additional revenue derived therefrom).

indirect cost.   See *overhead*.

industrial goods.   See *producers' goods*.

inflation.   A period, occasioned by rising prices and wages, when the *purchasing power* of the dollar is falling.

information returns.   Reports by employers on wages, salaries, dividends, or interest paid, filed with the Internal Revenue Service, showing the name of the one paid and the amount received; used to verify tax statements made by the one receiving the payment.

information system.   Information organized to facilitate decision-making, planning, control, and reporting.

inheritance tax.   See *estate tax*.

initial markup.   See *markon*.

insolvent.   Said of a business that is unable to pay its debts as they become due. Even though the firm's *assets* may exceed its *liabilities*, the nature of the assets are such that they cannot be readily converted into cash to meet the maturing obligations of the business. See also *bankruptcy*.

inspection order.   An authorization to an inspection department or group to perform an inspection operation.

installment plan.   The purchase (sale) of goods on credit for which a series of equal payments is made over a period of time. Title to the product may or may not remain with the seller until payments are completed. See also *conditional sales contract.*

institutional advertising.   Advertising for the primary purpose of selling the business, rather than the products or services it has to offer, i.e., advertising which emphasizes the business's activities or which seeks to improve its image; contrast with *direct advertising.*

insurance.   A *contract* for reimbursement of specific losses, purchased with insurance premiums, e.g., *business insurance.*

intangible assets.   Assets which have no substance or physical body, such as *goodwill, patents, franchises, copyrights, trademarks,* and *covenants not to compete.*

integration of industry.   Organizing the different processes in the production and distribution of goods and services under a single ownership or management. See also *vertical* and *horizontal integration.*

interest.   Payments a borrower pays a lender for the use of his or her money.

intermittent manufacturing process.   Goods manufactured to customer's order and specifications. Contrast with *repetitive manufacturing process* and *continuous manufacturing process.*

interstate commerce.   Commerce between the states and with foreign countries.

intrastate commerce.   Commerce occurring within a state.

inventory.   As a noun, the balance in an *asset* account, such as merchandise, supplies, raw materials, work in process, and finished goods; also called *stock* or stores. As a verb, to determine the number of units of goods on hand, or their cost, at a given time.

inventory carrying costs.   Same as inventory *possession costs.*

inventory turnover.   The number of times the *average inventory* has been sold or used up during a period; calculated by dividing the average inventory for a period into the *cost of goods sold* during that period. Sometimes called *stockturn.*

investment capital.   Same as *fixed capital.*

investment tax credit.   A reduction in income tax liability granted by the federal government to business firms that purchase new or used equipment.

invoice.   A bill rendered for products or services sold, showing quantity, price, terms, nature of delivery, and amount due.

involuntary bankruptcy.   *Bankruptcy* proceedings begun by petition of a *creditor.*

IRA.   Acronym for Individual Retirement Account, a *tax-sheltered* pension fund available to income receiver, including the self-employed.

job analysis.   A study of a job to determine the duties performed, the responsibilities and organizational relationships involved, and the human traits required.

jobber.   A *wholesaler;* usually sells in small lots.

job description.   A list of job duties (or description of what the job incumbent does); indicates working conditions, materials and equipment handled, and how the job is related to other jobs in the organization. Contrast with *job specifications.*

job evaluation.   Measuring and comparing relative difficulties and required skills for various jobs for the purpose of establishing fair and equitable wage and salary rates.

job shop.   One that is engaged in the *intermittent manufacturing process.*

job specifications.   Specifies for each job the skill, effort, aptitudes, experience, knowledge or education, and other personal requirements needed to perform the job satisfactorily. Contrast with *job description.*

job ticket.   An authorization to a worker to perform a machine or manual operation.

joint determination program.   See *set-aside program.*

journal.   An accounting record in which financial transactions are recorded in the order in which they occur; *a book of original entry,* from which the transactions are further recorded in a *ledger.*

judgment.   In law, a decision of a judge entered on the court's books.

judgment note.   A *promissory note* permitting *judgment* to be taken against the signer without a trail if he or she fails to pay the note.

jurisdictional strike.   A disagreement between two or more unions as to which union shall perform a given kind of work or which union shall be the representative of a given group of employees, with one of the unions striking to force the employer to yield to its demands.

Keogh plan.   A *tax-sheltered* pension plan for the self-employed.

key-employee insurance.   See *business insurance.*

landed cost.   List price less trade discounts plus the cost of transporting the goods to the buyer (freight-in).

last-in, first-out inventory valuation.   Assumes that the last units purchased or produced were the first ones sold, the remaining units being those purchased or produced at an earlier point in time.

leader pricing.   See *loss leader pricing.*

leadership.   The act or process of influencing subordinates to work willingly and enthusiastically toward the achievement of the firm's goals.

lead time.   See *procurement lead time.*

lease.   A contract, usually in writing, for the use or occupancy of property for a specified time.

ledger.   A book of *accounts.*

legal entity.   Any person or business enterprise which has, in the eyes of the law, the capacity to make a *contract* or agreement.

legal organization.   A proprietorship, partnership, corporation or other *legal entity;* also called *ownership organization.*

legal tender.   Currency in such denominations as the law authorizes a debtor to tender and requires a creditor to accept in payment of money obligations.

leverage.   See *financial leverage.*

leverage ratios.   Measures of a firm's debt load.

liabilities.   The claims of *creditors* against the *assets* of the business, i.e., what the business owes.

license.   Formal permission to carry on a certain activity or to use someone else's property.

LIFO.   See *last-in, first-out inventory valuation.*

limited-function wholesaler.   Term applied to a variety of wholesalers that have eliminated certain functions normally associated with wholesaling, such as the elimination of the delivery function by cash-and-carry wholesalers.

limited liability.   The liability of stockholders in a *corporation* (liability being limited to the stockholders' equity or investment in the business).

limited partner.   A partner not personally liable for debts of the *partnership.* Contrast with *general partner.*

linear organization structure.   The chain of command that runs from the top of the business organization to its lowest ranks. Term used to describe a large organization with several levels or "scales" of *line authority* (vertical organization structure), as differentiated from the relatively "flat" (horizontal) structure of smaller organizations.

line authority.   The power to command subordinates, for whose activities and performance the manager has *responsibility.* Contrast with *staff authority.*

line layout.   Layout of equipment by product, all processes or operations on a given product being performed in one department. Contrast with *functional layout.*

line of credit.   The maximum credit allowed to be outstanding on an individual customer account.

liquidation value.   The anticipated value of an asset that would be realized in case of liquidation of the business; the *market value.*

liquidity.   The degree to which assets can be converted into cash. See also *insolvency.*

liquidity ratios.   Ratios, such as the *current* and *acid-test ratios*, that measure the ability of a firm to meet its debts as they come due.

list price.   A printed price, as in a catalog, used as basis on which *trade discounts* are computed.

loan.   A business transaction between two legal entities whereby one party borrows funds from the other party, usually entailing the payment of *interest* by the borrower.

location affinities.   See *retail affinities.*

long-term.   Due more than one year hence.

long-term capital.   See *fixed capital.*

loss leader.   A popular, fast selling item priced at less than its *landed cost,* with the expectation that sales of other goods bearing higher *markups* will increase enough to compensate for the "loss" on the popular item.

lower of cost or market.   See *cost or market, whichever is lower.*

management.   The process of *planning, organizing, directing,* and *controlling* the activities of a business enterprise so as to attain stated objectives by the use of people and other resources; requires *decision-making* and *leadership.*

management consultant.   One who gives professional advice or services to line executives in a business organization.

management function.   See *management.* Contrast with *business function.*

management science.   The common body of knowledge (methods and procedures) underlying the art of *management.*

management succession.   Planning for the continuation of a business and/or the transfer of ownership.

manager.   One who undertakes the function of *management* at any level in the organization.

manufacturers' agent.   An *agent middleman* who sells the products of two or more (usually noncompetitive) client manufacturers in a specified territory. Differs from a *merchandise broker* in that his or her relationship to the manufacturer is a continuous one, and differs from a *selling agent* in that he or she is bound by the price policy of the manufacturer.

manufacturing cycle time.   See *procurement lead time.*

manufacturing enterprise.   A business firm that makes *finished goods* from *raw materials* by hand or machinery.

manufacturing order.   See *production order.*

margin.   See *gross margin.*

marginal income/cost.   The addition to cost or income resulting from the addition of one unit of production or sales; same as *incremental cost (or income).*

markdown.   A reduction of selling price below the original selling price (the markdown percentage being calculated as a percentage of the original selling price).

market.   The area in which buyers and sellers of a product or service are in communication with one another, and in which exchange takes place; a trading area. See also *trade-area survey.*

market demand.   See *demand.*

marketing.   The act or process of buying or selling in a market. Synonymous with *distribution*.

market value.   Same as *liquidation value*.

markon.   The difference between the cost of goods purchased and the original selling price set on the goods; same as *initial markup*.

markup.   The difference between merchandise cost and the selling price, commonly expressed as a percentage of the selling price; also called *gross margin*.

mass-production.   See *continuous manufacturing process*.

materials list.   See *bill of materials*.

materials requisition.   An authorization which identifies the type and quantity of materials to be withdrawn from stores.

materials reserve system.   See *reserve system of stock control*.

medium of exchange.   Something commonly accepted in exchange for goods and services and recognized as representing a standard of value.

mercantile credit.   See *trade credit*.

merchandise acceptance curve. See *fashion cycle*.

merchandise broker.   An *agent middleman* who acts for buyers and sellers but takes no title or possession of them; relationship to clients is noncontinuous.

merchandise mart.   A central place at which buyers (retailers) and sellers (wholesalers) gather together to buy and sell.

merchandisers.   Business firms that engage in the purchase or resale of goods; *wholesalers* and *retailers*.

merchandise turnover.   See *inventory turnover*.

merchandising.   The purchase and resale of consumer products.

merchant middleman.   A *middleman* who takes title to the goods he or she deals in and thus bears all the risks of ownership. Contrast with *agent middleman*.

merger.   Any of various methods of combining two or more business firms, such as *consolidation* and *statutory merger*.

merit rating.   (1) Reappraising the job qualifications of employees periodically for purposes of wage adjustments and promotions. (2) In unemployment compensation insurance, the variation in the premium rate for the abnormal or subnormal risk experience of the employer.

metric system.   A decimal system of weights and measures based on the meter and on the kilogram.

middleman.   An individual or firm that stands between prime *producer* and the *ultimate consumer* in the distribution of products. See *agent middleman* and *merchant middleman*.

minimum wage.   The lowest wage, established by law, which can be paid by the employer.

min-max system.   In inventory control, the issuance of a replenishment order when the *available stock* falls to or below a specified minimum, the replenishment order bringing the stock up to the specified maximum; the difference between the minimum and maximum quantities is the *economic ordering quantity*.

miscellaneous shop. One that is engaged in the *repetitive manufacturing process*.

model stock plan. Prepared and used by the retailer for *fashion goods* or merchandise, rather than staples; a breakdown of the "ideal" composition of the stock in terms of such factors as size, color, style, price line, etc. Contrast with *basic stock list*.

M.O.M. dating. Similar to *E.O.M. dating* except that all purchases are billed as of the fifteenth (middle) of the month instead of the end of the month, and cash discounts and net credit periods begin on that date.

monetary policy (federal). Efforts to modify the *business cycle* by controlling the supply of money and credit. Contrast with government *fiscal policy*.

monopoly. A market situation in which one or two firms so control the supply of a product as to be able to regulate its price.

morale. The mental and emotional attitudes of employees toward the work expected of them by the company and their loyalty to it.

mortgage. A claim given by the borrower to the lender against the borrower's property in return for a *loan*.

mortgage loan. A loan secured by a *mortgage* on property; when the mortgage is on personal (rather than real) property it is called a *chattel mortgage*.

mortgage note. A *promissory note* secured by a *mortgage* on real or personal property; same as a *mortgage loan*.

move order. An authorization to move work in process from one location in the plant to another.

multilevel distributorship. A marketing scheme in which one distributor recruits and sells to other distributors in a pyramid fashion.

multiplier method of pricing. A method of allocating the *indirect cost* of providing services when the amount of service (in terms of labor costs) varies from customer to customer. Contrast with *flat-rate pricing*.

negotiable instrument. *Promissory notes, checks,* and *bills of exchange* that are used as credit instruments and substitutes for cash.

net profit. *Net sales,* less *cost of goods sold* and *operating expenses* during a period; the earnings of a business.

net sales. *Gross sales* minus *returns and allowances*.

net worth. Total *assets* of the business less the total *liabilities;* same as *owner's equity*.

nontaxable exchange. See *tax-free exchange*.

note payable. A *promissory note* owed by the business.

note receivable. A *promissory note* owed to the business.

obsolescence.   The decline in *market value* of an asset caused by alternatives becoming available that will be more cost-effective.

occupancy expense.   Expense relating to the use of the real property; e.g., heat, light, rent or depreciation, and maintenance.

offering price.   The price at which the prospective entrepreneur is ready to buy a particular business.

100 percent location.   The retail site in a business district that has the greatest exposure to pedestrian traffic.

open account.   Credit that is not supported by written evidence of indebtedness; an *account receivable* or *account payable.*

open-end credit.   A *line of credit* that may be used over and over again up to a certain borrowing limit; a *revolving credit* account. Contrast with *closed-end credit.*

opening inventory.   See *beginning inventory.*

open to buy.   Total planned purchases for a period less receipts and merchandise on order.

operating expenses.   The costs incurred in operating a business; does not include *cost of goods sold.*

operating organization.   See *administrative organization.*

operating ratios.   Relationships between sales income and other items in an *operating statement.*

operating statement.   See *profit-and-loss statement.*

order control.   Control of the progress of each *production order* through the successive operations in its *manufacturing cycle.*

order of work.   A daily written memorandum of the important tasks that must be done listed in the order of priority; a *time management* tool. Contrast with the *routing* function in manufacturing.

order point.   See *reorder point.*

organizing.   The *management* function of dividing the work or activities of the business into manageable units.

outside staff.   Advice or counsel given to line executives by persons from outside the organization structure. See also *staff.*

overhead.   Any cost not specifically associated with the production of identifiable products and services; an *indirect cost,* often referred to as *burden.*

owner's equity.   The ownership right in the business; the monetary value of the business which exceeds the claims of its creditors; same as *net worth.*

ownership organization.   The business enterprise as a *legal entity.*

participation loan.   A loan extended by several banks or other lenders.

partnership.   Ownership of an unincorporated business by two or more persons.

parts list.   See *bill of materials.*

par value.   The face value appearing on a bond or stock certificate.

passive costs.   Same as *standby costs.*

patent.   An exclusive right granted by the federal government to an inventor for 17 years to sell or manufacture the invented product.

payback period.   The time that elapses before cash inflows from an investment equal the cash outflows.

payroll taxes.   Taxes assessed to fund *social insurance programs,* e.g., *unemployment taxes* and *social security taxes.*

pension.   A fixed sum paid regularly to an employee who has retired from the company because of age or disability.

percentage lease.   A *lease* of business property providing that the rental will be a percentage of the lessee's sales.

periodic inventory.   See *physical inventory.*

permit.   Same as *license.*

perpetual inventory.   The determination of the amount and value of stock on hand at any point in time by recording each addition to or withdrawal of stock as such transactions occur; also called *book inventory.* See also *physical inventory.*

personal property.   Property other than *real property* consisting of things temporary or movable.

petty cash fund.   A cash fund from which small expenses are paid.

physical inventory.   The determination of the amount and value of stock on hand by periodic actual count; also called *periodic inventory.*

piece rate.   An *incentive wage* plan.

piggyback service.   The service performed by *freight forwarders.*

placement.   The assignment of a work applicant to a suitable job in the business enterprise.

planning.   The *management* function of selecting the future courses of action for the business (goals, policies, strategies).

police power.   The inherent power of a government to exercise reasonable control over persons and property within its jurisdiction in the interest of the general security, health, safety, morals, and welfare except where specifically prohibited by statute.

policies.   Standing plans or guides to *direct* and *control* the activities of the business; guides to *decision-making.*

possession costs.   In inventory control, the costs of carrying an item in stock, comprised mainly of taxes, depreciation and obsolescence, shrinkage, insurance, and interest on investment.

posting.   The transfer of information from a *journal* to a *ledger.*

prepaid expense.   See *deferred expense.*

present value.   The value today of a sum of money to be received at some future date, discounted at some interest rate.

prestige pricing.   The pricing of a product at a higher-than-normal markup in the industry in order to establish it in consumers' minds as a "quality" product.

price cutting.   Pricing below cost for the purpose of eliminating competition.

price discrimination.   Charging different prices to different customers under similar conditions of sale.

price fixing.   Control of the price of a product or service by collusion of competitors.

price index.   A number used to indicate the change in price as compared with the price at some specified time usually taken as 100.

price lining.   Setting a number of prices within each merchandise classification, such as men's shirts selling for $9.95, $14.95, and $19.95.

price maintenance.   See *resale price maintenance.*

prime rate.   The *interest* rate for short-term loans charged by commercial banks to their most credit-worthy customers.

principal.   In an *agency* relationship, the person from whom an agent's authority is derived.

private brand.   *Brands* that are the property rights of *middlemen* in the channel of distribution.

private enterprise.   See *free enterprise.*

process layout.   Same as *functional layout.*

process time.   The time during which the material is being changed, whether it is a machining operation or a hand assembly.

procurement lead time.   The time which must be allowed between the day goods are ordered (purchase or production order) and the day delivery can be expected or the manufacturing process completed; *purchasing lead time* or *manufacturing cycle time.*

producer.   An individual or firm that grows or mines materials, or manufactures *raw materials* into articles of use.

producers' goods.   Goods used in the production of other goods; also called *industrial goods.* Contrast with *consumer goods.*

product differentiation.   The *brand*ing of a seller's products to differentiate them from those of competitors, and to promote consumer preference for the firm's products through advertising and its reputation for quality.

production.   Those business activities involved in the creation of goods or services capable of satisfying human wants; includes the purchasing of the "ingredients" used in producing a product or service (equipment, materials, labor) as well as product fabrication. A primary *business function.*

production control.   Directing or regulating production through the entire *manufacturing cycle* from the requisitioning of raw materials to the delivery of the finished product; involves the functions of *dispatching* and production *follow-up.*

production order.   A document conveying authority for the manufacture of specified parts or products in specified quantities; also called *manufacturing order.*

production planning.   In *mass production* industries, setting the overall level and rate of manufacturing output; in other industries, the *routing* and *scheduling* of individual *production orders.*

production pool.   An SBA program in which several small firms may merge their production facilities to bid on government procurement orders too large or complicated for any one of the firms to handle alone.

productivity.   The amount of work turned out by a worker (or a machine) per unit of time.

product layout.   Same as *line layout.*

product liability.   The legal liability of manufacturers, distributors, and retailers for the safety of the products they make or sell.

profit.   The compensation accruing to entrepreneurs for the assumption of risk in business ownership.

profit-and-loss statement.   A summary of the income and expenses of a business to show net profit or loss for the fiscal period. Also called: *earnings statement, income statement,* or *operating statement.*

profit contribution.   The difference between sales income and *variable costs,* plus *programmed costs* if any; same as *contribution margin.*

profit ratios.   Measures of a firm's earnings in relation to sales and investment.

profit sharing.   A system under which employees receive, in addition to their regular wages, a part of the profits earned by the business enterprise.

profit-volume income.   *Incremental income* less *incremental cost.*

pro forma financial statement.   A hypothetical financial statement based on a sales *forecast.*

programmed costs.   *Incremental costs* of a fixed or variable nature.

progressive income tax.   A tax system in which the tax rate increases as the taxpayer's income increases; based on the ability-to-pay principle.

promissory note.   An unconditional written promise to pay a specified sum of money on demand or on a specified date.

promotion.   The assignment of an employee to a job of superior position or rank in the organization.

property taxes.   Taxes levied on *personal property* and *real property.*

proprietorship.   Ownership of an unincorporated *business firm* by one person only.

prosperity.   The period of a *business cycle* when production and employment are highest.

public relations.   The art or science of developing reciprocal understanding and goodwill between a business firm and the public.

purchase order.   A document sent by the buyer to the seller indicating the kind and quality of goods desired.

purchasing agent.   An *agent middleman* who acts only for buyers, on a continuing basis.

purchasing lead time.   See *procurement lead time.*

purchasing power.   (1) The value of money in buying goods and services; varies inversely with the *price index* or level. (2) The potential personal or family income available for the purchase of *consumer goods.*

quantity discount.   A reduction in the cost of merchandise or other goods, based on the size of the purchase order.

quick assets.   *Current assets* exclusive of *inventories,* i.e., assets that can be converted readily into their money value.

raw material.   Material suitable for manufacture.

real property.   Land or anything permanently attached thereto.

rebate.   (1) Unearned interest which is returned to a debtor if his/her installment or other loan is paid off prior to the maturity date. (2) A refund of part of the price paid for a product.

receivership.   The appointment by a court of a person to manage a firm unable to pay its debts when due.

recession.   A mild form of *depression.* See *business cycle.*

recovery property.   Property that qualifies for depreciation and investment tax credit under the Accelerated Cost Recovery System.

red-circle zone.   A deteriorated urban core of high-risk area on which property insurance is either unavailable at any cost or available only at unreasonably high premium rates.

referee in bankruptcy.   A person appointed by a court in *bankruptcy* cases to investigate and report to the court on settlement of the matter.

refund.   See *rebate.*

regional shopping center.   A planned *shopping center* serving a very large trading area embracing several communities.

Regulation Z.   The regulation issued by the Federal Reserve Board which states the detailed disclosure rules under the Truth-in-Lending Law.

Reilly's law.   The hypothesis that two communities attract retail trade from an intermediate area in the vicinity of the breaking point (where consumers will purchase equal amounts of goods and services from each community) approximately in direct proportion to the population of the two communities, and in inverse proportion to the square of the distance from these two communities to the intermediate point.

remedial training.   Training concerned with the correction of faulty work habits. Contrast with *developmental training.*

reorder point.   The *available stock* level or point at which an inventory replenishment order is initiated.

reorganization.   A merger or acquisition in which the seller corporation transfers its stock or assets to the buyer corporation.

repetitive manufacturing process.   Large and diverse line of standard products manufactured not continuously but in lots of economic size. Contrast with *continuous manufacturing process* and *intermittent manufacturing process.*

replacement cost (or value).   (1) The cost of restoring damaged property to its original condition, or the cost of replacing lost, stolen, or damaged property. (2) The current fair market price to purchase another, similar asset (with the same future benefit or service potential).

replenishment lead time.   See *procurement lead time.*

resale price maintenance.   An agreement between a manufacturer and his/her retailers on the price at which the latter will sell the manufacturer's product. See *fair trade laws.*

reserve system of stock control.   A *perpetual inventory* record which deducts reserved stock in determining the amount of *available stock.*

resident buying office.   A *purchasing agent* that represents many retailers in the same line of business in the central market.

resources file.   A compilation of facts and observations about suppliers from whom a firm purchases its merchandise or other materials.

responsibility.   The obligation owed by subordinates to their superiors for exercising *authority* delegated to them in a way to achieve expected results; see also *accountability.*

restraint of trade.   Practices tending to "unreasonably" limit the freedom of business activities.

retail affinities.   Natural clusterings of stores with a community of interests, i.e., do well when located close to each other.

retailers.   *Merchant middlemen* engaged primarily in selling to *ultimate consumers.*

retail inventory method.   Estimating the *lower of cost or market* value of an inventory by using ratios of cost to selling price.

retail reductions.   The total of *markdowns*, discounts to employees and other groups, and inventory shortages.

retained earnings.   Net income over the life of a business less all income distributions.

return on investment.   *Net profit* divided by the *capital* invested by the owners of the business.

returns and allowances.   A reduction in the sales invoice price for goods returned by the purchaser because they were defective or were not exactly what was ordered.

revolving credit.   *Open-end credit;* same as a *line of credit.*

right of rescission.   Generally, the right to set a contract aside when the other party is guilty of breach. As granted in the Truth-in-Lending Law, the right of a credit customer to change his or her mind and cancel an installment contract under certain conditions.

risk management.   Involves risk reduction as well as insurance planning or risk transference.

R.O.G. dating.   The cash discount and net credit periods start only after the goods have been received.

ROI.   See *return on investment.*

routing.   Specifying the manufacturing operations on a part and the sequence of these operations, the material requirements (kind and quantity), machine and tool requirements, and the time allowance for each operation.

safety stock.   The amount of inventory required to avoid a *stockout* at a given level of probability.

sales finance company.   A firm principally engaged in financing consumer *installment purchases* of durable goods.

sales forecast.   See *forecast*.

sales promotion.   The coordination of all marketing activities having to do with the performance of the selling function.

sales tax.   A tax levied upon a product or service at the time of sale; a form of *excise tax*.

salvage value.   Actual or estimated value of an asset at the end of its *service life*.

SBIC.   Acronym for *Small Business Investment Company*.

scheduling.   Establishing the timing for the performance of an operation or task.

scrabbled merchandising.   The selling of items not usually associated with a retailer's primary lines; e.g., the selling of variety goods by drug stores.

season dating.   A form of *extra dating* to encourage purchase of seasonal merchandise well in advance of sales demand.

secondary boycott.   A strike by employees against their own employer to force him or her to cease business with another employer.

Section 1244 stock.   Stock issued under Section 1244 of the Internal Revenue Code, wherein an investor is allowed to treat losses on the stock of a *Small Business Corporation* as deductions against ordinary income while gains are treated as *capital gains*.

secular trend.   The average course followed by business and economic activities over a period of several *business cycles*.

securities.   *Stocks* and *bonds*.

self-employment taxes.   Social security taxes paid by employer in his or her own behalf.

selling agent.   An *agent middleman* who acts continuously for his or her client in selling the manufacturer's entire output, with wide discretion as to price. See also *manufacturers' agent*.

semi-term loan.   Short-term loans that are renewed by a commercial bank under favorable conditions; see also *term loan*.

semivariable cost.   A cost that increases with increases in volume but less than proportionately.

service business.   A business firm producing a service (intangible in nature), as opposed to a product.

service life.   The period of expected usefulness of a *fixed asset*, hence the period of time over which the asset is normally *depreciated*. Contrast with *cost recovery period*.

set-aside program.   An SBA program under which certain government procurement orders are earmarked for competitive bidding exclusively by small firms.

setup time.   The time required to prepare production equipment for performing a specified job.

shopping center.   A geographic cluster of retail stores collectively selling a wide variety of goods to which customers are drawn for the purpose of shopping; an example of a *generative location.*

shopping goods.   Goods which the customer, before buying, usually compares as to quality, price, and style, i.e., the customer "shops around."

short-term.   Due within a year.

small business.   One that is actively managed by its owner(s), highly personalized, largely local in its area of operations, of relatively small size within the industry, and largely dependent upon internal sources of capital to finance its growth.

Small Business Corporation.   A corporation that qualifies for special tax treatment under *Section 1244* and *Subchapter S* of the Internal Revenue Code.

Small Business Investment Company.   A privately owned investment company licensed by the Small Business Administration to provide long-term funds and equity capital to small businesses.

SMP program.   See *special multiperil policy.*

social insurance.   Insurance made compulsory by the federal or state government against the risks of unemployment, industrial accidents, sickness, and old age.

social security taxes.   Taxes levied by the federal government on both employers and employees to provide annuity payments and medical care to retired workers and their survivors; officially called *FICA taxes* (for Federal Insurance Contributions Act).

special multiperil policy.   A "package policy" covering most of the risks of the small business owner that formerly required separate insurance policies.

specialty goods.   Goods with unique characteristics and/or brand identification for which the buyer is willing to make a special purchase effort; same as *fashion goods.*

staff.   (1) Personnel who provide specialized, technical, or professional assistance (advice) to "line" personnel; see also *staff authority.* (2) In small organizations, the body of persons (personnel) employed in the firm.

staff authority.   The authority of "ideas," as opposed to the authority of power or "position"; a relationship in an organization where the incumbent's task is to give some other person advice or counsel. Within a staff person's own area of *responsibility,* however, he or she exercises *line authority.*

staffing.   The assignment of tasks to individuals qualified to perform them.

standard cost.   A measured cost established as a criterion or basis for comparison.

standby costs.   Costs that are fixed at the minimal level of plant capacity, and hence which can be disregarded in *marginal income/cost* management decisions under conditions of unused capacity.

staple goods.   Goods for which there is a fairly active demand and which the retailer finds necessary to carry in stock continuously.

statutory merger.   A *merger* in which the seller corporation loses its identity by its absorption into the buyer corporation.

stock.   (1) the *inventory* of goods of a merchant or manufacturer. (2) The proprietorship element in a *corporation* divided into shares giving to the owners an interest in its assets and earnings.

stockchasing.   See *expediting.*

stockout.   A situation in which inventory is depleted before orders on hand can be completed or customer demand fulfilled.

stockturn.   See *inventory turnover.*

stores.   See *inventory.*

storeskeeping.   The receipt, storage, maintenance, and issuing of goods or supplies.

straight-line depreciation.   Spreading the initial cost of a capital asset, less its *salvage value,* in equal amounts over the estimated *service life* of the asset.

Subchapter S corporation.   A *small business corporation* in which profits and losses are treated as ordinary income or loss to the individual stockholder, i.e., corporation earnings are taxed as "partnership income" to the stockholders; also known as a *tax-option corporation.*

subsidiary ledger.   A specialized ledger that contains the detailed accounts whose total is shown in a general ledger *control account.*

sum-of-the-digits.   (1) A method used by creditors for calculating partial refunds of finance charges, requiring the use of fractions, where the numerators correspond in descending order to the digits in the numbered installment period and the denominator is the sum of the digits. (2) A method used in depreciating fixed assets, where the numerators correspond in descending order to the digits in the numbered depreciation periods and the denominator is the sum of the digits.

supervisor.   One who oversees and coordinates (*directs*) the activities of subordinates.

supplier.   Any individual or firm from whom purchases are made.

suscipient location.   A location to which consumers are impulsively or coincidentally attracted from their place of residence for any purpose other than shopping. Contrast with *generative location.*

T-account.   A skeleton ledger account shaped like the letter "T," often used for demonstrating the effect of a series of financial transactions.

tangible assets.   Assets that can be seen or touched.

tangible net assets.   Same as *tangible net worth.*

tangible net worth.   The *net worth* of a business excluding intangible assets such as patents and goodwill.

tariff.   A customs duty on goods as they enter the U.S., i.e., a tax on *imports.*

tax credit.   A subtraction from income taxes otherwise payable, such as the *investment tax credit.* Contrast with *tax deduction.*

tax deduction.   A subtraction from reported income, thereby lowering the taxable income.

tax-free exchange.   An exchange of one asset for another that involves no recognition for tax purposes.

tax-option corporation.   See *Subchapter S corporation.*

tax shelter.   Current income on which income taxes are deferred to some future date, such as payments into a *Keogh plan* or an *IRA.*

tax withholding.   A method of collecting estimated taxes as the income is earned, rather than delaying payment until the end of the taxable year; deductions from salaries or wages are remitted by the employer, in the employee's name, to the taxing authority.

term loan.   A loan with a maturity date; also called a *time loan.* Contrast with *demand loan.*

thinning the assets.   Making the business more affordable for the prospective buyer by selling only part of the firm's assets and leasing the rest.

third-party liability.   Liability for bodily injury to nonemployees on the business premises (customers, pedestrians, deliverymen, and even trespassers).

tie-in contract.   An agreement which obligates the buyer to buy goods or services the buyer does not want in order to obtain those the buyer does want.

tight money.   High interest rates, caused by the Federal Reserve Board's curtailment of the supply of money and credit, making for more difficult borrowing.

time loan.   See *term loan.*

time management.   The endeavor to work smarter rather than harder or longer; a systematic procedure to help make one's job more productive.

time wage.   The payment for work performed at a standard rate for the hour or the day.

track sheet.   Means of dispatching or "feeding" of material onto a production line in the amounts and times specified in the production schedule.

trade acceptance.   A *bill of exchange* drawn by the seller of goods on the purchaser and accepted by the purchaser.

trade-area survey.   Provides information on which communities customers prefer to shop. Contrast with *consumer survey.*

trade association.   An association of business firms engaged in the same trade for interchange of information, establishment of standards, and other activities of common interest to the members.

trade center.   A place in which the products of various producers and distributors are exhibited and sold at wholesale.

trade credit.   Credit extended by one business to another to help finance the distribution of consumer and producers' goods. Contrast with *consumer credit*.

trade discount.   A discount allowed a *middleman* from a *list price*.

trade fair.   A gathering of buyers and sellers at a particular place and time for trade.

trade-in allowance.   The value of an item taken as part payment for a purchase.

trademark.   A distinctive name, sign, or symbol. Exclusive rights to use a trademark are granted by the federal government for 28 years and can be renewed for another 28 years.

trade mission.   A group sent to a foreign country to promote trade with that country.

trade name.   The name by which a product is known in the market; a *brand*.

trade publication.   A publication specializing in the dissemination of economic, marketing and management, and other information for those engaged in a particular occupation, business, or industry.

trade show.   See *trade fair*.

trading area.   See *market* and *trade-area survey*.

traffic analysis.   Determination of the amount of pedestrian or customer traffic that passes a given location at different times of the day.

transfer.   The assignment of an employee to a job equal in position or rank to the job previously held.

traveler's check.   A special kind of *cashier's check*.

trial balance.   A listing of all account balances to check the arithmetic accuracy (equality) of the entries made to the accounts.

trust.   Any large-scale business firm which is a *monopoly* or, in the eyes of the law, has a tendency toward it.

truth in lending.   See *Regulation Z*.

turnover ratios.   Ratios that measure the number of times that assets (such as inventories, accounts receivable, working capital, and investment capital) are replaced during the accounting period.

UCC.   See *Uniform Commercial Code*.

ultimate consumer.   One who buys goods and services for personal or family use or for household consumption.

undistributed profits tax.   See *excess profits tax*.

unemployment compensation.   Payments made to workers who are unemployed and who qualify for such payments under the law.

unemployment taxes.   Insurance premiums (taxes) collected by the federal and state governments from which *unemployment compensation* is paid; commonly called *FUTA taxes* (for Federal Unemployment Tax Act).

Uniform Commercial Code.   A code adopted by all the states to regulate sales transactions, negotiable commercial paper, and secured transactions in personal property.

unit control.   In inventory control, determination of proper inventory levels in terms of the number of units of each kind of inventory. Contrast with *dollar control.*

unsecured loan.   See *character loan.*

usury.   The charging of unlawful or illegal rates of *interest.*

value added by manufacture.   The cost of a product or *work in process,* minus the cost of the materials purchased for the product or work in process.

variable cost.   A cost that changes as the volume of business changes; such a cost, for example, is zero when the level of business activity is zero; also called a *controllable cost.* Contrast with *fixed cost.*

vendor.   See *supplier.*

venture.   An undertaking involving chance or risk.

venture capital.   Same as *equity capital.*

vertical integration.   A union or *merger* under one ownership of two or more firms engaged in successive processes or stages of production and marketing. Contrast with *horizontal integration.*

voluntary bankruptcy.   *Bankruptcy* proceedings begun by petition of a *debtor.*

voting stock.   Stock which gives the stockholder the right to vote at corporate meetings.

want slips.   Records or notations of customer requests for items that cannot be supplied from stock.

warranty.   A promise by a seller to correct deficiences in products sold.

wholesalers.   *Merchant middlemen* engaged primarily in selling to *retailers* for resale or to industrial, institutional, and commercial users; also called *distributors.* See also *full-service wholesalers* and *limited-function wholesalers.*

withholding taxes.   See *tax withholding.*

without recourse.   Assumption of collection risks on purchased receivables and other financial instruments.

with recourse.   Seller of receivables or other financial instruments held responsible for payment in event of default by debtor(s).

word processing.   A method of storing and manipulating text matter in a computer. Contrast with *data processing.*

work analysis.   A listing of all the activities that must be performed if the business is to achieve its planned objectives (or if a job is to be adequately performed). See also *job analysis.*

workers' compensation insurance.   *Insurance* which protects employers against their liability for accidents to employees; compulsory in all states.

working capital.   The difference between *current assets* and *current liabilities; often referred to as *circulating capital.*

work in process.   The *inventory* of partially completed products.

write-off.   The charging of an *asset* to *expense,* such as equipment depreciation and bad debts.

zoning regulations.   Local ordinances restricting the use of *real property* to residential, business, industrial, and other purposes.

Index

A-B-C inventory control, 134–35
Accelerated Cost Recovery System (ACRS), 97, 341–44
Accounting, 309–38, 339–49
  basic records, 312–23
  computerization, 333–34
  depreciation and inventory valuation, 339–49
  financial statements and their interpretation, 324–33
  importance of financial records, 309–11
  principles of internal control, 333
Accounting equation, 311–12
Active Corps of Executives (ACE), 79
Administered prices, 217–18
Administrative organization, 42–47, 50, 468–71
Advertising, 205–6, 225–30, 231–32, 286, 431–32
  see also Buying motives
Agency, law of, 391, 402–3, 409
Agent middleman, see Functional middlemen
Antitrust legislation, 10, 423–24
Arbitration of labor disputes, 433
Authority, delegation of, 46–47, 64–65

Bad-check losses, 395
Balance sheet, 324, 325–27, 476
Bankruptcy and debt settlements, 28, 438–39
Barometer of Small Business, 363
Basic stock list, 108, 138
Billing disputes, resolution of, 298–99
Bookkeeping, see Accounting
Brand names, regulation of, 430
Break-even analysis, 353–57

Budgeting:
  capital, 376–82
  cash, 372–76
  expenses, 31, 227–29, 360–65
Building requirements, 93–96
Bureau of International Commerce, 249, 252–53
Burglary/robbery protective measures, 393
  see also Property insurance
Business continuity, providing for, 68–69, 70
Business districts, 186–91
Business functions (areas of management), 43–44
  financing production and marketing activities, 259–392
    budgeting cash and capital expenditures, 372–83
    extending customer credit, 278–308
    maintaining financial records, 309–49
    profit planning and expense control, 350–71
    raising capital, 261–77
    risk management, 384–98
  marketing or distributing goods and services, 177–257
    advertising and sales promotion, 224–48
    market analysis and business location, 179–203
    pricing, see Pricing methods and strategies
    sales to foreign markets, 249–57
  production of goods and services, 91–176
    acquiring, training, and motivating employees, 145–68
    controlling inventories, 123–44

Business functions (*Cont.*)
  manufacturing, 169–76
  providing and maintaining physical fa-
    cilities, 93–106
  purchasing goods for resale or materials
    for manufacture, 107–22
Business law, 401–8
  agency, 402–3
  contracts, 401–2
  negotiable instruments, 404–5
  sales transactions, 403–4
Business plan, preparing a, 461–76
Buying a business, *see* Selling a business
Buying groups, cooperative, 113–14
Buying motives, customers', 224–25
Buy/lease decisions:
  business premises, 93–94
  equipment, 96–98

Capital:
  cost of, 16–18
  debt, 262–64
  equity, 18, 262–64
  estimating needs, 261, 472–74
  kinds of, 262–63
  sources of, 264–73, 474–75
  uses of, 262
Capital budgeting, 376–82
Capital gains, 20–21
Cash budgeting, 372–76
Cash discounts:
  on purchases, 115–16
  on sales, 301
Cash flow, importance of, 31, 372–76, 476
Cash flow statement, 376, 476
Census publications, 76–78, 252
Chambers of Commerce, 66, 67, 77, 183
Charge accounts, open-end or revolving, 282,
    289–90
Child labor legislation, 436
Coinsurance policy clause, 386–87
Collections on account, 296–99
Collective bargaining legislation, 432–33
Commercial banks as a source of capital,
    267–69
Commercial law, *see* Business law
Community obligations, 65–66, 70
Company name, choosing a, 430
Competition:
  as a factor in business location, 182–83
    see also Retail affinities
  as a factor in price setting, 206–7
  regulation of, 10, 423–25

Competitive weakness as a cause of failure,
    31
Computerized recordkeeping, 333–34
Congressional Committees on Small Business,
    11
Consequential (indirect) loss from property
    damage, 390
Consultants, management, 84–86
  see also Small Business Institute program
Consumer credit, 278–301
  control system, 290–94
  credit bureaus, 294–96
  credit cards, 300–301
  financing of, 299–300
  installment sales, 281–82, 287–88
  regulations, 282–86, 294–96, 298–99
  types of, 281–82
Contracts, law of, 401–2
Controlling as a management function, 49, 50
Cooperative buying groups, 113–14
Corporate form of organization, 412–14, 416
Cost control, *see* Expense budgeting
Credit:
  advantages and disadvantages of extend-
    ing, 30, 279–80
  advertising of terms, 286
  collections, 296–99
  consumer, 278, 280–301
  domestic trade, 115–16, 271–72, 278,
    301–4
  export trade, 253–55
  ratings, 294–96, 302
  regulations, 282–86, 290, 293, 294–96,
    298–99
Credit bureaus, *see* Credit-reporting agencies
Credit cards, 300–301
Credit-reporting agencies, 294–96, 302
Customer relations, 236–38

Debt vs. equity capital, 263–64
Definition of small business, 3–4
  see also Strategy of business size
Delegation of authority, 46–47, 64–65
Demand elasticity, 205–6
Depreciation methods and allowances, 97,
    339–44
Differential pricing, 218
Directing as a management function, 47–49,
    50
Dispatching of production orders, 171–72
Distribution, *see* Business functions
Double-declining-balance depreciation, 97,
    340

Downtown locations, 186–88
Dun & Bradstreet, Inc., 28, 29, 31, 34, 35, 82, 86, 302, 327, 361, 363, 440(*fn*)

Economic contributions of small business, 9–11
Economic Development Administration, 77, 273
Economic ordering quantities, 130–33
Economic security legislation, 444–47
Economy, role of small business in, *see* Role of small business in economy
Education for small business management, 57–58, 66–68, 70
Elasticity of demand, 205–6
Employee dishonesty, 393–94
Employee relations, *see* Personnel and employee relations
Employment practices, fair, 433–35
Employment records, 155
Employment taxes, *see* Payroll taxes
Entrepreneurship, *see* Starting a business
Environmental Protection Agency, 432
Equal credit opportunity, 290, 293
Equal employment opportunity, 147–54
see also Fair employment practices
Equal-pay-for-equal-work, 436–37
Equity vs. debt capital, 263–64
Exception principle in management, 64
Excise taxes, federal, 451–52
Expediting:
of production orders, 172
of purchase orders, 117
Expense budgeting, 31, 227–29, 360–65
Expense ratios, 362–65
Expenses in Retail Business, 363
Export-Import Bank, 252, 253–54
Exporting, 249–57

Factory layout, 100–103
Factory production, 169–76
flow control, 172–73
planning production orders, 170–71
production order control, 171–72
dispatching, 171–72
follow-up or expediting, 172
Failure in business, causes of, 28–31
see also Success factors in business management
Fair employment practices, 433–35
FAIR plan, 388
Fair trade laws, 210, 426–27
Federal Crime Insurance Program, 388–89

Federal Trade Commission, 21, 283, 424–25, 427, 429, 430, 431–32
FICA taxes, *see* Social security taxes
FIFO inventory valuation, 345, 346
Finance(ing), *see* Business functions
Finance charges, calculating, 287–90
Financial ratios, 327–33, 362–65
Financial statements, 324–33, 475–76
Fire and theft, protection from, 393–95
see also Property insurance
Flat-rate pricing, 216
Follow-up, *see* Expediting
Food and Drug Administration, 428
Forecasting, 109, 351
Foreign Credit Insurance Association, 254–55
Foreign trade, *see* Exporting *and* Importing
Franchising, 12–13, 24–25, 238–39
Functional middlemen, 111–12
FUTA taxes, *see* Unemployment taxes

General partnership form of organization, 410–12, 416
Gift and inheritance taxes, 20
Goodwill, valuation of, 486–88
Green River ordinances, 438
Gross-margin pricing, *see* Markups
Guild pricing, 215

Highway locations, 190–91

Importing, 114–15
Income statement, *see* Profit-and-loss statement
Income taxes, 19–20, 447–51
Incremental costs/income, *see* Marginal-income/cost analysis
Indirect loss from property damage, 390
Individual Retirement Account (IRA), 451
Information returns, tax, 450
Inheritance and gift taxes, 20
Innovation, 11, 42
see also Patent regulations and abuses
Installment sales, 281–82, 287–88
Insurance and risk management:
estimating fire and theft losses, 389–90
insurance planning, 254–55, 303–4, 384–89, 390–92, 471–72
consequential (indirect) loss, 390
death or disability of key personnel, 391–92
export credit, 254–55
legal liability, 390–91, 428–29

Insurance and risk management (*Cont.*)
    loss or damage of property, 386–90
        special multiperil policy, 392
        trade credit, 303–4
    loss reduction or prevention, 392–95
        bad checks, 395
        burglary and robbery, 393
        employee dishonesty, 393–94
        fire, 393
        shoplifting, 394–95
Interior displays, 233
International Council for Small Business, 58
International Franchise Association, 25
Inventory control, 30, 123–44
    A-B-C classification, 134–35
    dollar control vs. unit control, 125, 137–39
    min-max system, 128–34
    ordering quantities, 130–33
    perpetual inventory records, 126–27
    physical inventory counts, 127–28
    reordering points, 125, 134
Inventory needs, determining, 107–9, 467–68
Inventory records, 125–28
Inventory valuation, 344–47
    average-cost method, 345, 346
    FIFO method, 345, 346
    LIFO method, 345, 346
    retail method, 345–47
Investment criteria, 376–82
    payback period, 380–81
    present values, 377–80
    rate of return, 381–82
Investment tax credit, 97, 98

Job analysis, 43–44, 146–47
Job descriptions, 47, 146–47
Job evaluation, 158–59
Job specifications, 47, 146–47
Journal of Small Business Management, 58

Keogh pension plan, 450–51
Key-employee insurance, 391–92

Labeling, product, 428, 429–30
Labor legislation, 432–37
Layout of physical facilities, 95, 98–104
    in factories, 100–103
    in retail stores, 99–100
    in service establishments, 103
    in wholesale establishments, 103–4
Leadership and morale, 48–49, 161–63
Leasing:
    business premises, 183, 192
    equipment, 98

Legal forms of business organization, 409–22,
    471
    conventional corporation, 412–14, 416
    general partnership, 410–12, 416
    limited partnership, 412
    proprietorship, 410, 416
    tax-option corporation, 414–15, 417
Leverage ratios, 328, 332–33
Liability insurance, 390–91, 428–29
Licenses, state and local, 437
LIFO inventory valuation, 345, 346
Limited partnership form of organization,
    412
Liquidity ratios, 328, 330
Lobbying organizations, small business, 25–
    26
Locating the business, 179–203
    choosing the area or community, 179–83
        competitive businesses, 182–83
        demographic characteristics, 182
        economic base, 180–81
    choosing the building site, 183
    the retail location, 183–95
        basic factors in site selection, 191–95
        business districts, 186–91
        the trading area, 184–86
    requirements in other types of business:
        manufacturing, 197–98
        service businesses, 196
        wholesaling, 196–97
Loss-leader pricing, 207, 426

Management assistance, sources of, 58,
    66–68, 72–89
    government sources:
        Small Business Administration, 58, 66–
            68, 78–80
        U.S. Department of Commerce, 75–78
    nongovernment sources:
        lawyers/accountants, others, 86–87
        management consultants, 84–86
        suppliers and equipment manufacturers,
            86
        trade and other publications, 84
        trade associations, 80–83
Management consultants, 84–86
Management functions, basic, 39–52
    controlling, 49, 50
    directing, 47–49, 50
        coordinating, 47–48
        supervising, 49
    organizing, 42–44, 50
    planning, 39–42, 50
    staffing, 44–47, 50

Management succession, 68–69, 70
Manufacturing businesses, 5–7
  economic lot sizes, 133
  factory layout, 100–103
  inventory records, 126–27, 172
  location analysis, 197–98
  pricing methods and strategies, 216–18
  production planning and control, 169–76
Manufacturing processes, types of, 100–101
Marginal-income/cost analysis, 206, 228–29, 357–60
Market analysis, 179–83, 227, 462–64
Marketing, *see* Business functions
Markons, 213–14
Markups and markdowns, 209, 210–13
Merchandise control systems, 135–39
Merchandise marts, 114
Merchandise regulations, 428–31
Merchandising businesses, 7
  see also Retail businesses *and* Wholesale businesses
Merchant middlemen, 110–11
Mergers and consolidations, 20–21, 490
Metric system of weights and measures, 255–56
Middlemen, 110–12
Minimum-wage legislation, 22
Min-max system of inventory control, 128–34
Minority business enterprise, 77–78, 80, 273
Model stock plan, 108, 138
Morale and leadership, 48–49, 161–63
Mr. Businessman's (tax) *Kit*, 75
Multiplier pricing, 215–16

National Association of Franchised Businessmen, 25
National Federation of Independent Business, 26, 249
National Industrial Conference Board, 54
National Retail Merchants Association, 394
National Small Business Association, 24, 26
National Small Business Week, 11
Negotiable instruments, law of, 404–5
Neighborhood shopping areas, 188–89

OASDI, *see* Social security taxes
"One-man band" problem, 56–57
Open-to-buy, 137–38
Operating organization, *see* Administrative organization
Operating ratios, 363–65
Ordering quantities, 130–33, 136

Organizational forms:
  administrative, 42–47, 50, 468–71
  legal, 409–22, 471
Organizing as a management function, 42–44, 50
OSHA, *see* Safety and health, employee
Ownership organization, *see* Legal forms of business organization
Ownership succession, preparing for, 68–69, 70

Partnership forms of organization, 410–12, 416
Patent abuses, 23–24
Patent regulations, 431
Payback period on investment, 380–81
Payroll taxes, 444–47
Pensions, employee, 160–61
Permits to do business, 437
Perpetual inventory records, 126–27
Personal selling, 236–38
Personnel and employee relations, 43–44, 48–49, 145–68
  employee training, 156–57
  employment records, 155
  job analysis, 43–44, 146–47
  leadership and morale, 48–49, 161–163
  placement, 155–56
  recruitment and selection, 147–55
  remuneration, 158–61
  transfers and promotions, 157–58
Physical facilities, providing, 93–106, 466–67
  building requirements, 93–96
  obtaining the equipment, 96–98
  planning the layout, 98–104
    in factories, 100–103
    in service shops, 103
    in stores, 99–100
    in wholesale establishments, 103–4
Physical inventory counts, 127–28
Placement of employees, 155–56
Planning as a management function, 39–42, 50
Policy formulation, 40–42
Present-value investment criterion, 377–80
Prestige pricing, 208
Price lining, 209
Price regulations, 425–27
  price cutting, 426
  price discrimination, 425–26
  price fixing, 425
  resale price maintenance, 426–27

Pricing methods and strategies, 204–23, 426–27
  administered prices, 217–18
  differential pricing, 218
  in factories, 216–18
  factors in price setting, 204–8
  flat-rate pricing, 216
  gross-margin pricing (*see* Markups)
  guild pricing, 215
  loss-leader pricing, 207, 426
  markdowns, 209
  markons, 213–14
  markups, 205, 210–12
  multiplier pricing, 215–16
  prestige pricing, 208
  price lining, 209
  resale price maintenance, 426–27
  in retailing, 208–14
  in service establishments, 214–16
  in wholesaling, 214
  see also Price regulations
Problems of small business, external or environmental, 16–27
  capital shortages, 16–18
  franchising abuses, 24–25
  patent abuses, 23–24
  product liability, 22–23
  taxation and regulations, 19–22
Production, *see* Business functions
Product labeling, 428, 429–30
Product safety and liability, 22–23, 428–29
Product warranties, 429
Profit-and-loss statement, 324–25, 475–76
Profit planning, 109, 206, 227–29, 350–71
  break-even analysis, 353–57
  demand forecasting, 109, 351
  expense budgeting, 227–29, 360–65
  marginal-income/cost analysis, 206, 228–29, 357–60
Profit ratios, 328–30
Profit sharing, 160
Promotions and transfers, employee, 157–58
Property insurance, 386–90
Proprietorship form of organization, 410, 416
Public relations, 240–41
Purchasing goods and supplies, 107–22, 467–68
  determining inventory needs, 107–9, 467–68
  follow-up after purchase, 117
  locating and selecting suppliers, 109–15
  maintaining favorable relations with suppliers, 116

  receiving, checking, and marking goods, 116–17

Ratio analysis, 328–33, 362–65
Records:
  accounting, 309–11, 312–23
    see also Financial statements
  depreciation, 344
  employment, 155
  inventory, 125–28
  payroll, 318, 320
Recruitment and selection of employees, 147–55
Regulations, government, 10, 20–25, 147–54, 195, 210, 282–86, 290, 293–96, 298–99, 423–43, 448–53
  advertising, 431–32
  advertising of credit terms, 286
  bankruptcy and debt settlements, 438–39
  billing disputes, 298–299
  brand names, 430
  child labor, 436
  collective bargaining, 432–36
  company names, 430
  competition, 10, 423–25
  consumer credit terms, 282–86
  consumer-reporting agencies, 294–96
  environmental protection, 432
  equal credit opportunity, 290, 293
  equal employment opportunity, 147–54
  equal-pay-for-equal-work, 436–37
  fair employment practices, 433–35
  fair trade, 210, 426–27
  food, drugs, and cosmetics, 428
  franchising, 25
  Green River ordinances, 438
  labor, 432–37
  licenses and permits, 437
  merchandise, 428–31
  minimum wages, 22
  occupational safety and health, 22, 436
  patents, 431
  pricing, 425–27
  product labeling, 428, 429–30
  product safety and liability, 22–23, 428–29
  product warranties, 429
  tax withholding and remittance, 20, 448–50
  trademarks, 430–31
  wages, hours, and working conditions, 435–36
  zoning, 195, 437

Remuneration of employees, 158–61
  wage payment methods, 159
  wage supplements, 159–61
    pensions, 160–61
    profit sharing, 160
Rent-advertising relationship, 194
Reordering points, 125, 134
Reorganizations, tax-free, 490
Resale price maintenance, 426–27
  see also Administered prices
Responsibility, assignment of, 44–46
  see also Authority, delegation of
Restrictive ordinances, 195, 437, 438
Retail affinities, 194–95
Retail businesses:
  inventory control, 126, 136–39
  location analysis, 183–95
  pricing methods and strategies, 208–14
  store layout, 99–100
Retail method of inventory valuation, 345–47
Retail reductions, 137, 212–14
Return on investment, 381–82
Risk management and insurance, *see* Insurance and risk management
Robbery/burglary protective measures, 393
  see also Property insurance
Robert Morris Associates, 327, 363
Role of small business in economy, 3–15
  economic contributions, 9–11
  make-up or composition, 4–8
  predominance of small business, 4

Safety, product, 22, 23, 128, 29
Safety and health, employee, 22, 436
  see also Workers' compensation
Sales promotion, 205–6, 224–48, 286, 431–32, 462–64
  advertising, 205–6, 225–30, 231–32, 286, 431–32
  customers' buying motives, 224–25
  franchising and other methods of distribution, 238–39
  government assistance programs, 239
  market analysis, 227, 462–64
  personal selling and customer relations, 236–38
  public relations, 240–41
  special sales events, 233–36
  window and interior displays, 230, 233
Sales taxes, state and local, 452–53
Sales transactions, law of, 403–4
Section 1244 stock, 266
Self-Employed Individuals Tax Retirement Act, 450–51

Self-employment taxes, 446
Selling a business, 484–95
  setting the sales (purchase) price, 485–88
    valuation of goodwill, 486–88
    valuation of tangible assets, 485–86
  striking a "deal," 488–90
    installment sale (purchase), 489
    tax-free reorganization, 490
Service businesses, 8
  layout of physical facilities, 103
  location analysis, 196
  pricing methods and strategies, 214–16
Service Corps of Retired Executives (SCORE), 79
Shoplifting, 394–95
Shopping centers, controlled, 189–90
Small Business Administration, 10–11, 17, 58, 67–68, 78–80, 239, 253, 264, 269–70, 333, 475
  financial assistance, 17, 264, 269–70, 333, 475(*fn*)
  foreign-trade assistance, 253
  government-contract procurement, assistance in, 239
  legislative authority, 10–11
  management assistance, 58, 66–68, 78–80
  minority-business assistance, 80
Small business defined, 3–4
  see also Strategy of business size
Small Business Development Centers, 79
Small Business Institute (SBI) program, 79
Small Business Investment Companies (SBICs), 271
Social security taxes, 445–47
Society for the Advancement of Management, 58
Special Multiperil (insurance) Policy, 392
Special sales events, 233–36
Staffing as a management function, 44–47, 50
Starting a business, 461–83
  preparing the financial plan, 472–76
    capital requirements and sources, 472–75
    pro forma financial statements, 475–76
  preparing the marketing or distribution plan, 461–66
    market feasibility, 462–64
    marketing strategy, 464–66
  preparing the organization and staffing plan, 466–72
    administrative (operating) organization, 468–71

Starting a business (*Cont.*)
    insuring business risks, 471–72
    legal (ownership) organization, 471
    opening inventories, 467–68
    physical facilities, 466–67
Store layout, 99–100
Straight-line depreciation, 339–40
Strategy of business size, 53–55
Subchapter S corporation, 414–15, 417
Success factors in business management, 31–34
Sum-of-the-years'-digits depreciation, 340
Supervision, *see* Directing as a management function
Suppliers, locating and selecting, 86, 109–15
Survey of Current Business, 75

Tax calendar (*table*), 454–56
Taxes, 19–21, 444–58
    capital gains, 20–21
    income taxes, federal, 19–20, 447–51
        information returns, 450
        remitting withheld taxes, 20, 449–50
        withholding employees' taxes, 20, 448–49
    inheritance and gift taxes, 20
    payroll taxes, 444–47
        social security taxes, 445–47
        unemployment taxes, 445
    sales taxes, 451–53
        federal excise taxes, 451–52
        state and local sales taxes, 452–53
    self-employment taxes, 446
Tax Guide for Small Business, 74
Tax-option corporation, 414–15, 417
Theft and fire protection, 393–95
    see also Property insurance
Time management, 62–65, 69–70
Trade associations, 67, 80–83

Trade credit, 115–16, 271–72, 278, 301–4
Trademarks, 430–31
Trade publications, 84
Trade shows, 114
Trading areas, retail, 184–86
Training of employees, 156–57
Transfers and promotions, employee, 157–58
Turnover ratios, 328, 331–32

Unemployment taxes, 445
Uniform Commercial Code, 401, 403, 404
U.S. Department of Commerce, 75–78, 252
    census and other publications, 75–77, 252
    minority-business assistance, 77–78
    see also Bureau of International Commerce

Vocational education, federal/state programs in, 74
Voluntary chains, *see* Franchising

Wage payment methods, 159
Wages, hours, and working conditions, regulation of, 435–36
    see also Minimum-wage legislation
Warranties, product, 429
Wayside locations, 190–91
White House Committee on Small Business, 11
Wholesale businesses:
    inventory records, 126
    layout of physical facilities, 103–4
    location analysis, 196–97
    pricing methods, 214
Window displays, 230, 233
Withholding and remittance, tax, 20, 448–50
Work analysis, *see* Job analysis
Workers' compensation, 391, 444–45

Zoning regulations, 195, 437